Chevrolet Express and GMC Savana Full-size Vans Automotive Repair Manual

by Mike Stubblefield and John H Haynes

Member of the Guild of Motoring Writers

Models covered:

Chevrolet Express and GMC Savana Full-size vans 1996 through 2007

Does not include information specific to all-wheel drive, diesel or 8.1L engine models

(4M3 - 24081)

ABCDE
FGHIJ
KLMNO
P

Haynes Publishing Group
Sparkford Nr Yeovil
Somerset BA22 7JJ England

Haynes North America, Inc
861 Lawrence Drive
Newbury Park
California 91320 USA

Acknowledgements

Technical writers who contributed to this project include John Wegmann, Rob Maddox and Joe L. Hamilton. Wiring diagrams originated exclusively for Haynes North America, Inc. by Solution Builders.

© **Haynes North America, Inc. 2005, 2008**

With permission from J.H. Haynes & Co. Ltd.

A book in the Haynes Automotive Repair Manual Series

Printed in the U.S.A.

ISBN-13: 978-1-56392-719-5
ISBN-10: 1-56392-719-5

Library of Congress Catalog Card Number 2008927725

Contents

Haynes mechanic and photographer with a 1999 GMC Savana van

About this manual

Its purpose

The purpose of this manual is to help you get the best value from your vehicle. It can do so in several ways. It can help you decide what work must be done, even if you choose to have it done by a dealer service department or a repair shop; it provides information and procedures for routine maintenance and servicing; and it offers diagnostic and repair procedures to follow when trouble occurs.

We hope you use the manual to tackle the work yourself. For many simpler jobs, doing it yourself may be quicker than arranging an appointment to get the vehicle into a shop and making the trips to leave it and pick it up. More importantly, a lot of money can be saved by avoiding the expense the shop must pass on to you to cover its labor and overhead costs. An added benefit is the sense of satisfaction and accomplishment that you feel after doing the job yourself.

Using the manual

The manual is divided into Chapters. Each Chapter is divided into numbered Sections, which are headed in bold type between horizontal lines. Each Section consists of consecutively numbered paragraphs.

At the beginning of each numbered Section you will be referred to any illustrations which apply to the procedures in that Section. The reference numbers used in illustration captions pinpoint the pertinent Section and the Step within that Section. That is, illustration 3.2 means the illustration refers to Section 3 and Step (or paragraph) 2 within that Section.

Procedures, once described in the text, are not normally repeated. When it's necessary to refer to another Chapter, the reference will be given as Chapter and Section number. Cross references given without use of the word "Chapter" apply to Sections and/or paragraphs in the same Chapter. For example, "see Section 8" means in the same Chapter.

References to the left or right side of the vehicle assume you are sitting in the driver's seat, facing forward.

Even though we have prepared this manual with extreme care, neither the publisher nor the author can accept responsibility for any errors in, or omissions from, the information given.

NOTE

A **Note** provides information necessary to properly complete a procedure or information which will make the procedure easier to understand.

CAUTION

A **Caution** provides a special procedure or special steps which must be taken while completing the procedure where the Caution is found. Not heeding a Caution can result in damage to the assembly being worked on.

WARNING

A **Warning** provides a special procedure or special steps which must be taken while completing the procedure where the Warning is found. Not heeding a Warning can result in personal injury.

Introduction to the Chevrolet Express and GMC Savana vans

The Chevrolet and GMC full-size vans covered by this manual are conventional front engine/rear wheel drive layout.

Fuel-injected V6 and V8 engines are used for power.

The engine transmits power to the rear wheels through a 4-speed automatic transmission and a driveshaft to the rear axle.

These models feature independent front suspension with coil springs and shock absorbers at the front. At the rear, a solid rear axle is supported by leaf springs and shock absorbers.

The power-assisted steering is either rack-and-pinion or conventional recirculating-ball type. The rack-and-pinion steering unit is mounted on a crossmember in front of the engine and the conventional steering box is located on the left-side frame rail.

All models have a power-assisted brake system with disc brakes at the front and either disc or drum brakes at the rear. Some models are equipped with an Anti-lock Braking System (ABS).

Vehicle identification numbers

Modifications are a continuing and unpublicized process in vehicle manufacturing. Since spare parts manuals and lists are compiled on a numerical basis, the individual vehicle numbers are essential to correctly identify the component required.

Vehicle Identification Number (VIN)

This very important identification number is stamped on a plate attached to the left side of the dashboard just inside the windshield on the driver's side of the vehicle (see illustration). The VIN also appears on the Vehicle Certificate of Title and Registration. It contains information such as where and when the vehicle was manufactured, the model year and the body style.

VIN year and engine codes

Two particularly important pieces of information located in the VIN are the model year and engine codes. Counting from the left, the engine code is the eighth digit and the model year code is the 10th digit.

On the models covered by this manual the engine codes are:

W, X 4.3L V6
V 4.8L V8
M 5.0L V8
T 5.3L V8
R 5.7L V8
U 6.0L V8
J 7.4L V8

On the models covered by this manual the model year codes are:

U 1996
V 1997
W 1998
X 1999
Y 2000
1 2001
2 2002
3 2003
4 2004
5 2005
6 2006
7 2007

Equipment identification plate

This plate is located on the inside of the hood. It contains valuable information concerning the production of the vehicle as well as information on all production or special equipment.

The VIN plate is visible from outside of the vehicle, through the driver's side of the windshield

The Vehicle Safety Certification label is affixed to the end of the driver's door

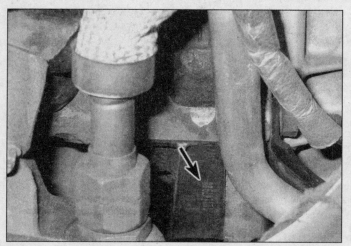

On V6 and most V8 engines the identification number is located on a pad at the left rear of the engine

Typical automatic transmission identification number locations

Safety Certification label

The Safety Certification label is affixed to the left front door **(see illustration)**. The plate contains the name of the manufacturer, the month and year of production, the Gross Vehicle Weight Rating (GVWR) and the safety certification statement. This label also contains the paint code. It is especially useful for matching the color and type of paint during repair work.

Engine identification number

The Engine Identification Number on all engines except the 7.4L V8 is stamped into the rear of the engine block on the left side, near the transmission bellhousing **(see illustration)**. On the 7.4L V8 engine it's located on a machined pad at the front of the engine block, below the right cyllinder head.

Transmission identification number

The ID number on automatic transmissions is stamped into the transmission case above the oil pan flange **(see illustration)**.

Buying parts

Replacement parts are available from many sources, which generally fall into one of two categories - authorized dealer parts departments and independent retail auto parts stores. Our advice concerning these parts is as follows:

Retail auto parts stores: Good auto parts stores will stock frequently needed components which wear out relatively fast, such as clutch components, exhaust systems, brake parts, tune-up parts, etc. These stores often supply new or reconditioned parts on an exchange basis, which can save a considerable amount of money. Discount auto parts stores are often very good places to buy materials and parts needed for general vehicle maintenance such as oil, grease, filters, spark plugs, belts, touch-up paint, bulbs, etc. They also usually sell tools and general accessories, have convenient hours, charge lower prices and can often be found not far from home.

Authorized dealer parts department: This is the best source for parts which are unique to the vehicle and not generally available elsewhere (such as major engine parts, transmission parts, trim pieces, etc.).

Warranty information: If the vehicle is still covered under warranty, be sure that any replacement parts purchased - regardless of the source - do not invalidate the warranty!

To be sure of obtaining the correct parts, have engine and chassis numbers available and, if possible, take the old parts along for positive identification.

Maintenance techniques, tools and working facilities

Maintenance techniques

There are a number of techniques involved in maintenance and repair that will be referred to throughout this manual. Application of these techniques will enable the home mechanic to be more efficient, better organized and capable of performing the various tasks properly, which will ensure that the repair job is thorough and complete.

Fasteners

Fasteners are nuts, bolts, studs and screws used to hold two or more parts together. There are a few things to keep in mind when working with fasteners. Almost all of them use a locking device of some type, either a lockwasher, locknut, locking tab or thread adhesive. All threaded fasteners should be clean and straight, with undamaged threads and undamaged corners on the hex head where the wrench fits. Develop the habit of replacing all damaged nuts and bolts with new ones. Special locknuts with nylon or fiber inserts can only be used once. If they are removed, they lose their locking ability and must be replaced with new ones.

Rusted nuts and bolts should be treated with a penetrating fluid to ease removal and prevent breakage. Some mechanics use turpentine in a spout-type oil can, which works quite well. After applying the rust penetrant, let it work for a few minutes before trying to loosen the nut or bolt. Badly rusted fasteners may have to be chiseled or sawed off or removed with a special nut breaker, available at tool stores.

If a bolt or stud breaks off in an assembly, it can be drilled and removed with a special tool commonly available for this purpose. Most automotive machine shops can perform this task, as well as other repair procedures, such as the repair of threaded holes that have been stripped out.

Flat washers and lockwashers, when removed from an assembly, should always be replaced exactly as removed. Replace any damaged washers with new ones. Never

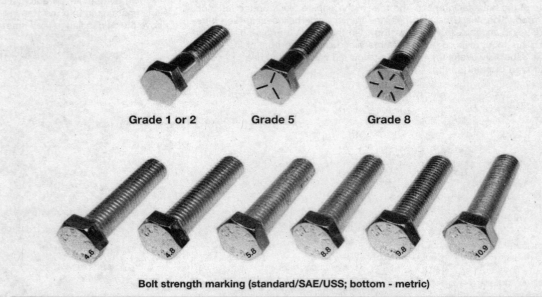

Bolt strength marking (standard/SAE/USS; bottom - metric)

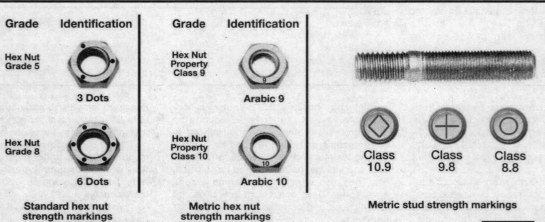

Standard hex nut strength markings

Metric hex nut strength markings

Metric stud strength markings

00-1 HAYNES

use a lockwasher on any soft metal surface (such as aluminum), thin sheet metal or plastic.

Fastener sizes

For a number of reasons, automobile manufacturers are making wider and wider use of metric fasteners. Therefore, it is important to be able to tell the difference between standard (sometimes called U.S. or SAE) and metric hardware, since they cannot be interchanged.

All bolts, whether standard or metric, are sized according to diameter, thread pitch and length. For example, a standard 1/2 - 13 x 1 bolt is 1/2 inch in diameter, has 13 threads per inch and is 1 inch long. An M12 - 1.75 x 25 metric bolt is 12 mm in diameter, has a thread pitch of 1.75 mm (the distance between threads) and is 25 mm long. The two bolts are nearly identical, and easily confused, but they are not interchangeable.

In addition to the differences in diameter, thread pitch and length, metric and standard bolts can also be distinguished by examining the bolt heads. To begin with, the distance across the flats on a standard bolt head is measured in inches, while the same dimension on a metric bolt is sized in millimeters (the same is true for nuts). As a result, a standard wrench should not be used on a metric bolt and a metric wrench should not be used on a standard bolt. Also, most standard bolts have slashes radiating out from the center of the head to denote the grade or strength of the bolt, which is an indication of the amount of torque that can be applied to it. The greater the number of slashes, the greater the strength of the bolt. Grades 0 through 5 are commonly used on automobiles. Metric bolts have a property class (grade) number, rather than a slash, molded into their heads to indicate bolt strength. In this case, the higher the number, the stronger the bolt. Property class numbers 8.8, 9.8 and 10.9 are commonly used on automobiles.

Strength markings can also be used to distinguish standard hex nuts from metric hex nuts. Many standard nuts have dots stamped into one side, while metric nuts are marked with a number. The greater the number of dots, or the higher the number, the greater the strength of the nut.

Metric studs are also marked on their ends according to property class (grade). Larger studs are numbered (the same as metric bolts), while smaller studs carry a geometric code to denote grade.

It should be noted that many fasteners, especially Grades 0 through 2, have no distinguishing marks on them. When such is the case, the only way to determine whether it is standard or metric is to measure the thread pitch or compare it to a known fastener of the same size.

Standard fasteners are often referred to as SAE, as opposed to metric. However, it should be noted that SAE technically refers to a non-metric fine thread fastener only. Coarse thread non-metric fasteners are referred to as

Metric thread sizes	Ft-lbs	Nm
M-6	6 to 9	9 to 12
M-8	14 to 21	19 to 28
M-10	28 to 40	38 to 54
M-12	50 to 71	68 to 96
M-14	80 to 140	109 to 154

Pipe thread sizes		
1/8	5 to 8	7 to 10
1/4	12 to 18	17 to 24
3/8	22 to 33	30 to 44
1/2	25 to 35	34 to 47

U.S. thread sizes		
1/4 - 20	6 to 9	9 to 12
5/16 - 18	12 to 18	17 to 24
5/16 - 24	14 to 20	19 to 27
3/8 - 16	22 to 32	30 to 43
3/8 - 24	27 to 38	37 to 51
7/16 - 14	40 to 55	55 to 74
7/16 - 20	40 to 60	55 to 81
1/2 - 13	55 to 80	75 to 108

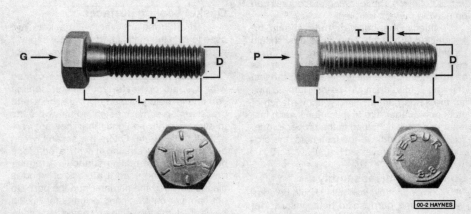

Standard (SAE and USS) bolt dimensions/ grade marks

G   Grade marks (bolt strength)
L   Length (in inches)
T   Thread pitch (number of threads per inch)
D   Nominal diameter (in inches)

Metric bolt dimensions/grade marks

P   Property class (bolt strength)
L   Length (in millimeters)
T   Thread pitch (distance between threads in millimeters)
D   Diameter

USS sizes.

Since fasteners of the same size (both standard and metric) may have different strength ratings, be sure to reinstall any bolts, studs or nuts removed from your vehicle in their original locations. Also, when replacing a fastener with a new one, make sure that the new one has a strength rating equal to or greater than the original.

Tightening sequences and procedures

Most threaded fasteners should be tightened to a specific torque value (torque is the twisting force applied to a threaded component such as a nut or bolt). Overtightening the fastener can weaken it and cause it to break, while undertightening can cause it to even-

tually come loose. Bolts, screws and studs, depending on the material they are made of and their thread diameters, have specific torque values, many of which are noted in the Specifications at the beginning of each Chapter. Be sure to follow the torque recommendations closely. For fasteners not assigned a specific torque, a general torque value chart is presented here as a guide. These torque values are for dry (unlubricated) fasteners threaded into steel or cast iron (not aluminum). As was previously mentioned, the size and grade of a fastener determine the amount of torque that can safely be applied to it. The figures listed here are approximate for Grade 2 and Grade 3 fasteners. Higher grades can tolerate higher torque values.

Fasteners laid out in a pattern, such as

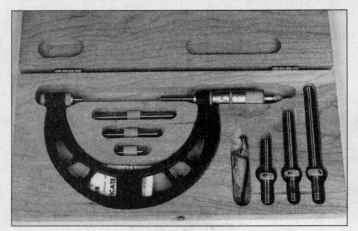

Micrometer set

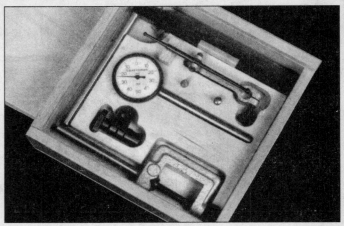

Dial indicator set

cylinder head bolts, oil pan bolts, differential cover bolts, etc., must be loosened or tightened in sequence to avoid warping the component. This sequence will normally be shown in the appropriate Chapter. If a specific pattern is not given, the following procedures can be used to prevent warping.

Initially, the bolts or nuts should be assembled finger-tight only. Next, they should be tightened one full turn each, in a criss-cross or diagonal pattern. After each one has been tightened one full turn, return to the first one and tighten them all one-half turn, following the same pattern. Finally, tighten each of them one-quarter turn at a time until each fastener has been tightened to the proper torque. To loosen and remove the fasteners, the procedure would be reversed.

Component disassembly

Component disassembly should be done with care and purpose to help ensure that the parts go back together properly. Always keep track of the sequence in which parts are removed. Make note of special characteristics or marks on parts that can be installed more than one way, such as a grooved thrust washer on a shaft. It is a good idea to lay the disassembled parts out on a clean surface in the order that they were removed. It may also be helpful to make sketches or take instant photos of components before removal.

When removing fasteners from a component, keep track of their locations. Sometimes threading a bolt back in a part, or putting the washers and nut back on a stud, can prevent mix-ups later. If nuts and bolts cannot be returned to their original locations, they should be kept in a compartmented box or a series of small boxes. A cupcake or muffin tin is ideal for this purpose, since each cavity can hold the bolts and nuts from a particular area (i.e. oil pan bolts, valve cover bolts, engine mount bolts, etc.). A pan of this type is especially helpful when working on assemblies with very small parts, such as the carburetor, alternator, valve train or interior dash and trim pieces. The cavities can be marked with paint or tape to identify the contents.

Whenever wiring looms, harnesses or connectors are separated, it is a good idea to identify the two halves with numbered pieces of masking tape so they can be easily reconnected.

Gasket sealing surfaces

Throughout any vehicle, gaskets are used to seal the mating surfaces between two parts and keep lubricants, fluids, vacuum or pressure contained in an assembly.

Many times these gaskets are coated with a liquid or paste-type gasket sealing compound before assembly. Age, heat and pressure can sometimes cause the two parts to stick together so tightly that they are very difficult to separate. Often, the assembly can be loosened by striking it with a soft-face hammer near the mating surfaces. A regular hammer can be used if a block of wood is placed between the hammer and the part. Do not hammer on cast parts or parts that could be easily damaged. With any particularly stubborn part, always recheck to make sure that every fastener has been removed.

Avoid using a screwdriver or bar to pry apart an assembly, as they can easily mar the gasket sealing surfaces of the parts, which must remain smooth. If prying is absolutely necessary, use an old broom handle, but keep in mind that extra clean up will be necessary if the wood splinters.

After the parts are separated, the old gasket must be carefully scraped off and the gasket surfaces cleaned. Stubborn gasket material can be soaked with rust penetrant or treated with a special chemical to soften it so it can be easily scraped off. **Caution:** *Never use gasket removal solutions or caustic chemicals on plastic or other composite components.* A scraper can be fashioned from a piece of copper tubing by flattening and sharpening one end. Copper is recommended because it is usually softer than the surfaces to be scraped, which reduces the chance of gouging the part. Some gaskets can be removed with a wire brush, but regardless of the method used, the mating surfaces must be left clean and smooth. If for some reason the gasket surface is gouged, then a gasket

sealer thick enough to fill scratches will have to be used during reassembly of the components. For most applications, a non-drying (or semi-drying) gasket sealer should be used.

Hose removal tips

Warning: *If the vehicle is equipped with air conditioning, do not disconnect any of the A/C hoses without first having the system depressurized by a dealer service department or a service station.*

Hose removal precautions closely parallel gasket removal precautions. Avoid scratching or gouging the surface that the hose mates against or the connection may leak. This is especially true for radiator hoses. Because of various chemical reactions, the rubber in hoses can bond itself to the metal spigot that the hose fits over. To remove a hose, first loosen the hose clamps that secure it to the spigot. Then, with slip-joint pliers, grab the hose at the clamp and rotate it around the spigot. Work it back and forth until it is completely free, then pull it off. Silicone or other lubricants will ease removal if they can be applied between the hose and the outside of the spigot. Apply the same lubricant to the inside of the hose and the outside of the spigot to simplify installation.

As a last resort (and if the hose is to be replaced with a new one anyway), the rubber can be slit with a knife and the hose peeled from the spigot. If this must be done, be careful that the metal connection is not damaged.

If a hose clamp is broken or damaged, do not reuse it. Wire-type clamps usually weaken with age, so it is a good idea to replace them with screw-type clamps whenever a hose is removed.

Tools

A selection of good tools is a basic requirement for anyone who plans to maintain and repair his or her own vehicle. For the owner who has few tools, the initial investment might seem high, but when compared to the spiraling costs of professional auto maintenance and repair, it is a wise one.

To help the owner decide which tools are

Dial caliper

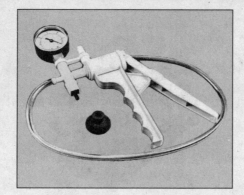

Hand-operated vacuum pump

Timing light

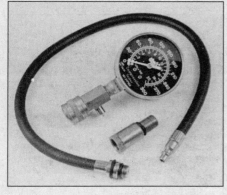

Compression gauge with spark plug hole adapter

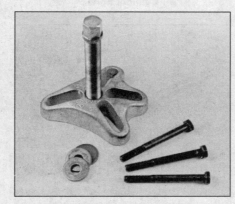

Damper/steering wheel puller

General purpose puller

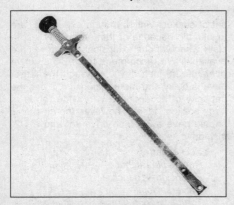

Hydraulic lifter removal tool

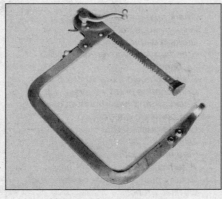

Valve spring compressor

Valve spring compressor

Ridge reamer

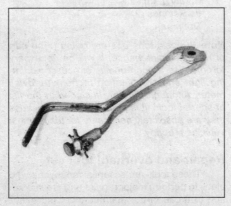

Piston ring groove cleaning tool

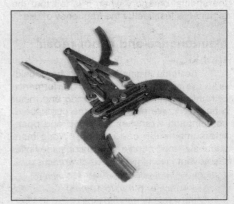

Ring removal/installation tool

Ring compressor

Cylinder hone

Brake hold-down spring tool

Torque angle gauge

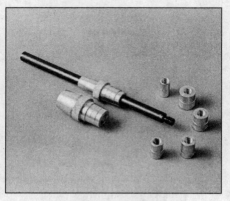

Clutch plate alignment tool

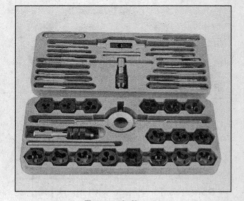

Tap and die set

needed to perform the tasks detailed in this manual, the following tool lists are offered: *Maintenance and minor repair, Repair/overhaul* and *Special*.

The newcomer to practical mechanics should start off with the *maintenance and minor repair* tool kit, which is adequate for the simpler jobs performed on a vehicle. Then, as confidence and experience grow, the owner can tackle more difficult tasks, buying additional tools as they are needed. Eventually the basic kit will be expanded into the *repair and overhaul* tool set. Over a period of time, the experienced do-it-yourselfer will assemble a tool set complete enough for most repair and overhaul procedures and will add tools from the special category when it is felt that the expense is justified by the frequency of use.

Maintenance and minor repair tool kit

The tools in this list should be considered the minimum required for performance of routine maintenance, servicing and minor repair work. We recommend the purchase of combination wrenches (box-end and open-end combined in one wrench). While more expensive than open end wrenches, they offer the advantages of both types of wrench.

Combination wrench set (1/4-inch to 1 inch or 6 mm to 19 mm)
Adjustable wrench, 8 inch
Spark plug wrench with rubber insert

Spark plug gap adjusting tool
Feeler gauge set
Brake bleeder wrench
Standard screwdriver (5/16-inch x 6 inch)
Phillips screwdriver (No. 2 x 6 inch)
Combination pliers - 6 inch
Hacksaw and assortment of blades
Tire pressure gauge
Grease gun
Oil can
Fine emery cloth
Wire brush
Battery post and cable cleaning tool
Oil filter wrench
Funnel (medium size)
Safety goggles
Jackstands (2)
Drain pan

Note: *If basic tune-ups are going to be part of routine maintenance, it will be necessary to purchase a good quality stroboscopic timing light and combination tachometer/dwell meter. Although they are included in the list of special tools, it is mentioned here because they are absolutely necessary for tuning most vehicles properly.*

Repair and overhaul tool set

These tools are essential for anyone who plans to perform major repairs and are in addition to those in the maintenance and minor repair tool kit. Included is a comprehensive set of sockets which, though expensive, are invaluable because of their versatility, especially when various extensions and drives are available. We recommend the 1/2-inch drive over the 3/8-inch drive. Although the larger drive is bulky and more expensive, it has the capacity of accepting a very wide range of large sockets. Ideally, however, the mechanic should have a 3/8-inch drive set and a 1/2-inch drive set.

Socket set(s)
Reversible ratchet
Extension - 10 inch
Universal joint
Torque wrench (same size drive as sockets)
Ball peen hammer - 8 ounce
Soft-face hammer (plastic/rubber)
Standard screwdriver (1/4-inch x 6 inch)
Standard screwdriver (stubby - 5/16-inch)
Phillips screwdriver (No. 3 x 8 inch)
Phillips screwdriver (stubby - No. 2)
Pliers - vise grip
Pliers - lineman's
Pliers - needle nose
Pliers - snap-ring (internal and external)
Cold chisel - 1/2-inch
Scribe
Scraper (made from flattened copper tubing)
Centerpunch
Pin punches (1/16, 1/8, 3/16-inch)
Steel rule/straightedge - 12 inch

*Allen wrench set (1/8 to 3/8-inch or
4 mm to 10 mm)*
A selection of files
Wire brush (large)
Jackstands (second set)
Jack (scissor or hydraulic type)

Note: *Another tool which is often useful is an electric drill with a chuck capacity of 3/8-inch and a set of good quality drill bits.*

Special tools

The tools in this list include those which are not used regularly, are expensive to buy, or which need to be used in accordance with their manufacturer's instructions. Unless these tools will be used frequently, it is not very economical to purchase many of them. A consideration would be to split the cost and use between yourself and a friend or friends. In addition, most of these tools can be obtained from a tool rental shop on a temporary basis.

This list primarily contains only those tools and instruments widely available to the public, and not those special tools produced by the vehicle manufacturer for distribution to dealer service departments. Occasionally, references to the manufacturer's special tools are included in the text of this manual. Generally, an alternative method of doing the job without the special tool is offered. However, sometimes there is no alternative to their use. Where this is the case, and the tool cannot be purchased or borrowed, the work should be turned over to the dealer service department or an automotive repair shop.

Valve spring compressor
Piston ring groove cleaning tool
Piston ring compressor
Piston ring installation tool
Cylinder compression gauge
Cylinder ridge reamer
Cylinder surfacing hone
Cylinder bore gauge
Micrometers and/or dial calipers
Hydraulic lifter removal tool
Balljoint separator
Universal-type puller
Impact screwdriver
Dial indicator set
*Stroboscopic timing light (inductive
pick-up)*
Hand operated vacuum/pressure pump
Tachometer/dwell meter
Universal electrical multimeter
Cable hoist
*Brake spring removal and installation
tools*
Floor jack

Buying tools

For the do-it-yourselfer who is just starting to get involved in vehicle maintenance and repair, there are a number of options available when purchasing tools. If maintenance and minor repair is the extent of the work to be done, the purchase of individual tools is satisfactory. If, on the other hand, extensive work is planned, it would be a good idea to purchase a modest tool set from one of the large retail chain stores. A set can usually be bought at a substantial savings over the individual tool prices, and they often come with a tool box. As additional tools are needed, add-on sets, individual tools and a larger tool box can be purchased to expand the tool selection. Building a tool set gradually allows the cost of the tools to be spread over a longer period of time and gives the mechanic the freedom to choose only those tools that will actually be used.

Tool stores will often be the only source of some of the special tools that are needed, but regardless of where tools are bought, try to avoid cheap ones, especially when buying screwdrivers and sockets, because they won't last very long. The expense involved in replacing cheap tools will eventually be greater than the initial cost of quality tools.

Care and maintenance of tools

Good tools are expensive, so it makes sense to treat them with respect. Keep them clean and in usable condition and store them properly when not in use. Always wipe off any dirt, grease or metal chips before putting them away. Never leave tools lying around in the work area. Upon completion of a job, always check closely under the hood for tools that may have been left there so they won't get lost during a test drive.

Some tools, such as screwdrivers, pliers, wrenches and sockets, can be hung on a panel mounted on the garage or workshop wall, while others should be kept in a tool box or tray. Measuring instruments, gauges, meters, etc. must be carefully stored where they cannot be damaged by weather or impact from other tools.

When tools are used with care and stored properly, they will last a very long time. Even with the best of care, though, tools will wear out if used frequently. When a tool is damaged or worn out, replace it. Subsequent jobs will be safer and more enjoyable if you do.

How to repair damaged threads

Sometimes, the internal threads of a nut or bolt hole can become stripped, usually from overtightening. Stripping threads is an all-too-common occurrence, especially when working with aluminum parts, because aluminum is so soft that it easily strips out.

Usually, external or internal threads are only partially stripped. After they've been cleaned up with a tap or die, they'll still work. Sometimes, however, threads are badly damaged. When this happens, you've got three choices:

1) *Drill and tap the hole to the next suitable oversize and install a larger diameter bolt, screw or stud.*
2) *Drill and tap the hole to accept a threaded plug, then drill and tap the plug to the original screw size. You can also buy a plug already threaded to the original size. Then you simply drill a hole to the specified size, then run the threaded plug into the hole with a bolt and jam nut. Once the plug is fully seated, remove the jam nut and bolt.*
3) *The third method uses a patented thread repair kit like Heli-Coil or Slimsert. These easy-to-use kits are designed to repair damaged threads in straight-through holes and blind holes. Both are available as kits which can handle a variety of sizes and thread patterns. Drill the hole, then tap it with the special included tap. Install the Heli-Coil and the hole is back to its original diameter and thread pitch.*

Regardless of which method you use, be sure to proceed calmly and carefully. A little impatience or carelessness during one of these relatively simple procedures can ruin your whole day's work and cost you a bundle if you wreck an expensive part.

Working facilities

Not to be overlooked when discussing tools is the workshop. If anything more than routine maintenance is to be carried out, some sort of suitable work area is essential.

It is understood, and appreciated, that many home mechanics do not have a good workshop or garage available, and end up removing an engine or doing major repairs outside. It is recommended, however, that the overhaul or repair be completed under the cover of a roof.

A clean, flat workbench or table of comfortable working height is an absolute necessity. The workbench should be equipped with a vise that has a jaw opening of at least four inches.

As mentioned previously, some clean, dry storage space is also required for tools, as well as the lubricants, fluids, cleaning solvents, etc. which soon become necessary.

Sometimes waste oil and fluids, drained from the engine or cooling system during normal maintenance or repairs, present a disposal problem. To avoid pouring them on the ground or into a sewage system, pour the used fluids into large containers, seal them with caps and take them to an authorized disposal site or recycling center. Plastic jugs, such as old antifreeze containers, are ideal for this purpose.

Always keep a supply of old newspapers and clean rags available. Old towels are excellent for mopping up spills. Many mechanics use rolls of paper towels for most work because they are readily available and disposable. To help keep the area under the vehicle clean, a large cardboard box can be cut open and flattened to protect the garage or shop floor.

Whenever working over a painted surface, such as when leaning over a fender to service something under the hood, always cover it with an old blanket or bedspread to protect the finish. Vinyl covered pads, made especially for this purpose, are available at auto parts stores.

Jacking and towing

Jacking

The jack supplied with the vehicle should only be used for raising the vehicle when changing a tire or placing jackstands under the frame. NEVER work under the vehicle or start the engine when the vehicle supported only by a jack.

The vehicle should be parked on level ground with the wheels blocked, the parking brake applied and the transmission in Park. If the vehicle is parked alongside the roadway, or in any other hazardous situation, turn on the emergency hazard flashers. If a tire is to be changed, loosen the lug nuts one-half turn before raising off the ground.

Place the jack under the vehicle in the indicated positions (see illustrations). Operate the jack with a slow, smooth motion until the wheel is raised off the ground. Remove the lug nuts, pull off the wheel, install the spare and thread the lug nuts back on with the beveled side facing in. Tighten the lug nuts snugly, lower the vehicle until some weight is on the wheel, tighten them completely in a criss-cross pattern and remove the jack. Note that some spare tires are designed for temporary use only - don't exceed the recommended speed, mileage or other restriction instructions accompanying the spare.

Towing

Equipment specifically designed for towing should be used and attached to the main structural members of the vehicle. Optional tow hooks may be attached to the frame at both ends of the vehicle; they are intended for emergency use only, such as rescuing a stranded vehicle. Do not use the tow hooks for highway towing. Stand clear when using tow straps or chains, as they could break and cause serious injury.

Safety is a major consideration when towing and all applicable state and local laws must be obeyed. In addition to a tow bar, a safety chain must be used for all towing.

These vehicles should not be towed with all four wheels on the ground; the rear wheels should be placed on a dolly. However, if it is absolutely necessary (due to the lack of proper equipment), the vehicle can be towed with the drive wheels on the ground, but do not exceed 35 mph or tow the vehicle farther than 50 miles. The best way to have the vehicle towed is on a flat-bed type carrier.

If any vehicle is to be towed with the front wheels on the ground and the rear wheels raised, the ignition key must be turned to the OFF position to unlock the steering column and a steering wheel clamping device designed for towing must be used or damage to the steering column lock may occur.

Front jacking point (under the frame rail)

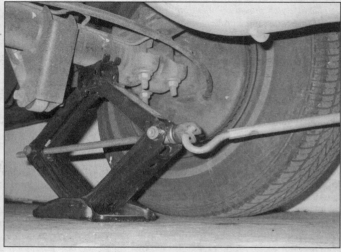

Rear jacking point (under the axle tube)

Booster battery (jump) starting

Observe these precautions when using a booster battery to start a vehicle:

a) *Before connecting the booster battery, make sure the ignition switch is in the Off position.*
b) *Turn off the lights, heater and other electrical loads.*
c) *Your eyes should be shielded. Safety goggles are a good idea.*
d) *Make sure the booster battery is the same voltage as the dead one in the vehicle.*
e) *The two vehicles MUST NOT TOUCH each other!*
f) *Make sure the transmission is IN Park.*
g) *If the booster battery is not a maintenance-free type, remove the vent caps and lay a cloth over the vent holes.*

Connect the red jumper cable to the positive (+) terminals of each battery **(see illustration)**.

Connect one end of the black jumper cable to the negative (-) terminal of the booster battery. The other end of this cable should be connected to a good ground on the vehicle to be started, such as a bolt or bracket on the body.

Start the engine using the booster battery, then, with the engine running at idle speed, disconnect the jumper cables in the reverse order of connection.

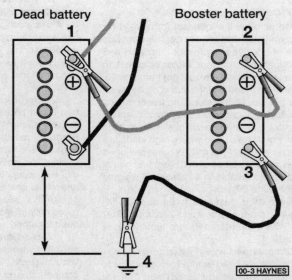

Make the booster battery cable connections in the numerical order shown (note that the negative cable of the booster battery is NOT attached to the negative terminal of the dead battery)

Automotive chemicals and lubricants

A number of automotive chemicals and lubricants are available for use during vehicle maintenance and repair. They include a wide variety of products ranging from cleaning solvents and degreasers to lubricants and protective sprays for rubber, plastic and vinyl.

Cleaners

Carburetor cleaner and choke cleaner is a strong solvent for gum, varnish and carbon. Most carburetor cleaners leave a dry-type lubricant film which will not harden or gum up. Because of this film it is not recommended for use on electrical components.

Brake system cleaner is used to remove brake dust, grease and brake fluid from the brake system, where clean surfaces are absolutely necessary. It leaves no residue and often eliminates brake squeal caused by contaminants.

Electrical cleaner removes oxidation, corrosion and carbon deposits from electrical contacts, restoring full current flow. It can also be used to clean spark plugs, carburetor jets, voltage regulators and other parts where an oil-free surface is desired.

Demoisturants remove water and moisture from electrical components such as alternators, voltage regulators, electrical connectors and fuse blocks. They are non-conductive and non-corrosive.

Degreasers are heavy-duty solvents used to remove grease from the outside of the engine and from chassis components. They can be sprayed or brushed on and, depending on the type, are rinsed off either with water or solvent.

Lubricants

Motor oil is the lubricant formulated for use in engines. It normally contains a wide variety of additives to prevent corrosion and reduce foaming and wear. Motor oil comes in various weights (viscosity ratings) from 0 to 50. The recommended weight of the oil depends on the season, temperature and the demands on the engine. Light oil is used in cold climates and under light load conditions. Heavy oil is used in hot climates and where high loads are encountered. Multi-viscosity oils are designed to have characteristics of both light and heavy oils and are available in a number of weights from 5W-20 to 20W-50.

Gear oil is designed to be used in differentials, manual transmissions and other areas where high-temperature lubrication is required.

Chassis and wheel bearing grease is a heavy grease used where increased loads and friction are encountered, such as for wheel bearings, balljoints, tie-rod ends and universal joints.

High-temperature wheel bearing grease is designed to withstand the extreme temperatures encountered by wheel bearings in disc brake equipped vehicles. It usually contains molybdenum disulfide (moly), which is a dry-type lubricant.

White grease is a heavy grease for metal-to-metal applications where water is a problem. White grease stays soft under both low and high temperatures (usually from -100 to +190-degrees F), and will not wash off or dilute in the presence of water.

Assembly lube is a special extreme pressure lubricant, usually containing moly, used to lubricate high-load parts (such as main and rod bearings and cam lobes) for initial start-up of a new engine. The assembly lube lubricates the parts without being squeezed out or washed away until the engine oiling system begins to function.

Silicone lubricants are used to protect rubber, plastic, vinyl and nylon parts.

Graphite lubricants are used where oils cannot be used due to contamination problems, such as in locks. The dry graphite will lubricate metal parts while remaining uncontaminated by dirt, water, oil or acids. It is electrically conductive and will not foul electrical contacts in locks such as the ignition switch.

Moly penetrants loosen and lubricate frozen, rusted and corroded fasteners and prevent future rusting or freezing.

Heat-sink grease is a special electrically non-conductive grease that is used for mounting electronic ignition modules where it is essential that heat is transferred away from the module.

Sealants

RTV sealant is one of the most widely used gasket compounds. Made from silicone, RTV is air curing, it seals, bonds, waterproofs, fills surface irregularities, remains flexible, doesn't shrink, is relatively easy to remove, and is used as a supplementary sealer with almost all low and medium temperature gaskets.

Anaerobic sealant is much like RTV in that it can be used either to seal gaskets or to form gaskets by itself. It remains flexible, is solvent resistant and fills surface imperfections. The difference between an anaerobic sealant and an RTV-type sealant is in the curing. RTV cures when exposed to air, while an anaerobic sealant cures only in the absence of air. This means that an anaerobic sealant cures only after the assembly of parts, sealing them together.

Thread and pipe sealant is used for sealing hydraulic and pneumatic fittings and vacuum lines. It is usually made from a Teflon compound, and comes in a spray, a paint-on liquid and as a wrap-around tape.

Chemicals

Anti-seize compound prevents seizing, galling, cold welding, rust and corrosion in fasteners. High-temperature ant-seize, usually made with copper and graphite lubricants, is used for exhaust system and exhaust manifold bolts.

Anaerobic locking compounds are used to keep fasteners from vibrating or working loose and cure only after installation, in the absence of air. Medium strength locking compound is used for small nuts, bolts and screws that may be removed later. High-strength locking compound is for large nuts, bolts and studs which aren't removed on a regular basis.

Oil additives range from viscosity index improvers to chemical treatments that claim to reduce internal engine friction. It should be noted that most oil manufacturers caution against using additives with their oils.

Gas additives perform several functions, depending on their chemical makeup. They usually contain solvents that help dissolve gum and varnish that build up on carburetor, fuel injection and intake parts. They also serve to break down carbon deposits that form on the inside surfaces of the combustion chambers. Some additives contain upper cylinder lubricants for valves and piston rings, and others contain chemicals to remove condensation from the gas tank.

Miscellaneous

Brake fluid is specially formulated hydraulic fluid that can withstand the heat and pressure encountered in brake systems. Care must be taken so this fluid does not come in contact with painted surfaces or plastics. An opened container should always be resealed to prevent contamination by water or dirt.

Weatherstrip adhesive is used to bond weatherstripping around doors, windows and trunk lids. It is sometimes used to attach trim pieces.

Undercoating is a petroleum-based, tar-like substance that is designed to protect metal surfaces on the underside of the vehicle from corrosion. It also acts as a sound-deadening agent by insulating the bottom of the vehicle.

Waxes and polishes are used to help protect painted and plated surfaces from the weather. Different types of paint may require the use of different types of wax and polish. Some polishes utilize a chemical or abrasive cleaner to help remove the top layer of oxidized (dull) paint on older vehicles. In recent years many non-wax polishes that contain a wide variety of chemicals such as polymers and silicones have been introduced. These non-wax polishes are usually easier to apply and last longer than conventional waxes and polishes.

Conversion factors

Length (distance)
Inches (in)	X	25.4	= Millimeters (mm)	X 0.0394	= Inches (in)
Feet (ft)	X	0.305	= Meters (m)	X 3.281	= Feet (ft)
Miles	X	1.609	= Kilometers (km)	X 0.621	= Miles

Volume (capacity)
Cubic inches (cu in; in³)	X	16.387	= Cubic centimeters (cc; cm³)	X 0.061	= Cubic inches (cu in; in³)
Imperial pints (Imp pt)	X	0.568	= Liters (l)	X 1.76	= Imperial pints (Imp pt)
Imperial quarts (Imp qt)	X	1.137	= Liters (l)	X 0.88	= Imperial quarts (Imp qt)
Imperial quarts (Imp qt)	X	1.201	= US quarts (US qt)	X 0.833	= Imperial quarts (Imp qt)
US quarts (US qt)	X	0.946	= Liters (l)	X 1.057	= US quarts (US qt)
Imperial gallons (Imp gal)	X	4.546	= Liters (l)	X 0.22	= Imperial gallons (Imp gal)
Imperial gallons (Imp gal)	X	1.201	= US gallons (US gal)	X 0.833	= Imperial gallons (Imp gal)
US gallons (US gal)	X	3.785	= Liters (l)	X 0.264	= US gallons (US gal)

Mass (weight)
Ounces (oz)	X	28.35	= Grams (g)	X 0.035	= Ounces (oz)
Pounds (lb)	X	0.454	= Kilograms (kg)	X 2.205	= Pounds (lb)

Force
Ounces-force (ozf; oz)	X	0.278	= Newtons (N)	X 3.6	= Ounces-force (ozf; oz)
Pounds-force (lbf; lb)	X	4.448	= Newtons (N)	X 0.225	= Pounds-force (lbf; lb)
Newtons (N)	X	0.1	= Kilograms-force (kgf; kg)	X 9.81	= Newtons (N)

Pressure
Pounds-force per square inch (psi; lbf/in²; lb/in²)	X	0.070	= Kilograms-force per square centimeter (kgf/cm²; kg/cm²)	X 14.223	= Pounds-force per square inch (psi; lbf/in²; lb/in²)
Pounds-force per square inch (psi; lbf/in²; lb/in²)	X	0.068	= Atmospheres (atm)	X 14.696	= Pounds-force per square inch (psi; lbf/in²; lb/in²)
Pounds-force per square inch (psi; lbf/in²; lb/in²)	X	0.069	= Bars	X 14.5	= Pounds-force per square inch (psi; lbf/in²; lb/in²)
Pounds-force per square inch (psi; lbf/in²; lb/in²)	X	6.895	= Kilopascals (kPa)	X 0.145	= Pounds-force per square inch (psi; lbf/in²; lb/in²)
Kilopascals (kPa)	X	0.01	= Kilograms-force per square centimeter (kgf/cm²; kg/cm²)	X 98.1	= Kilopascals (kPa)

Torque (moment of force)
Pounds-force inches (lbf in; lb in)	X	1.152	= Kilograms-force centimeter (kgf cm; kg cm)	X 0.868	= Pounds-force inches (lbf in; lb in)
Pounds-force inches (lbf in; lb in)	X	0.113	= Newton meters (Nm)	X 8.85	= Pounds-force inches (lbf in; lb in)
Pounds-force inches (lbf in; lb in)	X	0.083	= Pounds-force feet (lbf ft; lb ft)	X 12	= Pounds-force inches (lbf in; lb in)
Pounds-force feet (lbf ft; lb ft)	X	0.138	= Kilograms-force meters (kgf m; kg m)	X 7.233	= Pounds-force feet (lbf ft; lb ft)
Pounds-force feet (lbf ft; lb ft)	X	1.356	= Newton meters (Nm)	X 0.738	= Pounds-force feet (lbf ft; lb ft)
Newton meters (Nm)	X	0.102	= Kilograms-force meters (kgf m; kg m)	X 9.804	= Newton meters (Nm)

Vacuum
Inches mercury (in. Hg)	X	3.377	= Kilopascals (kPa)	X 0.2961	= Inches mercury
Inches mercury (in. Hg)	X	25.4	= Millimeters mercury (mm Hg)	X 0.0394	= Inches mercury

Power
Horsepower (hp)	X	745.7	= Watts (W)	X 0.0013	= Horsepower (hp)

Velocity (speed)
Miles per hour (miles/hr; mph)	X	1.609	= Kilometers per hour (km/hr; kph)	X 0.621	= Miles per hour (miles/hr; mph)

Fuel consumption*
Miles per gallon, Imperial (mpg)	X	0.354	= Kilometers per liter (km/l)	X 2.825	= Miles per gallon, Imperial (mpg)
Miles per gallon, US (mpg)	X	0.425	= Kilometers per liter (km/l)	X 2.352	= Miles per gallon, US (mpg)

Temperature
Degrees Fahrenheit = (°C x 1.8) + 32

Degrees Celsius (Degrees Centigrade; °C) = (°F - 32) x 0.56

*It is common practice to convert from miles per gallon (mpg) to liters/100 kilometers (l/100km), where mpg (Imperial) x l/100 km = 282 and mpg (US) x l/100 km = 235

DECIMALS to MILLIMETERS

Decimal	mm	Decimal	mm
0.001	0.0254	0.500	12.7000
0.002	0.0508	0.510	12.9540
0.003	0.0762	0.520	13.2080
0.004	0.1016	0.530	13.4620
0.005	0.1270	0.540	13.7160
0.006	0.1524	0.550	13.9700
0.007	0.1778	0.560	14.2240
0.008	0.2032	0.570	14.4780
0.009	0.2286	0.580	14.7320
		0.590	14.9860
0.010	0.2540		
0.020	0.5080		
0.030	0.7620		
0.040	1.0160	0.600	15.2400
0.050	1.2700	0.610	15.4940
0.060	1.5240	0.620	15.7480
0.070	1.7780	0.630	16.0020
0.080	2.0320	0.640	16.2560
0.090	2.2860	0.650	16.5100
		0.660	16.7640
0.100	2.5400	0.670	17.0180
0.110	2.7940	0.680	17.2720
0.120	3.0480	0.690	17.5260
0.130	3.3020		
0.140	3.5560		
0.150	3.8100		
0.160	4.0640	0.700	17.7800
0.170	4.3180	0.710	18.0340
0.180	4.5720	0.720	18.2880
0.190	4.8260	0.730	18.5420
		0.740	18.7960
0.200	5.0800	0.750	19.0500
0.210	5.3340	0.760	19.3040
0.220	5.5880	0.770	19.5580
0.230	5.8420	0.780	19.8120
0.240	6.0960	0.790	20.0660
0.250	6.3500		
0.260	6.6040		
0.270	6.8580	0.800	20.3200
0.280	7.1120	0.810	20.5740
0.290	7.3660	0.820	21.8280
		0.830	21.0820
0.300	7.6200	0.840	21.3360
0.310	7.8740	0.850	21.5900
0.320	8.1280	0.860	21.8440
0.330	8.3820	0.870	22.0980
0.340	8.6360	0.880	22.3520
0.350	8.8900	0.890	22.6060
0.360	9.1440		
0.370	9.3980		
0.380	9.6520		
0.390	9.9060		
		0.900	22.8600
0.400	10.1600	0.910	23.1140
0.410	10.4140	0.920	23.3680
0.420	10.6680	0.930	23.6220
0.430	10.9220	0.940	23.8760
0.440	11.1760	0.950	24.1300
0.450	11.4300	0.960	24.3840
0.460	11.6840	0.970	24.6380
0.470	11.9380	0.980	24.8920
0.480	12.1920	0.990	25.1460
0.490	12.4460	1.000	25.4000

FRACTIONS to DECIMALS to MILLIMETERS

Fraction	Decimal	mm	Fraction	Decimal	mm
1/64	0.0156	0.3969	33/64	0.5156	13.0969
1/32	0.0312	0.7938	17/32	0.5312	13.4938
3/64	0.0469	1.1906	35/64	0.5469	13.8906
1/16	0.0625	1.5875	9/16	0.5625	14.2875
5/64	0.0781	1.9844	37/64	0.5781	14.6844
3/32	0.0938	2.3812	19/32	0.5938	15.0812
7/64	0.1094	2.7781	39/64	0.6094	15.4781
1/8	0.1250	3.1750	5/8	0.6250	15.8750
9/64	0.1406	3.5719	41/64	0.6406	16.2719
5/32	0.1562	3.9688	21/32	0.6562	16.6688
11/64	0.1719	4.3656	43/64	0.6719	17.0656
3/16	0.1875	4.7625	11/16	0.6875	17.4625
13/64	0.2031	5.1594	45/64	0.7031	17.8594
7/32	0.2188	5.5562	23/32	0.7188	18.2562
15/64	0.2344	5.9531	47/64	0.7344	18.6531
1/4	0.2500	6.3500	3/4	0.7500	19.0500
17/64	0.2656	6.7469	49/64	0.7656	19.4469
9/32	0.2812	7.1438	25/32	0.7812	19.8438
19/64	0.2969	7.5406	51/64	0.7969	20.2406
5/16	0.3125	7.9375	13/16	0.8125	20.6375
21/64	0.3281	8.3344	53/64	0.8281	21.0344
11/32	0.3438	8.7312	27/32	0.8438	21.4312
23/64	0.3594	9.1281	55/64	0.8594	21.8281
3/8	0.3750	9.5250	7/8	0.8750	22.2250
25/64	0.3906	9.9219	57/64	0.8906	22.6219
13/32	0.4062	10.3188	29/32	0.9062	23.0188
27/64	0.4219	10.7156	59/64	0.9219	23.4156
7/16	0.4375	11.1125	15/16	0.9375	23.8125
29/64	0.4531	11.5094	61/64	0.9531	24.2094
15/32	0.4688	11.9062	31/32	0.9688	24.6062
31/64	0.4844	12.3031	63/64	0.9844	25.0031
1/2	0.5000	12.7000	1	1.0000	25.4000

Safety first!

Regardless of how enthusiastic you may be about getting on with the job at hand, take the time to ensure that your safety is not jeopardized. A moment's lack of attention can result in an accident, as can failure to observe certain simple safety precautions. The possibility of an accident will always exist, and the following points should not be considered a comprehensive list of all dangers. Rather, they are intended to make you aware of the risks and to encourage a safety conscious approach to all work you carry out on your vehicle.

Essential DOs and DON'Ts

DON'T rely on a jack when working under the vehicle. Always use approved jackstands to support the weight of the vehicle and place them under the recommended lift or support points.

DON'T attempt to loosen extremely tight fasteners (i.e. wheel lug nuts) while the vehicle is on a jack - it may fall.

DON'T start the engine without first making sure that the transmission is in Neutral (or Park where applicable) and the parking brake is set.

DON'T remove the radiator cap from a hot cooling system - let it cool or cover it with a cloth and release the pressure gradually.

DON'T attempt to drain the engine oil until you are sure it has cooled to the point that it will not burn you.

DON'T touch any part of the engine or exhaust system until it has cooled sufficiently to avoid burns.

DON'T siphon toxic liquids such as gasoline, antifreeze and brake fluid by mouth, or allow them to remain on your skin.

DON'T inhale brake lining dust - it is potentially hazardous (see *Asbestos* below).

DON'T allow spilled oil or grease to remain on the floor - wipe it up before someone slips on it.

DON'T use loose fitting wrenches or other tools which may slip and cause injury.

DON'T push on wrenches when loosening or tightening nuts or bolts. Always try to pull the wrench toward you. If the situation calls for pushing the wrench away, push with an open hand to avoid scraped knuckles if the wrench should slip.

DON'T attempt to lift a heavy component alone - get someone to help you.

DON'T rush or take unsafe shortcuts to finish a job.

DON'T allow children or animals in or around the vehicle while you are working on it.

DO wear eye protection when using power tools such as a drill, sander, bench grinder, etc. and when working under a vehicle.

DO keep loose clothing and long hair well out of the way of moving parts.

DO make sure that any hoist used has a safe working load rating adequate for the job.

DO get someone to check on you periodically when working alone on a vehicle.

DO carry out work in a logical sequence and make sure that everything is correctly assembled and tightened.

DO keep chemicals and fluids tightly capped and out of the reach of children and pets.

DO remember that your vehicle's safety affects that of yourself and others. If in doubt on any point, get professional advice.

Asbestos

Certain friction, insulating, sealing, and other products - such as brake linings, brake bands, clutch linings, torque converters, gaskets, etc. - may contain asbestos. Extreme care must be taken to avoid inhalation of dust from such products, since it is hazardous to health. If in doubt, assume that they do contain asbestos.

Fire

Remember at all times that gasoline is highly flammable. Never smoke or have any kind of open flame around when working on a vehicle. But the risk does not end there. A spark caused by an electrical short circuit, by two metal surfaces contacting each other, or even by static electricity built up in your body under certain conditions, can ignite gasoline vapors, which in a confined space are highly explosive. Do not, under any circumstances, use gasoline for cleaning parts. Use an approved safety solvent.

Always disconnect the battery ground (-) cable at the battery before working on any part of the fuel system or electrical system. Never risk spilling fuel on a hot engine or exhaust component. It is strongly recommended that a fire extinguisher suitable for use on fuel and electrical fires be kept handy in the garage or workshop at all times. Never try to extinguish a fuel or electrical fire with water.

Fumes

Certain fumes are highly toxic and can quickly cause unconsciousness and even death if inhaled to any extent. Gasoline vapor falls into this category, as do the vapors from some cleaning solvents. Any draining or pouring of such volatile fluids should be done in a well ventilated area.

When using cleaning fluids and solvents, read the instructions on the container carefully. Never use materials from unmarked containers.

Never run the engine in an enclosed space, such as a garage. Exhaust fumes contain carbon monoxide, which is extremely poisonous. If you need to run the engine, always do so in the open air, or at least have the rear of the vehicle outside the work area.

If you are fortunate enough to have the use of an inspection pit, never drain or pour gasoline and never run the engine while the vehicle is over the pit. The fumes, being heavier than air, will concentrate in the pit with possibly lethal results.

The battery

Never create a spark or allow a bare light bulb near a battery. They normally give off a certain amount of hydrogen gas, which is highly explosive.

Always disconnect the battery ground (-) cable at the battery before working on the fuel or electrical systems.

If possible, loosen the filler caps or cover when charging the battery from an external source (this does not apply to sealed or maintenance-free batteries). Do not charge at an excessive rate or the battery may burst.

Take care when adding water to a non maintenance-free battery and when carrying a battery. The electrolyte, even when diluted, is very corrosive and should not be allowed to contact clothing or skin.

Always wear eye protection when cleaning the battery to prevent the caustic deposits from entering your eyes.

Household current

When using an electric power tool, inspection light, etc., which operates on household current, always make sure that the tool is correctly connected to its plug and that, where necessary, it is properly grounded. Do not use such items in damp conditions and, again, do not create a spark or apply excessive heat in the vicinity of fuel or fuel vapor.

Secondary ignition system voltage

A severe electric shock can result from touching certain parts of the ignition system (such as the spark plug wires) when the engine is running or being cranked, particularly if components are damp or the insulation is defective. In the case of an electronic ignition system, the secondary system voltage is much higher and could prove fatal.

Troubleshooting

Contents

This section provides an easy reference guide to the more common problems which may occur during the operation of your vehicle. These problems and possible causes are grouped under various components or systems; i.e. Engine, Cooling System, etc., and also refer to the Chapter and/or Section which deals with the problem.

Remember that successful troubleshooting is not a mysterious black art practiced only by professional mechanics. It's simply the result of a bit of knowledge combined with an intelligent, systematic approach to the problem. Always work by a process of elimination, starting with the simplest solution and working through to the most complex - and never overlook the obvious. Anyone can forget to fill the gas tank or leave the lights on overnight, so don't assume that you are above such oversights.

Finally, always get clear in your mind why a problem has occurred and take steps to ensure that it doesn't happen again. If the electrical system fails because of a poor connection, check all other connections in the system to make sure that they don't fail as well. If a particular fuse continues to blow, find out why - don't just go on replacing fuses. Remember, failure of a small component can often be indicative of potential failure or incorrect functioning of a more important component or system.

Engine

1 Engine will not rotate when attempting to start

1   Battery terminal connections loose or corroded. Check the cable terminals at the battery. Tighten the cable or remove corrosion as necessary.
2   Battery discharged or faulty. If the cable connections are clean and tight on the battery posts, turn the key to the On position and switch on the headlights and/or windshield wipers. If they fail to function, the battery is discharged.
3   Automatic transmission not completely engaged in Park or Neutral or clutch pedal not completely depressed.
4   Broken, loose or disconnected wiring in the starting circuit. Inspect all wiring and connectors at the battery, starter solenoid and ignition switch.
5   Starter motor pinion jammed in flywheel ring gear. Remove starter and inspect pinion and flywheel at earliest convenience (Chapter 5).
6   Starter solenoid faulty (Chapter 5).
7   Starter motor faulty (Chapter 5).
8   Ignition switch faulty (Chapter 12).

2 Engine rotates but will not start

1   Fuel tank empty, fuel filter plugged or fuel line restricted.
2   Fault in the fuel injection system (Chapter 4).
3   Battery discharged (engine rotates slowly). Check the operation of electrical components as described in the previous Section.
4   Battery terminal connections loose or corroded (see previous Section).
5   Fuel pump faulty (Chapter 4).
6   Excessive moisture on, or damage to, ignition components (see Chapter 5).
7   Worn, faulty or incorrectly gapped spark plugs (Chapter 1).
8   Broken, loose or disconnected wiring in the starting circuit (see previous Section).
9   Broken, loose or disconnected wires at the ignition coil (Chapter 5).
10   Contaminated fuel.

3 Starter motor operates without rotating engine

1   Starter pinion sticking. Remove the starter (Chapter 5) and inspect.
2   Starter pinion or flywheel teeth worn or broken. Remove the flywheel/driveplate access cover and inspect.

4 Engine hard to start when cold

1   Battery discharged or low. Check as described in Section 1.

2   Fault in the fuel or electrical systems (Chapters 4 and 5).

5 Engine hard to start when hot

1   Air filter clogged (Chapter 1).
2   Fault in the fuel or electrical systems (Chapters 4 and 5).
3   Fuel not reaching the injectors (see Chapter 4).
4   Low cylinder compression (Chapter 2).

6 Starter motor noisy or excessively rough in engagement

1   Pinion or flywheel gear teeth worn or broken. Remove the cover at the rear of the engine (if equipped) and inspect.
2   Starter motor mounting bolts loose or missing.

7 Engine starts but stops immediately

1   Loose or faulty electrical connections at distributor, coil or alternator.
2   Fault in the fuel or electrical systems (Chapters 4 and 5).
3   Vacuum leak at the gasket surfaces of the intake manifold or throttle body. Make sure all mounting bolts/nuts are tightened securely and all vacuum hoses connected to the manifold are positioned properly and in good condition.
4   Restricted intake or exhaust systems (Chapter 4)
5   Contaminated fuel.

8 Engine lopes while idling or idles erratically

1   Vacuum leakage. Check the mounting bolts/nuts at the throttle body and intake manifold for tightness. Make sure all vacuum hoses are connected and in good condition. Use a stethoscope or a length of fuel hose held against your ear to listen for vacuum leaks while the engine is running. A hissing sound will be heard. A soapy water solution will also detect leaks.
2   Fault in the fuel or electrical systems (Chapters 4 and 5).
3   Plugged PCV valve or hose (see Chapters 1 and 6).
4   Air filter clogged (Chapter 1).
5   Fuel pump not delivering sufficient fuel to the fuel injectors (see Chapter 4).
6   Leaking head gasket. Perform a compression check (Chapter 2).
7   Camshaft lobes worn (Chapter 2).

9 Engine misses at idle speed

1   Spark plugs worn, fouled or not gapped

properly (Chapter 1).
2   Fault in the fuel or electrical systems (Chapters 4 and 5).
3   Faulty spark plug wires (Chapter 1).
4   Vacuum leaks at intake or hose connections. Check as described in Section 14.
5   Uneven or low cylinder compression. Check compression as described in Chapter 2.

10 Engine misses throughout driving speed range

1   Fuel filter clogged and/or impurities in the fuel system (Chapter 1).
2   Faulty or incorrectly gapped spark plugs (Chapter 1).
3   Fault in the fuel or electrical systems (Chapters 4 and 5).
4   Defective spark plug wires (Chapter 1).
5   Faulty emissions system components (Chapter 6).
6   Low or uneven cylinder compression pressures. Remove the spark plugs and test the compression with a gauge (Chapter 2).
7   Weak or faulty ignition system (Chapter 5).
8   Vacuum leaks at the throttle body, intake manifold or vacuum hoses (see Section 14).

11 Engine stalls

1   Idle speed incorrect. Refer to the VECI label.
2   Fuel filter clogged and/or water and impurities in the fuel system (Chapter 1).
3   Fault in the fuel system or sensors (Chapters 4 and 6).
4   Faulty emissions system components (Chapter 6).
5   Faulty or incorrectly gapped spark plugs (Chapter 1). Also check the spark plug wires (Chapter 1).
6   Vacuum leak at the throttle body, intake manifold or vacuum hoses. Check as described in Section 14.

12 Engine lacks power

1   Fault in the fuel or electrical systems (Chapters 4 and 5).
2   Faulty or incorrectly gapped spark plugs (Chapter 1).
3   Faulty coil (Chapter 5).
4   Brakes binding (Chapter 1).
5   Automatic transmission fluid level incorrect (Chapter 1).
6   Clutch slipping (Chapter 8).
7   Fuel filter clogged and/or impurities in the fuel system (Chapter 1).
8   Emissions control system not functioning properly (Chapter 6).
9   Use of substandard fuel. Fill the tank with the proper fuel.
10   Low or uneven cylinder compression pressures. Test with a compression tester,

which will detect leaking valves and/or a blown head gasket (Chapter 2).

11   Restriction in the intake or exhaust system (Chapter 4).

13   Engine backfires

1   Emissions system not functioning properly (Chapter 6).

2   Fault in the fuel or electrical systems (Chapters 4 and 5).

3   Faulty secondary ignition system (cracked spark plug insulator or faulty plug wires) (Chapters 1 and 5).

4   Vacuum leak at the throttle body, intake manifold or vacuum hoses. Check as described in Section 14.

5   Valves sticking (Chapter 2).

6   Crossed plug wires (Chapter 1).

14   Pinging or knocking engine sounds during acceleration or uphill

1   Incorrect grade of fuel. Fill the tank with fuel of the proper octane rating.

2   Fault in the fuel or electrical systems (Chapters 4 and 5).

3   Improper spark plugs. Also check the plugs and wires for damage (Chapter 1).

4   Faulty emissions system (Chapter 6).

5   Vacuum leak. Check as described in Section 14.

15   Engine continues to run after switching off

1   Idle speed too high. Refer to (Chapter 4).

2   Fault in the fuel or electrical systems (Chapters 4 and 5).

3   Excessive engine operating temperature. Probable causes of this are a low coolant level (see Chapter 1), malfunctioning thermostat, clogged radiator or faulty water pump (see Chapter 3).

Engine electrical system

16   Battery will not hold a charge

1   Alternator drivebelt defective or not adjusted properly (Chapter 1).

2   Electrolyte level low or battery discharged (Chapter 1).

3   Battery terminals loose or corroded (Chapter 1).

4   Alternator not charging properly (Chapter 5).

5   Loose, broken or faulty wiring in the charging circuit (Chapter 5).

6   Short in the vehicle wiring causing a continuous drain on the battery (refer to Chapter 12 and the Wiring Diagrams).

7   Battery defective internally.

17   Ignition light fails to go out

1   Fault in the alternator or charging circuit (Chapter 5).

2   Alternator drivebelt defective or not properly adjusted (Chapter 1).

18   Ignition light fails to come on when key is turned on

1   Instrument cluster warning light bulb defective (Chapter 12).

2   Alternator faulty (Chapter 5).

3   Fault in the instrument cluster printed circuit, dashboard wiring or bulb holder (Chapter 12).

Fuel system

19   Excessive fuel consumption

1   Dirty or clogged air filter element (Chapter 1).

2   Emissions system not functioning properly (Chapter 6).

3   Fault in the fuel or electrical systems (Chapters 4 and 5).

4   Low tire pressure or incorrect tire size (Chapter 1).

5   Restricted exhaust system (Chapter 4).

20   Fuel leakage and/or fuel odor

1   Leak in a fuel feed line (Chapter 4).

2   Tank overfilled.

3   Evaporative emissions system canister clogged (Chapter 6).

4   Vapor leaks from system lines (Chapter 4).

Cooling system

21   Overheating

1   Insufficient coolant in the system (Chapter 1).

2   Water pump drivebelt defective or not adjusted properly (Chapter 1).

3   Radiator core blocked or radiator grille dirty and restricted (see Chapter 3).

4   Thermostat faulty (Chapter 3).

5   Fan blades broken or cracked (Chapter 3).

6   Cooling system pressure cap not maintaining proper pressure (Chapter 3).

22   Overcooling

1   Thermostat faulty (Chapter 3).

2   Inaccurate temperature gauge (Chapter 12).

23   External coolant leakage

1   Deteriorated or damaged hoses or loose clamps. Replace hoses and/or tighten the clamps at the hose connections (Chapter 1).

2   Water pump seals defective. If this is the case, water will drip from the weep hole in the water pump body (Chapter 3).

3   Leakage from the radiator core or side tank(s). This will require the radiator to be professionally repaired (see Chapter 3 for removal procedures).

4   Engine drain plug(s) leaking (Chapter 1) or water jacket core plugs leaking (see Chapter 2).

24   Internal coolant leakage

Note: *Internal coolant leaks can usually be detected by examining the oil. Check the dipstick and inside of the valve cover for water deposits and an oil consistency like that of a milkshake.*

1   Leaking cylinder head gasket. Have the cooling system pressure tested.

2   Cracked cylinder bore or cylinder head. Dismantle the engine and inspect (Chapter 2).

3   Leaking intake manifold gasket.

25   Coolant loss

1   Too much coolant in the system (Chapter 1).

2   Coolant boiling away due to overheating (see Section 15).

3   External or internal leakage (see Sections 23 and 24).

4   Faulty pressure cap (Chapter 3).

26   Poor coolant circulation

1   Inoperative water pump. A quick test is to pinch the top radiator hose closed with your hand while the engine is idling, then let it loose. You should feel the surge of coolant if the pump is working properly (see Chapter 1).

2   Restriction in the cooling system. Drain, flush and refill the system (Chapter 1). If necessary, remove the radiator (Chapter 3) and have it reverse flushed.

3   Water pump drivebelt defective or not adjusted properly (Chapter 1).

4   Thermostat sticking (Chapter 3).

5   Drivebelt incorrectly routed, causing the pump to turn backwards (Chapter 1).

Automatic transmission

Note: *Due to the complexity of the automatic transmission, it's difficult for the home mechanic to properly diagnose and service this component. For problems other than the* *following, the vehicle should be taken to a dealer service department or a transmission shop.*

27 General shift mechanism problems

1   Chapter 7 deals with checking and adjusting the shift linkage on automatic transmissions. Common problems which may be attributed to poorly adjusted linkage are:

a) *Engine starting in gears other than Park or Neutral.*
b) *Indicator on shifter pointing to a gear other than the one actually being selected.*
c) *Vehicle moves when in Park.*

2   Refer to Chapter 7 to adjust the linkage.

28 Transmission will not downshift with accelerator pedal pressed to the floor

Throttle valve (TV) cable misadjusted (if equipped).

29 Transmission slips, shifts rough, is noisy or has no drive in forward or reverse gears

1   There are many probable causes for the above problems, but the home mechanic should be concerned with only one possibility - fluid level.

2   Before taking the vehicle to a repair shop, check the level and condition of the fluid as described in Chapter 1. Correct fluid level as necessary or change the fluid and filter if needed. If the problem persists, have a professional diagnose the probable cause.

30 Fluid leakage

1   Automatic transmission fluid is a deep red color. Fluid leaks should not be confused with engine oil, which can easily be blown by air flow to the transmission.

2   To pinpoint a leak, first remove all built-up dirt and grime from around the transmission. Degreasing agents and/or steam cleaning will achieve this. With the underside clean, drive the vehicle at low speeds so air flow will not blow the leak far from its source. Raise the vehicle and determine where the leak is coming from. Common areas of leakage are:

a) *Pan: Tighten the mounting bolts and/or replace the pan gasket as necessary (see Chapter 7).*
b) *Filler pipe: Replace the rubber seal where the pipe enters the transmission case.*
c) *Transmission oil lines: Tighten the connectors where the lines enter the transmission case and/or replace the lines.*

d) *Vent pipe: Transmission overfilled and/ or water in fluid (see checking procedures, Chapter 1).*
e) *Speedometer connector: Replace the O-ring where the speedometer sensor enters the transmission case (Chapter 7).*

Driveshaft

31 Oil leak at seal end of driveshaft

Defective transmission or transfer case oil seal. See Chapter 7 for replacement procedures. While this is done, check the splined yoke for burrs or a rough condition which may be damaging the seal. Burrs can be removed with crocus cloth or a fine whetstone.

32 Knock or clunk when the transmission is under initial load (just after transmission is put into gear)

1   Loose or disconnected rear suspension components. Check all mounting bolts, nuts and bushings (see Chapter 10).
2   Loose driveshaft bolts. Inspect all bolts and nuts and tighten them to the specified torque.
3   Worn or damaged universal joint bearings. Check for wear (see Chapter 8).

33 Metallic grinding sound consistent with vehicle speed.

Pronounced wear in the universal joint bearings. Check as described in Chapter 8.

34 Vibration

Note: *Before assuming that the driveshaft is at fault, make sure the tires are perfectly balanced and perform the following test.*

1   Install a tachometer inside the vehicle to monitor engine speed as the vehicle is driven. Drive the vehicle and note the engine speed at which the vibration (roughness) is most pronounced. Now shift the transmission to a different gear and bring the engine speed to the same point.
2   If the vibration occurs at the same engine speed (rpm) regardless of which gear the transmission is in, the driveshaft is NOT at fault since the driveshaft speed varies.
3   If the vibration decreases or is eliminated when the transmission is in a different gear at the same engine speed, refer to the following probable causes.
4   Bent or dented driveshaft. Inspect and replace as necessary (see Chapter 8).
5   Undercoating or built-up dirt, etc. on the driveshaft. Clean the shaft thoroughly and recheck.

6   Worn universal joint bearings. Remove and inspect (see Chapter 8).
7   Driveshaft and/or companion flange out of balance. Check for missing weights on the shaft. Remove the driveshaft (see Chapter 8) and reinstall 180-degrees from original position, then retest. Have the driveshaft professionally balanced if the problem persists.

Axles

35 Noise

1   Road noise. No corrective procedures available.
2   Tire noise. Inspect tires and check tire pressures (Chapter 1).
3   Rear wheel bearings loose, worn or damaged (Chapter 8).

36 Vibration

See probable causes under *Driveshaft*. Proceed under the guidelines listed for the driveshaft. If the problem persists, check the rear wheel bearings by raising the rear of the vehicle and spinning the rear wheels by hand. Listen for evidence of rough (noisy) bearings. Remove and inspect (see Chapter 8).

37 Oil leakage

1   Pinion seal damaged (see Chapter 8).
2   Axleshaft oil seals damaged (see Chapter 8).
3   Differential inspection cover leaking. Tighten the bolts or replace the gasket as required (see Chapters 1 and 8).

Brakes

Note: *Before assuming that a brake problem exists, make sure that the tires are in good condition and inflated properly (see Chapter 1), that the front end alignment is correct and that the vehicle is not loaded with weight in an unequal manner.*

38 Vehicle pulls to one side during braking

1   Defective, damaged or oil contaminated disc brake pads on one side. Inspect as described in Chapter 9.
2   Excessive wear of pad material or disc on one side. Inspect and correct as necessary.
3   Loose or disconnected front suspension components. Inspect and tighten all bolts to the specified torque (Chapter 10).
4   Defective caliper assembly. Remove the caliper and inspect for a stuck piston or other damage (Chapter 9).

5   Inadequate lubrication of front brake cali-per slide rails. Remove caliper and lubricate slide rails (Chapter 9).

39 Noise (high-pitched squeal with the brakes applied)

1   Disc brake pads worn out. The noise comes from the wear sensor rubbing against the disc (does not apply to all vehicles) or the actual pad backing plate itself if the material is completely worn away. Replace the pads with new ones immediately (Chapter 9). If the pad material has worn completely away, the brake discs should be inspected for damage as described in Chapter 9.
2   Missing or damaged brake pad insula-tors. Replace pad insulators (see Chapter 9).
3   Linings contaminated with dirt or grease. Replace pads.
4   Incorrect linings. Replace with correct linings.

40 Excessive brake pedal travel

1   Partial brake system failure. Inspect the entire system (Chapter 9) and correct as required.
2   Insufficient fluid in the master cylinder. Check (Chapter 1), add fluid and bleed the system if necessary (Chapter 9).

41 Brake pedal feels spongy when depressed

1   Air in the hydraulic lines. Bleed the brake system (Chapter 9).
2   Faulty flexible hoses. Inspect all system hoses and lines. Replace parts as necessary.
3   Master cylinder mounting bolts/nuts loose.
4   Master cylinder defective (Chapter 9).

42 Excessive effort required to stop vehicle

1   Power brake booster not operating prop-erly (Chapter 9).
2   Excessively worn pads. Inspect and replace if necessary (Chapter 9).
3   One or more caliper pistons seized or sticking. Inspect and replace as required (Chapter 9).
4   Brake pads contaminated with oil or grease. Inspect and replace as required (Chapter 9).
5   New pads installed and not yet seated. It will take a while for the new material to seat against the disc.

43 Pedal travels to the floor with little resistance

1   Little or no fluid in the master cylinder reservoir caused by leaking caliper piston(s), loose, damaged or disconnected brake lines. Inspect the entire system and correct as nec-essary.
2   Worn master cylinder seals (Chapter 9).

44 Brake pedal pulsates during brake application

1   Brake disc defective. Remove (Chap-ter 9) and check for excessive lateral runout and parallelism. Have the discs resurfaced or replace them with new ones.
2   Brake drum out-of-round. Have the drums resurfaced or replace them with new ones.

Suspension and steering systems

45 Vehicle pulls to one side

1   Tire pressures uneven (Chapter 1).
2   Defective tire (Chapter 1).
3   Excessive wear in suspension or steer-ing components (Chapter 10).
4   Front end in need of alignment.
5   Front brakes dragging. Inspect the brakes as described in Chapter 9.

46 Shimmy, shake or vibration

1   Tire or wheel out-of-balance or out-of-round. Have professionally balanced.
2   Loose, worn or out-of-adjustment front wheel bearings (Chapter 1).
3   Shock absorbers and/or suspension components worn or damaged (Chapter 10).

47 Excessive pitching and/or rolling around corners or during braking

1   Defective shock absorbers. Replace as a set (Chapter 10).
2   Broken or weak springs and/or suspen-sion components. Inspect as described in Chapter 10.

48 Excessively stiff steering

1   Lack of fluid in power steering fluid res-ervoir (Chapter 1).
2   Incorrect tire pressures (Chapter 1).
3   Lack of lubrication at steering joints (see Chapter 1).
4   Front end out of alignment.

5   Lack of power assistance (see Sec-tion 50).

49 Excessive play in steering

1   Loose front wheel bearings (Chapters 1 and 10).
2   Excessive wear in suspension or steer-ing components (Chapter 10).
3   Steering gearbox damaged or out of adjustment (Chapter 10).

50 Lack of power assistance

1   Steering pump drivebelt faulty or not adjusted properly (Chapter 1).
2   Fluid level low (Chapter 1).
3   Hoses or lines restricted. Inspect and replace parts as necessary.
4   Air in power steering system. Bleed the system (Chapter 10).

51 Excessive tire wear (not specific to one area)

1   Incorrect tire pressures (Chapter 1).
2   Tires out-of-balance. Have profession-ally balanced.
3   Wheels damaged. Inspect and replace as necessary.
4   Suspension or steering components excessively worn (Chapter 10).

52 Excessive tire wear on outside edge

1   Inflation pressures incorrect (Chapter 1).
2   Excessive speed in turns.
3   Front end alignment incorrect. Have pro-fessionally aligned.
4   Suspension arm bent or twisted (Chap-ter 10).

53 Excessive tire wear on inside edge

1   Inflation pressures incorrect (Chapter 1).
2   Front end alignment incorrect. Have pro-fessionally aligned.
3   Loose or damaged steering components (Chapter 10).

54 Tire tread worn in one place

1   Tires out-of-balance.
2   Damaged or buckled wheel. Inspect and replace if necessary.
3   Defective tire (Chapter 1).

Chapter 1
Tune-up and routine maintenance

Contents

Specifications

Recommended lubricants and fluids

Note: *Listed here are manufacturer recommendations at the time this manual was written. Manufacturers occasionally upgrade their fluid and lubricant specifications, so check with your local auto parts store for current recommendations, or refer to your owner's manual.*

Engine oil	API grade "certified for gasoline engines"
Viscosity	See accompanying chart
Fuel	Unleaded gasoline, 87 octane minimum
Automatic transmission fluid	
1996 through 2005 models	Dexron III automatic transmission fluid
2006 and later models	Dexron VI automatic transmission fluid

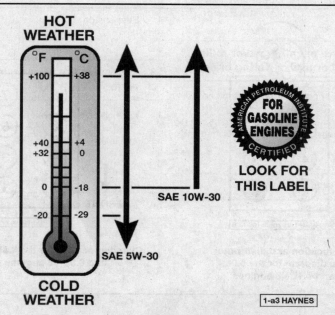

Engine oil viscosity chart - for best fuel economy and cold starting, select the lowest SAE viscosity grade for the expected temperature range

LOOK FOR THIS LABEL

1-a3 HAYNES

Recommended lubricants and fluids (continued)

Differential lubricant
  2001 and earlier models... SAE 80W-90 GL-5 gear lubricant
  2002 through 2005 models
    1500 .... SAE 75W-90 synthetic gear lubricant
    2500/3500 .... SAE 80W-90 GL-5 gear lubricant
  2006 and later models... 75W-90 synthetic gear lubricant
Power steering fluid .... GM hydraulic power steering fluid or equivalent
Brake fluid... DOT 3 brake fluid
Engine coolant... 50/50 mixture of DEX-COOL® antifreeze and distilled water
Parking brake mechanism grease .... NLGI Grade 2 GC or GC-LB chassis grease
Chassis lubrication grease .... NLGI Grade 2 GC or GC-LB chassis grease
Front wheel bearings .... NLGI Grade 2 GC or GC-LB wheel bearing grease

Capacities*

Engine oil (including filter)
  4.3L V6 engine.. 4.5 quarts
  4.8L V8, 5.3L V8 and 6.0L V8 engines... 6 quarts
  5.0L V8 and 5.7L V8 engines .... 5 quarts
  7.4L V8 engine
    1996 and 1997 models .... 7 quarts
    1998 and 1999 models .... 6.6 quarts
    2000 models .... 6 quarts
Automatic transmission (drain and refill)
  4L60-E/4L65-E.. 5 quarts
  4L80-E/4L85-E.. 7.7 quarts

Note: *The best way to determine the amount of fluid to add during a routine transmission fluid change is to measure the amount drained. It is important not to overfill the transmission. After draining the transmission, begin the refilling procedure by initially adding 3/4 of the amount drained, then adding 1/2-pint at a time until the level is correct on the dipstick.*

Cooling system
  Without rear heating
    4.3L V6 engine... 11 quarts
    4.8L V8 and 5.3L V8 engines.. 13.4 quarts
    6.0L V8 engines... 14.8 quarts
    5.0L V8 and 5.7L V8 engines.. 17 quarts
    7.4L V8 engine... 23 quarts
  With rear heating
    4.3L V6 engine... 14 quarts
    4.8L V8 and 5.3L V8 engines.. 16.4 quarts
    6.0L V8 engines... 17.8 quarts
    5.0L V8 and 5.7L V8 engines.. 20 quarts
    7.4L V8 engine... 26 quarts

All capacities approximate. Add as necessary to bring to appropriate level.

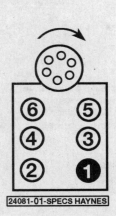

Cylinder location and distributor rotation diagram for the 4.3L V6 engines

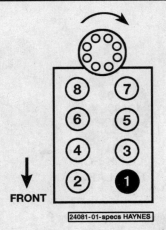

Cylinder location and distributor rotation diagram for the 5.0L, 5.7L and 7.4L V8 engines

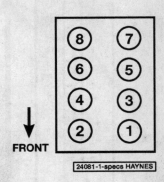

Cylinder location for the 4.8L, 5.3L and 6.0L V8 engines

Ignition system

Spark plugs*
    4.3L V6 engine
        1996
            Type.. AC CR43TS or equivalent
            Gap.. 0.035 inch
        1997 through 2006
            Type.. AC 41-932 or equivalent
            Gap.. 0.060 inch
        2007 and later models
            Type.. AC 41-993 or equivalent
            Gap.. 0.060 inch
    4.8L V8, 5.3L V8 and 6.0L V8 engines
        Type.. AC 41-985 or equivalent
        Gap.. 0.040 inch
    5.0L/5.7L/7.4LV8 engines
        Type.. AC 41-932 or equivalent
        Gap.. 0.060 inch
Firing order
    4.3L V6 engine 1-6-5-4-3-2
    4.8L V8, 5.3L V8 and 6.0L V8 engines.................................. 1-8-7-2-6-5-4-3
    5.0L V8 and 5.7L V8 engines 1-8-4-3-6-5-7-2
    7.4L V8 engine 1-8-4-3-6-5-7-2

If the spark plug gap listed on your VECI label differs from that shown here, use the information on the label.

Brakes

Disc brake pad lining thickness (minimum) .... 1/8 inch
Drum brake shoe lining thickness (minimum)............................. 1/16 inch

Torque specifications   **Ft-lbs** (unless otherwise indicated)

Engine oil drain plug
    All except 7.4L V8 engine 18
    7.4L V8 engine 20
Spark plugs.. 132 in-lbs
Wheel lug nuts... 140
Automatic transmission pan bolts
    4L60-E/4L65-E
        2003 and earlier models .... 84 to 120 in-lbs
        2004 and later models .... 141 in-lbs
    4L80-E/4L85-E 18

Typical engine compartment layout

1 Battery	5 Power steering reservoir	8 Engine oil dipstick
2 Engine coolant reservoir	6 Brake fluid reservoir	9 Automatic transmission fluid dipstick
3 Engine oil filler cap	7 Windshield washer fluid reservoir	10 Radiator cap
4 Air filter housing		

Typical engine underside components

1	Lower radiator hose	3	Engine oil drain plug	5	Exhaust pipe
2	Steering linkage grease fitting	4	Oil filter		

Typical rear underside components

1	*Exhaust pipe*	4	*Rear shock absorber*	6	*Driveshaft*
2	*Leaf spring*	5	*Fuel tank*	7	*Muffler*
3	*Differential cover*				

1 Maintenance schedule

The following maintenance intervals are based on the assumption that the vehicle owner will be doing the maintenance or service work, as opposed to having a dealer service department do the work. These are the minimum maintenance intervals recommended by the factory for vehicles that are driven daily. If you wish to keep your vehicle in peak condition at all times, you may wish to perform some of these procedures even more often. Because frequent maintenance enhances the efficiency, performance and resale value of your car, we encourage you to do so. If you drive in dusty areas, tow a trailer, idle or drive at low speeds for extended periods or drive for short distances (less than four miles) in below freezing temperatures, shorter intervals are also recommended.

When the vehicle is new, follow the maintenance schedule to the letter, record the maintenance performed in your owners manual and keep all receipts to protect the new vehicle warranty. In many cases the initial maintenance check is done at no cost to the owner (check with your dealer service department for more information).

Every 250 miles or weekly, whichever comes first

Check the engine oil level (Section 4)
Check the coolant level (Section 4)
Check the windshield washer fluid level (Section 4)
Check the brake fluid level (Section 4)
Check the power steering fluid level (Section 4)
Check the automatic transmission fluid level (Section 4)
Check the tires and tire pressures (Section 5)

Every 3000 miles or 3 months, whichever comes first

All items listed above, plus . . .
Change the engine oil and filter (Section 6)

Every 6000 miles or 6 months, whichever comes first

All items listed above, plus . . .
Check the seat belts (Section 7)
Inspect the windshield wiper blades (Section 8)
Check and service the battery (Section 9)
Lubricate the chassis (Section 10)
Check the rear axle lubricant level (Section 11)
Rotate the tires (Section 12)
Check the cooling system (Section 13)
Inspect underhood hoses (Section 14)

Every 15,000 miles or 12 months, whichever comes first

All items listed above, plus . . .
Check the fuel system (Section 15)
Check the brake system (Section 16)*
Check the air filter (Section 17)*

Every 30,000 miles or 24 months, whichever comes first

All items listed above, plus . . .
Replace the air filter (Section 17)*
Check the exhaust system (Section 18)
Replace the fuel filter (Section 19)
Change the brake fluid (Section 20)
Check and repack the front wheel bearings (2002 and earlier models only) (Section 21)
Check the steering and suspension (Section 22)
Service the cooling system (drain, flush and refill) (green-colored ethylene glycol anti-freeze only) (Section 23)

Every 60,000 miles or 48 months, whichever comes first

All items listed above, plus . . .
Check the engine drivebelt (Section 24)
Inspect the evaporative emissions control system (Section 25)

Every 100,000 miles or 60 months, whichever comes first

Service the cooling system (drain, flush and refill) (orange-colored DEX-COOL® anti-freeze only) (Section 23)
Replace the spark plugs (Section 26)
Inspect/replace the spark plug wires (Section 27)
Change the automatic transmission fluid and filter (Section 28)**
Check the Positive Crankcase Ventilation (PCV) system (Section 29)

*   This item is affected by "severe" operating conditions, as described below. If the vehicle is operated under severe conditions, perform all maintenance indicated with an asterisk (*) at half the indicated intervals.*

Severe conditions exist if you mainly operate the vehicle . . .
in dusty areas
towing a trailer
idling for extended periods
driving at low speeds when outside temperatures remain below freezing and most trips are less than four miles long

**   Perform this procedure at half the recommended interval if operated under one or more of the following conditions:*
in heavy city traffic where the outside temperature regularly reaches 90-degrees F or higher in hilly or mountainous terrain
frequent trailer towing
if the vehicle has been driven through deep water

4.2 The oil dipstick is located at the front of the engine compartment

2   Introduction

This Chapter is designed to help the home mechanic maintain his or her vehicle with the goals of maximum performance, economy, safety and reliability in mind.

Included is a master maintenance schedule, followed by procedures dealing specifically with each item on the schedule. Visual checks, adjustments, component replacement and other helpful items are included. Refer to **the accompanying illustrations** of the engine compartment and the underside of the vehicle for the locations of various components.

Servicing your vehicle in accordance with the mileage/time maintenance schedule and the step-by-step procedures will result in a planned maintenance program that should produce a long and reliable service life. Keep in mind that it's a comprehensive plan, so maintaining some items but not others at the specified intervals will not produce the same results.

As you service your vehicle, you will discover that many of the procedures can - and should - be grouped together because of the nature of the particular procedure you're performing or because of the close proximity of two otherwise unrelated components to one another.

For example, if the vehicle is raised for chassis lubrication, you should inspect the exhaust, suspension, steering and fuel systems while you're under the vehicle. When you're rotating the tires, it makes good sense to check the brakes since the wheels are already removed. Finally, let's suppose you have to borrow or rent a torque wrench. Even if you only need it to tighten the spark plugs, you might as well check the torque of as many critical fasteners as time allows.

The first step in this maintenance program is to prepare yourself before the actual work begins. Read through all the procedures you're planning to do, then gather up all the parts and tools needed. If it looks like you might run into problems during a particular job, seek advice from a mechanic or an experienced do-it-yourselfer.

Owner's Manual and VECI label information

Your vehicle Owner's Manual was written for your year and model and contains very specific information on component locations, specifications, fuse ratings, part numbers, etc. The Owner's Manual is an important resource for the do-it-yourselfer to have; if one was not supplied with your vehicle, it can generally be ordered from a dealer parts department.

Among other important information, the Vehicle Emissions Control Information (VECI) label contains specifications and procedures for tune-up adjustments (if applicable) and spark plugs (see Chapter 6 for more information on the VECI label). The information on this label is the exact maintenance data recommended by the manufacturer. This data often varies by intended operating altitude, local emissions regulations, month of manufacture, etc.

This Chapter contains procedural details, safety information and more ambitious maintenance intervals than you might find in the manufacturer's literature. However, you may also find procedures and specifications in your Owner's Manual or VECI label that differ with what's printed here. In these cases, the Owner's Manual or VECI label can be considered correct, since it is specific to your particular vehicle.

3   Tune-up general information

The term tune-up is used in this manual to represent a combination of individual operations rather than one specific procedure that will maintain a gasoline engine in proper tune.

If, from the time the vehicle is new, the routine maintenance schedule is followed closely and frequent checks are made of fluid levels and high wear items, as suggested throughout this manual, the engine will be kept in relatively good running condition and the need for additional work will be minimized.

More likely than not, however, there may be times when the engine is running poorly due to lack of regular maintenance. This is even more likely if a used vehicle, which has not received regular and frequent maintenance checks, is purchased. In such cases, an engine tune-up will be needed outside of the regular routine maintenance intervals.

The first step in any tune-up or diagnostic procedure to help correct a poor running engine is a cylinder compression check. A compression check (see Chapter 2C) will help determine the condition of internal engine components and should be used as a guide for tune-up and repair procedures. If, for instance, the compression check indicates serious internal engine wear, a conventional tune-up won't improve the performance of the engine and would be a waste of time and money. Because of its importance, the com-

pression check should be done by someone with the right equipment and the knowledge to use it properly.

The following procedures are those most often needed to bring a generally poor running engine back into a proper state of tune.

Minor tune-up
Check all engine related fluids (Section 4)
Clean, inspect and test the battery (Section 9)
Check the cooling system (Section 13)
Check all underhood hoses (Section 14)
Check the air filter (Section 17)
Check the drivebelt (Section 24)
Replace the spark plugs (Section 26)
Inspect the spark plug wires (Section 27)

Major tune-up
All items listed under Minor tune-up, plus . . .
Replace the air filter (Section 17)
Replace the spark plug wires (Section 27)
Check the ignition system (Chapter 5)
Check the charging system (Chapter 5)

4   Fluid level checks (every 250 miles or weekly)

Note: *The following are fluid level checks to be done on a 250 mile or weekly basis. Additional fluid level checks can be found in specific maintenance procedures that follow. Regardless of intervals, be alert to fluid leaks under the vehicle, which would indicate a fault to be corrected immediately.*

1   Fluids are an essential part of the lubrication, cooling, brake, power steering, transmission and windshield washer systems. Because the fluids gradually become depleted and/or contaminated during normal operation of the vehicle, they must be periodically replenished. See *Recommended lubricants and fluids* at the beginning of this Chapter before adding fluid to any of the following components. **Note:** *The vehicle must be on level ground when fluid levels are checked.*

Engine oil
Refer to illustrations 4.2, 4.4 and 4.6
2   The engine oil level is checked with a dipstick that extends through a tube and into the oil pan at the bottom of the engine (**see illustration**).
3   The oil level should be checked before the vehicle has been driven, or about 5 minutes after the engine has been shut off. If the oil is checked immediately after driving the vehicle, some of the oil will remain in the upper engine components, resulting in an inaccurate reading on the dipstick.
4   Pull the dipstick out of the tube and wipe all the oil from the end with a clean rag or paper towel. Insert the clean dipstick all the way back into the tube, then pull it out again. Note the oil at the end of the dipstick. Add oil as necessary to keep the level between the MIN and MAX marks or within the SAFE zone

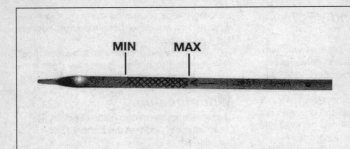

MIN   MAX

4.4 The oil level must be maintained between the marks at all times - it takes one quart of oil to raise the level from the MIN to MAX mark

4.6 Oil is added to the engine after unscrewing the oil filler cap - always make sure the tube and the bottom of the cap are clean before removing the cap to prevent dirt from contaminating the engine

on the dipstick **(see illustration)**.

5   It takes one quart of oil to raise the level from the lower hole to the upper hole on the dipstick. Do not overfill the engine by adding too much oil since this may result in oil-fouled spark plugs, oil leaks or oil seal failures.

6   Oil is added to the engine after unscrewing a cap from a tube connected to the valve cover **(see illustration)**. A funnel may help to reduce spills.

7   Checking the oil level is an important preventive maintenance step. A consistently low oil level indicates oil leakage through damaged seals, defective gaskets or past worn rings or valve guides. If the oil looks milky or has water droplets in it, the cylinder head gasket(s) may be blown or the head(s) or block may be cracked. The engine should be checked immediately. The condition of the oil should also be checked. Whenever you check the oil level, slide your thumb and index finger up the dipstick before wiping off the oil. If you see small dirt or metal particles clinging to the dipstick, the oil should be changed (see Section 6).

Engine coolant
Refer to illustration 4.9

Warning: *Do not allow antifreeze to come in contact with your skin or painted surfaces of the vehicle. Rinse off spills immediately with plenty of water. Antifreeze is highly toxic if ingested. Never leave antifreeze lying around in an open container or in puddles on the floor; children and pets are attracted by its sweet smell and may drink it. Check with local authorities on disposing of used anti-freeze. Many communities have collection centers that will see that antifreeze is disposed of safely.*

Note: *Non-toxic antifreeze is now manufactured and available at local auto parts stores, but even this type should be disposed of properly.*

Caution: *Never mix green-colored ethylene glycol anti-freeze and orange-colored "DEX-COOL®" silicate-free coolant because doing so will destroy the efficiency of the "DEX-COOL®" coolant which is designed to last for 100,000 miles or five years.*

8   All vehicles covered by this manual are equipped with a pressurized coolant recovery system. A coolant reservoir, located on the right side of the engine compartment, is connected by a hose to the base of the radiator filler neck. If the coolant heats up during engine operation, coolant can escape through the pressurized filler cap, then through the connecting hose into the reservoir. As the engine cools, the coolant is automatically drawn back into the cooling system to maintain the correct level.

9   The coolant level in the reservoir should be checked regularly. The level will vary with the temperature of the engine. When the engine is cold, the coolant level should be at or slightly above the FULL COLD mark on the tank. If it isn't, remove the cap from the reservoir **(see illustration)** and add coolant to bring the level up to the FULL COLD line. **Warning:** *Do not remove the radiator cap to check the coolant level when the engine is warm!* Use only the recommended coolant and water in the mixture ratio listed in this Chapter's Specifications. Do not use supplemental inhibitors or additives. If only a small amount of coolant is required to bring the system up to the proper level, water can be used. However, repeated additions of water will dilute the recommended antifreeze and water solution. In order to maintain the proper ratio of antifreeze and water, it is advisable to top up the coolant level with the correct mixture.

10   If the coolant level drops within a short time after replenishment, there may be a leak in the system. Inspect the radiator, hoses, engine coolant filler cap, drain plugs and water pump. If no leak is evident, have the radiator cap pressure tested. **Warning:** *Never remove the radiator cap or the coolant reservoir cap when the engine is running or has just been shut down, because the cooling system is*

hot. Escaping steam and scalding liquid could cause serious injury.

11   If it is necessary to open the radiator cap, wait until the system has cooled completely, then wrap a thick cloth around the cap and turn it to the first stop. If any steam escapes, wait until the system has cooled further, then remove the cap.

12   When checking the coolant level, always note its condition. It should be relatively clear. If it is brown or rust colored, the system should be drained, flushed and refilled. Even if the coolant appears to be normal, the corrosion inhibitors wear out with use, so it must be replaced at the specified intervals.

13   Do not allow antifreeze to come in contact with your skin or painted surfaces of the vehicle. Flush contacted areas immediately with plenty of water.

Windshield washer fluid
Refer to illustration 4.14

14   Fluid for the windshield washer system is located in a plastic reservoir in the left side of the engine compartment **(see illustration)**.

4.9 The coolant reservoir is located on the right side of the engine compartment

4.14 Flip open the cap to check the fluid level in the windshield washer tank

4.18 Never let the brake fluid level drop below the MIN marks

4.26 The power steering reservoir is located next to the
brake fluid reservoir

15   In milder climates, plain water can be used in the reservoir, but it should be kept no more than 2/3 full to allow for expansion if the water freezes. In colder climates, use windshield washer system antifreeze, available at any auto parts store, to lower the freezing point of the fluid. Mix the antifreeze with water in accordance with the manufacturer's directions on the container. **Caution:** *Don't use cooling system antifreeze - it will damage the vehicle's paint.*

16   To help prevent icing in cold weather, warm the windshield with the defroster before using the washer.

Brake fluid

Refer to illustration 4.18

17   The brake master cylinder is mounted on the upper left of the engine compartment firewall.

18   The translucent plastic reservoir allows the fluid inside to be checked without removing the cover **(see illustration)**. Be sure to wipe the top of the reservoir cap with a clean rag to prevent contamination of the brake system before removing the cover.

19   When adding fluid, pour it carefully into the reservoir to avoid spilling it on surrounding painted surfaces. Be sure the specified fluid is used, since mixing different types of brake fluid can cause damage to the system. See *Recommended lubricants and fluids* at the front of this Chapter or your owner's manual. **Warning:** *Brake fluid can harm your eyes and damage painted surfaces, so use extreme caution when handling or pouring it. Do not use brake fluid that has been standing open or is more than one year old. Brake fluid absorbs moisture from the air. Moisture in the system can cause a dangerous loss of brake performance.*

20   At this time, the fluid and master cylinder can be inspected for contamination. The system should be drained and refilled if deposits, dirt particles or water droplets are seen in the fluid.

21   After filling the reservoir to the proper level, make sure the cover is on tight to prevent fluid leakage.

22   The brake fluid level in the master cylinder will drop slightly as the pads at the wheels wear down during normal operation. If the master cylinder requires repeated additions to keep it at the proper level, it's an indication of leakage in the brake system, which should be corrected immediately. Check all brake lines and connections (see Section 16 for more information).

23   If, upon checking the master cylinder fluid level, you discover one or both reservoirs empty or nearly empty, the brake system should be bled and thoroughly inspected (see Chapter 9).

Power steering fluid

Refer to illustrations 4.26 and 4.27

24   Check the power steering fluid level periodically to avoid steering system problems, such as damage to the pump. **Caution:** *DO NOT hold the steering wheel against either stop (extreme left or right turn) for more than five seconds. If you do, the power steering pump could be damaged.*

25   For the check, the front wheels should be pointed straight ahead and the engine should be off.

26   The power steering reservoir, located inside of the engine compartment **(see illustration)**. Use a clean rag to wipe off the reservoir cap and the area around the cap. This will help prevent any foreign matter from entering the reservoir during the check.

27   Twist off the cap and check the temperature of the fluid at the end of the dipstick with your finger. Wipe off the fluid with a clean rag, reinsert the dipstick, then withdraw it and read the fluid level. The fluid should be at the proper level, depending on whether it was checked hot or cold **(see illustration)**. Never allow the fluid level to drop below the lower mark on the dipstick.

28   If additional fluid is required, pour the specified type directly into the reservoir, using a funnel to prevent spills.

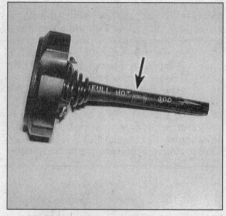

4.27 The power steering fluid dipstick
has marks on it so the fluid can be
checked hot or cold

29   If the reservoir requires frequent fluid additions, all power steering hoses, hose connections, steering gear and the power steering pump should be carefully checked for leaks.

Automatic transmission fluid

Refer to illustrations 4.32 and 4.35

30   The automatic transmission fluid level should be carefully maintained. Low fluid level can lead to slipping or loss of drive, while overfilling can cause foaming and loss of fluid.

31   With the parking brake set, start the engine, then move the shift lever through all the gear ranges, ending in Park. The fluid level must be checked with the vehicle level and the engine running at idle. **Note:** *Incorrect fluid level readings will result if the vehicle has just been driven at high speeds for an extended period, in hot weather in city traffic, or if it has been pulling a trailer. If any of these conditions apply, wait until the fluid has cooled (about 30 minutes).*

32   With the transmission at normal operating temperature, remove the dipstick from the

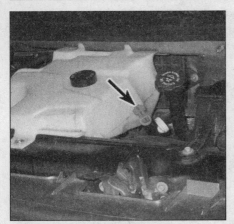

4.32 The automatic transmission dipstick is located next to the engine oil dipstick - flip up the handle before pulling out the dipstick

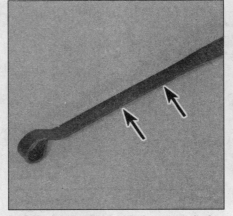

4.35 Check the fluid with the transmission at normal operating temperature - the level should be kept in the HOT range in the crosshatched area

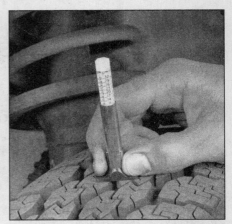

5.2 A tire tread depth indicator should be used to monitor tire wear - they are available at auto parts stores and service stations and cost very little

filler tube. The dipstick is located at the rear of the engine compartment on the passenger's side **(see illustration).**

33 Wipe the fluid from the dipstick with a clean rag and push it back into the filler tube until the cap seats.

34 Pull the dipstick out again and note the fluid level.

35 If the fluid is hot, the level should be in the crosshatched area, near the MAX line **(see illustration).** If additional fluid is required, add it directly into the tube using a funnel. It takes

about one pint to raise the level from the bottom of the crosshatched area to the MAX line with a hot transmission, so add the fluid a little at a time and keep checking the level until it's correct.

36 The condition of the fluid should also be checked along with the level. If the fluid at the end of the dipstick is a dark reddish-brown color, or if it smells burned, it should be changed. If you are in doubt about the condition of the fluid, purchase some new fluid and compare the two for color and smell.

5   Tire and tire pressure checks (every 250 miles or weekly)

Refer to illustrations 5.2, 5.3, 5.4a, 5.4b and 5.8

1   Periodic inspection of the tires may spare you the inconvenience of being stranded with a flat tire. It can also provide you with vital information regarding possible problems in the steering and suspension systems before major damage occurs.

UNDERINFLATION

CUPPING

Cupping may be caused by:
- Underinflation and/or mechanical irregularities such as out-of-balance condition of wheel and/or tire, and bent or damaged wheel.
- Loose or worn steering tie-rod or steering idler arm.
- Loose, damaged or worn front suspension parts.

OVERINFLATION

INCORRECT TOE-IN OR EXTREME CAMBER

FEATHERING DUE TO MISALIGNMENT

5.3 This chart will help you determine the condition of your tires, the probable cause(s) of abnormal wear and the corrective action necessary

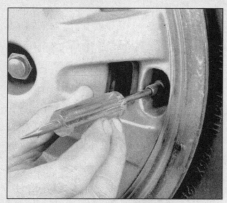

5.4a If a tire loses air on a steady basis, check the valve core first to make sure it's snug (special inexpensive wrenches are commonly available at auto parts stores

5.4b If the valve core is tight, raise the corner of the vehicle with the low tire and spray a soapy water solution onto the tread as the tire is turned slowly - slow leaks will cause small bubbles to appear

5.8 To extend the life of your tires, check the air pressure at least once a week with an accurate gauge (don't forget the spare!)

2   The original tires on this vehicle are equipped with 1/2-inch wide wear bands that will appear when tread depth reaches 1/16-inch, at which point the tires can be considered worn out. Tread wear can be monitored with a simple, inexpensive device known as a tread depth indicator **(see illustration)**.

3   Note any abnormal tread wear **(see illustration)**. Tread pattern irregularities such as cupping, flat spots and more wear on one side than the other are indications of front end alignment and/or balance problems. If any of these conditions are noted, take the vehicle to a tire shop or service station to correct the problem.

4   Look closely for cuts, punctures and embedded nails or tacks. Sometimes a tire will hold air pressure for a short time or leak down very slowly after a nail has embedded itself in the tread. If a slow leak persists, check the valve stem core to make sure it's tight **(see illustration)**. Examine the tread for an object that may have embedded itself in the tire or for a "plug" that may have begun to leak (radial tire punctures are repaired with a plug that's installed in a puncture). If a puncture is suspected, it can be easily verified by spraying a solution of soapy water onto the puncture area **(see illustration)**. The soapy solution will bubble if there's a leak. Unless the puncture is unusually large, a tire shop or service station can usually repair the tire.

5   Carefully inspect the inner sidewall of each tire for evidence of brake fluid leakage. If you see any, inspect the brakes immediately.

6   Correct air pressure adds miles to the lifespan of the tires, improves mileage and enhances overall ride quality. Tire pressure cannot be accurately estimated by looking at a tire, especially if it's a radial. A tire pressure gauge is essential. Keep an accurate gauge in the vehicle. The pressure gauges attached to the nozzles of air hoses at gas stations are often inaccurate.

7   Always check tire pressure when the tires are cold. Cold, in this case, means the vehicle has not been driven over a mile in the three hours preceding a tire pressure check. A pressure rise of four to eight pounds is not uncommon once the tires are warm.

8   Unscrew the valve cap protruding from the wheel or hubcap and push the gauge firmly onto the valve stem **(see illustration)**. Note the reading on the gauge and compare the figure to the recommended tire pressure shown on the placard on the driver's side door pillar. Be sure to reinstall the valve cap to keep dirt and moisture out of the valve stem mechanism. Check all four tires and, if necessary, add enough air to bring them up to the recommended pressure.

9   Don't forget to keep the spare tire inflated to the specified pressure (refer to your owner's manual or the tire sidewall).

---

6   Engine oil and filter change (every 3000 miles or 3 months)

Refer to illustrations 6.3, 6.9, 6.14 and 6.18
Note: *Some models may be equipped with an oil life indicator system that notifies the driver when the system deems it necessary to change the oil. A number of factors are taken into consideration to determine when the oil should be considered "worn out." Generally, this system will allow the vehicle to accumulate more miles between oil changes than the traditional 3000 mile interval, but we believe that frequent oil changes are "cheap insurance" and will prolong engine life. If you decide not to change your oil every 3000 miles and rely on the oil life indicator instead, make sure you don't exceed 7,500 miles before the oil is changed, regardless of what the oil life indicator shows.*

1   Frequent oil changes are the most important preventive maintenance procedures that can be done by the home mechanic. As engine oil ages, it becomes diluted and contaminated, which leads to premature engine wear.

2   Although some sources recommend oil filter changes every other oil change, we feel that the minimal cost of an oil filter and the relative ease with which it is installed dictate that a new filter be installed every time the oil

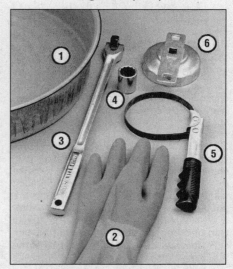

6.3 These tools are required when changing the engine oil and filter

1   **Drain pan** - It should be fairly shallow in depth, but wide in order to prevent spills

2   **Rubber gloves** - When removing the drain plug and filter, it is inevitable that you will get oil on your hands (the gloves will prevent burns)

3   **Breaker bar** - Sometimes the oil drain plug is pretty tight and a long breaker bar is needed to loosen it

4   **Socket** - To be used with the breaker bar or a ratchet (must be the correct size to fit the drain plug)

5   **Filter wrench** - This is a metal band-type wrench, which requires clearance around the filter to be effective

6   **Filter wrench** - This type fits on the bottom of the filter and can be turned with a ratchet or breaker bar (different size wrenches are available for different types of filters)

is changed.

3   Gather together all necessary tools and materials before beginning this procedure **(see illustration)**.

6.9 Use a proper size box-end wrench or socket to remove the oil drain plug and avoid rounding it off

6.14 Since the oil filter is on very tight, you'll need an oil filter wrench for removal - DO NOT use the wrench to tighten the new filter

6.18 Lubricate the oil filter gasket with clean engine oil before installing the filter on the engine

4   You should have plenty of clean rags and newspapers handy to mop up any spills. Access to the underside of the vehicle may be improved if the vehicle can be lifted on a hoist, driven onto ramps or supported by jackstands. **Warning:** *Do not work under a vehicle which is supported only by a bumper, hydraulic or scissors-type jack.*

5   If this is your first oil change, familiarize yourself with the locations of the oil drain plug and the oil filter.

6   Warm the engine to normal operating temperature. If the new oil or any tools are needed, use this warm-up time to gather everything necessary for the job. The correct type of oil for your application can be found in *Recommended lubricants and fluids* at the beginning of this Chapter.

7   With the engine oil warm (warm engine oil will drain better and more built-up sludge will be removed with it), raise and support the vehicle. Make sure it's safely supported!

8   Move all necessary tools, rags and newspapers under the vehicle. Set the drain pan under the drain plug. Keep in mind that the oil will initially flow from the pan with some force; position the pan accordingly.

9   Being careful not to touch any of the hot exhaust components, use a wrench to remove the drain plug near the bottom of the oil pan **(see illustration)**. Depending on how hot the oil is, you may want to wear gloves while unscrewing the plug the final few turns.

10   Allow the oil to drain into the pan. It may be necessary to move the pan as the oil flow slows to a trickle.

11   After all the oil has drained, wipe off the drain plug with a clean rag. Small metal particles may cling to the plug and would immediately contaminate the new oil.

12   Clean the area around the drain plug opening and reinstall the plug. Tighten the plug securely with the wrench. If a torque wrench is available, use it to tighten the plug to the torque listed in this Chapter's Specifications.

13   Move the drain pan into position under the oil filter.

14   Use the oil filter wrench to loosen the oil filter **(see illustration)**.

15   Completely unscrew the old filter. Be careful: it's full of oil. Empty the oil inside the filter into the drain pan, then lower the filter.

16   Compare the old filter with the new one to make sure they're the same type.

17   Use a clean rag to remove all oil, dirt and sludge from the area where the oil filter mounts to the engine. Check the old filter to make sure the rubber gasket isn't stuck to the engine. If the gasket is stuck to the engine (use a flashlight if necessary), remove it.

18   Apply a light coat of clean oil to the rubber gasket on the new oil filter **(see illustration)**.

19   Attach the new filter to the engine, following the tightening directions printed on the filter canister or packing box. Most filter manufacturers recommend against using a filter wrench due to the possibility of overtightening and damage to the seal.

20   Remove all tools, rags, etc. from under the vehicle, being careful not to spill the oil in the drain pan, then lower the vehicle.

21   Move to the engine compartment and locate the oil filler cap.

22   Pour the fresh oil through the filler opening. A funnel may be helpful.

23   Refer to the engine oil capacity in this Chapter's Specifications and add the proper amount of fresh oil into the engine. Wait a few minutes to allow the oil to drain into the pan, then check the level on the oil dipstick (see Section 4 if necessary). If the oil level is above the hatched area, start the engine and allow the new oil to circulate.

24   Run the engine for only about a minute and then shut it off. Immediately look under the vehicle and check for leaks at the oil pan drain plug and around the oil filter.

25   With the new oil circulated and the filter now completely full, recheck the level on the dipstick and add more oil as necessary.

26   During the first few trips after an oil change, make it a point to check frequently for leaks and proper oil level.

27   The old oil drained from the engine cannot be reused in its present state and should be disposed of. Check with your local auto parts store, disposal facility or environmental agency to see if they will accept the oil for recycling. After the oil has cooled it can be drained into a container (capped plastic jugs, topped bottles, milk cartons, etc.) for transport to one of these disposal sites. Don't dispose of the oil by pouring it on the ground or down a drain!

Oil Life Monitor

28   The Oil Life Monitor is a function of the PCM that tracks engine operating temperature and rpm. If the PCM determines that your engine's oil has been used long enough, an indicator that shows "Change Engine Oil" will light on the instrument panel.

29   When you change your engine oil and filter, whether you change it at the interval recommended in this Chapter or only when the light comes on, you will have to reset the system to make the indicator go out.

30   To reset, switch the ignition key to Run (engine not running) and depress/let up the throttle pedal quickly three times. The light should flash for five seconds, to let you know the system is reset properly.

7   Seat belt check (every 6000 miles or 6 months)

1   Check seat belts, buckles, latch plates and guide loops for obvious damage and signs of wear.

2   Where the seat belt receptacle bolts to the floor of the vehicle, check that the bolts are secure.

3   See if the seat belt reminder light comes on when the key is turned to the Run or Start position. A chime should also sound.

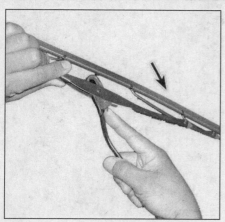

8.4 Depress the release lever and slide the wiper assembly down the wiper arm and out of the hook in the end of the arm

8   Wiper blade inspection and replacement (every 6000 miles or 6 months)

Refer to illustration 8.4

1   The windshield wiper and blade assembly should be inspected periodically for damage, loose components and cracked or worn blade elements.

2   Road film can build up on the wiper blades and affect their efficiency, so they should be washed regularly with a mild detergent solution.

3   If the wiper blade elements are cracked, worn or warped, or no longer clean adequately, they should be replaced with new ones.

4   Lift the arm assembly away from the glass for clearance, pry up on the release lever, then slide the wiper blade assembly out of the hook in the end of the arm **(see illustration)**.

5   Attach the new wiper to the arm. Connection can be confirmed by an audible click.

9   Battery check, maintenance and charging (every 6000 miles or 6 months)

Refer to illustrations 9.1, 9.5, 9.7a, 9.7b and 9.7c

Warning: *Certain precautions must be followed when checking and servicing the battery. Hydrogen gas, which is highly flammable, is always present in the battery cells, so keep lighted tobacco and all other open flames and sparks away from the battery. The electrolyte inside the battery is actually dilute sulfuric acid, which will cause injury if splashed on your skin or in your eyes. It will also ruin clothes and painted surfaces. When removing the battery cables, always detach the negative cable first and hook it up last!*

1   A routine preventive maintenance program for the battery in your vehicle is the only way to ensure quick and reliable starts. But

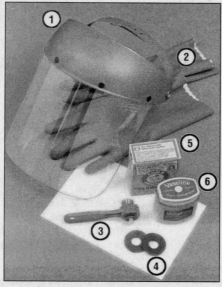

9.1 Tools and materials required for battery maintenance

1   **Face shield/safety goggles** - *When removing corrosion with a brush, the acidic particles can easily fly up into your eyes*

2   **Rubber gloves** - *Another safety item to consider when servicing the battery - remember that's acid inside the battery!*

3   **Battery terminal/cable cleaner** - *This wire brush cleaning tool will remove all traces of corrosion from the battery posts and cable clamps*

4   **Treated felt washers** - *Placing one of these on each post, directly under the cable clamps, will help prevent corrosion*

5   **Baking soda** - *A solution of baking soda and water can be used to neutralize corrosion*

6   **Petroleum jelly** - *A layer of this on the battery posts will help prevent corrosion*

before performing any battery maintenance, make sure that you have the proper equipment necessary to work safely around the battery **(see illustration)**.

2   There are also several precautions that should be taken whenever battery maintenance is performed. Before servicing the battery, always turn the engine and all accessories off and disconnect the cable from the negative terminal of the battery.

3   The battery produces hydrogen gas, which is both flammable and explosive. Never create a spark, smoke or light a match around the battery. Always charge the battery in a ventilated area.

4   Electrolyte contains poisonous and corrosive sulfuric acid. Do not allow it to get in your eyes, on your skin or on your clothes. Never ingest it. Wear protective safety glasses when working near the battery. Keep children away from the battery.

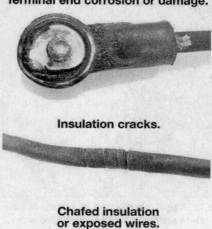

Terminal end corrosion or damage.

Insulation cracks.

Chafed insulation or exposed wires.

Burned or melted insulation.

9.5 Typical battery cable problems

5   Note the external condition of the battery. If the positive terminal and cable clamp on your vehicle's battery is equipped with a rubber protector, make sure that it's not torn or damaged. It should completely cover the terminal. Look for any corroded or loose connections, cracks in the case or cover or loose hold-down clamps. Also check the entire length of each cable for cracks and frayed conductors **(see illustration)**.

6   If corrosion, which looks like white, fluffy deposits is evident, particularly around the terminals, the battery should be removed for cleaning. Loosen the cable bolts with a wrench, being careful to remove the ground cable first, and slide them off the terminals. Then disconnect the hold-down clamp bolt and nut, remove the clamp and lift the battery from the engine compartment.

7   Clean the cable ends thoroughly with a battery brush or a terminal cleaner and a solution of warm water and baking soda. Wash the terminals and the side of the battery case with the same solution but make sure that the solution doesn't get into the battery. When cleaning the cables, terminals and battery case, wear safety goggles and rubber gloves to prevent any solution from coming in contact with your eyes or hands. Wear old clothes too - even diluted, sulfuric acid splashed onto

9.7a A tool like this one (available at auto parts stores) is used to clean the side-terminal type battery-cable contact area

9.7b Use the brush side of the tool to finish the job

9.7c Regardless of the type of tool used on the battery and cables, a clean, shiny surface should be the result

clothes will burn holes in them. If the terminals have been corroded, clean them up with a terminal cleaner **(see illustrations)**. Thoroughly wash all cleaned areas with plain water.

8   Make sure that the battery tray is in good condition and the hold-down clamp bolts are tight. If the battery is removed from the tray, make sure no parts remain in the bottom of the tray when the battery is reinstalled. When reinstalling the hold-down clamp bolts, do not overtighten them.

9   Any metal parts of the vehicle damaged by corrosion should be covered with a zinc-based primer, then painted.

10   Information on removing and installing the battery can be found in Chapter 5. Information on jump starting can be found at the front of this manual. For more detailed battery checking procedures, refer to the *Haynes Automotive Electrical Manual*.

Charging

Warning: *When batteries are being charged, hydrogen gas, which is very explosive and flammable, is produced. Do not smoke or allow open flames near a charging or a recently charged battery. Wear eye protection when near the battery during charging. Also, make sure the charger is unplugged before connecting or disconnecting the battery from the charger.*

11   Slow-rate charging is the best way to restore a battery that's discharged to the point where it will not start the engine. It's also a good way to maintain the battery charge in a vehicle that's only driven a few miles between starts. Maintaining the battery charge is particularly important in the winter when the battery must work harder to start the engine and electrical accessories that drain the battery are in greater use.

12   It's best to use a one or two-amp battery charger (sometimes called a "trickle" charger). They are the safest and put the least strain on the battery. They are also the least expensive. For a faster charge, you can use a higher amperage charger, but don't use one rated more than 1/10th the amp/hour rating of the battery. Rapid boost charges that claim

to restore the power of the battery in one to two hours are hardest on the battery and can damage batteries not in good condition. This type of charging should only be used in emergency situations.

13   The average time necessary to charge a battery should be listed in the instructions that come with the charger. As a general rule, a trickle charger will charge a battery in 12 to 16 hours.

14   Remove all the cell caps (if equipped) and cover the holes with a clean cloth to prevent spattering electrolyte. Disconnect the negative battery cable and hook the battery charger cable clamps up to the battery posts (positive to positive, negative to negative), then plug in the charger. Make sure it is set at 12-volts if it has a selector switch.

15   If you're using a charger with a rate higher than two amps, check the battery regularly during charging to make sure it doesn't overheat. If you're using a trickle charger, you can safely let the battery charge overnight after you've checked it regularly for the first couple of hours.

16   If the battery has removable cell caps, measure the specific gravity with a hydrometer every hour during the last few hours of the charging cycle. Hydrometers are available inexpensively from auto parts stores - follow the instructions that come with the hydrometer. Consider the battery charged when there's no change in the specific gravity reading for two hours and the electrolyte in the cells is gassing (bubbling) freely. The specific gravity reading from each cell should be very close to the others. If not, the battery probably has a bad cell(s).

17   Some batteries with sealed tops have built-in hydrometers on the top that indicate the state of charge by the color displayed in the hydrometer window. Normally, a bright-colored hydrometer indicates a full charge and a dark hydrometer indicates the battery still needs charging.

18   If the battery has a sealed top and no built-in hydrometer, you can hook up a digital voltmeter across the battery terminals to check the charge. A fully charged battery

should read 12.5 volts or higher.

19   Further information on the battery and jump-starting can be found in Chapter 5 and at the front of this manual.

10   Chassis lubrication (every 6000 miles or 6 months)

Refer to illustrations 10.1 and 10.2

1   Refer to *Recommended lubricants and fluids* at the front of this Chapter to obtain the necessary grease, etc. You'll also need

10.1 Materials required for chassis and body lubrication

1   **Engine oil** - *Light engine oil in a can like this can be used for door and hood hinges*

2   **Graphite spray** - *Used to lubricate lock cylinders*

3   **Grease** - *Grease, in a variety of types and weights, is available for use in a grease gun. Check the Specifications for your requirements*

4   **Grease gun** - *A common grease gun, shown here with a detachable hose and nozzle, is needed for chassis lubrication. After use, clean it thoroughly!*

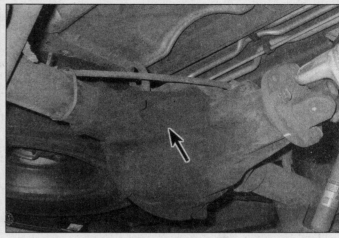

10.2 Wipe the dirt from the grease fittings before pushing the grease gun nozzle onto the fitting

11.2 Remove the filler plug to check the differential lubricant level

a grease gun **(see illustration).** If a suspension component has no grease fitting in place, this indicates the part is sealed and doesn't require periodic lubrication.

2   Look under the vehicle and locate the grease fittings **(see illustration).**

3   For easier access under the vehicle, raise it with a jack and place jackstands under the frame. Make sure it's safely supported by the stands. If the wheels are to be removed at this interval for tire rotation or brake inspection, loosen the lug nuts slightly while the vehicle is still on the ground.

4   Before beginning, force a little grease out of the nozzle to remove any dirt from the end of the gun. Wipe the nozzle clean with a rag.

5   With the grease gun and plenty of clean rags, crawl under the vehicle and begin lubricating the components.

6   Wipe one of the grease fittings clean and push the nozzle firmly over it. Pump the gun until the component is completely lubricated. On balljoints, stop pumping when the rubber seal is firm to the touch. Do not pump too much grease into the fitting as it could rupture the seal. For all other suspension and steering components, continue pumping grease into the fitting until it oozes out of the joint between the two components. If it escapes around the grease gun nozzle, the fitting is clogged or the nozzle is not completely seated on the fitting. Resecure the gun nozzle to the fitting and try again. If necessary, replace the fitting with a new one.

7   Wipe the excess grease from the components and the grease fitting. Repeat the procedure for the remaining fittings.

8   Clean the fitting and pump grease into the driveline universal joints until the grease can be seen coming out of the contact points. The other U-joints are sealed and do not require lubrication. **Note:** *Most replacement driveshaft U-joints aren't permanently sealed, and are sold with grease fittings. If your U-joints have been replaced, make sure you include them in your routine chassis lubrication.*

9   Also clean and lubricate the parking brake cable guides and levers. **Caution:** *Do not use chassis lubrication on the brake cables themselves. The grease will cause the cable housings to deteriorate.*

11   Differential lubricant level check (every 6,000 miles or 6 months)

Refer to illustration 11.2

1   The filler plug on the differential is a threaded metal type. If the vehicle is raised to gain access to the plug, be sure to support it safely on jackstands - DO NOT crawl under the vehicle when it's supported only by the jack. Be sure the vehicle is level or the check may not be accurate.

2   Using a ratchet and an extension, unscrew the plug from the filler hole in the differential housing or cover **(see illustration).**

3   The lubricant level should be at the bottom of the filler hole. If not, use a pump or squeeze bottle to add the recommended lubricant until it just starts to run out of the opening.

4   Install the plug securely into the filler hole.

12   Tire rotation (every 6,000 miles or 6 months)

Refer to illustrations 12.2a and 12.2b

1   The tires should be rotated at the specified intervals and whenever uneven wear is noticed.

2   Tires must be rotated in the recommended pattern **(see illustrations).**

3   Refer to the information in *Jacking and towing* at the front of this manual for the proper procedures to follow when raising the vehicle and changing a tire. If the brakes are to be checked, don't apply the parking brake as stated. Make sure the tires are blocked to prevent the vehicle from rolling as it's raised.

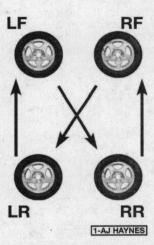

12.2a The recommended four-tire rotation pattern for non-directional radial tires

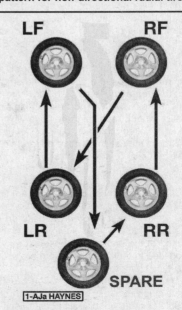

12.2b Five tire rotation pattern

4   Preferably, the entire vehicle should be raised at the same time. This can be done on a hoist or by jacking up each corner and then lowering the vehicle onto jackstands placed under the frame rails. Always use four jackstands and make sure the vehicle is safely supported.

5   After rotation, check and adjust the tire pressures as necessary. Tighten the lug nuts to the torque listed in this Chapter's Specifications.

13   Cooling system check (every 6,000 miles or 6 months)

Refer to illustration 13.4

Caution: *Never mix green-colored ethylene glycol anti-freeze and orange-colored "DEX-COOL®" silicate-free coolant because doing so will destroy the efficiency of the "DEX-COOL®" coolant which is designed to last for 100,000 miles or five years.*

1   Many major engine failures can be caused by a faulty cooling system.

2   The engine must be cold for the cooling system check, so perform the following procedure before the vehicle is driven for the day or after it has been shut off for at least three hours.

3   Remove the radiator cap by turning it to the left until it reaches a stop. If you hear a hissing sound (indicating there is still pressure in the system), wait until this stops. Now press down on the cap with the palm of your hand and continue turning to the left until the cap can be removed. Thoroughly clean the cap, inside and out, with clean water. Also clean the filler neck on the radiator. All traces of corrosion should be removed. The coolant inside the radiator should be relatively transparent. If it is rust colored, the system should be drained and refilled (see Section 23). If the coolant level is not up to the top, add additional antifreeze/coolant mixture (see Section 4).

4   Carefully check the large upper and lower radiator hoses along with the smaller diameter heater hoses which run from the engine to the firewall. Inspect each hose along its entire length, replacing any hose which is cracked, swollen or shows signs of deterioration. Cracks may become more apparent if the hose is squeezed **(see illustration)**. Regardless of condition, it's a good idea to replace hoses with new ones every two years.

5   Make sure all hose connections are tight. A leak in the cooling system will usually show up as white or rust colored deposits on the areas adjoining the leak. If wire-type clamps are used at the ends of the hoses, it may be a good idea to replace them with more secure screw-type clamps.

6   Use compressed air or a soft brush to remove bugs, leaves, etc. from the front of the radiator or air conditioning condenser. Be careful not to damage the delicate cooling fins or cut yourself on them.

7   Every other inspection, or at the first indication of cooling system problems, have the cap and system pressure tested. If you don't have a pressure tester, most gas stations and repair shops will do this for a minimal charge.

14   Underhood hose check and replacement (every 6000 miles or 6 months)

General

1   High temperatures in the engine compartment can cause the deterioration of the rubber and plastic hoses used for engine, accessory and emission systems operation. Periodic inspection should be made for cracks, loose clamps, material hardening and leaks. Information specific to the cooling system hoses can be found in Section 13.

2   Some, but not all, hoses are secured to their fittings with clamps. Where clamps are used, check to be sure they haven't lost their tension, allowing the hose to leak. If clamps aren't used, make sure the hose has not expanded and/or hardened where it slips over the fitting, allowing it to leak.

Vacuum hoses

3   It's quite common for vacuum hoses, especially those in the emissions system, to be color-coded or identified by colored stripes molded into them. Various systems require hoses with different wall thickness, collapse resistance and temperature resistance. When replacing hoses, be sure the new ones are made of the same material.

4   Often the only effective way to check a hose is to remove it completely from the vehicle. If more than one hose is removed, be sure to label the hoses and fittings to ensure correct installation.

5   When checking vacuum hoses, be sure to include any plastic T-fittings in the check. Inspect the fittings for cracks and the hose where it fits over the fitting for distortion, which could cause leakage.

6   A small piece of vacuum hose (1/4-inch inside diameter) can be used as a stethoscope to detect vacuum leaks. Hold one end of the hose to your ear and probe around vacuum hoses and fittings, listening for the "hissing" sound characteristic of a vacuum leak. **Warning:** *When probing with the vacuum hose stethoscope, be very careful not to come into contact with moving engine components such as the drivebelt, cooling fan, etc.*

Fuel hose

Warning: *Gasoline is extremely flammable, so take extra precautions when you work on any part of the fuel system. Don't smoke or allow open flames or bare light bulbs near the work area, and don't work in a garage where a gas-type appliance (such as a water heater or clothes dryer) is present. Since gasoline is carcinogenic, wear latex gloves when there's*

Check for a chafed area that could fail prematurely.

Check for a soft area indicating the hose has deteriorated inside.

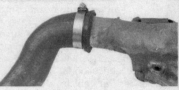

Overtightening the clamp on a hardened hose will damage the hose and cause a leak.

Check each hose for swelling and oil-soaked ends. Cracks and breaks can be located by squeezing the hose.

13.4 Hoses, like drivebelts, have a habit of failing at the worst possible time - to prevent the inconvenience of a blown radiator or heater hose, inspect them carefully as shown here

a possibility of being exposed to fuel, and, if you spill any fuel on your skin, rinse it off immediately with soap and water. Mop up any spills immediately and do not store fuel-soaked rags where they could ignite. When you perform any kind of work on the fuel system, wear safety glasses and have a Class B type fire extinguisher on hand. The fuel system is under pressure, so if any lines must be disconnected, the pressure in the system must be relieved first (see Chapter 4 for more information).

7   Check all rubber fuel lines for deterioration and chafing. Check especially for cracks in areas where the hose bends and just before fittings, such as where a hose attaches to the fuel filter and fuel injection unit.

8   High quality fuel line, specifically designed for high-pressure fuel injection applications, must be used for fuel line replacement. Never, under any circumstances, use regular fuel line, unreinforced vacuum line, clear plastic tubing or water hose for fuel lines.

9   Spring-type (pinch) clamps are commonly used on fuel lines. These clamps often lose their tension over a period of time, and can be "sprung" during removal. Replace all spring-type clamps with screw clamps whenever a hose is replaced.

Metal lines

10   Sections of metal line are routed along the frame, between the fuel tank and the engine. Check carefully to be sure the line has not been bent or crimped and no cracks have started in the line.
11   If a section of metal fuel line must be replaced, only seamless steel tubing should be used, since copper and aluminum tubing don't have the strength necessary to withstand normal engine vibration.
12   Check the metal brake lines where they enter the master cylinder and brake proportioning unit for cracks in the lines or loose fittings. Any sign of brake fluid leakage calls for an immediate and thorough inspection of the brake system.

15   Fuel system check (every 15,000 miles or 12 months)

Warning: *Gasoline is flammable, so take extra precautions when you work on any part of the fuel system. Don't smoke or allow open flames or bare light bulbs near the work area, and don't work in a garage where a gas-type appliance (such as a water heater or clothes dryer) is present. Since fuel is carcinogenic, wear latex gloves when there's a possibility of being exposed to fuel, and, if you spill any fuel on your skin, rinse it off immediately with soap and water. Mop up any spills immediately and do not store fuel-soaked rags where they could ignite. When you perform any kind of work on the fuel system, wear safety glasses and have a Class B type fire extinguisher on hand. The fuel system is under constant pressure, so, before any lines are disconnected, the fuel system pressure must be relieved (see Chapter 4).*
1   If you smell gasoline while driving or after the vehicle has been sitting in the sun, inspect the fuel system immediately.
2   Remove the fuel filler cap and inspect if for damage and corrosion. The gasket should have an unbroken sealing imprint. If the gasket is damaged or corroded, install a new cap.
3   Inspect the fuel feed line for cracks. Make sure that the connections between the fuel lines and the fuel injection system and between the fuel lines and the in-line fuel filter are tight. **Warning:** *Your vehicle is fuel injected, so you must relieve the fuel system pressure before servicing fuel system components. The fuel system pressure relief procedure is outlined in Chapter 4.*
4   Since some components of the fuel system - the fuel tank and part of the fuel feed line, for example - are underneath the vehicle, they can be inspected more easily with the vehicle raised on a hoist. If that's not possible, raise the vehicle and support it on jackstands.
5   With the vehicle raised and safely supported, inspect the gas tank and filler neck for punctures, cracks and other damage. The connection between the filler neck and the tank is particularly critical. Sometimes a rubber filler neck will leak because of loose clamps or deteriorated rubber. Inspect all fuel tank mounting brackets and straps to be sure that the tank is securely attached to the vehicle. **Warning:** *Do not, under any circumstances, try to repair a fuel tank (except rubber components). A welding torch or any open flame can easily cause fuel vapors inside the tank to explode.*
6   Carefully check all rubber hoses and metal lines leading away from the fuel tank. Check for loose connections, deteriorated hoses, crimped lines and other damage. Repair or replace damaged sections as necessary (see Chapter 4).

16   Brake check (every 15,000 miles or 12 months)

Warning: *Dust created by the brake system is harmful to your health. Never blow it out with compressed air and don't inhale any of it. An approved filtering mask should be worn when working on brakes. Do not, under any circumstances, use petroleum-based solvents to clean brake parts. Use brake system cleaner only!*
1   The brakes should be inspected every time the wheels are removed or whenever a defect is suspected. Indications of a potential brake system problem include the vehicle pulling to one side when the brake pedal is depressed, noises coming from the brakes when they are applied, excessive brake pedal travel, a pulsating pedal and leakage of fluid, usually seen on the inside of the tire or wheel. **Note:** *It is normal for a vehicle equipped with an Anti-lock Brake System (ABS) to exhibit brake pedal pulsations during severe braking conditions.*

Disc brakes

Refer to illustration 16.5

2   Disc brakes can be visually checked without removing any parts except the wheels. Remove the hub caps (if applicable) and loosen the front wheel lug nuts a quarter turn each.
3   Raise the front of the vehicle and place it securely on jackstands. **Warning:** *Never work under a vehicle that is supported only by a jack!*
4   Remove the front wheels. Now visible is the disc brake caliper which contains the pads. There is an outer pad and an inner pad. Both must be checked for wear.
5   Measure the thickness of the outer pad at each end of the caliper and the inner pad through the inspection hole in the caliper body **(see illustration).** Compare the measurement with the limit given in this Chapter's Specifications; if any brake pad thickness is less than specified, then all brake pads must be replaced (see Chapter 9).
6   If you're in doubt as to the exact pad thickness or quality, remove them for measurement and further inspection (see Chapter 9).
7   Check the disc for score marks, wear and burned spots. If any of these conditions exist, the disc should be removed for servicing or replacement (see Chapter 9).
8   Before installing the wheels, check all the brake lines and hoses for damage, wear, deformation, cracks, corrosion, leakage, bends and twists, particularly in the vicinity of the rubber hoses and calipers.
9   Install the front wheels, lower the vehicle and tighten the wheel lug nuts to the torque given in this Chapter's Specifications.

Drum brakes

Refer to illustrations 16.14 and 16.17

10   Remove the hub caps (if applicable) and loosen the wheel lug nuts a quarter turn each.
11   Raise the rear of the vehicle and support it securely on jackstands. **Warning:** *Never work under a vehicle that is supported only by a jack!* Block the front wheels to prevent the vehicle from rolling, however, do not apply the parking brake or it will lock the drums in place. Remove the rear wheels.

16.5 You will find an inspection hole like this in each caliper through which you can view the thickness of remaining friction material for the pads

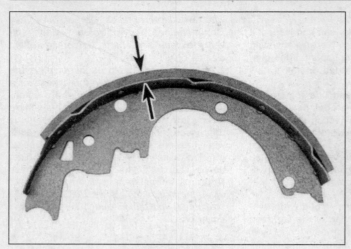

16.14 If the lining is bonded to the brake shoe, measure the lining thickness from the outer surface to the metal shoe, as shown here; if the lining is riveted to the shoe, measure from the lining outer surface to the rivet head

16.17 Carefully peel back the wheel cylinder boot and check for leaking fluid indicating that the cylinder must be replaced or rebuilt

12   Remove the brake drum as described in Chapter 9.

13   With the drum removed, carefully clean off any accumulations of dirt and dust using brake system cleaner. **Warning:** *DO NOT blow the dust out with compressed air and don't inhale any of it.*

14   Measure the thickness of the lining material on both leading and trailing brake shoes **(see illustration)**. Compare the measurement with the limit given in this Chapter's Specifications, if any brake shoe thickness is less than specified, then all brake shoes must be replaced (see Chapter 9).

15   Inspect the brake shoes for uneven wear patterns, cracks, glazing and delamination and replace if necessary. If the shoes have been saturated with brake fluid, oil or grease, this also necessitates replacement (see Chapter 9).

16   Make sure all the brake assembly springs are connected and in good condition.

17   Check the brake wheel cylinder for signs of fluid leakage. Carefully pry back the rubber dust boots on the wheel cylinder **(see illustration)**. Any leakage here is an indication that the wheel cylinders must be overhauled immediately (see Chapter 9). Also, check all hoses and connections for signs of leakage.

18   Clean the inside of the drum with brake system cleaner. Again, be careful not to breathe the dust.

19   Inspect the inside of the drum for cracks, score marks, deep scratches and "hard spots" which will appear as small discolored areas. If imperfections cannot be removed with fine emery cloth, the drum must be taken to an automotive machine shop for resurfacing.

20   Repeat the procedure for the remaining wheel.

21   Install the wheels, lower the vehicle and tighten the wheel lug nuts to the torque given in this Chapter's Specifications.

Parking brake

22   One method of checking the parking brake is to park the vehicle on a steep hill with the engine running (so you can apply the brakes if necessary) with the parking brake set and the transmission in Neutral. If the parking brake cannot prevent the vehicle from rolling, it needs adjustment (see Chapter 9).

17   Air filter check and replacement (every 15,000 miles or 12 months)

Refer to illustrations 17.1a and 17.1b

1   The air filter is located inside a housing in side of the engine compartment. To remove the air filter, loosen the clamp securing the inlet tube to the air filter cover, release the clamps that secure the two halves of the air cleaner housing together, then separate the cover halves and remove the air filter element **(see illustrations)**.

2   Inspect the outer surface of the filter element. If it is dirty, replace it. If it is only moderately dusty, it can be reused by blowing it

17.1a Loosen the intake hose clamp (A), release the clips securing the cover (B) . . .

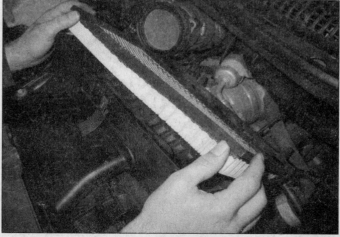

17.1b . . . then lift off the cover and remove the filter element

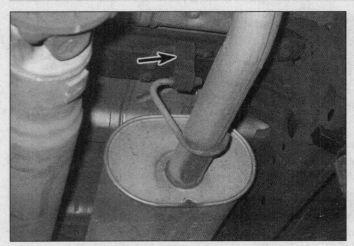

18.2 Be sure to check each exhaust system rubber hanger for damage

19.4 After relieving the fuel system pressure, squeeze the tabs to release the fuel lines (A), then remove the bracket bolt and remove the filter (B)

clear from the back to the front surface with compressed air. Because it is a pleated paper type filter, it cannot be washed or oiled. If it cannot be cleaned satisfactorily with compressed air, discard and replace it. While the cover is off, be careful not to drop anything down into the housing. **Caution:** *Never drive the vehicle with the air cleaner removed. Excessive engine wear could result and backfiring could even cause a fire under the hood.*

3   Wipe out the inside of the air cleaner housing.

4   Place the new filter into the air cleaner housing, making sure it seats properly.

5   Installation of the housing is the reverse of removal.

18 Exhaust system check (every 30,000 miles or 24 months)

Refer to illustration 18.2

1   With the engine cold (at least three hours after the vehicle has been driven), check the complete exhaust system from the engine to the end of the tailpipe. Ideally, the inspection should be done with the vehicle on a hoist to permit unrestricted access. If a hoist isn't available, raise the vehicle and support it securely on jackstands.

2   Check the exhaust pipes and connections for evidence of leaks, severe corrosion and damage. Make sure that all brackets and hangers are in good condition and tight **(see illustration).**

3   At the same time, inspect the underside of the body for holes, corrosion, open seams, etc. which may allow exhaust gases to enter the passenger compartment. Seal all body openings with silicone or body putty.

4   Rattles and other noises can often be traced to the exhaust system, especially the mounts and hangers. Try to move the pipes, muffler and catalytic converter. If the components can come in contact with the body or suspension parts, secure the exhaust system

with new mounts.

5   Check the running condition of the engine by inspecting inside the end of the tailpipe. The exhaust deposits here are an indication of engine state-of-tune. If the pipe is black and sooty or coated with white deposits, the engine may need a tune-up, including a thorough fuel system inspection and adjustment.

19 Fuel filter replacement (every 30,000 miles or 24 months)

Refer to illustration 19.4

Warning: *Gasoline is extremely flammable, so take extra precautions when you work on any part of the fuel system. Don't smoke or allow open flames or bare light bulbs near the work area, and don't work in a garage where a gas-type appliance (such as a water heater or clothes dryer) is present. Since fuel is carcinogenic, wear latex gloves when there's a possibility of being exposed to fuel, and, if you spill any fuel on your skin, rinse it off immediately with soap and water. Mop up any spills immediately and do not store fuel-soaked rags where they could ignite. When you perform any kind of work on the fuel system, wear safety glasses and have a Class B type fire extinguisher on hand.*

1   The fuel filter is mounted under the vehicle, in front of the gas tank.

2   Relieve the fuel system pressure (see Chapter 4).

3   If necessary, raise the vehicle and support it securely on jackstands. Inspect the fittings at both ends of the filter to see if they're clean. If more than a light coating of dust is present, clean the fittings before proceeding.

4   Release the clips holding the fuel lines to the filter **(see illustration).**

5   Detach the fuel hoses, one at a time, from the filter. Be prepared for fuel spillage.

6   After the lines are detached, check the fittings for damage and distortion. If they

were damaged in any way during removal, new ones must be used when the lines are reattached to the new filter (if new clips are packaged with the filter, be sure to use them in place of the originals).

7   Remove the fuel filter from the mounting clamp, while noting the direction the fuel filter is installed.

8   Install the new filter in the same direction. Carefully push each hose onto the filter until it's seated against the collar on the fitting, then install the clips. Make sure the clips are securely attached to the hose fittings - if they come off, the hoses could back off the filter and a fire could result!

9   Start the engine and check for fuel leaks.

20 Brake fluid change (every 30,000 miles or 24 months)

Warning: *Brake fluid can harm your eyes and damage painted surfaces, so use extreme caution when handling or pouring it. Do not use brake fluid that has been standing open or is more than one year old. Brake fluid absorbs moisture from the air. Excess moisture can cause a dangerous loss of braking effectiveness.*

1   At the specified intervals, the brake fluid should be drained and replaced. Since the brake fluid may drip or splash when pouring it, place plenty of rags around the master cylinder to protect any surrounding painted surfaces.

2   Before beginning work, purchase the specified brake fluid (see *Recommended lubricants and fluids* at the beginning of this Chapter).

3   Remove the cap from the master cylinder reservoir.

4   Using a hand suction pump or similar device, withdraw the fluid from the master cylinder reservoir.

5   Add new fluid to the master cylinder until

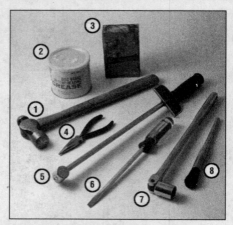

21.1 **Tools and materials needed for front wheel bearing maintenance**

1   **Hammer** - *A common hammer will do just fine*
2   **Grease** - *High-temperature grease that is formulated specially for front wheel bearings should be used*
3   **Wood block** - *If you have a scrap piece of 2x4, it can be used to drive the new seal into the hub*
4   **Needle-nose pliers** - *Used to straighten and remove the cotter pin in the spindle*
5   **Torque wrench** - *Used for preloading the bearing before adjustment*
6   **Screwdriver** - *Used to remove the seal from the hub (a long screwdriver is preferred)*
7   **Socket/breaker bar** - *Needed to loosen the nut on the spindle if it's extremely tight*
8   **Brush** - *Together with some clean solvent, this will be used to remove old grease from the hub and spindle*

it rises to the base of the filler neck.

6   Bleed the brake system as described in Chapter 9 at all four brakes until new and uncontaminated fluid is expelled from the

21.6 **Dislodge the dust cap by working around the outer edge with a hammer and chisel**

bleeder screw. Be sure to maintain the fluid level in the master cylinder as you perform the bleeding process. If you allow the master cylinder to run dry, air will enter the system.
7   Refill the master cylinder with fluid and check the operation of the brakes. The pedal should feel solid when depressed, with no sponginess. **Warning:** *Do not operate the vehicle if you are in doubt about the effectiveness of the brake system.*

---

21   Front wheel bearing check, repack and adjustment (every 30,000 miles or 24 months)

Refer to illustrations 21.1, 21.6, 21.7, 21.8, 21.11 and 21.15
Note: *This procedure applies to 2002 and earlier models only.*
1   In most cases the front wheel bearings will not need servicing until the brake pads are changed. However, the bearings should be checked whenever the front of the vehicle is raised for any reason. Several items, including a torque wrench and special grease, are

21.7 **Remove the cotter pin and discard it - use a new one when the hub is reinstalled**

required for this procedure **(see illustration).**
2   With the vehicle securely supported on jackstands, spin each wheel and check for noise, rolling resistance and freeplay.
3   Grasp the top of each tire with one hand and the bottom with the other. Move the wheel in-and-out on the spindle. If there's any noticeable movement, the bearings should be checked and then repacked with grease or replaced if necessary.
4   Remove the wheel.
5   Remove the brake caliper (see Chapter 9) and hang it out of the way on a piece of wire. **Caution:** *Don't depress the brake pedal while the caliper is removed.*
6   Pry the dust cap out of the hub using a screwdriver or hammer and chisel **(see illustration).**
7   Straighten the bent ends of the cotter pin, then pull the cotter pin out of the nut **(see illustration).** Discard the cotter pin and use a new one during reassembly.
8   Remove the spindle nut and washer from the end of the spindle **(see illustration).**
9   Pull the hub/disc assembly out slightly, then push it back into its original position. This

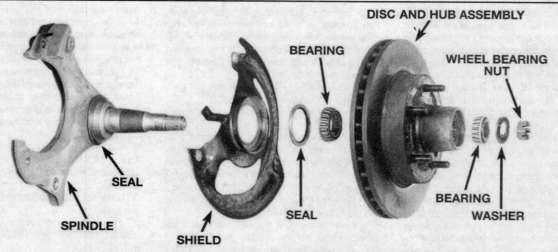

21.8 **Typical front wheel hub and bearing components (2002 and earlier models)**

21.11 Use a large screwdriver to pry the grease seal out of the rear of the hub

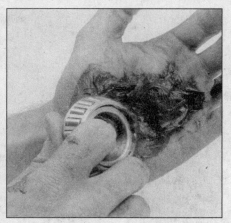

21.15 Work grease into the bearing rollers by pressing it against the palm of your hand

should force the outer bearing off the spindle enough so it can be removed.

10 Pull the hub/disc assembly off the spindle.

11 Use a screwdriver to pry the seal out of the rear of the hub **(see illustration)**. As this is done, note how the seal is installed.

12 Remove the inner wheel bearing from the hub.

13 Use solvent to remove all traces of the old grease from the bearings, hub and spindle. A small brush may prove helpful; however make sure no bristles from the brush embed themselves inside the bearing rollers. Allow the parts to air dry.

14 Carefully inspect the bearings for cracks, heat discoloration, worn rollers, etc. Check the bearing races inside the hub for wear and damage. If the bearing races are defective, the hubs should be taken to a machine shop with the facilities to remove the old races and press new ones in. Note that the bearings and races come as matched sets and old bearings should never be installed on new races.

15 Use high-temperature front wheel bearing grease to pack the bearings. Work the grease completely into the bearings, forcing it between the rollers, cone and cage from the back side **(see illustration)**.

16 Apply a thin coat of grease to the spindle at the outer bearing seat, inner bearing seat,

shoulder and seal seat.

17 Put a small quantity of grease inboard of each bearing race inside the hub.

18 Place the grease-packed inner bearing into the rear of the hub and put a little more grease outboard of the bearing.

19 Place a new seal over the inner bearing and tap the seal evenly into place with a hammer and block of wood until it's flush with the hub.

20 Carefully place the hub assembly onto the spindle and push the grease-packed outer bearing into position.

21 Install the washer and spindle nut. Tighten the nut only slightly (no more than 12 ft-lbs of torque).

22 Spin the hub in a forward direction to seat the bearings and remove any grease or burrs which could cause excessive bearing play later.

23 Check to see that the tightness of the spindle nut is still approximately 12 ft-lbs.

24 Loosen the spindle nut until it's just loose, no more.

25 Using your hand (not a wrench of any kind), tighten the nut until it's snug. Install a new cotter pin through the hole in the spindle and spindle nut. If the nut slots don't line up, loosen the nut slightly until they do. From the hand-tight position, the nut should not be

loosened more than one-half flat to install the cotter pin.

26 Bend the ends of the cotter pin until they're flat against the nut. Cut off any extra length which could interfere with the dust cap.

27 Install the dust cap, tapping it into place with a hammer.

28 Place the brake caliper near the rotor and carefully remove the wood spacer. Install the caliper (see Chapter 9).

29 Install the tire/wheel assembly on the hub and tighten the lug nuts.

30 Grasp the top and bottom of the tire and check the bearings in the manner described earlier in this Section.

31 Lower the vehicle.

22 Suspension and steering check (every 30,000 miles or 24 months)

Note: *The steering linkage and suspension components should be checked periodically. Worn or damaged suspension and steering linkage components can result in excessive and abnormal tire wear, poor ride quality and vehicle handling and reduced fuel economy. For detailed illustrations of the steering and suspension components, refer to Chapter 10.*

Shock absorber check
Refer to illustration 22.6

1 Park the vehicle on level ground, turn the engine off and set the parking brake. Check the tire pressures.

2 Push down at one corner of the vehicle, then release it while noting the movement of the body. It should stop moving and come to rest in a level position within one or two bounces.

3 If the vehicle continues to move up-and-down or if it fails to return to its original position, a worn or weak shock absorber is probably the reason.

4 Repeat the above check at each of the three remaining corners of the vehicle.

5 Raise the vehicle and support it securely on jackstands.

6 Check the shock absorbers for evidence of fluid leakage **(see illustration)**. A light film of fluid is no cause for concern. Make sure that any fluid noted is from the shocks and not from some other source. If leakage is noted, replace the shocks as a set.

7 Check the shocks to be sure that they are securely mounted and undamaged. Check the upper mounts for damage and wear. If damage or wear is noted, replace the shocks as a set (front or rear).

8 If the shocks must be replaced, refer to Chapter 10 for the procedure.

Steering and suspension check
Refer to illustrations 22.9a, 22.9b, 22.9c and 22.11

9 Visually inspect the steering and suspension components (front and rear) for damage

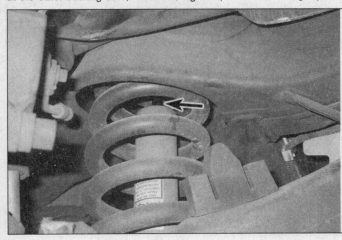

22.6 Check the shocks for leakage at the indicated area

22.9a Examine the mounting points for the upper . . .

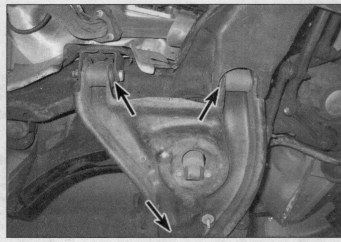

22.9b . . . and lower control arms on the front suspension

and distortion. Look for damaged seals, bushings and leaks of any kind. Examine the bushings where the control arms meet the chassis **(see illustrations)**.

10   Clean the lower end of the steering knuckle. Have an assistant grasp the lower edge of the tire and move the wheel in-and-out while you look for movement at the steering knuckle-to-control arm balljoint. If there is any movement the suspension balljoint(s) must be replaced.

11   Grasp each front tire at the front and rear edges, push in at the front, pull out at the rear and feel for play in the steering system components. If any freeplay is noted, check the idler arm and the tie-rod ends for looseness **(see illustration)**.

12   Additional steering and suspension system information and illustrations can be found in Chapter 10.

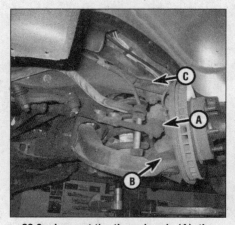

22.9c Inspect the tie-rod ends (A), the lower balljoint (B) and the upper balljoint (C)

22.11 With the steering wheel in the locked position and the vehicle raised, grasp the front tire as shown and try to move it back-and-forth - if any play is noted, check the idler arm and the tie-rod ends for looseness

---

23   Cooling system servicing (draining, flushing and refilling) (see Maintenance schedule for service intervals)

Warning 1: *Wait until the engine is completely cool before beginning this procedure.*
Warning 2: *Do not allow antifreeze to come in contact with your skin or painted surfaces of the vehicle. Rinse off spills immediately with plenty of water. Antifreeze is highly toxic if ingested. Never leave antifreeze lying around in an open container or in puddles on the floor; children and pets are attracted by its sweet smell and may drink it. Check with local authorities on disposing of used anti-freeze. Many communities have collection centers that will see that antifreeze is disposed of safely. Antifreeze is flammable under certain conditions - be sure to read the precautions on the container.*
Caution: *Never mix green-colored ethylene glycol anti-freeze and orange-colored "DEX-COOL®" silicate-free coolant because doing so will destroy the efficiency of the "DEX-*

COOL®" coolant, which is designed to last for 100,000 miles or five years.

Draining

Refer to illustrations 23.3 and 23.4

1   Periodically, the cooling system should be drained, flushed and refilled to replenish the antifreeze mixture and prevent formation of rust and corrosion, which can impair the performance of the cooling system and cause engine damage. When the cooling system is serviced, all hoses and the radiator cap should be checked and replaced if necessary.

2   Apply the parking brake and block the wheels. **Warning:** *If the vehicle has just been driven, wait several hours to allow the engine to cool down before beginning this procedure.*

3   Move a large container under the radiator drain to catch the coolant. Some models are equipped with a drain valve - it's located on the lower left side of the radiator **(see illustration)**. Attach a drain hose to the drain fitting and direct it into the container, then open the drain fitting (a pair of pliers may be required to turn it). On models without a drain fitting, detach the lower radiator hose from the radiator and direct the flow of coolant into the

container. **Note:** *On later models the radiator hoses are secured to the radiator fittings with retaining clips. Pull the clip from the hose*

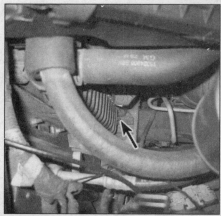

23.3 The radiator drain valve is located at the bottom of the radiator (viewed here from the top)

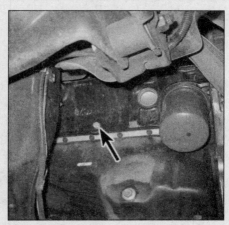

23.4 Cylinder block drain plug - there is one on each side of the block

fitting to release the hose from the radiator. Remove the radiator cap.

4   After coolant stops flowing out of the radiator, move the container under the engine block drain plugs - there's one on each side of the block (see illustration). Remove the plugs and allow the coolant in the block to drain.

5   While the coolant is draining, check the condition of the radiator hoses, heater hoses and clamps (refer to Section 13 if necessary).

6   Replace any damaged clamps or hoses. Apply Teflon pipe sealant to the drain plugs, then reinstall the drain plugs and tighten them securely.

Flushing

Refer to illustration 23.9

7   Once the system is completely drained, remove the thermostat from the engine (see Chapter 3). Then reinstall the thermostat housing without the thermostat. This will allow the system to be thoroughly flushed.

8   Reinstall the lower radiator hose or tighten the radiator drain plug. Turn your heating system controls to Hot, so that the heater core will be flushed at the same time as the rest of the cooling system.

9   Disconnect the upper radiator hose, then place a garden hose in the upper radiator inlet and flush the system until the water runs clear at the upper radiator hose (see illustration).

10   In severe cases of contamination or clogging of the radiator, remove the radiator (see Chapter 3) and have a radiator repair facility clean and repair it if necessary.

11   Many deposits can be removed by the chemical action of a cleaner available at auto parts stores. Follow the procedure outlined in the manufacturer's instructions. **Note:** *When the coolant is regularly drained and the system refilled with the correct antifreeze/water mixture, there should be no need to use chemical cleaners or descalers.*

Refilling

2002 and earlier models

12   To refill the system, install the thermostat and reconnect any radiator hoses.

13   Place the heater temperature control(s) in the maximum heat position.

14   Be sure to use the proper coolant listed in this Chapter's Specifications. Open the bleed valve (if equipped) on top of the thermostat housing, then slowly fill the radiator with the recommended mixture of antifreeze and water until a steady bubble free stream of coolant flows from the bleed valve, or on models not equipped with a bleed valve, until the coolant level is up to 1/2-inch from the bottom of the filler neck. Tighten the bleed valve securely. Add more coolant to the reservoir until it reaches the FULL COLD mark.

15   Run the engine until normal operating temperature is reached, then allow the engine to cool. With the engine cool, add coolant as necessary to bring the level to the FULL COLD mark on the reservoir.

16   Keep a close watch on the coolant level and various cooling system hoses during the first few miles of driving and check for any coolant leaks. Tighten the hose clamps and add more coolant mixture as necessary.

2003 and later models

17   To refill the system, install the thermostat and reconnect any radiator hoses.

18   Place the heater temperature control(s) in the maximum heat position.

19   Be sure to use the proper coolant listed in this Chapter's Specifications. Disconnect the upper radiator hose and the bleeder hose from the radiator, then using a funnel, slowly fill the upper radiator hose with the recommended mixture of antifreeze and water until a steady bubble free stream of coolant flows from the bleeder hose.

20   Reconnect the upper radiator hose and bleeder hose to the radiator.

21   Add more coolant to the radiator through the filler neck, until it is up to 1/2-inch from the base of the filler neck. Then add coolant to the reservoir until it reaches the FULL COLD mark.

22   Run the engine until normal operating temperature is reached, then allow the engine to cool. With the engine cool, add coolant as necessary to bring the level to the FULL COLD mark on the reservoir.

23   Keep a close watch on the coolant level and various cooling system hoses during the first few miles of driving and check for any coolant leaks. Tighten the hose clamps and add more coolant mixture as necessary.

---

24   Drivebelt check and replacement/ tensioner replacement (every 60,000 miles or 48 months)

Drivebelt check and replacement

Refer to illustrations 24.2a, 24.2b, 24.5a and 24.5b

1   A V-ribbed drivebelt (two on 2003 and later V8 models) is located at the front of the engine and plays an important role in the overall operation of the engine and accessories. Due to its function and material makeup, the belt is prone to failure after a period of time and should be inspected periodically. **Note:** *On 2003 and later V8 models with air conditioning, a separate belt for the air conditioning compressor is used.*

2   With the engine off, locate the drivebelt(s) at the front of the engine. Using your fingers (and a flashlight, if necessary), move along

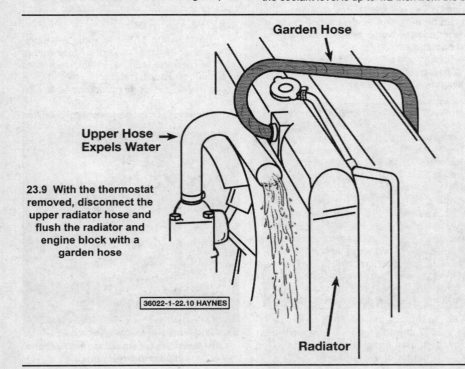

Garden Hose

Upper Hose Expels Water

23.9 With the thermostat removed, disconnect the upper radiator hose and flush the radiator and engine block with a garden hose

36022-1-22.10 HAYNES

Radiator

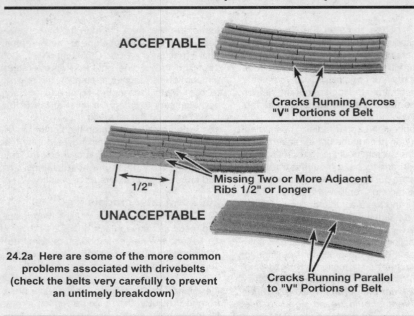

ACCEPTABLE

Cracks Running Across
"V" Portions of Belt

Missing Two or More Adjacent
Ribs 1/2" or longer

1/2"

UNACCEPTABLE

Cracks Running Parallel
to "V" Portions of Belt

24.2a Here are some of the more common
problems associated with drivebelts
(check the belts very carefully to prevent
an untimely breakdown)

24.2b The indexing mark (A) on the
tensioner arm must remain between the
limit marks (B) on the tensioner body
(2003 and later model V8 shown)

the belt, checking for cracks and separation of the belt plies **(see illustration)**. Also check for fraying and glazing, which gives the belt

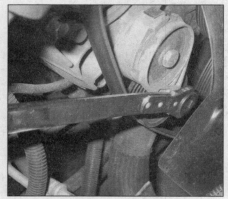

24.5a Rotate the tensioner arm to relieve
belt tension (1999 5.0L V8 shown)

a shiny appearance. Both sides of the belt should be inspected, which means you will have to twist the belt to check the underside. Check the pulleys for nicks, cracks, distortion and corrosion. Also check the tensioner; the belt should be replaced when the indexing mark nears or surpasses the limit mark on the tensioner body **(see illustration)**.

3 Check the ribs on the underside of the belt. They should be all the same depth, with none of the surface uneven.

4 The tension of the belt is automatically controlled by the tensioner, so no adjustment is necessary.

5 To replace the belt, use a breaker bar and socket to rotate the tensioner **(see illustrations)**. This will release the tension so the belt can be removed. When the belt is out of the way, release the tensioner slowly so you don't damage it.

6 Take the old belt with you when purchasing a new one to make a direct comparison for length, width and design.

7 When installing the new belt, make sure it is routed correctly. Also, the belt must completely engage the grooves in the pulleys.

Tensioner replacement

Refer to illustrations 24.8a, 24.8b and 24.8c

8 To replace the tensioner, remove the drivebelt, then unscrew the mounting bolt(s) and separate the tensioner from the engine **(see illustrations)**.

9 Installation is the reverse of the removal procedure. Be sure to tighten the fasteners securely.

25 Evaporative Emissions (EVAP) control system - check (every 60,000 miles or 48 months)

Refer to illustration 25.2

1 The function of the evaporative emissions control system is to draw fuel vapors from the gas tank and fuel system, store them in a charcoal canister and route them to the intake manifold during normal engine operation.

2 The most common symptom of a fault in

24.5b On 2003 and later V8 models with
air conditioning, the A/C belt tensioner is
best accessed from below - use a 3/8-inch
drive tool in the square hole to rotate
it for belt removal

24.8a To replace the drivebelt tensioner
on a 2002 or earlier model, remove the
drivebelt, then unscrew the bolt in the
center of the tensioner

24.8b Main belt tensioner mounting bolts
- 2003 and later models

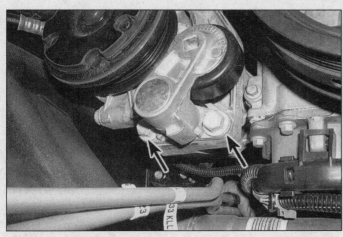

24.8c Air conditioning belt tensioner - 2003 and later V8 models

25.2 The EVAP canister is located in front of the fuel tank

the evaporative emissions system is a strong fuel odor. If a fuel odor is detected, inspect the EVAP canister, located in front of the fuel tank **(see illustration)**. Check the canister and all hoses for damage and deterioration.

3   The evaporative emissions control system is explained in more detail in Chapter 6.

26 Spark plug replacement (every 100,000 miles or 60 months)

Refer to illustrations 26.2, 26.5a, 26.5b, 26.6a, 26.6b, 26.8, 26.9 and 26.10

1   The spark plugs are threaded into the sides of the cylinder heads, adjacent to the

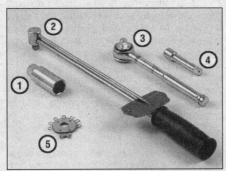

26.2 Tools required for changing spark plugs

1   **Spark plug socket** - *This will have special padding inside to protect the spark plug's porcelain insulator*
2   **Torque wrench** - *Although not mandatory, using this tool is the best way to ensure the plugs are tightened properly*
3   **Ratchet** - *Standard hand tool to fit the spark plug socket*
4   **Extension** - *Depending on model and accessories, you may need special extensions and universal joints to reach one or more of the plugs*
5   **Spark plug gap gauge** - *This gauge for checking the gap comes in a variety of styles. Make sure the gap for your engine is included*

exhaust ports.

2   In most cases, the tools necessary for spark plug replacement include a spark plug socket which fits onto a ratchet (spark plug sockets are padded inside to prevent damage to the porcelain insulators on the new plugs), various extensions and a gap gauge to check and adjust the gaps on the new plugs **(see illustration)**. A special plug wire removal tool is available for separating the wire boots from the spark plugs, but it isn't absolutely necessary. A torque wrench should be used to tighten the new plugs.

3   The best approach when replacing the spark plugs is to purchase the new ones in advance, adjust them to the proper gap and replace them one at a time. When buying the new spark plugs, be sure to obtain the correct plug type for your particular engine. This information can be found in the owner's manual and the Specifications at the front of this Chapter.

4   Allow the engine to cool completely before attempting to remove any of the plugs. While you're waiting for the engine to cool, check the new plugs for defects and adjust the gaps.

5   The gap is checked by inserting the proper-thickness gauge between the electrodes at the tip of the plug **(see illustration)**. The gap between the electrodes should be the same as the one specified on the Vehicle Emissions Control Information label or in this Chapter's Specifications. The wire should just slide between the electrodes with a slight amount of drag. If the gap is incorrect, use the adjuster on the gauge body to bend the curved side electrode slightly until the proper gap is obtained **(see illustration)**. If the side electrode is not exactly over the center electrode, bend it with the adjuster until it is. Check for cracks in the porcelain insulator (if any are found, the plug should not be used).

6   Loosen the front wheel lug nuts, raise the front of the vehicle and support it securely on jackstands, then remove the wheels and the inner fender splash shields. For easier access to the rear plugs, remove the engine cover (see Chapter 11). With the engine cool, remove the spark plug wire from one spark plug. Pull only on the boot at the end of the wire - do not pull on the wire. A plug wire removal tool should be used if available **(see illustrations)**.

26.5a Checking the spark plug gap using a wire-type gauge - if the wire does not slide between the electrodes with a slight drag, adjustment is required

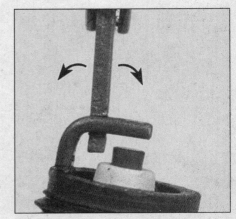

26.5b To change the gap, bend the side electrode only, as indicated by the arrows, and be very careful not to crack or chip the porcelain insulator surrounding the center electrode

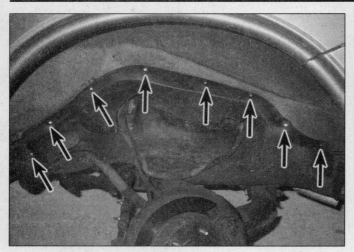

26.6a Remove the inner fender splash shield to gain access to the spark plugs

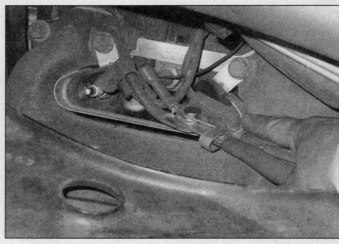

26.6b A tool like this one makes the job of removing the spark plug boots easier - twist it back-and-forth and pull only on the boot

7   If compressed air is available, use it to blow any dirt or foreign material away from the spark plug hole. The idea here is to eliminate the possibility of debris falling into the cylinder as the spark plug is removed.

8   Place the spark plug socket over the plug and remove it from the engine by turning it in a counterclockwise direction **(see illustration)**.

9   Compare the spark plug with the chart on the inside back cover of this manual to get an indication of the general running condition of the engine. Before installing the new plugs, it is a good idea to apply a thin coat of anti-seize compound to the threads **(see illustration)**.

10   Thread one of the new plugs into the hole until you can no longer turn it with your fingers, then tighten it with a torque wrench (if available) or the ratchet. It's a good idea to slip a short length of rubber hose over the end of the plug to use as a tool to thread it into place **(see illustration)**. The hose will grip the plug well enough to turn it, but will start to slip

if the plug begins to cross-thread in the hole - this will prevent damaged threads and the accompanying repair costs.

11   Before pushing the spark plug wire onto the end of the plug, inspect it following the procedures outlined in Section 27.

12   Attach the plug wire to the new spark plug, again using a twisting motion on the boot until it's seated on the spark plug.

13   Repeat the procedure for the remaining spark plugs, replacing them one at a time to prevent mixing up the spark plug wires.

---

27   Spark plug wires, distributor cap and rotor check and replacement (every 100,000 miles or 60 months)

Spark plug wires

Refer to illustration 27.6

1   The spark plug wires should be checked at the recommended intervals and whenever

new spark plugs are installed in the engine. 4.3L V6, 5.0L V8, 5.7L V8 and 7.4L V8 engines have spark plug wires that go from the plugs all the way to the distributor, while 4.8L V8, 5.3L V8 and 6.0L V8 engines have individual coils for each cylinder (no distributor is used) and short plug wires from each coil to the corresponding spark plug. For access to the plug wires, loosen the front wheel lug nuts, raise the front of the vehicle and support it securely on jackstands, then remove the wheels and the inner fender splash shields. Also remove the engine cover (see Chapter 11).

2   Begin this procedure by making a visual check of the spark plug wires while the engine is running. In a darkened garage (make sure there is adequate ventilation) start the engine and observe each plug wire. Be careful not to come into contact with any moving engine parts. If there is a break in the wire, you will see arcing or a small spark at the damaged area. If arcing is noticed, make a note to obtain new wires, then allow the engine to cool and check the distributor cap and rotor, if equipped (see Step 9).

3   Disconnect the plug wire from one spark plug (with the engine Off). To do this, grab the rubber boot, twist slightly and pull the wire free. Do not pull on the wire itself, only on the rubber boot. A boot-pulling tool is helpful **(see illustration 26.6b)**.

4   Check inside the boot for corrosion, which will look like a white crusty powder. Push the wire and boot back onto the end of the spark plug. It should be a tight fit on the plug. If it isn't, remove the wire and use a pair of pliers to carefully crimp the metal connector inside the boot until it fits securely on the end of the spark plug.

5   Using a clean rag, wipe the entire length of the wire to remove any built-up dirt and grease. Once the wire is clean, check for holes, burned areas, cracks and other damage. Don't bend the wire excessively or the conductor inside might break.

6   Disconnect the wire from the distributor

26.8 Use a socket and extension to unscrew the spark plugs - various length extensions and perhaps a flex-joint may be required to reach some plugs

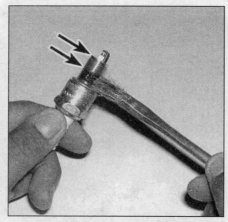

26.9 Apply a thin film of anti-seize compound to the spark plug threads, being careful not to get any near the electrodes (indicated by the arrows)

26.10 A length of rubber hose will save time and prevent damaged threads when installing the spark plugs

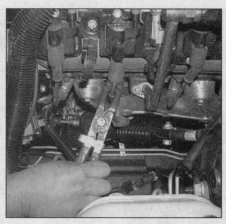

27.6 Use a spark plug boot pulling tool to remove each end of a spark plug wire - never pull on the wire itself

27.10 The ignition rotor should be checked for wear and corrosion (if in doubt about its condition, buy a new one)

cap or coil. Pull the wire straight out of the cap or coil. Pull only on the rubber boot during removal (see illustration). Check for corrosion and a tight fit in the same manner as the spark plug end. Reattach the wire to the distributor cap or individual coil.

7   Check the remaining spark plug wires one at a time, making sure they are securely fastened at both ends when the check is complete.

8   If new spark plug wires are required, purchase a new set for your specific engine model. Wire sets are available pre-cut, with the rubber boots already installed. Remove and replace the wires one at a time to avoid mix-ups in the firing order. The wire routing is extremely important, so be sure to note exactly how each wire is situated before removing it. On models equipped with a distributor, release the ignition wire loom clamps to exchange the wires, then snap the clamps back in place on the new wires. On models equipped with individual coils, there are two designs of plug wires, and the lengths are

different. Compare your old ones to the new ones to insure obtaining the correct replacements.

Distributor cap and rotor (4.3L V6, 5.0L V8, 5.7L V8 and 7.4L V8 engines only)

Refer to illustrations 27.10, 27.11 and 27.13

9   Remove the distributor cap screws. Pull up on the cap, with the wires attached, to separate it from the distributor, then position it to one side.

10   The rotor is now visible on the end of the distributor shaft. Check it carefully for cracks and carbon tracks. Make sure the center terminal spring tension is adequate and look for corrosion and wear on the rotor tip (see illustration). If in doubt about its condition, replace it with a new one.

11   If replacement is required, remove the two screws, then detach the rotor from the shaft and install a new one (see illustration).

12   The rotor is indexed to the shaft so it can

only be installed one way. It has an internal key that must line up with a slot in the end of the shaft (or vice versa).

13   Check the distributor cap for carbon tracks, cracks and other damage. Closely examine the terminals on the inside of the cap for excessive corrosion and damage (see illustration). Slight deposits are normal. Again, if in doubt about the condition of the cap, replace it with a new one. Be sure to apply a small dab of silicone dielectric grease to each terminal before installing the cap. Also, make sure the carbon brush (center terminal) is correctly installed in the cap - a wide gap between the brush and rotor will result in rotor burn-through and/or damage to the distributor cap.

14   To replace the cap, simply separate it from the distributor and transfer the spark plug wires, one at a time, to the new cap. Be very careful not to mix up the wires!

15   Reattach the cap to the distributor, then install the screws to hold it in place.

27.11 Remove the two screws to remove the rotor from the distributor

27.13 Inspect the inside of the cap for corrosion, carbon tracks and wear (check the outside of the cap for carbon tracks, too)

28.5 Remove the two fasteners securing the heat shield

28.10a Remove the filter from the transmission by pulling it straight down

28 Automatic transmission fluid and filter change (every 100,000 miles or 60 months)

Refer to illustrations 28.5, 28.10a, 28.10b and 28.12

1   At the specified intervals, the transmission fluid should be drained and replaced. Since the fluid will remain hot long after driving, perform this procedure only after the engine has cooled down completely.

2   Before beginning work, purchase the specified transmission fluid (see *Recommended lubricants and fluids* at the front of this Chapter) and a new filter and pan gasket.

3   Other tools necessary for this job include a floor jack, jackstands to support the vehicle in a raised position, a drain pan capable of holding at least eight quarts, newspapers and clean rags.

4   Raise the vehicle and support it securely on jackstands.

5   To access the pan bolts on the right side of the vehicle, remove the heat shield next to the catalytic converter **(see illustration)**.

6   Place the drain pan underneath the transmission pan. Remove the front and side pan mounting bolts, but only loosen the rear pan bolts approximately four turns.

7   Carefully pry the transmission pan loose with a screwdriver, allowing the fluid to drain.

8   Remove the remaining bolts, pan and gasket. Carefully clean the gasket surface of the transmission pan to remove all traces of the old gasket and sealant.

9   Drain the fluid from the transmission pan, clean the pan with solvent and dry it with compressed air, if available. **Note:** *Some models are equipped with magnets in the transmission pan to catch metal debris. Clean the magnet thoroughly. A small amount of metal material is normal at the magnet. If there is considerable debris, consult a dealer or transmission specialist.*

10   Remove the filter and filter seal from the valve body inside the transmission **(see illustrations)**. **Note:** *When removing the filter*

seal, be very careful not to gouge the delicate aluminum gasket surface on the valve body.

11   Install a new seal and filter. On many replacement filters, the seal is attached to the filter to simplify installation.

12   Make sure the gasket surface on the transmission pan is clean, then install a new gasket on the pan **(see illustration)**. Put the pan in place against the transmission and install all of the bolts. Working around the pan, tighten each bolt a little at a time to the torque listed in this Chapter's Specifications.

13   Reinstall the components removed for access to the pan bolts.

14   Lower the vehicle and add approximately 4 quarts of the specified type of automatic transmission fluid through the filler tube (see Section 4).

15   With the transmission in Park and the parking brake set, run the engine at a fast idle, but don't race it.

16   Move the gear selector through each range and back to Park, then let the engine idle for a few minutes. Check the fluid level. It

28.10b Use a seal removal tool to remove transmission seal from the valve body, then replace it with a new seal - be careful not to scratch the aluminum cavity

28.12 Clean the transmission pan, position the magnet back in place, and install the new pan gasket

will probably be low. Add enough fluid to bring the level to the proper mark on the dipstick. Be careful not to overfill.

17   Check under the vehicle for leaks during the first few trips. Check the fluid level again when the transmission is hot (see Section 4).

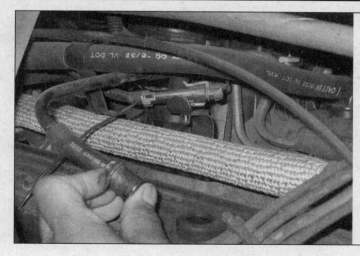

29.2 Pull out the PCV valve and check for vacuum with your finger

29   Positive Crankcase Ventilation (PCV) valve check and replacement (every 100,000 miles or 60 months)

Refer to illustration 29.2

1   The PCV valve is located in the valve cover. For access to the valve you'll have to remove the engine cover (see Chapter 11). **Note:** *For additional information on the PCV system, refer to Chapter 6.*

2   With the engine idling at normal operating temperature, pull the valve (with hose attached) from the rubber grommet in the cover **(see illustration).**

3   Place your finger over the valve opening. If there's no vacuum at the valve, check for a plugged hose, manifold port, or the valve itself. Replace any plugged or deteriorated hoses.

4   Turn off the engine and shake the PCV valve, listening for a rattle. If the valve doesn't rattle, replace it with a new one.

5   To replace the valve, pull it from the end of the hose, noting its installed position.

6   When purchasing a replacement PCV valve, make sure it's for your particular vehicle and engine size. Compare the old valve with the new one to make sure they're the same.

7   Push the valve into the end of the hose until it's seated.

8   Inspect the rubber grommet for damage and hardening. Replace it with a new one if necessary.

9   Push the PCV valve and hose securely into position.

Notes

Chapter 2 Part A
4.3L V6 and 5.0L, 5.7L and 7.4L V8 engines

Contents

Specifications

4.3L V6 engine

General
Displacement	262 cubic inches (4.3 liters)
Bore and stroke	4.012 x 3.480 inches
Cylinder numbers	
Left bank	1-3-5
Right bank	2-4-6
Firing order	1-6-5-4-3-2
Distributor rotation (viewed from above)	Clockwise

Camshaft
Journal diameter	
1996	1.8682 to 1.8696
1997	1.8682 to 1.8692
1988 and later	1.8677 to 1.8696 inch
Endplay	0.0010 to 0.0090 inch
Lobe lift	
1996	
Intake	0.274 to 0.278 inch
Exhaust	0.283 to 0.287 inch
1997	
Intake	0.286 to 0.290 inch
Exhaust	0.292 to 0.296 inch

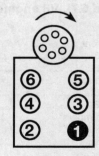

Cylinder location and distributor rotation diagram for the 4.3L V6 engine

Camshaft (continued)

Lobe lift
  1998 and 1999
    Intake
      L35 engine (VIN W)..   0.274 to 0.278 inch
      LF6 engine (VIN X)..   0.266 to 0.270 inch
    Exhaust
      L35 engine (VIN W)..   0.283 to 0.287 inch
      LF6 engine (VIN X)..   0.257 to 0.261 inch
  2000 through 2004
    Intake..   0.274 to 0.278 inch
    Exhaust...   0.283 to 0.287 inch
  2005 and later
    Intake..   0.270
    Exhaust...   0.279
Runout
  1996 through 2005 models ....   0.0026 inch
  2006 and later models...   0.0039 inch

Torque specifications

Ft-lbs (unless otherwise indicated)

Camshaft retainer bolt ....   106 in-lbs
Camshaft sprocket bolt...   18
Cylinder head bolts (in sequence - **see illustration 8.22a**)
  Step 1 (all bolts)   22
  Step 2
    Long bolts (1, 4, 5, 8 and 9)...   Tighten an additional 75-degrees
    Medium length bolts (12 and 13) ....   Tighten an additional 65-degrees
    Short bolts (11, 7, 3, 2, 6 and 10) ....   Tighten an additional 55-degrees
Driveplate-to-crankshaft bolts..   74
Upper intake manifold studs
  Step 1...   44 in-lbs
  Step 2...   80 in-lbs
Lower intake manifold bolts **(see illustration 6.29a)**
  Step 1...   27 in-lbs
  Step 2...   106 in-lbs
  Step 3...   132 in-lbs
Exhaust manifold bolt/stud
  Step 1...   132 in-lbs
  Step 2...   22
Oil pan mounting bolt/nut..   18
Oil pan baffle bolt..   106 in-lbs
Oil pump mounting bolt...   66
Rocker arm studs (1999 and earlier models)   35
Rocker arm nut (1999 and earlier models)...   20
Rocker arm bolts (2000 and later models)...   22
Rear main oil seal housing bolts...   106 in-lbs
Valve cover-to-cylinder head bolts...   106 in-lbs
Timing chain cover-to-block bolts ....   106 in-lbs
Vibration damper bolt   70

5.0L and 5.7L V8 engines

General

Displacement
  5.0L V8..   305 cubic inches (5.0 liters)
  5.7L V8..   356 cubic inches (5.7 liters)
Bore and stroke
  5.0L V8..   3.737 x 3.480 inches
  5.7L V8..   4.001 x 3.480 inches
Cylinder numbers
  Left bank   1-3-5-7
  Right bank   2-4-6-8
Firing order   1-8-4-3-6-5-7-2
Distributor rotation (viewed from above)...   Clockwise

Camshaft

Journal diameter...   1.8677 to 1.8697 inch
Endplay..   0.002 to 0.012 inch

**Cylinder location and distributor
rotation diagram
for the 5.0L, 5.7L and 7.4L
V8 engines**

Camshaft (continued)

Lobe lift	
Intake	0.274 to 0.278 inch
Exhaust	0.283 to 0.287 inch
Runout	0.0026 inch

Torque specifications

Ft-lbs (unless otherwise indicated)

Camshaft retainer bolt	106 in-lbs
Camshaft sprocket bolt	18
Cylinder head bolts (in sequence - **see illustration 8.22b**)	
Step 1 (all bolts)	22
Step 2	
Long bolts (1, 2, 5, 6, 9, 10 and 13)	Tighten an additional 75-degrees
Medium length bolts (14 and 17)	Tighten an additional 65-degrees
Short bolts (3, 4, 7, 8, 11, 12, 15 and 16)	Tighten an additional 55-degrees
Driveplate-to-crankshaft bolts	74
Upper intake manifold studs	
Step 1	44 in-lbs
Step 2	89 in-lbs
Lower intake manifold bolts (**see illustration 6.29a**)	
Step 1	27 in-lbs
Step 2	106 in-lbs
Step 3	132 in-lbs
Exhaust manifold bolt/stud	
Step 1	132 in-lbs
Step 2	22
Oil pan mounting bolts	106 in-lbs
Oil pan mounting nuts	18
Oil pump mounting bolt	
Step 1	15
Step 2	Tighten an additional 65-degrees
Valve cover-to-cylinder head bolts	106 in-lbs
Timing chain cover-to-block bolts	106 in-lbs
Vibration damper bolt	74

7.4L V8 engine

General

Displacement	454 cubic inches (7.4 liters)
Bore and stroke	4.25 x 4.00 inches
Cylinder numbers	
Left bank	1-3-5-7
Right bank	2-4-6-8
Firing order	1-8-4-3-6-5-7-2
Distributor rotation (viewed from above)	Clockwise

Camshaft

Journal diameter	1.9477 to 1.9497 inch
Endplay	0.002 to 0.012 inch
Lobe lift	
Intake	0.2801 to 0.2841 inch
Exhaust	0.2823 to 0.2863 inch
Runout	0.002 inch

Torque specifications

Ft-lbs (unless otherwise indicated)

Camshaft retainer bolt	106 in-lbs
Camshaft sprocket bolt	25
Cylinder head bolts* (in sequence - **see illustration 8.22c**)	
1997	
Step 1	30
Step 2	60
Step 3	85
1998	
Step 1	30
Step 2	60
Step 3	85
Step 4	
Long bolts (1, 2, 3, 6, 7, 8, 9, 12, 14 and 15)	92
Long bolts (13 and 16)	92
Short bolts (4, 5, 10 and 11)	89

Torque specifications (continued)

	Ft-lbs (unless otherwise indicated)
1999 and 2000	
Step 1 (all bolts)..	37
Step 2	
Long bolts (1, 2, 3, 6, 7, 8, 9, 12, 14 and 15)	Tighten an additional 150-degrees
Long bolts (13 and 16)	Tighten an additional 150-degrees
Short bolts (4, 5, 10 and 11)	Tighten an additional 90-degrees
Driveplate-to-crankshaft bolts..	65
Drivebelt pulley-to-vibration damper bolts	30
Upper intake manifold bolts **(see illustration 6.36)**	
Step 1..	72 in-lbs
Step 2..	156 in-lbs
Lower intake manifold bolts **(see illustration 6.29b and 6.29c)**	
Step 1..	22
Step 2..	30
Exhaust manifold center bolt	40
Exhaust manifold nuts (excluding center bolt).....................................	22
Oil pan mounting bolt	
Step 1..	18
Step 2..	18
Oil pump mounting bolt...	65
Rocker arm bolts	45
Valve cover-to-cylinder head bolts...	106 in-lbs
Timing chain cover-to-block bolts	106 in-lbs
Vibration damper bolt	110

Note: * *Use new cylinder head bolts*

1   General information

This Part of Chapter 2 is devoted to in-vehicle repair procedures for the 4.3L V6 and the 5.0L, 5.7L and 7.4L V8 engines. These engines utilize cast-iron blocks with cylinders arranged in a "V" shape angle between the two banks. The overhead valve cast iron cylinder heads are equipped with integral valve guides and seats. Hydraulic roller lifters actuate the valves through tubular pushrods and rocker arms. A balance shaft has been incorporated into the 4.3L V6 engine to smooth power pulsations. The balance shaft is located directly above the camshaft in the engine block and is driven off the camshaft. Refer to Chapter 2C for more information concerning the 4.3L V6 balance shaft.

To positively identify the engine, locate the Vehicle Identification Number (VIN) on the left front corner of the instrument panel. The VIN is visible from the outside of the vehicle through the windshield. The eighth character in the sequence is the engine designation. For example:

W, X = 4.3 liter V6 engine
M = 5.0 liter V8 engine
R = 5.7 liter V8 engine
J = 7.4 liter V8 engine

Information concerning engine removal and installation and engine overhaul can be found in Part C of this Chapter. The following repair procedures are based on the assumption that the engine is installed in the vehicle. If the engine has been removed from the vehicle and mounted on a stand, many of the steps outlined in this Part of Chapter 2 will not apply.

2   Repair operations possible with the engine in the vehicle

Many major repair operations can be accomplished without removing the engine from the vehicle.

Clean the engine compartment and the exterior of the engine with some type of pressure washer before any work is done. It will make the job easier and help keep dirt out of the internal areas of the engine.

Many of the in-vehicle engine repairs will require removal of the engine cover from inside the passenger compartment. Refer to Chapter 11 for the engine cover removal procedure. Also, many in-vehicle engine repairs will require air filter housing removal (see Chapter 4) and coolant reservoir removal (see Chapter 3).

If vacuum, exhaust, oil or coolant leaks develop, indicating a need for gasket or seal replacement, the repairs can generally be made with the engine in the vehicle. The intake and exhaust manifold gaskets, timing chain cover gasket, oil pan gasket, crankshaft oil seals and cylinder head gaskets are all accessible with the engine in place.

Exterior engine components, such as the intake and exhaust manifolds, the oil pan and oil pump, the water pump, the starter motor, the alternator, the distributor and the fuel system components can be removed for repair with the engine in place.

Since the cylinder heads can be removed without pulling the engine, valve component servicing can also be accomplished with the engine in the vehicle. Replacement of the timing chain and sprockets is also possible with the engine in the vehicle.

3   Top Dead Center (TDC) for number one piston - locating

Refer to illustrations 3.7 and 3.8

1   Top Dead Center (TDC) is the highest point in the cylinder that each piston reaches as it travels up the cylinder bore. Each piston reaches TDC on the compression stroke and again on the exhaust stroke, but TDC generally refers to piston position on the compression stroke.

2   Positioning the piston(s) at TDC is an essential part of many procedures such as distributor and timing chain/sprocket removal.

3   Before beginning this procedure, be sure to place the transmission in Neutral and apply the parking brake or block the rear wheels. Also, remove the engine cover (see Chapter 11), disable the ignition system by the disconnecting primary (low voltage) electrical connectors from the coil or the distributor (see Chapter 5), then remove the spark plugs (see Chapter 1).

4   In order to bring any piston to TDC, the crankshaft must be turned using one of the methods outlined below. When looking at the front of the engine, normal crankshaft rotation is clockwise.

a) *The preferred method is to turn the crankshaft with a socket and ratchet attached to the bolt threaded into the front of the crankshaft. Turn the bolt in a clockwise direction.*

b) *A remote starter switch, which may save some time, can also be used. Follow the instructions included with the switch. Once the piston is close to TDC, use a socket and ratchet as described in the previous step.*

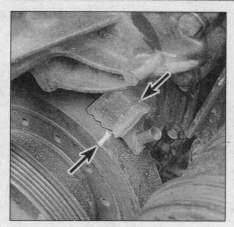

3.7 Align the timing mark on the vibration damper with the timing marks on the front cover . . .

3.8 . . . and check the position of the rotor. If the rotor is pointing to the mark you made on the distributor, the engine is at TDC compression for cylinder number one

c) *If an assistant is available to turn the ignition switch to the Start position in short bursts, you can get the piston close to TDC without a remote starter switch. Make sure your assistant is out of the vehicle, away from the ignition switch, then use a socket and ratchet as described in Paragraph (a) to complete the procedure.*

5   Scribe or paint a small mark on the distributor body directly below the number one spark plug wire terminal in the distributor cap.

6   Remove the distributor cap as described in Chapter 1 and position it aside with the spark plug wires attached.

7   Turn the crankshaft using one of the methods described above until the line on the vibration damper is aligned with the zero or "TDC" mark on the timing indicator **(see illustration)**.

8   If the engine is at TDC compression for cylinder number one, the rotor will be pointing at the mark that you made on the distributor body **(see illustration)**. If the rotor is 180-

degrees off, turn the crankshaft one complete revolution and line up the timing marks on the front cover and vibration damper.

9   After the number one piston has been positioned at TDC on the compression stroke, TDC for any of the remaining pistons can be located by turning the crankshaft (clockwise) 90-degrees (1/4-turn) at a time (V8 engines) or 120-degrees (1/3-turn) at a time (V6 engine) and following the firing order.

4   Valve covers - removal and installation

Note: *Not all steps apply to all models.*

Removal

1   Disconnect the cable from the negative terminal of the battery (see Chapter 5, Section 1).

2   Remove the air filter housing and air

intake duct (see Chapter 4).

3   Remove the engine cover (see Chapter 11).

Left side

Refer to illustrations 4.13a and 4.13b

4   Disconnect the spark plug wires from their clips and remove the spark plug wires from the spark plugs (see Chapter 1). Be sure each plug wire is labeled before removal to ensure correct reinstallation.

5   Remove the PCV valve and hose assembly or crankcase breather tube from the valve cover.

6   Remove the oil fill tube.

7   Remove the alternator rear bracket.

8   Disconnect the coolant gauge sender or coolant temperature sensor electrical connector (see Chapter 3).

9   Unbolt the air conditioning compressor from its bracket to give you some working room (see Chapter 3). On some models it may also be necessary to unbolt the bracket and move it forward **(see illustration 8.10)**.

10   Remove the power steering pump and bracket (see Chapter 10). Position the power steering pump off to the side without disconnecting the fluid lines. **Note:** *On some models it may not be necessary to remove the power steering pump. Loosen the power steering bracket bolts and move the assembly slightly for additional clearance.*

11   Remove the Secondary AIR injection pipe from the exhaust manifold (see Chapter 6), if equipped.

12   Remove the EGR pipe, if equipped (see Chapter 6).

13   Remove the valve cover bolts, then detach the cover from the cylinder head **(see illustrations)**. **Note:** *If the cover is stuck to the cylinder head, bump one end with a block of wood and a hammer to jar it loose. If that doesn't work, try to slip a flexible putty knife between the cylinder head and cover to break the gasket seal. Don't pry at the cover-to-head*

4.13a Remove the three retaining bolts from the center of the valve cover - 4.3L V6 engine

4.13b Remove the crankcase breather tube (1) and the retaining bolts (2) from the valve cover - 5.0L V8 engine shown

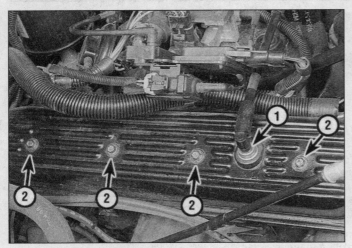

4.20 Details of the PCV valve (1) and the valve cover bolts (2) in the right side valve cover - 5.0L V8 engine shown

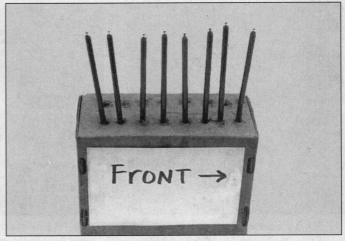

5.4 A perforated cardboard box can be used to store the pushrods to ensure that they're installed in their original positions - note the label indicating the front of the engine

joint or damage to the sealing surfaces may occur (leading to oil leaks in the future).

Right side

Refer to illustration 4.20

14   Remove the nuts and bolts securing the engine wiring harness to the upper intake manifold. Disconnect the connector from the ignition control module and position the engine wiring harness aside.

15   Remove the oil filler tube mounting bracket from the alternator and separate the oil filler tube from the valve cover.

16   Disconnect the spark plug wires from their clips and remove the spark plug wires from the spark plugs (see Chapter 1). Be sure each plug wire is labeled before removal to ensure correct reinstallation.

17   Disconnect the PCV valve and hose or crankcase breather tube from the valve cover.

18   Remove the AIR bypass hose, if equipped.

19   On 7.4L V8 engines, remove the throttle body and the throttle body studs (see Chapter 4).

20   Remove the valve cover bolts, then detach the cover from the cylinder head **(see illustration)**. **Note:** *If the cover is stuck to the cylinder head, bump one end with a block of wood and a hammer to jar it loose. If that doesn't work, try to slip a flexible putty knife between the cylinder head and cover to break the gasket seal. Don't pry at the cover-to-head joint or damage to the sealing surfaces may occur (leading to oil leaks in the future).*

Installation

21   The mating surfaces of each cylinder head and valve cover must be perfectly clean when the covers are installed. Use a gasket scraper to remove all traces of sealant and old gasket material, then clean the mating surfaces with lacquer thinner or acetone. If there's sealant or oil on the mating surfaces when the cover is installed, oil leaks may develop.

22   Clean the mounting bolt threads with a die to remove any corrosion and restore damaged threads. Make sure the threaded holes in the cylinder head are clean - run a tap into them to remove corrosion and restore damaged threads.

23   The gaskets should be mated to the covers before the covers are installed. Apply a thin coat of RTV sealant to the cover flange, then position the gasket inside the cover lip and allow the sealant to set up so the gasket adheres to the cover.

24   Install new valve cover bolt grommets to the valve cover and carefully position the cover(s) on the cylinder head and install the bolts.

25   Tighten the bolts in three or four steps to the torque listed in this Chapter's Specifications.

26   The remaining installation steps are the reverse of removal.

27   Start the engine and check carefully for oil leaks as the engine warms up.

---

5   Rocker arms and pushrods - removal, inspection and installation

---

Removal

Refer to illustration 5.4

1   Detach the valve cover(s) from the cylinder head(s) (see Section 4).

2   Beginning at the front of one cylinder head, loosen and remove the rocker arm stud nuts or bolts (7.4L V8 and 2000 and later 4.3L V6 models). Store them separately in marked containers to ensure that they will be reinstalled in their original locations. **Note:** *If the pushrods are the only items being removed, loosen each nut just enough to allow the rocker arms to be rotated to the side so the pushrods can be lifted out.*

3   Lift off the rocker arms and pivot balls

and store them in the marked containers with the nuts (they must be reinstalled in their original locations).

4   Remove the pushrods and store them separately to make sure they don't get mixed up during installation **(see illustration)**.

Inspection

5   Check each rocker arm for wear, cracks and other damage, especially where the pushrods and valve stems contact the rocker arm faces.

6   Make sure the hole at the pushrod end of each rocker arm is open.

7   Check each rocker arm pivot area for wear, cracks and galling. If the rocker arms are worn or damaged, replace them with new ones and use new pivot balls as well. On 2000 and later 4.3L V6 models, check the roller bearings in the rocker arm for free rotation.

8   Inspect the pushrods for cracks and excessive wear at the ends. Roll each pushrod across a piece of plate glass to see if it's bent (if it wobbles, it's bent).

Installation

Refer to illustrations 5.10 and 5.11

9   Lubricate the lower end of each pushrod with clean engine oil or moly-base grease and install them in their original locations. Make sure each pushrod seats completely in the lifter.

10   Apply moly-base grease to the ends of the valve stems and the upper ends of the pushrods before positioning the rocker arms over the studs **(see illustration)**.

11   Set the rocker arms in place, then install the pivot balls and nuts/bolts finger tight. Apply moly-base grease to the pivot balls to prevent damage to the mating surfaces before engine oil pressure builds up **(see illustration)**. Be sure to install each nut with the flat side against the pivot ball. **Note:** *On 2000 and later 4.3L V6 models, lubricate the roller bearings in the rocker arms with clean*

5.10 Lube the ends of the pushrods and the valve stems with moly-base grease prior to installation of the rocker arms

5.11 Moly-base grease applied to the pivot balls will ensure adequate lubrication until oil pressure builds up when the engine is started

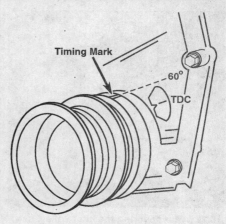

5.12 Before tightening the rocker arm nuts, position the crankshaft so that the timing mark is 60-degrees before TDC (V6 engine)

engine oil. If the rocker arm supports (below the rocker arms) were removed, make sure to reinstall them with the cast-in arrows pointing UP (away from the cylinder head) before installing the rocker arms.

4.3L V6 models

Refer to illustration 5.12

12   Rotate the crankshaft so that the timing mark on the vibration damper is 60-degrees before TDC **(see illustration)**. This is a neutral position in the engine rotation and will allow less valve spring tension as the rocker arms are tightened. Tighten the rocker arm nuts/bolts to the torque listed in this Chapter's Specifications.

5.0L and 5.7L V8 models

Refer to illustration 5.13

13   Rotate the engine to TDC for number 1 cylinder on the compression stroke (see Section 3). Tighten the rocker arm nuts on the number 1 cylinder intake and exhaust valves rocker arms until all play is removed from the

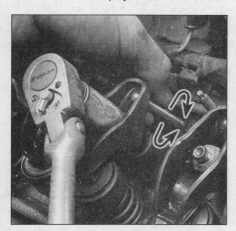

5.13 Rotate each pushrod as the rocker arm nut is tightened to determine the point at which all play is removed, then tighten each nut an additional 3/4 turn

pushrods. This can be determined by rotating the pushrod between the thumb and index finger before the nut is tightened **(see illustration)**. You will be able to feel the point at which all play is eliminated because a slight drag will be felt as you rotate the pushrod.

14   Tighten each nut an additional 3/4 turn (270 degrees) to center the lifters. Valve adjustment for cylinder number 1 is now complete.

15   With the engine still at TDC for cylinder number one, you can also adjust the intake valves for cylinders 2, 5 and 7, and the exhaust valves for cylinders 3, 4 and 8, using the same method.

16   Rotate the engine one complete revolution and line up the timing marks. With the engine in this position, adjust the intake valves for cylinders 3, 4, 6 and 8, and the exhaust valves for cylinders 2, 5, 6 and 7.

7.4L V8 models

17   Rotate the engine to TDC for number 1 cylinder on the compression stroke (see Section 3). Tighten the rocker arm bolts to the torque listed in this Chapter's Specifications.

All models

18   The remainder of the installation is the reverse of removal.

19   Start the engine and check for valve cover leaks and valvetrain noise.

---

6   Intake manifold - removal and installation

Warning: *Wait until the engine is completely cool before beginning this procedure.*
Note: *On the 4.3LV6 and the 5.0L/5.7L V8 engines, the upper and lower intake manifolds can be removed as a unit, by removing only the lower intake manifold bolts. For repairs or inspection of the fuel meter body or injectors, refer to Chapter 4.*

Removal

1   Relieve the fuel system pressure (see Chapter 4), then disconnect the cable from the negative terminal of the battery (see Chapter 5, Section 1).

2   Remove the engine cover (see Chapter 11).

3   Remove the air intake duct and detach the throttle cable and the cruise control cable from the throttle body (see Chapter 4).

4   Drain the cooling system and remove the drivebelt (see Chapter 1).

Upper intake manifold

5   Remove the Secondary AIR bypass hose(s), if equipped (see Chapter 6).

6   Label and disconnect the vacuum hoses and electrical connectors attached to the intake manifold and throttle body.

7   Remove the wiring harness brackets and clamps from the studs on the intake manifold and set the wiring harness aside.

8   Disconnect the fuel lines at the rear of the intake manifold (see Chapter 4).

9   Remove the crankcase vent tube from the throttle body or the PCV valve and hose from the valve cover (see Chapter 1).

10   On 7.4L V8 models, remove the throttle body (see Chapter 4).

11   Remove the EVAP canister purge solenoid valve (see Chapter 6).

12   Loosen the upper intake manifold mounting bolts a little at a time until they can be removed by hand.

13   Remove the upper intake manifold. As the upper intake manifold is lifted from the engine, be sure to disconnect anything still attached to the manifold.

Lower intake manifold

Note: *On some models it may be necessary to remove one of the valve covers (it doesn't matter which one) in order to get the intake manifold off (see Section 4).*

14   Remove the air conditioning compressor (see Chapter 3). Position the compressor off to the side without disconnecting the refriger-

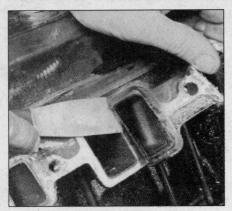

6.22 After covering the lifter valley, use a gasket scraper to remove all traces of sealant and old gasket material from the cylinder head and manifold mating surfaces

6.23 The bolt hole threads must be clean and dry to ensure accurate torque readings when the manifold mounting bolts are installed

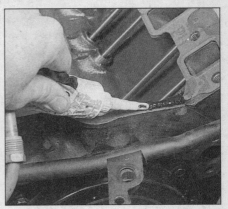

6.24 Apply a 3/16-inch bead of RTV sealant to the front and rear manifold mating surfaces of the engine block - be sure the beads extend up the cylinder heads 1/2-inch on each side

6.26 Be sure the gaskets are installed with the marks UP

ant lines. **Note:** *On some models it is possible to loosen the air conditioning compressor/ power steering pump bracket bolts and move the bracket forward with the components still attached.*

15   Remove the power steering pump and bracket (see Chapter 10). Position the power steering pump off to the side without disconnecting the fluid lines. **Note:** *Just as stated in the previous Step, you may be able to get away with simply loosening the bracket bolts and sliding the components forward.*

16   Remove any electrical connectors or ground straps that are attached to the manifold.

17   Refer to Chapter 5 and remove the distributor and alternator.

18   Remove the EGR pipe from the intake manifold and the exhaust manifold (see Chapter 6).

19   Remove the upper radiator hose from the intake manifold. Remove the coolant bypass hose from the intake manifold and the water pump (see Chapter 3). Also detach the heater hoses if they are attached to the manifold or are in the way.

20   Loosen the lower intake manifold mounting bolts in 1/4-turn increments in the reverse order of the tightening sequence until they

can be removed by hand **(see illustration 6.29a, 6.29b and 6.29c)**. Remove the lower intake manifold. The manifold will probably be stuck to the cylinder heads and force may be required to break the gasket seal. A pry bar can be positioned to pry up a casting projection at the front of the manifold to break the bond made by the gasket. **Caution:** *Do not pry between the block and manifold or the heads and manifold or damage to the gasket sealing surfaces may result and vacuum leaks could develop.*

21   As the manifold is lifted from the engine, be sure to disconnect any vacuum lines or electrical connectors still attached to the manifold.

Installation
Lower intake manifold

Refer to illustrations 6.22, 6.23, 6.24, 6.26, 6.29a and 6.29b

Note: *The mating surfaces of the cylinder heads, block and lower intake manifold must be perfectly clean when the manifold is installed. Gasket removal solvents in aerosol cans are available at most auto parts stores and may be helpful when removing old gasket material that is stuck to the heads and manifold. Be sure to follow the directions printed on the container.*

22   Use a gasket scraper to remove all traces of sealant and old gasket material, then clean the mating surfaces with lacquer thinner or acetone. If there's old sealant or oil on the mating surfaces when the manifold is installed, oil or vacuum leaks may develop. When working on the cylinder heads and block, cover the lifter valley with shop rags to keep debris out of the engine **(see illustration)**. Use a vacuum cleaner to remove any gasket material that falls into the intake ports in the cylinder heads.

23   Use a tap of the correct size to chase the threads in the bolt holes, then use compressed air (if available) to remove the debris from the holes **(see illustration)**. **Warning:** *Wear safety glasses or a face shield to pro-*

tect your eyes when using compressed air! Remove excessive carbon deposits and corrosion from the exhaust, EGR and coolant passages in the cylinder heads and manifold.

24   Apply a 3/16-inch wide bead of RTV sealant to the front and rear manifold mating surfaces of the block **(see illustration)**. Make sure the beads extend up the cylinder heads 1/2-inch on each side.

25   If the new manifold gaskets do not come equipped with a rubber sealing ring around the coolant passages, apply a thin coat of RTV sealant around the coolant passage holes on the cylinder head side of the new intake manifold gaskets. **Note:** *Factory replacement gaskets come equipped with a rubber sealant ring around the coolant passages and do not require extra RTV sealant around the coolant passages.*

26   Position the gaskets on the cylinder heads, with the ears at each end overlapping the bead of RTV sealant on the cylinder head. The upper side of each gasket should have a THIS SIDE UP label stamped into it to ensure correct installation **(see illustration)**.

27   Make sure all intake port openings, coolant passage holes and bolt holes are aligned correctly. Some gaskets may have small tabs which must be bent over until they're flush with the rear surface of each cylinder head.

28   Carefully set the manifold in place while the sealant is still wet. **Caution:** *Don't disturb the gaskets and don't move the manifold fore-and-aft after it contacts the sealant on the block.*

29   Following the recommended sequence, install the bolts (with thread-locking compound on the bolts) and tighten them to the torque listed in this Chapter's Specifications **(see illustrations)**.

30   The remaining installation steps are the reverse of removal.

31   Install the upper intake manifold, if removed.

32   Change the engine oil and filter and refill the cooling system (see Chapter 1).

33   Start the engine and check carefully for

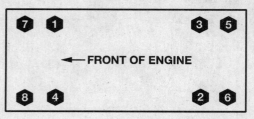

6.29a Lower intake manifold bolt tightening sequence on the 4.3L V6 and 5.0L, 5.7L V8 engines

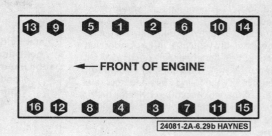

6.29b Lower intake manifold bolt tightening sequence on the 7.4L V8 engine - 1996 models

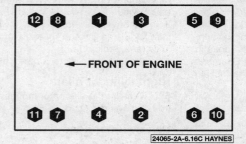

6.29c Lower intake manifold bolt tightening sequence on the 7.4L V8 engine - 1997 and later models

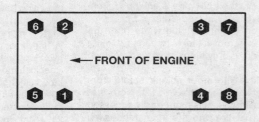

6.36 Upper intake manifold bolt tightening sequence on the 7.4L V8 engine

oil and coolant leaks at the intake manifold joints.

Upper intake manifold

Refer to illustration 6.36

34 Make sure all the fuel system components and the upper intake manifold are completely assembled and ready for installation (see Chapter 4). **Note:** *The fuel rail and fuel injection components on the 7.4L V8 engine are installed onto the lower intake manifold before the upper intake manifold is installed.*

35 Install a new rubber gasket into the upper intake manifold and carefully set the upper manifold in place. Do not allow the upper intake manifold to pinch the fuel injector lines between the lower intake manifold while lower-

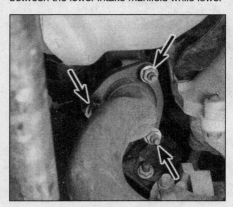

7.4 Access the exhaust pipe bolts/nuts from underneath the vehicle - on some models it may be easier to remove the wheel and fender splash shield and work through the fenderwell opening

ing the upper intake manifold into place.

36 Tighten the bolts to the torque listed in this Chapter's Specifications. On 7.4L V8 engines, follow the correct torque sequence **(see illustration)**.

37 The remaining installation steps are the reverse of removal. Start the engine and check carefully for oil and coolant leaks.

7 Exhaust manifolds - removal and installation

Removal

Refer to illustrations 7.4, 7.8 and 7.16

Warning: *Use caution when working around the exhaust manifolds - the sheetmetal heat shields can be sharp on the edges. Also, the engine should be cold when this procedure is followed.*

1 Disconnect the cable from the negative terminal of the battery (see Chapter 5, Sec-

tion 1). Remove the engine cover (see Chapter 11).

2 Raise the vehicle and support it securely on jackstands.

3 Working under the vehicle, apply penetrating oil to the exhaust pipe-to-manifold studs and nuts (they're usually rusty).

4 Remove the nuts retaining the exhaust pipe(s) to the manifold(s) **(see illustration)**.

Right side manifold

5 Remove the air filter housing (see Chapter 4).

6 Remove the Secondary AIR bypass hoses and valves, if equipped, from the exhaust manifold (see Chapter 6).

7 Detach the spark plug wires from the plugs, then remove the plug wire retaining bracket from the cylinder head and position them out of the way.

8 Remove the oil dipstick, unbolt the dipstick tube bracket and move the dipstick tube **(see illustration)**.

7.8 Right exhaust manifold mounting bolts and the oil dipstick tube mounting bolt (A)

9   Remove the inner splash shield from the fenderwell (see Chapter 11). Note that the exhaust manifold is more easily accessed with the front tire and the inner fenderwell removed, but it's not absolutely necessary.

10   Bend the lock tabs back (if equipped), then remove the mounting bolts and separate the exhaust manifold from the cylinder head. Remove the heat shields from the manifold after the bolts are removed.

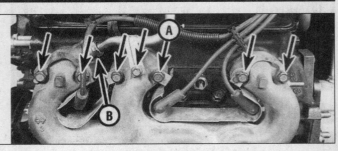

7.16 Left exhaust manifold mounting bolts and the EGR tube mounting nut (A) and tube fitting (B)

Left side manifold

11   Remove the Secondary AIR injection pipe, if equipped, from the exhaust manifold (see Chapter 6).

12   Remove the EGR pipe, if equipped, from the exhaust manifold (see Chapter 6).

13   Detach the spark plug wires from the plugs, then remove the plug wire retaining bracket from the cylinder head and position them out of the way.

14   Remove the inner splash shield from the fenderwell (see Chapter 11). Note that the exhaust manifold is more easily accessed with the front tire and the inner fenderwell removed, but it's not absolutely necessary.

15   Disconnect the electrical connector from the Engine Coolant Temperature (ECT) sensor (see Chapter 6).

16   Bend the lock tabs back (if equipped), then remove the mounting bolts and separate the exhaust manifold from the cylinder head **(see illustration)**. Remove the heat shields from the manifold after the bolts are removed.

Installation

17   Check the manifold for cracks and make sure the bolt threads are clean and undamaged. The manifold and cylinder head mating surfaces must be clean before the manifolds are reinstalled - use a gasket scraper to remove all carbon deposits.

18   Position the manifold on a bench and install the heat shields, bolts and gaskets onto the manifold. Retaining tabs surrounding

the gasket bolt holes will hold the assembly together as the manifold is installed. Place the manifold on the cylinder head and install the mounting bolts finger tight.

19   When tightening the mounting bolts, work from the center to the ends and be sure to use a torque wrench. Tighten the bolts in two steps to the torque listed in this Chapter's Specifications. If equipped, bend the locking tabs back against the bolt heads.

20   The remaining installation steps are the reverse of removal.

21   Start the engine and check for exhaust leaks.

---

8   Cylinder heads - removal and installation

Caution: *The engine must be completely cool when the cylinder heads are removed. Failure to allow the engine to cool off could result in cylinder head warpage. When cool, refer to Chapter 1 and drain the cooling system.*

Removal

1   If the vehicle is equipped with rear air conditioning and you're going to remove the left cylinder head, have the air conditioning system discharged by a licensed air conditioning technician.

2   Disconnect the cable from the negative

terminal of the battery (see Chapter 5, Section 1), then remove the engine cooling fan (see Chapter 3). Remove the valve cover(s) (see Section 4).

3   Remove the upper and lower intake manifolds (see Section 6), and exhaust manifolds (see Section 7).

4   Remove the pushrods (see Section 5).

Right cylinder head

5   Remove the alternator mounting bracket from the cylinder head.

Left cylinder head

Refer to illustration 8.10

6   Unbolt the engine ground wire at the rear of the cylinder head.

7   Remove the coolant gauge temperature sender, if equipped (see Chapter 3).

8   If equipped with rear air conditioning, unscrew the fitting nut and detach the auxiliary evaporator tube from the refrigerant line manifold at the air conditioning compressor.

9   Unbolt the air conditioning compressor from its bracket and position it to the side, without disconnecting the hoses.

10   Remove the air conditioning compressor/power steering pump mounting bracket from the left cylinder head **(see illustration)**.

11   Support the power steering pump and bracket out of the way with a length of wire or rope. Be careful not to let the bracket contact the radiator.

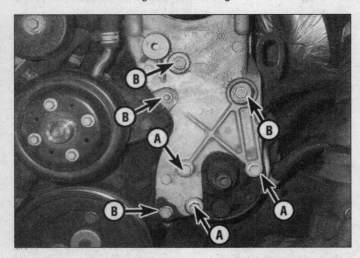

8.10 Location of the air conditioning compressor/power steering pump bracket mounting fasteners - 5.0L V8 engine shown

A   *Power steering pump mounting bolts*
B   *Bracket mounting bolts*

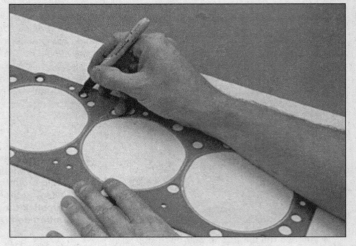

8.12 To avoid mixing up the cylinder head bolts, use a new gasket to transfer the bolt hole pattern to a piece of cardboard, then punch holes to accept the bolts

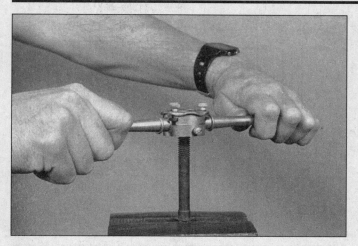

8.18 A die should be used to remove sealant and corrosion from the cylinder head bolt threads prior to installation

8.19a Locating dowels are used to position the cylinder head gaskets (and head) on the block

Both cylinder heads

Refer to illustration 8.12

12 Using a new cylinder head gasket, outline the cylinders and bolt pattern on a piece of cardboard **(see illustration)**. Be sure to indicate the front of the engine for reference. Punch holes at the bolt locations.

13 Loosen the cylinder head bolts in 1/4-turn increments until they can be removed by hand. Work from bolt-to-bolt in a pattern that's the reverse of the tightening sequence **(see illustration 8.22a, 8.22b or 8.22c)**. **Note:** *Don't overlook the row of bolts on the lower edge of each cylinder head, near the spark plug holes.* Store the bolts in the cardboard holder as they're removed; this will ensure that the bolts are reinstalled in their original holes.

14 Lift the cylinder head(s) off the engine. If resistance is felt, DO NOT pry between the cylinder head and block as damage to the mating surfaces will result. To dislodge the cylinder head, place a block of wood against the end of it and strike the wood block with a hammer. Store the cylinder heads on wood

blocks to prevent damage to the gasket sealing surfaces.

Installation

Refer to illustrations 8.18, 8.19a, 8.19b, 8.21, 8.22a, 8.22b and 8.22c

15 The mating surfaces of the cylinder heads and block must be perfectly clean when the cylinder heads are installed.

16 Use a gasket scraper to remove all traces of carbon and old gasket material, then clean the mating surfaces with lacquer thinner or acetone. If there's oil on the mating surfaces when the cylinder heads are installed, the gaskets may not seal correctly and leaks may develop. When working on the block, cover the lifter valley with shop rags to keep debris out of the engine. Use a vacuum cleaner to remove any debris that falls into the cylinders.

17 Check the block and cylinder head mating surfaces for nicks, deep scratches and other damage. If damage is slight, it can be removed with a file - if it's excessive, machin-

ing may be the only alternative.

18 Use a tap of the correct size to chase the threads in the cylinder head bolt holes. Mount each bolt in a vise and run a die down the threads to remove corrosion and restore the threads **(see illustration)**. Dirt, corrosion, sealant and damaged threads will affect torque readings.

19 Position the new gaskets over the dowel pins in the block **(see illustration)**. **Note:** *If a steel gasket is used, apply a thin, even coat of a sealant such as K&W Copper Coat to both sides prior to installation* **(see illustration)**. **Warning:** *Composition-type gaskets are used on some engines, with a thin, sheetmetal core. Be very careful when handling because the edges may be very sharp. Composition gaskets do not require sealant.*

20 Carefully position the cylinder heads on the block without disturbing the gaskets.

21 Before installing the cylinder head bolts, coat the threads with a non-hardening sealant such as Permatex no. 2 **(see illustration)**.

22 Install the bolts in their original locations and tighten them finger tight. Follow the rec-

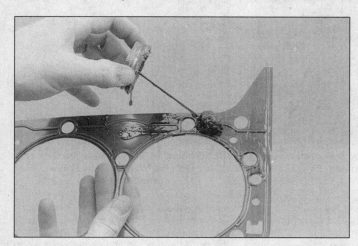

8.19b Steel gaskets should be coated with a sealant such as K&W Copper Coat before installation - composite gaskets do not use sealant

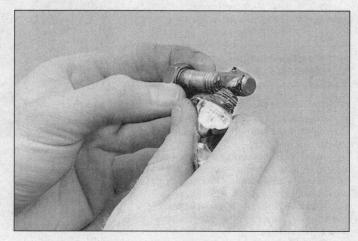

8.21 The cylinder head bolts MUST be coated with a non-hardening sealant (such as Permatex no. 2) before they're installed - coolant will leak past the bolts if this isn't done

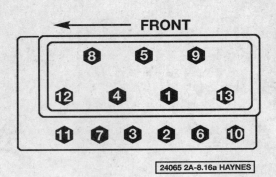

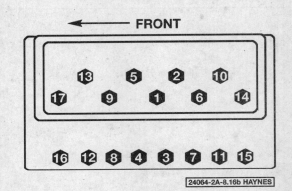

8.22a Cylinder head bolt tightening sequence on 4.3L V6 engines

8.22b Cylinder head bolt tightening sequence on the 5.0L and 5.7L V8 engines

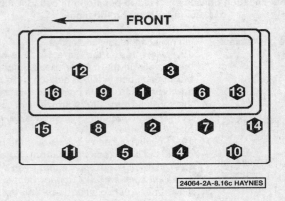

8.22c Cylinder head bolt tightening sequence on the 7.4L V8 engines

9.3 Remove the crankshaft pulley bolts and separate the pulley from the vibration damper

ommended sequence and tighten the bolts in several steps to the torque and angle of rotation listed in this Chapter's Specifications **(see illustrations)**.

23   The remaining installation steps are the reverse of removal.

24   Change the engine oil and filter (see Chapter 1), then start the engine and check carefully for oil and coolant leaks.

9   Vibration damper and pulley - removal and installation

Refer to illustrations 9.3, 9.5 and 9.6

1   Disconnect the cable from the negative terminal of the battery (see Chapter 5, Section 1).

2   Refer to Chapter 3 and remove the fan shroud and the engine cooling fan, then refer to Chapter 1 and remove the engine drivebelt.

3   Remove the bolts and separate the crankshaft pulley from the vibration damper **(see illustration)**.

4   Remove the large vibration damper-to-crankshaft bolt. To keep the crankshaft from turning, remove the starter (see Chapter 5) and have an assistant wedge a large screw-

9.5 Use a bolt-on-type puller to remove the vibration damper

driver against the ring gear teeth.

5   Using the proper puller, detach the vibration damper from the crankshaft **(see illustration)**. **Caution:** *Do not use a puller with jaws that grip the outer edge of the damper. The puller must be the type that utilizes bolts to apply force to the center of the damper hub*

9.6 The pulley keyway must be aligned with the Woodruff key in the crankshaft nose

only. Be careful not to lose the Woodruff key. **Caution:** *Insert a short bolt somewhat smaller than the damper bolt into the crankshaft for the tip of the tool to push against, or use an adapter on the end of the crankshaft for the puller screw to bear against to avoid damage to the threads in the crankshaft.*

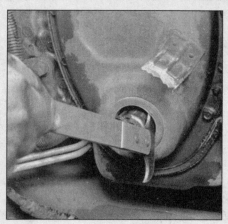

10.2 If you're replacing the seal with the timing chain cover installed, pry it out with a seal removal tool or a large screwdriver

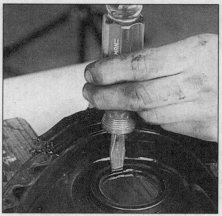

10.3 If you're replacing the seal with the timing chain cover removed, drive the old seal out from the inside with a hammer and punch or a screwdriver while supporting the cover near the seal bore,

10.5 Use a seal driver or large socket to drive the new seal into the cover

6   Make sure the woodruff key is in place, then position the vibration damper on the crankshaft and slide it on as far as it will go. Use a small dab of RTV sealant on the keyway of the damper before installation. Note that the slot (keyway) in the hub must be aligned with the Woodruff key in the end of the crankshaft **(see illustration)**.

7   Using a vibration damper installation tool, press the damper onto the crankshaft. Note that the crankshaft bolt can also be used to press the crankshaft balancer into position, but when doing so, use a liberal amount of clean engine oil on the bolt threads to prevent galling. Make sure the raised crown of the damper bolt washer is away from the crankshaft.

8   Tighten the crankshaft bolt to the torque listed in this Chapter's Specifications.

9   The remaining installation steps are the reverse of removal.

10   Crankshaft front oil seal - replacement

Refer to illustrations 10.2, 10.3, 10.5 and 10.6

1   Remove the crankshaft pulley and vibration damper (see Section 9).

2   Note how the seal is installed - the new one must be installed to the same depth and facing the same way. Carefully pry the oil seal out of the cover with a seal puller **(see illustration)**. **Caution:** *Be careful not to scratch, gouge or distort the area that the seal fits into or an oil leak will develop.* Wrap electrician's tape around the tip of the screwdriver to avoid damage to the crankshaft.

3   If the seal is being replaced with the timing chain cover removed, support the cover on top of two blocks of wood and drive the seal out from the backside with a hammer and punch **(see illustration)**. **Caution:** *Be careful not to scratch, gouge or distort the area that the seal fits into or a leak will develop.*

4   Clean the seal bore to remove any old

seal material and corrosion. Position the new seal in the bore with the seal lip (usually the side with the spring) facing IN (toward the engine). A small amount of oil applied to the outer edge of the new seal will make installation easier.

5   Drive the seal into the bore with a seal driver or a large socket and hammer until it's completely seated **(see illustration)**. Select a socket that's the same outside diameter as the seal and make sure the new seal is pressed into place until it bottoms against the cover flange.

6   Check the surface of the damper that the oil seal rides on. If the surface has been grooved from long-time contact with the seal, a press-on sleeve may be available to renew the sealing surface **(see illustration)**. This sleeve is pressed into place with a hammer and a block of wood and is commonly available from auto parts stores.

7   Lubricate the seal lips with engine oil and reinstall the vibration damper. Use a vibration damper installation tool to press the damper

10.6 If the sealing surface of the damper hub has a wear groove from contact with the seal, repair sleeves are available at most auto parts stores

onto the crankshaft.

8   Install the vibration damper-to-crankshaft bolt and tighten it to the torque listed in this Chapter's Specifications. Install the crankshaft pulley and tighten the bolts to the torque listed in this Chapter's Specifications.

9   The remainder of installation is the reverse of the removal.

11   Timing chain and sprockets - removal and installation

Warning: *Wait until the engine is completely cool before beginning this procedure*

Note: *Some 1996 and all 1997 and later 4.3L V6 and 5.0L, 5.7L V8 engines are equipped with a non-reusable plastic front cover. Once it is removed, it must be discarded or oil leaks could develop. 1998 and later 7.4L V8 engines are equipped with a reusable front cover and gasket; replace the front cover and gasket only if they have become damaged or worn.*

Removal

Refer to illustrations 11.5, 11.8 and 11.9

1   Disconnect the cable from the negative terminal of the battery (see Chapter 5, Section 1). Drain the cooling system (see Chapter 1).

2   Refer to Chapter 3 and remove the upper and lower fan shrouds, drivebelt, cooling fan and water pump.

3   Refer to Section 3 and position the number one piston at TDC on the compression stroke, then rotate the crankshaft an additional 360-degrees. **Caution:** *Once this has been done, DO NOT turn the crankshaft until the timing chain and sprockets have been reinstalled!*

4   Refer to Section 9 and remove the crankshaft pulley and vibration damper.

5   Remove the crankshaft position sensor and the nut retaining the wiring harness to the front cover **(see illustration)**.

6   Remove the oil pan (see Section 13).

11.5 Remove the crankshaft position sensor (lower arrow) and remove the nut (upper arrow) retaining the wiring harness to the cover stud

11.8 Before removing the sprockets or chain, remove the reluctor ring from the crankshaft

7   Remove the cover bolts and separate the timing chain cover from the block. It may be stuck - if so, use a putty knife or screwdriver to break the gasket seal. **Note:** *4.3L V6 and 5.0L, 5.7L V8 engines use a timing chain cover that is made of a composite material, which is not reusable. It is recommended to replace the front cover and the oil seal rather than try to reseal it and have it leak later.*

8   Remove the crankshaft position sensor reluctor ring **(see illustration)** just inside the front cover (see Chapter 6). Measure the timing chain freeplay. If it is more than 5/8-inch, the chain and both sprockets should be replaced. **Note:** *7.4L V8 engines require a special tool to remove the crankshaft position sensor reluctor ring.*

9   Remove the three bolts from the end of the camshaft, then detach the camshaft sprocket and chain as an assembly **(see illustration)**. **Note:** *On 4.3L V6 engines, the balance shaft drive gear will stay attached to the camshaft and the driven gear will stay attached to the balance shaft. If replacement of the timing chain is necessary, remove the sprocket on the crankshaft with a two or three-jaw puller, but be careful not to damage*

the threads in the end of the crankshaft.

Installation

Refer to illustration 11.13

10   Use a gasket scraper to remove all traces of old gasket material and sealant from the engine block. Clean the block sealing surfaces with lacquer thinner or acetone.

11   If a new timing chain is being installed, be sure to align the keyway in the crankshaft sprocket with the Woodruff key in the end of the crankshaft. Press the sprocket onto the crankshaft with the vibration damper bolt, a large socket and some washers, or tap it gently into place until it's completely seated. **Caution:** *If resistance is encountered, DO NOT hammer the sprocket onto the crankshaft. It may eventually move onto the shaft, but it may be cracked in the process and fail later, causing extensive engine damage.*

12   On 4.3L V6 engines, before installing the timing chain and camshaft sprocket, align the balance shaft gears (see Chapter 2C). The camshaft should be positioned with the balance shaft drive gear timing mark at 12 o'clock and the driven gear mark at 6 o'clock.

13   Check to make sure the crankshaft

sprocket timing mark is still in the 12 o'clock position. Loop the chain over the camshaft sprocket, mesh the chain with the crankshaft sprocket and position the camshaft sprocket on the camshaft with the timing mark in the 6 o'clock position. When correctly installed, the marks on the sprockets will be aligned as shown **(see illustration)**.

14   Apply a non-hardening thread locking compound to the camshaft sprocket bolt threads, then install and tighten them to the torque listed in this Chapter's Specifications. Lubricate the chain with clean engine oil.

15   Install the crankshaft position sensor reluctor ring. Be sure to install the reluctor with the dished side facing OUT!

16   Apply a thin layer of RTV sealant to the engine block sealing surface:

a)   *On 4.3L V6 and 5.0L/5.7L V8 engines, apply a small amount of sealant into the U-shaped channel at the bottom of the front cover. Position the new front cover and oil seal assembly on the engine block (the dowel pins and sealant will hold it in place). Composite covers do not have a gasket, they use sealant only - always purchase a new front cover and oil seal assembly to avoid sealing problems caused by the distortion of prying the old cover off.*

b)   *On 7.4L V8 engines, cut the tabs from a new front pan oil seal and use gasket sealer to hold the seal in the bottom of the front cover. Apply a 1/8 inch bead of RTV type gasket sealer to the junction of the oil pan and the front face of the block on each side.*

17   Install the cover retaining bolts and tighten them to the torque listed in this Chapter's Specifications.

18   Refer to the appropriate Sections and install the oil pan, vibration damper and the crankshaft position sensor. Be sure to use a **New** O-ring on the crankshaft position sensor.

19   The remaining installation steps are the reverse of removal.

11.9 Remove the three bolts from the end of the camshaft and remove the camshaft sprocket and chain as an assembly

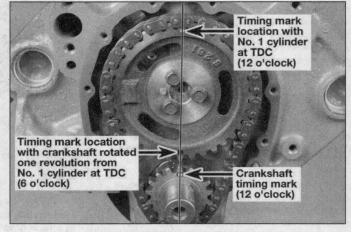

Timing mark location with No. 1 cylinder at TDC (12 o'clock)

Timing mark location with crankshaft rotated one revolution from No. 1 cylinder at TDC (6 o'clock)

Crankshaft timing mark (12 o'clock)

11.13 Crankshaft and camshaft timing marks (V8 engine shown, V6 similar)

12.3 When checking the camshaft lobe lift, the dial indicator plunger must be positioned directly above and in-line with the pushrod (use a short length of vacuum hose to hold the plunger over the pushrod end if you have difficulty keeping the plunger on the pushrod)

12.11 The lifters in an engine that has accumulated many miles may have to be removed with a special tool (arrow) - store them in an organized manner to make sure they're reinstalled in their original locations

12.13a The camshaft is retained by a thrust plate

12.13b Thread three long bolts into the end of the camshaft to use as a handle

12   Camshaft, bearings and lifters - removal, inspection and installation

Note: *The camshaft should always be thoroughly inspected before installation and camshaft endplay should always be checked prior to camshaft removal.*

Camshaft lobe lift check

Refer to illustration 12.3

1   To determine the extent of cam lobe wear, the lobe lift should be checked prior to camshaft removal. Refer to Section 3 and remove the valve covers.

2   Position the number one piston at TDC on the compression stroke (see Section 3).

3   Beginning with the number one cylinder, loosen the rocker arm nuts and pivot the rocker arms sideways. Mount a dial indicator on the engine and position the plunger against the top of the first pushrod **(see illustration)**.

4   Zero the dial indicator, then very slowly turn the crankshaft in the normal direction of rotation until the indicator needle stops and begins to move in the opposite direction. The point at which it stops indicates maximum cam lobe lift.

5   Record this figure for future reference, then reposition the piston at TDC on the compression stroke.

6   Move the dial indicator to the other number one cylinder pushrod and repeat the check. Be sure to record the results for each valve.

7   Repeat the check for the remaining valves. Since each piston must be at TDC on the compression stroke for this procedure, work from cylinder-to-cylinder following the firing order sequence.

8   After the check is complete, compare the results to the Specifications listed in this

Chapter. If camshaft lobe lift is less than specified, cam lobe wear has occurred and a new camshaft should be installed.

Removal

Refer to illustrations 12.11, 12.13a and 12.13b

9   Refer to the appropriate Sections and remove the intake manifold, the rocker arms, the pushrods and the timing chain and camshaft sprocket. On models with roller lifters, remove the lifter retainer (and on V8 engines, the lifter guides). Keep all of these parts in order; they must be returned to their original locations.

10   There are several ways to extract the lifters from the bores. A special tool designed to grip and remove lifters is manufactured by many tool companies and is widely available, but it may not be required in every case. On newer engines without a lot of varnish buildup, the lifters can often be removed with a small magnet or even with your fingers. A machinist's scribe with a bent end can be used to pull the lifters out by positioning the point under the retainer ring inside the top of each lifter. **Caution:** *Do not use pliers to remove the lifters unless you intend to replace them with new ones (along with the camshaft). The pliers will damage the precision machined and hardened lifters, rendering them useless.*

11   Before removing the lifters, arrange to store them in a clearly labeled box to ensure that they are reinstalled in their original locations. **Note:** *On engines equipped with roller lifters, the retainer must be removed before the lifters are withdrawn).* Remove the lifters and store them where they will not get dirty **(see illustration)**. Do not attempt to withdraw the camshaft with the lifters in place.

12   On 4.3L V6 engines, remove the balance shaft drive and driven gears (see Chapter 2C).

13   Remove the camshaft thrust plate **(see**

illustration). Thread 6-inch long 5/16 - 18 bolts into the camshaft sprocket bolt holes to use as a handle when removing the camshaft from the block **(see illustration)**.

14   Carefully pull the camshaft out. Support the cam near the block so the lobes do not nick or gouge the bearings as it is withdrawn.

Inspection

Refer to illustrations 12.16, 12.19a, 12.19b, 12.19c, 12.19d and 12.21

Camshaft and bearings

15   After the camshaft has been removed from the engine, cleaned with solvent and dried, inspect the bearing journals for uneven wear, pitting and evidence of seizure. If the journals are damaged, the bearing inserts in the block are probably damaged as well. Both the camshaft and bearings will have to be replaced. Replacement of the camshaft bearings requires special tools and techniques which place it beyond the scope of the home mechanic. The block will have to be removed from the vehicle and taken to an automotive machine shop for this procedure.

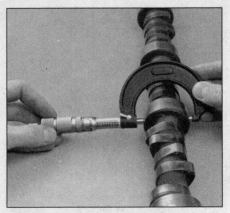

12.16 Check the diameter of each camshaft bearing journal to pinpoint excessive wear and out-of-round conditions

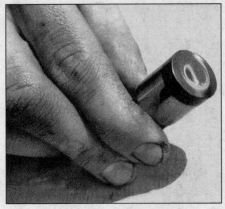

12.19a If the bottom of any lifter is worn concave, scratched or galled, replace the entire set with new lifters

12.19b The foot of each lifter should be slightly convex - the side of another lifter can be used as a straightedge to check it; if it appears flat, it is worn and must not be reused

16 Measure the bearing journals with a micrometer to determine if they are excessively worn or out-of-round (see illustration).
17 Check the camshaft lobes for heat discoloration, score marks, chipped areas, pitting and uneven wear. If the lobes are in good condition and if the lobe lift measurements are as specified, the camshaft can be reused.

Conventional lifters

18 Clean the lifters with solvent and dry them thoroughly without mixing them up.
19 Check each lifter wall, pushrod seat and foot for scuffing, score marks and uneven wear. Each lifter foot (the surface that rides on the cam lobe) must be slightly convex, although this can be difficult to determine by eye. If the base of the lifter is concave (see illustrations), the lifters and camshaft must be replaced. If the lifter walls are damaged or worn (which is not very likely), inspect the lifter bores in the engine block as well. If the pushrod seats are worn, check the pushrod ends.
20 If new lifters are being installed, a new camshaft must also be installed. If a new camshaft is installed, then use new lifters as well. Never install used lifters unless the origi-

nal camshaft is used and the lifters can be installed in their original locations.

Roller lifters

21 Check the rollers carefully for wear and damage and make sure they turn freely without excessive play (see illustration). The inspection procedure for conventional lifters also applies to roller lifters.
22 Used roller lifters can be reinstalled with a new camshaft and the original camshaft can be used if new lifters are installed.

Installation

Refer to illustrations 12.23 and 12.25

23 Lubricate the camshaft bearing journals and cam lobes with moly-base grease or engine assembly lube (see illustration).
24 Slide the camshaft into the engine. Support the cam near the block and be careful not to scrape or nick the bearings.
25 Turn the camshaft until the dowel pin is in the 9 o'clock position (see illustration).
26 On 4.3L V6 engines, install the balance shaft drive and driven gears (see Chapter 2C).
27 Refer to Section 11 and install the timing chain and sprockets.

12.19c If the lifters are pitted or rough, they shouldn't be reused

28 Lubricate the lifters with clean engine oil and install them in the block. If the original lifters are being reinstalled, be sure to return them to their original locations. If a new camshaft was installed, be sure to install new lifters as well.
29 The remaining installation steps are the reverse of removal.

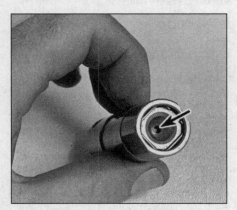

12.19d Check the pushrod seat in the top of each lifter for wear

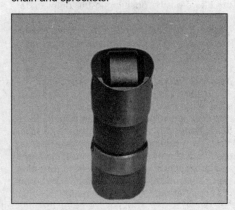

12.21 The roller on roller lifters must turn freely - check for wear and excessive play as well

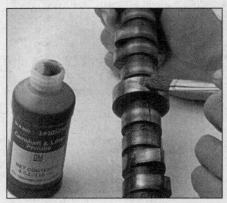

12.23 Lubricate the camshaft journals and lobes with camshaft and lifter assembly lube before installation to provide initial lubrication

12.25 After the camshaft is in place, turn it until the dowel pin is in the 9 o'clock position as shown here

13.16 Before tightening the oil pan bolts, measure the gap between the bellhousing and the oil pan in three places - if the gap is greater than 0.011 the oil pan will have to move towards the bellhousing - ideally the oil pan should be flush with the bellhousing

30   Before starting and running the engine, change the oil and install a new oil filter (see Chapter 1).

13   Oil pan - removal and installation

Refer to illustrations 13.16 and 13.17

Removal

1   Disconnect the cable from the negative terminal of the battery (see Chapter 5, Section 1).
2   Raise the vehicle and support it securely on jackstands. Refer to Chapter 1 and drain the engine oil and remove the oil filter. Remove the engine cover (see Chapter 11).
3   Remove the oil dipstick tube.
4   Install an engine support fixture.
5   Disconnect the exhaust pipes from the exhaust manifolds and the rear portion of the exhaust system and remove it from the vehicle (see Chapter 4). This step is not absolutely necessary, but it will help facilitate removal of the oil pan.
6   On 7.4L engines, remove the engine mounts. The engine must remain in a fixed position, supported by an engine hoist or engine support fixture. It may be necessary to remove the engine cooling fan (see Chapter 3) and raise the engine slightly for additional clearance for oil pan removal.
7   Remove the starter motor (see Chapter 5).
8   Remove the torque converter cover from the transmission.
9   Remove the oil pan nut and bracket retaining the transmission oil cooler lines.
10   Remove the oil pan bolts and nuts.
11   Remove the oil pan reinforcements on each side of the oil pan.
12   Lower the pan from the engine. The pan will probably stick to the engine, so strike the pan with a rubber mallet until it breaks the gasket seal. **Caution:** *Before using force on the oil pan, be sure all the bolts have been*

removed. Carefully slide the oil pan out, to the rear. **Note:** *It may be necessary to turn the crankshaft a little to reposition the crank throws so that they are out of the way.*

Installation

13   Wash out the oil pan with solvent.
14   Thoroughly clean the mounting surfaces of the oil pan and engine block of old gasket material and sealer. Wipe the gasket surfaces clean with a rag soaked in lacquer thinner or acetone. **Note:** *On models with a low-oil-level sensor, if a new oil pan is being installed, also install a new oil level sensor (don't transfer the old sensor to the new pan).*
15   Apply a 3/16-inch wide, one inch long bead of RTV sealant to the corners where the front cover meets the block and at the rear where the rear main oil seal retainer meets the block. Then attach the new gasket to the pan, install the pan and tighten the bolts/studs finger-tight.
16   On 4.3L V6 engines, the alignment of the

rear face of the aluminum pan to the rear of the block is important. Measure between the rear face of the pan and the front face of transmission bellhousing with feeler gauges. Clearance should ideally be flush, but up to 0.011-inch is allowable **(see illustrations)**.
17   Tighten the oil pan bolts to the torque listed in this Chapter's Specifications using a criss-cross pattern. **Note:** *On V6 models, use the recommended bolt tightening sequence* **(see illustration)**.
18   The remainder of installation is the reverse of removal.
19   Add the proper type and quantity of oil (see Chapter 1), start the engine and check for leaks before placing the vehicle back in service.

14   Oil pump - removal and installation

Refer to illustrations 14.2 and 14.3

1   Remove the oil pan (see Section 13).
2   While supporting the oil pump, remove the pump-to-rear main bearing cap bolt **(see illustration)**.

13.17 Bolt tightening sequence for the cast aluminum oil pan on the 4.3L V6 engine

24071-2B-12.15BHAYNES

14.2 Unscrew the bolt holding the oil pump to the rear main bearing cap, then remove the pump

14.3 Make sure the nylon sleeve is in place between the oil pump and driveshaft

15.2 Before removing the driveplate, mark its relationship to the crankshaft

3   Lower the pump and remove it along with the pump driveshaft. Note that on most models a hard nylon sleeve is used to align the oil pump driveshaft and the oil pump shaft. Make sure this sleeve is in place on the oil pump driveshaft **(see illustration)**. If it is not there, check the oil pan for the pieces of the sleeve, clean them out of the pan, then get a new sleeve for the oil pump driveshaft.

4   Check the screen and the pickup tube for any damage or looseness. It must fit very tight onto the oil pump.

5   If a new oil pump is installed, make sure the pump driveshaft is mated with the shaft inside the pump.

6   Position the pump on the engine and make sure the slot in the upper end of the driveshaft is aligned with the tang on the lower end of the distributor shaft. The distributor drives the oil pump, so it is absolutely essential that the components mate properly.

7   Install the mounting bolt and tighten it to the torque listed in this Chapter's Specifications.

8   Install the oil pan.

15   Driveplate - removal and installation

Removal

Refer to illustration 15.2

1   Raise the vehicle and support it securely on jackstands, then refer to Chapter 7 and remove the transmission.

2   Mark the relationship between the driveplate and the crankshaft with a marker or similar device, then remove the bolts that secure the driveplate to the crankshaft **(see illustration)**. If the crankshaft turns, wedge a screwdriver in the ring gear teeth to jam the driveplate. **Note:** *If there is a retaining ring between the bolts and the driveplate, note which side faces the driveplate when removing it.*

3   Remove the driveplate from the crank-

shaft. Since the driveplate is fairly heavy, be sure to support it while removing the last bolt. **Caution:** *When removing a flywheel, wear gloves to protect your fingers - the edges of the ring gear teeth may be sharp.*

4   Clean the driveplate to remove grease and oil. Inspect the surface for cracks, and check for cracked and broken ring gear teeth. Lay the driveplate on a flat surface to check for warpage.

5   Clean and inspect the mating surfaces of the driveplate and the crankshaft. If the rear main oil seal is leaking, replace it before reinstalling the driveplate (see Section 16).

Installation

6   Position the driveplate against the crankshaft. Be sure to align the marks made during removal. Note that some engines have an alignment dowel or staggered bolt holes to ensure correct installation. Before installing the bolts, apply non-hardening thread locking compound to the threads and place the retaining ring (if equipped) in position on the driveplate.

7   Wedge a screwdriver through the ring gear teeth to keep the driveplate from turning as you tighten the bolts to the torque listed in this Chapter's Specifications. With the transmission on the bench, inspect the front pump seal/O-ring for leaking, now would be a very good time to replace it.

8   The remainder of installation is the reverse of the removal procedure.

16   Rear main oil seal - replacement

4.3L V6 and 5.0L, 5.7L V8 engines

Refer to illustration 16.2

1   All V6 and small block V8 engines use a one-piece rear main oil seal which is installed in a bolt-on housing. Replacing this seal requires removal of the transmission and

16.2 Carefully pry the old seal out - do not damage the surface of the crankshaft

torque converter and driveplate. Refer to Chapter 7 for the transmission removal procedures.

2   Although the seal can be removed by prying it out of the housing by inserting a screwdriver into the notches provided **(see illustration)**, installation with the housing still mounted on the block requires the use of a special tool, which attaches to the threaded holes in the crankshaft flange and then presses the new seal into place.

3   If the special installation tool is not available, remove the oil pan (see Section 13) and the bolts securing the housing to the block, then detach the housing and gasket. Whenever the housing is removed from the block a new seal and gasket must be installed.

4   Remove the oil pan (see Section 13).

5   Insert a screwdriver blade into the notches in the seal housing and pry out the old seal. Be sure to note how far it's recessed into the housing bore before removal so the new seal can be installed to the same depth.

6   Clean the housing thoroughly, then apply a thin coat of engine oil to the new seal. Set

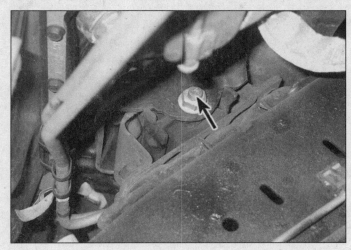

17.9a Location of the right-side engine mount through-bolt nut

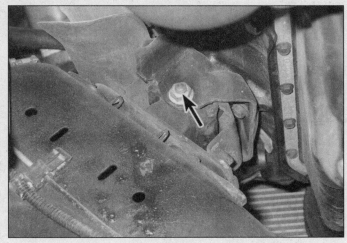

17.9b Location of the left-side engine mount through-bolt nut

the seal squarely into the recess in the housing, then, using a piece of wood that extends to each side of the housing, use a hammer to press the seal into place.

7   Carefully slide the seal over the crankshaft and bolt the seal housing to the block. Be sure to use a new gasket, but don't use any gasket sealant.

8   The remainder of installation is the reverse of the removal procedure.

7.4 liter V8 engine

Note: *We recommend using a special seal installation tool for this procedure. If the tool is not available, you may be able to install the seal using a piece of pipe with a diameter slightly smaller than the outer diameter of the seal or a blunt punch and a hammer.*

9   This engine uses a one-piece rear main oil seal, but, unlike the V6 and small block V8 engines, there is no bolt-on housing for the seal. The seal is pressed into a bore machined into the rear main bearing cap and engine block. Remove the transmission and driveplate (see Section 15).

10   Pry out the old seal with a hooked tool or a large screwdriver. **Caution:** *To prevent an oil leak after the new seal is installed, be very careful not to scratch or otherwise damage the crankshaft sealing surface or the bore in the bearing cap/engine block.*

11   Clean the crankshaft and seal bore in the block/bearing cap thoroughly and de-grease these areas by wiping them with a rag soaked in lacquer thinner or acetone. Lubricate the lip and outer diameter of the new seal with engine oil. **Note:** *When installing the new seal, the lip of the seal must face the front of the engine.*

12   If a special tool is available, install the

new seal on the tool and position the tool against the crankshaft. Thread the attaching screws into the crankshaft, then tighten the screws securely with a screwdriver. Turn the tool handle until it bottoms, then remove the tool.

13   If a special tool is not available, tap the new seal into place using a hammer and a piece of pipe or a blunt punch. Work around the seal, tapping it evenly into place until it bottoms.

14   The remainder of installation is the reverse of removal.

---

17   Engine mounts - check and replacement

---

1   Engine mounts seldom require attention, but broken or deteriorated mounts should be replaced immediately or the added strain placed on the driveline components may cause damage.

Check

2   During the check, the engine must be raised slightly to remove the weight from the mounts.

3   Raise the vehicle and support it securely on jackstands, then position the jack under the engine oil pan. Place a large block of wood between the jack head and the oil pan, then carefully raise the engine just enough to take the weight off the mounts. **Caution:** *Do not use the jack to support the entire weight of the engine.*

4   Check the mounts to see if the rubber is cracked, hardened or separated from the metal plates. Sometimes the rubber will split right down the center.

5   Check for relative movement between the mount plates and the engine or frame (use a large screwdriver or prybar to attempt to move the mounts). If movement is noted, check the tightness of the mount fasteners first before condemning the mounts. Usually when engine mounts are broken, they are very obvious as the engine will easily move away from the mount when pried or under load.

Replacement

Refer to illustrations 17.9a and 17.9b

6   Disconnect the cable from the negative terminal of the battery (see Chapter 5, Section 1).

7   Remove the coolant reservoir (see Chapter 3) and the air filter housing (see Chapter 4).

8   Attach an engine hoist to the top of the engine for lifting; do not use a jack under the oil pan to support the entire weight of the engine or the oil pump pick-up could be damaged. **Note:** *If a hoist is not available, casting lugs on each side of the engine block can be used to support the entire weight of the engine while the engine mounts are being replaced.*

9   Remove the engine mount through-bolts **(see illustrations).**

10   Remove the engine mount-to-frame bracket bolts.

11   Raise the engine slightly until the engine mount can be unbolted from the block. Unbolt the mount from the engine block and remove it from the vehicle.

12   Installation is the reverse of removal. Use non-hardening thread-locking compound on the mount bolts and be sure to tighten them securely.

Notes

Chapter 2 Part B
4.8L, 5.3L and 6.0L V8 engines

Contents

Specifications

General

Displacement
4.8L	293 cubic inches
5.3L	325 cubic inches
6.0L	364 cubic inches

Bore and stroke
4.8L	3.779 x 3.268 inches
5.3L	3.779 x 3.622 inches
6.0L	4.001 x 3.622 inches

Cylinder numbers (front-to-rear)
Left (driver's) side	1-3-5-7
Right side	2-4-6-8
Firing order	1-8-7-2-6-5-4-3

Camshaft

Journal diameters	2.164 to 2.166 inches
Camshaft endplay	0.001 to 0.012 inch

Lobe lift

4.8L and 5.3L engines
Intake	0.268 inch
Exhaust	0.274 inch

6.0L engine
Intake	0.274 inch
Exhaust	0.281 inch

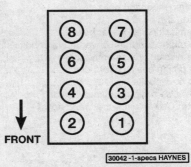

30042-1-specs HAYNES

Cylinder numbering - 4.8L, 5.3L and 6.0L V8 engines

Torque specifications

	Ft-lbs (unless otherwise indicated)
Camshaft sprocket bolts	26
Camshaft retainer bolts	
Hex head bolts	18
Torx head bolts	132 in-lbs
Crankshaft balancer bolt	
Step 1 (use old bolt)	240
Step 2* (use new bolt)	37
Step 3 (use new bolt)	Turn an additional 140-degrees
Coolant bleed pipe bolts	106 in-lbs
Cylinder head bolts** (in sequence - **see illustration 8.18**)	
2003 and 2004 models	
Step 1	
All 11mm bolts	22
Step 2	
All 11mm bolts	Turn an additional 90-degrees
Step 3	
11mm bolts (1 through 8)	Turn an additional 90-degrees
11mm bolts (9 and 10)	Turn an additional 50-degrees
Step 4	
All 8 mm bolts (11 through 15)	22
2005 and later models	
Step 1	
All 11mm bolts (1 through 10)	22
Step 2	
All 11mm bolts (1 through 10)	Turn an additional 90-degrees
Step 3	
All 11mm bolts (1 through 10)	Turn an additional 70-degrees
Step 4	
All 8 mm bolts (11 through 15)	22
Driveplate bolts	
Step 1	15
Step 2	37
Step 3	74
Engine crossmember bolts	89
Engine valley cover bolts	18
Exhaust manifold bolts	
Step 1	132 in-lbs
Step 2	18
Exhaust manifold heat shield bolt	80 in-lbs
Exhaust pipe flange nuts	20 to 25
Intake manifold bolts (in sequence - **see illustration 6.19**)	
Step 1	44 in-lbs
Step 2	89 in-lbs
Lifter retainer bolts	106 in-lbs
Oil pan baffle bolts	106 in-lbs
Oil pan drain plug	18
Oil pan rear access plugs	80 in-lbs
Oil pan bolts	
Step 1 (to engine and front cover)	18
Step 2 (to rear cover)	106 in-lbs
Oil cooler adapter cover bolts	106 in-lbs
Oil pump mounting bolts	18
Rocker arm bolts	22
Transmission side cover bolts	106 in-lbs
Transmission torque converter cover bolts/studs	37
Transmission crossmember bolts	74
Front timing chain cover bolts	18
Valve cover bolts	106 in-lbs

*Note: *Use a new crankshaft balancer bolt*
**Note: *Use new cylinder head bolts*

1   General information

This Part of Chapter 2 is devoted to in-vehicle repair procedures for the 4.8L, 5.3L and 6.0L V8 engines. These engines utilize cast-iron blocks with eight cylinders arranged in a "V" shape at a 90-degree angle between the two banks. All V8 cylinder heads utilize an overhead valve arrangement. The 4.8L and 5.3L engines use aluminum cylinder heads with pressed-in valve guides and hardened valve seats, while 6.0L V8 engines use cast iron cylinder heads with integral valve guides and pressed-in valve seats. Hydraulic roller lifters actuate the valves through tubular pushrods and rocker arms. The oil pump is mounted at the front of the engine behind the timing chain cover and is driven by the crankshaft.

To positively identify these engines, locate the Vehicle Identification Number (VIN) on the left front corner of the instrument panel. The VIN is visible from the outside of the vehicle through the windshield. The eighth character in the sequence is the engine designation:

V = 4.8 liter V8 engine
T = 5.3 liter V8 engine
U = 6.0 liter V8 engine

Information concerning engine removal and installation and engine overhaul can be found in Part C of this Chapter. The following repair procedures are based on the assumption that the engine is installed in the vehicle. If the engine has been removed from the vehicle and mounted on a stand, many of the steps outlined in this Part of Chapter 2 will not apply.

2   Repair operations possible with the engine in the vehicle

Many major repair operations can be accomplished without removing the engine from the vehicle.

Many of the in-vehicle engine repairs will require removal of the engine cover from inside the passenger compartment. Refer to Chapter 11 for the engine cover removal procedure. Also, many in-vehicle engine repairs will require air filter housing removal (see Chapter 4) and coolant reservoir removal (see Chapter 3).

Clean the engine compartment and the exterior of the engine with some type of pressure washer before any work is done. A clean engine will make the job easier and will help keep dirt out of the internal areas of the engine.

If oil or coolant leaks develop, indicating a need for gasket or seal replacement, the repairs can generally be made with the engine in the vehicle. The oil pan gasket, the cylinder head gaskets, intake and exhaust manifold gaskets, timing chain cover gaskets and the crankshaft oil seals are all accessible with the engine in place.

Exterior engine components, such as the water pump, the starter motor, the alterna-tor, the distributor and the fuel injection components, as well as the intake and exhaust manifolds, can be removed for repair with the engine in place.

Since the cylinder heads can be removed without removing the engine, valve component servicing can also be accomplished with the engine in the vehicle.

Replacement of, repairs to or inspection of the timing chain and sprockets and the oil pump are all possible with the engine in place.

In extreme cases caused by a lack of necessary equipment, repair or replacement of piston rings, pistons, connecting rods and rod bearings is possible with the engine in the vehicle. However, this practice is not recommended because of the cleaning and preparation work that must be done to the components involved.

3   Top Dead Center (TDC) for number one piston - locating

1   Top Dead Center (TDC) is the highest point in the cylinder that each piston reaches as it travels up the cylinder bore. Each piston reaches TDC on the compression stroke and again on the exhaust stroke, but TDC generally refers to piston position on the compression stroke.

2   Positioning the piston(s) at TDC is an essential part of procedures such as timing chain/sprocket and camshaft replacement.

3   Before beginning this procedure, be sure to place the transmission in Park and apply the parking brake or block the rear wheels. Also, disable the ignition system by disconnecting the primary electrical connectors at the ignition coil packs, then remove the spark plugs (see Chapter 1).

4   In order to bring any piston to TDC, the crankshaft must be turned using one of the methods outlined below. When looking at the front of the engine, normal crankshaft rotation is clockwise.

a)   *The preferred method is to turn the crankshaft with a socket and ratchet attached to the bolt threaded into the front of the crankshaft. Turn the bolt in a clockwise direction.*

b)   *A remote starter switch, which may save some time, can also be used. Follow the instructions included with the switch. Once the piston is close to TDC, use a socket and ratchet as described in the previous paragraph.*

c)   *If an assistant is available to turn the ignition switch to the Start position in short bursts, you can get the piston close to TDC without a remote starter switch. Make sure your assistant is out of the vehicle, away from the ignition switch, then use a socket and ratchet as described in Paragraph (a) to complete the procedure.*

5   Install a compression gauge in the number one spark plug hole and rotate the crank-shaft using one of the methods described above until pressure registers on the gauge. Pressure at the spark plug hole indicates that the cylinder has started the compression stroke. Once the compression stroke has begun, TDC for the number one cylinder is obtained when the piston reaches the top of the cylinder on the compression stroke.

6   To bring the piston to the top of the cylinder, insert a long screwdriver into the number one spark plug hole until it touches the top of the piston. **Note:** *Make sure to wrap the tip of the screwdriver with tape to avoid scratching the top of the piston and the cylinder walls.* Use the screwdriver (as a feeler gauge) to tell where the top of the piston is located in the cylinder while slowly rotating the crankshaft by hand. As the piston rises the screwdriver will be pushed out. The point at which the screwdriver stops moving outward is TDC. **Note:** *Always hold the screwdriver upright while the engine is being rotated so that the screwdriver will not get wedged as the piston travels upward.* This will be *approximate* TDC for number 1 piston.

7   These engines are not equipped with external components (vibration damper, fly-wheel, timing hole, etc.) that are marked to identify the position of number 1 TDC. Therefore the only method to double-check the *exact* location of TDC number 1 is to remove the timing chain cover to access timing chain sprockets (see Section 11), or with the use of a degree wheel on the crankshaft vibration damper and a positive stop threaded into the spark plug hole, as would be used in the process of degreeing a camshaft (these tools may be available for rent at some auto parts stores).

8   If you go past TDC, rotate the crankshaft counterclockwise until the piston is approximately one inch below TDC, then slowly rotate the crankshaft clockwise again until TDC is reached.

9   After the number one piston has been positioned at TDC on the compression stroke, TDC for any of the remaining pistons can be located by turning the crankshaft (clockwise) 90-degrees (1/4-turn) at a time and following the firing order.

4   Valve covers - removal and installation

Removal

1   Disconnect the cable from the negative terminal of the battery (see Chapter 5, Section 1).

2   Remove the air filter housing and air intake duct (see Chapter 4).

3   Remove the engine cover (see Chapter 11).

Left side

Refer to illustration 4.7

4   Detach the clips securing the engine wir-

4.7 Valve cover mounting bolts (left side shown)

4.16 Position the new gasket in the valve cover groove

ing harness to the valve cover and position the engine wiring harness aside.
5   Remove the ignition coils from the valve cover (see Chapter 5). Be sure each plug wire is labeled before removal to ensure correct reinstallation.
6   Disconnect the PCV hose from the valve cover.
7   Remove the valve cover bolts **(see illustration)**, then detach the cover from the cylinder head. **Note:** *If the cover is stuck to the cylinder head, bump one end with a block of wood and a hammer to jar it loose. If that doesn't work, try to slip a flexible putty knife between the cylinder head and cover to break the gasket seal. Don't pry at the cover-to-head joint or damage to the sealing surfaces may occur (leading to oil leaks in the future).*

Right side

8   Remove the oil filler tube bracket and separate the oil filler tube from the valve cover and engine compartment.
9   Remove the upper portion of the transmission filler tube, if it's in the way.
10   Disconnect the electrical connectors from the ignition coils and the EGR valve. Unclip the wiring harness from the ignition coil bracket and lay it aside.

11   Remove the ignition coils from the valve cover (see Chapter 5). Be sure each plug wire is labeled before removal to ensure correct reinstallation.
12   Disconnect the fresh air inlet hose from the valve cover (see Chapter 6).
13   Remove the valve cover bolts **(see illustration 4.7)**, then detach the cover from the cylinder head. **Note:** *If the cover is stuck to the cylinder head, bump one end with a block of wood and a hammer to jar it loose. If that doesn't work, try to slip a flexible putty knife between the cylinder head and cover to break the gasket seal. Don't pry at the cover-to-head joint or damage to the sealing surfaces may occur (leading to oil leaks in the future).*

Installation

Refer to illustration 4.16

14   The mating surfaces of each cylinder head and valve cover must be perfectly clean when the covers are installed. Use a gasket scraper to remove all traces of sealant and old gasket material, then clean the mating surfaces with lacquer thinner or acetone. If there's sealant or oil on the mating surfaces when the cover is installed, oil leaks may develop.

15   Clean the mounting bolt threads with a die to remove any corrosion and restore damaged threads. Make sure the threaded holes in the cylinder head are clean - run a tap into them to remove corrosion and restore damaged threads.
16   The gaskets should be mated to the covers before the covers are installed. Position the gasket inside the cover groove **(see illustration)**. If the gasket will not stay in place in the cover groove, apply a thin coat of RTV sealant to the cover flange, then allow the sealant to set up so the gasket adheres to the cover.
17   Inspect the valve cover bolt grommets for damage. If the grommets aren't damaged they can be reused. Carefully position the valve cover(s) on the cylinder head and install the bolts and grommets.
18   Tighten the bolts evenly in three or four steps to the torque listed in this Chapter's Specifications.
19   The remaining installation steps are the reverse of removal.
20   Start the engine and check carefully for oil leaks as the engine warms up.

5   Rocker arms and pushrods - removal, inspection and installation

Removal

Refer to illustrations 5.2 and 5.3

1   Refer to Section 4 and detach the valve covers from the cylinder heads.
2   Loosen the rocker arm pivot bolts one at a time and detach the rocker arms and bolts, then detach the pivot support pedestal **(see illustration)**. Keep track of the rocker arm positions, since they must be returned to the same locations. Store each set of rocker components separately in a marked plastic bag to ensure that they're reinstalled in their original locations.
3   Remove the pushrods and store them separately to make sure they don't get mixed up during installation **(see illustration)**.

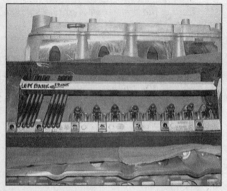

5.2 Remove the mounting bolts (A) and rocker arms, then remove the pivot support pedestal (B)

5.3 Store the pushrods and rocker arms in order to ensure they are reinstalled in their original locations - note the arrow indicating the front of the engine

Inspection

Refer to illustration 5.4

4   Check each rocker arm for wear, cracks and other damage, especially where the push-rods and valve stems contact the rocker arm **(see illustration)**.

5   Check the pivot bearings for binding and roughness. If the bearings are worn or damaged, replacement of the entire rocker arm will be necessary. **Note:** *Keep in mind that there is no valve adjustment on these engines, so excessive wear or damage in the valve train can easily result in excessive valve clearance, which in turn will cause valve noise when the engine is running.* Also check the rocker arm pivot support pedestal for cracks and other obvious damage.

6   Make sure the hole at the pushrod end of each rocker arm is open.

7   Inspect the pushrods for cracks and excessive wear at the ends, also check that the oil hole running through each pushrod is not clogged. Roll each pushrod across a piece of plate glass to see if it's bent (if it wobbles, it's bent).

Installation

Refer to illustration 5.9

8   Lubricate the lower end of each pushrod with clean engine oil or engine assembly lube and install them in their original locations. Make sure each pushrod seats completely in the lifter socket.

9   Apply engine assembly lube to the ends of the valve stems and to the upper ends of the pushrods to prevent damage to the mating surfaces on initial start-up **(see illustration)**. Also apply clean engine oil to the pivot shaft and bearing of each rocker arm and install the rocker arms loosely in their original locations. DO NOT tighten the bolts at this time!

10   Rotate the crankshaft until the number one piston is at TDC (see Section 3). When the number one piston is at TDC, tighten the intake valve rocker arms for the Number 1, 3, 4, and 5

cylinders and the exhaust rocker arms for the Number 1, 2, 7, and 8 cylinders. Tighten each of the specified rocker arm bolts to the torque listed in this Chapter's Specifications.

11   Rotate the crankshaft 360-degrees. Tighten the intake valve rocker arms for the Number 2, 6, 7, and 8 cylinders and the exhaust rocker arms for the Number 3, 4, 5, and 6 cylinders. Tighten each of the rocker arm bolts to the torque listed in this Chapter's Specifications.

12   Refer to Section 4 and install the valve covers. Start the engine, listen for unusual valve train noses and check for oil leaks at the valve cover gaskets.

---

6   Intake manifold - removal and installation

Warning: *Wait until the engine is completely cool before starting this procedure.*

Removal

Refer to illustrations 6.8a and 6.8b

1   Disconnect the cable from the negative terminal of the battery (see Chapter 5, section 1).

2   Remove the engine cover (see Chapter 11).

3   Clamp off the coolant hoses leading to the throttle body.

4   Remove the air filter housing and the throttle body (see Chapter 4). Remove the accelerator and cruise control brackets from the intake manifold.

5   Relieve the fuel system pressure (see Chapter 4).

6   Remove the engine oil fill tube.

7   Remove the transmission fluid fill tube bracket from the cylinder head.

8   Disconnect the electrical connectors from the fuel injectors, EGR valve, EVAP solenoid, the MAP sensor and from the sensors on the throttle body. Label each connector clearly

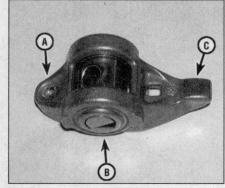

5.4 Rocker arm wear points

A   *Pushrod socket*
B   *Pivot bearings*
C   *Valve stem contact point*

5.9 Lubricate the pushrod ends and the valve stems with engine assembly lube before installing the rocker arms

to aid in the reassembly process. Detach the large wiring harness brackets from the studs on the top of the intake manifold and lay the harness aside **(see illustrations)**.

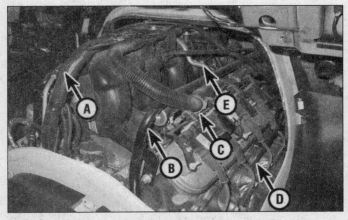

6.8a Intake manifold component details - right side shown

A   *Transmission wiring harness*
B   *Transmission fluid fill tube*
C   *Engine control components wiring harness*
D   *Oil dipstick tube*
E   *Fuel line*

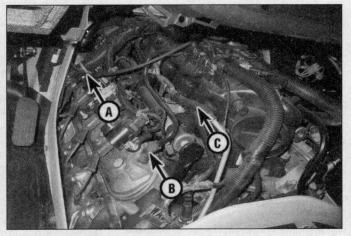

6.8b Intake manifold component details - left side shown

A   *Wiring harness*
B   *PCV valve and tube*
C   *Fuel line*

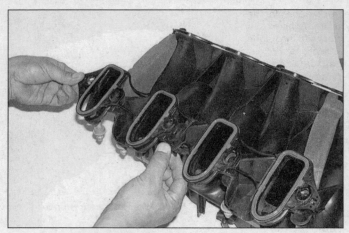

6.17 Align the tabs on the intake gaskets with the tabs on the manifold and snap the gasket into place

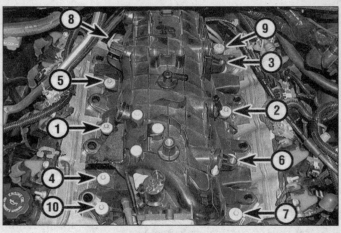

6.19 Intake manifold bolt tightening sequence

9   Remove the fuel rails and injectors as an assembly (see Chapter 4). The two fuel rails can be pulled straight up with the injectors still attached, but it will take some force to dislodge the injectors from the intake manifold. **Note:** *This Step is not absolutely necessary, but it will help prevent subsequent damage to the fuel injectors as the intake manifold is removed.*

10   Remove the EGR valve and pipe assembly from the engine (see Chapter 6).

11   Disconnect and label any remaining electrical connectors or vacuum hoses connected to the intake manifold.

12   Loosen the intake manifold mounting bolts in 1/4-turn increments in the reverse order of the tightening sequence until they can be removed by hand **(see illustration 6.19)**.

13   The manifold might be stuck to the cylinder heads and force may be required to break the gasket seal. A prybar can be positioned between the front of the manifold and the valley tray to break the bond made by the gasket. **Caution:** *Do not pry between the manifold and the heads or damage to the gasket sealing surfaces may result and vacuum leaks could develop. Also, don't use too much force - the manifold is made of a plastic composite and could crack.*

14   Remove the intake manifold. As the manifold is lifted from the engine, be sure to check for and disconnect anything still attached to the manifold.

Installation

Refer to illustrations 6.17 and 6.19

Note: *The mating surfaces of the cylinder heads, block and manifold must be perfectly clean when the manifold is installed.*

15   Carefully remove all traces of old gasket material. Note that the intake manifold is made of a composite material and the cylinder heads on 4.8L and 5.3L engines are made of aluminum, therefore aggressive scraping is not suggested and will damage the sealing surfaces. After the gasket surfaces are cleaned and free of any gasket material wipe

the mating surfaces with a cloth saturated with safety solvent. If there is old sealant or oil on the mating surfaces when the manifold is installed, oil or vacuum leaks may develop. Use a vacuum cleaner to remove any gasket material that falls into the intake ports in the heads.

16   Use a tap of the correct size to chase the threads in the bolt holes, then use compressed air (if available) to remove the debris from the holes. **Warning:** *Wear safety glasses or a face shield to protect your eyes when using compressed air.*

17   Position the new gaskets on the intake manifold **(see illustration)**. Note that the gaskets are equipped with installation tabs that must snap into place on the intake manifold. The words "Manifold Side" may appear on the gasket, If so, this will ensure proper installation. Make sure the gaskets snap into place and all intake port openings align.

18   Carefully set the manifold in place.

19   Apply medium-strength threadlocking compound to the threads of the bolts. Install the bolts and tighten them following the recommended sequence **(see illustration)** to the torque listed in this Chapter's Specifications. Do not overtighten the bolts or gasket leaks may develop.

20   The remaining installation steps are the reverse of removal. Check the coolant level, adding as necessary (see Chapter 1). Start the engine and check carefully for vacuum leaks at the intake manifold joints.

7   Exhaust manifolds - removal and installation

Refer to illustrations 7.5, 7.9 and 7.10

Removal

Warning: *Use caution when working around the exhaust manifolds - the sheetmetal heat shields can be sharp on the edges. Also, the engine should be cold when this procedure is followed.*

1   Disconnect the cable from the negative terminal of the battery (see Chapter 5, Section 1).

2   Remove the engine cover (see Chapter 11).

3   Raise the vehicle and support it securely on jackstands.

4   Working under the vehicle, apply penetrating oil to the exhaust pipe-to-manifold studs and nuts (they're usually rusty). Disconnect the electrical connector for the oxygen sensor.

5   Remove the nuts retaining the exhaust pipe(s) to the manifold(s) **(see illustration)**.

6   Detach the spark plug wires and remove the spark plugs from the side being worked on (see Chapter 1).

7   If both manifolds are being removed, detach all the spark plug wires and remove all the spark plugs.

Right side manifold

8   Remove the inner splash shield from the fenderwell (see Chapter 11). Note that the exhaust manifold is more easily accessed with the front wheel and the inner fenderwell removed, but it's not absolutely necessary.

9   Remove the oil dipstick, unbolt the dip-

7.5 Remove the exhaust pipe-to-manifold nuts

7.9 Remove the oil dipstick tube mounting bolt (A) and tube - (B) indicates the secondary air injection check valve and pipe assembly on the right manifold

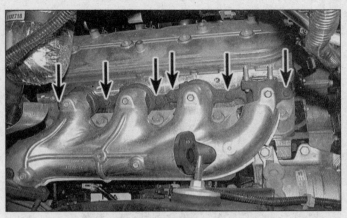

7.10 Exhaust manifold fastener locations (right side shown, left side similar)

stick tube bracket and move the dipstick tube **(see illustration)**.
10 Remove the EGR valve and pipe assembly (see Chapter 6). Remove the mounting bolts and separate the exhaust manifold from the cylinder head **(see illustration)**. Remove the heat shields from the manifold after the manifold has been removed.

Left side manifold
11 Remove the EGR pipe from the exhaust manifold (see Chapter 6).
12 Remove the inner splash shield from the fenderwell (see Chapter 11). Note that the exhaust manifold is more easily accessed with the front tire and the inner fenderwell removed, but it's not absolutely necessary.
13 Remove the mounting bolts and separate the exhaust manifold from the cylinder head. Remove the heat shields from the manifold after the manifold has been removed.

Installation
14 Check the manifold for cracks and make sure the bolt threads are clean and undamaged. The manifold and cylinder head mat-

ing surfaces must be clean before the manifolds are reinstalled - use a gasket scraper to remove all carbon deposits and gasket material. **Note:** *The cylinder heads on 4.8L and 5.3L engines are made of aluminum, therefore aggressive scraping is not suggested and will damage the sealing surfaces.*
15 Install the heat shields, then install the bolts and gaskets onto the manifold. Retaining tabs surrounding the gasket bolt holes should hold the assembly together as the manifold is installed.
16 Place the manifold on the cylinder head and install the mounting bolts finger tight.
17 When tightening the mounting bolts, work from the center to the ends and be sure to use a torque wrench. Tighten the bolts in two steps to the torque listed in this Chapter's Specifications. If required, bend the exposed end of the exhaust manifold gasket back against the cylinder head.
18 The remaining installation steps are the reverse of removal. Always use new O-rings and gaskets on the EGR valve and pipe assembly.
19 Start the engine and check for exhaust leaks.

8 Cylinder heads - removal and installation

Warning: *Wait until the engine is completely cool before beginning this procedure.*
Note: *It will be necessary to purchase a new set of head bolts for this procedure.*

Removal
Refer to illustrations 8.4, 8.5, 8.8 and 8.10
1 Disconnect the cable from the negative terminal of the battery (see Chapter 5, Section 1). Drain the cooling system (see Chapter 1).
2 Remove the valve covers (see Section 4).
3 Remove the intake manifold (see Section 6).
4 Remove the bolts and remove the coolant air bleed pipes from the cylinder heads **(see illustration)**.
5 Remove the knock sensors (see Chapter 6) and the engine valley cover from the center of the engine **(see illustration)**.
6 Detach both exhaust manifolds from the

8.4 The coolant bleed pipe is retained by two bolts at the front and two bolts at the rear of the cylinder heads

8.5 Location of the mounting bolts on the engine valley cover

8.8 Alternator/power steering pump mounting bracket bolts - remove the bolts and lay the bracket aside with the components attached

8.10 Using a prybar inserted into an intake port to break the head loose - do not use excessive force or damage to the head may result

cylinder heads (see Section 7).

7   Remove the rocker arms and pushrods (see Section 5). **Caution:** *Again, as mentioned in Section 5, keep all the parts in order so they are reinstalled in the same location.*

8   Disconnect the wiring from the back of the alternator, then remove the power steering pump/alternator mounting bracket from the engine. Lay the bracket aside (with the components attached), without disconnecting the lines from the steering pump **(see illustration)**.

9   Loosen the head bolts in 1/4-turn increments in the reverse order of the tightening sequence **(see illustration 8.18)** until they can be removed by hand. **Note:** *There will be different length and size head bolts for different locations. Make a note of the different sizes and lengths and where they go when removing the bolts to ensure correct installation of the new bolts.*

10   Lift the heads off the engine. If resistance is felt, do not pry between the head and block as damage to the mating surfaces will result. To dislodge the head, place a pry bar or long screwdriver into the intake port and carefully pry the head off the engine **(see illustration)**. Store the heads on blocks of wood to prevent damage to the gasket sealing surfaces.

Installation

Refer to illustrations 8.15, 8.18, 8.19 and 8.20

11   The mating surfaces of the cylinder heads and block must be perfectly clean when the heads are installed. Gasket removal solvents are available at auto parts stores and may prove helpful.

12   Use a gasket scraper to remove all traces of carbon and old gasket material, then wipe the mating surfaces with a cloth saturated with lacquer thinner or acetone. **Note:** *The cylinder heads on 4.8L and 5.3L engines are made of aluminum, therefore aggressive scraping is not suggested and will damage the sealing surfaces.* If there is oil on the mating surfaces when the heads are installed, the gaskets may not seal correctly and leaks may develop. When working on the block, use a vacuum cleaner to remove any debris that falls into the cylinders.

13   Check the block and head mating sur-

faces for nicks, deep scratches and other damage. If damage is slight, it can be removed with emery cloth. If it is excessive, machining may be the only alternative.

14   Use a tap of the correct size to chase the threads in the head bolt holes in the block. If a tap is not available, spray a liberal amount of brake cleaner into each hole. Use compressed air (if available) to remove the debris from the holes. **Warning:** *Wear safety glasses or a face shield to protect your eyes when using compressed air.* All cylinder head bolts must be replaced with **New** bolts.

15   Position the new gaskets over the dowels in the block **(see illustration)**.

16   Carefully position the heads on the block without disturbing the gaskets.

17   Before installing the 8mm head bolts, coat the threads with a medium-strength threadlocking compound. Then install the **New** 8mm head bolts (bolts 11 through 15).

18   Install **New** 11 mm head bolts (bolts 1 through 10) and tighten them finger tight. Following the recommended sequence **(see illustration)**, tighten all of the bolts in four steps to the torque listed in this Chapter's Specifi-

8.15 Position the head gasket over the dowels at each end of the cylinder head with the mark facing the front of the vehicle

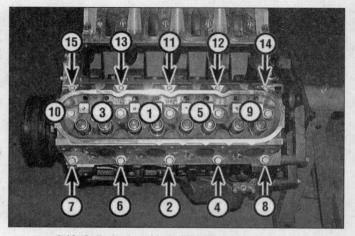

8.18 Cylinder head bolt TIGHTENING sequence

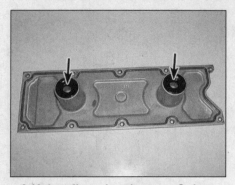

8.19 Install new knock sensor O-rings into the engine valley cover

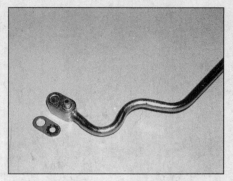

8.20 Be sure to use new gaskets at each cylinder head-to-coolant bleed pipe joint

9.5 Use a strap wrench to hold the crankshaft balancer while removing the center bolt (a chain-type wrench may be used if you wrap a section of old drivebelt or rag around the balancer first)

cations. **Warning:** *DO NOT use the old head bolts - always replace them with new ones.*
19   Install the engine valley cover **(see illustration)**. Tighten the bolts to the torque listed in this Chapter's Specifications.
20   Install the coolant bleed pipe, using new gaskets, onto the cylinder heads **(see illustration)**. Tighten the bolts to the torque listed in this Chapter's Specifications.
21   The remaining installation steps are the reverse of removal.
22   Refill the cooling system and change the engine oil and filter (see Chapter 1). Start the engine and check for proper operation and coolant or oil leaks.

---

9   Crankshaft balancer - removal and installation

Refer to illustrations 9.5, 9.6 and 9.9
Note: *This procedure requires a special balancer installation tool that is available through specialized tool manufacturers only, and a new crankshaft balancer bolt. Read through the entire procedure and obtain the tool and materials before proceeding.*

1   Disconnect the cable from the negative terminal of the battery (see Chapter 5, section 1).
2   Raise the front of the vehicle and support it securely on jackstands. Then apply the parking brake.
3   Remove the drivebelt (see Chapter 1) and the engine cooling fan (see Chapter 3).
4   Working under the vehicle, remove the splash shield from below the engine, if equipped.
5   Use a strap wrench around the crankshaft pulley to hold it while using a breaker bar and socket to remove the crankshaft pulley center bolt **(see illustration)**.
6   Pull the balancer off the crankshaft with a puller **(see illustration)**. **Caution:** *The jaws of the puller must only contact the hub of the balancer - not the outer ring.* **Note:** *A long Allen-head bolt should be inserted into the crankshaft nose for the puller's tapered tip to push against, or use an adapter on the end of the crankshaft for the puller screw to bear against to avoid damage to the threads in the crankshaft.*
7   Position the crankshaft pulley/balancer on the crankshaft and slide it on as far as it will go. Note that the slot (keyway) in the hub

must be aligned with the Woodruff key in the end of the crankshaft.
8   Using the specialized crankshaft balancer installation tool, press the crankshaft pulley/balancer onto the crankshaft.
9   Install the old crankshaft balancer bolt and tighten the crankshaft bolt to 240 ft-lbs. Remove the old bolt and measure the distance from the snout of the crankshaft to the balancer hub **(see illustration)**. When properly installed, the balancer hub should extend 3/32 to 11/64-inch past the crankshaft snout. If the measurement is incorrect, reinstall the balancer installation tool and press the balancer on the crankshaft until the measurement is correct.
10   Install a **New** crankshaft balancer bolt and tighten it in two steps to the torque and angle of rotation listed in this Chapter's Specifications.
11   The remaining installation steps are the reverse of removal.

9.6 The use of a three jaw puller will be necessary to remove the crankshaft balancer - always place the puller jaws around the hub, not the outer ring

9.9 Before the new crankshaft bolt is installed and tightened, the balancer must be measured for proper installation - when properly installed, the balancer hub should extend 3/32 to 11/64-inch past the crankshaft snout

10.2 Carefully pry the old seal out of the timing chain cover - don't damage the crankshaft in the process

10.4 Drive the new seal into place with a large socket and hammer

10.5 If the sealing surface of the pulley hub has a wear groove from contact with the seal, repair sleeves are available at most auto parts stores

10 Crankshaft front oil seal - removal and installation

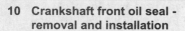

Refer to illustrations 10.2, 10.4 and 10.5

1   Remove the crankshaft balancer (see Section 9).

2   Note how the seal is installed - the new one must be installed to the same depth and facing the same way. Carefully pry the oil seal out of the cover with a seal puller or a large screwdriver **(see illustration)**. Be very careful not to distort the cover or scratch the crankshaft! Wrap electrician's tape around the tip of the screwdriver to avoid damage to the crankshaft.

3   If the seal is being replaced with the timing chain cover removed, support the cover on top of two blocks of wood and drive the seal out from the backside with a hammer and punch. **Caution:** *Be careful not to scratch, gouge or distort the area that the seal fits into or a leak will develop.*

4   Apply clean engine oil or multi-purpose grease to the outer edge of the new seal, then install it in the cover with the lip (spring side) facing IN. Drive the seal into place **(see illustration)** with a seal driver or a large socket

and a hammer. Make sure the seal enters the bore squarely and stops when the front face is at the proper depth.

5   Check the surface on the balancer hub that the oil seal rides on. If the surface has been grooved from long-time contact with the seal, a press-on sleeve may be available to renew the sealing surface **(see illustration)**. This sleeve is pressed into place with a hammer and a block of wood and is commonly available at auto parts stores for various applications.

6   Lubricate the balancer hub with clean engine oil and reinstall the crankshaft balancer as described in Section 9.

7   The remainder of installation is the reverse of the removal.

11 Timing chain - removal, inspection and installation

Removal and inspection

Refer to illustrations 11.6, 11.9 and 11.12

1   Disconnect the cable from the negative terminal of the battery (see Chapter 5, Section 1).

2   Drain the cooling system and engine oil (see Chapter 1).

3   Remove the upper and lower fan shrouds (see Chapter 3), drivebelt, cooling fan and water pump.

4   Remove the crankshaft balancer (see Section 9).

5   Remove the oil pan (see Section 13).

6   Remove the timing chain cover mounting bolts and separate the timing chain cover from the block **(see illustration)**. The cover may be stuck; if so, use a putty knife to break the gasket seal. Since the cover is made of aluminum it can easily be damaged, so DO NOT attempt to pry it off.

7   Remove the oil pick-up tube and the oil pump (see Section 14).

8   Measure the timing chain freeplay. If it is more than 5/8 inch, the chain and both sprockets should be replaced.

9   Loosen the camshaft sprocket bolts one turn, then screw the crankshaft balancer bolt into the end of the crankshaft and rotate the crankshaft in the normal direction of rotation (clockwise) until the timing marks align **(see illustration)**.

10   Remove the three bolts from the end of the camshaft, then detach the camshaft

11.6 Timing chain cover mounting bolts

11.9 Timing chain alignment marks

11.12 The sprocket on the crankshaft can be removed with a two or three-jaw puller

11.15 Slip the chain and camshaft sprocket in place over the crankshaft sprocket with the camshaft sprocket timing mark at the bottom

11.19 Install the front cover with a new gasket onto the engine block LOOSELY - the cover must be aligned properly before final installation

sprocket and chain as an assembly.

11   Inspect the camshaft and crankshaft sprockets for damage or wear.

12   If replacement of the timing chain is necessary, remove the sprocket on the crankshaft with a two-or three-jaw puller, but be careful not to damage the threads in the end of the crankshaft **(see illustration)**.

Installation

Refer to illustrations 11.15, 11.19 and 11.20

Note: *Timing chains must be replaced as a set with the camshaft and crankshaft sprockets. Never put a new chain on old sprockets.*

13   Use a gasket scraper to remove all traces of old gasket material and sealant from the cover and engine block.

14   Align the crankshaft sprocket with the Woodruff key and press the sprocket onto the crankshaft (if removed) with the crankshaft balancer bolt, a large socket and some washers or tap it gently into place until it is completely seated. **Caution:** *If resistance is encountered, do not hammer the sprocket onto the crankshaft. It may eventually move onto the shaft, but it may be cracked in the process and fail later, causing extensive engine damage.*

15   Loop the new chain over the camshaft sprocket, then turn the sprocket until the timing mark is at the bottom **(see illustration)**. Mesh the chain with the crankshaft sprocket and position the camshaft sprocket on the end of the camshaft. If necessary, turn the camshaft so the dowel in the camshaft fits into the hole in the sprocket with the timing mark in the 6 o'clock position **(see illustration 11.9)**. When the chain is installed, the timing marks MUST align as shown.

16   Apply a non-hardening thread locking compound to the camshaft sprocket bolt threads and tighten the bolts to the torque listed in this Chapter's Specifications.

17   Lubricate the chain with clean engine oil.

18   Install the oil pump and the oil pick up tube onto the engine (see Section 14). Now would be a good time to replace the crankshaft front oil seal (see Section 10).

19   Install the timing chain cover on the engine loosely using a new gasket **(see illustration)**.

20   Align the timing chain cover as follows:

a) *Install the crankshaft balancer on the engine as described in Section 9. This Step will align the front oil seal with the balancer hub.*

b) *Place a straightedge on the engine block oil pan rail. Measure the distance on each side of the block from the oil pan rail to the timing chain cover with a feeler gauge* **(see illustration)**. *This Step measures the difference between the sealing surface of the oil pan and the sealing surface of the timing chain cover in relationship to each other.*

c) *Tilt the front timing cover as necessary to achieve an even measurement on each side. This Step properly aligns the front timing cover to oil pan sealing surfaces. Typically 0.000 to 0.020 inch is an acceptable tolerance.* **Note:** *Ideally the timing chain cover should be flush with the oil pan rail, but because of the differences in seal thickness, this may not always be obtainable. That is why there is a tolerance of 0.000 to 0.020 inch. Always let the front seal center itself around the crankshaft balancer hub and tilt the cover from side to side to even up the measurement at both oil pan rails. Never push downward on the front timing cover in an attempt to make the oil pan sealing surface flush, as this will distort the front oil seal and eventually lead to an oil leak!*

d) *With the timing chain cover properly aligned, tighten the cover bolts to the torque listed in this Chapter's Specifications.*

21   Apply a thin layer of RTV sealant to the areas where the timing chain cover and cylinder block meet, then install the oil pan as described in Section 13.

22   The remaining installation steps are the reverse of removal.

23   Add coolant and oil to the engine (see Chapter 1). Run the engine and check for oil and coolant leaks.

11.20 With the crankshaft balancer in place and the front cover bolts installed LOOSELY, measure the distance between the oil pan rail and the front cover sealing surface on each side - then adjust the cover so the measurements are even on both sides before tightening the cover bolts

12 Camshaft and lifters - removal, inspection and installation

Note 1: *The camshaft lobe lift should be checked before removal (refer to Steps 7 through 12).*

Note 2: *If the camshaft is being replaced, always install new lifters as well. Do not use old lifters on a new camshaft.*

Removal

Refer to illustrations 12.2a, 12.2b and 12.4

1   Refer to the appropriate Sections and remove the intake manifold, valve covers, rocker arms, pushrods, timing chain and the cylinder heads. Also remove the radiator and air conditioning condenser (see Chapter 3) and the camshaft position sensor (see Chapter 6).

12.2a The roller lifters are held in place by retainers - remove the retainer bolts and remove the retainers and the lifters as an assembly - note that each retainer houses four individual lifters and they must be installed back in their original locations if they're going to be reused

12.2b Once the lifters and retainers are removed from the block they can be marked (for location and installation purposes) and inspected

2   Before removing the lifters, arrange to store them in a clearly labeled box to ensure that they're reinstalled in their original locations. Remove the lifter retainers and lifters and store them where they won't get dirty **(see illustrations)**. DO NOT attempt to withdraw the camshaft with the lifters in place.

3   If the lifters are built up with gum and varnish they may not come out with the retainer. If so, there are several ways to extract the lifters from the bores. A special tool designed to grip and remove lifters is manufactured by many tool companies and is widely available, but it may not be required in every case. On newer engines without a lot of varnish buildup, the lifters can often be removed with a small magnet or even with your fingers. A machinist's scribe with a bent end can be used to pull the lifters out by positioning the point under the retainer ring in the top of each lifter. **Caution:** *Don't use pliers to remove the lifters unless you intend to replace them with new ones. The pliers will damage the precision machined and hardened lifters, rendering them useless.*

4   Remove the bolts and the camshaft retainer plate, noting which direction faces the block **(see illustration)**.

5   Thread three 6-inch long bolts into the camshaft sprocket bolt holes to use as a "handle" when removing the camshaft from the block.

6   Carefully pull the camshaft out. Support the cam near the block so the lobes don't nick or gouge the bearings as it's withdrawn.

Inspection

Camshaft lobe lift check

Refer to illustrations 12.8, 12.14a and 12.14b

7   The first and easiest method to check camshaft lobe lift is through the use of a dial indicator with the camshaft installed in the engine block and the rocker arms and spark plugs removed. **Note:** *The following method can also be used if the cylinder heads and*

or pushrods have been removed by simply mounting the dial indicator on the deck surface of the engine block and placing the plunger against the top surface of the lifter on the cylinder you're checking.

8   Beginning with the number one cylinder, mount a dial indicator on the engine and position the plunger against the top surface of the pushrod or lifter. Position the number one cylinder at TDC on the compression stroke (see Section 3). The plunger should be directly above and in line with the pushrod **(see illustration)**.

9   Zero the dial indicator, then very slowly turn the crankshaft in the normal direction of rotation (clockwise) until the indicator needle stops and begins to move in the opposite direction. The point at which it stops indicates maximum cam lobe lift.

10   Record this figure for future reference, then reposition the piston at TDC on the compression stroke again.

11   Move the dial indicator to the other number one cylinder pushrod or lifter and repeat

the check. Be sure to record the results for each valve.

12   Repeat the check for the remaining valves. Since each piston must be at TDC on the compression stroke for this procedure, work from cylinder-to-cylinder following the firing order sequence.

13   The second method for measuring camshaft lobe lift is obtained through the use of a micrometer with the camshaft removed from the engine block.

14   Using this method, measure the camshaft lobe height and the base circle **(see illustrations)**. The difference between the two measurements is the lobe lift (lobe height - base circle = lobe lift). Record this figure for future reference and repeat the check on the remaining camshaft lobes.

15   After the lobe lift check is complete, compare the results to the Specifications listed in this Chapter. If the lobe lift is less than specified, cam lobe wear has occurred and a new camshaft should be installed.

12.4 Remove the bolts and take off the camshaft retainer plate, noting which side faces the block

12.8 Checking camshaft lobe lift with the camshaft installed in the engine - always make sure the dial indicator plunger is directly in line with the pushrod or lifter

12.14a If the camshaft is removed from the engine, lobe lift can be obtained by measuring camshaft lobe height . . .

12.14b . . . and by measuring the camshaft base circle - the difference between the two measurements equals lobe lift

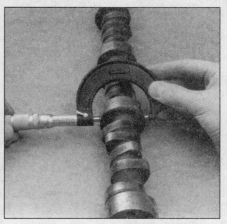

12.17 Check the diameter of each camshaft bearing journal to pinpoint the excessive wear and out-of-round conditions

Bearing journals, lobes and bearings

Refer to illustration 12.17
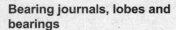

16   After the camshaft has been removed from the engine, cleaned with solvent and dried, inspect the bearing journals for uneven wear, pitting and evidence of seizure. If the journals are damaged, the bearing inserts in the block are probably damaged as well. Both the camshaft and bearings will have to be replaced. **Note:** *Camshaft bearing replacement requires special tools and expertise that place it beyond the scope of the average home mechanic. The tools for bearing removal and installation are available at stores that carry automotive tools, possibly even found at a tool rental business. It is advisable though, if the bearings are bad and the procedure is beyond your ability, take the engine block to an automotive machine shop to ensure that the job is done correctly.*
17   Measure the bearing journals with a micrometer to determine if they are excessively worn or out-of-round **(see illustration)**.
18   Check the camshaft lobes for heat discoloration, score marks, chipped areas, pitting and uneven wear. If the lobes are in good

condition and if the lobe lift measurements recorded earlier are as specified, the camshaft can be reused.

Lifters

Refer to illustrations 12.19 and 12.20

19   Clean the lifters with solvent and dry them thoroughly without mixing them up. Check each lifter wall and pushrod seat and for score marks and uneven wear **(see illustration)**. If the lifter walls are damaged or worn (which is not very likely), inspect the lifter bores in the engine block as well. If the pushrod seats are worn, check the pushrod ends.
20   Check the rollers carefully for wear and damage and make sure they turn freely without excessive play **(see illustration)**.
21   Used roller lifters can not be reinstalled with a new camshaft, but the original camshaft can be used if new lifters are installed. Always use new lifters when installing a new camshaft.

Installation

Refer to illustration 12.22

22   Lubricate the camshaft bearing journals and cam lobes with camshaft and lifter

assembly lube **(see illustration)**.
23   Slide the camshaft into the engine. Support the cam near the block and be careful not to scrape or nick the bearings.
24   Turn the camshaft until the dowel pin is in the 3 o'clock position, and install the camshaft thrust plate, tighten the bolts to the torque listed in this Chapter's Specifications. Make sure the gasket surface on the camshaft thrust plate and the engine block are free from oil and dirt.
25   Install the timing chain and sprockets (see Section 11). Also install the camshaft position sensor using a new O-ring (see Chapter 6).
26   Lubricate the lifters with clean engine oil and install them in the lifter retainers. Be sure to align the flats on the lifters with the flats in the lifter retainers. Install the retainer and lifters into the engine block as an assembly. If the original lifters are being reinstalled, be sure to return them to their original locations. If a new camshaft is being installed, install new lifters as well. Tighten the lifter retainer bolts to the torque listed in this Chapter's Specifications.

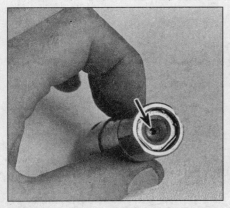

12.19 Check the pushrod seal in the top of each lifter for wear

12.20 The roller on hydraulic lifters must turn freely - check for wear and excessive play as well

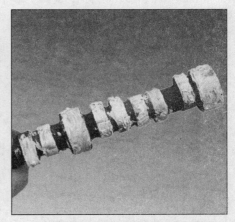

12.22 Be sure to apply camshaft assembly lube to the cam lobes and bearing journals before installing the camshaft

13.3 Remove the bolts and the lower control arm support crossmember

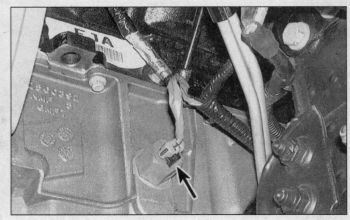

13.7 The oil level sensor is located on the passenger side of the oil pan

27   The remaining installation steps are the reverse of removal.

28   Before starting and running the engine, change the oil and install a new oil filter (see Chapter 1).

13   Oil pan - removal and installation

Removal

Refer to illustrations 13.3 and 13.7

1   Disconnect the cable from the negative terminal of the battery (see Chapter 5, Section 1).

2   Raise the vehicle and support it securely on jackstands, then refer to Chapter 1 and drain the engine oil and remove the oil filter.

3   Remove the lower control arm crossmember from below the oil pan **(see illustration)**.

4   Disconnect the front exhaust pipes from the exhaust manifolds and remove them from the vehicle. This step is not absolutely necessary, but it will help facilitate removal of the oil pan.

5   Remove the starter motor (see Chapter 5). Also remove the transmission side cov-

ers, if equipped, from the engine block at the transmission bellhousing (see Chapter 7).

6   Remove the wiring harness bracket from the front of the oil pan and the bracket on the passenger side of the oil pan securing the transmission oil cooler lines and the starter motor wiring.

7   Disconnect the electrical connector from the oil level sensor **(see illustration)**.

8   Remove the transmission to oil pan bolts (see Chapter 7).

9   If the vehicle is equipped with an engine oil cooler, remove the engine oil cooler lines and adapter from the driver's side of the oil pan.

10   On models equipped with the 4L80-E automatic transmission, remove the torque converter cover bolts, and on models with the 4L60-E automatic, remove the stud and bolt on the right side.

11   Remove all the oil pan bolts, then lower the pan from the engine. The pan will probably stick to the engine, so strike the pan with a rubber mallet until it breaks the gasket seal. **Caution:** *Before using force on the oil pan, be sure all the bolts have been removed.* Carefully slide the oil pan down and out, to the rear.

Installation

Refer to illustrations 13.12 and 13.15

12   Drill out the rivets securing the oil pan gasket to the oil pan and remove the old gasket **(see illustration)**. Wash out the oil pan with solvent.

13   Thoroughly clean the mounting surfaces of the oil pan and engine block of old gasket material and sealant. Wipe the gasket surfaces clean with a rag soaked in lacquer thinner, acetone or brake system cleaner.

14   Apply a 3/16-inch wide, one inch long bead of RTV sealant to the corners of the block where the front cover and the rear cover meet the engine block. Then attach the new gasket to the pan, install the pan and tighten the bolts finger-tight. Be sure the oil gallery passages in the pan and the gasket are aligned properly. **Note:** *Oil pan gasket rivets do not need to be installed on assembly.*

15   The alignment of the rear face of the aluminum pan to the rear of the block is important. Measure between the rear face of the pan and the front face of the transmission bellhousing with feeler gauges. Clearance should ideally be flush, but a gap of up to 0.010-inch is allowable. If the clearance is

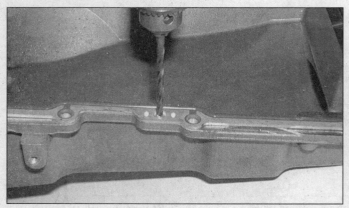

13.12 The manufacturer uses rivets to hold the gasket to the oil pan during assembly - carefully drill them out (it isn't necessary to rivet the new gasket to the oil pan)

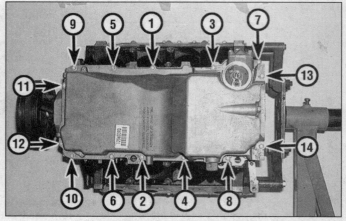

13.15 Oil pan TIGHTENING sequence

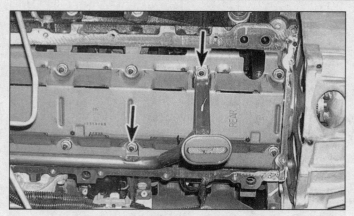

14.2a Oil pick-up tube-to-main stud retaining nuts

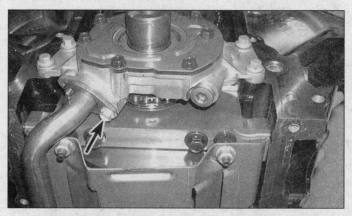

14.2b Remove the bolt securing the oil pick-up tube to the oil pump and remove it from the engine

OK, tighten the pan bolts/studs in sequence to the torque listed in this Chapter's Specifications (see illustration). If the clearance is not acceptable, install the two lower oil pan-to-bellhousing bolts and tighten them finger tight. This should draw the oil pan flush with the bellhousing. Caution: *The rear of the oil pan should never protrude rearward of the bellhousing plane of the block.*

16   The remainder of installation is the reverse of removal. Torque the oil pan bolts to the Specifications listed in this Chapter.

17   Add the proper type and quantity of oil (see Chapter 1), start the engine and check for leaks before placing the vehicle back in service.

14 Oil pump - removal, inspection and installation

Removal

Refer to illustrations 14.2a, 14.2b and 14.3

1   Refer to the Section 11, Steps 1 through 6 and remove the timing chain cover.

2   Remove the oil pump pick-up tube mounting nuts and bolts and lower the pick-up tube and screen assembly from the vehicle (see illustrations).

3   Remove the oil pump retaining bolts and slide the pump off the end of the crankshaft (see illustration).

Inspection

Refer to illustration 14.4

4   Remove the oil pump cover and withdraw the rotors from the pump body (see illustration). Clean the components with solvent, dry them thoroughly and inspect for any obvious damage. Also check the bolt holes for damaged threads and the splined surfaces on the crankshaft sprocket for any apparent damage. If any of the components are scored, scratched or worn, replace the entire oil pump assembly. At the time of writing there were no serviceable parts available.

Installation

Refer to illustration 14.8

5   Prime the pump by pouring clean motor oil into the pick-up tube hole, while turning the pump by hand.

6   Position the oil pump over the end of the crankshaft and align the teeth on the crankshaft sprocket with the teeth on the oil pump drive gear. Making sure the pump is fully seated against the block.

14.3 Oil pump mounting bolts

7   Install the oil pump mounting bolts and tighten them to the torque listed in this Chapter's Specifications.

8   Install a new O-ring on the oil pump pick-up tube, then fasten it to the oil pump and the engine block main studs (see illustration). Caution: *Be absolutely certain that the pick-up tube-to-oil pump bolts are properly tightened so that no air can be sucked into the oiling system at this connection.*

9   Install and align the timing chain cover, then install the oil pan. Refer to Sections 11

14.4 Oil pump cover-to-oil pump housing mounting bolts

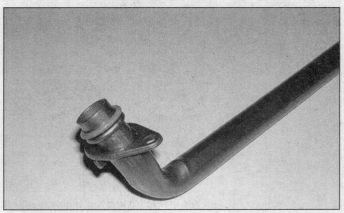

14.8 Always install a new O-ring on the oil pump pick up tube

16.3 Carefully pry the old seal out with a screwdriver at the notches provided in the rear cover

16.4 The rear oil seal can be pressed into place with a seal installation tool, a section of pipe or a blunt object shown here - in any case be sure the seal is installed squarely into the seal bore and flush with the rear cover

and 13 for the installation procedures.

10   The remainder of installation is the reverse of removal.

11   Add oil and coolant as necessary. Run the engine and check for oil and coolant leaks. Also check the oil pressure as described in Chapter 2C.

15   Driveplate - removal and installation

The driveplate replacement for 4.8L, 5.3L and 6.0L V8 engines is identical to the driveplate replacement procedure for the 4.3L V6 and 5.0L, 5.7L and 7.4L V8 engines. Refer to Chapter 2, Part A for the procedure, but use the torque figures in this Chapter's Specifications. **Note:** *If the spacer between the driveplate and the crankshaft must be removed and it's stuck, insert bolts (M11 bolts, 1.5 mm long) into the two threaded holes in the spacer. Tightening the bolts will force the*

spacer off the crankshaft.

16   Rear main oil seal - replacement

Refer to illustrations 16.3 and 16.4

Note: *If you're installing a new rear seal during a complete engine overhaul, refer to the "Rear main oil seal housing" procedure in Chapter 2C.*

1   Remove the transmission (see Chapter 7).

2   Remove the driveplate (see Section 15).

3   Pry the oil seal from the rear cover with a screwdriver **(see illustration)**. Be careful not to nick or scratch the crankshaft or the seal bore. Be sure to note how far it's recessed into the housing bore before removal so the new seal can be installed to the same depth. Thoroughly clean the seal bore in the block with a shop towel. Remove all traces of oil and dirt.

4   Lubricate the outside diameter of the

seal and install the seal over the end of the crankshaft. Make sure the lip of the seal points toward the engine. Preferably, a seal installation tool (available at most auto parts store) should be used to press the new seal back into place. If the proper seal installation tool is unavailable, use a large socket and carefully drive the new seal squarely into the seal bore and flush with the rear cover **(see illustration)**.

5   Install the driveplate (see Section 15).

6   Install the transmission (see Chapter 7).

17   Engine mounts - check and replacement

Refer to illustrations 17.1a and 17.1b

Refer to Chapter 2, Part A for this procedure but use the accompanying illustrations for the engine mount location **(see illustrations)**.

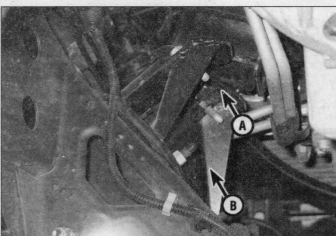

17.1a Location of the engine mount (A) and the engine mount support bracket (B) on the left side

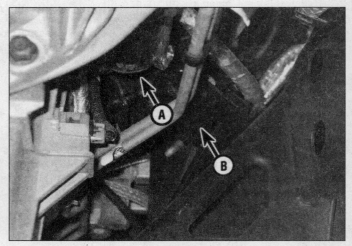

17.1b Location of the engine mount (A) and the engine mount support bracket (B) on the right side

Chapter 2 Part C
General engine overhaul procedures

Contents

Specifications

General

Displacement
4.3L V6	262 cubic inches
4.8L V8	293 cubic inches
5.0L V8	305 cubic inches
5.3L V8	325 cubic inches
5.7L V8	356 cubic inches
6.0L V8	364 cubic inches
7.4L V8	454 cubic inches

Bore and stroke
4.3L V6	4.012 x 3.480 inches
4.8L V8	3.779 x 3.268 inches
5.0L V8	3.737 x 3.480 inches
5.3L V8	3.779 x 3.622 inches
5.7L V8	4.001 x 3.480 inches
6.0L V8	4.001 x 3.622 inches
7.4L V8	4.250 x 4.000 inches

Cylinder compression pressure
Minimum	100 psi
Maximum variation between cylinders	25-percent from highest reading

Oil pressure (minimum)
1000 rpm	6 psi
2000 rpm	18 psi
4000 rpm	24 psi

Balance shaft (4.3L V6 engine)

Rear bearing journal diameter	1.4994 to 1.5000 inches
Rear bearing journal oil clearance	1.0020 to 1.0035 inch

Torque specifications*

Ft-lbs (unless otherwise indicated)

Balance shaft retainer bolts (4.3L V6 engine)	106 in-lbs
Balance shaft drive gear bolt (4.3L V6 engine)	
Step 1	15
Step 2	Turn an additional 35-degrees
Connecting rod cap bolts/nuts	
4.3L V6 engine	
Step 1	20
Step 2	Turn an additional 70-degrees
5.0L/5.7L V8 engines	
Step 1	20
Step 2	Turn an additional 55-degrees
4.8L, 5.3L, 6.0L V8 engines	
Step 1	15
Step 2	Turn an additional 75-degrees
7.4 V8 engines	47
Main bearing cap bolts	
4.3L V6 engine	
Step 1	15
Step 2	Turn an additional 73-degrees
5.0L/5.7L V8 engines	
Two bolt main bearing caps	
Step 1	15
Step 2	Turn an additional 73-degrees
Four bolt main bearing caps	
Step 1	15
Step 2	Turn an additional 43-degrees
Step 3	Turn an additional 73-degrees
4.8L, 5.3L, 6.0L V8 engines **(see illustration 11.19)**	
Inner bolts (1 through 10)	
Step 1	15
Step 2	Turn an additional 80-degrees
Outer stud nuts (11 through 20)	
Step 1	15
Step 2	Turn an additional 50-degrees
Side bolts **(21 through 30)...	18
7.4 V8 engines	
Step 1 (inner bolts)	102
Step 2 (outer bolts)	102
Rear main seal housing bolts	
4.3L V6 and 5.0L/5.7L V8 engines...	106 in-lbs
4.8L, 5.3L, 6.0L V8 engines	18

Refer to Part A or B for additional torque specifications.
*** Use new bolts*

1.1 An engine block being bored. An engine rebuilder will use special machinery to recondition the cylinder bores

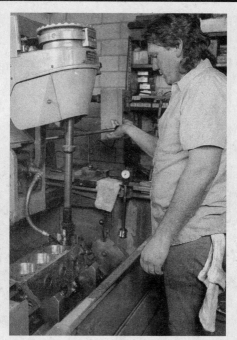

1.2 If the cylinders are bored, the machine shop will normally hone the engine on a machine like this

1.3 A crankshaft having a main bearing journal ground

1.4 A machinist checks for a bent connecting rod, using specialized equipment

1 General information - engine overhaul

Refer to illustrations 1.1, 1.2, 1.3, 1.4, 1.5 and 1.6

Included in this portion of Chapter 2 are general information and diagnostic testing procedures for determining the overall mechanical condition of your engine.

The information ranges from advice concerning preparation for an overhaul and the purchase of replacement parts and/or components to detailed, step-by-step procedures covering removal and installation.

The following Sections have been written to help you determine whether your engine needs to be overhauled and how to remove and install it once you've determined it needs to be rebuilt. For information concerning in-vehicle engine repair, see Chapter 2A or 2B.

It's not always easy to determine when, or if, an engine should be completely overhauled, because a number of factors must be considered.

High mileage is not necessarily an indication that an overhaul is needed, while low mileage doesn't preclude the need for an overhaul. Frequency of servicing is probably the most important consideration. An engine that's had regular and frequent oil and filter changes, as well as other required maintenance, will most likely give many thousands of miles of reliable service. Conversely, a neglected engine may require an overhaul very early in its service life.

Excessive oil consumption is an indication that piston rings, valve seals and/or valve guides are in need of attention. Make sure that oil leaks aren't responsible before deciding that the rings and/or guides are bad. Perform a cylinder compression check to determine the extent of the work required (see Section 3). Also check the vacuum readings under various conditions (see Section 4).

Check the oil pressure with a gauge installed in place of the oil pressure sending unit and compare it to this Chapter's Specifications (see Section 2). If it's extremely low, the bearings and/or oil pump are probably worn out.

Loss of power, rough running, knocking or metallic engine noises, excessive valve train noise and high fuel consumption rates may also point to the need for an overhaul, especially if they're all present at the same time. If a complete tune-up doesn't remedy the situation, major mechanical work is the only solution.

An engine overhaul involves restoring the internal parts to the specifications of a new engine. During an overhaul, the piston rings are replaced and the cylinder walls are reconditioned (rebored and/or honed) **(see illustrations 1.1 and 1.2)**. If a rebore is done by an automotive machine shop, new oversize pistons will also be installed. The main bearings, connecting rod bearings and camshaft bearings are generally replaced with new ones and, if necessary, the crankshaft may be reground to restore the journals **(see illustration 1.3)**. Generally, the valves are serviced as well, since they're usually in less-than-perfect condition at this point. While the engine is being overhauled, other components, such as the distributor, starter and alternator, can be rebuilt as well. The end result should be similar to a new engine that will give many trouble free miles. **Note:** *Critical cooling system components such as the hoses, drivebelts, thermostat and water pump should be replaced with new parts when an engine is overhauled. The radiator should be checked carefully to ensure that it isn't clogged or leaking* (see Chapter 3). *If you purchase a rebuilt engine or short block, some rebuilders will not warranty their engines unless the radiator has been professionally flushed. Also, we don't recommend overhauling the oil pump - always install a new one when an engine is rebuilt.*

Overhauling the internal components on today's engines is a difficult and time-consuming task which requires a significant amount of specialty tools and is best left to a professional engine rebuilder **(see illustrations 1.4, 1.5 and 1.6)**. A competent engine rebuilder will handle the inspection of your old parts and offer advice concerning the reconditioning or replacement of the original engine, never purchase parts or have machine work done on other components until the block has been thoroughly inspected by a professional machine shop. As a general rule, time is the primary cost of an overhaul, especially since the vehicle may be tied up for a mini-

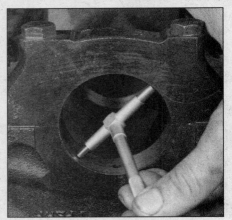

1.5 A bore gauge being used to check the main bearing bore

1.6 Uneven piston wear like this indicates a bent connecting rod

2.2a Location of the oil pressure sending unit on a 4.3L V6 engine

mum of two weeks or more. Be aware that some engine builders only have the capability to rebuild the engine you bring them while other rebuilders have a large inventory of rebuilt exchange engines in stock. Also be aware that many machine shops could take as much as two weeks time to completely rebuild your engine depending on shop workload. Sometimes it makes more sense to simply exchange your engine for another engine that's already rebuilt to save time.

2 Oil pressure check

Refer to illustrations 2.2a, 2.2b and 2.2c

1   Low engine oil pressure can be a sign of an engine in need of rebuilding. A "low oil pressure" indicator (often called an "idiot light") is not a test of the oiling system. Such indicators only come on when the oil pressure is dangerously low. Even a factory oil pressure gauge in the instrument panel is only a relative indication, although much better for driver information than a warning light. A better test is with a mechanical (not electrical) oil pressure gauge.

2   Remove the engine cover (see Chapter 11) and locate the oil pressure indicator

sending unit - it's located on the rear of the engine block, behind the intake manifold **(see illustrations)**.

3   Unscrew and remove the oil pressure sending unit and then screw in the hose for your oil pressure gauge. If necessary, install an adapter fitting. Use Teflon tape or thread sealant on the threads of the adapter and/or the fitting on the end of your gauge's hose.

4   Connect an accurate tachometer to the engine, according to the tachometer manufacturer's instructions.

5   Check the oil pressure with the engine running (normal operating temperature) at the specified engine speed, and compare it to this Chapter's Specifications. If it's extremely low, the bearings and/or oil pump are probably worn out.

3 Cylinder compression check

Refer to illustration 3.6

1   A compression check will tell you what mechanical condition the upper end of your engine (pistons, rings, valves, head gaskets) is in. Specifically, it can tell you if the compression is down due to leakage caused by worn

piston rings, defective valves and seats or a blown head gasket. **Note:** *The engine must be at normal operating temperature and the battery must be fully charged for this check.*

2   Begin by cleaning the area around the spark plugs before you remove them (compressed air should be used, if available). The idea is to prevent dirt from getting into the cylinders as the compression check is being done.

3   Disable the ignition system by unplugging the primary (low voltage) electrical connector from the distributor or from the ignition coil assemblies (see Chapter 5). Disable the fuel system by removing the fuel pump relay (see Chapter 4).

4   Remove all of the spark plugs from the engine (see Chapter 1).

5   Block the throttle wide open.

6   Install a compression gauge in the spark plug hole **(see illustration)**.

7   Crank the engine over at least seven compression strokes and watch the gauge. The compression should build up quickly in a healthy engine. Low compression on the first stroke, followed by gradually increasing pressure on successive strokes, indicates worn piston rings. A low compression reading on the first stroke, which doesn't build up during

2.2b Location of the oil pressure sending unit on a 5.0L V8 engine

2.2c Location of the oil pressure sending unit on a 5.3L V8 engine

3.6 Use a compression gauge with a threaded fitting for the spark plug hole, not the type that requires hand pressure to maintain the seal

successive strokes, indicates leaking valves or a blown head gasket (a cracked head could also be the cause). Deposits on the undersides of the valve heads can also cause low compression. Record the highest gauge reading obtained.

8   Repeat the procedure for the remaining cylinders and compare the results to this Chapter's Specifications.

9   Add some engine oil (about three squirts from a plunger-type oil can) to each cylinder, through the spark plug hole, and repeat the test.

10   If the compression increases after the oil is added, the piston rings are definitely worn. If the compression doesn't increase significantly, the leakage is occurring at the valves or head gasket. Leakage past the valves may be caused by burned valve seats and/or faces or warped, cracked or bent valves.

11   If two adjacent cylinders have equally low compression, there's a strong possibility that the head gasket between them is blown. The appearance of coolant in the combustion chambers or the crankcase would verify this condition.

12   If one cylinder is slightly lower than the others, and the engine has a slightly rough idle, a worn lobe on the camshaft could be the cause.

13   If the compression is unusually high, the combustion chambers are probably coated with carbon deposits. If that's the case, the cylinder head(s) should be removed and decarbonized.

14   If compression is way down or varies greatly between cylinders, it would be a good idea to have a leak-down test performed by an automotive repair shop. This test will pinpoint exactly where the leakage is occurring and how severe it is.

---

4   Vacuum gauge diagnostic checks

Refer to illustrations 4.4 and 4.6

A vacuum gauge provides inexpensive but valuable information about what is going on in the engine. You can check for worn rings or cylinder walls, leaking head or intake manifold gaskets, restricted exhaust, stuck or burned valves, weak valve springs, improper ignition or valve timing and ignition problems.

Unfortunately, vacuum gauge readings are easy to misinterpret, so they should be used in conjunction with other tests to confirm the diagnosis.

Both the absolute readings and the rate of needle movement are important for accurate interpretation. Most gauges measure vacuum in inches of mercury (in-Hg). The following references to vacuum assume the diagnosis is being performed at sea level. As elevation increases (or atmospheric pressure decreases), the reading will decrease. For every 1,000 foot increase in elevation above approximately 2,000 feet, the gauge readings will decrease about one inch of mercury.

Connect the vacuum gauge directly to

the intake manifold vacuum, not to ported (throttle body) vacuum **(see illustration)**. Use a T-fitting to access the vacuum signal. Be sure no hoses are left disconnected during the test or false readings will result.

Before you begin the test, allow the engine to warm up completely. Block the wheels and set the parking brake. With the transmission in Park, start the engine and allow it to run at normal idle speed. **Warning:** *Keep your hands and the vacuum gauge clear of the fans.*

Read the vacuum gauge; an average, healthy engine should normally produce about 17 to 22 in-Hg with a fairly steady needle **(see illustration)**. Refer to the following vacuum gauge readings and what they indicate about the engine's condition:

1   A low, steady reading usually indicates a leaking gasket between the intake manifold and cylinder head(s) or throttle body, a leaky vacuum hose, late ignition timing or incorrect camshaft timing. Check ignition timing with a timing light and eliminate all other possible causes, utilizing the tests provided in this Chapter before you remove the timing chain cover to check the timing marks.

2   If the reading is three to eight inches below normal and it fluctuates at that low reading, suspect an intake manifold gasket leak at an intake port or a faulty fuel injector.

3   If the needle has regular drops of about two-to-four inches at a steady rate, the valves

4.4 A simple vacuum gauge can be handy in diagnosing engine condition and performance

are probably leaking. Perform a compression check or leak-down test to confirm this.

4   An irregular drop or down-flick of the needle can be caused by a sticking valve or an ignition misfire. Perform a compression check or leak-down test and read the spark plugs.

5   A rapid vibration of about four in-Hg vibration at idle combined with exhaust smoke indicates worn valve guides. Perform a leak-down test to confirm this. If the rapid vibration occurs with an increase in engine speed,

Low, steady reading   Low, fluctuating needle   Regular drops

Irregular drops   Rapid vibration

Large fluctuation   Slow fluctuation

STD-O-OBR HAYNES

4.6 Typical vacuum gauge readings

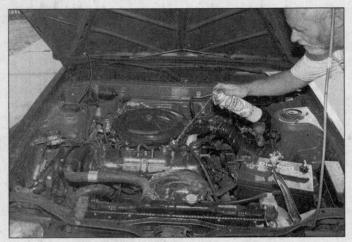

6.1 After tightly wrapping water-vulnerable components, use a spray cleaner on everything, with particular concentration on the greasiest areas, usually around the valve cover and lower edges of the block. If one section dries out, apply more cleaner

6.2 Depending on how dirty the engine is, let the cleaner soak in according to the directions and then hose off the grime and cleaner. Get the rinse water down into every area you can get at; then dry important components with a hair dryer or paper towels

check for a leaking intake manifold gasket or head gasket, weak valve springs, burned valves or ignition misfire.

6   A slight fluctuation, say one inch up and down, may mean ignition problems. Check all the usual tune-up items and, if necessary, run the engine on an ignition analyzer.

7   If there is a large fluctuation, perform a compression or leak-down test to look for a weak or dead cylinder or a blown head gasket.

8   If the needle moves slowly through a wide range, check for a clogged PCV system, incorrect idle fuel mixture, throttle body or intake manifold gasket leaks.

9   Check for a slow return after revving the engine by quickly snapping the throttle open until the engine reaches about 2,500 rpm and let it shut. Normally the reading should drop to near zero, rise above normal idle reading (about 5 in-Hg over) and then return to the previous idle reading. If the vacuum returns slowly and doesn't peak when the throttle is snapped shut, the rings may be worn. If there is a long delay, look for a restricted exhaust system (often the muffler or catalytic converter). An easy way to check this is to temporarily disconnect the exhaust ahead of the suspected part and redo the test.

5   Engine rebuilding alternatives

The do-it-yourselfer is faced with a number of options when purchasing a rebuilt engine. The major considerations are cost, warranty, parts availability and the time required for the rebuilder to complete the project. The decision to replace the engine block, piston/connecting rod assemblies and crankshaft depends on the final inspection results of your engine. Only then can you make a cost effective decision whether to have your engine overhauled or simply purchase an exchange engine for your vehicle.

Some of the rebuilding alternatives include:

Individual parts - If the inspection procedures reveal that the engine block and most engine components are in reusable condition, purchasing individual parts and having a rebuilder rebuild your engine may be the most economical alternative. The block, crankshaft and piston/connecting rod assemblies should all be inspected carefully by a machine shop first.

Short block - A short block consists of an engine block with a crankshaft and piston/connecting rod assemblies already installed. All new bearings are incorporated and all clearances will be correct. The existing valve train components, cylinder head and external parts can be bolted to the short block with little or no machine shop work necessary.

Long block - A long block consists of a short block plus an oil pump, oil pan, cylinder

6.3 Get an engine stand sturdy enough to firmly support the engine while you're working on it. Stay away from three-wheeled models: they have a tendency to tip over more easily, so get a four-wheeled unit

head, valve cover, camshaft and valve train components, timing sprockets and chain or gears and timing cover. All components are installed with new bearings, seals and gaskets incorporated throughout. The installation of manifolds and external parts is all that's necessary.

Low mileage used engines - Some companies now offer low mileage used engines which is a very cost effective way to get your vehicle up and running again. These engines often come from vehicles which have been in totaled in accidents or come from other countries which have a higher vehicle turn over rate. A low mileage used engine also usually has a similar warranty like the newly remanufactured engines.

Give careful thought to which alternative is best for you and discuss the situation with local automotive machine shops, auto parts dealers and experienced rebuilders before ordering or purchasing replacement parts.

6   Engine removal - methods and precautions

Refer to illustrations 6.1, 6.2, and 6.3

If you've decided that an engine must be removed for overhaul or major repair work, several preliminary steps should be taken. Read all removal and installation procedures carefully prior to committing to this job.

Locating a suitable place to work is extremely important. Adequate work space, along with storage space for the vehicle, will be needed. If a shop or garage isn't available, at the very least a flat, level, clean work surface made of concrete or asphalt is required.

Cleaning the engine compartment and engine before beginning the removal procedure will help keep tools clean and organized (see illustrations 6.1 and 6.2).

An engine hoist will also be necessary. Make sure the hoist is rated in excess of the combined weight of the engine and transmission. Safety is of primary importance, considering the potential hazards involved in removing the engine from the vehicle.

If you're a novice at engine removal, get at least one helper. One person cannot easily do all the things you need to do to remove a big heavy engine and transmission assembly from the engine compartment. Also helpful is to seek advice and assistance from someone who's experienced in engine removal.

Plan the operation ahead of time. Arrange for or obtain all of the tools and equipment you'll need prior to beginning the job **(see illustration 6.3)**. Some of the equipment necessary to perform engine removal and installation safely and with relative ease are (in addition to an engine hoist) a heavy duty floor jack (preferably fitted with a transmission jack head adapter), complete sets of wrenches and sockets as described in the front of this manual, wooden blocks, plenty of rags and cleaning solvent for mopping up spilled oil, coolant and gasoline.

Plan for the vehicle to be out of use for quite a while. A machine shop can do the work that is beyond the scope of the home mechanic. Machine shops often have a busy schedule, so before removing the engine, consult the shop for an estimate of how long it will take to rebuild or repair the components that may need work.

7   Engine - removal and installation

Warning 1: *Gasoline is extremely flammable, so take extra precautions when you work on any part of the fuel system. Don't smoke or allow open flames or bare light bulbs near the work area, and don't work in a garage where a gas-type appliance (such as a water heater or clothes dryer) is present. Since gasoline is carcinogenic, wear fuel-resistant gloves when there's a possibility of being exposed to fuel, and, if you spill any fuel on your skin, rinse it off immediately with soap and water. Mop up any spills immediately and do not store fuel-soaked rags where they could ignite. The fuel system is under constant pressure, so, if any fuel lines are to be disconnected, the fuel pressure in the system must be relieved first (see Chapter 4 for more information). When you perform any kind of work on the fuel system, wear safety glasses and have a Class B type fire extinguisher on hand.*
Warning 2: *The air conditioning system is under high pressure. Do not loosen any hose fittings or remove any components until after the system has been discharged. Air conditioning refrigerant must be properly discharged into an EPA-approved recovery/recycling unit at a dealer service department or an automotive air conditioning repair facility. Always wear eye protection when disconnecting air conditioning system fittings.*
Warning 3: *The engine must be completely cool before beginning this procedure.*

Removal

Refer to illustration 7.15

1   Have the air conditioning system discharged by an automotive air conditioning technician.
2   Relieve the fuel system pressure (see Chapter 4).
3   Disconnect the cable from the negative terminal of the battery (see Chapter 5, Section 1).
4   Remove the air filter housing and air intake duct (see Chapter 4).
5   Remove the engine cover (see Chapter 11).
6   Drain the cooling system and remove the drivebelts (see Chapter 1).
7   Remove the hood, the radiator grille, the front bumper and the radiator support (see Chapter 11).
8   If equipped, remove the air conditioning condenser and automatic transmission oil cooler (see Chapter 3).
9   Remove the coolant reservoir, the radiator, the upper and lower fan shrouds and the engine cooling fan (see Chapter 3).
10   Disconnect the accelerator cable or accelerator pedal position sensor (APPS) (see Chapter 4) and throttle valve cable (see Chapter 7).
11   Remove the power steering pump and brackets without disconnecting the power steering fluid hoses and tie it out of the way (see Chapter 10).
12   Remove the alternator (see Chapter 5).
13   Remove the air conditioning compressor (see Chapter 3).
14   Remove the upper intake manifold (see Chapter 2A or 2B).
15   Label and disconnect all wires from the engine **(see illustration)**. Masking tape and/ or a touch-up paint applicator work well for marking items. **Note:** *Take instant photos or sketch the locations of components and brackets to help with reassembly.*
16   Disconnect the fuel lines at the engine (see Chapter 4) and plug the lines to prevent fuel loss.
17   Remove the transmission fluid level indicator tube and dipstick.
18   Remove the engine oil dipstick tube.
19   Raise the vehicle and support it securely on jackstands.
20   Drain the engine oil (see Chapter 1).
21   Remove the transmission cooler lines and brackets (see Chapter 7) and the engine oil cooler lines and brackets, if equipped (see Chapter 3).
22   Remove the exhaust manifolds (see Chapter 2A or 2B).
23   Disconnect the wires from the starter solenoid and remove the starter (see Chapter 5).
24   Lower the vehicle.
25   If you're working on a 4.8L, 5.3L or 6.0L engine, remove the intake manifold (see Chapter 2B).
26   Support the engine from above with a hoist. Attach the hoist chain to the engine lifting brackets. If no brackets are present, you

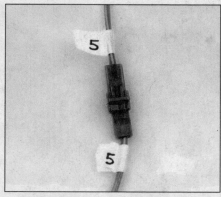

7.15 Label both ends of each wire or vacuum connection before disconnecting them

will have to obtain some, or fasten the chains to some substantial part of the engine - one that is strong enough to take the weight, but in a location that will provide good balance. If you're attaching a chain to the stud on the engine, or are using a bolt passing through the chain and into a threaded hole, place a washer between the nut or bolt head and the chain and tighten the nut or bolt securely.
27   Remove the torque converter bolts (see Chapter 7).
28   Support the transmission with a floor jack (place a block of wood on the jack head to protect the transmission). Remove the transmission-to-engine bolts (see Chapter 7).
29   Use the hoist to take the weight off the engine mounts, and remove the engine mount through-bolts (2002 and earlier models) or mount-to-mount bracket bolts (2003 and later models) (see Chapter 2A or 2B).
30   Check to make sure everything is disconnected, then slowly lift the engine out of the vehicle. The engine will probably need to be tilted and/or maneuvered as it's lifted out, so have an assistant handy. **Warning:** *Do not place any part of your body under the engine when it is supported only by a hoist or other lifting device.*
31   Remove the driveplate and mount the engine on an engine stand or set the engine on the floor and support it so it doesn't tip over. Then disconnect the engine hoist.

Installation

32   Check the engine mounts. If they're worn or damaged, replace them.
33   Inspect the torque converter seal and bushing.
34   Attach the hoist to the engine, remove the engine from the engine stand and install the flywheel (see Chapter 2A or 2B).
35   Carefully guide the engine into place, lowering it slowly and moving it back into the engine compartment until the engine mounts can be secured.
36   With the engine still supported by the hoist, use a jack with a piece of wood on top to support the oil pan, allowing you to control of the angle of the rear of the engine for alignment with the transmission.

9.6 Remove the two Torx bolts and the balance shaft retainer

9.7 A small slide hammer must be threaded into the front of the balance shaft to pull the balance shaft and front bearing out of the block

37   Install the transmission-to-engine bolts and tighten them securely. **Caution:** *DO NOT use the bolts to force the transmission and engine together!*
38   Tighten all the bolts on the engine mounts and remove the hoist and jack.
39   Reinstall the remaining components in the reverse order of removal.
40   Add coolant, oil, power steering and transmission fluid as needed (see Chapter 1).
41   Run the engine and check for proper operation and leaks. Shut off the engine and recheck the fluid levels.

8   Engine overhaul - disassembly sequence

1   It's much easier to remove the external components if it's mounted on a portable engine stand. A stand can often be rented quite cheaply from an equipment rental yard. Before the engine is mounted on a stand, the driveplate should be removed from the engine.
2   If a stand isn't available, it's possible to remove the external engine components with it blocked up on the floor. Be extra careful not to tip or drop the engine when working without a stand.
3   If you're going to obtain a rebuilt engine, all external components must come off first, to be transferred to the replacement engine. These components include:
    Driveplate
    Ignition system components
    Emissions-related components
    Engine mounts and mount brackets
    Intake/exhaust manifolds
    Fuel injection components
    Oil filter
    Spark plug wires and spark plugs
    Thermostat and housing assembly
    Water pump
Note: *When removing the external components from the engine, pay close attention to*

details that may be helpful or important during installation. Note the installed position of gaskets, seals, spacers, pins, brackets, washers, bolts and other small items.
4   If you're going to obtain a short block (assembled engine block, crankshaft, pistons and connecting rods), then remove the timing chain, cylinder heads, oil pan, oil pump pick-up tube, oil pump and water pump from your engine so that you can turn in your old short block to the rebuilder as a core. See *Engine rebuilding alternatives* for additional information regarding the different possibilities to be considered.

9   Balance shaft and bearings (4.3L V6 engine) - removal, inspection and installation

Removal
Refer to illustrations 9.6 and 9.7
Note 1: *If the balance shaft is to be removed, the balance shaft gear bolt should be removed before the timing chain is removed, so that the shaft is held while the bolt is loosened.*
Note 2: *The balance shaft and the balance shaft front bearing are serviced only as an assembly. Do not remove the balance shaft bearing only.*
1   Disconnect the cable from the negative terminal of the battery (see Chapter 5, Section 1).
2   Remove the air filter housing and air intake duct (see Chapter 4).
3   Drain the cooling system and remove the drivebelts (see Chapter 1).
4   Remove the coolant reservoir (see Chapter 3).
5   Remove the timing chain (see Chapter 2A).
6   Remove the two bolts and the balance shaft retainer at the front of the block **(see illustration)**.
7   The balance shaft front bearing fits tightly

into the block; use a slide-hammer threaded into the front of the balance shaft to knock it out **(see illustration)**.

Inspection
8   Inspect the balance shaft and measure the rear bearing journal diameter in the same manner as the camshaft. If the journal diameter doesn't fall within the values listed in this Chapter's Specifications, replace the balance shaft, bearing and bushing as a set. The balance shaft rides in a bearing at the front of the block and a bushing at the rear.
9   The rear bushing is similar to a camshaft bearing, pressed into the rear of the block. It must be installed by a machine shop with the proper tools, to the proper depth and with the oil hole aligned.
10   Inspect the balance shaft drive gear (the one behind the camshaft gear), and the balance shaft driven gear (bolted to the front of the balance shaft) for signs of wear, pitting, broken teeth or rough operation. As with the balance shaft and its bearings, the two balance shaft gears are serviced only as a set.

Installation
Refer to illustrations 9.12 and 9.16
Note: *The balance shaft is installed after the camshaft. Refer to the camshaft installation procedure in Part A of this Chapter.*
11   Lubricate the balance shaft bearing journals with clean engine oil or engine assembly lube.
12   Slide the balance shaft into the engine. Support the balance shaft near the block and be careful not to scrape or nick the rear bearing. Using a bearing driver or large socket, gently drive the shaft into the block until the front bearing is seated **(see illustration)**.
13   Install the balance shaft retainer and two bolts and tighten them to the torque listed in this Chapter's Specifications.
14   Install the balance shaft driven gear and tighten the bolt to the torque listed in this Chapter's Specifications.

9.12 Drive the balance shaft and front bearing into the block until the bearing retainer can be bolted into place

9.16 Position the balance shaft drive and driven gears with the timing marks aligned as shown

15   Rotate the camshaft so that, with the balance shaft drive gear temporarily installed, the timing mark is straight up at the 12 o'clock position. Remove the drive gear.

16   Rotate the balance shaft until the timing mark on the driven gear is facing straight down at the 6 o'clock position. Reinstall the balance shaft drive gear to the camshaft and make sure both balance shaft gears are aligned **(see illustration)**.

17   Install the timing chain, sprockets and cover (see Part A of this Chapter).

10 Pistons and connecting rods - removal and installation

Removal

Refer to illustrations 10.1, 10.3 and 10.4

Note: *Prior to removing the piston/connecting rod assemblies, remove the cylinder heads and oil pan (see Chapter 2A or 2B).*

1   Use your fingernail to feel if a ridge has formed at the upper limit of ring travel (about 1/4-inch down from the top of each cylinder). If carbon deposits or cylinder wear have produced ridges, they must be completely removed with a special tool **(see illustration)**. Follow the manufacturer's instructions provided with the tool. Failure to remove the ridges before attempting to remove the piston/connecting rod assemblies may result in piston breakage.

2   After the cylinder ridges have been removed, turn the engine so the crankshaft is facing up.

3   Before the main bearing cap assembly and connecting rods are removed, check the connecting rod endplay with feeler gauges. Slide them between the first connecting rod and the crankshaft throw until the play is removed **(see illustration)**. Repeat this procedure for each connecting rod. The endplay is equal to the thickness of the feeler gauge(s). Check with an automotive machine shop for the endplay service limit (a typical end play limit should measure between 0.005 to 0.015 inch [0.127 to 0.369 mm]). If the play

exceeds the service limit, new connecting rods will be required. If new rods (or a new crankshaft) are installed, the endplay may fall under the minimum allowable. If it does, the rods will have to be machined to restore it. If necessary, consult an automotive machine shop for advice.

4   Check the connecting rods and caps for identification marks. If they aren't plainly marked, use paint or marker **(see illustration)** to clearly identify each rod and cap (1, 2, 3, etc., depending on the cylinder they're associated with). Do not interchange the rod caps. Install the exact same rod cap onto the same connecting rod. **Caution:** *Do not use a punch and hammer to mark the connecting rods or they may be damaged.*

5   Loosen each of the connecting rod cap bolts/nuts 1/2-turn at a time until they can be removed by hand. **Note:** *On models equipped with rod bolts, new connecting rod cap bolts must be used when reassembling the engine, but save the old bolts for use when checking the connecting rod bearing oil clearance.*

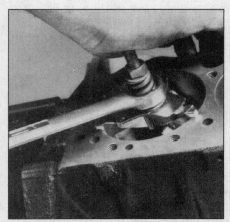

10.1 Before you try to remove the pistons, use a ridge reamer to remove the raised material (ridge) from the top of the cylinders

10.3 Checking the connecting rod endplay (side clearance)

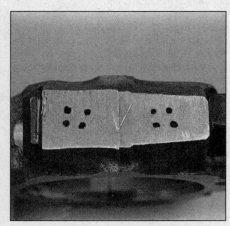

10.4 If the connecting rods or caps are not marked, use permanent ink or paint to mark the caps to the rods by cylinder number (for example, this would be number 4 cylinder connecting rod)

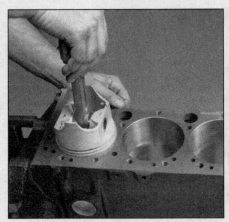

10.13 Install the piston ring into the cylinder then push it down into position using a piston so the ring will be square in the cylinder

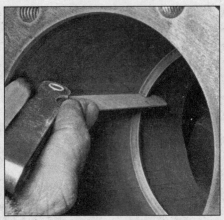

10.14 With the ring square in the cylinder, measure the ring end gap with a feeler gauge

10.15 If the ring end gap is too small, clamp a file in a vise as shown and file the piston ring ends - be sure to remove all raised material

6   Remove the number one connecting rod cap and bearing insert. Don't drop the bearing insert out of the cap.

7   Remove the bearing insert and push the connecting rod/piston assembly out through the top of the engine. Use a wooden or plastic hammer handle to push on the upper bearing surface in the connecting rod. If resistance is felt, double-check to make sure that all of the ridge was removed from the cylinder.

8   Repeat the procedure for the remaining cylinders. **Note:** *If the connecting rod caps are retained by bolts instead of nuts, discard the old rod cap bolts. Use new bolts when reassembling the engine.*

9   After removal, reassemble the connecting rod caps and bearing inserts in their respective connecting rods and install the cap bolts finger tight. Leaving the old bearing inserts in place until reassembly will help prevent the connecting rod bearing surfaces from being accidentally nicked or gouged.

10   The pistons and connecting rods are now ready for inspection and overhaul at an automotive machine shop.

Piston ring installation

Refer to illustrations 10.13, 10.14, 10.15, 10.19a, 10.19b and 10.22

11   Before installing the new piston rings, the ring end gaps must be checked. It's assumed that the piston ring side clearance has been checked and verified correct.

12   Lay out the piston/connecting rod assemblies and the new ring sets so the ring sets will be matched with the same piston and cylinder during the end gap measurement and engine assembly.

13   Insert the top (number one) ring into the first cylinder and square it up with the cylinder walls by pushing it in with the top of the piston **(see illustration)**. The ring should be near the bottom of the cylinder, at the lower limit of ring travel.

14   To measure the end gap, slip feeler gauges between the ends of the ring until a gauge equal to the gap width is found **(see**

illustration). The feeler gauge should slide between the ring ends with a slight amount of drag. A typical ring gap should fall between 0.010 and 0.020 inch [0.25 to 0.50 mm] for compression rings and up to 0.030 inch [0.76 mm] for the oil ring steel rails. If the gap is larger or smaller than specified, double-check to make sure you have the correct rings before proceeding.

15   If the gap is too small, it must be enlarged or the ring ends may come in contact with each other during engine operation, which can cause serious damage to the engine. If necessary, increase the end gaps by filing the ring ends very carefully with a fine file. Mount the file in a vise equipped with soft jaws, slip the ring over the file with the ends contacting the file face and slowly move the ring to remove material from the ends. When performing this operation, file only by pushing the ring from the outside end of the file towards the vise **(see illustration)**.

16   Excess end gap isn't critical unless it's greater than 0.040 inch (1.01 mm). Again, double-check to make sure you have the correct ring type.

17   Repeat the procedure for each ring that

will be installed in the first cylinder and for each ring in the remaining cylinders. Remember to keep rings, pistons and cylinders matched up.

18   Once the ring end gaps have been checked/corrected, the rings can be installed on the pistons.

19   The oil control ring (lowest one on the piston) is usually installed first. It's composed of three separate components. Slip the spacer/expander into the groove **(see illustration)**. If an anti-rotation tang is used, make sure it's inserted into the drilled hole in the ring groove. Next, install the upper side rail in the same manner **(see illustration)**. Don't use a piston ring installation tool on the oil ring side rails, as they may be damaged. Instead, place one end of the side rail into the groove between the spacer/expander and the ring land, hold it firmly in place and slide a finger around the piston while pushing the rail into the groove. Finally, install the lower side rail.

20   After the three oil ring components have been installed, check to make sure that both the upper and lower side rails can be rotated smoothly inside the ring grooves.

10.19a Installing the spacer/expander in the oil ring groove

10.19b DO NOT use a piston ring installation tool when installing the oil control side rails

10.22 Use a piston ring installation tool to install the number 2 and the number 1 (top) rings - be sure the directional mark on the piston ring(s) is facing toward the top of the piston

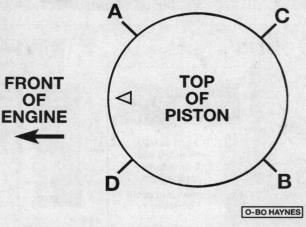

10.30 Position the piston ring end gaps as shown here before installing the piston/connecting rod assemblies into the engine

A   *Top compression ring gap*
B   *Second compression ring and oil ring spacer gap*
C   *Upper oil ring gap*
D   *Lower oil ring gap*

21   The number two (middle) ring is installed next. It's usually stamped with a mark which must face up, toward the top of the piston. Do not mix up the top and middle rings, as they have different cross-sections. **Note:** *Always follow the instructions printed on the ring package or box - different manufacturers may require different approaches.*

22   Use a piston ring installation tool and make sure the identification mark is facing the top of the piston, then slip the ring into the middle groove on the piston **(see illustration)**. Don't expand the ring any more than necessary to slide it over the piston.

23   Install the number one (top) ring in the same manner. Make sure the mark is facing up. Be careful not to confuse the number one and number two rings.

24   Repeat the procedure for the remaining pistons and rings.

Installation

25   Before installing the piston/connecting rod assemblies, the cylinder walls must be perfectly clean, the top edge of each cylinder bore must be chamfered, and the crankshaft must be in place.

26   Remove the cap from the end of the number one connecting rod (refer to the marks made during removal). Remove the original bearing inserts and wipe the bearing surfaces of the connecting rod and cap with a clean, lint-free cloth. They must be kept spotlessly clean.

Connecting rod bearing oil clearance check

Refer to illustrations 10.30, 10.33, 10.35, 10.37 and 10.41

27   Clean the back side of the new upper bearing insert, then lay it in place in the connecting rod.

28   Make sure the tab on the bearing fits into

the recess in the rod. Don't hammer the bearing insert into place and be very careful not to nick or gouge the bearing face. Don't lubricate the bearing at this time **(see illustration)**.

29   Clean the back side of the other bearing insert and install it in the rod cap. Again, make sure the tab on the bearing fits into the recess in the cap, and don't apply any lubricant. It's critically important that the mating surfaces of the bearing and connecting rod are perfectly clean and oil free when they're assembled.

30   Position the piston ring gaps at the intervals around the piston as shown **(see illustration)**.

31   Lubricate the piston and rings with clean engine oil and attach a piston ring compressor to the piston. Leave the skirt protruding about 1/4-inch to guide the piston into the cylinder. The rings must be compressed until they're flush with the piston.

32   Rotate the crankshaft until the number one connecting rod journal is at BDC (bottom dead center) and apply a liberal coat of

engine oil to the cylinder walls. Refer to the TDC locating procedure in Chapter 2A or 2B for additional information.

33   With the arrow, notch or mark on the top of the piston facing the front of the engine, gently insert the piston/connecting rod assembly into the number one cylinder bore and rest the bottom edge of the ring compressor on the engine block **(see illustration)**.

34   Tap the top edge of the ring compressor to make sure it's contacting the block around its entire circumference.

35   Gently tap on the top of the piston with the end of a wooden or plastic hammer handle **(see illustration)** while guiding the end of the connecting rod into place on the crankshaft journal. The piston rings may try to pop out of the ring compressor just before entering the cylinder bore, so keep some downward pressure on the ring compressor. Work slowly, and if any resistance is felt as the piston enters the cylinder, stop immediately. Find out what's hanging up and fix it before proceeding. Do

10.33 The arrow, notch or mark must face the front of the engine - 5.3L V8 engine shown

10.35 Use a plastic or wooden hammer handle to push the piston into the cylinder

ENGINE BEARING ANALYSIS

Debris

Babbitt bearing embedded with debris from machinings

Microscopic detail of debris

Microscopic detail of gouges

Overplated copper alloy bearing gouged by cast iron debris

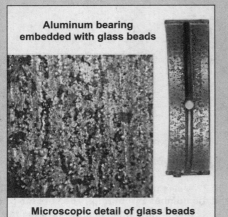

Aluminum bearing embedded with glass beads

Microscopic detail of glass beads

Damaged lining caused by dirt left on the bearing back

Misassembly

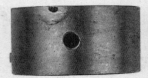

Result of a lower half assembled as an upper - blocking the oil flow

Excessive oil clearance is indicated by a short contact arc

Polished and oil-stained backs are a result of a poor fit in the housing bore

Result of a wrong, reversed, or shifted cap

Overloading

Damage from excessive idling which resulted in an oil film unable to support the load imposed

Damaged upper connecting rod bearings caused by engine lugging; the lower main bearings (not shown) were similarly affected

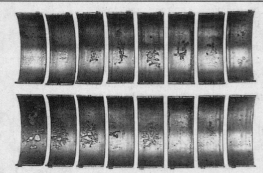

The damage shown in these upper and lower connecting rod bearings was caused by engine operation at a higher-than-rated speed under load

Misalignment

A warped crankshaft caused this pattern of severe wear in the center, diminishing toward the ends

A poorly finished crankshaft caused the equally spaced scoring shown

A tapered housing bore caused the damage along one edge of this pair

A bent connecting rod led to the damage in the "V" pattern

Lubrication

Result of dry start: The bearings on the left, farthest from the oil pump, show more damage

Result of a low oil supply or oil starvation

Severe wear as a result of inadequate oil clearance

Corrosion

Microscopic detail of corrosion

Corrosion is an acid attack on the bearing lining generally caused by inadequate maintenance, extremely hot or cold operation, or inferior oils or fuels

Microscopic detail of cavitation

Example of cavitation - a surface erosion caused by pressure changes in the oil film

Damage from excessive thrust or insufficient axial clearance

Bearing affected by oil dilution caused by excessive blow-by or a rich mixture

10.37 Place Plastigage on each connecting rod bearing journal parallel to the crankshaft centerline

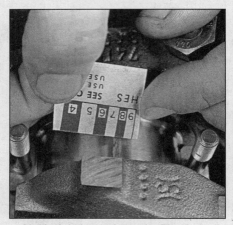

10.41 Use the scale on the Plastigage package to determine the bearing oil clearance - be sure to measure the widest part of the Plastigage and use the correct scale; it comes with both standard and metric scales

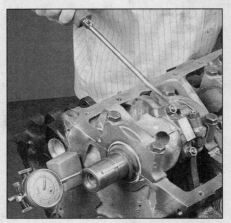

11.1 Checking crankshaft endplay with a dial indicator

not, for any reason, force the piston into the cylinder - you might break a ring and/or the piston.

36   Once the piston/connecting rod assembly is installed, the connecting rod bearing oil clearance must be checked before the rod cap is permanently installed.

37   Cut a piece of the appropriate size Plastigage slightly shorter than the width of the connecting rod bearing and lay it in place on the number one connecting rod journal, parallel with the journal axis **(see illustration)**.

38   Clean the connecting rod cap bearing face and install the rod cap. Make sure the mating mark on the cap is on the same side as the mark on the connecting rod **(see illustration 10.4)**.

39   Install the old rod bolts/nuts, at this time, and tighten them to the torque listed in this Chapter's Specifications. **Note:** *Use a thin-wall socket to avoid erroneous torque readings that can result if the socket is wedged between the rod cap and the bolt or nut. If the socket tends to wedge itself between the fastener and the cap, lift up on it slightly until it no longer contacts the cap. DO NOT rotate the crankshaft at any time during this operation.*

40   Remove the fasteners and detach the rod cap, being very careful not to disturb the Plastigage. Discard the cap bolts at this time as they cannot be reused.

41   Compare the width of the crushed Plastigage to the scale printed on the Plastigage envelope to obtain the oil clearance **(see illustration)**. The connecting rod oil clearance is usually about 0.001 to 0.002 inch. Consult an automotive machine shop for the clearance specified for the rod bearings on your engine.

42   If the clearance is not as specified, the bearing inserts may be the wrong size (which means different ones will be required). Before deciding that different inserts are needed, make sure that no dirt or oil was between the bearing inserts and the connecting rod or cap when the clearance was measured. Also, recheck the journal diameter. If the Plastigage was wider at one end than the other, the journal may be tapered. If the clearance still

exceeds the limit specified, the bearing will have to be replaced with an undersize bearing. **Caution:** *When installing a new crankshaft always use a standard size bearing.*

Final installation

43   Carefully scrape all traces of the Plastigage material off the rod journal and/or bearing face. Be very careful not to scratch the bearing - use your fingernail or the edge of a plastic card.

44   Make sure the bearing faces are perfectly clean, then apply a uniform layer of clean moly-base grease or engine assembly lube to both of them. You'll have to push the piston into the cylinder to expose the face of the bearing insert in the connecting rod.

45   Slide the connecting rod back into place on the journal, install the rod cap, install the nuts or bolts and tighten them to the torque listed in this Chapter's Specifications. Again, work up to the torque in three steps.

46   Repeat the entire procedure for the remaining pistons/connecting rods.

47   The important points to remember are:
   a) *Keep the back sides of the bearing inserts and the insides of the connecting rods and caps perfectly clean when assembling them.*
   b) *Make sure you have the correct piston/rod assembly for each cylinder.*
   c) *The mark on the piston must face the front of the engine.*
   d) *Lubricate the cylinder walls liberally with clean oil.*
   e) *Lubricate the bearing faces when installing the rod caps after the oil clearance has been checked.*

48   After all the piston/connecting rod assemblies have been correctly installed, rotate the crankshaft a number of times by hand to check for any obvious binding.

49   As a final step, check the connecting rod endplay again. If it was correct before disassembly and the original crankshaft and rods

were reinstalled, it should still be correct. If new rods or a new crankshaft were installed, the endplay may be inadequate. If so, the rods will have to be removed and taken to an automotive machine shop for resizing.

11   Crankshaft - removal and installation

Removal

Refer to illustrations 11.1 and 11.3

Note: *The crankshaft can be removed only after the engine has been removed from the vehicle. It's assumed that the flywheel or driveplate, crankshaft pulley, timing chain, oil pan, oil pump, oil filter and piston/connecting rod assemblies have already been removed. The rear main oil seal retainer must be unbolted and separated from the block before proceeding with crankshaft removal.*

1   Before the crankshaft is removed, measure the endplay. Mount a dial indicator with the indicator in line with the crankshaft and just touching the end of the crankshaft as shown **(see illustration)**.

2   Pry the crankshaft all the way to the rear and zero the dial indicator. Next, pry the crankshaft to the front as far as possible and check the reading on the dial indicator. The distance traveled is the endplay. A typical crankshaft endplay will fall between 0.003 to 0.010 inch. If it is greater than that, check the crankshaft thrust washer/bearing assembly surfaces for wear after it's removed. If no wear is evident, new main bearings should correct the endplay. Refer to Step 11 for the location of the thrust washer/bearing assembly on each engine.

3   If a dial indicator isn't available, feeler gauges can be used. Gently pry the crankshaft all the way to the front of the engine. Slip feeler gauges between the crankshaft and the front face of the thrust bearing or washer to determine the clearance **(see illustration)**.

4   Loosen the main bearing cap bolts 1/4-turn at a time each, until they can be removed by hand.

5   Gently tap the main bearing caps/bedplate assembly with a soft-face hammer around the perimeter of the assembly. Pull the main bearing cap/bedplate assembly straight up and off the cylinder block. Try not to drop the bearing inserts if they come out with the assembly.

6   Carefully lift the crankshaft out of the engine. It may be a good idea to have an assistant available, since the crankshaft is quite heavy and awkward to handle. With the bearing inserts in place inside the engine block and main bearing caps, reinstall the main bearing cap assembly onto the engine block and tighten the bolts finger tight. Make sure you install the main bearing cap assembly with the arrow facing the front end (timing chain) of the engine.

Installation

7   Crankshaft installation is the first step in engine reassembly. It's assumed at this point that the engine block and crankshaft have been cleaned, inspected and repaired or reconditioned.

8   Position the engine block with the bottom facing up.

9   Remove the mounting bolts and lift off the main bearing cap assembly.

10   If they're still in place, remove the original bearing inserts from the block and from the main bearing cap assembly. Wipe the bearing surfaces of the block and main bearing cap assembly with a clean, lint-free cloth. They must be kept spotlessly clean. This is critical for determining the correct bearing oil clearance.

Main bearing oil clearance check

Refer to illustrations 11.17, 11.19 and 11.21

11 Without mixing them up, clean the back sides of the new upper main bearing inserts (with grooves and oil holes) and lay one in each main bearing saddle in the block. Each upper bearing has an oil groove and oil hole in it. **Caution:** *The oil holes in the block must line up with the oil holes in the upper bearing inserts.* Locate the thrust washers.

a) *On 4.3L V6 engines, the thrust washer/ bearing assembly is located on the number 4 (rear) main journal.*

b) *On 5.0L, 5.7L and 7.4L V8 engines, the thrust washer/bearing assembly is located on the number 5 (rear) main journal.*

c) *On 4.8L, 5.3L and 6.0L V8 engines, the thrust washer/main bearing assembly is located on the number 3 journal (middle)*

The thrust washer/bearing assemblies must be installed in the correct journal. Clean the back sides of the lower main bearing inserts and lay them in the corresponding location in the main bearing cap assembly. Make sure the tab on the bearing insert fits into the recess in the block or main bearing cap assembly. The upper bearings with the oil holes are installed into the engine block while the lower bearings without the oil holes are installed in the

11.3 Checking crankshaft endplay with feeler gauges at the thrust bearing journal

main bearing caps. **Caution:** *Do not hammer the bearing insert into place and don't nick or gouge the bearing faces. DO NOT apply any lubrication at this time.*

12   Clean the faces of the bearing inserts in the block and the crankshaft main bearing journals with a clean, lint-free cloth.

13   Check or clean the oil holes in the crankshaft, as any dirt here can go only one way - straight through the new bearings.

14   Once you're certain the crankshaft is clean, carefully lay it in position in the cylinder block.

15   Before the crankshaft can be permanently installed, the main bearing oil clearance must be checked.

16   Cut several strips of the appropriate size of Plastigage. They must be slightly shorter than the width of the main bearing journal.

17   Place one piece on each crankshaft main bearing journal, parallel with the journal axis as shown **(see illustration).**

18   Clean the faces of the bearing inserts in the main bearing caps. Hold the bearing inserts in place and install the caps onto the crankshaft and cylinder block. DO NOT disturb the Plastigage. Make sure you install the main bearing caps with the arrow facing the front (timing chain end) of the engine.

19   Apply clean engine oil to all bolt threads prior to installation, then install all bolts finger-

11.17 Place the Plastigage onto the crankshaft bearing journal as shown

tight. Tighten main bearing cap bolts. On 4.3L V6 and 5.0L, 5.7L, 7.4L V8 engines, tighten the main bearing cap bolts, starting in the center and working towards the ends to the torque listed in this Chapter's Specifications. On 4.8L, 5.3L and 6.0L V8 engines, follow the correct torque sequence **(see illustration).** Don't rotate the crankshaft at any time during this operation! **Note:** *On 4.8L, 5.3L and 6.0L V8 engines, the main bearing tightening procedure requires five steps. First tighten the inner bolts (bolts 1 through 10) in two steps to the torque and angle of rotation listed in this Chapter's Specifications, then tighten the outer bolts (bolts 11 through 20) in two steps to the torque and angle of rotation listed in this Chapter's Specifications. The fifth step is tightening the side bolts, but DO NOT use the new side bolts during the oil clearance check.*

20   Remove the bolts in the *reverse* order of the tightening sequence and carefully lift the main bearing cap assembly straight up and off the block. Do not disturb the Plastigage or rotate the crankshaft. If the main bearing caps are difficult to remove, tap it gently from side-to-side with a soft-face hammer to loosen it.

21   Compare the width of the crushed Plastigage on each journal to the scale printed on the Plastigage envelope to determine the main bearing oil clearance **(see illustration).**

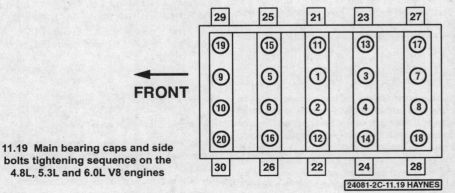

FRONT

11.19 Main bearing caps and side bolts tightening sequence on the 4.8L, 5.3L and 6.0L V8 engines

24081-2C-11.19 HAYNES

COMMON ENGINE OVERHAUL TERMS

B

Backlash - The amount of play between two parts. Usually refers to how much one gear can be moved back and forth without moving the gear with which it's meshed.

Bearing Caps - The caps held in place by nuts or bolts which, in turn, hold the bearing surface. This space is for lubricating oil to enter.

Bearing clearance - The amount of space left between shaft and bearing surface. This space is for lubricating oil to enter.

Bearing crush - The additional height which is purposely manufactured into each bearing half to ensure complete contact of the bearing back with the housing bore when the engine is assembled.

Bearing knock - The noise created by movement of a part in a loose or worn bearing.

Blueprinting - Dismantling an engine and reassembling it to EXACT specifications.

Bore - An engine cylinder, or any cylindrical hole; also used to describe the process of enlarging or accurately refinishing a hole with a cutting tool, as to bore an engine cylinder. The bore size is the diameter of the hole.

Boring - Renewing the cylinders by cutting them out to a specified size. A boring bar is used to make the cut.

Bottom end - A term which refers collectively to the engine block, crankshaft, main bearings and the big ends of the connecting rods.

Break-in - The period of operation between installation of new or rebuilt parts and time in which parts are worn to the correct fit. Driving at reduced and varying speed for a specified mileage to permit parts to wear to the correct fit.

Bushing - A one-piece sleeve placed in a bore to serve as a bearing surface for shaft, piston pin, etc. Usually replaceable.

C

Camshaft - The shaft in the engine, on which a series of lobes are located for operating the valve mechanisms. The camshaft is driven by gears or sprockets and a timing chain. Usually referred to simply as the cam.

Carbon - Hard, or soft, black deposits found in combustion chamber, on plugs, under rings, on and under valve heads.

Cast iron - An alloy of iron and more than two percent carbon, used for engine blocks and heads because it's relatively inexpensive and easy to mold into complex shapes.

Chamfer - To bevel across (or a bevel on) the sharp edge of an object.

Chase - To repair damaged threads with a tap or die.

Combustion chamber - The space between the piston and the cylinder head, with the piston at top dead center, in which air-fuel mixture is burned.

Compression ratio - The relationship between cylinder volume (clearance volume) when the piston is at top dead center and cylinder volume when the piston is at bottom dead center.

Connecting rod - The rod that connects the crank on the crankshaft with the piston. Sometimes called a con rod.

Connecting rod cap - The part of the connecting rod assembly that attaches the rod to the crankpin.

Core plug - Soft metal plug used to plug the casting holes for the coolant passages in the block.

Crankcase - The lower part of the engine in which the crankshaft rotates; includes the lower section of the cylinder block and the oil pan.

Crank kit - A reground or reconditioned crankshaft and new main and connecting rod bearings.

Crankpin - The part of a crankshaft to which a connecting rod is attached.

Crankshaft - The main rotating member, or shaft, running the length of the crankcase, with offset throws to which the connecting rods are attached; changes the reciprocating motion of the pistons into rotating motion.

Cylinder sleeve - A replaceable sleeve, or liner, pressed into the cylinder block to form the cylinder bore.

D

Deburring - Removing the burrs (rough edges or areas) from a bearing.

Deglazer - A tool, rotated by an electric motor, used to remove glaze from cylinder walls so a new set of rings will seat.

E

Endplay - The amount of lengthwise movement between two parts. As applied to a crankshaft, the distance that the crankshaft can move forward and back in the cylinder block.

F

Face - A machinist's term that refers to removing metal from the end of a shaft or the face of a larger part, such as a flywheel.

Fatigue - A breakdown of material through a large number of loading and unloading cycles. The first signs are cracks followed shortly by breaks.

Feeler gauge - A thin strip of hardened steel, ground to an exact thickness, used to check clearances between parts.

Free height - The unloaded length or height of a spring.

Freeplay - The looseness in a linkage, or an assembly of parts, between the initial application of force and actual movement. Usually perceived as slop or slight delay.

Freeze plug - See Core plug.

G

Gallery - A large passage in the block that forms a reservoir for engine oil pressure.

Glaze - The very smooth, glassy finish that develops on cylinder walls while an engine is in service.

H

Heli-Coil - A rethreading device used when threads are worn or damaged. The device is installed in a retapped hole to reduce the thread size to the original size.

I

Installed height - The spring's measured length or height, as installed on the cylinder head. Installed height is measured from the spring seat to the underside of the spring retainer.

J

Journal - The surface of a rotating shaft which turns in a bearing.

K

Keeper - The split lock that holds the valve spring retainer in position on the valve stem.

Key - A small piece of metal inserted into matching grooves machined into two parts fitted together - such as a gear pressed onto a shaft - which prevents slippage between the two parts.

Knock - The heavy metallic engine sound, produced in the combustion chamber as a result of abnormal combustion - usually detonation. Knock is usually caused by a loose or worn bearing. Also referred to as detonation, pinging and spark knock. Connecting rod or main bearing knocks are created by too much oil clearance or insufficient lubrication.

L

Lands - The portions of metal between the piston ring grooves.

Lapping the valves - Grinding a valve face and its seat together with lapping compound.

Lash - The amount of free motion in a gear train, between gears, or in a mechanical assembly, that occurs before movement can begin. Usually refers to the lash in a valve train.

Lifter - The part that rides against the cam to transfer motion to the rest of the valve train.

M

Machining - The process of using a machine to remove metal from a metal part.

Main bearings - The plain, or babbit, bearings that support the crankshaft.

Main bearing caps - The cast iron caps, bolted to the bottom of the block, that support the main bearings.

O

O.D. - Outside diameter.

Oil gallery - A pipe or drilled passageway in the engine used to carry engine oil from one area to another.

Oil ring - The lower ring, or rings, of a piston; designed to prevent excessive amounts of oil from working up the cylinder walls and into the combustion chamber. Also called an oil-control ring.

Oil seal - A seal which keeps oil from leaking out of a compartment. Usually refers to a dynamic seal around a rotating shaft or other moving part.

O-ring - A type of sealing ring made of a special rubberlike material; in use, the O-ring is compressed into a groove to provide the sealing action.

Overhaul - To completely disassemble a unit, clean and inspect all parts, reassemble it with the original or new parts and make all adjustments necessary for proper operation.

P

Pilot bearing - A small bearing installed in the center of the flywheel (or the rear end of the crankshaft) to support the front end of the input shaft of the transmission.

Pip mark - A little dot or indentation which indicates the top side of a compression ring.

Piston - The cylindrical part, attached to the connecting rod, that moves up and down in the cylinder as the crankshaft rotates. When the fuel charge is fired, the piston transfers the force of the explosion to the connecting rod, then to the crankshaft.

Piston pin (or wrist pin) - The cylindrical and usually hollow steel pin that passes through the piston. The piston pin fastens the piston to the upper end of the connecting rod.

Piston ring - The split ring fitted to the groove in a piston. The ring contacts the sides of the ring groove and also rubs against the cylinder wall, thus sealing space between piston and wall. There are two types of rings: Compression rings seal the compression pressure in the combustion chamber; oil rings scrape excessive oil off the cylinder wall.

Piston ring groove - The slots or grooves cut in piston heads to hold piston rings in position.

Piston skirt - The portion of the piston below the rings and the piston pin hole.

Plastigage - A thin strip of plastic thread, available in different sizes, used for measuring clearances. For example, a strip of plastigage is laid across a bearing journal and mashed as parts are assembled. Then parts are disassembled and the width of the strip is measured to determine clearance between journal and bearing. Commonly used to measure crankshaft main-bearing and connecting rod bearing clearances.

Press-fit - A tight fit between two parts that requires pressure to force the parts together. Also referred to as drive, or force, fit.

Prussian blue - A blue pigment; in solution, useful in determining the area of contact between two surfaces. Prussian blue is commonly used to determine the width and location of the contact area between the valve face and the valve seat.

R

Race (bearing) - The inner or outer ring that provides a contact surface for balls or rollers in bearing.

Ream - To size, enlarge or smooth a hole by using a round cutting tool with fluted edges.

Ring job - The process of reconditioning the cylinders and installing new rings.

Runout - Wobble. The amount a shaft rotates out-of-true.

S

Saddle - The upper main bearing seat.

Scored - Scratched or grooved, as a cylinder wall may be scored by abrasive particles moved up and down by the piston rings.

Scuffing - A type of wear in which there's a transfer of material between parts moving against each other; shows up as pits or grooves in the mating surfaces.

Seat - The surface upon which another part rests or seats. For example, the valve seat is the matched surface upon which the valve face rests. Also used to refer to wearing into a good fit; for example, piston rings seat after a few miles of driving.

Short block - An engine block complete with crankshaft and piston and, usually, camshaft assemblies.

Static balance - The balance of an object while it's stationary.

Step - The wear on the lower portion of a ring land caused by excessive side and back-clearance. The height of the step indicates the ring's extra side clearance and the length of the step projecting from the back wall of the groove represents the ring's back clearance.

Stroke - The distance the piston moves when traveling from top dead center to bottom dead center, or from bottom dead center to top dead center.

Stud - A metal rod with threads on both ends.

T

Tang - A lip on the end of a plain bearing used to align the bearing during assembly.

Tap - To cut threads in a hole. Also refers to the fluted tool used to cut threads.

Taper - A gradual reduction in the width of a shaft or hole; in an engine cylinder, taper usually takes the form of uneven wear, more pronounced at the top than at the bottom.

Throws - The offset portions of the crankshaft to which the connecting rods are affixed.

Thrust bearing - The main bearing that has thrust faces to prevent excessive endplay, or forward and backward movement of the crankshaft.

Thrust washer - A bronze or hardened steel washer placed between two moving parts. The washer prevents longitudinal movement and provides a bearing surface for thrust surfaces of parts.

Tolerance - The amount of variation permitted from an exact size of measurement. Actual amount from smallest acceptable dimension to largest acceptable dimension.

U

Umbrella - An oil deflector placed near the valve tip to throw oil from the valve stem area.

Undercut - A machined groove below the normal surface.

Undersize bearings - Smaller diameter bearings used with re-ground crankshaft journals.

V

Valve grinding - Refacing a valve in a valve-refacing machine.

Valve train - The valve-operating mechanism of an engine; includes all components from the camshaft to the valve.

Vibration damper - A cylindrical weight attached to the front of the crankshaft to minimize torsional vibration (the twist-untwist actions of the crankshaft caused by the cylinder firing impulses). Also called a harmonic balancer.

W

Water jacket - The spaces around the cylinders, between the inner and outer shells of the cylinder block or head, through which coolant circulates.

Web - A supporting structure across a cavity.

Woodruff key - A key with a radiused backside (viewed from the side).

11.21 Use the scale on the Plastigage package to determine the bearing oil clearance - be sure to measure the widest part of the Plastigage and use the correct scale; it comes with both standard and metric scales

12.7 It will be necessary to install the rear main oil seal into the housing first, then install a new gasket and the seal housing onto the engine block - be sure to lubricate the seal lip and carefully work the seal over the crankshaft with a blunt tool

Check with an automotive machine shop for the oil clearance for your engine.

22   If the clearance is not as specified, the bearing inserts may be the wrong size (which means different ones will be required). Before deciding if different inserts are needed, make sure that no dirt or oil was between the bearing inserts and the cap assembly or block when the clearance was measured. If the Plastigage was wider at one end than the other, the crankshaft journal may be tapered. If the clearance still exceeds the limit specified, the bearing insert(s) will have to be replaced with an undersize bearing insert(s). **Caution:** *When installing a new crankshaft always install a standard bearing insert set.*

23   Carefully scrape all traces of the Plastigage material off the main bearing journals and/or the bearing insert faces. Be sure to remove all residue from the oil holes. Use your fingernail or the edge of a credit card - don't nick or scratch the bearing faces.

Final installation

24   Carefully lift the crankshaft out of the cylinder block.

25   Clean the bearing insert faces in the cylinder block, then apply a thin, uniform layer of moly-base grease or engine assembly lube to each of the bearing surfaces. Be sure to coat the thrust faces as well as the journal face of the thrust washer.

26   Make sure the crankshaft journals are clean, then lay the crankshaft back in place in the cylinder block.

27   Clean the bearing insert faces and then apply the same lubricant to them. Clean the engine block thoroughly. The surfaces must be free of oil residue.

28   Assemble the main bearing caps and bearings and install each main bearing cap onto the crankshaft and cylinder block. Make sure the arrow faces the front of the engine.

29   Prior to installation, apply clean engine oil to all bolt threads wiping off any excess,

then install all bolts finger-tight.

30   Pry the crankshaft slightly back and forth in the block to seat the thrust bearings. Tighten all main bearing cap bolts as described in Step 19 to specifications. **Note:** *On 4.8L, 5.3L and 6.0L V8 engines, install new main bearing cap side bolts and tighten the bolts to the torque listed in this Chapter's Specifications. Be sure to tighten both side bolts on a main bearing cap before proceeding to the next cap and always install new side bolts or oil leaks may develop.*

31   Recheck crankshaft endplay with a feeler gauge or a dial indicator. The endplay should be correct if the crankshaft thrust faces aren't worn or damaged and if new bearings have been installed.

32   Rotate the crankshaft a number of times by hand to check for any obvious binding. It should rotate with a running torque of 50 in-lbs or less. If the running torque is too high, correct the problem at this time.

33   Install the new rear main oil seal (see Chapter 2A and 2B).

12   Rear main oil seal and housing - installation

Refer to illustrations 12.7 and 12.9.

1   All engines covered by this manual, except the 7.4L V8, are equipped with a one-piece rear main seal and a seal housing that bolts to the rear of the engine block. Although the rear main seal housings on 4.3L V6 and V8 engines differ in appearance, seal installation is essentially the same with the exception of installing the seal housing onto the engine block. 4.3L V6 engines use alignment dowels on the rear of the block to automatically center the seal housing over the end of the crankshaft. V8 engines are not equipped with alignment dowels on the rear of the block and therefore must be aligned manually prior to tightening of the rear seal housing.

2   The crankshaft must be installed first and the main bearing caps bolted in place, then the new seal should be installed in the housing and the housing bolted to the block.

3   Before installing the crankshaft, check

the seal contact surface very carefully for scratches and nicks that could damage the new seal lip and cause oil leaks. If the crankshaft is damaged, the only alternative is a new or different crankshaft.

4   The old seal can be removed from the housing by inserting a large screwdriver into the three notches provided and prying it out (see Chapter 2A or 2B).

5   Be sure to note how far it's recessed into the housing bore before removing it; the new seal will have to be recessed an equal amount. Be very careful not to scratch or otherwise damage the bore in the housing or oil leaks could develop.

6   Make sure the housing is clean, then apply a thin coat of engine oil to the outer edge of the new seal. The seal must be pressed squarely into the housing bore, so hammering it into place is not recommended. If you don't have access to a press, sandwich the housing and seal between two smooth pieces of wood and press the seal into place with the jaws of a large vise. The pieces of wood must be thick enough to distribute the force evenly around the entire circumference of the seal. Work slowly and make sure the seal enters the bore squarely.

7   On 4.3L V6 engines, make sure the dowel pins are in place before installing the housing. Lubricate the seal lips with small amount of clean engine oil and slide the rear seal/housing over the rear of the crankshaft **(see illustration)**. Be sure to use a new gasket between the rear seal housing and the engine block - no sealant is required.

4.3L V6 and 5.0L/5.7L V8 engines

8   Tighten the bolts a little at a time until the seal housing is fully seated against the engine block, then tighten them to the torque listed in this Chapter's Specifications.

4.8L, 5.3L and 6.0L V8 engines

9   Install the rear seal housing retaining bolts on the engine loosely and align the rear housing as follows:

a) Place a straightedge on the engine block oil pan rail. Measure the distance on each side of the block from the oil pan rail to the seal housing with a feeler gauge **(see illustration)**. *This Step measures the difference between the sealing surface of the oil pan and the sealing surface of the rear seal housing.*

b) Tilt the rear seal housing as necessary to achieve an even measurement on each side. *This Step properly aligns the rear seal housing to oil pan sealing surfaces. Typically 0.000 to 0.020 inch is an acceptable tolerance.* **Note:** *Ideally the rear seal housing should be flush with the oil pan rail, but because of the differences in seal thickness, this may not always be obtainable. That is why there is a tolerance of 0.000 to 0.020 inch. Always let the rear seal center itself around the crankshaft, then tilt the housing from side-to-side to even up the measurement at both oil pan rails. Never push downward on the rear seal housing in an attempt to make the oil pan sealing surface flush, as this will distort the rear oil seal and eventually lead to an oil leak!*

c) With the rear seal housing properly aligned, tighten the housing bolts to the torque listed in this Chapter's Specifications.

12.9 With the rear seal housing in place and the bolts installed loosely, measure the distance between the oil seal housing and the oil pan rail on each side - then adjust the housing so the measurements are even on both sides before tightening the cover bolts

13   Engine overhaul - reassembly sequence

1   Before beginning engine reassembly, make sure you have all the necessary new parts, gaskets and seals as well as the following items on hand:

Common hand tools
A 1/2-inch drive torque wrench
New engine oil
Gasket sealant
Thread locking compound

2   If you obtained a short block it will be necessary to install the cylinder head, the oil pump and pick-up tube, the oil pan, the water pump, the timing chain and timing cover, and the valve cover (see Chapter 2A or 2B). In order to save time and avoid problems, the external components must be installed in the following general order:

Thermostat and housing cover
Water pump
Intake and exhaust manifolds
Fuel injection components
Emission control components
Spark plugs
Distributor or ignition coils
Oil filter
Engine mounts and mount brackets
Driveplate

14   Initial start-up and break-in after overhaul

Warning: *Have a fire extinguisher handy when starting the engine for the first time.*

1   Once the engine has been installed in the vehicle, double-check the engine oil and coolant levels.

2   With the spark plugs out of the engine and the ignition system and fuel pump disabled (see Section 3), crank the engine until oil pressure registers on the gauge or the light goes out.

3   Install the spark plugs, hook up the plug wires and restore the ignition system and fuel pump functions.

4   Start the engine. It may take a few moments for the fuel system to build up pressure, but the engine should start without a great deal of effort.

5   After the engine starts, it should be allowed to warm up to normal operating temperature. While the engine is warming up, make a thorough check for fuel, oil and coolant leaks.

6   Shut the engine off and recheck the engine oil and coolant levels.

7   Drive the vehicle to an area with minimum traffic, accelerate from 30 to 50 mph, then allow the vehicle to slow to 30 mph with the throttle closed. Repeat the procedure 10 or 12 times. This will load the piston rings and cause them to seat properly against the cylinder walls. Check again for oil and coolant leaks.

8   Drive the vehicle gently for the first 500 miles (no sustained high speeds) and keep a constant check on the oil level. It is not unusual for an engine to use oil during the break-in period.

9   At approximately 500 to 600 miles, change the oil and filter.

10   For the next few hundred miles, drive the vehicle normally. Do not pamper it or abuse it.

11   After 2000 miles, change the oil and filter again and consider the engine broken in.

Notes

Chapter 3
Cooling, heating and air conditioning systems

Contents

Specifications

General

Coolant capacity	See Chapter 1
Radiator pressure cap rating	15 psi
Refrigerant type	R-134a
Refrigerant capacity	
2002 and earlier	
Standard	2.0 pounds
With rear air conditioning	3.5 pounds
2003 and later	
Standard	2.0 pounds
With rear air conditioning	3.0 pounds

Torque specifications

Ft-lbs (unless otherwise indicated)

Thermostat housing nuts/bolts	
V6 and 5.0L/5.7L V8 engines	18
7.4L engine	30
4.8L/5.3L/6.0L V8 engines	132 in-lbs
Water pump attaching bolts	
4.3L, 5.0L, 5.7L and 7.4L engines	31
4.8L, 5.3L and 6.0L engines	
Step 1	132 in-lbs
Step 2	22
Water pump pulley bolts (4.3L, 5.0L, 5.7L and 7.4L engines)	18

1   General information

Refer to illustrations 1.1 and 1.2

Engine cooling system

All vehicles covered by this manual employ a pressurized engine cooling system with thermostatically controlled coolant circulation. An impeller-type water pump mounted on the engine block pumps coolant through the engine. The coolant flows around each cylinder and toward the rear of the engine. Cast-in coolant passages direct coolant around the intake and exhaust ports, near the spark plug areas and in close proximity to the exhaust valve guides.

A wax-pellet type thermostat controls engine coolant temperature. During warm up, the closed thermostat prevents coolant from circulating through the radiator. As the engine nears normal operating temperature, the thermostat opens and allows hot coolant to travel through the radiator, where it's cooled before returning to the engine.

The cooling system is sealed by a pressure-type radiator cap, which raises the boiling point of the coolant and increases the cooling efficiency of the radiator. If the system pressure exceeds the cap pressure relief value, the excess pressure in the system forces the spring-loaded valve inside the cap off its seat and allows the coolant to escape through the overflow tube into a coolant reservoir. When the system cools the excess coolant is automatically drawn from the reservoir back into the radiator. The coolant reservoir serves as both the point at which fresh coolant is added to the cooling system to maintain the proper fluid level and as a holding tank for overheated coolant. This type of cooling system is known as a closed design because coolant that escapes past the pressure cap is saved and reused.

Engine cooling fan and clutch

These models are equipped with a cooling fan that pulls outside air through the radiator and air conditioning condenser. The fan is controlled by a clutch (on which it is mounted) and its pulley is driven by the engine drivebelt from the crankshaft pulley. As the need for engine cooling increases (slow vehicle speed and high load), the clutch will engage and the fan will move air. The opposite occurs when the demand for engine cooling decreases.

Heating system

The heating system consists of a blower fan and heater core located in the heater box, the hoses connecting the heater core to the engine cooling system and the heater/air conditioning control head on the dashboard. Hot engine coolant is circulated through the heater core. When the heater mode is activated, a flap door opens to expose the heater box to the passenger compartment. A fan switch on the control head activates the blower motor, which forces air through the core, heating the air. In the case of front and rear (dual) heating systems, there are two individual systems installed; one in front and one in the rear.

Air conditioning system

The air conditioning system consists of a condenser mounted in front of the radiator, an evaporator mounted adjacent to the heater core, a compressor mounted on the engine, an accumulator and the plumbing connecting all of the above components.

A blower fan forces the warmer air of the passenger compartment through the evaporator core (sort of a radiator-in-reverse), transferring the heat from the air to the refrigerant. The liquid refrigerant boils off into low pressure vapor, taking the heat with it when it leaves the evaporator. In the case of dual A/C systems, a separate evaporator is used for the rear air conditioner.

2   Antifreeze - general information

Refer to illustration 2.5

Warning: *Do not allow antifreeze to come in contact with your skin or painted surfaces of the vehicle. Rinse off spills immediately with plenty of water. Antifreeze is highly toxic if ingested. Never leave antifreeze lying around in an open container or in puddles on the floor; children and pets are attracted by its sweet smell and may drink it. Check with local authorities about disposing of used antifreeze. Many communities have collection centers which will see that antifreeze is disposed of safely. Never dump used antifreeze on the ground or pour it into drains.*
Caution: *The manufacturer recommends using only DEX-COOL coolant for these systems. DEX-COOL is a long-lasting coolant designed for 100,000 miles or 5 years. Never mix green-colored ethylene glycol anti-freeze and orange-colored "DEX-COOL" silicate-free coolant because doing so will destroy the efficiency of the "DEX-COOL".*
Note: *Non-toxic antifreeze is now manufactured and available at local auto parts stores, but even this type must be disposed of properly.*

The cooling system should be filled with a water/ethylene glycol based antifreeze solution, which will prevent freezing down to at least -20-degrees F (even lower in cold climates). It also provides protection against corrosion and increases the coolant boiling point. Some engines in these vehicles have aluminum heads. The manufacturer recommends that the correct type of coolant be used and strongly urges that coolant types not be mixed (see Chapter 1 Specifications).

Drain, flush and refill the cooling system using the schedule found in Chapter 1. These models are filled with a long-life "DEX-COOL" coolant, which the manufacturer claims is good for five years.

Before adding antifreeze to the system, inspect all hose connections. Antifreeze can leak through very minute openings.

2.5 Use a hydrometer (available at most auto parts stores) to test the condition of your coolant

The exact mixture of antifreeze to water, which you should use, depends on the relative weather conditions. The mixture should contain at least 50-percent antifreeze, but should never contain more than 70-percent antifreeze. Consult the mixture ratio chart on the container before adding coolant.

Hydrometers are available at most auto parts stores to test the coolant **(see illustration).** Use antifreeze that meets factory specifications for engines with aluminum cylinder heads (if equipped) (see Chapter 1).

3   Thermostat - check and replacement

Check

1   Before assuming the thermostat is to blame for a cooling system problem, check the coolant level, drivebelt tension (see Chapter 1) and temperature gauge (or light) operation.
2   If the engine seems to be taking a long time to warm up (based on heater output or temperature gauge operation), the thermostat is probably stuck open. Replace the thermostat with a new one.
3   If the engine runs hot, use your hand to check the temperature of the radiator hose that leads from the thermostat to the radiator. The thermostat is positioned in different locations depending on the engine: On 4.3L V6 engines and 5.0L/5.8L and 7.4L engines, feel the upper radiator hose. On 4.8L/5.3L and 6.0L V8 engine, feel the lower radiator hose. If the hose isn't hot, but the engine is, the thermostat is probably stuck closed, preventing the coolant inside the engine from circulating through the radiator. Replace the thermostat.
Caution: *Don't drive the vehicle without a thermostat. The computer may stay in open loop and emissions and fuel economy will suffer.*
4   If the radiator hose is hot, it means the coolant is flowing and the thermostat is open. Consult the *Troubleshooting* section at the front of this manual for cooling system diagnosis.

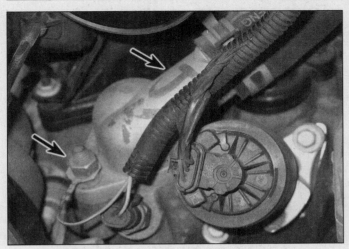

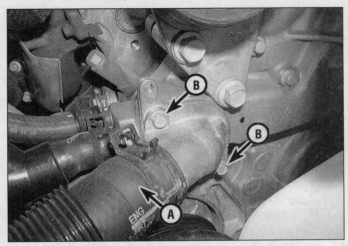

3.8a A typical V6 or 2002 and earlier V8 thermostat housing, showing one mounting fastener (the hidden fastener is on the other side)

3.8b 2003 and later V8 engine thermostat housing details

A   Lower radiator hose   B   Thermostat housing bolts

Replacement

Refer to illustrations 3.8a, 3.8b, 3.11 and 3.14

Warning: *The engine must be completely cool when this procedure is performed.*

5   Remove the air filter housing and air intake duct (see Chapter 4).

6   Drain the cooling system (see Chapter 1). If the coolant is relatively new or in good condition, save it and reuse it. Read the **Warning** in Section 2.

7   Remove the coolant reservoir (see Section 5).

8   On 4.3L V6 engines and 2002 and earlier V8 engines, follow the upper radiator hose to the engine to locate the thermostat housing cover **(see illustration)**. On 2003 and later V8 engines, the thermostat housing is located on the water pump, at the end of the lower radiator hose **(see illustration)**.

9   Loosen the hose clamp, then detach the hose from the fitting. If it's stuck, grasp it near the end with a pair of adjustable pliers and twist it to break the seal, then pull it off. If the hose is old or deteriorated, cut it off and install a new one.

10   If the outer surface of the large fitting that mates with the hose is deteriorated (corroded, pitted, etc.) it may be damaged further by hose removal. If it is, the thermostat housing cover will have to be replaced.

11   Remove the thermostat housing cover fasteners **(see illustration 3.8a or 3.8b)** and remove the cover. If it is stuck, tap it with a soft-face hammer to jar it loose. Be prepared for some coolant to spill as the gasket seal is broken. On 2003 and later V8 engines, the thermostat and housing are assembled as a single unit **(see illustration)**.

12   Note how the thermostat is installed (with the spring end directed towards the engine), then remove it. (On 2003 and later V8 engines the thermostat can't be removed from the housing - they must be replaced together.)

13   Remove all traces of old gasket material and/or sealant from the housing cover. On 2003 and later V8 engines, the housing assembly is sealed by a single O-ring which is included with the replacement unit.

14   On V6 and 2002 and earlier V8 engines, install a new rubber seal over the thermostat

(see illustration).

15   On V6 and 2002 and earlier V8 engines, install the new thermostat. Make sure the spring end is directed into the engine.

16   Install the housing cover and bolts. Tighten the bolts to the torque listed in this Chapter's Specifications.

17   Reattach the hose and tighten the hose clamp securely. Install all components that were removed for access.

18   Refill the cooling system (see Chapter 1).

19   Start the engine and allow it to reach normal operating temperature, then check for leaks and proper thermostat operation (as described in Steps 3 and 4).

---

4   Engine cooling fan and clutch - check and replacement

Warning: *Keep hands, tools and clothing away from the fan. To avoid injury or damage DO NOT operate the engine with a damaged fan. Do not attempt to repair fan blades - replace a damaged fan with a new one.*

Check

1   All models are equipped with thermostatically controlled fan clutches.

2   Begin the clutch check with a lukewarm engine (start it when cold and let it run for two minutes only).

3   Remove the key from the ignition switch for safety purposes.

4   Turn the fan blades and note the resistance. There should be moderate resistance, depending on temperature.

5   Drive the vehicle until the engine is warmed up. Shut it off and remove the key.

6   Turn the fan blades and again note the resistance. There should be a noticeable increase in resistance.

7   If the fan clutch fails this check or is locked up solid, replacement is indicated.

3.11 Thermostat and housing assembly for 2003 and later model V8 engines

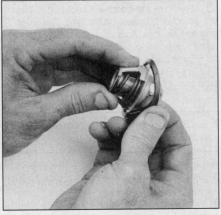

3.14 Install a new rubber seal around the thermostat (V6 and 2002 and earlier V8 engines)

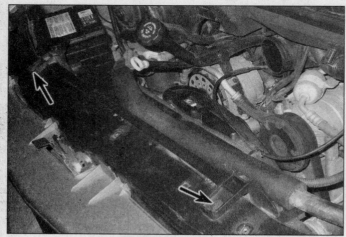

4.10a The top fasteners to the upper radiator shroud

4.10b The lower fasteners (right side) of the upper radiator shroud

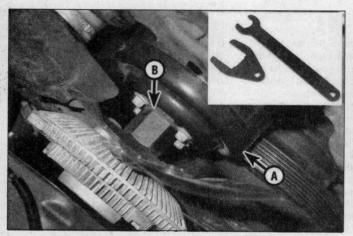

4.11a The water pump drive pulley (A) is held (with a special wrench that fits over the pulley nuts) while the drive hub nut (B) is turned counterclockwise (V6 and 2002 and earlier V8 models)

4.11b On 2003 and later V8 models, a strap wrench can be used to immobilize the water pump pulley while the hub nut is loosened

8   If excessive fluid is leaking from the hub or lateral play over 1/4-inch is noted, replace the fan clutch. **Warning:** *If the fan is damaged in any way, don't attempt to repair it. Replace the fan with a new one.*

Replacement

Refer to illustrations 4.10a, 4.10b, 4.11a, 4.11b and 4.13

9   Remove the air cleaner assembly and intake duct (see Chapter 4). Also remove the coolant reservoir (see Section 5). **Note:** *If you're careful, you may be able to simply remove the fasteners and position the reservoir out of the way without disconnecting the hoses.*

10   Detach any hoses attached to the upper fan shroud and position them aside. Remove the upper fan shroud **(see illustration)**. It's only necessary to remove the upper portion for many service operations.

11   Special fan wrenches, available at most auto parts stores, are needed to remove the cooling fan assembly. The fan clutch is attached to the drive hub with a large nut.

Hold the water pump pulley while loosening the clutch nut with the right size wrench. Turn the drive hub nut counterclockwise to loosen it **(see illustrations)**.

12   Lift the fan assembly up and out of the engine compartment.

13   Remove the fasteners securing the fan to the fan clutch **(see illustration)**. **Caution:** *To prevent silicone fluid from contaminating the fan drive bearing lubricant, the clutch should be kept in an upright position.*

14   Installation is the reverse of removal. Be sure to tighten all fasteners securely.

5   Coolant reservoir - removal and installation

Refer to illustration 5.2
Warning: *Wait until the engine is completely cool before beginning this procedure.*

1   Refer to the coolant **Warning** in Section 2, then detach the overflow hose from the radiator filler neck. Immediately plug the hose to prevent coolant spillage.

2   Remove the mounting bolt in front **(see illustration)**.

3   Lift the reservoir forward to clear the tabs in the rear and then remove it from the engine compartment. The reservoir can now be drained into an approved container.

4   Prior to installation make sure the res-

4.13 Fan-to-fan clutch bolts

5.2 The reservoir is held by a single bolt and two tabs that go into the cowl

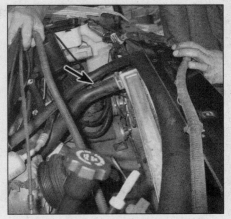

6.2 Typical upper radiator hose location

6.3 Typical lower radiator hose location

ervoir is clean and free of debris which could be drawn into the radiator (wash it with soapy water and a brush if necessary, then rinse thoroughly).

5   Installation is the reverse of removal. Top up the cooling system with the proper type and mixture of coolant (see Chapter 1) and check for leaks.

6 Radiator - removal and installation

Refer to illustrations 6.2, 6.3, 6.4a, 6.4b, 6.7 and 6.10

Warning: *The engine must be completely cool when this procedure is performed.*

1   Drain the cooling system (see Chapter 1). Remove the air cleaner assembly and intake duct (see Chapter 4). Also remove the coolant reservoir (see Section 5).

2   Disconnect the upper radiator hose and, on models so equipped, the heater outlet hose from the radiator **(see illustration).**

3   Disconnect the vent pipe hose (if equipped) and the lower radiator hose from the radiator **(see illustration).**

4   Carefully disconnect the transmission cooler lines from the right side of the radiator **(see illustrations).** To disconnect the lines from the radiator, simply unsnap the plastic collar from the quick-connect fitting, then pry off the quick-connect fitting retaining clip and remove the lines. **Note:** *Do not remove the clips by pulling straight out. Hold one side in with your fingers while using a pick (with a bent tip) to pull the other side out, then rotate the clip off. Install clips the same way, not straight on.* Plug the ends of the lines to prevent fluid from leaking out after you disconnect them. Have a drip pan ready to catch any spills. Always be sure to inspect the O-rings on the cooler lines before reinstallation.

5   If equipped with an engine oil cooler, disconnect the lines on the opposite side of the radiator, as described in the previous step. Also disconnect the engine oil cooler lines from the lower fan shroud (if applicable).

6   Remove the upper fan shroud (see Section 4). **Note:** *The radiator is secured by the upper fan shroud and will be loose once the shroud is removed.*

7   Remove the lower fan shroud **(see illustration).**

8   Remove the radiator from the engine compartment.

6.4a Transmission cooler lines (right side of radiator)

9   Prior to installing the radiator, replace any damaged radiator hoses and hose clamps.

10   Installation is the reverse of removal. Guide the radiator into the lower rubber mounts until it seats properly **(see illustration).** Install the cooler line retaining clips onto the quick connect fittings before installing the

6.4b The retaining clip is exposed when the plastic collar is moved aside

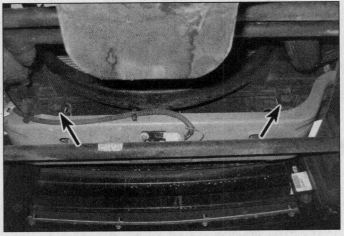

6.7 Mounting bolt locations for the lower fan shroud

lines, then snap the cooler lines into place on the fittings. Be sure to reinstall the plastic collars on the fittings to lock the retaining clips in place.

10   After installation, refill the cooling system (see Chapter 1), then check the engine oil and automatic transmission fluid levels.

7   Water pump - check and replacement

Warning: *Wait until the engine is completely cool before starting this procedure.*

Check

Refer to illustration 7.2

1   Water pump failure can cause overheating and serious damage to the engine. There are three ways to check the operation of the water pump while it is installed on the engine. If any one of the following quick-checks indicates water pump problems, it should be replaced immediately.

2   A seal protects the water pump impeller shaft bearing from contamination by engine coolant. If this seal fails, a weep hole in the water pump snout will leak coolant **(see illustration)** (an inspection mirror can be used to look at the underside of the pump if the hole isn't on top). If the weep hole is leaking, shaft bearing failure will follow. Replace the water pump immediately.

3   The water pump impeller shaft bearing can also prematurely wear out. When the bearing wears out, it emits a high-pitched squealing sound. If such a noise is coming from the water pump during engine operation, the shaft bearing has failed - replace the water pump immediately. **Note:** *Do not confuse belt noise with bearing noise.*

4   To identify excessive bearing wear, remove the drivebelt (see Chapter 1), grasp the water pump pulley and try to force it up-and-down or from side-to-side. If the pulley

6.10 Be sure to check the rubber mounts before installing the radiator

7.2 If coolant leaks from the weep hole, replace the water pump

can be moved either horizontally or vertically, the bearing is nearing the end of its service life. Replace the water pump.

5   It is possible for a water pump to be bad, even if it doesn't howl or leak water. Sometimes the fins on the back of the impeller can corrode away until the pump is no longer effective. The only way to check for this is to remove the pump for examination.

Replacement

Refer to illustrations 7.10, 7.11 and 7.12

6   Drain the coolant (see Chapter 1).

7   Remove the air cleaner assembly and intake duct (see Chapter 4).

8   Remove the upper radiator shroud and fan/clutch assembly (see Section 4).

9   Remove the drive belt (see Chapter 1).

10   On 4.3L, 5.0L, 5.7L and 7.4L engines, remove the water pump pulley, detach the lower radiator hose, the heater hose and the coolant by-pass hose from the water pump **(see illustration)**. **Note:** *To detach the pulley you will need to hold the pulley with a strap wrench or equivalent to remove the bolts.*

11   On 4.8L, 5.3L and 6.0L engines, remove the lower radiator hose and the thermostat housing (see Section 3). Also remove the upper radiator hose and the heater hoses from the water pump housing **(see illustration).**

12   Unbolt the water pump **(see illustration).** It may be necessary to tap the pump with a soft-face hammer to break the gasket seal. Inspect the pump's impeller blades on the backside for corrosion. If any fins are missing or badly corroded, replace the pump with a new one.

13   Clean the sealing surfaces of all gasket material on both the water pump and block.

14   Apply a thin layer of RTV sealant to both sides of the new gasket and install the gasket on the water pump.

15   Place the water pump in position and install the bolts finger tight. Use caution to ensure that the gasket doesn't slip out of position. Tighten the bolts to the torque listed in this Chapter's Specifications. **Note:** *On 4.3L, 5.0L, 5.7L and 7.4L engines, use RTV sealant on the water pump bolt threads.*

7.10 4.3L V6 and 5.0L, 5.7L and 7.4L V8 water pump details

    A   Water pump pulley bolts   C   Water pump mounting
    B   Hose connections   bolts

7.11 Water pump heater hose connections on 4.8L, 5.3L, and 6.0L engines

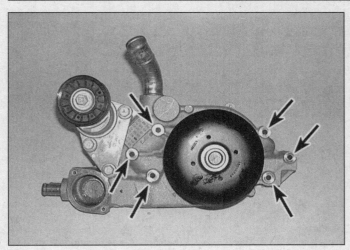

7.12 Water pump mounting bolt locations on 4.8L, 5.3L, and 6.0L engines

8.1 Coolant temperature sending unit (5.0L V8 engine shown)

16   The remainder of the installation procedure is the reverse of removal.

17   Add coolant to the specified level (see Chapter 1), start the engine and check for the proper coolant level. Be sure to bleed the cooling system of air as described in Chapter 1. Also check for coolant leaks around the water pump and hoses.

8   Coolant temperature gauge sending unit - check and replacement

Warning: *Wait until the engine is completely cool before beginning this procedure.*

Note: *1996 through 2000 models are equipped with a coolant temperature sending unit and an engine coolant temperature sensor (ECT). 2001 and later models are only equipped with an engine coolant temperature sensor (ECT). The following check and replacement procedure applies to the coolant temperature sending unit on 2000 and earlier models only. Refer to Chapter 6 for information on the engine coolant temperature (ECT) sensor.*

Check

Refer to illustration 8.1

1   The coolant temperature indicator system consists of a temperature gauge mounted in the instrument panel and a coolant temperature sending unit mounted in the left bank of the engine block **(see illustration).**

2   If an overheating indication occurs, check the coolant level in the system and then make sure all connectors in the wiring harness between the sending unit and the temperature gauge are tight.

3   If the gauge is inoperative, test the circuit by briefly grounding the wire to the sending unit while the ignition is On (engine not running for safety). The gauge needle should deflect to full hot. If the gauge checks out okay, replace the sending unit.

4   If the gauge doesn't respond in the test outlined in Step 3, have the temperature gauge wiring circuit checked by a dealer service department or other qualified automotive repair facility.

Replacement

5   If the sending unit must be replaced, simply unscrew it from the engine and quickly install the replacement. Use a conductive sealant on the threads (not Teflon tape). Make sure the engine is cool before removing the defective sending unit. There will be some coolant loss as the unit is removed, so be prepared to catch it. Check the coolant level after the replacement part has been installed.

9   Blower motor resistor and blower motor- replacement

Blower motor resistor
Front air conditioning systems

Refer to illustrations 9.1

1   Disconnect the electrical connector from

9.1 Blower motor resistor electrical connector and mounting screws (front A/C system)

the blower resistor **(see illustration). Note:** *The blower motor resistor assembly contains a relay for the blower motor that cannot be serviced separately.*

2   Disconnect the electrical connector from the blower motor **(see illustration 9.10).**

3   Remove the blower motor resistor mounting screws and then the resistor.

4   Installation is the reverse of removal.

Rear air conditioning systems

Refer to illustration 9.6

5   Remove the left rear quarter trim panel (see Chapter 11).

6   Disconnect the electrical connector from the blower resistor **(see illustration).**

7   Remove the blower motor resistor mounting screws and then the resistor.

8   Installation is the reverse of removal.

Blower motor

Front air conditioning systems

Refer to illustrations 9.10 and 9.13

9   Remove the coolant reservoir (see Section 5)

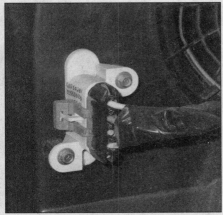

9.6 The rear blower motor resistor mounting screws and electrical connector

9.10 The front blower motor electrical connector and mounting screws

9.13 Remove the clip to remove the fan from the motor shaft

10   Disconnect the electrical connector from the blower motor **(see illustration)**.

11   Detach the cooling hose and remove the blower motor retaining screws.

12   Pull the blower motor straight out to remove it.

13   If you're replacing the blower motor with a new one, remove the fan from the motor **(see illustration)**.

14   Install the fan onto the new motor and install the blower motor into the heater housing.

15   The rest of the installation is the reverse of removal.

Rear air conditioning systems

Refer to illustration 9.17

16   Remove the rear air conditioning and heater housing from the vehicle (see Section 11).

17   Remove the relay bracket and move it aside **(see illustration)**.

18   Disconnect the electrical connector from the blower motor.

19   Detach the cooling hose and remove the blower motor retaining screws.

20   Pull the blower motor straight out to remove it.

21   If you're replacing the blower motor with a new one, remove the fan from the motor **(see illustration 9.13)**.

22   Install the fan onto the new motor and install the blower motor into the heater housing.

23   The rest of the installation is the reverse of removal.

---

10   Heater/air conditioning control assembly - removal and installation

---

Front heater/air conditioning control assembly

Refer to illustrations 10.2 and 10.4

Warning: *The models covered by this manual are equipped with Supplemental Restraint systems (SRS), more commonly known as airbags. Always disable the airbag system before working in the vicinity of any airbag system component to avoid the possibility of accidental deployment of the airbag, which could cause personal injury (see Chapter 12).*

1   Remove the main instrument panel bezel (see Chapter 11).

2   Remove the control assembly retaining screw **(see illustration)**.

3   Move the control assembly outward on the left side to release the retaining tab on the right.

4   Carefully disconnect the electrical and vacuum connectors and then remove the control assembly **(see illustration)**. **Note:** *The connectors have locking tabs that keep them connected. These tabs must be released*

9.17 Rear blower motor details

A   Blower motor electrical connector
B   Mounting screw details (two shown - one hidden under relay bracket.
C   Cooling hose
D   Relay bracket

10.2 The mounting screw is exposed when the bezel is removed

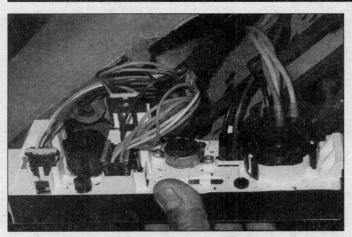

10.4 The electrical and vacuum connectors for the control assembly

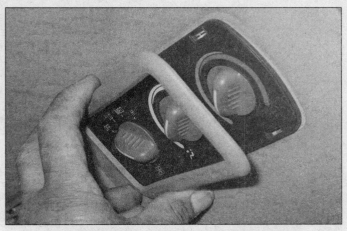

10.6 Removing the rear heater control assembly trim

before the connectors can be separated.
5   Installation is the reverse the removal. Be sure that all connectors are replaced correctly.

Rear heater/air conditioning control assembly
Refer to illustrations 10.6 and 10.8
6   Carefully remove the rear control assembly trim bezel **(see illustration).**
7   Release the control assembly by inserting a screwdriver into the tab slots and moving the tabs inward while carefully pulling on the control panel.
8   Disconnect the electrical connector and remove the control panel from the vehicle **(see illustration).**
9   Installation is the reverse of removal. Be sure the control assembly snaps securely back into place.

11   Heater core - removal and installation

Warning 1: *The models covered by this manual are equipped with Supplemental*

Restraint systems (SRS), more commonly known as airbags. Always disable the airbag system before working in the vicinity of any airbag system component to avoid the possibility of accidental deployment of the airbag, which could cause personal injury (see Chapter 12).
Warning 2: *The air conditioning system is under high pressure. DO NOT loosen any fittings or remove any components until after the system has been discharged. Air conditioning refrigerant must be properly discharged into an EPA-approved container at a dealer service department or an automotive air conditioning repair facility. Always wear eye protection when disconnecting air conditioning system fittings.*
1   Disconnect the cable from the negative battery terminal (see Chapter 5, Section 1).
2   Drain the cooling system (see Chapter 1).

Front heater core
Refer to illustrations 11.4, 11.6, 11.7, 11.8, 11.9 and 11.10
3   Remove the coolant reservoir (see Section 5).
4   Disconnect the heater hoses at the heater core inlet and outlet pipes on the

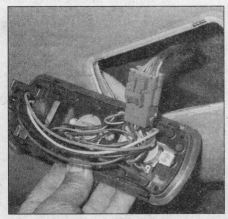

10.8 Once the retaining tabs are released, the connector is accessible

engine side of the firewall (passenger side) **(see illustration)** and plug the open fittings.
5   If the hoses are stuck to the pipes, cut them off and replace them with new ones upon installation.
6   Remove the passenger side kick panel **(see illustration).**
7   Remove the air duct that is in front of the heater core cover **(see illustration).**
8   Remove the screws to the heater core

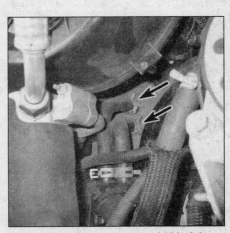

11.4 The heater hoses are behind the receiver/drier, flush with the firewall

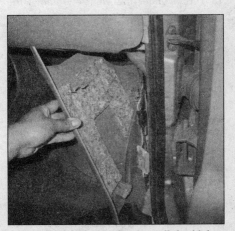

11.6 Carefully, but firmly, pull the kick panel to release the fasteners

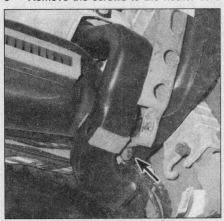

11.7 Remove this screw and detach the air duct

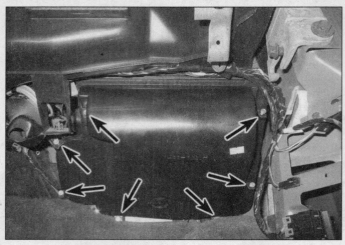

11.8 The heater core cover fastener locations

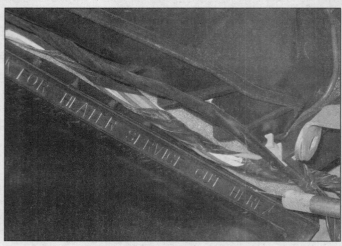

11.9 Carefully cut the edge of the heater core cover

11.10 The heater core retainer fasteners

11.16 Remove the fasteners to the upright air duct

cover **(see illustration)**.

9   Carefully cut along the top edge of the cover **(see illustration)** then remove it.

10   Remove the heater core retainers **(see illustration)**, then detach the heater core from the housing.

11   Installation is the reverse of removal. **Note:** *When reinstalling the heater core, make sure any original insulating/sealing materials are in place around the heater core pipes and around the core.*

12   Refill the cooling system (see Chapter 1).

13   Start the engine and check for proper operation.

Rear heater core

Refer to illustrations 11.16, 11.17, 11.18, 11.19, 11.20 and 11.21

Note: *The following procedure involves removing the air conditioning and heater housing assembly.*

14   Have the air conditioning system discharged by a dealer service department or by an automotive air conditioning shop before proceeding (see **Warning** above).

15   Remove the left rear quarter trim panel (see Chapter 11).

16   Remove the upright air duct from the housing **(see illustration)**.

17   Disconnect the electrical connectors to the HVAC housing **(see illustration)**.

18   From under the vehicle, remove the

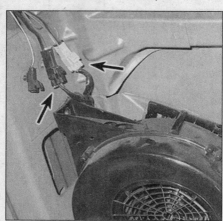

11.17 The connectors for the HVAC housing

cover to the housing assembly plumbing **(see illustration)**.

19   Remove the heater and air conditioning hoses and the mounting nuts to the housing assembly **(see illustration)**.

20   From inside the vehicle, remove the fasteners to the housing assembly **(see illustra-**

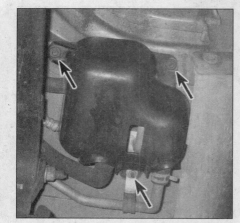

11.18 The housing assembly plumbing cover fastener locations

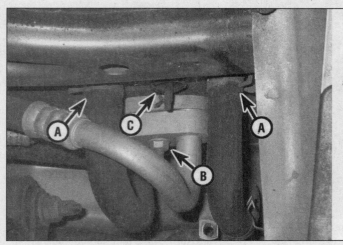

11.19 Housing assembly plumbing and mounting details

A   Heater hoses
B   Nut securing refrigerant lines
C   Mounting nut for housing assembly (one shown - the other is hidden behind the A/C hose assembly)

11.20 Housing assembly fastener locations

tion) and then lift it out of the vehicle. **Note:** *When removing the housing assembly, the horizontal air duct should separate from the housing. Remove the air duct if necessary.*

21   Remove the bottom of the housing assembly **(see illustration)** and then remove the heater core.

22   Installation is the reverse of removal. **Note:** *When reinstalling the heater core, make sure any original insulating/sealing materials are in place around the heater core pipes and around the core.*

23   Check the coolant level, adding coolant as necessary (see Chapter 1). Have the air conditioning system charged by the shop that discharged it.

24   Start the engine and check for proper operation. Recheck the coolant level.

---

12   Air conditioning and heating system - check and maintenance

---

Refer to illustration 12.1

Warning: *The air conditioning system is under high pressure. Do not loosen any hose fittings or remove any components until after the system has been discharged by a dealer*

service department or service station. Always wear eye protection when disconnecting air conditioning system fittings.

1 The following maintenance checks should be performed on a regular basis to ensure the air conditioner continues to operate at peak efficiency.

 a) *Check the compressor drivebelt. If it's worn or deteriorated, replace it (see Chapter 1).*
 b) *Check the drivebelt tension and, if necessary, adjust it (see Chapter 1).*
 c) *Check the system hoses. Look for cracks, bubbles, hard spots and deterioration. Inspect the hoses and all fittings for oil bubbles and seepage. If there's any evidence of wear, damage or leaks, replace the hose(s).*
 d) *Inspect the condenser fins for leaves, bugs and other debris. Use a "fin comb" or compressed air to clean the condenser.*
 e) *Make sure the system has the correct refrigerant charge.*
 f) *Check the evaporator housing drain tube* **(see illustration)** *for blockage.*

2   It's a good idea to operate the system for about 10 minutes at least once a

month, particularly during the winter. Long term non-use can cause hardening, and subsequent failure, of the seals.

3   Because of the complexity of the air conditioning system and the special equipment necessary to service it, in-depth troubleshooting and repairs are not included in this manual (refer to the *Haynes Automotive Heating and Air Conditioning Repair Manual*). However, simple checks and component replacement procedures are provided in this Chapter.

4   The most common cause of poor cooling is simply a low system refrigerant charge. If a noticeable drop in cool air output occurs, the following quick check will help you determine if the refrigerant level is low.

Checking the refrigerant charge

5   Warm the engine up to normal operating temperature.

6   Place the air conditioning temperature selector at the coldest setting and the blower at the highest setting. Open the vehicle doors (to make sure the air conditioning system doesn't cycle off as soon as it cools the passenger compartment).

11.21 Remove these screws to access the heater core

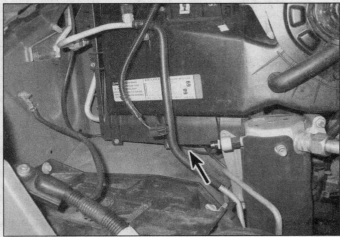

12.1 Look for the evaporator drain tube on the firewall just below the housing assembly - make sure it isn't clogged

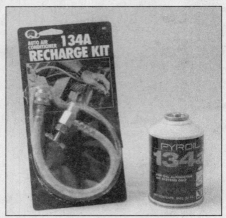

12.9 A basic charging kit for R-134a systems is available at most auto parts stores - it must say R-134a (not R-12) and so must the can of refrigerant

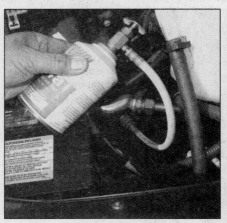

12.12 Cans of R-134A refrigerant (available at auto parts stores) can be added to the low side of the air conditioning system with a simple recharging kit

12.15 Insert a thermometer in the center vent, turn on the air conditioning system and wait for it to cool down; depending on the humidity, the output air should be 30 to 40-degrees cooler than the ambient air temperature

7   With the compressor engaged - the clutch will make an audible click and the center of the clutch will rotate - feel the evaporator inlet and outlet lines at the firewall. The inlet (small diameter) line should feel warm and the outlet (large diameter) line should feel cold. If so, the system is properly charged.

8   Place a thermometer in the dashboard vent nearest the evaporator and operate the system until the indicated temperature is around 40 to 45-degrees F. If the ambient (outside) air temperature is very high, say 110-degrees F, the duct air temperature may be as high as 60-degrees F, but generally the air conditioning is 30 to 40-degrees F cooler than the ambient air. **Note**: *Humidity of the ambient air also affects the cooling capacity of the system. Higher ambient humidity lowers the effectiveness of the air conditioning system.*

Adding refrigerant

Refer to illustrations 12.9, 12.12, and 12.15

9   Buy an automotive charging kit at an auto parts store **(see illustration)**. A charging kit includes a 12- or 14-ounce can of refrigerant, a tap valve and a short section of hose that can be attached between the tap valve and the system low side service valve. Because one can of refrigerant may not be sufficient to bring the system charge up to the proper level, it's a good idea to buy an additional can. Make sure that one of the cans contains red refrigerant dye. If the system is leaking, the red dye will leak out with the refrigerant and help you pinpoint the location of the leak. **Caution:** *There are two types of refrigerant used in automotive systems; R-12 - which has been widely used on earlier models and the more environmentally-friendly R-134a used in all models covered by this manual. These two refrigerants (and their appropriate refrigerant oils) are not compatible and must never be mixed or components will be damaged. Use only R-134a refrigerant in the models covered by this manual.*

10   Hook up the charging kit by following the

manufacturer's instructions. **Warning:** *DO NOT hook the charging kit hose to the system high side! The fittings on the charging kit are designed to fit only on the low side of the system.*

11   Back off the valve handle on the charging kit and screw the kit onto the refrigerant can, making sure first that the O-ring or rubber seal inside the threaded portion of the kit is in place. **Warning**: *Wear protective eyewear when dealing with pressurized refrigerant cans.*

12   Remove the dust cap from the low-side charging connection and attach the quick-connect fitting on the kit hose **(see illustration)**.

13   Warm up the engine and turn on the air conditioner. Keep the charging kit hose away from the fan and other moving parts. **Note:** *The charging process requires the compressor to be running. Your compressor may cycle off if the pressure is low due to a low charge. If the clutch cycles off, you can disconnect the A/C pressure switch (located on the receiver-dryer), and attach a jumper wire across the two terminals of the connector (not the terminals of the switch itself). This will keep the compressor ON.*

14   Turn the valve handle on the kit until the stem pierces the can, then back the handle out to release the refrigerant. You should be able to hear the rush of gas. Add refrigerant to the low side of the system until both the accumulator surface and the evaporator inlet pipe feel about the same temperature. Allow stabilization time between each addition.

15   If you have an accurate thermometer, place it in the center air conditioning vent **(see illustration)** and then note the temperature of the air coming out of the vent. A fully-charged system which is working correctly should cool down to about 40-degrees F. Generally, an air conditioning system will put out air that is 30 to 40-degrees F cooler than the ambient air. For example, if the ambient (outside) air temperature is very high (over 100-degrees F), the temperature of air coming out of the registers should be 60 to 70-degrees F.

16   When the can is empty, turn the valve handle to the closed position and release the connection from the low-side port. Replace the dust cap. **Caution:** *Never add more than 1-1/2 cans (models without rear A/C) or two cans (models with rear A/C) of refrigerant to the system.*

17   Remove the charging kit from the can and store the kit for future use with the piercing valve in the UP position, to prevent inadvertently piercing the can on the next use.

Heating systems

18   If the carpet under the heater core is damp, or if antifreeze vapor or steam is coming through the vents, the heater core is leaking. Remove it (see Section 12) and install a new unit (most radiator shops will not repair a leaking heater core).

19   If the air coming out of the heater vents isn't hot, the problem could stem from any of the following causes:

a) *The thermostat is stuck open, preventing the engine coolant from warming up enough to carry heat to the heater core. Replace the thermostat (see Section 3).*

b) *There is a blockage in the system, preventing the flow of coolant through the heater core. Feel both heater hoses at the firewall. They should be hot. If one of them is cold, there is an obstruction in one of the hoses or in the heater core, or the heater control valve is shut. Detach the hoses and back flush the heater core with a water hose. If the heater core is clear but circulation is impeded, remove the two hoses and flush them out with a water hose.*

c) *If flushing fails to remove the blockage from the heater core, the core must be replaced (see Section 12).*

Eliminating air conditioning odors

20   Unpleasant odors that often develop in

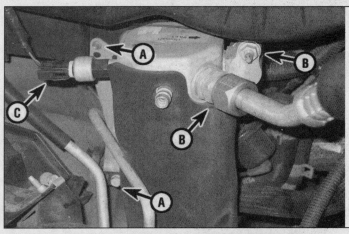

13.3 Accumulator details (5.0L V8 shown, others similar):

A *Mounting bolts*
B *Refrigerant line connections*
C *Pressure cycling switch connector*

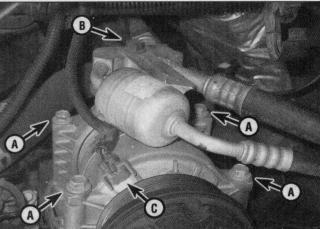

14.5a Air conditioning compressor details (4.3L V6 and 2002 and earlier V8 models):

A *Mounting bolts*
B *Refrigerant line fitting manifold bolt*
C *Clutch connector*

3   Disconnect the refrigerant inlet and outlet lines **(see illustration)**. Cap or plug the open lines immediately to prevent the entry of dirt or moisture.
4   Disconnect the electrical connector from the pressure cycling switch.
5   Loosen the mounting bolt(s) on the mounting bracket and then remove the accumulator.
6   If you are replacing the accumulator with a new one, add one ounce of fresh refrigerant oil to the new unit (oil must be R-134a compatible).
7   Installation is the reverse of removal. When installing the refrigerant lines, use new O-rings and coat them with clean refrigerant oil.
8   Have the system evacuated, recharged and leak tested by the shop that discharged it.

14 Air conditioning compressor - removal and installation

Removal
Refer to illustrations 14.5a and 14.5b
Warning: *The air conditioning system is under high pressure. Do not loosen any hose fittings or remove any components until after the system has been discharged. Air conditioning refrigerant must be properly discharged into an EPA-approved recovery/re-cycling unit at a dealer service department or an automotive air conditioning repair facility. Always wear eye protection when disconnecting air conditioning system fittings.*
Caution: *When replacing the compressor with a new one, the amount of oil inside of it must be adjusted. Be sure to read the can before adding any oil to the system to make sure it is compatible with the R-134a system.*
Note 1: *The accumulator (see Section 13) should be replaced whenever the compressor is replaced.*
Note 2: *Whenever the compressor is replaced because of internal damage, the expansion (orifice) tube should also be replaced (see Section 16).*
1   Have the refrigerant discharged and recovered by an air conditioning technician (see Warning above). Disconnect the cable from the negative battery terminal (see Chapter 5, Section 1).
2   Remove the air intake duct and air filter housing (see Chapter 4).
3   Remove the drivebelt(s) (see Chapter 1).
4   If you're working on a 2003 or later V8 model, loosen the right front wheel lug nuts, then raise the front of the vehicle and support it securely on jackstands. Remove the wheel and the inner fender splash shield.
5   Disconnect the electrical connectors: the clutch connector in front and a high pressure switch in the rear of the compressor. Clean the compressor thoroughly around the refrigerant line fittings **(see illustrations)**.

air conditioning systems are caused by the growth of a fungus, usually on the surface of the evaporator core. The warm, humid environment there is a perfect breeding ground for mildew to develop.
21   The evaporator core on most vehicles is difficult to access, and factory dealerships have a lengthy, expensive process for eliminating the fungus by opening up the evaporator case and using a powerful disinfectant and rinse on the core until the fungus is gone. You can service your own system at home, but it takes something much stronger than basic household germ-killers or deodorizers.
22   Aerosol disinfectants for automotive air conditioning systems are available in most auto parts stores, but remember when shopping for them that the most effective treatments are also the most expensive. The basic procedure for using these sprays is to start by running the system in the RECIRC mode for ten minutes with the blower on its highest speed. Use the highest heat mode to dry out the system and keep the compressor from engaging by disconnecting the wiring connector at the compressor (see Section 14).
23   Make sure that the disinfectant can comes with a long spray hose. Point the nozzle through the air recirculation door so that it protrudes inside the evaporator housing and then spray according to the manufacturer's recommendations. Try to cover

the whole surface of the evaporator core, by aiming the spray up, down and sideways. Follow the manufacturer's recommendations for the length of spray and waiting time between applications.
24   Once the evaporator has been cleaned, the best way to prevent the mildew from coming back again is to make sure your evaporator housing drain tube is clear **(see illustration 12.1)**.

13 Air conditioning accumulator - removal and installation

Refer to illustration 13.3
Warning: *The air conditioning system is under high pressure. DO NOT loosen any fittings or remove any components until after the system has been discharged. Air conditioning refrigerant must be properly discharged into an EPA approved recovery/recycling unit at a dealer service department or an automotive air conditioning repair facility. Always wear eye protection when disconnecting air conditioning system fittings.*
1   Have the refrigerant discharged and recovered by an air conditioning technician (see **Warning** above).
2   Remove the coolant reservoir (see Section 5) and the battery (see Chapter 5).

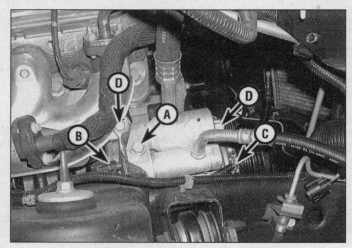

14.5b Air conditioning compressor details (2003 and later V8 models):

A   *Refrigerant line mounting bolt*
B   *High pressure switch connector*
C   *Compressor clutch electrical connector*
D   *Compressor mounting bolts (lower two bolts not visible)*

15.4 Air conditioning condenser details (5.0L V8 shown, others similar):

A   *Mounting bolts*
B   *Refrigerant line connections (the left one is hidden behind the radiator support - it can be accessed from the other side)*

6   Disconnect the suction and discharge lines from the compressor. Both lines are mounted to the compressor with a manifold secured by one bolt. Plug the open fittings to prevent the entry of dirt and moisture, and discard the seals between the plate and compressor.

7   Remove the compressor mounting bolts. Detach the compressor from the mounting bracket and remove the compressor from the engine compartment. **Note:** *On 4.8L, 5.3L and 6.0L engines, the compressor mounting bolts can be accessed from the bottom of the vehicle and through the wheel well.*

Installation

8   If a new compressor is being installed, pour the oil from the old compressor into a graduated container and add that exact amount of new refrigerant oil to the new compressor. Also follow any directions included with the new compressor. **Note:** *Some replacement compressors come with refrigerant oil in them. Follow the directions with the compressor regarding the draining of excess oil prior to installation.* **Caution:** *The oil used must be labeled as compatible with R-134a refrigerant systems.*

9   Installation is the reverse of removal. When installing the line fitting manifold bolt to the compressor, use new seals and tighten the bolt securely. **Note:** *Do not lubricate the new seals.*

10   If you're working on a 2003 or later V8 model, tighten the wheel lug nuts to the torque listed in the Chapter 1 Specifications.

11   Have the system evacuated, recharged and leak tested by the shop that discharged it.

15   Air conditioning condenser - removal and installation

Refer to illustration 15.4

Warning: *The air conditioning system is under high pressure. DO NOT loosen any fittings or remove any components until after the system has been discharged. Air conditioning refrigerant must be properly discharged into an EPA-approved recovery/recycling unit at a dealer service department or an automotive air conditioning repair facility. Always wear eye protection when disconnecting air conditioning system fittings.*

Caution: *When replacing entire components, additional refrigerant oil must be added to them. Be sure to read the can before adding any oil to the system, to make sure it is compatible with the R-134a system.*

Note: *The accumulator should be replaced if the condenser was damaged (see Section 13).*

1   Have the refrigerant discharged and recovered by an air conditioning technician (see Warning above).

2   Remove the radiator grille (see Chapter 11).

3   If you're working on a 2002 or earlier model, remove the hood latch (see Chapter 11).

4   Disconnect the refrigerant lines from the condenser **(see illustration)**. Plug the open ends of the condenser and the disconnected refrigerant lines to prevent entry of dirt or moisture. **Note:** *On 2003 and later models, discard the sealing washers on the refrigerant hoses.*

5   On 2003 and later models, remove the outside air temperature sensor electrical connector (located directly in front of the con-

denser near the bottom). Then remove the mounting bracket for the sensor (located near the hood latch).

6   Remove the condenser mounting bolts and then the condenser.

7   If the original condenser will be reinstalled, store it in a way that prevents the refrigerant oil from draining out. If a new condenser is being installed, pour one ounce of R-134a-compatible refrigerant oil into it prior to installation.

8   Installation is the reverse of removal. On 2003 and later models, be sure to use new sealing washers before connecting the hoses to the condenser.

9   Have the system evacuated, recharged and leak tested by the shop that discharged it.

16   Air conditioning expansion (orifice) tube - removal and installation

Refer to illustrations 16.2 and 16.5

Warning: *The air conditioning system is under high pressure. DO NOT loosen any fittings or remove any components until after the system has been discharged. Air conditioning refrigerant must be properly discharged into an EPA-approved recovery/recycling unit at a dealer service department or an automotive air conditioning repair facility. Always wear eye protection when disconnecting air conditioning system fittings.*

1   Have the refrigerant discharged and recovered by an air conditioning technician (see **Warning** above).

2   Open the hood and locate the expansion orifice tube fitting **(see illustration)**.

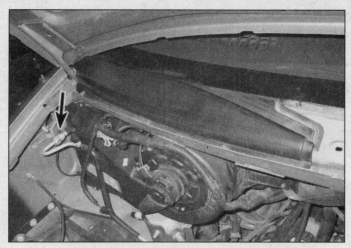

16.2 The expansion tube fitting is located on the small line leading to the evaporator core

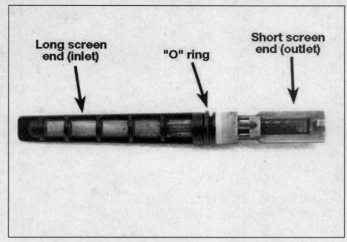

16.5 The expansion tube is equipped with a tapered mesh screen that must be cleaned and must not have any holes or damage

3   Hold the stationary fitting (on the line coming from the condenser) with one wrench, then loosen the other fitting with another wrench.

4   The expansion tube is a tube with a fixed-diameter orifice and a mesh filter at each end. When you separate the pipe at the fitting you will see one end of the orifice tube inside the pipe leading to the evaporator. Use needle-nose pliers to remove the orifice tube. **Note:** *If the orifice tube is stuck, carefully apply heat with a hair dryer to loosen it. Do not overheat the pipe.*

5   The orifice tube acts to meter the refrigerant, changing it from a high-pressure liquid to a low-pressure gas. It is possible to reuse the orifice tube if **(see illustration):**

   a) *The screens aren't plugged with grit or foreign material*
   b) *Neither screen is torn*
   c) *The plastic housing over the screens is intact*

   d) *The brass orifice inside the plastic housing is unrestricted*

6   Installation is the reverse of removal. Be sure to insert the expansion tube with the shorter end in first, toward the evaporator. **Caution:** *Always use a new O-ring when installing the expansion (orifice) tube and lubricate it with the proper refrigerant oil.*

7   Reconnect the refrigerant line and tighten the fitting securely, then have the system evacuated, recharged and leak-tested by the shop that discharged it.

17 Auxiliary engine oil cooler - removal and installation

Note: *Auxiliary engine coolers are found on vehicles with larger engines designed for heavy duty applications.*

1   The auxiliary engine oil cooler is located just below or in front of the A/C condenser.

2   Disconnect the quick connect fittings to the cooler, then plug the lines and fittings to prevent leakage. **Note:** *The fittings are similar to those used for the transmission oil cooler line connections; refer to Section 6 (radiator removal) for procedures on releasing this kind of connector.*

3   Remove the air baffle from under the vehicle (if equipped). **Note:** *Baffle removal is not necessary if your auxiliary cooler is mounted in front of the A/C condenser.*

4   Remove the mounting bolts to the cooler.

5   Installation is the reverse of removal. Make certain that all connections are secure.

6   Start the vehicle and check for leaks. Stop the engine and wait a few minutes, then check the engine oil level, adding as necessary (see Chapter 1).

Notes

Chapter 4
Fuel and exhaust systems

Contents

Specifications

General

Fuel pressure (engine running at idle speed)

4.3L V6 and 5.0L/5.7L V8 engines	60 to 66 psi
7.4L V8 engine	56 to 62 psi
4.8L, 5.3L and 6.0L V8 engines	55 to 62 psi

Torque specifications

Ft-lbs (unless otherwise indicated)

Throttle body mounting bolts/studs

4.3L V6 engine	
1996 through 1998	18 in-lbs
1999 on	80 in-lbs
5.0L and 5.7L V8 engines	18
7.4L V8 engine	18
4.8L, 5.3L and 6.0L V8 engines	89 in-lbs

Fuel rail mounting bolts/studs

4.8L, 5.3L and 6.0L V8 engine	
Crossover tube-to-right fuel rail retainer screw	34 in-lbs
Fuel rail mounting bolts	89 in-lbs
7.4L V8 engine	
Fuel rail mounting bolts	89 in-lbs
Fuel rail mounting stud	18

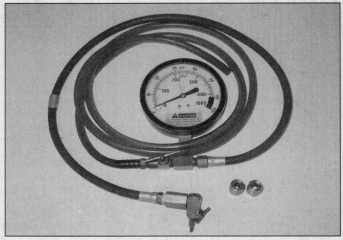

2.3 To depressurize the fuel system, remove the fuel pump relay, which is located inside the fuse and relay box in the engine compartment (this is the relay location on a 1999 model with a 5.0L V8; be sure to check the underside of the fuse box cover for the relay location on your model)

3.3 To check the fuel pressure, you'll need a fuel pressure gauge capable of reading the fuel pressure within the specified operating system pressure, a hose to connect the gauge to the fuel pressure test port and an adapter suitable for connecting the hose to the Schrader valve type test port

1   General information

Warning: *Gasoline is extremely flammable, so take extra precautions when you work on any part of the fuel system. Don't smoke or allow open flames or bare light bulbs near the work area, and don't work in a garage where a gas-type appliance (such as a water heater or a clothes dryer) is present. Since gasoline is carcinogenic, wear latex gloves when there's a possibility of being exposed to fuel, and, if you spill any fuel on your skin, rinse it off immediately with soap and water. Mop up any spills immediately and do not store fuel-soaked rags where they could ignite. The fuel system is under constant pressure, so, if any fuel lines are to be disconnected, the fuel pressure in the system must be relieved first. When you perform any kind of work on the fuel system, wear safety glasses and have a Class B type fire extinguisher on hand.*

All models covered by this manual are equipped with Sequential Fuel Injection (SFI). SFI systems use timed impulses to sequentially inject the fuel directly into the intake ports of each cylinder in the same sequence as the firing order. The Powertrain Control Module (PCM) controls the injectors. The PCM monitors various engine parameters and delivers the correct amount of fuel, in firing order sequence, into the intake ports. For more information about the fuel injection system, see Section 11.

The fuel pump is located in the roof of the fuel tank and protrudes down into the fuel inside the fuel tank. You must lower the fuel tank before you can remove the fuel pump from the fuel tank. The fuel level sending unit is an integral component of the fuel pump and it must be accessed in the same manner.

There are two fuel filters. A nylon mesh fuel "sock" or strainer is located at the lower (inlet) end of the fuel pump/fuel level sending unit. The strainer is an extended-life part and does not need to be replaced at scheduled maintenance intervals. It should only be replaced if diagnostic testing indicates the need to do so. The main fuel filter, which looks like a small metal canister, is located under the vehicle, between the fuel tank and the engine compartment. It must be replaced at the specified service interval (see Chapter 1).

The exhaust system consists of the two exhaust manifolds and, on most models, a single catalytic converter, exhaust pipe and muffler. Some 7.4L and 6.0L models are equipped with two catalysts, two separate exhaust pipes and two mufflers. All of these components are replaceable. For further information regarding the catalytic converter, refer to Chapter 6.

2   Fuel pressure relief procedure

Refer to illustration 2.3
Warning: *See the **Warning** in Section 1.*
1   Remove the fuel filler cap (this will relieve any pressure that has built-up in the tank).
2   Locate the fuse and relay box in the engine compartment, then remove the splash shield and the fuse box cover (see Section 3 in Chapter 12).
3   Remove the fuel pump relay **(see illustration)** from the engine compartment fuse and relay box. (You can locate any relay by looking at the relay guide printed on the underside of the fuse box cover.)
4   Turn the ignition key to START and crank over the engine for several seconds. It will either start momentarily and immediately stall, or it won't start at all.
5   Turn the ignition key to the OFF position.
6   Disconnect the cable from the negative terminal of the battery before beginning work on the fuel system.
7   After all work on the fuel system has been completed, install the fuel pump relay. The CHECK ENGINE light or MALFUNCTION INDICATOR light might come on during operation because the engine was cranked with the fuel pump relay unplugged. The light will probably go out after a period of normal operation. If it doesn't, you'll have to clear the Diagnostic Trouble Code (DTC) with a generic scan tool (see Chapter 6) or have the DTC cleared by a dealer service department or other qualified repair shop.

3   Fuel pump/fuel pressure - check

Warning: *See the **Warning** in Section 1.*

Preliminary check
1   The fuel pump is located inside the fuel tank, which muffles its sound when the engine is running. But you *can* actually hear the fuel pump. Sit inside the vehicle with the windows closed, turn the ignition key to ON (*not* START) and listen carefully for the soft whirring sound made by the fuel pump as it's briefly turned on by the PCM to pressurize the fuel system prior to starting the engine. You will only hear a soft whirring sound for a second or two, but that sound tells you that the pump is working. If you can't hear the pump from inside the vehicle, remove the fuel filler cap, depress the spring-loaded door inside the fuel filler neck, then have an assistant turn the ignition switch to ON while you listen for the sound of the pump operating for a couple of seconds. If the pump does not come on when the ignition key is turned to ON, check the fuel pump fuse and relay (both of which are located in the engine compartment fuse and relay box). If the fuse and relay are okay, check the wiring back to the fuel pump. If the fuse, relay and wiring are okay, the fuel pump is probably defective. If the pump runs *continuously* with the ignition

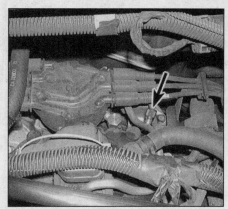

3.4a Fuel pressure test port location for the 4.3L V6 engine

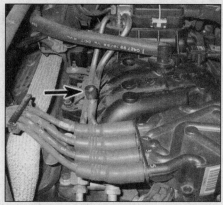

3.4b Fuel pressure test port location for 5.0L (shown) and 5.7L V8 engines

3.4c Fuel pressure test port location for 4.8L, 5.3L (shown) and 6.0L V8 engines

key in its ON position, the Powertrain Control Module (PCM) is probably defective. Have the PCM checked by a dealer service department or other qualified repair shop.

Pressure check

Refer to illustration 3.3, 3.4a, 3.4b and 3.4c

Note: *In order to perform the fuel pressure test, you will need a fuel pressure gauge capable of measuring high fuel pressure. You'll also need suitable fittings or adapters to attach it to the fuel rail.*

Caution: *Do not pinch the vehicle's fuel lines shut or damage to the line may occur.*

2   Relieve the fuel system pressure (see Section 2).

3   For this check, you'll need to obtain a fuel pressure gauge with a hose and an adapter suitable for connecting it to the Schrader valve type test port on the fuel feed line or fuel rail **(see illustration)**.

4   The test port is located on the fuel supply line on 4.3L V6 and 5.0L and 5.7L V8 engines **(see illustrations)**. On 4.8L, 5.3L, 6.0L and 7.4L V8 engines it's located on the fuel rail **(see illustration)**.

5   Unscrew the threaded cap from the test

4.2 The metal fuel lines (and plastic EVAP lines) are secured to the underside of the vehicle by small plastic clips. This one is typical

port and connect the fuel pressure gauge hose to the test port.

6   Start the engine and check the pressure on the gauge, comparing your reading with the pressure listed in this Chapter's Specifications.

7   If the fuel pressure is not within specifications, check the following:

a) *If the pressure is lower than specified, check for a restriction in the fuel system. If the fuel feed line is okay, try replacing the fuel filter (see Chapter 1), then repeat the pressure check. If the pressure is still too low, either the fuel pressure regulator or fuel pump is defective, or the inlet strainer on the pump is clogged.*

b) *If the fuel pressure is higher than specified, check the fuel return line for an obstruction. If the line is okay, replace the fuel pressure regulator (see Section 14).*

4 Fuel lines and fittings - repair and replacement

Refer to illustration 4.2

Warning 1: *Gasoline is extremely flammable, so take extra precautions when you work on any part of the fuel system. See the **Warning** in Section 2.*

Warning 2: *Before disconnecting any fuel line fittings, relieve the fuel system pressure (see Section 2) and equalize tank pressure by removing the fuel filler cap. This procedure will merely relieve the increased pressure necessary for the engine to run - remember that fuel will still be present in the system components, so you should be ready for fuel spills when disconnecting fuel line fittings.*

1   Always relieve the fuel pressure (see Section 2) before servicing fuel lines or fittings, then disconnect the cable from the negative battery terminal before proceeding (see Chapter 5, Section 1).

2   The fuel supply and return lines run from the fuel tank to the fuel meter body (4.3L V6 and 5.0L and 5.7L V8 engines) or to the fuel rail (4.8L, 5.3L, 6.0L and 7.4L V8 engines).

The Evaporative Emission Control (EVAP) system vapor lines connect the fuel tank to the EVAP canister and connect the canister to the canister purge solenoid on the intake manifold. The fuel and EVAP lines are secured to the underbody with small plastic brackets that are attached to the vehicle floorpan **(see illustration)**. To detach the lines from these brackets, spread the clips of the bracket apart and pull the line out.

3   Whenever you're working under the vehicle, be sure to inspect all fuel and EVAP lines for leaks, kinks, dents and other damage. Always replace a damaged fuel or EVAP line immediately. Leaking fuel and EVAP lines will result in loss of fuel and excessive air pollution (the leaking raw fuel emits unburned hydrocarbon vapors into the atmosphere).

4   If you find signs of dirt in the lines during disassembly, disconnect all lines and blow them out with compressed air. Inspect the fuel strainer on the lower end of the fuel pump for damage and deterioration. And inspect the fuel filter (see Chapter 1).

Steel tubing

5   Because fuel lines used on fuel-injected vehicles are under fairly high pressure, it is critical that they be replaced with lines of equivalent specification. Never use copper or aluminum tubing to replace steel tubing. These materials cannot withstand normal vehicle vibration.

6   Some steel fuel lines have threaded fittings. When loosening these fittings to service or replace components:

a) *Hold the stationary fitting with one wrench while loosening or tightening the tubing nut with another.*

b) *If you're going to replace one of these fittings, use original equipment parts or parts that meet original equipment standards.*

Plastic tubing

7   Some of the fuel and EVAP lines on the vehicles covered in this manual are plastic. If you ever have to replace a plastic line, use only plastic tubing meeting original equip-

4.12 Pull the end of the retainer off the fuel line, then disengage the other end from the female side of the fitting

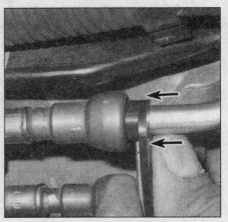

4.13a Insert the fuel line separator tool into the female side of the fitting, push it into the fitting until it releases the locking tabs inside the fitting . . .

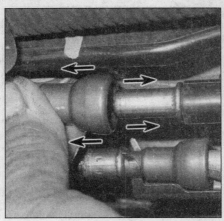

4.13b . . . then pull the two halves of the fitting apart

ment standards. **Caution:** *When removing or installing plastic fuel line tubing, be careful not to bend or twist it too much, which can*

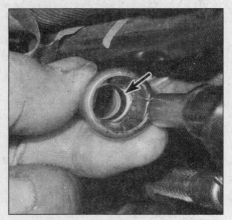

4.14 Inspect the O-ring inside the female side of the fitting; if it's cracked, torn or deteriorated, replace it

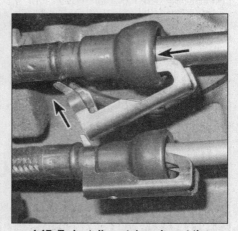

4.17 To install a retainer, insert the hooked end into the female side of the fitting, then push the clip end onto the fuel line until it snaps into place (when you're done, your retainer should look like the one already installed on the lower fitting)

damage it. And damaged fuel lines MUST be replaced! Also, be aware that the plastic fuel tubing is NOT heat resistant, so keep it away from excessive heat. Nor is it acid-proof, so don't wipe it off with a shop rag that has been used to wipe off battery electrolyte. If you accidentally spill or wipe electrolyte on plastic fuel tubing, replace the tubing.

Flexible hoses

Warning: *Use only original equipment replacement hoses or their equivalent. Unapproved hoses might fail when subjected to the high operating pressures of the fuel system.*

8   Don't route fuel hoses within four inches of exhaust system components or within ten inches of a catalytic converter. Make sure that no flexible hoses are installed directly against the vehicle, particularly in places where there is any vibration. If allowed to touch some vibrating part of the vehicle, a hose can easily become chafed and it might start leaking. A good rule of thumb is to maintain a minimum of 1/4-inch clearance around a hose (or metal line) to prevent contact with the vehicle underbody.

Fuel line and EVAP line fittings

9   The vehicles covered in this manual use two kinds of fuel line quick-connect fittings (metal or plastic) for most connections at the fuel pump, the fuel tank, under the vehicle and in the engine compartment. (A third type of plastic quick-connect fitting is used only at the EVAP canister and on the vent hose connection at the fuel tank for the EVAP canister vent solenoid.)

10   The procedure for releasing each type of fuel line fitting is different. But a few rules of thumb apply to all fittings:

1) *Inspect the fitting for dirt. If the fitting is dirty, clean it off before disassembling it. The seals in the fitting will stick to the fuel line as they age. Twist the fitting on the line, then push and pull the fitting until it moves freely.*

2) *Always disconnect all fuel line fittings from a fuel system component before removing the component.*
3) *When disconnecting a quick-connect fitting, inspect the condition of the retainer before reconnecting the fitting. The best strategy with respect to retainers is to simply replace the retainer every time that you disconnect the fitting.*
4) *When you disconnect a fitting with an O-ring inside, inspect the O-ring before reconnecting the fitting. Fuel line fittings are under the same pressure as the rest of the fuel system, so to avoid leaks (and fires!) make VERY SURE that the O-ring is good condition. Even better, simply replace it.*
5) *In most cases, the fitting itself is a non-removable part of the fuel line, so you might have to replace an entire fuel line if a fitting is damaged or defective.*

Metal collar quick-connect fittings

Disconnection

Refer to illustrations 4.12, 4.13a and 4.13b

Note: *You'll need a special tool set (J37088-A, or a suitable equivalent) to disconnect these fittings.*

11   Relieve the fuel system pressure (see Section 2).

12   Pull off the clip end of the retainer, then remove it from the fitting **(see illustration)**.

13   Using a fuel line separator tool of the proper size (available at most auto parts stores), insert the tool into the female side of the fitting, then push it into the fitting to release the locking tabs and pull the fitting apart **(see illustrations)**.

Reconnection

Refer to illustrations 4.14 and 4.17

14   Inspect the O-ring **(see illustration)**. If it's dried out, cracked, torn or otherwise deteriorated, replace it.

15   Apply a few drops of clean engine oil to the male pipe end.

16   Push both sides of the fitting together until the retaining tabs snap into place. Pull

4.19a To release a plastic quick-connect fitting, depress the tabs on the connector housing with a small screwdriver, then continue pressing on them . . .

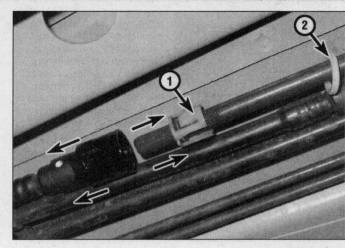

4.19b . . . until the two fuel lines are disconnected, then remove and discard the old retainer (1) and the indicator ring (2) (the indicator ring is used only during factory assembly; there is no need to reinstall it)

on both sides of the fitting to verify that it's securely connected.

17   Install the retainer, making sure it clips into place **(see illustration)**.

18   Start the engine and check for fuel leaks.

Plastic collar quick-connect fittings

Disconnection
Refer to illustrations 4.19a and 4.19b

19   To release this type of quick-connect fitting, depress the tabs of the retainer **(see illustration)**. Once the retainer is released, continue pressing on the tabs while pulling the two fuel lines apart **(see illustration)**.

20   Remove and discard the old retainer from the male side of the fitting.

21   Remove and discard the indicator ring from the male side of the fitting.

Reconnection
Refer to illustrations 4.22 and 4.23

22   Inspect the O-ring inside the female side of the fitting **(see illustration)**. If it's dried out, cracked, torn or deteriorated, replace it.

23   Insert a new retainer in the female side of the fitting. Make sure that the release tabs are aligned with the "windows" of the connec-

tor **(see illustration)**.

24   Apply a few drops of engine oil to the tip of the male fuel line.

25   Push both sides of the fitting together until the retainer release tabs snap into place.

26   Pull on both sides of the fitting to verify that it's securely connected.

27   Start the engine and check for fuel leaks.

5   Fuel tank - removal and installation

Refer to illustrations 5.5, 5.7 and 5.9
Warning: *See the* **Warning** *in Section 1.*

1   Relieve the fuel system pressure (see Section 2).

2   Disconnect the cable from the negative battery terminal (see Chapter 5, Section 1).

3   Raise the vehicle and place it securely on jackstands.

4   Remove the fuel tank shield, if equipped.

5   Loosen the hose clamps for the fuel filler neck hose **(see illustration)** and disconnect the hose from the filler neck pipe.

6   If the fuel tank still has a lot of fuel in it, siphon it from the tank now. Using a siphoning kit (available at most auto part stores), siphon the fuel from the tank, through the filler neck

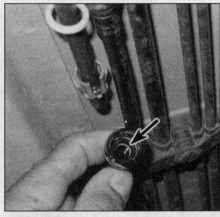

4.22 Inspect the O-ring inside the female side of the fitting; if it's cracked, torn or deteriorated, replace it

hose, into an approved gasoline container.
Warning: *Never start the siphoning action by mouth!*

7   Support the fuel tank with a transmission jack or with a floor jack **(see illustration)**. If you're going to use a floor jack, be sure to put a piece of wood between the jack head and the fuel tank to protect the tank.

4.23 Install a new retainer in the female side of the fitting; make sure that the release tabs are aligned with the windows in the connector

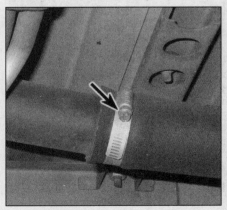

5.5 To disconnect the fuel filler neck hose from the filler neck pipe, loosen this hose clamp

5.7 Support the fuel tank with a jack, then remove the fuel tank strap bolts and swing the straps down out of the way

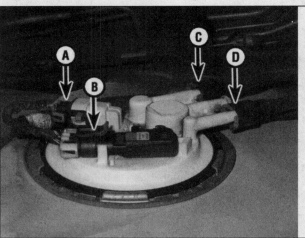

5.9 Lower the fuel tank far enough to access the fuel pump/fuel level sending unit electrical connectors and fuel line quick-connect fittings, then disconnect them (if you need help with the quick-connect fittings, see Section 4):

A   *Fuel pump/fuel level sending unit connector*
B   *Fuel tank pressure sensor connector*
C   *Fuel delivery line quick-connect fitting*
D   *Fuel return line quick-connect fitting*

8   Remove the fuel tank retaining strap bolts **(see illustration 5.7)** and swing the straps down and out of the way (remove them if necessary).

9   Carefully lower the fuel tank just far enough to disconnect the electrical connectors and fuel line quick-connect fittings from the fuel pump/fuel level sending unit **(see illustration)**.

10 Lower the fuel tank to the floor, then disconnect the EVAP line fitting.

11 Installation is basically the reverse of removal. Please note the following guidelines:

a) *If the fuel tank is being replaced, remove the necessary components from the old fuel tank and install them on the new tank. If you need help with any of the EVAP hoses, refer to Chapter 6.*

b) *Tighten the fuel tank retaining bolts securely.*

6   Fuel tank cleaning and repair - general information

1   The fuel tank installed in the vehicles covered by this manual is not repairable. If the fuel tank becomes damaged, it must be replaced.

2   Cleaning the fuel tank (due to fuel contamination) should be performed by a professional with the proper training to carry out this critical and potentially dangerous work. Even after cleaning and flushing, explosive fumes may remain inside the fuel tank.

3   If the fuel tank is removed from the vehicle, it should not be placed in an area where sparks or open flames could ignite the fumes coming out of the tank. Be especially careful inside a garage where a gas-type appliance is located.

7   Fuel pump/fuel level sending unit - removal and installation

Refer to illustrations 7.8 and 7.9
Warning: *See the* **Warning** *in Section 1.*

1   The fuel pump/fuel level sending unit module includes the electric fuel pump assembly (including the fuel pump inlet strainer) and the fuel level sending unit. This section covers the removal and installation of the complete module, which is removed as a complete assem-

bly. But you can replace the components separately. The procedure for *replacing* the fuel pump and the fuel level sending unit is in Section 8.

2   Relieve the fuel system pressure (see Section 2).

3   Disconnect the cable from the negative battery terminal (see Chapter 5, Section 1).

4   Raise the vehicle and place it securely on jackstands.

5   Remove the fuel tank (see Section 5).

6   To prevent dirt from entering the fuel tank, clean the area surrounding the fuel pump/fuel level sending unit.

7   Disconnect the electrical connectors and fuel lines from the fuel pump/fuel level sending unit **(see illustration 5.9)**.

8   Release the locking tab and use a pair of large pliers to turn the lockring counterclockwise and unscrew it **(see illustration)**.

9   Carefully remove the fuel pump/fuel level sending unit from the tank **(see illustration)**.

10 Inspect the large rubber gasket that seals the mounting hole for the fuel pump/fuel level sending unit. If it's cracked, torn, deteriorated or otherwise damaged, replace it.

11 The fuel pump inlet filter or strainer is attached to the bottom of the fuel pump. Anytime you remove the fuel pump for any reason, always inspect the inlet filter. If it's dirty, remove it and scrub it thoroughly with clean solvent and an old toothbrush (don't use a wire brush to clean the inlet filter - you'll damage it if you do). If you're unable to clean the inlet filter, replace it.

12 Installation is the reverse of removal.

8   Fuel pump/fuel level sending unit - replacement

Refer to illustrations 8.2, 8.3 and 8.4
Warning: *See the* **Warning** *in Section* 1.

1   Remove the fuel tank and the fuel pump/fuel level sending unit (see Sections 5 and 7, respectively).

2   Disconnect the fuel level sending unit

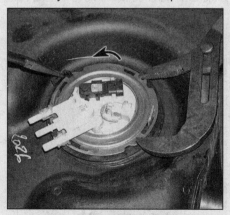

7.8 Release the locking tab and loosen the fuel pump/fuel level sending unit retaining ring by rotating it counterclockwise

7.9 Carefully remove the fuel pump/fuel level sending unit from the tank. Tilt the unit as necessary in order to protect the float arm (for the fuel level sending unit) from damage

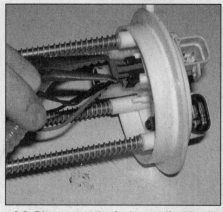

8.2 Disconnect the fuel pump/fuel level sending unit electrical connector from the fuel pump module cover

electrical connector from the fuel pump/fuel level sending unit cover **(see illustration)**.
3   Remove the sending unit retaining clip **(see illustration).**
4   Pinch the tabs together **(see illustration)** and slide the fuel level sending unit off the fuel pump module. Note the routing of the wiring for installation.
5   Installation is the reverse of removal.

9   Air filter housing and air intake duct - removal and installation

4.3L V6 and 5.0L, 5.7L and 7.4L V8 models

Air filter housing
Refer to illustration 9.2
1   Remove the air filter housing cover and the air filter element (see Chapter 1).
2   Remove the air filter housing bolts **(see illustration)** and remove the air filter housing.

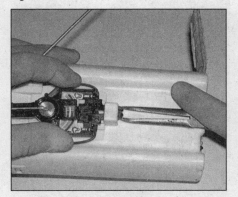

8.4 Pinch the tabs together and remove the fuel level sending unit from the fuel pump module

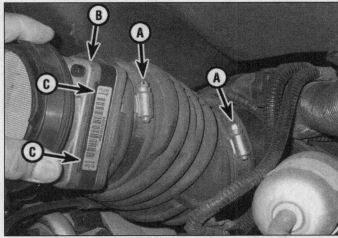

9.6 Air intake duct and MAF sensor details on 4.3L V6 and 5.0L, 5.7L or 7.4L V8 models

A   Hose clamp
B   MAF sensor
C   Directional arrows on the bar code label

3   Installation is the reverse of removal.

Air intake duct
Refer to illustration 9.6
4   Remove the air filter housing cover and the air filter element (see Chapter 1).
5   Remove the air filter housing **(see illustration 9.2)**.
6   Loosen the hose clamp **(see illustration)** and remove the air intake duct.
7   If you're going to disconnect the Mass Air Flow (MAF) sensor from the air intake duct, note the directional arrows on the bar code label on the edge of the MAF sensor. When you install the MAF sensor again, these arrows must face toward the throttle body.
8   Installation is the reverse of removal.

4.8L, 5.3L and 6.0L V8 models

Air filter housing
Refer to illustration 9.9
9   Remove the Connector Position Assurance (CPA) retainer from the MAF sensor electrical connector **(see illustration 11.6 in Chapter 6)**, then disconnect the MAF sensor

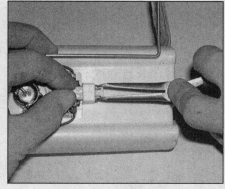

8.3 Remove the sending unit retaining clip

connector **(see illustration)**.
10   Loosen the hose clamp screws to detach the air filter housing from the air intake duct elbow.
11   Remove the air filter housing mounting bolts and remove the air filter housing.
12   Installation is the reverse of removal.

9.2 To detach the air filter housing from a 4.3L V6 or 5.0L, 5.7L or 7.4L V8 model, remove these three bolts

9.9 To detach the air filter housing from a 4.8L, 5.3L or 6.0L V8 model, disconnect the MAF sensor electrical connector (1), loosen the air intake duct elbow hose clamp screws (2) and remove the air filter housing mounting bolts (3)

9.13 To detach the air intake duct elbow from the air filter housing and from the air intake duct on a 4.8L, 5.3L or 6.0L V8 model, loosen these hose clamp screws and pull off the elbow

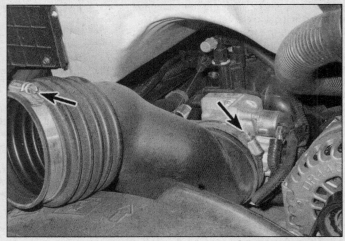

9.14 To remove the air intake duct from a 4.8L, 5.3L or 6.0L V8 engine, loosen these hose clamps screws and pull off the duct

Air intake duct elbow and air intake duct

Refer to illustrations 9.13 and 9.14

13   Loosen the hose clamp screws **(see illustration)** that connect the air intake duct elbow to the air filter housing and remove the air intake duct elbow.

14   Loosen the hose clamp screws **(see illustration)** and remove the air intake duct.

15   Inspect the condition of the air intake duct. Look for cracks, tears, deterioration and other damage. If the air intake duct is damaged in any way, replace it. A leaking air intake duct will allow the introduction of "false air" (unmetered air) into the air intake manifold, which will cause the air/fuel mixture to become excessively lean. A lean air/fuel mixture can cause rough running at idle, and even misfires if the leak is big enough.

16   Installation is the reverse of removal.

10   Accelerator cable - replacement

Refer to illustrations 10.2, 10.3, 10.5 and 10.6
Note: *All engines use a conventional accelerator cable except for 2004 and later 4.8L, 5.3L and 6.0L V8 engines with the Throttle Actuator Control (TAC) system.*

1   Remove the air intake duct (see Section 9) and the engine cover (see Chapter 11).

2   Using a pair of needle-nose pliers, squeeze the locking tangs of the accelerator cable together and disengage the cable from the cable bracket **(see illustration)**.

3   Disengage the cable end from the throttle cam **(see illustration)**.

4   Trace the accelerator cable to the firewall and note its routing. Detach the cable from any clamps, clips or brackets.

5   Working underneath the dash, disconnect the accelerator cable from the accelerator pedal **(see illustration)**.

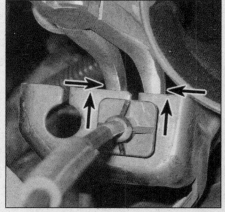

10.2 Using a pair of needle-nose pliers, squeeze the two sides of the cable housing together, then slide the housing straight up to disengage it from the cable bracket

10.3 To disengage the cable end from the throttle cam, rotate the cam and align the cable with the slot in the cam, then slide the cable and the end plug out

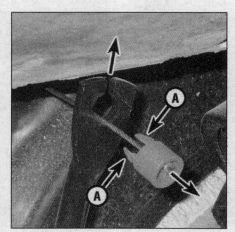

10.5 To disengage the cable from the pedal arm, squeeze the two tangs (A) together, then pull the end plug toward you and pass the cable through the slot in the arm

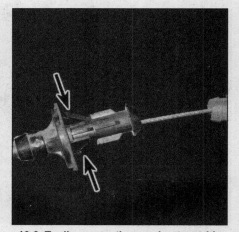

10.6 To disengage the accelerator cable from its hole in the firewall, squeeze these two tangs together and pull the cable through the hole from the engine compartment side

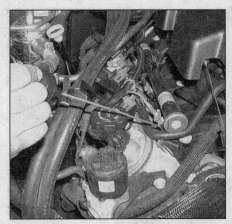

12.7 On 4.8L, 5.3L (shown) and 6.0L V8 engines, use a stethoscope to determine whether the injectors are operating correctly. They should make a steady clicking sound that rises and falls with engine speed

6   Disengage the accelerator cable from its hole in the firewall **(see illustration)**.
7   Pull the cable through the firewall and into the engine compartment.
8   Installation is the reverse of removal.

11 Fuel injection system - general information

The Sequential Fuel Injection (SFI) system consists of three sub-systems: air intake, engine control and fuel delivery. The system is controlled by the Powertrain Control Module (PCM), which uses an array of information sensors to calculate the correct air/fuel ratio for various operating conditions.

The fuel injection system and the engine control system are closely linked in function and design. For more information about the PCM and its information sensors, refer to Chapter 6.

Air intake system

The air intake system consists of the air filter housing (which houses the air filter element), the Mass Air Flow (MAF) sensor, the air intake duct, the throttle body and the intake manifold. The procedures for removing and installing the air filter housing, the air intake duct and the throttle body are in this Chapter. The procedure for replacing the air filter element is in Chapter 1. The procedure for removing and installing the intake manifold is in Chapter 2. The MAF sensor measures the amount of air drawn into the engine. For more information about the MAF sensor, refer to Chapter 6.

When the engine is idling, the air/fuel ratio is controlled by the Idle Air Control (IAC) system, which consists of the Powertrain Control Module (PCM) and the IAC valve. The IAC system regulates the amount of airflow past the throttle plate and into the intake manifold, thus increasing or decreasing the engine idle

12.8 On 4.8L, 5.3L (shown) and 6.0L V8 engines, measure the resistance of each injector across the two terminals of the injector

speed. The PCM uses the information that it receives from various information sensors to adjust the idle according to the demands of the engine and driver. Refer to Chapter 6 for more information on the IAC valve.

Emissions and engine control system

The emissions and engine control system is described in detail in Chapter 6.

Fuel delivery system

The fuel delivery system consists of the fuel pump, the fuel pressure regulator, the fuel meter body or fuel rail, and the fuel injectors. Fuel is pumped to the fuel meter body or fuel rail by an electric in-tank fuel pump. Fuel is drawn through an inlet "sock" or fuel strainer at the lower end of the pump, flows through the fuel delivery line, through the fuel filter and is delivered to the fuel meter body or fuel rail.

All 4.3L V6 and 5.0L/5.7L V8 engines are equipped with Central Sequential Fuel Injection (SFI). In the Central SFI system, six or eight injectors and the fuel pressure regulator are all housed inside an assembly known as the fuel meter body. The end of each injector is connected to a poppet nozzle by a nylon tube. The injectors, tubes and poppet nozzles are serviced as an assembly. The fuel meter body is located underneath the upper intake manifold, which you must remove to access the fuel meter body and any component mounted in or on the fuel meter body.

All 4.8L, 5.3L, 6.0L and 7.4L V8 engines are equipped with a conventional fuel rail. On these models, the injectors are located between the fuel rail and each intake port. The fuel pressure regulator is mounted on the fuel rail.

The injectors used on all models are solenoid-actuated pintle types consisting of a solenoid, plunger, needle valve and housing. When current is applied to the solenoid coil, the needle valve raises and pressurized fuel sprays out the nozzle. The amount of fuel injected is determined by the injector "pulse

width," i.e. the length of time that the injector is open.

On all models, the fuel pressure regulator maintains a constant fuel pressure to the injectors. Inside the pressure regulator is a spring-loaded diaphragm that opens when fuel pressure exceeds its designed threshold, routing excess fuel back to the fuel tank through the fuel return line.

The fuel pump relay is located in the engine compartment fuse and relay box. The PCM controls the relay by supplying battery voltage to the relay coil. When energized, the fuel pump relay connects battery voltage to the fuel pump. When the engine is neither cranking nor running, there is no signal from the Camshaft Position (CMP) or Crankshaft Position (CKP) sensors to the PCM, which de-energizes the fuel pump relay.

12 Fuel injection system - check

Refer to illustrations 12.7 and 12.8
Note: *The following procedure is based on the assumption that the fuel pressure is adequate* (see Section 3).
1   Remove the engine cover (see Chapter 11). Inspect all electrical connectors that are related to the system. Check the ground wire connections on the intake manifold for tightness. Loose connectors and poor grounds can cause many problems that resemble more serious malfunctions.
2   Verify that the battery is fully charged, as the control unit and sensors depend on an accurate supply of voltage in order to properly meter the fuel.
3   Inspect the air filter element (see Chapter 1). A dirty or partially blocked filter will severely impede performance and economy.
4   Check the related fuses. If a blown fuse is found, replace it and see if it blows again. If it does, search for a grounded wire in the harness.
5   Inspect the condition of all vacuum hoses connected to the intake manifold.
6   Remove the air intake duct and air resonator box (if equipped) and inspect the mouth of the throttle body for dirt, carbon or other residue build-up. If it's dirty, clean it with carburetor cleaner spray, a shop towel and a toothbrush, if necessary.
7   On 4.8L, 5.3L, 6.0L and 7.4L V8 engines, place an automotive stethoscope against each injector **(see illustration)**, one at a time, with the engine running, and listen for a clicking sound, which indicates that the injectors are operating. If you don't have a stethoscope, place the tip of a screwdriver against the injector and listen through the handle. (This test doesn't apply to 4.3L V6 and 5.0L and 5.7L V8 engines.)
8   On 4.8L, 5.3L, 6.0L and 7.4L V8 engines, disconnect the injector electrical connectors and measure the resistance of each injector **(see illustration)**. Compare the measurements of all eight injectors. If the resistance for any injectors is significantly different from

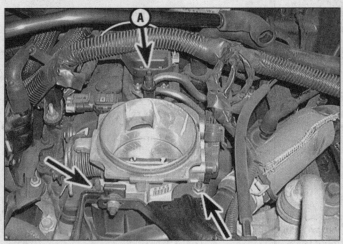

13.6a To detach the throttle body from the intake manifold on a 4.3L V6 (shown) or a 5.0L or 5.7L V8 engine, unscrew the air intake duct adapter stud (A), then remove all three throttle body mounting nuts (one of which, not visible, is below the air intake duct adapter stud)

13.6b To detach the throttle body from the intake manifold on a 4.8L, 5.3L (shown) or a 6.0L V8 engine, remove these three mounting nuts

the other injectors, that injector is probably defective. (This test doesn't apply to 4.3L V6 and 5.0L and 5.7L V8 engines.)

9   Any further testing of the fuel injection system should be performed at a dealer service department or other qualified repair shop.

10   For more information about the engine control system, refer to Chapter 6.

13   Throttle body - removal and installation

Refer to illustrations 13.6a and 13.6b

1   Disconnect the cable from the negative terminal of the battery (see Chapter 5, Section 1).

2   Remove the engine cover (see Chapter 11) and the air intake duct (see Section 9).

3   Disconnect the electrical connectors from the Throttle Position (TP) sensor and from the Idle Air Control (IAC) valve (see Chapter 6).

4   Disconnect the accelerator cable (see Section 10) and, if equipped, the cruise control cable from the throttle body. Disconnect the cruise control cable using the same procedure you used to disconnect the accelerator cable. Also remove the accelerator cable bracket mounting nuts and remove the bracket. **Note:** *There is no accelerator cable on 2004 and 2005 4.8L, 5.3L and 6.0L V8 engines with the Throttle Actuator Control (TAC) system.*

5   On 4.8L, 5.3L and 6.0L V8 models, disconnect the coolant hoses from the throttle body. On all models, disconnect any vacuum hoses from the throttle body. Inspect the vacuum hoses for cracks, tears and deterioration. If any of them are damaged, replace them.

6   Remove the throttle body mounting bolts **(see illustrations)** and remove the throttle body.

7   Remove the throttle body gasket and discard it.

8   Wipe off the gasket mating surfaces of the throttle body and the intake manifold. **Caution:** *Do NOT use spray carburetor cleaners or silicone lubricants on any part of the throttle body.*

9   Install a new throttle body gasket.

10   Installation is otherwise the reverse of removal. Be sure to tighten the throttle body mounting bolts to the torque listed in this Chapter's Specifications.

14   Fuel pressure regulator - removal and installation

Refer to illustrations 14.5a, 14.5b and 14.7

1   Relieve the fuel system pressure (see Section 2).

2   Disconnect the cable from the negative battery terminal (see Chapter 5, Section 1).

3   Remove the engine cover (see Chapter 11).

4   On 4.3L V6 and 5.0L and 5.7L V8 engines, remove the upper intake manifold (see Chapter 2A).

5   Remove the pressure regulator retaining clip and detach the fuel pressure regulator from the fuel meter body or fuel rail **(see illustrations)**.

6   If you're *replacing* the fuel pressure regulator, take the old regulator and the retaining clip with you to the auto parts store. These regulators all look the same but there are several different calibrations, depending on the application. Make SURE that you get the exact same replacement regulator and retaining clip.

7   Replace all of the pressure regulator O-rings **(see illustration)**. Lubricate them with a light film of engine oil. Don't overlook the smaller O-ring, which might still be in the fuel meter body or fuel rail.

14.5a To detach the fuel pressure regulator from the fuel meter body on a 4.3L V6 or a 5.0L/5.7L V8, remove this retaining clip

15   Fuel meter body - removal and installation

Warning: *See the* **Warning** *in Section 1.*

Note 1: *This procedure applies to 4.3L V6 and 5.0L/5.7L V8 engines. All other engines use a conventional fuel rail (see Section 16).*

Note 2: *When replacing components of the fuel meter body/injector assembly, refer to the identification numbers on the fuel meter body and injectors. Fuel injectors are calibrated with different flow rates and must not be interchanged with injectors from a different application.*

Removal

Refer to illustrations 15.4, 15.5a, 15.5b, 15.6, 15.7, 15.8a, 15.8b, 15.9 and 15.10

1   Relieve the fuel system pressure (see Section 2).

2   Disconnect the cable from the negative battery terminal (see Chapter 5, Section 1).

3   Remove the engine cover (see Chapter 11).

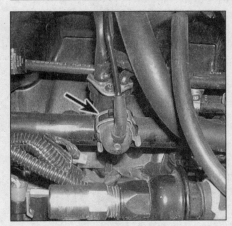

14.5b To detach the fuel pressure regulator from the fuel rail on a 4.8L, 5.3L or 6.0L V8, remove this retaining clip

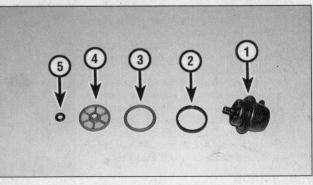

14.7 Fuel pressure regulator components

1 *Fuel pressure regulator*
2 *Back-up ring*
3 *Large O-ring*
4 *Filter disc*
5 *Small O-ring*

4   Remove the retaining clip and disconnect the electrical connector from the fuel meter body **(see illustration)**.
5   Disconnect the fuel supply and return

lines from the fittings at the rear of the engine **(see illustration)**. Remove the bracket bolt. Loosen the nuts attaching the fuel lines to the fuel meter body and remove the lines **(see illustration)**.
6   Remove the throttle body (see Section 13) and the accelerator cable bracket. Remove the ignition coil/module assembly (see Chapter 5). Remove the EVAP canister purge solenoid (see Chapter 6). Remove the rest of the upper intake manifold mounting

bolts **(see illustration)** and carefully remove the upper intake manifold. **Caution:** *Do not clean the composite upper intake manifold with solvent.*
7   Detach the poppet nozzles by squeezing the tabs together and pulling the nozzle straight out of the intake manifold **(see illustration)**. **Note:** *Apply a numbered tag to each nozzle or line with the corresponding cylinder number.*
8   Pry the bracket locking tabs away from

15.4 Remove the retaining clip and disconnect the electrical connector from the fuel meter body (4.3L V6 engine shown, 5.0L and 5.7L V8 engines similar)

15.5a Disconnect the fuel supply and return lines from the fittings (4.3L V6 engine shown, 5.0L and 5.7L V8 engines similar)

15.5b Remove the fuel line nuts and retainers and remove the fuel lines from the fuel meter body (4.3L V6 engine shown, 5.0L and 5.7L V8 engines similar)

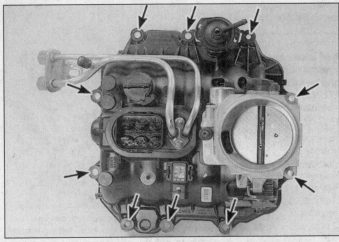

15.6 Upper intake manifold bolt locations on a 4.3L V6 engine (upper intake manifold removed for clarity)

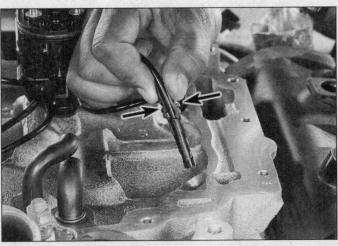

15.7 Squeeze the tabs and pull the poppet nozzle out of the intake manifold (4.3L V6 engine shown, 5.0L and 5.7L V8 engines similar)

the fuel meter body and pull the assembly off the bracket (**see illustrations**). Place the assembly on a clean work bench.

9   Remove the fuel injector hold-down plate nuts and remove the plate from the fuel meter body (**see illustration**).

10   While pulling down on the injector tube fitting, push the injector out of the fuel meter body with a dull screwdriver (**see illustration**). Be careful not to damage the electrical terminals. **Caution:** *Do not attempt to remove the fuel line or poppet nozzle from the injector. They are serviced as a complete assembly.*

Installation

11   Replace the injector O-rings. Apply a light coat of clean engine oil to the O-rings and press the injector into the fuel meter body until seated. Make sure the electrical terminals are properly aligned and the fuel tubes and nozzles are properly routed.

12   Install the injector hold-down plate and nuts.

13   Install the fuel meter body onto the intake manifold bracket. Install the poppet nozzles into the intake manifold, snapping them into place. Gently pull up on the fuel tube to ensure the nozzles are properly seated.

14   Inspect the fuel meter body and upper intake manifold seals for damage. Install new seals, if necessary. Install the upper intake manifold. Apply thread locking compound to the upper intake manifold bolts and tighten the bolts to the torque listed in the Chapter 2A Specifications section. Install the EVAP purge valve and ignition coil/module assembly.

15   Inspect the fuel line O-rings and retainers for damage. Replace the O-rings and retainers, if necessary. Install the fuel lines onto the fuel meter body. Apply thread locking compound to the fuel line bracket bolt and install the bracket.

16   Install the throttle body (see Section 13). Be sure to use a new throttle body gasket.

17   The remainder of installation is the reverse of removal.

18   When you're done, turn the ignition switch to ON but not to START. This activates the fuel pump for about two seconds, which builds up fuel pressure in the fuel lines and

15.8a Using two large screwdrivers or prybars, pry the locking tabs away from the fuel meter body . . .

the fuel meter body. Turn the ignition switch on and off several times, then check the fuel lines and fuel meter body for fuel leakage.

---

16   Fuel rail and injectors - removal and installation

Warning: *See the* **Warning** *in Section 1.*
Note 1: *This procedure applies to 4.8L, 5.3L, 6.0L and 7.4L V8 engines only.*
Note 2: *When replacing components of the fuel rail/injector assembly, be sure to write down the identification numbers on the fuel rail and injectors, or take the entire assembly with you so that the parts department can supply you with the correct part(s). The fuel injectors are calibrated with different flow rates and must not be interchanged with injectors from a different application.*

Removal

Refer to illustrations 16.9, 16.10, 16.11, 16.12a and 16.12b

1   Relieve the fuel system pressure (see Section 2).

2   Disconnect the cable from the negative battery terminal (see Chapter 5, Section 1).

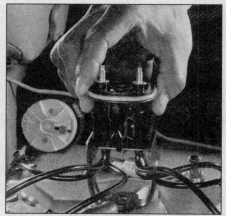

15.8b . . . and remove the fuel meter body along with the fuel lines and poppet nozzles from the intake manifold (4.3L V6 engine shown, 5.0L and 5.7L V8 engines similar)

3   Remove the air intake duct (see Section 9).

4   Remove the engine cover (see Chapter 11).

5   On 7.4L V8 engines, remove the upper intake manifold (see Chapter 2A).

6   Disconnect the accelerator cable and, if equipped, cruise control cable from the throttle body. Disengage the cables from the cable bracket and set the cables aside.

7   On 4.8L, 5.3L and 6.0L V8 engines, remove the upper engine wiring harness retainer nut and detach the upper engine wiring harness. On all engines, detach any wiring harnesses that will interfere with fuel rail removal and set them aside. If it's necessary to disconnect any electrical connectors in order to set aside a wiring harness, be sure to label the connectors to simplify reassembly.

8   Disconnect the vacuum hose from the fuel pressure regulator. Clearly label, then disconnect, any other vacuum hoses that are in the way.

9   Disconnect the fuel injector electrical

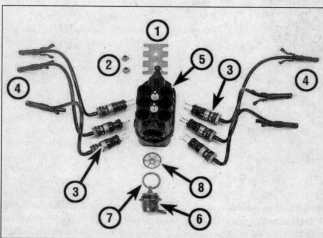

15.9 Fuel meter body components (4.3L V6 engine shown, 5.0L and 5.7L V8 engines similar)

1   *Fuel injector hold-down plate*
2   *Nuts*
3   *Fuel injectors*
4   *Poppet nozzles*
5   *Fuel meter body*
6   *Fuel pressure regulator*
7   *O-ring*
8   *Filter screen*

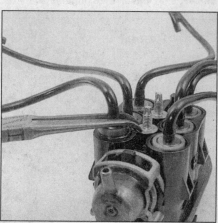

15.10 To remove an injector from the fuel meter body, pull on the tube fitting while pushing out the injector (4.3L V6 engine shown, 5.0L and 5.7L V8 engines similar)

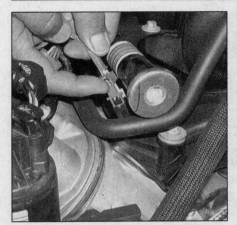

16.9 Pull up the retainer, push in the tab and disconnect the electrical connector from the fuel injector (5.3L V8 shown, 4.8L and 6.0L V8 similar)

16.10 Using the correct fuel line disconnection tool, disconnect the fuel supply and return lines (5.3L V8 shown, 4.8L and 6.0L V8 similar)

connectors **(see illustration). Note:** *If you feel there could be any confusion when putting things back together, apply a numbered tag to each connector with the corresponding cylinder number.* **Caution:** *On some models, the injector connectors are equipped with*

Connector Position Assurance (CPA) retainers. Use your fingers to release these retainers. Using pliers could damage them.
10   Disconnect the fuel supply and return lines from the fuel rail **(see illustration)**. Disconnect the vacuum line from the fuel pres-

sure regulator.
11   Clean any debris from around the injectors. Remove the fuel rail mounting bolts and/or studs **(see illustration)**. On 4.8L, 5.3L and 6.0L V8 engines loosen, but don't remove, the crossover tube retaining screw at the right (passenger) side fuel rail. Gently rock the fuel rail and injectors to loosen the injectors. Remove the fuel rail and fuel injectors as an assembly.
12   Remove the retaining clip and remove the injector(s) from the fuel rail assembly **(see illustrations)**. Remove and discard the O-rings and seals. **Note:** *Whether you're replacing an injector or a leaking O-ring, it's a good idea to remove all the injectors from the fuel rail and replace all the O-rings.*

Installation

13   Coat the new O-rings with clean engine oil and install them on the injector(s), then insert each injector into its corresponding bore in the fuel rail. Install the injector retaining clip.
14   Install the injector and fuel rail assembly on the intake manifold and fully seat the injectors. Apply thread locking compound to the fuel rail mounting bolts and tighten them to the torque listed in this Chapter's Specifications. On 4.8L, 5.3L and 6.0L V8 engines, tighten the crossover tube retainer screw at the right-side fuel rail.
15   Connect the fuel supply and return lines and make sure they're securely installed.
16   Connect the electrical connectors to each injector, referring to the numbered tags.
17   The remainder of installation is the reverse of removal.
18   After the fuel rail/injector assembly installation is complete, turn the ignition switch to On, but don't operate the starter (this activates the fuel pump for about two seconds, which builds up fuel pressure in the fuel lines and the fuel rail). Cycle the ignition On and Off several times, then check the fuel lines, fuel rail and injectors for fuel leakage.

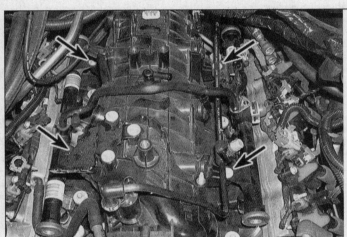

16.11   Remove the fuel rail mounting bolts (5.3L V8 shown, 4.8L and 6.0L V8 similar)

17   Exhaust system servicing - general information

Refer to illustrations 17.1 and 17.2
Warning: *The vehicle's exhaust system generates very high temperatures and must be allowed to cool down completely before touching any of the components. Be especially careful around the catalytic converter, which stays hot longer than other exhaust components.*
1   The exhaust system consists of the exhaust manifolds, the exhaust pipes, the catalytic converter(s), an extension pipe (on some models), the muffler, the tailpipe, various exhaust heat shields and all connecting flanges and clamps. The exhaust system is isolated from the vehicle body and from chassis components by a series of rubber hangers. Inspect these hangers periodically for cracks or other signs of deterioration, and

16.12a Remove the fuel injector retaining clip . . .

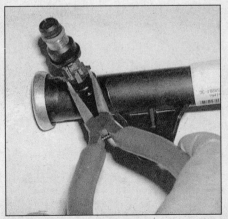

16.12b . . . and pry the injector out of the fuel rail with pliers (5.3L V8 shown, 4.8L and 6.0L V8 similar)

17.1 Inspect the rubber hangers for damage

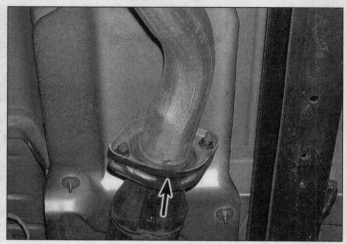

17.2 Inspect the exhaust system connections for leakage

replace them as necessary **(see illustration)**. Some exhaust components are also supported by brackets bolted to the underside of the vehicle. Make sure that these brackets are tightly fastened to the exhaust system and to the vehicle and that they're neither cracked nor corroded.

2   Conduct regular inspections of the exhaust system to keep it safe and quiet **(see illustration)**. Look for any damaged or bent parts, open seams, holes, loose connections, excessive corrosion or other defects which could allow exhaust fumes to enter the vehicle. Do not repair deteriorated exhaust system components; replace them with new parts.

3   If the exhaust system components are extremely corroded, or rusted together, you'll need welding equipment and a cutting torch to remove them. The convenient strategy at this point is to have a muffler repair shop remove the corroded sections with a cutting torch. If you want to save money by doing it yourself, but you don't have a welding outfit and cutting torch, simply cut off the old components with a hacksaw. If you have compressed air, there

are special pneumatic cutting chisels (available from specialty tool manufacturers) that can also be used. If you decide to tackle the job at home, be sure to wear safety goggles to protect your eyes from metal chips and wear work gloves to protect your hands.

4   Replacement of exhaust system components is basically a matter of removing the heat shields, disconnecting the component and installing a new one. The heat shields and exhaust system hangers must be reinstalled in the original locations or damage could result. Due to the high temperatures and exposed locations of the exhaust system components, rust and corrosion can seize parts together. Penetrating oils are available to help loosen frozen fasteners. However, in some cases it may be necessary to cut the pieces apart with a hacksaw or cutting torch. (Only persons experienced in this work should employ this latter method.) Here are some simple guidelines to follow when repairing the exhaust system:

a) *Work from the back to the front when removing exhaust system components.*

b) *Apply penetrating oil to the exhaust system component fasteners to make them easier to remove.*

c) *While you're waiting for the penetrant to loosen up the exhaust system fasteners, always disconnect the electrical connector for the downstream oxygen sensor and remove the sensor before removing the exhaust pipe section that includes the catalytic converter.*

c) *Use new gaskets, hangers and clamps when installing exhaust systems components.*

d) *Apply anti-seize compound to the threads of all exhaust system fasteners during reassembly.*

e) *Be sure to allow sufficient clearance between newly installed parts and all points on the underbody to avoid overheating the floor pan and possibly damaging the interior carpet and insulation. Pay particularly close attention to the catalytic converter and heat shield.*

Chapter 5
Engine electrical systems

Contents

Specifications

General

Battery voltage
Engine off	12.0 to 13.2 volts
Engine running	13.5 to 15 volts

Firing order
V6	1-6-5-4-3-2

V8 engines
5.0, 5.7L and 7.4L	1-8-4-3-6-5-7-2
4.8L, 5.3L and 6.0L	1-8-7-2-6-5-4-3

Torque specifications

Ft-lbs

Alternator mounting bolts
4.3L V6 and 5.0L, 5.7L and 7.4L V8
Front (long) mounting bolts	37
Rear (short) mounting bolt	18
4.8L, 5.3L and 6.0L V8	37
Distributor hold-down bolt	20

Starter motor mounting bolts
4.3L V6 and 5.0L, 5.7L and 7.4L V8	33
4.8L, 5.3L and 6.0L V8	37

1   General information, precautions and battery disconnection

General information

The engine electrical systems include all ignition, charging and starting components. Because of their engine-related functions, these components are discussed separately from body electrical devices such as the lights, the instruments, etc. (which are included in Chapter 12).

Precautions

Always observe the following precautions when working on the electrical system:

a) *Be extremely careful when servicing engine electrical components. They are easily damaged if checked, connected or handled improperly.*

b) *Never leave the ignition switched on for long periods of time when the engine is not running.*

c) *Never disconnect the battery cables while the engine is running.*

d) *Maintain correct polarity when connecting battery cables from another vehicle during jump starting - see the "Booster battery (jump) starting" section at the front of this manual.*

e) *Always disconnect the negative battery cable before working on the electrical system.*

It's also a good idea to review the safety-related information regarding the engine electrical systems located in the *"Safety first!"* section at the front of this manual, before beginning any operation included in this Chapter.

Battery disconnection

All models

Caution: *On models equipped with the Theft-lock audio system, be sure the lockout feature is turned off before performing any procedure which requires disconnecting the battery (see the front of this manual).*

Several systems on the vehicle require battery power to be available at all times, either to ensure their continued operation (such as the clock) or to maintain control unit memories (such as that in the engine management system's Powertrain Control Module) which would be wiped out if the battery were to be disconnected. Therefore, whenever the battery is to be disconnected, first note the following to ensure that there are no unforeseen consequences of this action:

a) *First, on any vehicle with power door locks, it is a wise precaution to remove the key from the ignition and to keep it with you, so that it does not get locked inside if the power door locks should engage accidentally when the battery is reconnected!*

b) *The engine management system's PCM will lose the information stored in its memory when the battery is disconnected. This includes idling and operating values, and any fault codes detected (see Chapter 6). Whenever the battery is disconnected, the information relating to idle speed control and other operating values will have to be re-programmed into the unit's memory. The PCM does this by itself, but until then, there may be surging, hesitation, erratic idle and a generally inferior level of performance. To allow the PCM to relearn these values, start the engine and run it as close to idle speed as possible until it reaches its normal operating temperature, then run it for approximately two minutes at 1200 rpm. Next, drive the vehicle as far as necessary - approximately 5 miles of varied driving conditions is usually sufficient - to complete the relearning process.*

Devices known as "memory-savers" can be used to avoid some of the above problems. Precise details vary according to the device used. Typically, it is plugged into the cigarette lighter, and is connected by its own wires to a spare battery; the vehicle's own battery is then disconnected from the electrical system, leaving the "memory-saver" to pass sufficient current to maintain audio unit security codes and PCM memory values, and also to run permanently live circuits such as the clock, all the while isolating the battery in the event of a short-circuit occurring while work is carried out. **Warning:** *Some of these devices allow a considerable amount of current to pass, which can mean that many of the vehicle's systems are still operational when the main battery is disconnected. If a "memory-saver" is used, ensure that the circuit concerned is actually "dead" before carrying out any work on it!*

Models with an auxiliary battery

Some models are equipped with an auxiliary battery located under the vehicle, mounted in a carrier attached to the frame rail. When performing any service which requires battery disconnection on a vehicle equipped with an auxiliary battery, you'll have to disconnect the negative cable from the auxiliary battery as well as the main battery under the hood.

THEFTLOCK anti-theft audio system

1   Some of these models are equipped with THEFTLOCK audio systems, which include an anti-theft feature that will render the stereo inoperative if stolen. If the power source to the stereo is cut with the anti-theft feature activated, the stereo will be inoperative. Even if the power source is immediately re-connected, the stereo will not function.

2   If your vehicle is equipped with this anti-theft system, do not disconnect the battery, remove the stereo or disconnect related components unless you have either turned off the feature or have the individual ID (code) number for the stereo.

Disabling the anti-theft feature

3   Press the stereo's 1 and 4 buttons at the same time for five seconds with the ignition on and the radio power off. The display will show SEC, indicating the unit is in the secure mode (anti-theft feature enabled).

4   Press the MN button. The display will show "000".

5   Press the MN button until the last two numbers are the same as your secret code.

6   Press HR until the first one or two numbers displayed match your code. The numbers will be displayed as entered.

7   Press AM/FM. If the display shows "_ _ _" you have successfully disabled the anti-theft feature. If SEC is displayed, the code you entered was incorrect and the anti-theft feature is still enabled.

Unlocking the stereo after a power loss

8   When the power is restored to the stereo, the stereo won't turn on and LOC will appear on the display. Enter your ID code as follows, without pausing more than 15 seconds between Steps.

9   Turn the ignition switch to ON, but leave the stereo off.

10   Press the MN button. "000" should display.

11   Press the HR button to make the last two numbers match your code, then release the button.

12   Press the HR button until the first one or two numbers match your code.

13   Press AM/FM. SEC should appear, indicating the stereo is unlocked. If LOC appears, the numbers you entered were not correct and the stereo is still inoperative.

14   You should have the code written down in a secure place, for use in unlocking the THEFTLOCK feature. **Note:** *When performing the above procedures, you are allowed only eight tries. After that, the system shuts down for an hour, with the radio displaying "INOP." At the end of that period, you have another three tries, after which you will have to bring the vehicle to your dealer for activation.*

2   Battery - emergency jump starting

Refer to the *Booster battery (jump) starting* procedure at the front of this manual.

3   Battery - check, removal and installation

Warning: *Hydrogen gas is produced by the battery, so keep open flames and lighted cigarettes away from it at all times. Always wear eye protection when working around a battery. Rinse off spilled electrolyte immediately* with large amounts of water.

Caution: *Always disconnect the negative cable first and hook it up last or you might accidentally short the battery with the tool that you're using to loosen the cable clamps.*

Check

Refer to illustrations 3.2 and 3.3

1   To check the battery state of charge, look at the indicator eye on the top of the battery (the eye is the top of a hydrometer that's built into the battery). If the indicator eye is green, the battery is 75 to 100 percent charged. If the indicator eye is black, the battery is 0 to 75 percent charged. If the indicator eye is clear (or bright), the battery electrolyte level is low. All factory-installed batteries are the *maintenance-free* type, i.e. the cell caps cannot be removed, so no water can be added. If the indicator eye is clear on a maintenance-free battery, replace the battery. If the maintenance-free battery has been replaced by a *low-maintenance* battery with removable cell caps, remove the caps and add enough water to bring it up to the correct level (which should be marked on the outside of the battery case. (If there are no MINIMUM and MAXIMUM lines on the battery case, add enough water to each cell so that the plates are fully immersed). Wait a few hours for the electrolyte in the plates to go back into solution, then charge the battery (see Chapter 1). **Note:** *A low-electrolyte/low-water condition is often a symptom of overcharging, so after recharging the battery, check the alternator charging voltage (see Section 11) and, if necessary, replace the alternator (see Section 12). Otherwise, the same condition will reoccur.*

2   Perform an open-voltage circuit test using a voltmeter **(see illustration)**. **Note:** *To obtain an accurate voltage measurement, you must first remove the battery's surface charge. To remove the surface charge, turn on the high beams for ten seconds, then turn them off and let the vehicle stand for two minutes.* With the engine and all accessories off, touch the negative probe of the voltmeter to

3.2 To test the open circuit voltage of the battery, connect a voltmeter to the battery as shown. A fully charged battery should have at least 12.4 volts

the negative terminal of the battery and the positive probe to the positive terminal of the battery. The battery voltage should be 12.4 volts or more. If the battery is less than the specified voltage, charge the battery before proceeding to the next test. Do not proceed with the battery load test unless the battery charge is correct.

3   Perform a battery load test. An accurate check of the battery condition can only be performed with a battery load tester (available at most auto parts stores). This test evaluates the ability of the battery to operate the starter and other accessories during periods of heavy amperage draw (load). The tool utilizes a carbon pile to increase the load demand (amperage draw) on the battery. Install a special battery load-testing tool onto the terminals **(see illustration)**. Load test the battery according to the tool manufacturer's instructions. Typically a load of 50-percent of the cold cranking amperage rating is applied during the test. The cold cranking amperage rating can usually be found on the battery label. Maintain the load on the battery for a maximum of 15 seconds. The battery voltage should not drop below

3.3 Connect a battery load tester to the battery and check the battery condition under load following the tool manufacturer's instructions

9.6 volts during the test. If the battery condition is weak or defective, the tool will indicate this condition immediately. **Note:** *Cold temperatures will cause the voltage readings to drop slightly. Follow the chart given in the tool manufacturer's instructions to compensate for cold climates. Minimum load voltage for freezing temperatures (32-degrees F) should be approximately 9.1 volts.*

Removal and installation

Main (underhood) battery

Refer to illustrations 3.5 and 3.6

4   If you're working on a 2003 or later model, remove the coolant reservoir mounting bolt and move the reservoir towards the driver's side of the vehicle to make room for battery removal (see Chapter 3).

5   Disconnect the cable from the negative battery terminal **(see illustration)**, then disconnect the cable from the positive terminal (see Section 1).

6   Remove the battery hold-down bolt and hold-down clamp **(see illustration)**.

7   Lift out the battery. Be careful - it's heavy.

3.5 When disconnecting the battery cables, always disconnect the cable from the negative terminal (1) first, then (and only then) disconnect the cable from the positive terminal (2)

3.6 After the battery cables are disconnected, remove the battery hold-down bolt and the hold-down clamp

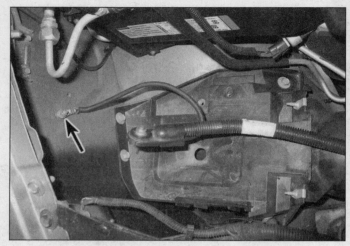

4.4a To disconnect the body ground cable from the right front fender, remove this bolt

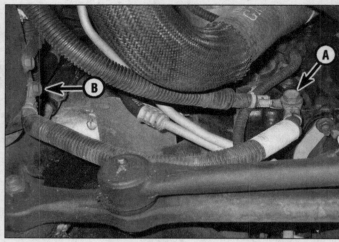

4.4b To disconnect the ground cables from the engine, remove bolt A. To disconnect the frame ground cable from the left frame rail, remove bolt B

Note: *Battery straps and handlers are available at most auto parts stores for a reasonable price. They make it easier to remove and carry the battery.*

8   While the battery is out, inspect the tray and surrounding area for corrosion. Clean the battery tray, then use baking soda to neutralize any deposits to prevent further oxidation. Spray the area with a rust-inhibiting paint.

9   If corrosion has leaked down past the battery tray, remove the tray for further cleaning.

10   If you are replacing the battery, make sure you get one that's identical, with the same dimensions, amperage rating, cold cranking rating, etc.

11   Installation is the reverse of removal.

Auxiliary battery

12   Refer to Steps 5 through 11, but keep in mind that depending on the ride height of the vehicle, it may be necessary to raise the vehicle and support it securely on jackstands for clearance.

4   Battery cables - check and replacement

Refer to illustrations 4.4a, 4.4b, 4.4c, 4.4d and 4.4e

1   Periodically inspect the entire length of each battery cable for damage, cracked or burned insulation and corrosion. Poor battery cable connections can cause starting problems and decreased engine performance.

2   Check the cable-to-terminal connections at the ends of the cables for cracks, loose wire strands and corrosion. The presence of white, fluffy deposits under the insulation at the cable terminal connection is a sign that the cable is corroded and should be replaced. Check the terminals for distortion, missing mounting bolts and corrosion.

3   When removing the cables, always disconnect the cable from the negative battery terminal first and hook it up last or the battery could be accidentally shorted by the tool you're using to loosen the cable clamps.

Even if you're only replacing the cable for the positive terminal, be sure to disconnect the cable from the negative battery terminal first (see Section 1).

4   Disconnect the old cables from the battery, then trace each of them to their opposite ends and disconnect them from the ground terminals, alternator, fuse box and starter solenoid **(see illustrations)**. Note the routing of each cable to ensure correct installation. If a cable is bundled with another wiring harness, cut the electrical tape tying them together, remove any protective sheathing and separate them.

5   If you are replacing either or both of the battery cables, take them with you when buying new cables. It is vitally important that you replace the cables with identical parts. Cables have characteristics that make them easy to identify: positive cables are usually red and larger in cross-section; ground cables are usually black and smaller in cross-section.

6   Clean the threads of the solenoid or ground connection with a wire brush to

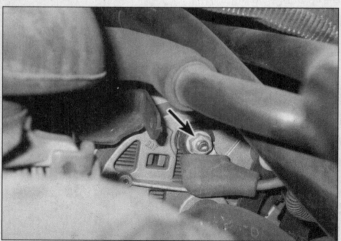

4.4c To disconnect the battery positive cable from the alternator, remove this nut and slide the cable eyelet off the stud terminal

4.4d To disconnect the positive battery cable from the engine compartment fuse and relay box, remove this nut and slide the cable eyelet off the stud terminal

4.4e To disconnect the positive battery cable from the starter solenoid, remove these two nuts and slide the cable eyelets off the stud terminals

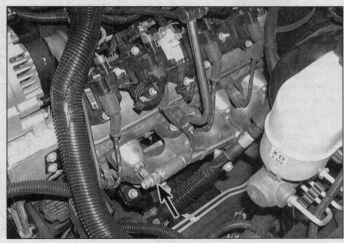

6.5 To use a calibrated ignition tester, simply disconnect a spark plug wire, connect it to the tester, clip the tester to a convenient ground and crank over the engine. If there's enough power to fire the plug, sparks will be visible between the electrode tip and the tester body

remove rust and corrosion. Apply a light coat of battery terminal corrosion inhibitor or petroleum jelly to the threads to prevent future corrosion.

7 Attach the cable to the solenoid or ground connection and tighten the mounting nut/bolt securely.

8 Before connecting a new cable to the battery, make sure that it reaches the battery post without having to be stretched.

9 Connect the positive cable first, followed by the negative cable.

5 Ignition system - general information

4.3L V6 and 5.0L, 5.7L and 7.4L V8 engines

The Distributor Ignition (DI) system consists of the battery, the Ignition Control Driver (ICD) module (later shortened to Ignition Control Module, or ICM), the ignition coil, the distributor, the spark plug wires, the spark plugs, the knock sensor(s), the Camshaft Position (CMP) sensor, the Crankshaft Position (CKP) sensor, the Manifold Absolute Pressure (MAP) sensor and the Powertrain Control Module (PCM). (For more information about the CMP sensor, CKP sensor, knock sensors, MAP sensor, TP sensor and PCM, refer to Chapter 6.)

On older Chevy and GMC electronic ignition systems, ignition timing and spark advance was controlled by the ignition control module. But as tailpipe emissions regulations were tightened by the Federal government under OBD-II, conventional electronic ignition systems were unable to control ignition timing and spark advance precisely enough to produce good performance, fuel economy *and* low emissions. So all of these engines are now equipped with a computer-controlled

system known as the Ignition Control (IC) system, in which the PCM controls ignition timing and spark advance. The base ignition timing is not adjustable on any model. The PCM controls the ignition system by opening and closing the ground path for the ICD module or ICM. Although the ICD module/ICM actually triggers the primary side of the coil on and off, it is no longer "calling the shots." It's now under the complete control of the PCM, which, using data from the information sensors mentioned above, alters the ignition timing many times a second in response to such factors as engine speed, coolant temperature and vacuum pressure in the intake manifold. (Refer to Chapter 6 for additional information on information sensors.)

The distributor on these engines is used only as a means of distributing spark and operating the CMP sensor. Because the distributor has no influence on spark timing, it's not adjustable on V6 engines. You *can*, however, adjust the position of the distributor on V8s, but only because the likelihood of "crossfire" between the high-tension terminals and spark plug wires is greater than on the V6 because of their close proximity.

4.8L, 5.3L and 6.0L V8 engines

The Electronic Ignition (EI) system consists of eight individual ignition coils, four per cylinder head. A single mounting bracket, which is bolted to the valve cover, secures each gang of four coils. Each coil is connected to its corresponding spark plug by a short spark plug wire. There is no distributor on these engines.

When buying a new coil for one of these engines, make sure that you get the correct unit. Coils manufactured by Melco are a square design while those from Delphi are a round design. The two brands of coils are not interchangeable because they use two different spark plug wire lengths and different

mounting brackets. The solid state driver that was housed in the ICD module or ICM, and mounted next to the coil, on the older style coil described above is an integral part of the ignition coil on these units. However, the PCM still fires the coils in firing order sequence by turning the ground path for the driver inside each coil on and off, which turns the primary winding inside the coils on and off. The EI system is otherwise similar in function and operation to the DI system described above.

6 Ignition system - check

Refer to illustration 6.5

Warning 1: *Because the ignition system generates high voltage, use extreme caution when servicing ignition components. This includes not just the ignition coil, but all ignition components and test equipment.*

Warning 2: *The following procedure requires cranking the engine during testing. When cranking the engine, make sure that no meter lead, loose clothing, long hair, etc. becomes contacts any moving parts (drivebelt, cooling fan, etc.).*

1 Before proceeding with the ignition system, check the following items:

a) *Make sure the battery cable clamps, where they connect to the battery, are clean and tight.*

b) *Test the condition of the battery (see Section 3). If it does not pass all the tests, replace it with a new battery.*

c) *Check the ignition system wiring and connections for tightness, damage, corrosion or any other signs of a bad connection.*

d) *Check the related fuses inside the engine compartment fuse and relay box (see Chapter 12). If they're burned, determine the cause and repair the circuit.*

2   If the engine turns over but won't start or has a severe misfire, perform the following steps using a calibrated ignition tester to make sure there is sufficient secondary ignition voltage to fire the spark plugs.

3   Disable the fuel system by removing the fuel pump relay, which is located in the engine compartment fuse and relay box (see Section 2 in Chapter 4).

4   Disconnect each spark plug wire and attach a calibrated ignition tester to verify that the coil is firing each spark plug.

5   Attach a calibrated ignition system tester (available at most auto parts stores) to the spark plug boot and clip the tester to a bolt or metal bracket on the engine **(see illustration)**. Note whether a bright blue, well-defined spark occurs (a weak spark or an intermittent spark is the same as no spark at all).

6   If sparks occur during cranking, sufficient voltage is reaching the plug to fire it. Repeat this test for each spark plug to verify that the coil is OK. However, be aware that even if the ignition coil(s) can fire the spark tester, the plugs themselves might be fouled, so remove and inspect the plugs too (see Chapter 1).

7   If no sparks occur during cranking at one cylinder, inspect the primary wire connection at the coil from which you're not getting any spark. Make sure that it's clean and tight.

8   If no sparks or intermittent sparks occur during cranking at all cylinders, the ignition control module or the PCM is probably defective. Have the ignition control module and PCM checked out by a dealer service department (testing these modules is beyond the scope of the do-it-yourselfer).

9   If the spark plug is in good shape, the coil might be defective, but no further testing is possible at home. Have the coil checked out by a dealer service department or other qualified repair shop (again, this procedure is beyond the scope of the home mechanic).

10   Any additional testing of the ignition system must be done by a dealer service department or by an independent repair shop with the right tools.

7   Ignition Control Driver (ICD) module or Ignition Control Module (ICM) - replacement

Refer to illustration 7.3
Note: *The following procedure applies only to 4.3L V6 and 5.0L, 5.7L and 7.4L V8 engines.*
1   Remove the engine cover (see Chapter 11). And if you still need more room to work, disconnect the air intake duct or resonator from the throttle body (see Chapter 4).
2   On 4.3L V6 and 5.0L/5.7L V8 engines the ICD module or ICM is mounted alongside the ignition coil on a bracket, which is located on the right side of the intake manifold. On 7.4L V8 engines, the ignition coil, ICD module (or ICM) and mounting bracket is virtually identical to the setup used on the V6 and smaller V8s, but it's located at the *rear* of the

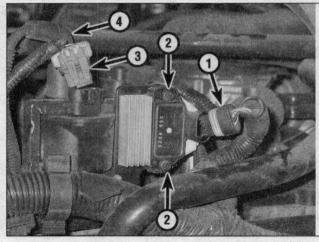

7.3 Ignition Control Driver (ICM) module/ Ignition Control Module (ICM) details (coil/module on a 5.0L V8 engine shown, 4.3L V6 and 5.7L V8 engines similar)

1   *ICM electrical connector*
2   *Mounting screws*
3   *Ignition coil electrical connector*
4   *High-tension cable*

intake manifold, right in front of the distributor. On most of these engines, you should be able to remove the ignition control module without removing the ignition coil mounting bracket from the engine. However, if it's easier for you to detach the coil, control module and mounting bracket as a single assembly, then detach the module from the bracket, that's okay too.
3   Disconnect the electrical connector from the ignition control module **(see illustration)**.
4   Remove the ignition control module mounting screws and remove the module from the coil/module mounting bracket.
5   Installation is the reverse of removal. **Note:** *The heat sink (the component with the cooling fins on it) is also secured to the coil/ module mounting bracket by the same screws as the module. This component is critical to the operation of the module, so don't forget to install it along with the new module.*

8   Ignition coil - replacement

1   Disconnect the cable from the negative battery terminal (see Section 1).
2   Remove the engine cover (see Chapter 11). If you need more room to work, remove the air intake duct or resonator from the throttle body (see Chapter 4). On 7.4L V8 engines, push the engine wiring harness aside to gain access to the ignition coil.

4.3L V6 and 5.0L, 5.7L and 7.4L V8 engines
Refer to illustrations 8.4 and 8.5
3   Disconnect the electrical connectors from the ignition coil and from the ignition control module and disconnect the high-tension cable from the coil high-tension terminal **(see illustration 7.3)**.
4   Remove the ignition coil/module bracket mounting bolts **(see illustration)** and remove the coil, module and mounting bracket from the engine as a single assembly.
5   Place the coil/module/mounting bracket assembly on a workbench. If you haven't already done so, remove the Ignition Control Driver (ICD) module or Ignition Control Mod-

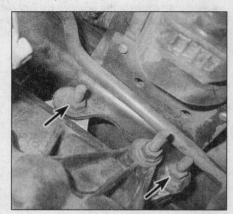

8.4 To detach the ignition coil/ignition control module mounting bracket, remove these two nuts, then slide the bracket off the mounting studs

ule (ICM) from the mounting bracket **(see illustration 7.3)**. The coil is attached to the bracket by a pair of rivets **(see illustration)**. To separate the coil from the bracket, drill out the centers of both rivets with an appropriate drill bit, then use a punch to knock out the rivets.

8.5 To detach the ignition coil from its mounting bracket, drill out the centers of these two rivets, then knock out the rivets with a punch

8.8 To remove a single ignition coil from the coil mounting bracket, disconnect the electrical connector (1) and the high-tension cable (2), then remove the mounting bolts (3)

8.10 To remove the entire ignition coil assembly from the valve cover, disconnect all coil electrical connectors and high-tension cables, then remove these five nuts

6   Attach the ignition coil to the bracket using screws. **Note:** *Screws should be provided with the new ignition coil.* Reattach the ignition module to the bracket (see **Note** regarding the heat sink in Section 7, Step 5.)

7   Installation is otherwise the reverse of removal.

4.8L, 5.3L and 6.0L V8 engines

Refer to illustrations 8.8 and 8.10

8   Disconnect the electrical connector from the ignition coil **(see illustration)** that you wish to replace.

9   Remove the ignition coil mounting bolts and remove the coil from the coil mounting bracket.

10   If you want to remove all of the coils from the valve cover, disconnect the electrical connectors from all the coils, then remove the coil mounting bracket nuts **(see illustration)** and lift the coil assembly from the valve cover.

11   Installation is the reverse of removal.

9   Distributor - removal and installation

Note: *The following procedure applies to 4.3L V6 and 5.0L, 5.7L and 7.4L V8 engines.*

Removal

Refer to illustration 9.6

1   Disconnect the cable from the negative battery terminal (see Section 1).

2   Remove the air intake duct or resonator from the throttle body (see Chapter 4).

3   Rotate the crankshaft to position the number one cylinder at TDC on the compression stroke (see Chapter 2A).

4   Disconnect the electrical connector from the distributor.

5   Disconnect the coil high-tension cable from the distributor cap. Remove the cap from the distributor and position the cap aside with the spark plug wires still connected. (If you're

unfamiliar with any of these steps, refer to *Spark plug wires, distributor cap and rotor check and replacement* in Chapter 1.)

6   The distributor rotor should be pointing at the high-tension terminal for the No. 1 cylinder. To verify that the rotor is pointing at the No. 1 terminal, hold the distributor cap directly above the rotor (with the cap oriented exactly the same way that it would be if it were actually installed) and eyeball the alignment of the rotor tip and the No. 1 terminal. When you have verified that the rotor is indeed pointing right at No. 1, make a mark on the edge of the distributor body directly below the and in line with the rotor tip **(see illustration).**

7   Mark the position of the distributor base to the engine to ensure the distributor can be re-installed in exactly the same position as originally installed.

8   Remove the distributor hold-down bolt and clamp.

9   To remove the distributor, pull it straight up. As you pull up the distributor, the rotor will turn approximately 42-degrees in a counterclockwise direction. Put a second mark below the point at which the rotor stops moving. This mark will be handy when installing the distributor.

10   Once you've removed the distributor, do NOT turn the crankshaft, or you will have to reposition the No. 1 piston at TDC before you can install the distributor.

Installation

11   If you rotated the crankshaft while the distributor was removed, you must reposition the number one piston at TDC before you can install the distributor (see Chapter 2A).

12   Turn the rotor until it points approximately 42-degrees counterclockwise from the mark that you made in Step 6. It should now be aligned with the second mark that you made in Step 9. (If you're installing a new distributor, make all three marks on the new unit in exactly the same place that you put the marks on the old distributor in Steps 6, 7 and 9.) Also make sure that the oil pump drive gear is correctly aligned with the tab on the distributor shaft. If necessary, use a long screwdriver to turn the oil pump drive shaft.

13   Insert the distributor into the engine block. As the distributor gear engages the camshaft the rotor will rotate about 42-degrees in a clockwise direction. When fully seated the rotor must align with the mark that you made in Step 6. The distributor must be

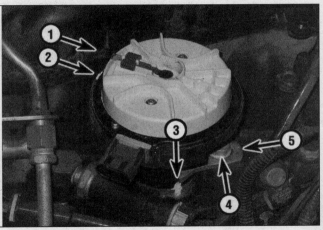

9.6 Distributor removal details (5.0L V8 shown, 4.3L V6 and 5.7L and 7.4L V8 similar)

1   *Rotor tip*
2   *Make a mark directly below the rotor tip on the distributor body*
3   *Make a mark on the distributor base and the manifold*
4   *Hold-down bolt*
5   *Hold-down clamp*

installed in precisely the same position that it was in before removal. If necessary, rotate the distributor base slightly until the marks that you made on the distributor base and the intake manifold in Step 7 are aligned. Now look at the rotor again. Make sure that the rotor is still aligned with the alignment mark that you made in Step 6. If it isn't, remove the distributor and install it again. **Caution:** *If the distributor is installed incorrectly, the engine will run poorly, the Malfunction Indicator Light (MIL) will come on and the Powertrain Control Module (PCM) will set a Diagnostic Trouble Code (see Chapter 6).*

14   Install the distributor hold-down clamp and tighten the bolt to the torque listed in this Chapter's Specifications.

15   The remainder of installation is the reverse of removal.

10   Charging system - general information and precautions

The charging system consists of the battery, the alternator, the charge indicator light, the voltage gauge and the wiring between these components. The charging system supplies electrical power for the ignition system, the lights, the radio, etc. The alternator is driven by a serpentine drivebelt at the front of the engine.

The ignition switch turns the charging system on and off. The system remains on as long as the engine is running. Voltage is supplied to the alternator field terminal on the backside of the alternator. The voltage regulator inside the alternator regulates the current output of the alternator (there is no external voltage regulator).

When the engine is started, the charge indicator light should come on briefly, then go out. If the charge indicator light does not go out after a second or two, there is a problem with the charging system (see Section 11).

When the engine is running, the voltage gauge on the instrument cluster indicates electrical system voltage. If the battery is charged, the indicator needle should be within the normal range. If the needle moves outside the normal range and stays there during normal driving, inspect the charging system (see Section 11). If the voltage gauge is defective, replace the instrument cluster (see Chapter 12). The voltage gauge cannot be serviced separately from the cluster.

The charging system doesn't ordinarily require periodic maintenance. However, you should inspect the drivebelt, the battery, the charging system wiring harness and all connections at the intervals outlined in Chapter 1. Be very careful when making electrical circuit connections to the alternator or the charging system circuit and note the following:

a) *When reconnecting wires to the alternator from the battery, be sure to observe correct polarity. Reversing these wires could damage the alternator and/or the battery.*

b) *Before using arc-welding equipment to repair any part of the vehicle, disconnect the wires from the alternator and the battery terminals.*

c) *Never start the engine with a battery charger connected.*

d) *Always disconnect both battery cables before using a battery charger.*

e) *The alternator is turned by the drivebelt, which can cause serious injury if your hands, hair or clothes become entangled in it while the engine is running.*

f) *Because the alternator is connected directly to the battery, it could arc or cause a fire if overloaded or shorted out.*

g) *Wrap a plastic bag over the alternator and secure it with rubber bands before steam-cleaning the engine.*

11   Charging system - check

Refer to illustration 11.2

Note: *These vehicles are equipped with an On-Board Diagnostic-II (OBD-II) system that is useful for detecting charging system problems because it can provide you with the Diagnostic Trouble Code (DTC) that will indicate the general nature of the problem. Refer to Chapter 6 for a list of the DTCs used by the PCM on these vehicles and for the procedure you'll need to use to obtain DTCs.*

1   If a malfunction occurs in the charging circuit, do not immediately assume that the alternator is causing the problem. First check the following items:

a) *The battery cables where they connect to the battery. Make sure the connections are clean and tight.*

b) *The battery electrolyte specific gravity (by observing the charge indicator on the battery). If it is low, charge the battery.*

c) *Inspect the external alternator wiring and connections.*

d) *Check the drivebelt condition and tension (see Chapter 1).*

e) *Check the alternator mounting bolts for tightness.*

f) *Run the engine and check the alternator for abnormal noise.*

2   Using a voltmeter, check the battery voltage with the engine off **(see illustration)**. It should be approximately 12.4 to 12.6 volts with a fully charged battery.

3   Start the engine and check the battery voltage again. It should now be greater than the voltage recorded in Step 2, but not more than 15 volts.

4   If the indicated voltage reading is less or more than the specified charging voltage, have the charging system checked at a dealer service department or other properly equipped repair facility. **Note:** *Many auto parts stores will bench test an alternator off the vehicle. Refer to your local auto parts store regarding their policy - many will perform this service free of charge.*

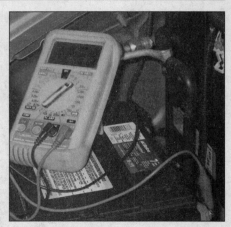

11.2 To check the charging voltage, attach the voltmeter leads to the battery terminals - check the battery voltage with the engine off, then start the engine and record the voltage reading at idle

12   Alternator - removal and installation

4.3L V6 and 5.0L, 5.7L and 7.4L V8 engines

Refer to illustrations 12.6a, 12.6b, 12.7a, 12.7b and 12.8

1   Disconnect the cable from the negative terminal of the battery (see Section 1).

2   Remove the coolant reservoir (see Chapter 3).

3   Remove the air filter housing (see Chapter 4).

4   Remove the upper fan shroud (see Chapter 3).

5   Remove the drivebelt (see Chapter 1).

6   Remove the heater hose pipe retaining bolts from the alternator support bracket **(see illustrations)** and push the hose and pipe aside. Then remove the dipstick tube, engine oil filler tube and transmission fluid filler tube retaining bolts from the support bracket and lift everything up as far as possible to provide enough clearance to remove the alternator. Finally, remove the support bracket mounting bolt and stud and remove the support bracket.

7   Remove the two front alternator mounting bolts and the single rear mounting bolt **(see illustrations)**.

8   Lift the alternator off its mounting bracket, turn it over so that you can access the electrical connectors on the backside, then disconnect the battery cable from the B+ output terminal and the field wire electrical connector from the field terminal **(see illustration)**.

9   If you are replacing the alternator, take the old one with you when purchasing a replacement unit. Make sure the new/rebuilt unit looks identical to the old alternator. Look at the terminals - they should be the same in number, size and location as the terminals on the old alternator. Finally, look at the identification numbers - they will be stamped into

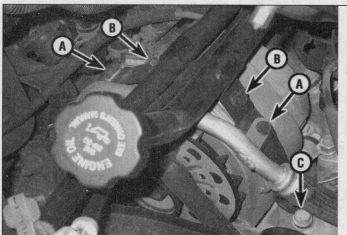

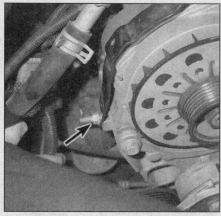

12.6a To detach the heater hose pipe from the alternator and bracket, remove bolts A. To detach the dipstick tube, engine oil filler tube and transmission fluid filler tube, remove bolts B. To detach the support bracket itself, remove the bolt (C) from lower left end of the bracket . . .

12.6b . . . and the right bolt/stud from the lower right end of the bracket (5.0L V8 shown, 4.3L V6 and 5.7L and 7.4L V8s similar)

11 Installation is the reverse of removal. Tighten the mounting bolts to the torque listed in this Chapter's Specifications.

12 When you're done check the charging voltage (see Section 11) to verify that the alternator is operating correctly.

4.8L, 5.3L and 6.0L V8 engines
Refer to illustrations 12.15 and 12.16

13 Disconnect the cable from the negative battery terminal (see Section 1).

14 Remove the drivebelt (see Chapter 1).

15 Disconnect the battery cable from the B+ output terminal and the field wire electrical connector from the field terminal on the back-side of the alternator **(see illustration)**.

16 Remove the alternator mounting bolts **(see illustration)** and remove the alternator from the engine.

17 If you are replacing the alternator, take the old one with you when purchasing a replacement unit. Make sure the new/rebuilt unit looks identical to the old alternator. Look

12.7a To detach the alternator from its mounting bracket, remove the two front mounting bolts (5.0L V8 shown, 4.3L V6 and 5.7L and 7.4L V8s similar) . . .

12.7b . . . and the rear mounting bolt (4.3L V6 shown, 5.0L, 5.7L and 7.4L V8s similar)

the housing or printed on a tag attached to the housing. Make sure the numbers are the same on both alternators.

10 Some new and remanufactured alter-

nators do not have a pulley installed, so you may have to switch the pulley from the old unit to the new/rebuilt one. When buying an alternator, find out the shop's policy regarding pulleys; some shops will perform this service free of charge.

12.8 Disconnect the battery cable from the B+ output terminal and the field wire electrical connector from the field terminal, then remove the alternator (5.0L V8 shown, 4.3L V6 and 5.7L and 7.4L V8s similar)

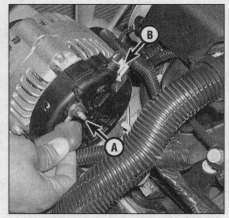

12.15 Disconnect the battery cable (A) from the B+ output terminal and the field wire electrical connector (B) from the field terminal (5.3L V8 engine shown, 4.8L and 6.0L V8 engines similar)

12.16 To detach the alternator from the alternator mounting bracket, remove these bolts (5.3L V8 engine shown, 4.8L and 6.0L V8 engines similar)

14.3 To use an inductive ammeter, hold the ammeter over the positive or negative cable while an assistant cranks over the engine

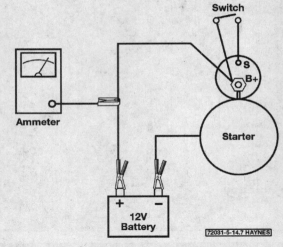

14.4 Starter motor bench-testing setup

at the terminals - they should be the same in number, size and location as the terminals on the old alternator. Finally, look at the identification numbers - they will be stamped into the housing. Make sure the numbers are the same on both alternators.

18   Many new/rebuilt alternators do not have a pulley installed, so you may have to switch the pulley from the old unit to the new/rebuilt one. When buying an alternator, find out the shop's policy regarding pulleys; some shops will perform this service free of charge.

19   Installation is the reverse of removal. Tighten the mounting bolts to the torque listed in this Chapter's Specifications.

20   When you're done check the charging voltage (see Section 11) to verify that the alternator is operating correctly.

13   Starting system - general description and precautions

General description

The starting system consists of the starter relay, the starter motor and starter solenoid assembly, the battery, the battery cables, the ignition switch and key lock cylinder, the Park/Neutral Position (PNP) switch and the wiring connecting these components. All starter motors are located on the lower part of the engine, near the transmission bellhousing, where they can engage the ring gear on the flexplate.

The starting system has two separate circuits: A low-amperage control circuit, which operates on less than 20 amps, and a high-amperage supply circuit that delivers between 150 and 350 amps to the starter motor. The low-amp control circuit includes the ignition switch, the PNP switch, the starter relay, the coil inside the starter solenoid and the wire harness connecting these components. The high-amp supply circuit consists of the battery, the battery cables, the contact disc in the

starter solenoid and the starter motor itself.

The PNP switch is installed in series between the starter relay ground terminal and ground. The PNP switch is normally open to prevent the starter relay from being energized unless the shift lever is in the NEUTRAL or PARK position. When the ignition switch is turned to START, battery voltage is supplied through the low-amperage control circuit to the battery terminal of the starter relay coil if the shift lever is in the NEUTRAL or PARK position. If it isn't, the starter circuit remains open and the engine won't start.

When the starter relay coil is energized, the normally-open relay contacts close and connect the relay common supply terminal to the relay's normally-open terminal. The closed relay contacts energize the windings of the starter solenoid pull-in coil, which pulls in the solenoid plunger, which pulls the shift lever in the starter motor, which engages the starter's overrunning clutch and pinion gear with the starter's ring gear. As the solenoid plunger reaches the end of its travel, the solenoid contact disc completes the high-current starter supply circuit and energizes the solenoid plunger hold-in coil. Current flows from the solenoid battery terminal to the starter motor and energizes the starter.

The starter motors used on vehicles powered by 4.3L V6 and 5.0L, 5.7L and 7.4L V8 engines are rebuildable, but we don't recommend doing so. Why? Because remanufactured starters are relatively inexpensive and because it's a lot easier to simply remove the old starter and install a rebuilt unit. And rebuilding a starter is not really something that the home mechanic is equipped to do. So going with a rebuilt unit is a far more sensible alternative. The starter motors used on vehicles powered by 4.8L, 5.3L and 6.0L V8 engines are not rebuildable because no parts are available. They're sold as complete new or remanufactured assemblies. If any part of the starter motor fails, including the starter solenoid, the entire assembly must be replaced.

Precautions

Always observe the following precautions when working on the starting system:

a) *Excessive cranking of the starter motor can overheat it and cause serious damage. Never operate the starter motor for more than 15 seconds at a time without pausing to allow it to cool for at least two minutes.*

b) *The starter is connected directly to the battery and could arc or cause a fire if mishandled, overloaded or shorted.*

c) *Always detach the cable from the negative terminal of the battery before working on the starting system.*

14   Starter motor and circuit - check

Refer to illustrations 14.3 and 14.4

1   If a malfunction occurs in the starting circuit, do not immediately assume that the starter is causing the problem. First, check the following items:

a) *Make sure the battery cable clamps, where they connect to the battery, are clean and tight.*

b) *Check the condition of the battery cables (see Section 4). Replace any defective battery cables with new parts.*

c) *Test the condition of the battery (see Section 3). If it does not pass all the tests, replace it with a new battery.*

d) *Check the starter motor wiring and connections.*

e) *Check the starter motor mounting bolts for tightness.*

f) *Check the related fuses in the engine compartment fuse box (see Chapter 12). If they're blown, determine the cause and repair the circuit.*

g) *Check the ignition switch circuit for correct operation (see the wiring diagrams at the end of Chapter 12).*

h) *Check the starter relay (see Chapter 12).*

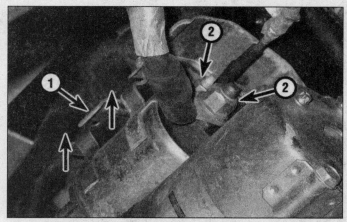

15.3 To remove the starter motor solenoid shield (1), simply push it straight up until it pops off the solenoid. Then remove the two nuts (2) from the solenoid terminals and disconnect the electrical leads from the solenoid

15.5 To detach the starter motor from the engine, remove these two bolts (5.0L engine shown, 4.3L V6 and 5.7L and 7.4L V8 engines similar)

i) Check the adjustment of the Park/Neutral Position (PNP) switch (see Chapter 6).

2 If the starter does not activate when the ignition switch is turned to the start position, check for battery voltage to the starter solenoid. This will determine if the solenoid is receiving the correct voltage from the ignition switch. Connect a 12-volt test light or a voltmeter to the starter solenoid positive terminal. While an assistant turns the ignition switch to the start position, observe the test light or voltmeter. The test light should shine brightly or battery voltage should be indicated on the voltmeter. If voltage is not available to the starter solenoid, refer to the wiring diagrams in Chapter 12 and check the fuses and starter relay in series with the starting system. If voltage is available but there is no movement from the starter motor, remove the starter from the engine (see Section 15) and bench test the starter (see Step 4).

3 If the starter turns over slowly, check the starter cranking voltage and the current draw from the battery. This test must be performed with the starter assembly on the engine. Crank the engine over (for 10 seconds or less) and observe the battery voltage. It should not drop below 9.6 volts. Also, check the current draw with an ammeter **(see illustration)**. Typically a starter should not exceed 160 amps. If the starter motor amperage draw is excessive, have it tested by a dealer service department or other qualified repair shop. There are several conditions that may affect the starter cranking potential. The battery must be in good condition and the battery cold-cranking rating must not be underrated for the particular application. Be sure to check the battery specifications carefully. The battery terminals and cables must be clean and not corroded. Also, in cases of extreme cold temperatures, make sure the battery and/or engine block is warmed before performing the tests.

4 If the starter is receiving voltage but does not activate, remove and check the starter motor assembly on the bench. Most

likely the solenoid is defective. In rare cases, the engine might be seized, so be sure to try and rotate the crankshaft pulley (see Chapter 2) before proceeding. With the starter assembly mounted in a vise on the bench, install one jumper cable from the positive terminal of a test battery to the B+ terminal on the starter **(see illustration)**. Install another jumper cable from the negative terminal of the battery to the body of the starter. Install a starter switch and apply battery voltage to the solenoid S terminal (for 10 seconds or less) and observe the solenoid plunger, shift lever and overrunning clutch extend and rotate the pinion drive. If the pinion drive extends but does not rotate, the solenoid is operating but the starter motor is defective. If there is no movement but the solenoid clicks, the solenoid and/or the starter motor is defective. If the solenoid plunger extends and rotates the pinion drive, the starter assembly is operating properly.

15 Starter motor - removal and installation

1 Disconnect the cable from the negative terminal of the battery (see Section 1).
2 Raise the vehicle and support it securely on jackstands.

4.3L V6 and 5.0L, 5.7L and 7.4L V8 engines

Refer to illustrations 15.3 and 15.5

3 On 4.3L V6 and 5.0L/5.7L V8 engines, remove the solenoid heat shield **(see illustration)** from the solenoid by simply pulling it straight up. (You can't remove the shield on 7.4L V8 engines until after you've removed the starter motor/solenoid assembly from the engine.)

4 Remove the nuts that secure the battery cable and the switch lead to the stud terminals on the starter solenoid, then disconnect both wires from the terminals. **Note:** If you

15.8 To detach the right bellhousing cover from the engine, remove this bolt

have difficulty disconnecting the battery cable or the switch cable from the solenoid terminals, leave them connected until you detach the starter from the transmission bellhousing and move it to a position where you can access the wiring connectors more easily.

5 Remove the starter motor mounting bolts **(see illustration)** and shims (if equipped). **Caution:** *The starter motor is fairly heavy, so be sure to support it while removing it. Do NOT allow it to hang by the wiring harness.*

6 If you're removing the starter motor from a 7.4L engine, and are planning to *replace* the starter, you'll need to remove the heat shield from the solenoid and install it on the new starter assembly. Remove the two mounting bolts from the rear end of the shield and the nut from the front end of the shield, then detach the heat shield from the solenoid.

7 Installation is the reverse of removal. Be sure to tighten the starter mounting bolts to the torque listed in this Chapter's Specifications.

4.8L, 5.3L and 6.0L V8 engines

Refer to illustrations 15.8, 15.9 and 15.12

8 Remove the right bellhousing cover retaining bolt **(see illustration)**.

15.9 To detach the starter motor from the engine, remove these two bolts (4.8L, 5.3L and 6.0L V8 engines)

15.12 Once you have the starter positioned so that you can disconnect the electrical leads, remove the nuts and disconnect the battery cable from the larger solenoid terminal (A) and the switch lead from the smaller terminal (B)

9   Remove the starter motor mounting bolts **(see illustration)**.

10   Disconnect the electrical connector from the oil level sensor (see Section 13 in Chapter 2B).

11   Move the starter motor toward the front of the vehicle until the starter pinion housing clears the transmission bellhousing. **Caution:** *The starter motor is fairly heavy, so be sure to support it while removing it. Do NOT allow it to hang by the wiring harness.*

12   Disconnect the battery cable and electrical connector from the terminals on the starter motor solenoid **(see illustration)**.

13   Installation is the reverse of removal. Be sure to tighten the starter motor mounting bolts to the torque listed in this Chapter's Specifications.

Chapter 6
Emissions and engine control systems

Contents

Specifications

Torque specifications

Ft-lbs (unless otherwise indicated)   **Nm**

Note: *One foot-pound (ft-lb) of torque is equivalent to 12 inch-pounds (in-lbs) of torque. Torque values below approximately 15 foot-pounds are expressed in inch-pounds, because most foot-pound torque wrenches are not accurate at these smaller values.*

Engine Coolant Temperature (ECT) sensor
- 4.3L V6 and 5.0L, 5.7L and 7.4L V8 .... 120 in-lbs
- 4.8L, 5.3L and 6.0L V8 .... 180 in-lbs

Knock sensor
- 4.3L V6
  - 1996 through 2000 (screw-in type) .... 168 in-lbs
  - 2000 on (single mounting bolt) 18
- 5.0L, 5.7L and 7.4L V8 (screw-in type) .... 168 in-lbs
- 4.8L, 5.3L and 6.0L V8 (screw-in type) .... 180 in-lbs

Oxygen sensors
- 4.3L V6 and 5.0L, 5.7L and 7.4L V8
  - 1996 through 1999 30
  - 2000 on 31
- 4.8L, 5.3L and 6.0L V8 31

1   General information

Refer to illustration 1.7

To prevent pollution of the atmosphere from incompletely burned and evaporating gases, and to maintain good driveability and fuel economy, a number of emission control systems are incorporated on the vehicles covered in this manual. These emission control systems and their components are an integral part of the engine management system. The engine management system also includes all the government mandated diagnostic features of the second generation of on-board diagnostics, which is known as On-Board Diagnostics II (OBD-II).

At the center of the engine management and OBD-II systems is the on-board computer, which is known as the Powertrain Control Module (PCM). Using a variety of information sensors, the PCM monitors all of the important engine operating parameters (temperature, speed, load, etc.). It also uses an array of output actuators - such as the ignition coils, the fuel injectors, the Idle Air Control (IAC) motor, the Torque Converter Clutch (TCC) and various solenoids and relays - to respond to and alter these parameters as necessary to maintain optimal performance, economy and emissions. The principal emission control systems used on the vehicles covered in this manual include the:

Catalytic converters
Evaporative Emission Control (EVAP) system
Exhaust Gas Recirculation (EGR) system
Positive Crankcase Ventilation (PCV) system
Secondary Air Injection (AIR) system
Torque Converter Clutch (TCC) system

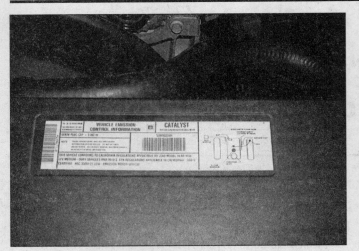

1.7 The Vehicle Emission Control Information (VECI) label, located in the engine compartment, contains information on the emission devices installed on your vehicle and a vacuum hose routing schematic

2.2 Scan tools, or scanners, like these from Actron and AutoXray are powerful diagnostic aids. They're programmed with comprehensive diagnostic information, and they can tell you just about anything that you want to know about your engine management system

The Sections in this Chapter include general descriptions and component replacement procedures for most of the information sensors and output actuators, as well as the important components that are part of the systems listed above. Refer to Chapter 4 for more information on the air induction, fuel delivery and injection systems and exhaust systems, and to Chapter 5 for information on the ignition system. Refer to Chapter 1 for any scheduled maintenance for emission-related systems and components.

The procedures in this Chapter are intended to be practical, affordable and within the capabilities of the home mechanic. The diagnosis of most engine and emission control functions and driveability problems requires specialized tools, equipment and training. When servicing emission devices or systems becomes too difficult or requires special test equipment, consult a dealer service department.

Although engine and emission control systems are very sophisticated on late-model vehicles, you can do most of the regular maintenance and some servicing at home with common tune-up and hand tools and relatively inexpensive digital multimeters. Because of the Federally mandated extended warranty that covers the emission control system, check with a dealer about warranty coverage before working on any emission-related systems. After the warranty has expired, you might want to perform some of the component replacement procedures in this Chapter to save money. Remember that the most frequent cause of emission and driveability problems is a loose electrical connector or a broken wire or vacuum hose, so before jumping to conclusions the first thing you should always do is to inspect all electrical connections, electrical wiring and vacuum hoses related to a system.

Pay close attention to any special precautions given in this Chapter. Remember that illustrations of various system components might not exactly match the component installed on the vehicle on which you're working because of changes made by the manufacturer during production or from year to year.

A Vehicle Emission Control Information (VECI) label **(see illustration)** is located in the engine compartment. This label contains emission-control and engine tune-up specifications and adjustment information. It also includes a vacuum hose routing diagram for emission-control components. When servicing the engine or emission systems, always check the VECI label in your vehicle. If any information in this manual contradicts what you read on the VECI label on your vehicle, always defer to the information on the VECI label.

2   On-Board Diagnostic (OBD) system and Diagnostic Trouble Codes (DTCs)

Scan tool information
Refer to illustration 2.2

1   Hand-held scanners are handy for analyzing the engine management systems used on late-model vehicles. Because extracting the Diagnostic Trouble Codes (DTCs) from an engine management system is now the first step in troubleshooting many computer-controlled systems and components, even the most basic generic scan tools are capable of access a computer's DTCs. More powerful scan tools can also perform many of the diagnostics once associated with expensive factory scan tools. If you're planning to obtain a generic scan tool for your vehicle, make sure that it's compatible with the year, make and model of the vehicle(s) on which

you plan to use it. Some of the more versatile scan tools accept removable cartridges, each of which contains the diagnostics for a particular manufacturer. An aftermarket generic scanner should work with any model covered by this manual. But before purchasing a scan tool, contact the manufacturer of the scanner you're planning to buy and verify that it will work properly with the system you want to scan. If you don't plan to purchase a scan tool and don't have access to one, you can have the codes extracted by a dealer service department or by an independent repair shop.

2   With the advent of the Federally mandated emission control system known as On-Board Diagnostics-II (OBD-II), specially designed scanners were developed. Several tool manufacturers have released OBD-II scan tools for the home mechanic **(see illustration)**.

OBD-II system general description

3   All vehicles covered by this manual are equipped with the OBD-II system. This system consists of the on-board computer, known as the Powertrain Control Module (PCM), and information sensors that monitor various functions of the engine and send a constant stream of data to the PCM during engine operation. Unlike earlier on-board diagnostics systems, the OBD-II system doesn't just monitor everything, store Diagnostic Trouble Codes (DTCs) and illuminate a light on the instrument panel when there's a problem. *It even predicts the probable failure of systems and components when their data starts to become suspicious!*

4   The PCM is the "brain" of the electronically controlled OBD-II system. It receives data from a number of information sensors and switches. Based on the data that it receives from the sensors, the PCM con-

stantly alters engine operating conditions to optimize driveability, performance, emissions and fuel economy. It does so by turning on and off and by controlling various output actuators such as relays, solenoids, valves and other devices. The PCM can only be accessed with an OBD-II scan tool plugged into the 16-pin Data Link Connector (DLC), which is located underneath the driver's end of the dashboard, near the steering column.

5   If your vehicle is still under warranty, virtually every fuel, ignition and emission control component in the OBD-II system is covered by a Federally mandated emissions warranty that is longer than the warranty covering the rest of the vehicle. Vehicles sold in California and in some other states have even longer emissions warranties than other states. Read your owner's manual for the terms of the warranty protecting the emission-control systems on your vehicle. It isn't a good idea to "do-it-yourself" at home while the vehicle emission systems are still under warranty because owner-induced damage to the PCM, the sensors and/or the control devices might VOID this warranty. So as long as the emission systems are still warranted, take the vehicle to a dealer service department if there's a problem.

Information sensors

6   **Accelerator Pedal Position Sensor (APPS)** - The APPS provides the PCM with a variable voltage signal that's proportional to the position (angle) of the accelerator pedal. The PCM uses this data to control the position of the throttle plate inside an *electronically-controlled* (no accelerator cable) throttle body used on these models. The APPS is used only on 2004 and 2005 4.8L, 5.3L and 6.0L V8 engines with the Throttle Actuator Control (TAC) system. These models actually have *two* APPS units, which are located on and are integral components of the accelerator pedal assembly.

7   **Camshaft Position (CMP) sensor** - The CMP sensor is a Hall effect switching device that produces a square-wave (LOW-HIGH) voltage signal that the PCM uses to monitor the position of the camshaft. The signal from the CMP sensor enables the PCM to determine the position of the camshaft (and therefore the valve train) so that it can time the firing sequence of the fuel injectors. The PCM also uses the signal from the CMP sensor and the signal from the Crankshaft Position (CKP) sensor to distinguish between fuel injection and spark timing. On 4.3L V6 and 5.0L, 5.7L and 7.4L V8 engines, the CMP sensor is mounted inside the distributor. On 4.8L, 5.3L and 6.0L V8 engines it's located on top of and at the rear of the engine block "valley" between the cylinder heads and is mounted in the same location as the distributor on older engines.

8   **Crankshaft Position (CKP) sensor** - Like the CMP sensor, the CKP sensor is a Hall effect device. The PCM uses data from the CKP sensor to calculate engine speed and crankshaft position, which enables it to synchronize ignition timing with fuel injector timing, to control spark knock and to detect misfires. On 4.3L V6 and 5.0L, 5.7L and 7.4L V8 engines, the CKP sensor is located on the front of the engine, on the timing chain cover. On 4.8L, 5.3L and 6.0L V8 engines the CKP sensor is located on the right rear part of the engine block, near the starter.

9   **Engine Coolant Temperature (ECT) sensor** - The ECT sensor is a Negative Temperature Coefficient (NTC) "thermistor" (temperature-sensitive variable resistor). In an NTC-type thermistor, the resistance of the thermistor decreases as the coolant temperature increases, so the voltage output of the ECT sensor increases. Conversely, the resistance of the thermistor increases as the coolant temperature decreases, so the voltage of the ECT sensor decreases. The PCM uses this variable voltage signal to calculate the temperature of the engine coolant. The ECT sensor tells the PCM when the engine is sufficiently warmed up to go into closed-loop operation and helps the PCM control the air/fuel mixture ratio and ignition timing. On 4.3L V6 and 5.0L, 5.7L and 7.4L V8 engines the ECT sensor is located at the upper front of the engine, to the right of the EGR valve (except on 7.4L V8s, which don't use EGR). On 4.8L, 5.3L and 6.0L engines the ECT sensor is located at the front of the end of the left cylinder head, right above the spark plug.

10   **EVAP system fuel tank pressure sensor** - The EVAP system fuel tank pressure sensor is located on top of the fuel tank, on the fuel pump/fuel level sending unit module. It monitors the pressure of unburned fuel vapors inside the fuel tank and provides a voltage signal to the PCM that's proportional to the pressure. In cold weather, the vapors inside the tank cool off and contract. Because the tank is a closed system, it could be damaged by a radical difference in pressure between the relative vacuum inside and the ambient (outside) air pressure. If the pressure inside the tank drops below a specified threshold, the PCM opens the vent valve and allows ambient air to enter the tank, equalizing the pressure. In hot weather, the vapors inside the fuel tank expand. If the pressure *exceeds* a specified threshold while the vehicle is parked, the expanding pressure inside the tank forces the vapors out of the tank, through the EVAP line and into the EVAP canister, where they're absorbed by the activated charcoal inside the canister. If the pressure inside the fuel tank becomes excessive while the vehicle is in operation, the PCM energizes the EVAP purge solenoid to open, allowing intake manifold vacuum to draw excess fuel vapors from the canister and from the fuel tank into the manifold, where they're mixed with the incoming air/fuel mixture and burned up in combustion.

11   **Input Shaft Speed (ISS) sensor** - The ISS sensor is used on 4L80-E and 4L85-E automatic transmissions. The ISS sensor is located on the left side of the transmission. There are two speed sensors on the left side of the transmission; the other one is the Output Shaft Speed (OSS) sensor. The ISS sensor is the unit closer to the front of the transmission. The ISS sensor is a magnetic pick-up coil that generates an alternating current (AC) signal output to the (PCM) that's proportional to the speed of rotation of the input shaft. The PCM uses this signal to determine the correct transmission gear ratio and to detect a problem with the Vehicle Speed Sensor (VSS) signal. The PCM also compares the ISS signal to the Output Shaft Speed (OSS) sensor signal to determine whether the Torque Converter Clutch (TCC) is slipping, or is starting to slip.

12   **Intake Air Temperature (IAT) sensor** - The IAT sensor is a Negative Temperature Coefficient (NTC) "thermistor" (temperature-sensitive variable resistor) that monitors the temperature of the air entering the engine and sends a variable voltage signal to the PCM (see the explanation for how an NTC-type thermistor works in the ECT sensor description above). The voltage signal from the IAT sensor is one of the parameters used by the PCM to determine injector pulse-width (the duration of each injector's "on-time") and to adjust spark timing (to prevent spark knock). On 4.3L V6 and 5.0L, 5.7L and 7.4L V8 engines the IAT sensor is located on the air intake duct. On 4.8L, 5.3L and 6.0L V8 engines the IAT sensor is one-half of the dual-function Intake Air Temperature/Mass Air Flow (IAT/MAF) sensor, which is located between the air filter housing and the air intake duct.

13   **Knock Sensor (KS)** - The Knock Sensor (KS) is a "piezoelectric" crystal that oscillates in proportion to engine vibration. (The term *piezoelectric* refers to the property of certain crystals that produce a voltage when subjected to a mechanical stress.) The oscillation of the piezoelectric crystal produces a voltage output that is monitored by the PCM, which retards the ignition timing when the oscillation exceeds a certain threshold. When the engine is operating normally, the Knock Sensor (KS) oscillates consistently and its voltage signal is steady. When detonation occurs, engine vibration increases, and the oscillation of the Knock Sensor (KS) exceeds a design threshold. (Detonation is an uncontrolled explosion, after the spark occurs at the spark plug, which spontaneously combusts the remaining air/fuel mixture, resulting in a "pinging" or "slapping" sound.) If allowed to continue, detonation is annoying, and engine performance is diminished. On 4.3L V6 engines the knock sensor is located on the upper rear part of the engine, next to the distributor. On 5.0L, 5.7L and 7.4L V8 engines, the knock sensor is located on the right side of the block, just ahead of the starter motor. On 4.8L, 5.3L and 6.0L V8 engines there are two knock sensors, both of which are located in the valley between the cylinder heads.

14   **Manifold Absolute Pressure (MAP) sensor** - As the altitude increases, the air becomes thinner. Because the air density

changes with altitude, the PCM needs to know whether the vehicle is at sea level or at some higher elevation. Altitude and barometric pressure are inversely proportional: as the altitude increases, the barometric pressure decreases. The MAP sensor monitors the pressure or vacuum downstream from the throttle plate, inside the intake manifold. The MAP sensor measures intake manifold pressure and vacuum on the absolute scale, i.e. from zero psi, not from sea-level atmospheric pressure (14.7 psi). The MAP sensor converts the absolute pressure into a variable voltage signal that changes with the pressure or vacuum. The PCM uses this signal to calculate intake manifold pressure or vacuum, barometric pressure, engine load, injector pulse-width, spark advance, shift points, idle speed and deceleration fuel shut-off. On 4.3L V6 and 5.0L, 5.7L and 7.4L V8 engines the MAP sensor is located on the intake manifold. On 4.8L, 5.3L and 6.0L engines the MAP sensor is located on the intake manifold.

15   Output Shaft Speed (OSS) sensor - The OSS sensor, which is used on 4L80-E and 4L85-E automatic transmissions, is a magnetic pick-up coil that generates an alternating current (AC) signal output to the PCM that's proportional to the speed of rotation of the output shaft. The PCM uses this signal to determine the correct transmission gear ratio, and to detect a problem with the Vehicle Speed Sensor (VSS) signal. The PCM also compares the OSS signal to the ISS signal to determine whether the Torque Converter Clutch (TCC) is slipping or is starting to slip. The OSS is located on the left side of the transmission. There are two speed sensors on the left side of the transmission; the other one is the Input Shaft Speed (ISS) sensor. The OSS sensor is the unit closer to the rear of the transmission.

16   Oxygen sensors - An oxygen sensor is a galvanic battery that generates a small variable voltage signal in proportion to the difference between the oxygen content in the exhaust stream and the oxygen content in the ambient air. The PCM uses the voltage signal from the upstream oxygen sensor to maintain a "stoichiometric" air/fuel ratio of 14.7:1 by constantly adjusting the "on-time" of the fuel injectors. On all 1996 through 2000 models there are *two* oxygen sensors: the *upstream* sensor is located just ahead of the junction between the two downpipes connecting the exhaust manifolds to the (single) catalytic converter, and a *downstream* oxygen sensor is located behind the catalyst. On 2001 and later 4.3L V6 models there are three oxygen sensors: one in each downpipe between the exhaust manifolds and the catalyst, and a third sensor behind the catalyst. On 2001 and 2002 5.0L and 5.7L V8 models, and on all 4.8L, 5.3L and 6.0L V8 models, there are four oxygen sensors: one in each downpipe between the manifolds and the catalytic converters (there are two catalysts on these models) and one behind each catalyst.

17   Park Neutral Position (PNP) switch

- The manufacturer still calls this sensor a PNP switch, but it's actually a **Transmission Range (TR) sensor**. The PNP switch/TR sensor is located at the end of the manual shaft, on the side of the automatic transmission on all transmissions. The PNP switch/TR sensor performs the same functions as any other PNP switch: it prevents the engine from starting in any gear other than Park or Neutral, and it closes the circuit for the back-up lights when the shift lever is moved to Reverse. But the PNP switch/TR sensor is also connected to the PCM, which monitors the voltage output signal from the switch in order to calculate the position of the manual lever. Thus the PCM is able to determine the gear selected and the correct pressure for the electronic pressure control system of the transaxle.

18   Throttle Position (TP) sensor - The TP sensor is a potentiometer that receives constant voltage input from the PCM and sends back a voltage signal that varies in relation to the opening angle of the throttle plate inside the throttle body. This voltage signal tells the PCM when the throttle is closed, half-open, wide open or anywhere in between. The PCM uses this data, along with information from other sensors, to calculate injector "pulse width" (the interval of time during which an injector solenoid is energized by the PCM). The TP sensor is located on the throttle body, on the end of the throttle plate shaft, on all 1996 through 2003 engines.

The electronic throttle body used on 2004 and later 4.8L, 5.3L and 6.0L V8 engines, which are equipped with a PCM-controlled Throttle Actuator Control (TAC) system, uses *two* TP sensors. Both TP sensors are an integral part of the throttle body's TAC motor assembly and cannot be serviced separately.

19   Vehicle Speed Sensor (VSS) - The VSS is a magnetic pick-up coil that monitors output shaft rotating speed on 4L60-E and 4L80-E automatic transmissions. The sensor is positioned right over the park gear. When the vehicle is moving the park gear lugs rotate past the speed sensor, which generates a pulsing alternating current (AC) voltage. The frequency of this AC voltage output increases as the speed goes up and decreases as the speed goes down. This signal is processed by the PCM. The PCM uses the VSS signal to calculate vehicle speed. The VSS is located on the extension housing.

Output actuators

20   EVAP purge solenoid - The EVAP purge solenoid is a PCM-controlled solenoid that controls the purging of evaporative emissions from the EVAP canister to the intake manifold. The EVAP purge solenoid is never turned on during cold start warm-ups or during hot start time delays. But once the engine reaches a specified temperature and enters closed-loop operation, the PCM energizes the canister purge solenoid during certain operating conditions, which allows the fuel vapors stored in the EVAP canister to be drawn into the intake

manifold, where they're mixed with intake air, then burned along with the normal air/fuel mixture. The PCM regulates the flow rate of the vapors by controlling the pulse-width of the solenoid (the length of time during which the solenoid is turned on) in accordance with operating conditions. On 4.3L V6 and 5.0L and 5.7L V8 models, the EVAP purge solenoid is located in the engine compartment, on the right side of the intake manifold, in front of the distributor. On 7.4L V8 models, the EVAP purge solenoid is located on the forward left side of the intake manifold. On 4.8L, 5.3L and 6.0L V8 models, the EVAP purge solenoid is located on the front end of the intake manifold, near the throttle body.

21   EVAP vent valve - When the fuel inside the fuel tank expands during hot weather, the fuel tank becomes pressurized by the expanding hydrocarbon (HC) vapors inside the tank. If there were no place for these vapors to go, they could damage the fuel tank and/or fuel line fittings. The EVAP canister absorbs these HC vapors. When the fuel inside the tank contracts during cold weather, the pressure inside the fuel tank drops, sometimes lower than atmospheric pressure. The EVAP vent valve allows ambient air to enter the fuel tank and the EVAP system (including the canister) so that the pressure inside and outside is equalized. (The vent valve is a one-way valve, so no HC vapors are allowed to escape to the atmosphere.) The vent valve, which is controlled by the PCM, also closes the system during leak testing by the PCM. The vent valve is located underneath the vehicle, next to the ABS hydraulic control unit. You have to remove the ABS rock shield to access it.

22   Exhaust Gas Recirculation (EGR) valve - The EGR valve "leaks" a small amount of burned exhaust gases back into the intake manifold in order to "dilute" the incoming air/fuel mixture under certain high-load conditions during which the engine combustion chamber temperature exceeds 2500 degrees and begins to produce substantial amount of Oxides of Nitrogen (NOx). The EGR valve is a PCM-controlled device that regulates how much exhaust gas is recirculated back into the intake manifold. On 4.3L V6 and 5.0L and 5.7L V8 engines, the EGR valve is located at the front end of the intake manifold. On 7.4L V8 engines, the EGR valve is located on the left side of the intake manifold. On 4.8L, 5.3L and 6.0L V8 engines, the EGR valve is located at the front end of the right cylinder head.

23   Fuel injectors - The fuel injectors, which spray a fine mist of fuel into the intake ports, where it is mixed with incoming air, are inductive coils under PCM control. On 4.3L V6 and 5.0L and 5.7L V8 engines, the injectors are installed inside the fuel metering body, which is mounted underneath the upper intake manifold. On 7.4L, 4.8L, 5.3L and 6.0L V8 engines, the injectors are installed between the fuel rail and the intake ports that connect the intake manifold runners to the combustion chambers. For more information about the injectors, see Chapter 4.

2.28 The Data Link Connector (DLC), or diagnostic connector, is located under the instrument panel

24   **Idle Air Control (IAC) valve** - The IAC valve controls the amount of air allowed to bypass the throttle plate when the throttle plate is at its (nearly closed) idle position. The IAC valve is controlled by the PCM. When the engine is placed under an additional load at idle (high power steering pressure or running the air conditioning compressor during low-speed maneuvers, for example), the engine can run roughly, stumble and even stall. To prevent this from happening, the PCM opens the IAC valve to increase the idle speed enough to overcome the extra load imposed on the engine. The IAC valve is mounted on the throttle body on all models.

25   **Ignition coils** - The ignition coils, which provide the high-voltage current for the spark plugs, are under the control of the Powertrain Control Module (PCM). For more information about the ignition coils refer to Chapter 5.

26   **Secondary Air Injection (AIR)** solenoid valve - Some 1996 through 2000 7.4L V8 engines and 2000 through 2002 4.3L V6 and 5.7L V8 engines are equipped with a PCM-controlled Secondary Air Injection (AIR) system that pumps air into the exhaust manifolds under certain conditions. Introducing extra air into the exhaust manifolds helps to burn off any residual unburned hydrocarbons (HC) and carbon monoxide (CO). 7.4L V8 models use a belt-driven pump. 4.3L V6 and 5.7L V8 models employ an electric pump. All AIR-equipped models are equipped with a PCM-controlled solenoid valve that, when energized by the PCM, directs low-pressure air from the pump through a pair of check valves (one for each cylinder head) and into the exhaust manifolds. See Section 22 for more information about the AIR system.

Obtaining and clearing Diagnostic Trouble Codes (DTCs)

27   All models covered by this manual are equipped with on-board diagnostics. When the PCM recognizes a malfunction in a monitored emission control system, component or circuit, it turns on the Malfunction Indicator Light (MIL) on the dash. The PCM will continue to display the MIL until the problem is fixed and the Diagnostic Trouble Code (DTC) is cleared from the PCM's memory. You'll need a scan tool to access any DTCs stored in the PCM. Before outputting any DTCs stored in the PCM, thoroughly inspect ALL electrical connectors and hoses. Make sure that all electrical connections are tight, clean and free of corrosion. And make sure that all hoses are correctly connected, fit tightly and are in good condition (no cracks or tears). Also, make sure that the engine is tuned up. A poorly running engine is probably one of the biggest causes of emission-related malfunctions. Often, simply giving the engine a good tune-up will correct the problem.

Accessing the DTCs

Refer to illustration 2.28

28   On the vehicles covered in this manual, all of which are equipped with On-Board Diagnostic II (OBD-II) systems, the Diagnostic Trouble Codes (DTCs) can only be accessed with a scan tool. Professional scan tools are expensive, but relatively inexpensive generic scan tools **(see illustration 2.2)** are available at most auto parts stores. Simply plug the connector of the scan tool into the Data Link Connector (DLC) or diagnostic connector, which is located under the lower edge of the dash, near the parking brake release handle **(see illustration)**. Then follow the instructions included with the scan tool to extract the DTCs.

29   Once you have outputted all of the stored DTCs look them up on the accompanying DTC chart.

30   After troubleshooting the source of each DTC make any necessary repairs or replace the defective component(s).

Clearing the DTCs

31   Clear the DTCs with the scan tool in accordance with the instructions provided by the scan tool's manufacturer.

Diagnostic Trouble Codes

32   The accompanying tables are a list of the Diagnostic Trouble Codes (DTCs) that can be accessed by a do-it-yourselfer working at home (there are many, many more DTCs available to dealerships with proprietary scan tools and software, but those codes cannot be accessed by a generic scan tool). If, after you have checked and repaired the connectors, wire harness and vacuum hoses (if applicable) for an emission-related system, component or circuit, the problem persists, have the vehicle checked by a dealer service department.

OBD-II Diagnostic Trouble Codes (DTCs)

Note: *Not all trouble codes apply to all models.*

Code	Possible cause
P0016	Crankshaft Position (CKP) sensor, signal incorrect or mismatch
P0030	Upstream oxygen sensor (left cylinder bank) circuit, heater performance (4.3L V6; 4.8L, 5.3L and 6.0L V8)
P0036	Upstream oxygen sensor (left cylinder bank) circuit, heater performance (4.8L, 5.3L and 6.0L V8)
P0050	Downstream oxygen sensor, heater control circuit (right cylinder bank)
P0053	Upstream oxygen sensor, heater resistance (left cylinder bank)
P0054	Downstream oxygen sensor, heater resistance (left cylinder bank)
P0056	Downstream oxygen sensor, heater control circuit (left cylinder bank)
P0059	Upstream oxygen sensor, heater resistance (right cylinder bank)
P0060	Downstream oxygen sensor, heater resistance (right cylinder bank)
P0068	MAF sensor circuit, difference between actual air flow and predicted speed density greater than expected

Code	Possible cause
P0068	Throttle body airflow performance
P0101	Mass Air Flow (MAF) sensor performance
P0102	Mass Air Flow (MAF) sensor circuit, frequency of output signal too low
P0103	Mass Air Flow (MAF) sensor circuit, frequency of output signal too high
P0106	Manifold Absolute Pressure (MAP) sensor performance, signal out of range
P0107	Manifold Absolute Pressure (MAP) sensor circuit, voltage too low
P0108	Manifold Absolute Pressure (MAP) sensor circuit, voltage too high
P0112	Intake Air Temperature (IAT) sensor circuit, voltage too low (temperature too high)
P0113	Intake Air Temperature (IAT) sensor circuit, voltage too high (temperature too low)
P0116	Temperature difference between ECT and IAT sensors not within calibrated range
P0116	Engine Coolant Temperature (ECT) sensor performance
P0117	Engine Coolant Temperature (ECT) sensor circuit, voltage too low (temperature too high)
P0118	Engine Coolant Temperature (ECT) sensor circuit, voltage too high (temperature too low)
P0120	Throttle Position (TP) sensor 1 circuit, siganal or reference voltage out of range (models with TAC)
P0121	Throttle Position (TP) sensor performance, signal voltage out of range
P0122	Throttle Position (TP) sensor circuit, voltage too low
P0123	Throttle Position (TP) sensor circuit, voltage too high
P0125	Engine Coolant Temperature (ECT) sensor takes too long to reach closed-loop temperature
P0128	Engine Coolant Temperature (ECT) sensor doesn't meet minimum thermostat regulating temperature
P0131	Upstream oxygen sensor (left cylinder bank), circuit voltage too low
P0132	Upstream oxygen sensor (left cylinder bank), circuit voltage too high
P0133	Upstream oxygen sensor (left cylinder bank), slow response
P0134	Upstream oxygen sensor (left cylinder bank) circuit, insufficient activity
P0135	Upstream oxygen sensor (left cylinder bank), heater performance
P0136	Downstream oxygen sensor (left cylinder bank) circuit, signal out of range
P0137	Downstream oxygen sensor (left cylinder bank) circuit, low voltage
P0138	Downstream oxygen sensor (left cylinder bank) circuit, high voltage
P0140	Downstream oxygen sensor (left cylinder bank) circuit, insufficient activity
P0141	Downstream oxygen sensor (left cylinder bank) circuit, heater performance
P0143	Downstream oxygen sensor (left cylinder bank) circuit, low voltage
P0144	Downstream oxygen sensor (left cylinder bank) circuit, high voltage
P0146	Downstream oxygen sensor (left cylinder bank) circuit, insufficient activity
P0147	Downstream oxygen sensor (left cylinder bank), heater performance
P0151	Upstream oxygen sensor (right cylinder bank) circuit voltage too low

Code	Possible cause
P0152	Upstream oxygen sensor (right cylinder bank), circuit voltage too high
P0153	Upstream oxygen sensor (right cylinder bank), slow response
P0154	Upstream oxygen sensor (right cylinder bank) circuit, insufficient activity
P0155	Upstream oxygen sensor (right cylinder bank), heater performance
P0156	Downstream oxygen sensor (right cylinder bank) circuit, signal out of range
P0157	Downstream oxygen sensor (right cylinder bank) circuit, low voltage
P0158	Downstream oxygen sensor (right cylinder bank) circuit, high voltage
P0160	Downstream oxygen sensor (right cylinder bank) circuit, insufficient activity
P0161	Downstream oxygen sensor (right cylinder bank), heater performance
P0171	Fuel trim system lean at upstream oxygen sensor (left cylinder bank)
P0172	Fuel trim system rich at upstream oxygen sensor (left cylinder bank)
P0174	Fuel trim system lean at upstream oxygen sensor (right cylinder bank)
P0175	Fuel trim system rich at upstream oxygen sensor (right cylinder bank)
P0200	Fuel injector control circuit, incorrect voltage
P0218	Transmission fluid temperature too high
P0220	Throttle Position (TP) sensor 2 signal or reference voltage outside normal range (models with TAC)
P0230	Fuel pump relay control circuit
P0300	Engine misfire detected, non-specific
P0301	Engine misfire detected, cylinder #1
P0302	Engine misfire detected, cylinder #2
P0303	Engine misfire detected, cylinder #3
P0304	Engine misfire detected, cylinder #4
P0305	Engine misfire detected, cylinder #5
P0306	Engine misfire detected, cylinder #6
P0307	Engine misfire detected, cylinder #7
P0308	Engine misfire detected, cylinder #8
P0315	Crankshaft Position (CKP) system variation values not stored in PCM memory or not learned
P0325	Knock sensor circuit malfunction
P0327	Knock sensor or knock sensor 1 signal frequency outside normal range or low
P0332	Knock sensor or knock sensor 2 signal frequency outside normal range or low
P0335	No signal from Crankshaft Position (CKP) sensor for more than three seconds
P0336	Crankshaft Position (CKP) sensor signal incorrect for more than three seconds
P0337	Crankshaft Position (CKP) sensor circuit, low duty cycle
P0338	Crankshaft Position (CKP) sensor circuit, high duty cycle

Code	Possible cause
P0339	Crankshaft Position (CKP) sensor circuit intermittent
P0341	Camshaft Position (CMP) sensor signal not present or mismatch with CKP signal
P0342	Camshaft Position (CMP) signal, low voltage
P0343	Camshaft Position (CMP) signal, high voltage
P0351	Ignition Control (IC) circuit out of range
P0351	Ignition coil 1 control circuit
P0352	Ignition coil 2 control circuit
P0353	Ignition coil 3 control circuit
P0354	Ignition coil 4 control circuit
P0355	Ignition coil 5 control circuit
P0356	Ignition coil 6 control circuit
P0357	Ignition coil 7 control circuit
P0358	Ignition coil 8 control circuit
P0404	Exhaust Gas Recirculation (EGR) system, open position performance
P0410	Secondary Air Injection (AIR) system
P0420	Catalyst system (left cylinder bank), low efficiency
P0430	Catalyst system (right cylinder bank), low efficiency
P0440	Evaporative Emission (EVAP) system
P0442	Evaporative Emission (EVAP) control system, small leak detected
P0443	Evaporative Emission (EVAP) control system, purge solenoid control circuit
P0446	Evaporative Emission (EVAP) control system, vent system performance
P0449	Evaporative Emission (EVAP) control system, vent solenoid control circuit
P0451	Fuel Tank Pressure (FTP) sensor performance
P0452	Fuel tank Pressure (FTP) sensor circuit, low voltage
P0453	Fuel Tank Pressure (FTP) sensor circuit, high voltage
P0455	Evaporative Emission (EVAP) control system, large leak detected
P0461	Fuel level sensor 1 performance
P0462	Fuel level sensor 1 circuit, voltage too low
P0463	Fuel level sensor 1 circuit, voltage too high
P0464	Fuel level sensor 1 circuiit, intermittent voltage
P0496	Evaporative Emission (EVAP) system, excessive (intake manifold) vacuum present
P0500	Vehicle Speed Sensor (VSS) circuit
P0502	Vehicle Speed Sensor (VSS) circuit, low voltage
P0503	Vehicle Speed Sensor (VSS) circuit, intermittent voltage

Code	Possible cause
P0506	Idle speed performance lower than expected or out of range
P0507	Idle speed performance higher than expected or out of range
P0522	Engine Oil Pressure (EOP) sensor circuit, low voltage
P0523	Engine Oil Pressure (EOP) sensor circuit, high voltage
P0562	System voltage too low
P0563	System voltage too high
P0567	Cruise control resume switch circuit
P0568	Cruise control set switch circuit
P0571	Cruise control brake switch circuit
P0601	Powertrain Control Module (PCM) or Transmission Control Module (TCM) Read Only Memory (ROM)
P0602	Powertain Control Module (PCM) or Transmission Control Module (TCM) not programmed
P0603	Powertrain Control Module (PCM) or Transmission Control Module (TCM) long-term memory reset
P0604	Powertrain Control Module (PCM) or Transmission Control Module (TCM) Random Access Memory (RAM)
P0605	Powertrain Control Module (PCM) Read-Only Memory (ROM)
P0606	Powertrain Control Module (PCM) internal performance
P0608	Vehicle speed output circuit
P0609	Rear wheel speed sensor circuit
P060B	Powertrain Control Module (PCM) analog-to-digital performance
P061C	Powertrain Control Module (PCM) engine speed performance
P062C	Powertrain Control Module (PCM) vehicle speed performance
P062F	Internal Powertrain Control Module (PCM) Electronically Erasable Programmable Read-Only Memory (EEPROM) error
P0622	Alternator F terminal circuit
P0641	5-volt reference circuit, out of range or low voltage
P0650	Incorrect voltage on the Malfunction Indicator Lamp (MIL) control circuit
P0651	5-volt reference 2 circuit
P0705	Transmission Range (TR) switch circuit
P0706	Transmission Range (TR) switch performance
P0711	Transmission Fluid Temperature (TFT) sensor performance
P0712	Transmission Fluid Temperature (TFT) sensor circuit, low voltage
P0713	Transmission Fluid Temperature (TFT) sensor circuit, high voltage
P0716	Input Speed Sensor (ISS) performance
P0717	Input Speed Sensor (ISS) circuit, low voltage
P0719	Brake switch circuit, low voltage
P0722	Output Speed Sensor (OSS) circuit, low voltage

Code	Possible cause
P0723	Output Speed Sensor (OSS) circuit, intermittent
P0724	Brake switch circuit, high voltage
P0730	Incorrect gear ratio
P0740	Torque Converter Clutch (TCC) enable solenoid control circuit
P0741	Torque Converter Clutch (TCC) system, stuck off
P0742	Torque Converter Clutch (TCC) system, stuck on
P0748	Pressure Control (PC) solenoid control circuit
P0751	1-2 Shift Solenoid (SS) valve performance, no first or fourth gear
P0752	1-2 Shift Solenoid (SS) valve performance, no second or third gear
P0753	1-2 Shift Solenoid (SS) control circuit
P0756	2-3 Shift Solenoid (SS) valve performance, no first or second gear
P0757	2-3 Shift Solenoid (SS) valve performance, no third or fourth gear
P0758	2-3 Shift Solenoid (SS) control circuit
P0785	3-2 Shift Solenoid (SS) control circuit
P0856	Traction control torque request circuit
P0894	Transmission component slipping
P0961	Line Pressure Control (PC) solenoid system peformance
P0973	1-2 Shift Solenoid (SS) control circuit, low voltage
P0974	1-2 Shift Solenoid (SS) control circuit, high voltage
P0976	2-3 Shift Solenoid (SS) control circuit, low voltage
P0977	2-3 Shift Solenoid (SS) control circuit, high voltage

3   Accelerator Pedal Position (APP) sensors - replacement

2004 and later models with 4.8L, 5.3L and 6.0L V8 engines are equipped with the Throttle Actuator Control (TAC) system, which is an all-electronic (no accelerator cable) throttle control system. Instead of an accelerator cable, which provides a direct mechanical link between the position of the accelerator pedal and the position of the throttle plate inside the throttle body, TAC-equipped vehicles use a pair of Accelerator Pedal Position (APP) sensors at the accelerator pedal assembly to monitor the angle of the accelerator pedal. Each APP sensor is a potentiometer with three wires. The PCM provides each sensor with a 5-volt reference circuit and a low reference circuit. Each sensor has a signal circuit through which it provides the PCM with a voltage signal proportional to pedal movement. The PCM uses this information to open and close the throttle plate inside the throttle body. To replace either APP sensor on these vehicles, you must replace the entire accelerator

pedal assembly. The two APP sensors cannot be replaced separately from each other and they can't be replaced separately from the pedal assembly. Replacing the pedal assem-

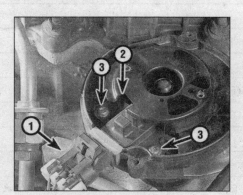

4.4 To remove the CMP sensor on a 4.3L V6 or a 5.0L, 5.7L or 7.4L V8, disconnect the electrical connector (1), align the square slot (2) in the reluctor with the sensor, then remove the two screws (3)

bly is simple and straightforward: simply disconnect the electrical connector and remove the pedal assembly mounting nuts. Unfortunately, you must check the throttle-opening and throttle-closing range with a proprietary factory scan tool when you're done, so we don't recommend tackling this job at home.

4   Camshaft Position (CMP) sensor - replacement

1   Disconnect the cable from the negative battery terminal (see Chapter 5, Section 1).
2   Remove the engine cover (see Chapter 11).

4.3L V6 and 5.0L, 5.7L and 7.4L V8 engines

Refer to illustration 4.4

Note: *The CMP sensor is located inside the distributor.*

3   Disconnect the spark plug wires and the ignition coil wire from the distributor cap, then remove the distributor cap and the rotor (see

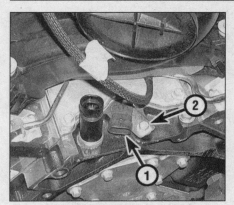

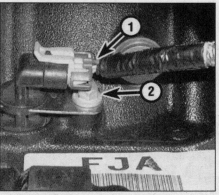

4.9 To remove the CMP sensor from a 4.8L, 5.3L or 6.0L V8, disconnect the electrical connector (1) and remove the CMP sensor mounting bolt (2) (5.3L V8 shown, other engines similar)

5.3 To detach the CKP sensor from the timing chain cover on a 4.3L V6 (shown) or a 5.0L, 5.7L or 7.4L V8, disconnect the electrical connector (1) and remove the sensor mounting bolt (2)

5.10 To detach the CKP sensor from the engine block on a 4.8L, 5.3L (shown) or 6.0L V8, disconnect the electrical connector (1) and remove the sensor mounting bolt (2)

Chapter 1).

4   Disconnect the CMP sensor electrical connector **(see illustration)**.

5   Rotate the crankshaft until the square slot in the reluctor is aligned with the CMP sensor.

6   Remove the sensor mounting screws and remove the CMP sensor.

7   When installing the CMP sensor, make sure that the square slot in the reluctor is aligned with the CMP sensor.

8   Installation is otherwise the reverse of removal. Be sure to tighten the CMP sensor mounting screws securely.

4.8L, 5.3L and 6.0L V8 engines

Refer to illustration 4.9

Note: *The CMP sensor is located on top and at the rear of the engine block valley.*

9   Disconnect the electrical connector from the CMP sensor **(see illustration)**.

10   Remove the CMP sensor mounting bolt and remove the CMP sensor.

11   Installation is the reverse of removal. Be sure to tighten the CMP sensor mounting bolt securely.

---

5   Crankshaft Position (CKP) sensor - replacement

1   Disconnect the cable from the negative battery terminal (see Chapter 5, Section 1).

2   Raise the front end of the vehicle and place it securely on jackstands.

4.3L V6 and 5.0L, 5.7L and 7.4L V8 engines

Refer to illustration 5.3

Note: *The CKP sensor is located on the front of the engine, on the timing chain cover.*

3   Disconnect the electrical connector from the CKP sensor **(see illustration)**.

4   Remove the CKP sensor mounting bolt **(see illustration 5.3)** and remove the sensor from the engine.

5   Remove the CKP sensor O-ring and

inspect it for cracks, tears and deterioration. If it's damaged, replace it.

6   Apply a small amount of engine oil to the O-ring and install the CKP sensor. Be sure to tighten the CKP sensor mounting bolt securely.

7   Installation is otherwise the reverse of removal.

8   When you're done, start the engine and note whether the Malfunction Indicator Light (MIL) is illuminated. If so, it's probably Diagnostic Trouble Code (DTC) 1336 - "CKP system variation not learned" - which means that the Powertrain Control Module (PCM) will need a little while to relearn the variation between the CKP and the CMP sensors, information that it needs to detect a misfire. A dealer technician can perform the "CKP system variation learn" procedure with a proprietary factory scan tool, then clear the DTC from the PCM's memory. At home, you can clear the DTC with an aftermarket scan tool but you can't perform the CKP system variation learn procedure. However, you should experience little or no effect on the driveability of the vehicle. If you *do* notice any difference in driveability, and if it persists for more than a few miles, have a dealer service department or other qualified repair shop perform the CKP system variation learn procedure for you and, if you don't have a scan tool at home, have the dealer or repair shop technician clear the DTC too.

4.8L, 5.3L and 6.0L V8 engines

Refer to illustration 5.10

Note: *The CKP sensor is located at the rear of the right side of the engine block, near the starter motor.*

9   Remove the starter motor (see Chapter 5).

10   Disconnect the CKP sensor electrical connector from the main engine harness **(see illustration)**.

11   Remove the CKP sensor mounting bolt **(see illustration 5.10)** and remove the sensor.

12   Installation is the reverse of removal. Be

sure to tighten the CMP sensor mounting bolt securely.

13   When you're done, start the engine and note whether the Malfunction Indicator Light (MIL) is illuminated. If so, it's probably Diagnostic Trouble Code (DTC) 0315 - "CKP system variation not learned" - which means that the Powertrain Control Module (PCM) will need a little while to relearn the variation between the CKP and the CMP sensors, information that it needs to detect a misfire. A dealer technician can perform the "CKP system variation learn" procedure with a proprietary factory scan tool, then clear the DTC from the PCM's memory. At home, you can clear the DTC with an aftermarket scan tool but you can't perform the CKP system variation learn procedure. However, you should experience little or no effect on the driveability of the vehicle. If you *do* notice any difference in driveability, and if it persists for more than a few miles, have a dealer service department or other qualified repair shop perform the CKP system variation learn procedure for you and, if you don't have a scan tool at home, have the dealer or repair shop technician clear the DTC too.

---

6   Engine Coolant Temperature (ECT) sensor - replacement

Warning: *Wait until the engine is completely cool before beginning this procedure.*

1   Disconnect the cable from the negative battery terminal (see Chapter 5, Section 1).

2   Drain the cooling system down to below the level of the sensor (see Chapter 1).

4.3L V6 and 5.0L, 5.7L and 7.4L V8 engines

Refer to illustrations 6.4a, 6.4b and 6.6

Note: *The ECT sensor is located at the front of the intake manifold, to the right of the EGR valve, on 1996 through 1999 4.3L V6 engines and on all 5.0L and 5.7L V8 engines. (It's in the same location on 7.4L engines, but there's*

6.4a To remove the ECT sensor from a 1996 through 1999 4.3L V6 (shown) or from any 5.0L, 5.7L or 7.4L V8, disconnect the electrical connector and unscrew the sensor from the coolant passage in the intake manifold

6.4b To remove the ECT sensor from the left cylinder head of a 2000 and later 4.3L V6 engine, disconnect the electrical connector and unscrew the sensor from the head

6.6 To prevent coolant from leaking past the threads of the ECT sensor, wrap them with Teflon tape

no EGR valve.) On 2000 and later 4.3L V6 engines the ECT sensor is located on the left side of the left cylinder head.

3   If you're replacing the ECT sensor on a 2000 or later 4.3L V6 engine, raise the front of the vehicle and place it securely on jackstands.

4   Disconnect the electrical connector from the ECT sensor **(see illustrations)**.

5   Using a deep socket, carefully unscrew the ECT sensor from the intake manifold.

6   To prevent leakage and thread corrosion, wrap the threads of the ECT sensor with Teflon sealing tape **(see illustration)** before installing the sensor. (Seal the sensor threads whether you're installing the old sensor or a new unit.)

7   Installation is otherwise the reverse of removal. Be sure to tighten the ECT sensor to the torque listed in this Chapter's Specifications.

8   When you're done, be sure to refill the cooling system (see Chapter 1).

4.8L, 5.3L and 6.0L V8 engines

Refer to illustration 6.10

Note: *The ECT sensor is located on the left side of the left cylinder head, near the front of the head.*

9   Raise the front of the vehicle and place it securely on jackstands.

10   Disconnect the electrical connector from the ECT sensor **(see illustration)**.

11   Using a deep socket, carefully unscrew the ECT sensor from the intake manifold.

12   To prevent leakage and thread corrosion, wrap the threads of the ECT sensor with Teflon sealing tape **(see illustration 6.6)** before installing the sensor. (Seal the sensor threads whether you're installing the old sensor or a new unit.)

13   Installation is otherwise the reverse of removal. Be sure to tighten the ECT sensor to the torque listed in this Chapter's Specifications.

14   When you're done, be sure to refill the cooling system (see Chapter 1).

7   Input Shaft Speed (ISS) and Output Shaft Speed (OSS) sensors - replacement

Refer to illustration 7.4

Note: *ISS and OSS sensors are located on the left side of 4L80-E and 4L85-E automatic transmissions; the ISS sensor near the front of the transmission and the OSS near the rear. ISS and OSS sensors are not used on 4L60-E and 4L65-E automatics, which are equipped instead with a single Vehicle Speed Sensor (VSS) (see Section 15 for the replacement procedure for the VSS).*

1   Disconnect the cable from the negative battery terminal (see Chapter 5, Section 1).

2   Raise the vehicle and support it securely on jackstands.

3   The ISS and OSS sensors are identical in appearance (and are replaced exactly the same way), so make sure that you've correctly identified the sensor that you wish to replace.

4   Disconnect the electrical connector from the ISS or OSS sensor **(see illustration)**.

5   Place a drain pan underneath the sensor

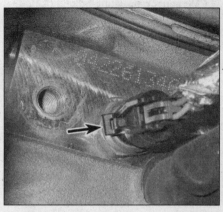

6.10 To remove the ECT sensor from the left cylinder head of a 4.8L, 5.3L or 6.0L V8, disconnect the electrical connector and unscrew the sensor from the head

that you're going to replace. Remove the sensor mounting bolt and pull out the sensor.

6   Installation is the reverse of removal.

7   When you're done, check the transmission fluid level (see Chapter 1) and add fluid as necessary.

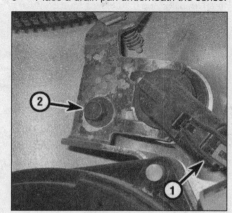

7.4 To remove an ISS or OSS sensor, disconnect the electrical connector (1) and remove the sensor mounting bolt (2) (ISS sensor shown, OSS sensor similar)

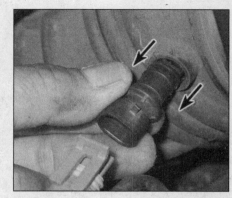

8.2 To remove the IAT sensor from the air intake duct on a 4.3L V6 or a 5.0L, 5.7L or 7.4L V8 engine, simply disconnect the electrical connector, then grasp the sensor firmly and carefully pull it out of its mounting hole in the intake duct

8 Intake Air Temperature (IAT) sensor - replacement

1   Disconnect the cable from the negative battery terminal (see Chapter 5, Section 1).

4.3L V6 and 5.0L, 5.7L and 7.4L V8 engines

Refer to illustration 8.2

Note: *The IAT sensor is located on the air intake duct.*

2   Disconnect the electrical connector from the IAT sensor **(see illustration)**.

3   To remove the IAT sensor, grasp it firmly and carefully pull it out of the air intake duct.

4   Inspect the IAT sensor mounting hole in the air intake duct for cracks, tears and deterioration. If the mounting hole is damaged, replace the air intake duct.

5   Installation is the reverse of removal.

4.8L, 5.3L and 6.0L V8 engines

6   The IAT sensor is an integral component of the Mass Air Flow (MAF) sensor (see Section 11).

9 Knock sensor(s) - replacement

1   Disconnect the cable from the negative battery terminal (see Chapter 5, Section 1).

4.3L V6 engine

Note: *The knock sensor is located on the rear part of the engine block, to the left of the distributor. On 1996 through 2000 models, the knock sensor is a threaded unit that is screwed into the block. On 2001 and later models, the knock sensor is in the same location but is bolted to the block.*

2   Remove the engine cover (Chapter 11).

3   Disconnect the electrical connector from the knock sensor.

4   Remove the knock sensor from the block. On 1996 through 2000 models, simply unscrew the knock sensor with a socket. On 2001 and later models, remove the knock

sensor mounting bolt.

5   Installation is the reverse of removal. Be sure to tighten the knock sensor or the knock sensor mounting bolt to the torque listed in this Chapter's Specifications. **Caution 1:** *Do NOT use thread sealant or thread locking compound on the threads of the knock sensor or the knock sensor mounting bolt.* **Caution 2:** *Over- or under-tightening the knock sensor or the knock sensor mounting bolt will affect knock sensor performance, which might affect the PCM's ability to prevent knocking.*

5.0L, 5.7L and 7.4L V8 engines

Refer to illustration 9.7

Note: *The knock sensor is located on the right side of the block, just ahead of the starter motor.*

6   Raise the front of the vehicle and place it securely on jackstands.

7   Disconnect the electrical connector from the knock sensor **(see illustration)**.

8   Unscrew and remove the knock sensor.

9   Installation is the reverse of removal. Be sure to tighten the knock sensor to the torque listed in this Chapter's Specifications. **Caution 1:** *Do NOT use thread sealant or thread locking compound on the threads of the knock sensor.* **Caution 2:** *Over- or under-tightening the knock sensor will affect knock sensor performance, which might affect the PCM's ability to prevent knocking.*

4.8L, 5.3L and 6.0L V8 engines

Refer to illustration 9.12

Note: *The two knock sensors are located on top of the engine, underneath the intake manifold. You have to remove the intake manifold to access either knock sensor.*

10   Remove the engine cover (Chapter 11).

11   Remove the intake manifold (see Chapter 2B).

12   Disconnect the electrical connector(s) from the knock sensor(s) **(see illustration)**.

13   Unscrew and remove the knock sensor(s).

14   Installation is the reverse of removal. Be sure to tighten the knock sensor(s) to

9.7 To remove the knock sensor from the engine block on a 5.0L or 5.7L V8 engine, disconnect the electrical connector from the knock sensor, then unscrew the sensor with an appropriate wrench or socket

the torque listed in this Chapter's Specifications. **Caution 1:** *Do NOT use thread sealant or thread locking compound on the threads of the knock sensor(s).* **Caution 2:** *Over- or under-tightening the knock sensor bolt will affect knock sensor performance, which might affect the PCM's ability to prevent knocking.*

10 Manifold Absolute Pressure (MAP) sensor - replacement

Refer to illustrations 10.3a and 10.3b

Note: *On 4.3L V6 and 5.0L, 5.7L and 7.4L V8 engines, the MAP sensor is located on the right side of the intake manifold. On 4.8L, 5.3L and 6.0L V8s, the MAP sensor is located on the rear part of the intake manifold.*

1   Disconnect the cable from the negative battery terminal (see Chapter 5, Section 1).

2   Remove the engine cover (Chapter 11).

3   Disconnect the electrical connector from the MAP sensor **(see illustrations)**.

9.12 To remove either knock sensor from a 4.8L, 5.3L or 6.0L V8 engine, disconnect the electrical connector, then unscrew the sensor with an appropriate deep socket

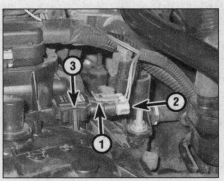

10.3a MAP sensor details - 4.3L V6, 5.0L (shown), 5.7L and 7.4L V8 engines
1   *Connector release tab*
2   *Electrical connector*
3   *Mounting bracket*

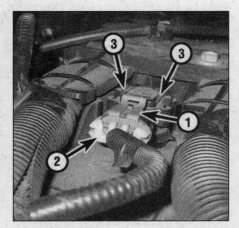

10.3b MAP sensor details - 4.8L (shown), 5.3L or 6.0L V8 engines
1   *Connector release tab*
2   *Electrical connector*
3   *Mounting bracket*

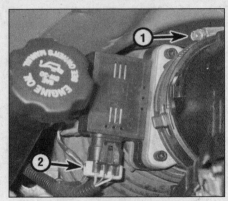

11.2 To detach the MAF sensor from the air filter housing on a 4.3L V6 or 5.0L (shown), 5.7L or 7.4L V8, loosen the clamp screw (1), separate the sensor from the housing cover, then disconnect the electrical connector (2)

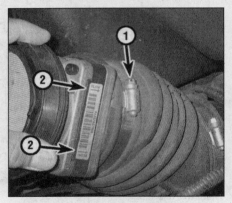

11.3 To detach the MAF sensor from the intake duct on a 4.3L V6 or 5.0L (shown), 5.7L or 7.4L V8, loosen the clamp screw (1), then remove the sensor. The arrows (2) on the bar code must point toward the duct when installing the sensor

11.6 To disconnect the electrical connector from the MAF sensor on 4.8L, 5.3L or 6.0L V8, pry off the Connector Position Assurance (CPA) retainer, if equipped, then disconnect the connector

11.7 To remove the air intake duct elbow from a 4.8L, 5.3L or 6.0L V8, loosen these hose clamp screws and remove the elbow

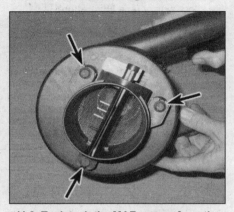

11.9 To detach the MAF sensor from the air filter housing on a 4.8L, 5.3L or 6.0L V8, remove these three bolts

7   Loosen the three hose clamp screws **(see illustration)** and remove the air intake duct elbow.
8   Remove the air filter housing (see Chapter 4).
9   To detach the MAF sensor from the air filter housing, remove the three mounting bolts **(see illustration)** and separate the sensor from the filter housing.
10   Installation is the reverse of removal. Be sure to tighten the MAF sensor mounting bolts securely.

---

12   Oxygen sensors - general description and replacement

General description

1   The oxygen in the exhaust reacts with the elements inside the oxygen sensor to produce a voltage output that varies from 0.1 volt (high oxygen, lean mixture) to 0.9 volt (low oxygen, rich mixture). The pre-converter oxygen sensor (mounted in the exhaust system before the catalytic converter) provides a feedback signal to the PCM that indicates the amount of leftover oxygen in the exhaust. The PCM monitors this variable voltage continuously to determine the required fuel injector pulse width and to control the engine air/fuel ratio. A mixture ratio of 14.7 parts air to 1 part fuel is the ideal ratio for minimum exhaust emissions, as well as the best combination for fuel economy and engine performance. Based on oxygen sensor signals, the PCM tries to maintain this air/fuel ratio of 14.7:1 at all times.
2   The post-converter oxygen sensor (mounted in the exhaust system after the catalytic converter) has no effect on PCM control of the air/fuel ratio. However, the post-converter sensor is identical to the pre-converter sensor and operates in the same way. The PCM uses the post-converter signal to monitor the efficiency of the catalytic converter. A post-converter oxygen sensor will produce a slower fluctuating voltage signal that reflects

4   Insert a pair of small screwdrivers between each side of the MAP sensor and its mounting bracket and carefully pry the sensor loose from the mounting bracket. (You might encounter a little resistance because of the accordion-pleated seal on the pipe that protrudes from the underside of the sensor into the manifold.)
5   Remove the MAP sensor O-ring and inspect it for cracks, tears and deterioration. If the O-ring is damaged, replace it.
6   Installation is the reverse of removal.

---

11   Mass Air Flow (MAF) sensor - replacement

1   Disconnect the cable from the negative battery terminal (see Chapter 5, Section 1).

4.3L V6 and 5.0L, 5.7L and 7.4L V8 engines

Refer to illustrations 11.2 and 11.3
Note: *The MAF sensor is located between the air filter housing and the air intake duct.*

2   To detach the MAF sensor from the air filter housing cover, loosen the hose clamp screw **(see illustration)** and carefully separate the MAF sensor from the cover.
3   To detach the MAF sensor from the air intake duct, loosen the hose clamp screw **(see illustration)** and carefully separate the MAF sensor from the intake duct.
4   Note the directional arrows on the bar code label on the edge of the MAF sensor. These arrows indicate the direction of air flowing through the MAF sensor. When you install the old MAF sensor, or a new unit, make sure that these directional arrows are facing toward the air intake duct.
5   Installation is otherwise the reverse of removal.

4.8L, 5.3L and 6.0L V8 engines

Refer to illustrations 11.6, 11.7 and 11.9
Note: *The MAF sensor is located between the air filter housing and the air intake duct.*
6   Remove the Connector Position Assurance (CPA) retainer, if equipped **(see illustration)**, then disconnect the MAF sensor electrical connector.

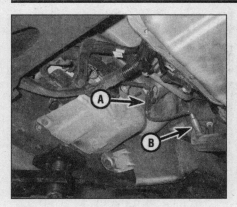

12.8a Typical left cylinder bank upstream oxygen sensor setup: electrical connector (A) and upstream sensor (B) (5.0L V8 shown, other engines similar)

12.8b Typical right cylinder bank upstream oxygen sensor. On some sensors, such as this one, the electrical connector might not be obvious. To find it, trace the electrical lead from the sensor to the connector (5.0L V8 engine shown, other engines similar)

12.8c Typical downstream (post-catalyst) oxygen sensor. Again, if the connector for the sensor isn't visible, just trace the electrical lead from the sensor to the connector

the lower oxygen content in the post-catalyst exhaust.

3   Oxygen sensor configuration varies depending on the model and on where it is sold, i.e. "Federal" (49-State) model or "California" model. On vehicles equipped with the Federal (49-State) emissions package and on some California models, there is one upstream and one downstream oxygen sensor. On these vehicles, the upstream oxygen sensor is located in the exhaust pipe ahead of the catalyst and the downstream sensor is located on the pipe behind the catalyst. On some vehicles equipped with the California emissions package (those with two catalysts, one for each cylinder bank) there are two upstream sensors (one in each exhaust pipe between the exhaust manifold and the catalyst) and two downstream sensors (one behind each catalyst).

4   An oxygen sensor produces no voltage when it is below its normal operating temperature of about 600-degrees F. During this warm-up period, the PCM operates in an open-loop fuel control mode. It does not use the oxygen sensor signal as a feedback indication of residual oxygen in the exhaust. Instead, the PCM controls fuel metering based on the inputs of other sensors and its own programs.

5   An oxygen sensor depends on four conditions in order to operate correctly:

a) *Electrical* - The low voltage generated by the sensor requires good, clean connections. Always check the connectors whenever an oxygen sensor problem is suspected or indicated.

b) *Outside air supply* - The sensor needs air circulation to the internal portion of the sensor. Whenever the sensor is installed, make sure that the air passages are not restricted.

c) *Correct operating temperature* - The PCM will not react to the sensor signal until the sensor reaches approximately 600-degrees F. This factor must be considered when evaluating the performance of the sensor.

d) *Unleaded fuel* - Unleaded fuel is essential for correct sensor operation.

6   The PCM can detect several different oxygen sensor problems and set Diagnostic Trouble Codes (DTCs) to indicate the specific fault (see Section 2). When an oxygen sensor DTC occurs, the PCM disregards the oxygen sensor signal voltage and reverts to open-loop fuel control as described previously.

Replacement

Refer to illustrations 12.8a, 12.8b and 12.8c

Note: *Since the exhaust pipe contracts when cool, the oxygen sensor may be hard to loosen. To make sensor removal easier, start*

the engine and let it run for a minute or two, then turn it off.

7   Raise the vehicle and place it securely on jackstands.

8   Locate the upstream or downstream oxygen sensor **(see illustrations)**, trace the sensor's electrical lead to the sensor electrical connector and disconnect it.

9   Remove the upstream or downstream oxygen sensor. On some models you can remove the sensors with a wrench. But if there isn't room to put a wrench on a sensor, use an oxygen sensor socket (available at most auto parts stores). Because an oxygen sensor socket is turned by a ratchet, it will fit into tight spaces where there isn't enough room to turn a wrench.

10   If necessary, clean the threads inside the sensor mounting hole in the exhaust pipe with an appropriate tap.

11   If you're installing the old sensor, clean off the threads, then apply a coat of anti-seize compound to the threads before installing the sensor. If you're installing a new sensor, do NOT apply anti-seize compound; new sensors are already coated with anti-seize.

12   Installation is otherwise the reverse of removal. Be sure to tighten the oxygen sensor to the torque listed in this Chapter's Specifications.

13   Park/Neutral Position (PNP) switch - replacement

Refer to illustrations 13.4, 13.6a, 13.6b and 13.8

1   Disconnect the cable from the negative terminal of the battery (see Chapter 5, Section 1).

2   Apply the parking brake and put the shift lever in NEUTRAL.

3   Raise the vehicle and place it securely on jackstands.

4   Unplug the electrical connectors from the PNP switch **(see illustration)**.

5   Disconnect the shift cable from the manual lever (see Chapter 7).

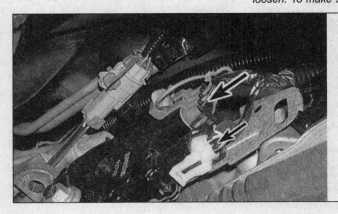

13.4 Disconnect the electrical connectors from the PNP switch

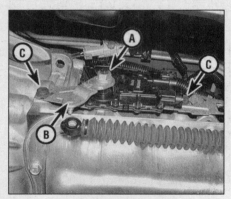

13.6a To detach the PNP switch from the transmission, remove the manual lever retaining nut (A), the manual lever (B) and the PNP switch mounting bolts (C)

13.6b If you accidentally move the manual lever out of the NEUTRAL position while removing it, be sure to install the lever on the manual shaft and to reposition it in NEUTRAL before removing the PNP switch

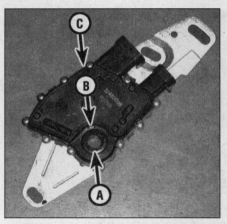

13.8 When installing a new PNP switch, put it in the NEUTRAL position by aligning the two raised ridges (A) on the rotating part of the switch with the two alignment marks (B) and with the groove (C) on the edge of the switch

6   Remove the manual lever retaining nut and remove the manual lever from the manual shaft **(see illustration)**. Note: *Be careful not to move the manual lever from the NEUTRAL position while removing it. If you accidentally move the lever, install the manual lever on the manual shaft again and reposition the lever at NEUTRAL before removing the PNP switch* **(see illustration)**.
7   Remove the switch retaining bolts and detach the switch from the transmission **(see illustration 13.6a)**.
8   If you're installing a new switch, align the slots on the switch (where the shaft is inserted) with the alignment marks on the switch and the notch in the edge of the switch **(see illustration)**. Then install the switch onto the manual shaft.
9   If you're installing the old switch, simply align the flats of the shift shaft with the flats of the PNP switch and install the switch.
10   Installation is otherwise the reverse of removal.
11   When you're done, verify that the engine will start only in PARK or NEUTRAL. If it starts in any other gear, readjust the switch. To readjust the switch, loosen the switch mounting bolts and turn the switch slightly one way

or the other until the engine now only starts in PARK or NEUTRAL, then tighten the mounting bolts securely.

---

14   Throttle Position (TP) sensor - replacement

---

1   Disconnect the cable from the negative battery terminal (see Chapter 5, Section 1).

4.3L V6 and 5.0L, 5.7L and 7.4L V8 engines
Refer to illustrations 14.4, 14.5 and 14.6
Note: *The TP sensor is located on the throttle body.*
2   Remove the engine cover (see Chapter 11).
3   Remove the air intake duct (see Chapter 4).
4   Disconnect the electrical connector from the TP sensor **(see illustration)**.
5   Remove the TP sensor mounting screws **(see illustration)** and remove the TP sensor from the throttle body.

6   When installing the TP sensor on the throttle body, align the sensor so that the flat surface on the inside of the TP sensor rotating ring is aligned with the flat surface on the throttle shaft **(see illustration)**. If the sensor fits flush against the throttle body, then you've installed the sensor correctly. If the sensor doesn't fit flush against the throttle body, then the locating flats on the inside of the rotating ring and the end of the throttle shaft are not correctly aligned. Pull off the sensor, align the flats and try installing it again.
7   Installation is otherwise the reverse of removal. Be sure to tighten the TP sensor mounting screws securely.

4.8L, 5.3L and 6.0L V8 engines
Refer to illustrations 14.9 and 14.10
Note: *The TP sensor is located on the throttle body.*
8   Remove the air intake duct (see Chapter 4).
9   Disconnect the electrical connector from the TP sensor **(see illustration)**.

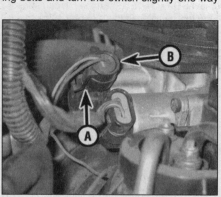

14.4 To disconnect the electrical connector from the TP sensor on a 4.3L V6 or 5.0L, 5.7L or 7.4L V8 engine, pry the lock tab (A) loose, then pull off the connector (B)

14.5 To detach the TP sensor from the throttle body on a 4.3L V6, 5.0L (shown), 5.7L or 7.4L V8 engine, remove these two mounting screws

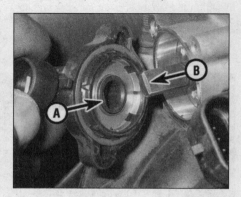

14.6 To install the TP sensor, align the flat surface (A) inside the rotating ring with the flat surface (B) on the end of the throttle shaft (5.0L V8 shown, other engines similar)

14.9 On 4.8L, 5.3L (shown) and 6.0L V8 engines, the TP sensor (A) is located on the left side of the throttle body, near the alternator. To remove it, disconnect the electrical connector (B) . . .

10   Remove the TP sensor mounting screws (see illustration).
11   When installing the TP sensor on the throttle body, align the sensor so that the flat surface on the inside of the TP sensor rotating ring is aligned with the flat surface on the throttle shaft (see illustration 14.6). If the sensor fits flush against the throttle body, then you've installed the sensor correctly. If the sensor doesn't fit flush against the throttle body, then the locating flats on the inside of the rotating ring and the end of the throttle shaft are not correctly aligned. Pull off the sensor, align the flats and try installing it again.
12   Installation is otherwise the reverse of removal. Be sure to tighten the TP sensor mounting screws securely.

15   Vehicle Speed Sensor (VSS) - replacement

Refer to illustration 15.4
Note: *The VSS is located on the right side of the extension housing on 4L60-E and 4L65-E transmissions. The VSS is not used on 4L80-E and 4L85-E transmissions, both of which are instead equipped with an Input Shaft Speed (ISS) and Output Shaft Speed (OSS) sensor (see Section 7 for the replacement procedure for these two sensors.)*
1   Disconnect the cable from the negative battery terminal (see Chapter 5, Section 1).
2   Raise the vehicle and place it securely on jackstands.
3   Place a drain pan under the VSS to catch any spilled transmission fluid.
4   Disconnect the electrical connector from the VSS (see illustration).
5   Remove the VSS mounting bolt and remove the VSS from the transmission. If the VSS is difficult to remove, grasp it firmly and wiggle it from side-to-side while working it out of the transmission.
6   If the VSS is equipped with an O-ring, remove the O-ring and inspect it for cracks, tears and deterioration. If the O-ring is damaged, replace it. If you're going to install a

14.10 . . . then remove these two mounting screws

new VSS, replace the O-ring even if the old O-ring looks okay.
7   Installation is the reverse of removal.
8   Check the level of the transmission fluid and refill as necessary (see Chapter 1).

16   Powertrain Control Module (PCM) - removal and installation

1996 through 2000 models
Refer to illustrations 16.1, 16.3a, 16.3b and 16.4
Caution: *Avoid static electricity damage to the Powertrain Control Module by grounding yourself to the body of the vehicle before touching the PCM and using a special anti-static pad on which to store the PCM or ECM once it's removed.*
Note 1: *Anytime the PCM is replaced with a new unit, it must be reprogrammed with a scan tool by a dealership service department or other qualified repair shop.*
Note 2: *Anytime the battery is disconnected, stored operating parameters may be lost from the PCM, causing the engine to run rough for a period of time while the PCM relearns the information.*

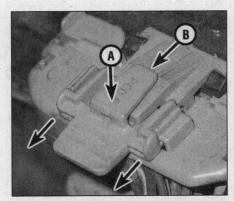

16.3a To remove the Connector Position Assurance (CPA) retainer (A) from each PCM electrical connector, pry up the connector locking tab (B) and slide off the retainer

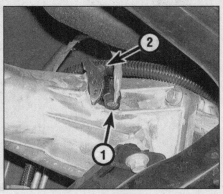

15.4 To remove the VSS, disconnect the electrical connector (1) and remove the sensor mounting bolt (2)

16.1 On 1996 through 2000 models, the PCM is located on the left side of the engine compartment, below the brake master cylinder

1   The PCM (see illustration) is located at the left side of the engine compartment, below the brake master cylinder.
2   Disconnect the cable from the negative terminal of the battery (see Chapter 5, Section 1).
3   Carefully disconnect the PCM electrical connectors (see illustrations).

16.3b To disconnect each electrical connector from the PCM, push down on this lock tab, then pull off the connector

16.4 To detach the PCM from its mounting bracket on 1996 through 2000 models, pry off both spring clips with a screwdriver

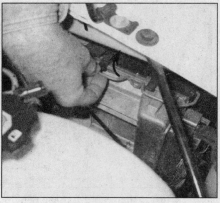

16.8 To detach the PCM from its mounting bracket on 2001 and later models, lift up this spring latch. Then carefully rotate the PCM so that the electrical connectors are facing up and disconnect the connectors

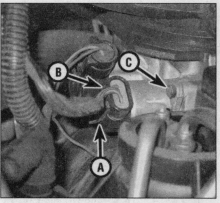

17.3 Release the lock tab (A) and disconnect the IAC valve electrical connector (B). To detach the IAC valve from the throttle body, remove the two mounting screws (C) (only one screw shown)

4   Remove the spring clips **(see illustration)** and carefully remove the PCM from its mounting bracket.

5   Installation is the reverse of removal.

2001 and later models
Refer to illustration 16.8

6   The PCM is located in the left front corner of the engine compartment, right behind the windshield washer fluid reservoir.

7   Disconnect the cable from the negative terminal of the battery (see Chapter 5, Section 1). Remove the air filter housing (see Chapter 4).

8   To detach the PCM from its mounting bracket, swing up the spring latch **(see illustration)**.

9   Carefully rotate the PCM so that the electrical connectors are facing up, then disconnect all connectors **(see illustrations 16.3a and 16.3b)** and remove the PCM.

10   Installation is the reverse of removal.

---

17 Idle Air Control (IAC) valve - replacement

1   Disconnect the cable from the negative terminal of the battery (see Chapter 5, Section 1).

2   Remove the engine cover (see Chapter 11).

4.3L V6 and 5.0L, 5.7L and 7.4L V8 engines
Refer to illustrations 17.3 and 17.7
Note: *The IAC valve is located on the throttle body.*

3   Disconnect the electrical connector from the IAC valve **(see illustration)**.

4   Remove the IAC valve mounting screws **(see illustration 17.3)** and remove the IAC valve.

5   Remove the IAC valve O-ring. Always use a new O-ring when installing the IAC valve.

6   Inspect the surface of the IAC valve pintle, the seating surface for the IAC valve mounting flange and the surface of the air passage inside the throttle body for heavy carbon deposits. If necessary, clean the IAC valve pintle, the flange mounting surface and the air passage with aerosol carburetor cleaner, a shop towel and a soft brush. Do NOT immerse the IAC valve in carb cleaner

(or in any liquid cleaner). If you're unable to clean the air passage adequately, remove the throttle body (see Chapter 4) and clean it thoroughly.

7   If you're installing a new IAC valve, measure the distance from the tip of the pintle valve to the IAC valve mounting flange **(see illustration)**. If the distance is more than 1-1/8 inch, press in the pintle by hand until the distance is less than 1-1/8 inch. **Caution:** *Do NOT try to press in the pintle on a used IAC valve. The force necessary to do so could damage the IAC valve.*

8   Install a new O-ring and lubricate it with a light coat of clean engine oil.

9   Installation is the reverse of removal.

10   When you're done, reset the IAC valve as follows:

a) *Start the engine and allow it to run for about 20 seconds.*

b) *Turn the ignition key to OFF for 10 seconds.*

c) *Start the engine again.*

d) *Verify that the idle speed is correct.*

17.7 Before installing a new IAC valve, measure the distance from the tip of the pintle to the mounting flange. If the distance is more than 1-1/8 inch, press in the pintle until the distance is correct

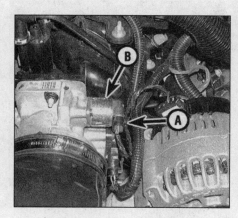

17.11 Disconnect the electrical connector (A) from the IAC valve (B) (4.8L, 5.3L and 6.0L V8 engines)

17.12 To detach the IAC valve from the throttle body on a 4.8L, 5.3L (shown) or 6.0L V8 engine, remove these two mounting screws

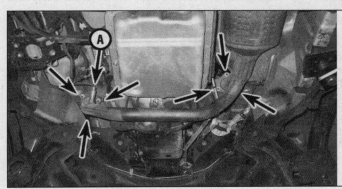

18.6a Trace the electrical lead from the upstream oxygen sensor (A) to its connector and unplug it, then remove the sensor. Then remove all six flange nuts and bolts

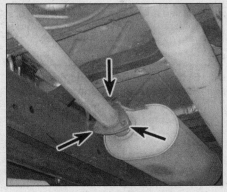

18.6b Disconnect the downstream oxygen sensor electrical connector and remove the sensor, then remove the catalyst pipe-to-muffler flange nuts and bolts

4.8L, 5.3L and 6.0L V8 engines

Refer to illustrations 17.11 and 17.12

Note: *The IAC valve is located on the throttle body.*

11   Disconnect the electrical connector from the IAC valve **(see illustration)**.

12   Remove the IAC valve mounting screws **(see illustration)** and remove the IAC valve.

13   Remove the IAC valve O-ring. Always use a new O-ring when installing the IAC valve.

14   Inspect the surface of the IAC valve pintle, the seating surface for the IAC valve mounting flange and the surface of the air passage inside the throttle body for heavy carbon deposits. If necessary, clean the IAC valve pintle, the flange mounting surface and the air passage with aerosol carburetor cleaner, a shop towel and a soft brush. Do NOT immerse the IAC valve in carb cleaner (or in any liquid cleaner). If you're unable to clean the air passage adequately, remove the throttle body (see Chapter 4) and clean it thoroughly.

15   If you're installing a new IAC valve, measure the distance from the tip of the pintle valve to the IAC valve mounting flange **(see illustration 17.7)**. If the distance is more than 1-1/8 inch, press in the pintle by hand until the distance is less than 1-1/8 inch. **Caution:** *Do NOT try to press in the pintle on a used IAC valve. The force necessary to do so could damage the IAC valve.*

16   Install a new O-ring and lubricate it with a light coat of clean engine oil.

17   Installation is the reverse of removal.

---

18 Catalytic converter - general description, check and replacement

Note: *Because of a Federally-mandated extended warranty which covers emission-related components such as the catalytic converter, check with a dealer service department before replacing the converter at your own expense.*

General description

1   A catalytic converter (or catalyst) is an emission control device in the exhaust system that reduces certain pollutants in the exhaust gas stream. There are two types of converters.

An oxidation catalyst reduces hydrocarbons (HC) and carbon monoxide (CO). A reduction catalyst reduces oxides of nitrogen (NOx). A catalyst that can reduce *all three pollutants* is known as a "Three-Way Catalyst" (TWC). All models covered by this manual are equipped with TWCs.

Check

2   The test equipment for a catalytic converter (a "loaded-mode" dynamometer and 5-gas analyzer) is expensive. If you suspect that the converter on your vehicle is malfunctioning, take it to a dealer or authorized emission inspection facility for diagnosis and repair.

3   Whenever you raise the vehicle to service underbody components, inspect the converter for leaks, corrosion, dents and other damage. Carefully inspect the welds and/or flange bolts and nuts that attach the front and rear ends of the converter to the exhaust system. If you note any damage, replace the converter.

4   Although catalytic converters don't break too often, they can become clogged or even plugged up. The easiest way to check for a restricted converter is to use a vacuum gauge to diagnose the effect of a blocked exhaust on intake vacuum.

a) *Connect a vacuum gauge to an intake manifold vacuum source (see Chapter 2).*

b) *Warm the engine to operating temperature, place the transaxle in Park (automatic models) or Neutral (manual models) and apply the parking brake.*

c) *Note the vacuum reading at idle and jot it down.*

d) *Quickly open the throttle to near its wide-open position and then quickly get off the throttle and allow it to close. Note the vacuum reading and jot it down.*

e) *Do this test three more times, recording your measurement after each test.*

f) *If your fourth reading is more than one in-Hg lower than the reading that you noted at idle, the exhaust system might be restricted (the catalytic converter could be plugged, OR an exhaust pipe or muffler could be restricted).*

Replacement

Refer to illustrations 18.6a and 18.6b

Warning: *Make sure that the exhaust system*

is completely cooled down before proceeding. If the vehicle has just been driven, the catalytic converter can be hot enough to cause serious burns.

Note: *The photos accompanying this procedure are of a 1999 5.0L V8 model with a single catalyst, short pipes welded to either end of the catalyst, with three-hole mounting flanges at the front end of the forward pipe and at the rear end of the rear pipe. Most models use a similar setup. However, some models with a 7.4L or 6.0L V8 are equipped with two catalysts, two exhaust pipes and two mufflers. But the procedure for removing either catalyst on one of these models is similar to the procedure outlined below.*

5   Raise the vehicle and place it securely on jackstands.

6   Spray a liberal amount of penetrant onto the threads of the exhaust manifold-to-catalyst pipe nuts and bolts and the catalyst pipe-to-exhaust pipe nuts and bolts behind the catalyst **(see illustrations)**, then wait awhile for the penetrant to loosen things up.

7   While you're waiting for the penetrant to do its work, disconnect the electrical connectors for the upstream and downstream oxygen sensor and remove both oxygen sensors (see Section 12).

8   Unscrew the exhaust manifold-to-catalyst pipe flange nuts and bolts. If they're still difficult to loosen, spray the threads with some more penetrant, wait awhile and try again.

9   Unscrew the e clamp that secures the slip joint between the exhaust pipe behind the catalytic converter and the pipe ahead of the muffler, back off the nut. If it's still difficult to loosen, spray the threads with some more penetrant, wait awhile and try again.

10   Remove the catalytic converter assembly. Remove and discard the old flange gasket.

11   Installation is the reverse of removal. Be sure to use a new flange gasket at the exhaust manifold mounting flange. Use new bolts at the front flange. Although the slip joint clamp doesn't get as overheated as the exhaust manifold flange bolts, it's still a good idea to use a new clamp. Coat the threads

of the clamp and the exhaust manifold bolts with anti-seize compound to facilitate future removal. Tighten the fasteners securely.

19   Evaporative emissions control (EVAP) system - general description and component replacement

General description

1   The **Evaporative Emissions Control (EVAP) system** prevents fuel system vapors (which contain unburned hydrocarbons) from escaping into the atmosphere. On warm days, vapors trapped inside the fuel tank expand until the pressure reaches a certain threshold, at which point the fuel vapors are routed from the fuel tank through the fuel vapor vent valve and the fuel vapor control valve to the EVAP canister, where they're stored temporarily, until they can be consumed by the engine during normal operation. When the conditions are right (engine warmed up, vehicle up to speed, moderate or heavy load on the engine, etc.) the Powertrain Control Module (PCM) opens the canister purge solenoid, which allows the fuel vapors to be drawn from the canister into the intake manifold, where they mix with the air/fuel mixture before being consumed in the combustion chambers. This system is complex and virtually impossible to troubleshoot without the right tools and training. However, the following description should give you a good idea of how the system works and where the components are located:

2   The **EVAP canister**, which contains activated carbon, is the repository for storing the fuel vapors. You'll have to raise the vehicle to inspect or replace the canister but it's designed to be maintenance-free and should last the life of the vehicle. On 1996 through 2002 models, the EVAP canister is located on top of the forward part of the fuel tank. On 2003 and later models, the EVAP canister is located underneath the vehicle, just in front of the fuel tank.

3   The **EVAP canister vent valve** is normally open. But it seals off the EVAP system for inspection and maintenance (I/M 240) testing and for OBD-II leak and pressure tests. The vent valve is located under the vehicle, near the EVAP canister. On 1996 through 2002 models with ABS, it's near the hydraulic control unit for the ABS system, which is located ahead of the EVAP canister.

4   The **EVAP system fuel tank pressure sensor**, which is located on top of the fuel tank, on the fuel pump/fuel level sending unit module, monitors the pressure of unburned fuel vapors inside the fuel tank and provides a voltage signal to the PCM that's proportional to the pressure. In cold weather, the vapors inside the tank cool off and contract. Because the tank is a closed system, it could be damaged by a radical difference in pressure between the relative vacuum inside and the ambient (outside) air pressure. If the pres-

sure inside the tank drops below a specified threshold, the PCM opens the vent valve and allows ambient air to enter the tank, equalizing the pressure. In hot weather, the vapors inside the fuel tank expand. If the pressure *exceeds* a specified threshold while the vehicle is parked, the expanding pressure inside the tank forces the vapors out of the tank, through the EVAP line and into the EVAP canister, where they're absorbed by the activated charcoal inside the canister. If the pressure inside the fuel tank becomes excessive while the vehicle is in operation, the PCM energizes the EVAP purge solenoid to open, allowing intake manifold vacuum to draw excess fuel vapors from the canister and from the fuel tank into the manifold, where they're mixed with the incoming air/fuel mixture and burned up in combustion.

5   The **EVAP canister purge solenoid**, which is under the control of the Powertrain Control Module (PCM), regulates the flow of vapors being purged from the EVAP canister into the intake manifold. The canister purge solenoid is normally closed. It opens only when directed to do so by the PCM, which uses the availability of intake manifold vacuum and data from various information sensor inputs to determine when and how long to open the valve. The interval of time during which the purge valve is opened by the PCM is known as its "duty cycle." The canister purge solenoid valve is located in the engine compartment, where it is attached to the side of the fuse and relay box. On 4.3L V6 and 5.0L and 5.7L engines, the EVAP canister purge solenoid is located on the right side of the intake manifold. On 7.4L engines, the purge solenoid is located on the left front side of the intake manifold. On 4.8L, 5.3L and 6.0L V8 engines, the purge solenoid is located on top of the intake manifold, at the front, right behind the throttle body.

General system checks

6   The most common symptom of a faulty EVAP system is a strong fuel odor (particularly during hot weather). If you smell fuel while driving or (more likely) right after you park the vehicle and turn off the engine, check the fuel filler cap first. Make sure that it's screwed onto the fuel filler neck all the way. If the odor persists, inspect all EVAP hose connections, both in the engine compartment and under the vehicle. You'll have to raise the vehicle and place it securely on jackstands to inspect most of the EVAP system, since it's located under the vehicle. Be sure to inspect each hose attached to the canister for damage and leakage along its entire length. Repair or replace as necessary. Inspect the canister for damage and look for fuel leaking from the bottom. If fuel is leaking or the canister is otherwise damaged, replace it.

7   Poor idle, stalling, and poor driveability can be caused by a defective fuel vapor vent valve or canister purge solenoid, a damaged canister, cracked hoses, or hoses connected to the wrong tubes. Fuel loss or fuel odor can

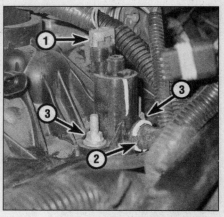

19.11a To remove the canister purge solenoid on 4.3L V6, 5.0L (shown), 5.7L or 7.4L V8 engines, disconnect the electrical connector (1), the purge hose (2) and remove the mounting nuts (3)

be caused by fuel leaking from fuel lines or hoses, a cracked or damaged canister, or a defective vapor valve.

8   To check for excessive fuel vapor pressure in the fuel tank, remove the gas cap and listen for the sound of pressure release. If the fuel tank emits a "whooshing" sound when you open the filler cap, fuel tank vapor pressure is excessive. Inspect the canister vapor hoses and the canister inlet port for blockage or collapsed hoses. Also inspect the hose for the EVAP canister vent valve. A complete test can only be done with a proprietary OBD-II scan tool (see Section 2), which will run a series of checks to detect excessive pressure. You'll have to take the vehicle to a dealer service department to have the EVAP system professionally diagnosed.

Component replacement

EVAP canister purge solenoid
Refer to illustrations 19.11a and 19.11b
Note: *On 4.3L V6 and 5.0L and 5.7L engines, the EVAP canister purge solenoid is located on the right side of the intake manifold. On 7.4L engines, the purge solenoid is located on the left front side of the intake manifold. On 4.8L, 5.3L and 6.0L V8 engines, the purge solenoid is located on top of the intake manifold, at the front, right behind the throttle body.*

9   Disconnect the cable from the negative battery terminal (see Chapter 5, Section 1).
10   Remove the engine cover (Chapter 11).
11   Disconnect the electrical connector from the EVAP canister purge solenoid **(see illustrations)**.
12   Disconnect the EVAP purge hose from the purge solenoid.
13   On 4.3L V6, 5.0L, 5.7L and 7.4L V8 engines, remove the EVAP canister purge solenoid mounting nuts and remove the solenoid.
14   On 4.8L, 5.3L and 6.0L V8 engines, remove the EVAP canister purge solenoid mounting bolt and insulator and remove the solenoid.

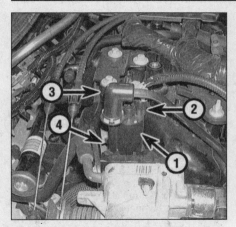

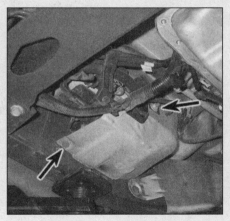

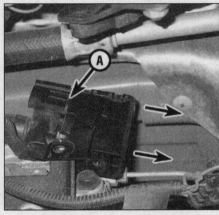

19.11b To detach the EVAP canister purge solenoid (1) from the intake manifold of a 4.8L, 5.3L (shown) or 6.0L V8 engine, disconnect the electrical connector (2), the purge hose (3) and remove the mounting bolt (4)

19.18 If a 1996 through 2002 vehicle is equipped with ABS, remove the rock shield for the hydraulic control unit to access the EVAP vent valve

19.19 To separate the vent valve from its mounting bracket on a 1996 through 2002 model, pry open the locking tang (A), firmly grasp the bracket and the valve and pull the valve out of the bracket

15   Installation is the reverse of removal. On 4.8L, 5.3L and 6.0L V8 engines, don't forget to install the insulator on the purge solenoid before installing the mounting bolt. And be sure to tighten the purge solenoid mounting nuts or bolt to the torque listed in this Chapter's Specifications.

EVAP canister vent valve

16   Disconnect the cable from the negative battery terminal (see Chapter 5, Section 1).
17   Raise the vehicle and place it securely on jackstands.

1996 through 2002 models
Refer to illustrations 19.18, 19.19 and 19.20
Note: *The EVAP canister vent valve is located under the left side of the vehicle, right behind the engine compartment, in front of the EVAP canister. On vehicles equipped with ABS, the vent valve mounting bracket is secured by one of the fasteners for the hydraulic control unit rock shield.*

18   If the vehicle is equipped with ABS, remove the rock shield for the ABS hydraulic control unit **(see illustration)**.
19   Pry open the tang on the vent valve mounting bracket **(see illustration)** and slide the vent valve out of its mounting bracket.
20   Disconnect the electrical connector and the EVAP vent hose from the vent valve **(see illustration)** and remove the valve.
21   Installation is the reverse of removal.

2003 and later models
Refer to illustrations 19.22 and 19.23
Note: *The EVAP canister vent valve is located to the left of the EVAP canister, which is mounted in front of the fuel tank.*
22   Locate the EVAP canister vent valve next to the EVAP canister **(see illustration)**.
23   Disconnect the EVAP canister vent valve electrical connector and the EVAP vent hose from the vent valve **(see illustration)**.
24   Cut the cable tie that secures the EVAP canister vent valve and remove the valve.

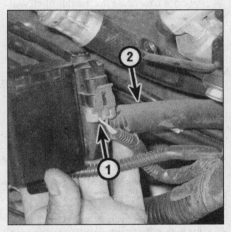

19.20 To remove the vent valve on a 1996 through 2002 model, disconnect the electrical connector (1) and the EVAP vent hose (2) from the vent valve

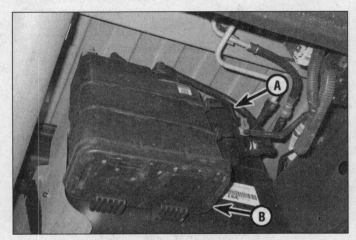

19.22 On 2003 and later models, the EVAP canister vent valve (A) is located right next to the EVAP canister (B), which is located just in front of the fuel tank

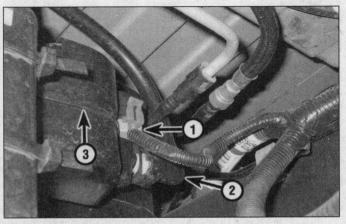

19.23 To remove the EVAP canister vent valve on a 2003 and later model, disconnect the electrical connector (1), disconnect the EVAP vent hose (2) and cut the cable tie (3) that secures the vent valve

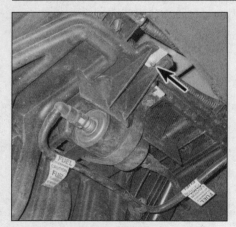

19.28 To detach the EVAP canister from the fuel tank on a 1996 through 2002 model, remove this bolt, then push the canister retaining strap aside

25   Using a new cable tie, secure the EVAP canister vent valve. Installation is otherwise the reverse of removal.

EVAP canister

26   Disconnect the cable from the negative battery terminal (see Chapter 5, Section 1).
27   Raise the vehicle and place it securely on jackstands.

1996 through 2002 models
Refer to illustrations 19.28 and 19.29
Note: *The EVAP canister is located under the left side of the vehicle, on top of the fuel tank.*
28   Remove the EVAP canister retaining strap bolt **(see illustration)**, then push the retaining strap aside.
29   Rotate the EVAP canister to access the three EVAP hose connections and disconnect all three hoses from the EVAP canister **(see illustration)**. If you're unfamiliar with the hose fittings, refer to Section 4 in Chapter 4.
30   Remove the EVAP canister.

31   Installation is the reverse of removal.

2003 and later models
Refer to illustration 19.33
32   The EVAP canister and the EVAP canister vent valve are located side by side, right in front of the fuel tank **(see illustration 19.22)**.
33   Disconnect all three hoses from the EVAP canister **(see illustration)**. If you're unfamiliar with the hose fittings, refer to Section 4 in Chapter 4.
34   Cut the cable tie that secures the EVAP canister and remove the canister.
35   Secure the EVAP canister with a new cable tie. Installation is otherwise the reverse of removal.

---

20   Exhaust Gas Recirculation (EGR) system - general description and component replacement

---

General description

1   Oxides of nitrogen, nitrogen oxide, or simply NOx, is a compound that is formed in the combustion chambers when the oxygen and nitrogen in the incoming air mix together. NOx is a natural byproduct of high combustion chamber temperatures (2500 degrees Fahrenheit and higher). When NOx is emitted from the tailpipe, it mixes with reactive organic compounds (ROCs), hydrocarbons (HC) and sunlight to form ozone and photochemical smog.
2   The EGR system reduces NOx by recirculating exhaust gases from the exhaust manifold, through the EGR valve and intake manifold, then back to the combustion chambers, where it mixes with the incoming air/fuel mixture before being consumed. These recirculated exhaust gases "dilute" the incoming air/fuel mixture, which cools the combustion chambers, thereby reducing NOx emissions.

3   The EGR system consists of the Powertrain Control Module (PCM), the EGR valve and various information sensors that the PCM uses to determine when to open the EGR valve. When the PCM closes the power/control circuit for the EGR valve, a solenoid inside the EGR valve is energized. This creates an electromagnetic field, which causes an armature to pull up, lifting the pintle off its seat. The exhaust gas then flows from the exhaust manifold port to the intake manifold.
4   Once activated by the PCM, the EGR valve uses a position feedback circuit to control the position of the pintle valve. The feedback circuit, which functions like a potentiometer, puts out a variable output voltage signal with an operating range between 0.5 and 5.4 volts. This variable output enables the PCM to control the position of the pintle with a high degree of precision. A pintle position sensor monitors the position of the pintle, and the PCM adjusts the current to match the actual pintle position to the optimal pintle position.
5   If there is too much EGR flow at idle, cruise or during cold running conditions, the engine will stop after a cold start, stop at idle after deceleration, surge during cruising speeds or idle roughly. If there is too little EGR flow, combustion chamber temperature can become too high during acceleration or under a heavy load, which can cause spark knock (detonation) and/or engine overheating.

Component replacement

4.3L V6 and 5.0L and 5.7L V8 engines

EGR valve
Refer to illustration 20.7
Note: *The EGR valve is located on top of the intake manifold, at the front of the engine.*
6   Disconnect the cable from the negative battery terminal (see Chapter 5, Section 1).
7   Disconnect the electrical connector from the EGR valve **(see illustration)**.

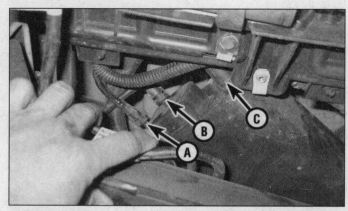

19.29 Before you can remove the EVAP canister from the top of the fuel tank on a 1996 through 2002 model, you must disconnect these three hoses (if you don't know how to disconnect the fittings, see Section 4 in Chapter 4)

A *Purge line (to canister purge solenoid)*	B *Vapor line (from fuel tank)*
	C *Vent line (to vent valve)*

19.33 To remove the EVAP canister on a 2003 and later model, disconnect these three hoses:

A *Purge line (to canister purge solenoid)*	B *Vapor line (from fuel tank)*
	C *Vent line (to vent valve)*

8   **Caution:** *Before removing the EGR valve, carefully note its orientation. It's a good idea to scribe a line across the valve and its mounting flange to ensure that the valve is installed in exactly the same position it was in before removal. If you accidentally install the EGR valve after it has been rotated 180-degrees, the valve will not operate correctly.* Remove the EGR valve mounting bolts and remove the EGR valve.

9   Remove and discard the EGR valve gasket. Thoroughly clean off the gasket mating surfaces of the EGR valve and the manifold. Be sure to remove all old gasket material.

10   Installation is the reverse of removal. Be sure to use a new gasket and tighten the EGR valve mounting bolts securely.

EGR pipe

Refer to illustrations 20.12 and 20.14

11   Remove the air filter housing and the air intake duct (see Chapter 4).

12   Unscrew the EGR pipe fitting from intake manifold **(see illustration)**.

13   Remove the engine cover (see Chapter 11).

14   Unscrew the EGR pipe fitting from the exhaust manifold **(see illustration)** and remove the EGR pipe.

15   Installation is the reverse of removal.

7.4L V8 engine

EGR valve

16   The EGR valve is the same unit that's used on 4.3L V6 and 5.0L and 5.7L V8 engines, except that it's located on the left side of the intake manifold, so remove the engine cover for better access (see Chapter 11). The procedure for removing and installing the EGR valve is identical to the procedure for removing and installing the EGR valve on 4.3L V6 and 5.0L and 5.7L V8 engines (see Steps 6 through 10). **Caution:** *Before removing the EGR valve, carefully*

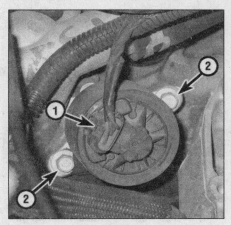

20.7 To remove the EGR valve from a 4.3L V6 or 5.0L (shown) or 5.3L V8, disconnect the electrical connector (1) and remove the EGR valve mounting bolts (2)

note its orientation. It's a good idea to scribe a line across the valve and its mounting flange to ensure that the valve is installed in exactly the same position it was in before removal. If you accidentally install the EGR valve after it has been rotated 180 degrees, the valve will fit but it will not operate correctly.

EGR pipe

17   Remove the engine cover (see Chapter 11).

18   The upper end of the EGR pipe is connected to the same mounting flange as the EGR valve. Unscrew the pipe fitting and disconnect the pipe from the EGR valve mounting flange.

19   The lower end of the EGR pipe is bolted to the exhaust manifold with two bolts. Remove both bolts and remove the EGR pipe. Remove and discard the EGR pipe gasket.

20   Installation is the reverse of removal. Be sure to use a new gasket at the exhaust mani-

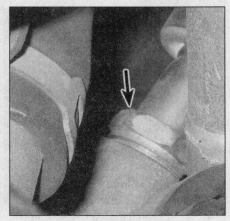

20.12 Unscrew the EGR pipe fitting from the intake manifold (4.3L V6 and 5.0L and 5.7L V8 engines)

fold and tighten the bolts at the exhaust manifold and the fitting at the EGR valve mounting flange securely.

4.8L, 5.3L and 6.0L V8 engines

EGR valve

Refer to illustrations 20.21 and 20.22
Note: *The EGR valve is located on a mounting flange that's bolted to the front end of the right cylinder head.*

21   Disconnect the electrical connector from the EGR valve **(see illustration)**.

22   **Caution:** *Before removing the EGR valve, carefully note its orientation. It's a good idea to scribe a line across the valve and its mounting flange to ensure that the valve is installed in exactly the same position it was in before removal. If you accidentally install the EGR valve after it has been rotated 180-degrees, the valve will fit but it will not operate correctly.* Remove the EGR valve

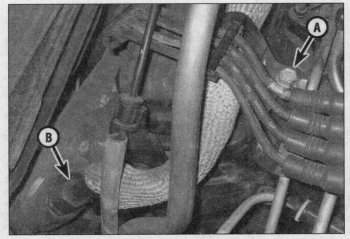

20.14 Remove the bolt (A) from the EGR pipe clip, then unscrew the EGR pipe fitting (B) from the exhaust manifold (4.3L V6 and 5.0L and 5.7L V8 engines)

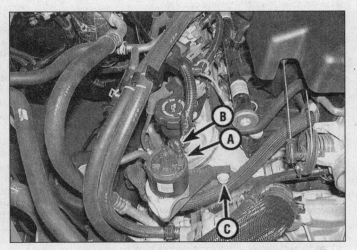

20.21 On 4.8L, 5.3L and 6.0L V8 engines, the EGR valve (A) is located at the front end of the right cylinder head. First, disconnect the electrical connector (B). If you're going to remove or replace the EGR pipe, you must remove the EGR valve, then remove the mounting bracket bolt (C)

20.22 To detach the EGR valve from its mounting flange, remove these two bolts

20.26 To disconnect the upper end of the EGR pipe from the intake manifold on a 4.8L, 5.3L (shown) or 6.0L V8 engine, remove these two flange bolts

20.28 To disconnect the lower end of the EGR pipe from the exhaust manifold on a 4.8L, 5.3L (shown) or 6.0L V8 engine, remove these two flange bolts

mounting bolts **(see illustration)** and remove the EGR valve.

23   Remove and discard the EGR valve gasket. Thoroughly clean off the gasket mating surfaces of the EGR valve and the EGR mounting flange. Be sure to remove all old gasket material.

24   Installation is the reverse of removal.

EGR pipe

Refer to illustration 20.26 and 20.28

25   Remove the EGR valve (see Steps 21 through 23).

26   Remove the flange bolts **(see illustration)** and disconnect the EGR pipe from the intake manifold.

27   Remove the bolt that attaches the EGR valve mounting flange/EGR pipe mounting bracket to the front of the right cylinder head **(see illustration 20.21).**

28   Remove the flange bolts **(see illustration)** and disconnect the EGR pipe from the exhaust manifold.

29   Installation is the reverse of removal. Be sure to tighten the flange bolts to the torque listed in this Chapter's Specifications.

30   When installing the EGR valve, be sure to use a new EGR valve gasket and tighten the EGR valve mounting bolts securely.

21 Positive Crankcase Ventilation (PCV) system - general description and check

General description

Refer to illustration 21.2a, 21.2b, 21.3a and 21.3b

Note: *For specific information on how to replace the PCV valves on the engines covered by this manual, see Chapter 1.*

1   The Positive Crankcase Ventilation (PCV) system reduces hydrocarbon emissions by scavenging crankcase vapors, which are rich in unburned hydrocarbons. The PCV system used by the vehicles covered in this manual is somewhat different from conventional PCV systems because it doesn't rely on intake manifold vacuum to scavenge blow-by

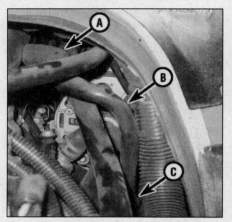

21.2a On 4.3L V6 and 5.0L (shown) and 5.7L V8 engines, the PCV fresh air inlet hose connects the air intake duct/resonator to the right valve cover

A   Rubber elbow
B   Fresh air inlet hose
C   Rubber grommet

gases from the engine crankcase. In a conventional PCV system, a pressure differential in the crankcase is produced by intake manifold vacuum, which is accomplished by connecting the crankcase to a manifold vacuum source with a hose between the valve cover and the throttle body or intake manifold. Intake manifold vacuum draws crankcase vapors into the intake manifold, where they mix with the air/fuel mixture before being consumed in the combustion chambers. A fresh air inlet hose, which connects the air intake duct or the air resonator box to the valve cover, allows fresh air to be drawn into the crankcase by the same intake vacuum source, thus equalizing the pressure in the bottom end. The result is a continuous loop of fresh air drawn into the crankcase, where it mixes with crankcase vapors before being drawn into the manifold by intake vacuum. A PCV valve regulates the flow of gases into the intake manifold in proportion to the amount of intake vacuum available. At idle, when intake vacuum is very high, the PCV valve restricts the flow of vapors

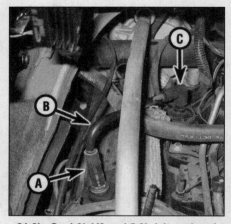

21.2b On 4.3L V6 and 5.0L (shown) and 5.7L V8 engines, the crankcase ventilation hose connects the left valve cover to the intake manifold

A   PCV valve
B   Crankcase ventilation hose
C   Rubber elbow

so that the engine doesn't run poorly. As the throttle plate opens and intake vacuum begins to diminish, the PCV valve opens more to allow vapors to flow more freely.

2   On 4.3L V6 and 5.0L, 5.7L and 7.4L V8 engines, the PCV system consists of a fresh air inlet hose **(see illustration)** that connects the air intake duct to the right valve cover and a crankcase ventilation hose **(see illustration)** that connects the left valve cover to the intake manifold. The PCV valve is located at the valve cover end of the crankcase ventilation hose.

3   On 4.8L, 5.3L and 6.0L V8 engines, the PCV system consists of a fresh air inlet hose **(see illustration)** that connects an elbow pipe on the right valve cover to another elbow pipe on the intake manifold and a crankcase ventilation hose **(see illustration)** that connects the left valve cover to the intake manifold. The PCV valve is located at the valve cover end of the crankcase ventilation hose.

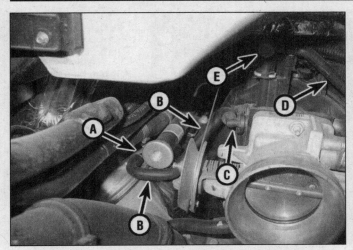

21.3a On 4.8L (shown), 5.3L and 6.0L V8 engines, the fresh air inlet hose connects the throttle body to the right valve cover and the crankcase ventilation hose connects the left valve cover to the intake manifold (see next illustration for the rest of the crankcase ventilation hose):

A	Metal elbow on right valve cover	D	Crankcase ventilation hose
B	Fresh air inlet hose	E	Plastic elbow at intake manifold
C	Plastic or metal elbow at throttle body		

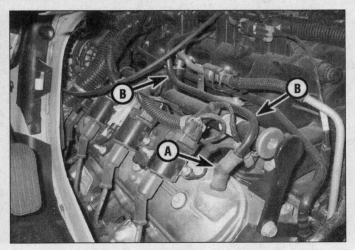

21.3b On 4.8L (shown), 5.3L and 6.0L V8 engines, the crankcase ventilation hose connects the left valve cover to the intake manifold (see previous illustration for the rest of the crankcase ventilation hose):

| A | PCV valve | B | Crankcase ventilation hose |

Check

4   An engine that is operated without a properly functioning crankcase ventilation system can be damaged. So anytime you're servicing the engine, be sure to inspect the PCV system hose(s) for cracks, tears, deterioration and other damage. Disconnect the hose(s) and inspect it/them for damage and obstructions. If a hose is clogged, clean it out. If you're unable to clean it satisfactorily, replace it.

5   A plugged PCV hose might cause any or all of the following conditions: A rough idle, stalling or a slow idle speed, oil leaks or sludge in the engine. So if the engine is running roughly, stalling and *idling at a lower than normal speed*, or is losing oil, or has oil in the throttle body or air intake manifold plenum, or has a build-up of sludge, a PCV system hose might be clogged. Repair or replace the hose(s) as necessary.

6   A leaking PCV hose might cause any or all of the following conditions: a rough idle, stalling or a high idle speed. So if the engine is running roughly, stalling and *idling at a higher than normal speed*, a PCV system hose might be leaking. Repair or replace the hose(s) as necessary.

7   Here's an easy functional check of the PCV system on a vehicle with a fresh air inlet hose and a crankcase ventilation hose with a PCV valve in it:

1   *Disconnect the crankcase ventilation hose (the crankcase ventilation hose, or simply "the PCV hose," is the hose that connects the PCV valve to the intake manifold).*

2   *Start the engine and let it warm up to its normal idle.*

3   *Verify that there is vacuum at the PCV hose. If there is no vacuum, look for a plugged hose or a clogged port or pipe on the intake manifold. Also look for a hose that collapses when it's blocked (i.e. when vacuum is applied). Replace clogged or deteriorated hoses.*

4   *Remove the engine oil dipstick and install a vacuum gauge on the upper end of the dipstick tube.*

5   *Pinch off or plug the PCV system's fresh air inlet hose.*

6   *Run the engine at 1500 rpm for 30 seconds, then read the vacuum gauge while the engine is running at 1500 rpm.*

7   *If there's vacuum present, the crankcase ventilation system is operating correctly.*

8   *If there's NO vacuum present, the engine might be drawing in outside air. The PCV system won't function correctly unless the engine is a sealed system. Inspect the valve cover(s), oil pan gasket or other sealing areas for leaks.*

9   *If the vacuum gauge indicates positive pressure, look for a plugged hose or engine blow-by.*

8   If the PCV system is functioning correctly, but there's evidence of engine oil in the throttle body or air filter housing, it could be caused by excessive crankcase pressure. Have the crankcase pressure tested by a dealer service department.

9   In the PCV system, excessive blow-by (caused by worn rings, pistons and/or cylinders, or by constant heavy loads) is discharged into the intake manifold and con-

sumed. If you discover heavy sludge deposits or a dilution of the engine oil, even though the PCV system is functioning correctly, look for other causes (see Troubleshooting and Chapter 2C) and correct them as soon as possible.

---

22   Secondary Air Injection (AIR) system - general description, check and component replacement

General description

Note: *Some 2000 and later 4.3L V6, 2000 through 2002 5.7L V8 and 1996 through 2000 7.4L V8 engines are equipped with a Secondary Air Injection (AIR) system.*

1   The air injection exhaust emission control system reduces the level of unburned hydrocarbons (HC) and carbon monoxide (CO) in the exhaust gases by injecting outside air into the hot exhaust gases flowing through the exhaust manifolds. When fresh air is mixed with the hot exhaust gases, oxidation is increased, reducing the concentration of hydrocarbons and carbon monoxide and converting them into harmless carbon dioxide and water. The system does not interfere with the NOx emission controls of the engine.

4.3L V6 engines
Refer to illustration 22.3

2   On 4.3L V6 engines, the AIR system consists of the electric AIR pump, the vacuum control solenoid, the shut-off valve, the check valves, and the hoses and pipes connecting all of these components.

3   **AIR pump** - The AIR pump **(see illustration)** draws in filtered outside air and pumps it into the exhaust manifolds. The pump is turned on and off by a relay. The ground path for the PCM-controlled pump relay is through the PCM. When the PCM closes the ground path, battery voltage is applied to the pump.

4   **AIR vacuum control solenoid** - The AIR vacuum control solenoid controls the AIR shut-off valve. When the PCM turns on the AIR system, it also grounds the vacuum control solenoid, which allows intake manifold vacuum to reach the AIR shut-off valve.

5   **AIR shut-off valve** - The AIR shut-off valve is operated by vacuum. When the AIR system is operating, intake manifold vacuum is applied to the shut-off valve, which opens the valve and allows air from the AIR pump to reach the check valves.

6   **AIR check valves** - The AIR check valves allow air from the AIR pump to flow to the exhaust manifolds but prevent the backflow of exhaust gases into the AIR system.

5.7L V8 engines

7   On 5.7L V8 engines, the AIR system consists of the electric AIR pump, the check valves and the hoses and pipes connecting these components.

8   **AIR pump** - The AIR pump **(see illustration 22.3)** draws in filtered outside air and pumps it into the exhaust manifolds. The pump is turned on and off by a relay. The ground path for the PCM-controlled pump relay is through the PCM. When the PCM closes the ground path, battery voltage is applied to the pump.

9   **AIR check valves** - The AIR check valves allow air from the AIR pump to flow to the exhaust manifolds but prevent the backflow of exhaust gases into the AIR system.

7.4L V8 engines

10   On 7.4L V8 engines, the AIR system consists of the belt-driven AIR pump, the PCM-controlled electric clutch, the AIR valve, the check valves, and the hoses and pipes connecting all of these components.

11   **AIR pump** - The belt-driven pump draws in filtered outside air and pumps it into the exhaust manifolds. The electric clutch on the pump is energized by a relay, which is turned on and off by the PCM. Under normal operating conditions, noise from the pump rises in pitch as engine speed increases. Do not attempt to lubricate the air injection pump with oil or any spray penetrant. Lubricating the pump will damage it.

12   **AIR check valves** - The AIR check valves allow air from the AIR pump to flow to the exhaust manifolds but prevent the backflow of exhaust gases into the AIR system.

All engines

13   When the coolant temperature is 45-degrees F. or more, or when the vehicle is decelerating (high intake vacuum, rich air/fuel mixture, lots of unburned hydrocarbons and carbon monoxide in the exhaust), the PCM energizes the AIR pump relay, which energizes the

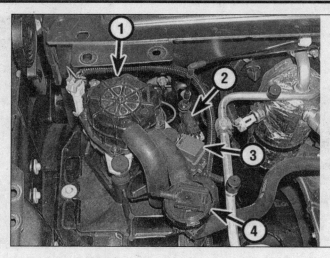

22.3 A typical electric AIR pump assembly:

1   *AIR pump*
2   *Vacuum control solenoid*
3   *AIR pump solenoid relay*
4   *AIR shut-off valve*

electric clutch, at which point the pump begins pumping air into the exhaust system.

14   The PCM may turn off the AIR pump's electric clutch when the system is in closed-loop operation, when one or more Diagnostic Trouble Codes (DTCs) are set by the PCM, when the system is in the power-enrichment mode for too long, when intake manifold vacuum is low or when the rise in intake vacuum is too quick (rapid deceleration).

Check

15   Checking the PCM-controlled, electric-pump-equipped AIR systems used on 4.3L V6 and 5.7L V8 engines is beyond the scope of the home mechanic. However, there are some simple things you can do to check the belt-driven pump used on 7.4L V8 engines. And the check valves on all AIR systems work the same way, so you can check them yourself on any of the AIR systems discussed above. If these simple checks fail to identify the problem, have the AIR system checked out by a dealer service department or other qualified repair shop.

AIR pump

16   On 7.4L V8 engines, check the drivebelt tension (see Chapter 1).

17   Disconnect the air supply hose from the pressure relief valve.

18   If you can feel airflow at the pump outlet with the engine running at idle, and if the airflow increases as the engine speed increases, then the pump is operating satisfactorily.

19   If you feel little or no airflow, replace the pump with a rebuilt or new unit.

20   If you note evidence of exhaust gases at the outlet port, one or both of the check valves is defective. If the pump is already inoperative, then make SURE that you inspect the check valves before installing a new pump.

Check valves

21   Disconnect the hose, pipe or tube from the intake side of each check valve.

22   Start the engine and verify that no exhaust gases are backflowing through either check valve. If there is any sign of leakage, replace the check valve(s).

Component replacement

4.3L V6 engine

AIR check valve/pipe

23   If you're going to remove the AIR check valve/pipe assembly for the left cylinder head, remove the air filter housing (see Chapter 4). If you're going to remove the AIR check valve/pipe assembly for the right cylinder head, remove the coolant reservoir (see Chapter 3).

24   Loosen the spring clamp, then disconnect the reactor hose from the reactor pipe.

25   Remove the reactor pipe assembly retaining bolts and remove the reactor pipe assembly.

26   Remove the reactor pipe assembly gasket.

27   Loosen the pipe locknut, then separate the check valve from the reactor pipe.

28   Installation is the reverse of removal. Be sure to tighten all fasteners securely.

AIR shut-off valve

29   Raise the vehicle and place it securely on jackstands.

30   Disconnect the vacuum line from the shut-off valve.

31   Loosen the spring clamp, disconnect the inlet and outlet hoses from the shut-off valve, then remove the shut-off valve.

32   Installation is the reverse of removal.

AIR pump

33   Raise the vehicle and place it securely on jackstands.

34   Disconnect the cable from the negative battery terminal (see Chapter 5, Section 1).

35   Loosen the spring clamps, then disconnect the inlet and outlet hoses from the AIR pump.

36   Disconnect the electrical connectors from the AIR pump and from the AIR valve.

37   Remove the AIR pump mounting bolts, then remove the pump.

38   Installation is the reverse of removal. Be sure to tighten all fasteners securely.

AIR solenoid valve

39   Remove the AIR pump (See Steps 32 through 36).

40   Remove the solenoid valve retaining screw from the mounting bracket and remove the solenoid valve.
41   Installation is the reverse of removal.

5.7L V8 engine

AIR injection pump
42   Disconnect the AIR pump electrical connector.
43   Disconnect the AIR output hose from the AIR valve.
44   Remove the bolt that secures the AIR pump to its mounting plate and remove the pump.
45   Installation is the reverse of removal. Be sure to tighten all fasteners securely.

AIR check valve/pipe
46   Remove the bolt for the AIR crossover bracket (left cylinder head).

47   Disconnect the AIR crossover hose (left cylinder head).
48   Disconnect the AIR pump output hose from the AIR valve.
49   Disconnect the right cylinder head AIR pipe from the AIR valve.
50   Remove the AIR valve mounting bolt and separate the valve from the bracket.
51   Installation is the reverse of removal. Be sure to tighten all fasteners securely.

7.4L V8

AIR injection pump
52   Remove the accessory drivebelt (see Chapter 1).
53   Disconnect the AIR pump electrical connector.
54   Disconnect the AIR air filter hose from the pump.
55   Disconnect the AIR output hose from the

pump.
56   Remove the pump mounting bolts and remove the pump.
57   Installation is the reverse of removal. Be sure to tighten all fasteners securely.

Secondary AIR injection check valve/pipe
58   Remove the bolt for the secondary AIR injection crossover bracket (left cylinder head).
59   Disconnect the AIR crossover hose (left cylinder head).
60   Disconnect the AIR pump output hose from the AIR valve.
61   Disconnect the right cylinder head AIR pipe from the AIR valve.
62   Remove the AIR valve mounting bolt and separate the valve from the bracket.
63   Installation is the reverse of removal. Be sure to tighten all fasteners securely.

Notes

Chapter 7
Automatic transmission

Contents

Specifications

General
Transmission fluid type .... See Chapter 1

Torque specifications   **Ft-lbs**
Transmission fluid pan bolts .... See Chapter 1
Torque converter-to-driveplate bolts 46
Transmission-to-engine bolts 34

1   General information

All vehicles covered by this manual come equipped with a four-speed automatic transmission. Due to the complexity of the automatic transmissions and the need for specialized equipment to perform most service operations, this Chapter contains only general diagnosis, routine maintenance, adjustment and removal and installation procedures.

The models covered by this manual use either a 4L60-E/4L65-E or a 4L80-E/4L85-E electronic four-speed automatic transmission.

These transmissions are equipped with a torque converter clutch (TCC) that engages in fourth gear, and in third gear when the overdrive switch is turned off. The TCC provides a direct connection between the engine and the drive wheels for improved efficiency and economy. The TCC consists of a solenoid controlled by the Powertrain Control Module (PCM) that locks the converter in third or fourth when the vehicle is cruising on level ground and the engine is fully warmed up. Some models are also equipped with an auxiliary transmission cooler that is mounted in front of the radiator and air conditioning condenser.

If the transmission requires major repair work, it should be left to a dealer service department or an automotive or transmission repair shop. You can, however, remove and install the transmission yourself and save the expense, even if the repair work is done by a transmission shop. Note that a faulty transmission should not be removed before the vehicle has been assessed by a knowledgeable technician equipped with the proper tools, as troubleshooting must be performed with the transmission installed in the vehicle.

2   Diagnosis - general

Note: *Automatic transmission malfunctions may be caused by five general conditions: poor engine performance, improper adjustments, hydraulic malfunctions, mechanical malfunctions or malfunctions in the Powertrain Control Module or its signal network. Diagnosis of these problems should always begin with a check of the easily repaired items: fluid level and condition (see Chapter 1), and shift cable adjustment (see Section 3). Next, perform a road test to determine if the problem has been corrected or if more diagnosis is necessary. Because the transmission relies on many sensors in the engine control system, and since the transmission shift points are controlled by the Powertrain Control Module, you'll also want to check to see if any trouble codes have been stored in the PCM (see Chapter 6 for a list of trouble codes and how to extract them). If the problem persists after the preliminary tests and corrections are completed, additional diagnosis should be done by a dealer service department or transmission repair shop. Refer to the Troubleshooting section at the front of this manual for transmission problem diagnosis.*

Preliminary checks

1   Drive the vehicle to warm the transmission to normal operating temperature.
2   Check the fluid level as described in Chapter 1:

 a) *If the fluid level is unusually low, add enough fluid to bring the level within the designated area of the dipstick, then check for external leaks.*
 b) *If the fluid level is abnormally high, drain off the excess, then check the drained fluid for contamination by coolant. The presence of engine coolant in the automatic transmission fluid indicates that a failure has occurred in the internal radiator walls that separate the coolant from the transmission fluid (see Chapter 3).*
 c) *If the fluid is foaming, drain it and refill the transmission, then check for coolant in the fluid or a high fluid level.*

3   Check the engine idle speed. **Note:** *If the engine is malfunctioning, do not proceed with the preliminary checks until it has been repaired and runs normally.*
4   Inspect the shift control cable (see Section 3). Make sure that it's properly adjusted and that it operates smoothly.
5   Check the Park/Neutral Position (PNP) switch adjustment (see Chapter 6).

Fluid leak diagnosis

6   Most fluid leaks are easy to locate visually. Repair usually consists of replacing a seal or gasket. If a leak is difficult to find, the following procedure may help.
7   Identify the fluid. Make sure it's transmission fluid and not engine oil or brake fluid (automatic transmission fluid is a deep red color).

8   Try to pinpoint the source of the leak. Drive the vehicle several miles, then park it over a large sheet of cardboard. After a minute or two, you should be able to locate the leak by determining the source of the fluid dripping onto the cardboard.
9   Make a careful visual inspection of the suspected component and the area immediately around it. Pay particular attention to gasket mating surfaces. A mirror is often helpful for finding leaks in areas that are hard to see.
10   If the leak still cannot be found, clean the suspected area thoroughly with a degreaser or solvent, then dry it.
11   Drive the vehicle for several miles at normal operating temperature and varying speeds. After driving the vehicle, visually inspect the suspected component again.
12   Once the leak has been located, the cause must be determined before it can be properly repaired. If a gasket is replaced but the sealing flange is bent, the new gasket will not stop the leak. The bent flange must be straightened.
13   Before attempting to repair a leak, check to make sure that the following conditions are corrected or they may cause another leak. **Note:** *Some of the following conditions cannot be fixed without highly specialized tools and expertise. Such problems must be referred to a transmission shop or a dealer service department.*

Gasket leaks

14   Check the pan periodically. Make sure the bolts are tight, no bolts are missing, the gasket is in good condition and the pan is flat (dents in the pan may indicate damage to the valve body inside).
15   If the pan gasket is leaking, the fluid level or the fluid pressure may be too high, the vent may be plugged, the pan bolts may be too tight, the pan sealing flange may be warped, the sealing surface of the transmission housing may be damaged, the gasket may be damaged or the transmission casting may be cracked or porous. If sealant instead of gasket material has been used to form a seal between the pan and the transmission housing, it may be the wrong sealant.

Seal leaks

16   If a transmission seal is leaking, the fluid level or pressure may be too high, the vent may be plugged, the seal bore may be damaged, the seal itself may be damaged or improperly installed, the surface of the shaft protruding through the seal may be damaged or a loose bearing may be causing excessive shaft movement.
17   Make sure the dipstick tube seal is in good condition and the tube is properly seated. Periodically check the area around the speedometer gear or vehicle speed sensor for leakage. If transmission fluid is evident, check the O-ring for damage. Also inspect the driveshaft oil seal for leakage.

Case leaks

18   If the case itself appears to be leak-

ing, the casting is porous and will have to be repaired or replaced.
19   Make sure the oil cooler hose fittings are tight and in good condition. The transmission oil cooler lines on these models are equipped with quick connect fittings - always inspect the O-rings if a leak is suspected.

Fluid comes out vent pipe or fill tube

20   If this condition occurs, the transmission is overfilled, there is coolant in the fluid, the case is porous, the dipstick is incorrect, the vent is plugged or the drain back holes are plugged.

3   Shift cable - check, replacement and adjustment

Warning: *The models covered by this manual are equipped with a Supplemental Restraint System (SRS), more commonly known as airbags. Always disarm the airbag system before working in the vicinity of any airbag system component to avoid the possibility of accidental deployment of the airbag, which could cause personal injury (see Chapter 12). Do not use a memory saving device to preserve the PCM's memory when working on or near airbag system components.*

Check

1   Firmly apply the parking brake and try to momentarily operate the starter in each shift lever position. The starter should only operate when the shift lever is in the PARK or NEUTRAL positions. If the starter operates in any position other than PARK or NEUTRAL, adjust the shift cable (see below). If, after adjustment, the starter still operates in positions other than PARK or NEUTRAL, the Park/Neutral Position switch is defective (see Chapter 6).

Replacement

Refer to illustrations 3.6, 3.7, 3.11, 3.12 and 3.13
2   Disconnect the cable from the negative terminal of the battery (see Chapter 5, Section 1).
3   Remove the steering column trim covers, the knee bolster from below the steering column, and the engine cover (see Chapter 11).
4   Place the transmission in PARK and apply the parking brake.
5   Block the rear wheels so the vehicle will not accidentally roll in either direction.
6   Working at the steering column, disengage the shift cable from the cable bracket **(see illustration)**.
7   Working at the steering column, disconnect the shift cable end from the lever ballstud **(see illustration)**.
8   Remove the air filter housing (see Chapter 4).
9   Remove the shift cable clips from the front and rear of the engine compartment.

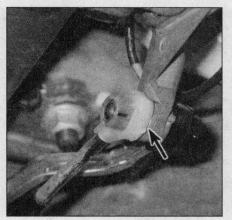

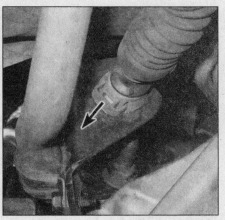

3.6 Use a screwdriver to disengage the shift cable retaining clip from the cable bracket

3.7 Carefully pry the shift cable end (grommet) from the shift lever mounted on the steering column

3.11 Pry the shift cable retaining clip from the cable housing at the transmission to release it from the bracket

10 Raise the vehicle and support it securely on jackstands.
11 Remove the shift cable from the bracket on the transmission **(see illustration)**.
12 Pry the shift cable end from the transmission shift lever **(see illustration)**.
13 Remove the rubber grommet from the cable at the engine compartment firewall **(see illustration)** and slide the cable through the opening.
14 Install the cable by reversing the removal procedure, making sure the grommet seats properly in the firewall, then adjust the cable. **Note:** *If a new cable is being installed, remove the shipping tab from the cable adjuster button.*

Adjustment
Refer to illustration 3.18 and 3.20
15 Make sure the driver's shift lever and the transmission shift lever are both in the Park position.
16 Remove the shift cable end from the transmission shift lever **(see illustration 3.12)**. **Note:** *Double-check the position of the shift lever. It must be situated in the*

Park detent.
17 On earlier models, slide the cover towards the end of the shift cable to expose the cable button. On later models, slide the lock tab to the side to release the shift cable adjuster.
18 Push the button on the shift cable out **(see illustration)**.
19 Push the shift cable end onto the shift lever ballstud until it snaps into place.
20 Press the adjustment button IN **(see illustration)**. The cable will lock into the correct position. **Note:** *On late models, engage the lock tab to set the correct shift cable adjustment.*
21 Install the shift cable end cover and lock tab, if equipped.

4 Park/Lock system - description and component replacement

Warning: *The models covered by this manual are equipped with a Supplemental Restraint System (SRS), more commonly known as airbags. Always disarm the airbag system*

3.12 Pry the cable end off the transmission shift lever ballstud

before working in the vicinity of any airbag system component to avoid the possibility of accidental deployment of the airbag, which could cause personal injury (see Chapter 12). Do not use a memory saving device to preserve the PCM's memory when working on or near airbag system components.

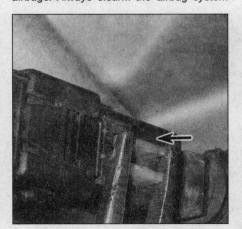

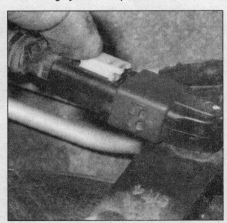

3.13 Push the rubber grommet through the firewall and remove the cable

3.18 Working on the backside of the assembly, use needle-nose pliers to push the shift cable button out towards the other side

3.20 Press the adjustment button to lock the shift cable, then slide the cover back into place

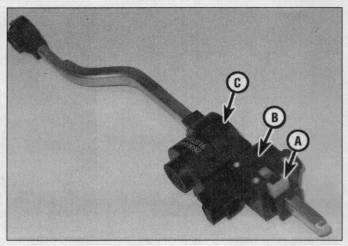

4.8 Details of the Brake Transmission Shift Interlock (BTSI) solenoid assembly

A   *Shift lever*
B   *BTSI solenoid link/mounting pin*
C   *BTSI solenoid*

4.9 Pry the BTSI solenoid actuator tab out (A), press the block (B) and slide the block assembly away from the solenoid (C) - BTSI assembly removed for clarity

Description

1   The Park/Lock system prevents the shift lever from being moved out of Park unless the brake pedal is depressed. It also prevents the ignition key from being removed from the ignition switch unless the shift lever is in the Park position. When the car is started, the BTSI (Brake Transmission Shift Interlock) solenoid is energized, locking the shift lever in Park; when the brake pedal is depressed, the solenoid is de-energized, unlocking the shift lever so that it can be moved into some other gear.

BTSI solenoid replacement

2   Remove the steering column covers (see Chapter 11).
3   Unplug the electrical connector from the solenoid **(see illustration 4.8)**.
4   Pry off each end of the BTSI solenoid assembly from its mounting pins **(see illustration 4.8)** and remove it from the steering column.
5   Installation is the reverse of removal.

BTSI adjustment

Refer to illustrations 4.8 and 4.9
6   Remove the steering column covers (see Chapter 11).
7   Place the shift lever in the Park position.
8   Disconnect the BTSI solenoid electrical connector **(see illustration)**.
9   Pull out the tab from the BTSI solenoid block **(see illustration)**.
10   Press the BTSI solenoid block down and simultaneously slide the assembly away from the BTSI solenoid as far as possible **(see illustration 4.9)**.
11   Push the tab in to lock the BTSI solenoid into position. Be sure to push the locking tab into the BTSI solenoid housing until it clicks back into place.
12   Install the electrical connector.
13   Check the operation of the Park/Lock system and make sure the ignition key cannot be removed without the shift lever in Park. Also make sure the shift lever can't be moved out of Park unless the brake pedal is

depressed (with the ignition key On).
14   The remainder of the installation is the reverse of removal.

5   Extension housing oil seal - replacement

Refer to illustrations 5.4 and 5.5
1   Oil leaks frequently occur due to wear of the extension housing oil seal. Replacement of this seal is relatively easy, since it can be performed without removing the transmission from the vehicle.
2   The extension housing oil seal is located at the extreme rear of the transmission, where the driveshaft is attached. If leakage at the seal is suspected, raise the vehicle and support it securely on jackstands. If the seal is leaking, transmission lubricant will be built up on the front of the driveshaft and may be dripping from the rear of the transmission.
3   Remove the driveshaft (see Chapter 8).

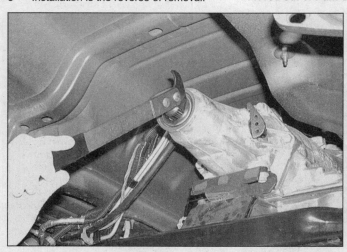

5.4 Carefully pry the old seal out of the extension housing - don't damage the splines on the output shaft

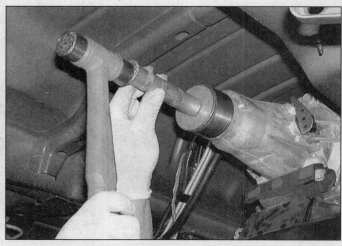

5.5 Drive the new seal into place with a seal driver or a large socket and hammer

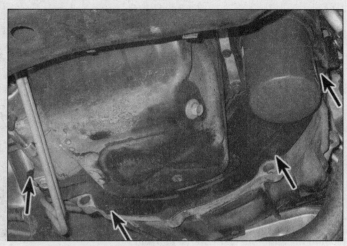

7.2 To check the transmission mount, insert a large screwdriver or prybar between the crossmember and the transmission and try to pry the transmission up - it should move very little

8.6a Remove the bellhousing cover mounting bolts - 1999 model shown

4   Using a seal removal tool or a large screwdriver, carefully pry the oil seal out of the rear of the transmission **(see illustration)**. Do not damage the splines on the transmission output shaft.

5   Using a seal driver or a very large deep socket as a drift, install the new oil seal **(see illustration)**. Drive it into the bore squarely and make sure it's completely seated.

6   Lubricate the splines of the transmission output shaft and the outside of the driveshaft yoke with lightweight grease, then install the driveshaft (see Chapter 8). Be careful not to damage the lip of the new seal.

6   Transmission fluid cooler - removal and installation

1   Drain the transmission fluid (see Chapter 1).

2   Remove the radiator grille (see Chapter 11).

3   Remove the transmission fluid lines at the transmission fluid cooler.

4   Remove the transmission fluid cooler upper mounting bolts.

5   Raise the vehicle and support it on jackstands.

6   Remove the transmission fluid cooler lower mounting bolts.

7   Separate the transmission fluid cooler from the radiator supports.

8   Installation is the reverse of removal.

7   Transmission mount - check and replacement

Check
Refer to illustration 7.2

1   Raise the vehicle and support it securely on jackstands.

2   Insert a large screwdriver or prybar into the space between the transmission extension housing and the crossmember and try to

pry the transmission up slightly **(see illustration)**.

3   The transmission should not move much at all - if the mount is cracked or torn, replace it.

Replacement

4   To replace the mount, remove the bolts or nuts attaching the mount to the crossmember and the bolts attaching the mount to the transmission.

5   Raise the transmission slightly with a jack and remove the mount.

6   Installation is the reverse of the removal procedure. Be sure to tighten all nuts and bolts securely.

8   Automatic transmission - removal and installation

Removal
Refer to illustrations 8.6a, 8.6b, 8.13, 8.16, 8.19a and 8.19b
Caution: *The transmission and torque converter must be removed as a single assem-*

bly. If you try to leave the torque converter attached to the driveplate, the converter driveplate, pump bushing and oil seal will be damaged. The driveplate is not designed to support the load, so none of the weight of the transmission should be allowed to rest on the plate during removal.

1   Remove the engine cover (see Chapter 11).

2   Disconnect the cable from the negative terminal of the battery (see Chapter 5, Section 1). Raise the vehicle and support it securely on jackstands.

3   Drain the transmission fluid (see Chapter 1).

4   Remove all exhaust components that will interfere with transmission removal (see Chapter 4).

5   Remove the shift cable from the transmission (see Section 3).

6   Remove the inspection cover **(see illustration)** at the bottom of the bellhousing and mark the relationship of the torque converter to the driveplate so they can be installed in the same position **(see illustration)**.

7   Remove the starter motor (see Chapter 5).

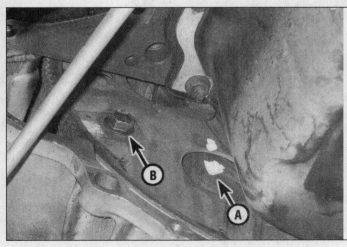

8.6b Mark the relationship between the torque converter and the driveplate (A) - (B) is one of the torque converter-to-driveplate bolts

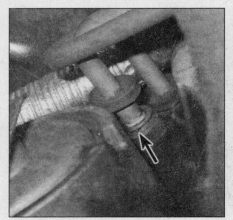

8.13 Pull the clip from the fitting, carefully moving the clip from side-to-side to avoid spreading it apart excessively

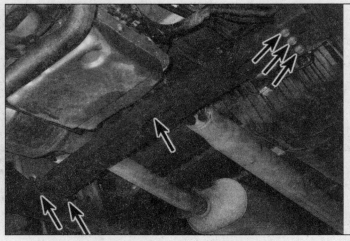

8.16 Location of the crossmember mounting bolts and the transmission mount nut (2002 and earlier models shown - 2003 and later models slightly different)

8   Remove the transmission vent hose and the dipstick tube.

9   Remove the torque converter-to-driveplate bolts **(see illustration 8.6b)**. Turn the crankshaft for access to each bolt. **Note:** *On 4.3L V6 engines, remove the starter opening shield to access the driveplate bolts.*

10   Remove the driveshaft (see Chapter 8).

11   Working on the left side of the transmission, unplug the electrical connectors from the Park/Neutral position switch (see Chapter 6). Remove the bolt securing the wiring harness bracket to the left side of the transmission.

12   Unplug the electrical connectors from the transmission solenoid and the vehicle speed sensor (see Chapter 6).

13   Disconnect the transmission fluid cooler lines from the transmission **(see illustration)**. To disconnect the lines from the transmission, pull back the plastic collar then remove the retaining clip from the slot in the fitting. Plug the ends of the lines to prevent fluid from leaking out after you disconnect them. Always be sure to inspect the plastic caps on the transmission fluid cooler lines before reinstallation.

14   Support the engine with a floor jack and block of wood placed under the oil pan. Don't raise the jack - it's just there to support the engine when the transmission is removed.

15   Support the transmission with a jack - preferably a jack made for this purpose (available at most tool rental yards). Safety chains will help steady the transmission on the jack.

16   Remove the nut securing the transmission mount to the crossmember and the crossmember mounting bolts and nuts. Then raise the transmission slightly and remove the crossmember **(see illustration)**. **Note:** *On 2003 and later models, remove the brake combination valve bracket and the fuel filter bracket from the crossmember and the transmission and position them off to the side.*

17   Remove the transmission heat shield, if equipped.

18   Remove the rear air conditioning line bracket from the transmission bellhousing, if equipped.

19   Remove the bolts securing the transmission to the engine **(see illustrations)**. A long extension and a U-joint socket will greatly simplify this step. **Note:** *The upper bolts are easier to remove after the transmission has*

been lowered (see the next Step).

20   Lower the engine and transmission slightly. Remove the dipstick tube bracket bolt and pull the tube out of the transmission. Don't lose the tube seal (it can be reused if it's still in good shape).

21   Clamp a small pair of locking pliers on the bellhousing case through the lower inspection hole. Clamp the pliers just in front of the torque converter, behind the driveplate. The pliers will prevent the torque converter from falling out while you're removing the transmission. Move the transmission to the rear to disengage it from the engine block dowel pins and make sure the torque converter is detached from the driveplate. Lower the transmission with the jack.

Installation

22   Prior to installation, make sure the torque converter is securely engaged in the pump. If you've removed the converter, apply a small amount of transmission fluid on the torque converter rear hub, where the transmission front seal rides. Install the torque converter onto the front input shaft of the transmission while rotating the converter back and forth.

8.19a Location of the transmission bolts accessible on the right side of the engine compartment

8.19b Location of the transmission bolts accessible on the left side of the engine compartment

It should engage into the transmission front pump in stages. To make sure the converter is fully engaged, lay a straightedge across the transmission-to-engine mating surface and make sure the converter lugs are at least 3/4-inch below the straightedge. Reinstall the locking pliers to hold the converter in this position.

23   With the transmission secured to the jack, raise it into position.

24   Turn the torque converter to line up the holes with the holes in the driveplate. The marks on the torque converter and driveplate made in Step 6 must line up.

25   Move the transmission forward carefully until the dowel pins and the torque converter are engaged. Make sure the transmission mates with the engine with no gap. If there's a gap, make sure there are no wires or other objects pinched between the engine and transmission and also make sure the torque converter is completely engaged in the transmission front pump. Try to rotate the converter - if it doesn't rotate easily, it's probably not fully engaged in the pump. If necessary, lower the transmission and install the converter fully.

26   Install the transmission dipstick tube and seal into the transmission housing, then install the transmission-to-engine bolts and tighten them securely. As you're tightening the bolts, make sure that the engine and transmission mate completely at all points. If not, find out why. **Caution:** *Never try to force the engine and transmission together with the bolts or you'll break the transmission case!*

27   Raise the rear of the transmission and install the transmission crossmember.

28   Remove the jacks supporting the transmission and the engine.

29   Install the torque converter-to-driveplate bolts, then tighten them to the torque listed in this Chapter's Specifications. Install the bellhousing cover. **Note:** *Install all of the bolts before tightening any of them.*

30   Install the starter motor (see Chapter 5).

31   Install new retaining rings onto the quick-connect fittings, if necessary. **Note:** *Don't push the retaining rings onto the fittings. Instead, hook one of the ends of the clip into a slot in the fitting, then rotate the other end of the ring into the other slot. If the retaining ring isn't installed like this, it may become spread-out and won't be able to retain the cooler lines securely.* Connect the transmission fluid cooler lines to the fittings, making sure they click into place, then push the plastic caps onto the fittings.

32   Connect the transmission electrical connectors.

33   Install the inspection cover.

34   Install the driveshaft (see Chapter 8).

35   Install any exhaust system components that were removed or disconnected (see Chapter 4).

36   Install and adjust the shift cable (see Section 3).

37   Remove the jackstands and lower the vehicle.

38   Fill the transmission with the specified fluid (see Chapter 1), run the engine and check for fluid leaks.

9   Automatic transmission overhaul - general information

In the event of a fault occurring, it will be necessary to establish whether the fault is electrical, mechanical or hydraulic in nature, before repair work can be contemplated. Diagnosis requires detailed knowledge of the transmission's operation and construction, as well as access to specialized test equipment, and so is deemed to be beyond the scope of this manual. It is therefore essential that problems with the automatic transmission are referred to a dealer service department or other qualified repair facility for assessment.

Note that a faulty transmission should not be removed before the vehicle has been assessed by a knowledgeable technician equipped with the proper tools, as troubleshooting must be performed with the transmission installed in the vehicle.

Notes

Chapter 8
Driveline

Contents

Specifications

Torque specifications

Driveshaft-to-differential companion flange	75
Driveshaft-to-differential yoke	
2002 and earlier models	15
2003 and later models	18
Pinion shaft lock bolt	
8.6-inch axle	27
9.5-inch axle	37
9.75-inch axle	20
Wheel lug nuts	See Chapter 1

1   General information

The information in this Chapter deals with the components from the rear of the engine to the front wheels, except for the transmission, which is dealt with in Chapter 7. For the purposes of this Chapter, these components are grouped into two categories - driveshaft and axle.

Since nearly all the procedures covered in this Chapter involve working under the vehicle, make sure it's securely supported on sturdy jackstands or on a hoist where the vehicle can be easily raised and lowered.

2   Driveshaft - general information

The driveshaft runs between the transmission and the rear axle (differential). The driveshaft has a splined sliding sleeve at the front connecting to the output shaft of the transmission. The purpose of this device is to accommodate, by retraction or extension, the varying shaft length caused by the movement of the rear axle as the rear suspension deflects. The attachment of the driveshaft to the axle may be connected by a bolted flange or strap type clamps that connect the driveshaft to the axle pinion yoke. The type of connection used depends on the axle type.

The driveshaft is finely balanced during manufacture and it is recommended that care be used when universal joints are replaced to help maintain this balance. Mark each individual yoke or flange in relation to the one

3.2 Mark the relationship of the rear driveshaft to the differential pinion flange or yoke

3.3 Insert a screwdriver or prybar through the yoke to prevent the shaft from turning when you loosen the bolts

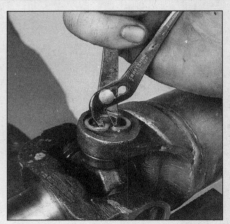

4.3 Use a small pair of pliers to remove the snap-rings from the ends of the universal joint yokes

4.4 To remove the U-joint from the driveshaft, use a vise as a press - the small socket will push the cross and bearing cap into the large socket

4.5 Locking pliers can be used to remove the bearing caps from the yoke

opposite in order to maintain the balance. Do not drop the assembly during servicing operations.

3   Driveshaft - removal and installation

Removal

Refer to illustrations 3.2 and 3.3

1   Raise the vehicle and support it securely on jackstands.

2   Use chalk or a scribe to "index" the relationship of the driveshaft to the differential axle assembly mating flange or yoke. This ensures correct alignment when the driveshaft is reinstalled **(see illustration)**.

3   Remove the bolts securing the driveshaft flange or universal joint clamps to the differential pinion flange or yoke **(see illustration)**.

4   Mark the relationship of the transmission to the slip yoke

5   Pry the universal joint away from its mating flange or yoke. Be careful not to let the caps fall off of the universal joint (which would cause contamination and loss of the needle

bearings). Lower the rear of the driveshaft.

6   Wrap tape around the universal joint bearings at the axle end of the driveshaft so they won't fall off. Slide the front of the driveshaft out of the transmission.

Installation

7   Installation is the reverse of removal. If the shaft cannot be lined up due to the components of the differential or transmission having been rotated, put the vehicle in Neutral or rotate one wheel to allow the original alignment to be achieved. Make sure the universal joint caps are properly placed in the flange seat or yoke. Tighten the fasteners to the torque listed in this Chapter's Specifications.

4   Universal joints - replacement

Note: *Always purchase a universal joint service kit for your model vehicle before beginning this procedure. Also, read through the entire procedure before beginning work.*

1   Remove the driveshaft (Section 2).

Outer snap-ring type

Refer to illustrations 4.3, 4.4, 4.5 and 4.6

2   Place the driveshaft on a workbench equipped with a vise.

3   Remove the snap-rings with a small pair of pliers **(see illustration)**.

4   Support the cross (also called a spider or trunnion) on a short piece of pipe or a large socket and use another socket to press out the cross by closing the vise **(see illustration)**.

5   Press the cross through as far as possible, then grip the bearing cup with locking pliers and remove it **(see illustration)**.

6   A universal joint repair kit will contain a new trunnion, seals, bearings, cups and snap-rings **(see illustration)**.

7   Inspect the bearing cup housing in the driveshaft for wear and damage.

8   If the bearing cup housings in the yoke are so worn that the cups are a loose fit in the yokes, the driveshaft will have to be replaced

with a new one.

9   Make sure the dust seals are properly located on the trunnion so the cavities face the trunnion.

10   Using a vise, press one bearing cup into the yoke approximately 1/4-inch.

11   Use multi-purpose grease to hold the needle rollers in place in the cup.

12   Insert the trunnion into the partially installed bearing cup, taking care not to dislodge the needle rollers.

13   Stick the needle bearings into the opposite cup, hold the trunnion in correct alignment and press both cups into place by slowly and carefully closing the jaws of the vise.

14   Use a socket slightly smaller in diameter than the cups to press them into the yoke. Press in one side, install the snap-ring, then press the other side to shift the trunnion assembly tight against the installed snap-ring and install the other snap-ring.

15   Repeat the operations for the remaining two bearing cups.

Injected plastic (inner snapring) type

Refer to illustrations 4.16 and 4.19

16   If this is the first time the joint is being

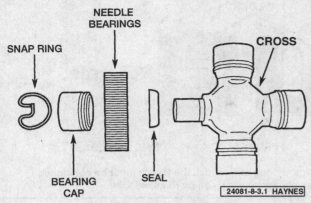

4.6 Outer snap-ring type U-joint

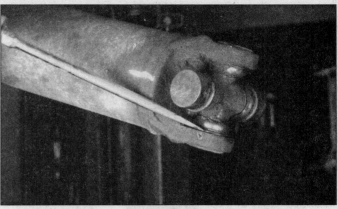

4.16 Remove the inner snap-rings from the U-joint by tapping them off with a screwdriver and hammer

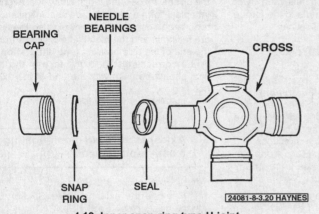

4.19 Inner snap-ring type U-joint

6.3 Remove the pinion shaft lock bolt

rebuilt it will not be necessary to remove the snap-rings, because there aren't any; the pressing operation will shear the molded plastic retaining material. If the driveshaft has previously had the original U-joints replaced with snap-ring types, remove the snap-rings before pressing the bearing cups out **(see illustration)**.

17 Press out the bearing cups as described in Steps 3 through 5.

18 Remove the trunnion (cross) and clean all plastic material from the yoke. Use a small punch to remove the plastic from the injection holes.

19 Reassembly is the same as for the outer snap-ring joint described in Steps 9 through 14, except that the snap-rings are on the inner part of each bearing cup **(see illustration)**.

5   Axles - general information

All axles are hypoid gear types with cast carriers and pressed-in axle tubes. Some models are equipped with limited slip or locking differentials designed to give better traction when one wheel has more traction than the other.

Two types of axleshafts are used: semi- and full-floating.

Semi-floating axleshafts are supported at the outer end of the axle by bearings pressed into the outer end of the axle tube, and are retained in the differential splines by a C-clip.

Full-floating axleshafts ride in the differential splines at their inner ends and is bolted to the wheel hub at the outer end. They are held in place by a hub-mounted flange which can be unbolted, allowing the axleshaft to be removed with the wheel in place.

6   Axleshaft - removal and installation

Semi-floating axleshaft
Removal
Refer to illustrations 6.3, 6.4, 6.5a and 6.5b

1   Loosen the rear wheel lug nuts. Raise the rear of the vehicle, support it securely on jackstands and block the front wheels. Remove the wheel and brake disc or drum (see Chapter 9).

2   Remove the differential cover and allow the lubricant to drain into a container (see Chapter 1).

3   Remove the lock screw **(see illustration)**.

6.4 Withdraw the pinion shaft for access to the C-locks (don't turn the axleshafts after the shaft has been pulled out, or the spider gears may become mispositioned)

4   On models with a conventional differential (non-locking), remove the pinion shaft. On models with a locking differential, withdraw the pinion shaft part way, then rotate the differential until the shaft touches the case, providing enough clearance for access to the C-locks **(see illustration)**.

5   Have an assistant push in on the outer

6.5a Push the axle flange in, then remove the C-lock from the inner end of the axleshaft

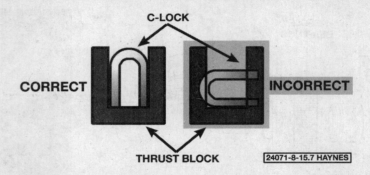

6.5b On models with a locking differential, the C-lock must be positioned as shown before it can be removed

flanged end of the axleshaft while you remove the C-lock from the groove in the inner end of the shaft **(see illustration)**. **Note:** *On models with a locking differential, use a screwdriver to rotate the C-lock until the open end points in* **(see illustration)**.

6   With the C-lock removed, withdraw the axleshaft, taking care not to damage the oil seal, but note that it is a good idea to replace the seal whenever the axleshaft is removed (see Section 7). Some models have a thrust washer in the differential; make sure it doesn't fall out when the axleshaft is removed.

Installation

7   To install, carefully insert the axleshaft into the housing and seat it securely in the differential.

8   Install the C-lock in the axleshaft groove and pull out on the flange to lock it.

9   Insert the pinion shaft, align the hole in the shaft with the lock screw hole and install the lock screw. **Note:** *Apply a non-hardening, thread-locking compound to the threads of the lock screw before installing it.* Tighten the lock screw to the torque listed in this Chapter's Specifications.

10   Install the cover and fill the differential

with the lubricant specified in Chapter 1.

11   Install the brake disc or drum, see Chapter 9. Install the wheel and lug nuts, then lower the vehicle. Tighten the lug nuts to the torque listed in the Chapter 1 Specifications.

Full-floating axleshaft

Refer to illustration 6.12

12   Remove the bolts that attach the axleshaft flange to the hub **(see illustration)**.

13   Tap the flange with a soft-face hammer to loosen the shaft, then grip the rib in the face of the flange with a pair of locking pliers. Twist the shaft slightly in both directions and withdraw it from the housing. Place a drip pan under the outer end of the axle to catch any lubricant which might leak out while the axle is removed.

14   Installation is the reverse of removal. Be sure to hold the axleshaft level to engage the splines at the inner end with those in the differential side gear. Always use a new gasket on the flange and keep both the flange and hub mating surface free of grease and oil.

---

7   Axleshaft oil seal (semi-floating axle) - replacement

Refer to illustrations 7.2 and 7.3

1   Remove the axleshaft (see Section 5).

2   Pry the oil seal from the end of the axle

housing **(see illustration)**.

3   Apply a film of multi-purpose grease to the oil seal recess and tap the new seal evenly into place with a hammer and seal installation tool, large socket or piece of pipe so the lips are facing in and the metal face is visible from the end of the axle housing **(see illustration)**. When correctly installed, the face of the oil seal should be flush with the end of the axle housing.

4   Install the axleshaft (see Section 6).

---

8   Axleshaft bearing (semi-floating axle) - replacement

Refer to illustrations 8.2, 8.3 and 8.4

1   Remove the axleshaft (see Section 6) and the oil seal (see Section 7).

2   A bearing puller which grips the bearing from behind will be required for this job **(see illustration)**.

3   Attach a slide hammer to the puller and extract the bearing from the axle housing **(see illustration)**.

4   Clean out the bearing recess and drive in the new bearing with a bearing installer positioned against the outer bearing race **(see illustration)**. Make sure the bearing is tapped in to the full depth of the recess.

5   Install a new oil seal (see Section 7), then install the axleshaft (see Section 6).

6.12 Remove the axleshaft flange-to-hub bolts

7.2 Prying out the axleshaft oil seal with a seal removal tool

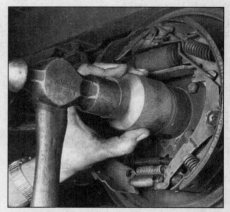

7.3 Using a large socket to install the axleshaft oil seal - drive the seal in until it's flush with the bore

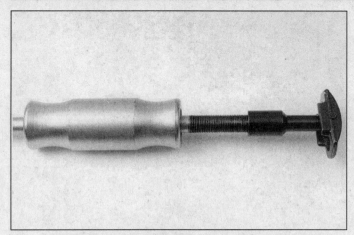

8.2 A typical slide hammer and axleshaft bearing remover attachment

8.3 Removing the axleshaft bearing with a slide hammer

9   Rear hub, wheel bearing and seal (full-floating axle) - removal, bearing/seal replacement and installation

Removal

Refer to illustrations 9.4a, 9.4b and 9.5
1   Remove the axleshaft (see Section 6).
2   Loosen the rear wheel lug nuts, raise the rear of the vehicle and support it securely on jackstands. Block the front wheels and remove the rear wheels.
3   On models equipped with disc brakes, remove the brake caliper and disc (see Chapter 9). On models equipped with drum brakes, remove the brake drum (see Chapter 9).
4   Remove the retaining ring and key from the end of the axle housing **(see illustrations).**
5   Remove the adjusting nut, using a special socket **(see illustration).**
6   Pull the hub assembly straight off the axle tube.
7   Remove and discard the oil seal from the back of the hub.
8   To further disassemble the hub, use a hammer and a long bar or drift punch to knock

out the inner bearing, cup (race) and oil seal.
9   Remove the outer retaining ring, then knock the outer bearing and cup from the hub.
10   Clean the old sealing compound from the seal bore in the hub.
11   Use solvent to clean the bearings, hub and axle tube. A small brush may prove useful; make sure no bristles from the brush embed themselves in the bearing rollers. Now spray the bearings with brake system cleaner, which will remove the solvent and allow the bearings to dry much more rapidly.
12   Carefully inspect the bearings for cracks, wear and damage. Check the axle tube flange, studs and hub splines for damage and corrosion. Check the bearing cups (races) for pitting or scoring. Worn or damaged components must be replaced with new ones.
13   Inspect the brake drum or disc (see Chapter 9).
14   Lubricate the bearings and the axle tube contact areas with wheel bearing grease. Work the grease completely into the bearings, forcing it between the rollers, cone and cage.
15   Reassemble the hub by reversing the disassembly procedure. Use only the proper size bearing driver when installing the new bearing cups (races).

8.4 Using a bearing driver to tap the bearing evenly into the axle housing

Installation
16   Make sure the axle housing oil deflector is in position. Place the hub assembly on the axle tube, taking care not to damage the oil seals.
17   Install the adjusting nut and adjust the bearings as described below.

9.4a Remove the retaining ring . . .

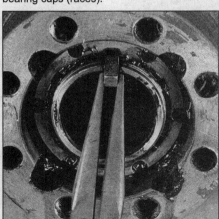

9.4b . . . then remove the key from the hub

9.5 Rear axle hub locknut tool available at most auto parts stores

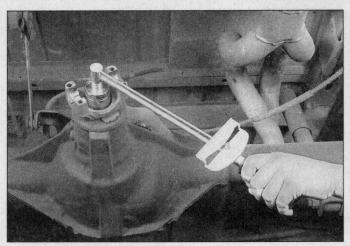

10.3 Use an inch-pound torque wrench to check the torque required to rotate the differential pinion

10.4 Before removing the nut, mark the position of the flange to the shaft and count the number of exposed threads

Adjustment

18   Rotate the hub, making sure it turns freely.

19   While rotating the hub in the normal direction of rotation (forward), tighten the adjusting nut to 50 ft-lbs with a torque wrench. Again, this will require the special socket, which is available at most auto parts stores.

20   Back the nut off 1/4-turn, then tighten the nut hand-tight with the special socket.

21   Turn the nut to align the closest slot in the nut with the keyway in the spindle, then install the key.

22   Install the retaining ring in the end of the spindle.

23   Wiggle the hub assembly; you shouldn't be able to detect any play, but the hub should turn freely (there shouldn't be any preload on the bearings, but there shouldn't be any freeplay, either).

24   Install the axleshaft (see Section 6) and lower the vehicle.

10   Pinion oil seal - replacement

Refer to illustrations 10.3, 10.4, 10.5, 10.8 and 10.9

1   Loosen the rear wheel lug nuts. Raise the rear of the vehicle and support it securely on jackstands. Block the front wheels to keep the vehicle from rolling off the stands. Remove the wheels.

2   Disconnect the driveshaft from the differential pinion flange and fasten it out of the way (see Section 3).

3   Rotate the pinion a few times by hand. Use a beam-type or dial-type inch-pound torque wrench to check the torque required to rotate the pinion **(see illustration)**. Record it for use later.

4   Mark the relationship of the pinion flange to the shaft **(see illustration),** then count and write down the number of exposed threads on the shaft.

5   Use a chain wrench to keep the companion flange from moving while the self-locking pinion nut is loosened **(see illustration).**

6   Remove the pinion nut.

7   Withdraw the flange. It may be necessary to use a two-jaw puller engaged behind the flange to draw it off. Do not attempt to pry or hammer behind the flange or hammer on the end of the pinion shaft.

8   Pry out the old seal and discard it **(see illustration).**

9   Lubricate the lips of the new seal and fill the space between the seal lips with wheel bearing grease, then tap it evenly into position with a seal installation tool or a large socket **(see illustration).** Make sure it enters the housing squarely and is tapped in to its full depth.

10   Install the pinion flange, lining up the marks made in Step 4. If necessary, tighten the pinion nut to draw the flange into place. Do not try to hammer the flange into position.

11   Apply a bead of RTV sealant to the ends of the splines visible in the center of the flange so oil will be sealed in.

12   Install the washer and a new pinion nut. Tighten the nut until the number of threads recorded in Step 4 are exposed.

10.5 A chain wrench can be used to prevent the companion flange from turning when removing the pinion nut

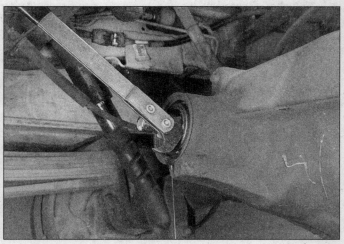

10.8 Pry out the old pinion seal

10.9 Use a seal installation tool or large socket to tap the pinion oil seal evenly into place

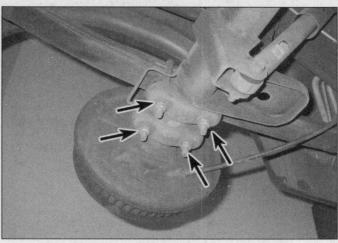

11.10 The rear axle is retained to each leaf spring by two U-bolts and four nuts

13 Measure the torque required to rotate the pinion and tighten the nut in small increments (no more than 5 ft-lbs) until it matches the figure recorded in Step 3. To compensate for the drag of the new oil seal, the nut should be tightened a little more until the rotational torque of the pinion exceeds the earlier recording by 5 in-lbs.

14 Reinstall all components removed previously by reversing the removal steps, tightening all fasteners to their specified torque values.

11 Axle assembly - removal and installation

Removal

Refer to illustration 11.10

1 Raise the rear of the vehicle and support it with jackstands placed under the frame rails.

2 Remove the rear wheels.

3 Disconnect the driveshaft from the rear axle (see Section 3).

4 Disconnect the ABS sensor, if equipped.

5 Disconnect the parking brake cable from the parking brake lever (see Chapter 9).

6 Unscrew the vent hose fitting to detach the brake line junction block from the axle tube.

7 Disconnect the brake lines from the clips and brackets on the axle housing. Remove the rear brake calipers, if equipped (see Chapter 9). **Caution:** *Tie the calipers up with wire to keep any strain off the flexible brake lines.*

8 Support the rear axle with a floor jack. If the rear differential is offset to one side, you'll have to use two jacks - one placed under each axle tube.

9 Remove the lower mounting bolts securing the rear shocks to the axle (see Chapter 10).

10 With the jack(s) supporting the axle, remove the nuts and U-bolts securing the axle to the springs **(see illustration).**

11 Lower the axle assembly and remove it from under the vehicle.

Installation

12 Installation is the reverse of the removal procedure.

13 Tighten the U-bolt nuts to the torque listed in the Chapter 10 Specifications. Tighten the caliper mounting bolts to the torque listed in the Chapter 9 Specifications. If necessary, check and fill the axle with the specified lubricant (see Chapter 1).

Notes

Chapter 9
Brakes

Contents

Specifications

General
Brake fluid type .... See Chapter 1

Disc brakes
Brake pad minimum thickness .... See Chapter 1
Disc lateral runout limit .... 0.003 inch
Disc minimum thickness .... Cast into disc

Drum brakes
Maximum drum diameter .... Cast into drum
Shoe lining minimum thickness .... See Chapter 1

Torque specifications   Ft-lbs
Brake hose-to-caliper inlet fitting bolt 32
Brake master cylinder mounting nuts 27
Caliper mounting bolts
  Front
    2002 and earlier models 38
    2003 and later models 80
  Rear
    1500 31
    2500/3500 80
Caliper mounting bracket bolts
  Front
    1500 129
    2500/3500 221
  Rear
    1500 148
    2500/3500 221
Power brake booster mounting nuts 26

2.2 The ABS hydraulic control unit is located under this heat shield

1   General information

General

The vehicles covered by this manual are equipped with a hydraulically operated brake system. The front brakes are disc type and the rear brakes are either drum or disc type. Both the front and rear disc brakes automatically compensate for disc and pad wear. As the pads wear down, the pistons gradually protrude farther from the calipers, but don't retract as far, automatically compensating for the thinner pads. Rear drum brakes have automatic adjusters which compensate for wear of the brake shoes.

Hydraulic system

The hydraulic system consists of two separate circuits, split front-to-rear. The master cylinder has separate reservoirs for the two circuits, and, in the event of a leak or failure in one hydraulic circuit, the other circuit will remain operative and a warning indicator will light up on the instrument panel when a substantial amount of brake fluid is lost, showing that a failure has occurred.

Power brake booster

The power brake booster uses either engine manifold vacuum or hydraulic pressure from the power steering pump to provide assistance to the brakes. It is mounted on the firewall in the engine compartment, directly behind the master cylinder.

Parking brake

The parking brake operates the rear brakes only, through cable actuation. It's activated by a pedal mounted under the left end of the instrument panel. The parking brake on rear disc brake models uses brake shoes and small brake drums integral with the rear brake discs.

Service

After completing any operation involving disassembly of any part of the brake sys-

tem, always test drive the vehicle to check for proper braking performance before resuming normal driving. When testing the brakes, perform the tests on a clean, dry, flat surface. Conditions other than these can lead to inaccurate test results.

Test the brakes at various speeds with both light and heavy pedal pressure. The vehicle should stop evenly without pulling to one side or the other.

Tires, vehicle load and wheel alignment are factors which also affect braking performance.

2   Anti-lock Brake System (ABS) - general information

General information

Refer to illustration 2.2

1   The anti-lock brake system is designed to maintain vehicle steerability, directional stability and optimum deceleration under severe braking conditions on most road surfaces. It does so by monitoring the rotational speed of each wheel and controlling the brake line pressure to each wheel during braking. This prevents the wheels from locking up.

2   The ABS system has three main components - the wheel speed sensors, the electronic control unit (ECU) and the hydraulic unit **(see illustration)**. Four wheel speed sensors - one at each wheel - send a variable voltage signal to the control unit, which monitors these signals, compares them to its program and determines whether a wheel is about to lock up. When a wheel is about to lock up, the control unit signals the hydraulic unit to reduce hydraulic pressure (or not increase it further) at that wheel's brake caliper. Pressure modulation is handled by electrically-operated solenoid valves.

3   If a problem develops within the system, an "ABS" warning light will glow on the dashboard. Sometimes, a visual inspection of the ABS system can help you locate the problem. Carefully inspect the ABS wiring harness. Pay particularly close attention to the harness and connections near each wheel. Look for signs of chafing and other damage caused by incorrectly routed wires. If a wheel sensor harness is damaged, the sensor must be replaced. **Warning:** *Do NOT try to repair an ABS wiring harness. The ABS system is sensitive to even the smallest changes in resistance. Repairing the harness could alter resistance values and cause the system to malfunction. If the ABS wiring harness is damaged in any way, it must be replaced.* **Caution:** *Make sure the ignition is turned off before unplugging or reattaching any electrical connections.*

Diagnosis and repair

4 If a dashboard warning light comes on and stays on while the vehicle is in operation, the ABS system requires attention. Although special electronic ABS diagnostic testing tools are necessary to properly diagnose the system,

you can perform a few preliminary checks before taking the vehicle to a dealer service department.

  a) *Check the brake fluid level in the reservoir.*
  b) *Verify that the computer electrical connectors are securely connected.*
  c) *Check the electrical connectors at the hydraulic control unit.*
  d) *Check the fuses.*
  e) *Follow the wiring harness to each wheel and verify that all connections are secure and that the wiring is undamaged.*

5   If the above preliminary checks do not rectify the problem, the vehicle should be diagnosed by a dealer service department or other qualified repair shop. Due to the complex nature of this system, all actual repair work must be done by a qualified automotive technician.

3   Disc brake pads - replacement

Warning: *Disc brake pads must be replaced on both front wheels or both rear wheels at the same time - never replace the pads on only one wheel. Also, the dust created by the brake system is harmful to your health. Never blow it out with compressed air and don't inhale any of it. An approved filtering mask should be worn when working on the brakes. Do not, under any circumstances, use petroleum-based solvents to clean brake parts. Use brake system cleaner only!*

Preliminary steps (all models)

Refer to illustrations 3.4 and 3.5
Caution: *Don't depress the brake pedal with the caliper removed.*

1   Remove the cap from the brake fluid reservoir. Remove about two-thirds of the fluid from the reservoir, then reinstall the cap. **Warning:** *Brake fluid is poisonous - never siphon it by mouth. Use a suction gun or old poultry baster. If a baster is used, never again use it for the preparation of food.* **Caution:** *Brake fluid will damage paint. If any fluid is spilled, wash it off immediately with plenty of clean, cold water.*

2   Loosen the wheel lug nuts, raise the end of the vehicle you're working on and support it securely on jackstands. Block the wheels that remain on the ground.

3   Remove the wheels. Work on one brake assembly at a time, using the assembled brake for reference if necessary.

4   Position a drain pan under the brake assembly and clean the caliper and surrounding area with brake system cleaner **(see illustration)**.

5   Push the piston back into its bore using a C-clamp **(see illustration)**. As the piston(s) is depressed to the bottom of the caliper bore, the fluid level in the master cylinder will rise as the brake fluid is displaced. Make sure it doesn't overflow. If necessary, siphon off some more of the fluid.

3.4 Before disassembling the brake, wash it thoroughly with brake system cleaner and allow it to dry - position a drain pan under the brake to catch the residue - DO NOT use compressed air to blow off brake dust!

3.5 To make room for the new pads, use a C-clamp to depress the piston(s) into the caliper before removing the caliper and pads - do this a little at a time, keeping an eye on the fluid level in the master cylinder to make sure it doesn't overflow

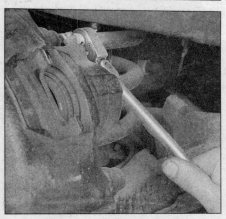

3.6 Remove the two caliper mounting bolts

3.7a Lift the caliper and pads straight up off the brake disc . . .

2002 and earlier models

Refer to illustrations 3.6, 3.7a, 3.7b, 3.8 and 3.11

6   Remove the two caliper mounting bolts **(see illustration)**.

7   Lift the caliper off the disc and remove the outer pad **(see illustrations)**.

8   Pull the inner pad out of the caliper and remove it **(see illustration)**. Fasten the caliper out of the way with a piece of wire to prevent damage to the brake hose.

9   Remove the mounting bolt seals, then use a scribe or similar tool to extract the rubber bushings from inside the caliper ears.

10   Clean the caliper and mounting bolts and check them for corrosion and damage. Replace the bolts with new ones if they're significantly corroded or damaged. Inspect the brake disc carefully as outlined in Section 5. If machining is necessary, follow the information in that Section to remove the disc.

11   Begin reassembly by installing the new rubber bushings and seals in the caliper **(see illustration)**. Fill the space between the bushings with silicone grease. It's also a good idea

to apply anti-squeal compound to the backing plates of the new brake pads **(see illustration 3.19d)**.

12   Position the inner pad, with the clip, in the caliper so the wear indicator is facing the rear of the caliper.

13   Position the outer pad in the caliper so the tab at the bottom of the pad is engaged in the cutout in the caliper.

14   Hold the caliper in position over the disc, push the mounting bolts through the bushings and thread them into the bracket. Tighten them to the torque listed in this Chapter's specifications.

15   Install the brake pads on the opposite wheel, then install the wheels and lower the vehicle. Add brake fluid to the reservoir until it's full (see Chapter 1).

16   Pump the brakes several times to seat the pads against the disc, then check the fluid level again.

17   Check the operation of the brakes before driving the vehicle in traffic. Try to avoid heavy brake applications until the brakes have been applied lightly several times to seat the pads.

2003 and later models

Refer to illustrations 3.19a through 3.19h

Note: *This procedure applies to the front and rear brake pads.*

18   Remove the caliper lower mounting bolt, then pivot the caliper up to expose the brake pads.

19   Follow the accompanying photo

3.7b . . . then remove the outer brake pad from the caliper

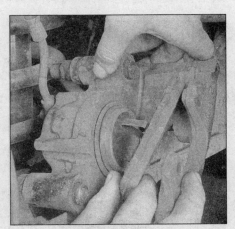

3.8 Pull the inner pad and clip out of the caliper

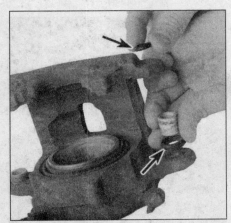

3.11 Make sure the caliper bushings are lubricated

3.19a Remove the inner brake pad

3.19b Remove the outer brake pad

3.19c Remove the upper and lower pad retainers from the caliper mounting bracket; if they are cracked or distorted, replace them

sequence for the actual pad replacement procedure **(see illustrations 3.19a through 3.19h).** Be sure to stay in order and read the caption under each illustration.

20 When reinstalling the caliper, be sure to tighten the mounting bolt(s) to the torque listed in this Chapter's Specifications. Tighten the wheel lug nuts to the torque listed in the

Chapter 1 Specifications.
21 After the job has been completed, firmly depress the brake pedal a few times to bring the pads into contact with the disc. Check the level of the brake fluid, adding some if necessary (see Chapter 1). Check the operation of the brakes carefully before placing the vehicle into normal service.

4 Disc brake caliper - removal and installation

Refer to illustration 4.2
Warning: *The dust created by the brake system is harmful to your health. Never blow it out with compressed air and don't inhale any of it. An approved filtering mask should be worn when working on the brakes. Do not, under any circumstances, use petroleum-based solvents to clean brake parts. Use brake system cleaner only!*

Removal

1 Loosen the front or rear wheel lug nuts, raise the front or rear of the vehicle and place it securely on jackstands. Block the wheels at the opposite end. Remove the front or rear wheel.
2 Remove the inlet fitting bolt and disconnect the brake hose from the caliper. Discard

3.19d Apply anti-squeal compound to the back of both pads (let the compound "set up" a few minutes before installing them)

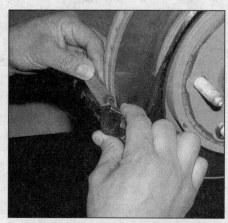

3.19e Install the upper and lower pad retainers on the caliper mounting bracket

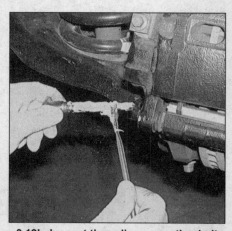

3.19h Inspect the caliper mounting bolt for scoring and corrosion, then lubricate it with high-temperature brake grease. If it was dry, pivot the caliper up again, slide the upper mounting bolt out of the bracket and lubricate it, too.

3.19f Install the inner brake pad . . .

3.19g . . . and the outer brake pad

4.2 There is a sealing washer on either side of the brake hose inlet fitting; be sure to replace these with new ones when reconnecting the hose

5.2 The brake pads on this vehicle were obviously neglected - they wore down completely and cut deep grooves into the disc (wear this severe means the disc must be replaced)

5.3a To check disc runout, mount a dial indicator as shown and rotate the disc

the old sealing washers **(see illustration).** Plug the brake hose immediately to keep contaminants and air out of the brake system and to prevent losing any more brake fluid than is necessary. **Note:** *If you are simply removing the caliper for access to other components, leave the brake hose connected and suspend the caliper with a length of wire - don't let it hang by the hose.*

3   Remove the caliper mounting bolts and detach the caliper from the mounting bracket. When removing a rear caliper on some models, it may be necessary hold the slide pins with an open-end wrench to prevent them from turning when the mounting bolts are unscrewed.

Installation

4   Installation is the reverse of removal. Don't forget to use new sealing washers on each side of the brake hose inlet fitting and be sure to tighten the fitting bolt and the caliper mounting bolts to the torque listed in this Chapter's Specifications.

5   Bleed the brake system (see Section 11). **Note:** *If the brake hose was not dis-*

connected, bleeding won't be required. Make sure there are no leaks from the hose connections. Test the brakes carefully before returning the vehicle to normal service.

5   Brake disc - inspection, removal and installation

Inspection
Refer to illustrations 5.2, 5.3a, 5.3b, 5.4a and 5.4b

1   Loosen the wheel lug nuts, raise the vehicle and support it securely on jackstands. Apply the parking brake. Remove the wheels.

2   Visually inspect the disc surface for score marks and other damage **(see illustration).** Light scratches and shallow grooves are normal after use and won't affect brake operation. Deep grooves require disc removal and refinishing by an automotive machine shop. Be sure to check both sides of the disc.

3   To check disc runout, place a dial indicator at a point about 1/2-inch from the outer edge of the disc **(see illustration).** Set the indicator to zero and turn the disc. The indicator reading should not exceed the runout limit listed in this Chapter's Specifications. If it does, the disc should be refinished by an automotive machine shop. **Note:** *When replacing the brake pads it's a good idea to have the discs refinished regardless of the dial indicator reading, as this will impart a smooth finish and ensure a perfectly flat surface, eliminating any brake pedal pulsation or other undesirable symptoms. At the very least, if you elect not to have the discs resurfaced, remove the glaze from the surface with emery cloth or sandpaper, using a swirling motion* **(see illustration).**

4   The disc must not be machined to a thickness less than the specified minimum thickness, which is cast into the disc **(see illustration).** The disc thickness can be checked with a micrometer **(see illustration).**

Removal and installation
5   Remove the brake calipers (don't disconnect the brake hoses) and hang them out of the way (see Section 4).

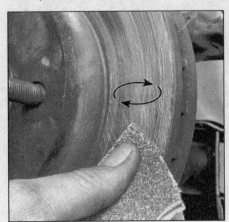

5.3b Using a swirling motion, remove the glaze from the disc surface with sandpaper or emery cloth

5.4a The minimum (discard) thickness of the brake disc is cast into the disc (typical)

5.4b Measure the brake disc thickness at several points with a micrometer

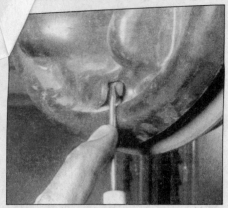

6.4a If the drum is difficult to remove, you may have to retract the brake shoes: Remove the rubber plug from the backing plate . . .

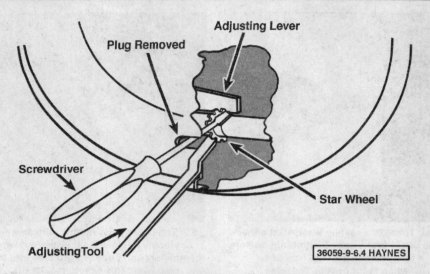

6.4b . . . insert a small screwdriver through the hole, push the adjusting lever off the star wheel and rotate the star adjuster with a brake adjustment tool or another screwdriver

6   On 2003 and later models, remove the caliper mounting bracket.

7   On front discs, remove the grease cap, wheel bearing retainer nut, spindle nut, outer bearing retainer washer and outer wheel bearing, then remove the disc/hub (see *Front wheel bearing check, repack and adjustment* in Chapter 1).

8   If you're removing a rear disc, simply slide disc off the wheel studs.

9   Installation is the reverse of removal. Tighten the caliper mounting bracket to the torque listed in this Chapter's Specifications.

10   Lower the vehicle and tighten the wheel lug nuts to the torque listed in the Chapter 1 Specifications.

6   Drum brake shoes (models with rear drum brakes) - replacement

Refer to illustrations 6.4a, 6.4b and 6.6a through 6.6z

Warning: *Drum brake shoes must be replaced on both wheels at the same time - never replace the shoes on only one wheel. Also, the dust created by the brake system is*

6.5 Wash the drum brake assembly with brake system cleaner so you don't inhale any brake dust

harmful to your health. Never blow it out with compressed air and don't inhale any of it. An approved filtering mask should be worn when working on the brakes. Do not, under any circumstances, use petroleum-based solvents to clean brake parts. Use brake system cleaner only!

Caution: *Whenever the brake shoes are replaced, the return and hold-down springs*

should also be replaced. Due to the continuous heating/cooling cycle the springs are subjected to, they can lose tension over a period of time and may allow the shoes to drag on the drum and wear at a much faster rate than normal.

1   Loosen the wheel lug nuts, raise the rear of the vehicle and support it securely on jackstands. Block the front wheels to keep the

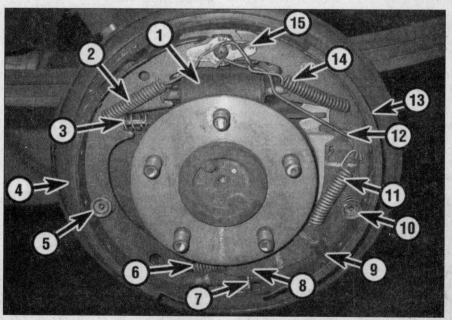

6.6a Rear drum brake components (left side shown)

1	Wheel cylinder	9	Lever return spring
2	Return spring	10	Hold-down spring and pin
3	Parking brake strut and spring	11	Return spring
4	Primary shoe	12	Actuator link
5	Hold-down spring and pin	13	Secondary shoe
6	Adjuster screw shoe spring	14	Return spring
7	Adjuster wheel	15	Anchor plate
8	Adjuster lever		

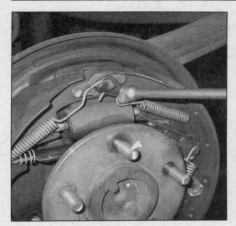

6.6b Remove the secondary shoe return spring from the actuator link

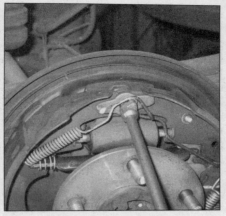

6.6c Remove the primary shoe return spring from the anchor plate pin

6.6d Spread the bottoms of the shoes apart and remove the adjuster screw assembly

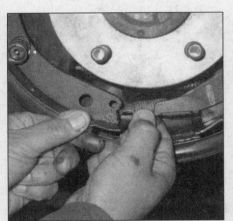

6.6e Remove the adjuster screw spring

6.6f Remove the primary shoe hold-down spring and pin (push the retainer in and turn it 90-degrees to release it from the pin)

6.6g Remove the primary brake shoe

vehicle from rolling.

2   Release the parking brake.

3   Remove the wheel. **Note:** *All four rear brake shoes must be replaced at the same time, but to avoid mixing up parts, work on only one brake assembly at a time.* **Note:** *If the brake drum cannot be easily pulled off the axle and shoe assembly, make sure the parking brake is completely released. If the drum*

still cannot be pulled off, the brake shoes will have to be retracted. This is done by first removing the plug from the brake backing plate **(see illustrations)**. With the plug removed, pull the lever off the adjuster star wheel with a hooked tool while turning the adjuster wheel with another screwdriver, mov-

ing the shoes away from the drum. The drum should now come off.

5   Clean the brake shoe assembly with brake system cleaner before beginning work **(see illustration)**.

6   Follow the accompanying illustrations for the brake shoe replacement procedure **(see illustrations 6.6a through 6.6z)**. Be sure to stay in order and read the caption under each illustration.

6.6h Remove the actuator link from the anchor pin

6.6i Remove the secondary shoe holddown spring and retainer

6.6j Disengage the parking brake strut from the secondary shoe

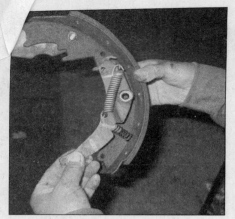

6.6k Separate the adjuster lever from the secondary shoe

6.6l Remove the clip from the pin on the parking brake lever and detach the lever from the old shoe

6.6m Lubricate the brake shoe contact areas with high-temperature grease. Now is a good time to check the wheel cylinder for fluid leakage

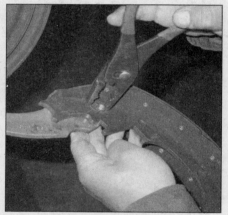

6.6n Transfer the parking brake lever to the new secondary shoe and secure it with a new clip

6.6o Position the secondary shoe on the backing plate, making sure the wheel cylinder pushrod seats properly in its notch, insert the hold-down pin through the backing plate and brake shoe . . .

6.6p . . . then install the adjuster lever

7   Before reinstalling the drum, it should be checked for cracks, score marks, deep scratches and hard spots, which will appear as small discolored areas. If the hard spots cannot be removed with fine emery cloth or if any of the other conditions listed above exist, the drum must be taken to an auto-

motive machine shop to have it resurfaced. **Note:** *Professionals recommend resurfacing the drums each time a brake job is done. Resurfacing will eliminate the possibility of out-of-round drums. If the drums are worn so*

much that they can't be resurfaced without exceeding the maximum allowable diameter (stamped or cast into the drum), then new ones will be required. At the very least, if you elect not to have the drums resurfaced, remove the glaze from the surface with emery cloth using a swirling motion.

8   Install the brake drum on the axle flange. Using a screwdriver inserted through the

6.6q Install the hold-down spring and retainer

6.6r Install the lever return spring

6.6s Attach the actuator link to the anchor plate pin

6.6t Install the parking brake strut, making sure it properly engages the secondary shoe and parking brake lever

6.6u Make sure the parking brake strut and wheel cylinder pushrod properly engage the primary shoe, then install the hold-down pin

6.6v Secure the primary shoe with the hold-down spring and retainer

6.6w Install the adjuster screw spring . . .

6.6x . . . and the adjuster screw

adjust the brakes until satisfactory pedal action is obtained.

11   Check the operation of the brakes carefully before driving the vehicle.

---

7   Wheel cylinder (models with rear drum brakes) - removal and installation

---

Note: *If replacement is indicated (usually because of fluid leakage or sticky operation), it is recommended that the wheel cylinders be replaced, not overhauled. Always replace the wheel cylinders in pairs - never replace just one of them.*

Removal

Refer to illustration 7.4

1   Raise the rear of the vehicle and support it securely on jackstands. Block the front wheels to keep the vehicle from rolling.

2   Remove the brake shoe assembly (see Section 6).

3   Remove all dirt and foreign material from around the wheel cylinder.

adjusting hole in the brake drum **(see illustration 6.4b),** turn the adjuster star wheel until the brake shoes drag on the drum as the drum is rotated, then back off the star wheel until the shoes don't drag. Reinstall the plug in the drum.

9   Mount the wheel and install the lug nuts. Lower the vehicle and tighten the lug nuts to the torque listed in the Chapter 1 Specifications.

10   Make a number of forward and reverse stops and operate the parking brake to

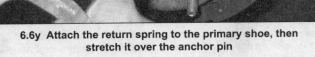

6.6y Attach the return spring to the primary shoe, then stretch it over the anchor pin

6.6z Attach the return spring to the secondary shoe, then attach it to the actuator link

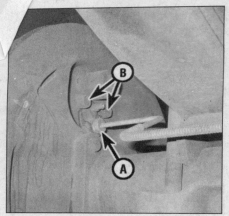

7.4 Completely loosen the brake line fitting (A), then remove the two wheel cylinder mounting bolts (B)

8.3 The parking brake shoe is secured at the bottom by a screw and a clip

8.4 Lift one end of the parking brake shoe over the axle flange, then "wind" the rest of the shoe over the flange

4   Disconnect the brake line **(see illustration).** Don't pull the brake line away from the wheel cylinder.
5   Remove the wheel cylinder mounting bolts.
6   Detach the wheel cylinder from the brake backing plate and immediately plug the brake line to prevent fluid loss and contamination.

Installation

7   Place the wheel cylinder in position and install the bolts finger tight. Connect the brake line to the cylinder, being careful not to cross thread the fitting. Tighten the wheel cylinder mounting bolts to the torque listed in this Chapter's Specifications. Now tighten the brake line fitting securely.
8   Install the brake shoe assembly (see Section 6).
9   Bleed the brakes (see Section 11).
10   Check the operation of the brakes carefully before driving the vehicle.

---

8   Parking brake shoes (models with rear disc brakes) - replacement

Refer to illustrations 8.3, 8.4 and 8.6
Warning: *The dust created by the brake system is harmful to your health. Never blow it out with compressed air and don't inhale any of it. An approved filtering mask should be worn when working on the brakes. Do not, under any circumstances, use petroleum-based solvents to clean brake parts. Use brake system cleaner only!*

1   Loosen the rear wheel lug nuts, raise the rear of the vehicle and support it securely on jackstands. Release the parking brake. Block the front wheels to prevent the vehicle from rolling, then remove the rear wheels.
2   Remove the brake caliper (see Section 4), mounting bracket and the brake disc (see Section 5). Loosen the nut on the parking brake equalizer to provide some slack in the cables.
3   Wash the brake assembly with brake

8.6 Make sure the ends of the shoe seat in the adjuster screw slot (A) and the tappet slot (B); C is the adjuster screw star wheel

system cleaner. Remove the screw and clip securing the bottom of the shoe **(see illustration),** then slide the shoe up and off of the actuator.
4   Lift one end of the shoe over the axle flange, then work the shoe over the flange and remove it **(see illustration).**
5   Before installing the new shoe, turn the adjuster screw star wheel in, then make sure the slots in the adjusting screw and the tappet are parallel with the backing plate.
6   To install the shoe, reverse the removal procedure. Make sure the ends of the shoe seat properly in the slots in the adjuster screw and tappet **(see illustration).**
7   When installing the new shoe and lining assembly, turn the adjuster screw until the shoe lining just drags on the braking surface inside the disc. Then remove the disc and back-off the adjuster screw until the shoe lining doesn't drag when the disc is installed and turned. The actual clearance between the lining surface of the shoe and the braking surface inside the disc should be 0.026-inch.
8   Installation is otherwise the reverse of the removal procedure. Be sure to tighten the caliper bracket bolts and the caliper mount-

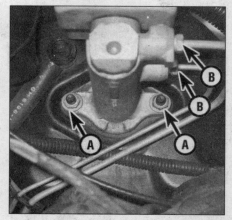

9.4 Master cylinder mounting details

A   Mounting nuts
B   Brake line fittings

ing bolts to the torque listed in this Chapter's Specifications, and the wheel lug nuts to the torque listed in the Chapter 1 Specifications.

---

9   Master cylinder - removal and installation

Removal

Refer to illustration 9.4
1   The master cylinder is located in the engine compartment, mounted to the power brake booster.
2   Remove as much fluid as you can from the reservoir with a syringe, such as an old turkey baster. **Warning:** *If a baster is used, never again use it for the preparation of food.*
3   Place rags under the fluid fittings and prepare caps or plastic bags to cover the ends of the lines once they are disconnected. **Caution:** *Brake fluid will damage paint. Cover all body parts and be careful not to spill fluid during this procedure.*
4   Loosen the fittings at the ends of the brake lines where they enter the master cylinder **(see illustration).** To prevent rounding

9.8 The best way to bleed air from the master cylinder before installing it on the vehicle is with a pair of bleeder tubes that direct brake fluid into the reservoir during bleeding

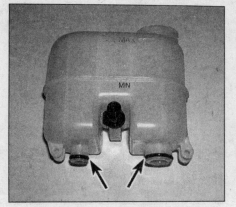

9.22 After the reservoir has been removed, replace the O-rings with new ones

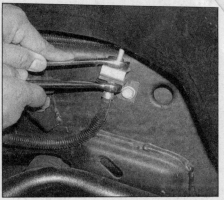

10.3a Using a flare-nut wrench, unscrew the threaded fitting on the brake line, while holding the hose end stationary with an open-end wrench . . .

off the corners on these nuts, the use of a flare-nut wrench, which wraps around the nut, is preferred. Pull the brake lines slightly away from the master cylinder and plug the ends to prevent contamination.

5   Disconnect the electrical connector at the brake fluid level switch on the master cylinder reservoir, if equipped, then remove the nuts attaching the master cylinder to the power booster. Pull the master cylinder off the studs and out of the engine compartment. Again, be careful not to spill the fluid as this is done.

6   If a new master cylinder is being installed, remove the reservoir from the master cylinder and transfer it to the new master cylinder (see Step 18). **Note:** *Be sure to install new seals when transferring the reservoir.*

Installation
Refer to illustration 9.8

7   Bench bleed the new master cylinder before installing it. Mount the master cylinder in a vise, with the jaws of the vise clamping on the mounting flange.

8   Attach a pair of master cylinder bleeder tubes to the outlet ports of the master cylinder **(see illustration).**

9   Fill the reservoir with brake fluid of the recommended type (see Chapter 1).

10   Slowly push the pistons into the master cylinder (a large Phillips screwdriver can be used for this) - air will be expelled from the pressure chambers and into the reservoir. Because the tubes are submerged in fluid, air can't be drawn back into the master cylinder when you release the pistons.

11   Repeat the procedure until no more air bubbles are present.

12   Remove the bleed tubes, one at a time, and install plugs in the open ports to prevent fluid leakage and air from entering. Install the reservoir cap.

13   Install the master cylinder over the studs on the power brake booster and tighten the attaching nuts only finger tight at this time. **Note:** *Be sure to install a new O-ring into the*

sleeve of the master cylinder.

14   Thread the brake line fittings into the master cylinder. Since the master cylinder is still a bit loose, it can be moved slightly in order for the fittings to thread in easily. Do not strip the threads as the fittings are tightened.

15   Fully tighten the mounting nuts, then the brake line fittings. Tighten the nuts to the torque listed in this Chapter's Specifications.

16   Fill the master cylinder reservoir with fluid, then bleed the master cylinder and the brake system as described in Section 11. To bleed the cylinder on the vehicle, have an assistant depress the brake pedal and hold the pedal to the floor. Loosen the fitting to allow air and fluid to escape. Repeat this procedure on both fittings until the fluid is clear of air bubbles. **Caution:** *Have plenty of rags on hand to catch the fluid - brake fluid will ruin painted surfaces. After the bleeding procedure is completed, rinse the area under the master cylinder with clean water.*

17   Test the operation of the brake system carefully before placing the vehicle into normal service. **Warning:** *Do not operate the vehicle if you are in doubt about the effectiveness of the brake system. It is possible for air to become trapped in the anti-lock brake system hydraulic control unit, so, if the pedal continues to feel spongy after repeated bleedings or the BRAKE or ANTI-LOCK light stays on, have the vehicle towed to a dealer service department or other qualified shop to be bled with the aid of a scan tool.*

Reservoir/O-ring replacement
Refer to illustration 9.22

Note: *The brake fluid reservoir can be replaced separately from the master cylinder body if it becomes damaged. If there is leakage between the reservoir and the master cylinder body, the O-rings on the reservoir can be replaced.*

18   Remove as much fluid as possible from the reservoir with a suction gun, large syringe or a poultry baster. **Warning:** *If a poultry baster is used, never again use it for the preparation of food.*

19   Place rags under the master cylinder to absorb any fluid that may spill out once the reservoir is detached from the master cylinder. **Caution:** *Brake fluid will damage paint. Cover all body parts and be careful not to spill fluid during this procedure.*

20   On some early models, the reservoir is attached to the master cylinder by two roll pins. Using a hammer and a small punch, drive out the roll pins that retain the reservoir to the master cylinder.

21   Pull the reservoir out of the master cylinder body.

22   If you are simply replacing the O-rings, carefully pry the old O-rings off and install new ones **(see illustration).**

23   Lubricate the reservoir O-rings with clean brake fluid, then press the reservoir into place on the master cylinder body and secure it with new roll pins.

24   Refill the reservoir with the recommended brake fluid (see Chapter 1) and check for leaks.

25   Bleed the master cylinder (see Step 16).

10   Brake hoses and lines - inspection and replacement

1   About every six months, with the vehicle raised and placed securely on jackstands, the flexible hoses which connect the steel brake lines with the front and rear brake assemblies should be inspected for cracks, chafing of the outer cover, leaks, blisters and other damage. These are important and vulnerable parts of the brake system and inspection should be complete. A light and mirror will be needed for a thorough check. If a hose exhibits any of the above defects, replace it with a new one.

Flexible hoses
Refer to illustrations 10.3a and 10.3b

2   Clean all dirt away from the ends of the hose.

3   To disconnect a brake hose from the brake line, unscrew the metal tube nut with a

nut wrench, then remove the U-clip from
female fitting at the bracket and remove
he hose from the bracket (see illustrations).
4   Disconnect the hose from the caliper,
discarding the sealing washers on either side
of the fitting.
5   Using new sealing washers, attach the
new brake hose to the caliper.
6   To reattach a brake hose to the metal
line, insert the end of the hose through the
frame bracket, make sure the hose isn't
twisted, then attach the metal line by tightening the tube nut fitting securely. Install the
U-clip at the frame bracket. Note: *The weight
of the vehicle must be on the suspension, so
the vehicle should not be raised while positioning the hose.*
7   Carefully check to make sure the suspension or steering components don't make
contact with the hose. Have an assistant push
down on the vehicle and also turn the steering
wheel lock-to-lock during inspection.
8   Bleed the brake system (see Section
11).

Metal brake lines

9   When replacing brake lines, be sure to
use the correct parts. Don't use copper tubing
for any brake system components. Purchase
steel brake lines from a dealer parts department or auto parts store.
10   Prefabricated brake line, with the tube
ends already flared and fittings installed, is
available at auto parts stores and dealer parts
departments. These lines can be bent to the
proper shapes using a tubing bender.
11   When installing the new line make sure
it's well supported in the brackets and has
plenty of clearance between moving or hot
components.
12   After installation, check the master cylinder fluid level and add fluid as necessary.
Bleed the brake system as outlined in Section
11 and test the brakes carefully before placing
the vehicle into normal operation.

11   Brake hydraulic system - bleeding

Refer to illustration 11.8
Warning 1: *If air has found its way into the
hydraulic control unit, the system must be
bled with the use of a scan tool. If the brake
pedal feels "spongy" even after bleeding the
brakes, or the ABS light on the instrument
panel does not go off, or if you have any
doubts whatsoever about the effectiveness
of the brake system, have the vehicle towed
to a dealer service department or other repair
shop equipped with the necessary tools for
bleeding the system.*
Warning 2: *Wear eye protection when bleeding the brake system. If the fluid comes in
contact with your eyes, immediately rinse
them with water and seek medical attention.*
Note: *Bleeding the brake system is necessary
to remove any air that's trapped in the system*

**10.3b . . . then remove the U-clip and
detach the hose from the bracket**

*when it's opened during removal and installa-
tion of a hose, line, caliper, wheel cylinder or
master cylinder.*
1   It will probably be necessary to bleed the
system at all four brakes if air has entered the
system due to low fluid level, or if the brake
lines have been disconnected at the master
cylinder.
2   If a brake line was disconnected only at
a wheel, then only that caliper or wheel cylinder must be bled.
3   If a brake line is disconnected at a fitting
located between the master cylinder and any
of the brakes, that part of the system served
by the disconnected line must be bled.
4   Remove any residual vacuum (or hydraulic pressure) from the brake power booster
by applying the brake several times with the
engine off.
5   Remove the master cylinder reservoir
cap and fill the reservoir with brake fluid. Reinstall the cap. **Note:** *Check the fluid level often
during the bleeding operation and add fluid as
necessary to prevent the fluid level from falling low enough to allow air bubbles into the
master cylinder.*
6   Have an assistant on hand, as well as
a supply of new brake fluid, an empty clear
plastic container, a length of plastic, rubber or
vinyl tubing to fit over the bleeder valve and a
wrench to open and close the bleeder valve.
7   Beginning at the right rear wheel, loosen
the bleeder screw slightly, then tighten it to a
point where it's snug but can still be loosened
quickly and easily.
8   Place one end of the tubing over the
bleeder screw fitting and submerge the other
end in brake fluid in the container (see illustration).
9   Have the assistant slowly depress the
brake pedal and hold it in the depressed position.
10   While the pedal is held depressed, open
the bleeder screw just enough to allow a flow
of fluid to leave the valve. Watch for air bubbles to exit the submerged end of the tube.
When the fluid flow slows after a couple of
seconds, tighten the screw and have your
assistant release the pedal.
11   Repeat Steps 9 and 10 until no more

**11.8 When bleeding the brakes, a hose
is connected to the bleed screw at
the caliper or wheel cylinder and then
submerged in brake fluid - air will be
seen as bubbles in the tube and
container (all air must be expelled
before moving to the next wheel)**

air is seen leaving the tube, then tighten the
bleeder screw and proceed to the left rear
wheel, the right front wheel and the left front
wheel, in that order, and perform the same
procedure. Be sure to check the fluid in the
master cylinder reservoir frequently.
12   Never use old brake fluid. It contains
moisture which can boil, rendering the brake
system inoperative.
13   Refill the master cylinder with fluid at the
end of the operation.
14   Check the operation of the brakes. The
pedal should feel solid when depressed, with
no sponginess. If necessary, repeat the entire
process. **Warning:** *Do not operate the vehicle
if you are in doubt about the effectiveness
of the brake system. It is possible for air to
become trapped in the anti-lock brake system
hydraulic control unit, so, if the pedal continues to feel spongy after repeated bleedings
or the BRAKE or ANTI-LOCK light stays on,
have the vehicle towed to a dealer service
department or other qualified shop to be bled
with the aid of a scan tool.*

12   Power brake booster - check, removal and installation

Check
Vacuum booster

Operating check
1   Depress the pedal and start the engine.
If the pedal goes down slightly, operation is
normal.
2   Depress the brake pedal several times
with the engine running and make sure that
there is no change in the pedal reserve distance.

Airtightness check
3   Start the engine and turn it off after one
or two minutes. Depress the brake pedal
several times slowly. If the pedal goes down

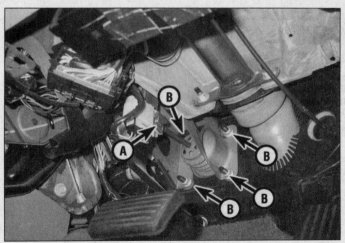

12.13 Pry off the clip retaining the brake light switch and the booster pushrod to the pin on the brake pedal (A), then unscrew the booster mounting nuts (B)

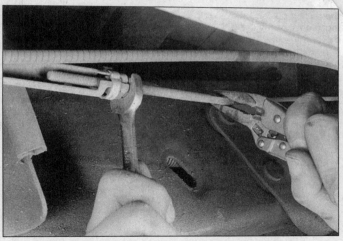

13.4 Hold the cable with locking pliers and turn the adjuster nut with a wrench

farther the first time but gradually rises after the second or third depression, the booster is airtight.

4   Depress the brake pedal while the engine is running, then stop the engine with the pedal depressed. If there is no change in the pedal reserve travel after holding the pedal for 30 seconds, the booster is airtight.

Hydraulic booster

5   Turn the engine off, then depress the brake pedal several times to deplete the pressure in the accumulator.

6   Push down on the brake pedal, exerting approximately 40 pounds of force, then start the engine. If the booster is working properly, the brake pedal will sink towards the floor then rise back up against your foot.

7   If the booster does not work as described, check the fluid level in the power steering reservoir, adding as necessary. Also check the hoses from the power steering pump to the booster for kinks. If everything checks out OK, the booster or power steering pump is defective. Have the power steering pump output pressure checked. If the pump is developing sufficient pressure, replace the booster.

Removal

Refer to illustration 12.13

8   If you're working on a model with a hydraulic booster, pump the brake pedal several times to deplete the pressure in the accumulator.

9   If you're working on a model with a vacuum booster, detach the vacuum hose from the booster.

10   If you're working on a model with a hydraulic booster, detach the pressure and return lines from the booster. Cap the lines to prevent fluid leakage.

11   If you're working on a model with a hydraulic booster, remove the master cylinder without detaching the brake lines. Pull it forward and position it aside. Be careful not to bend or kink the brake lines.

12   If you're working on a model with a vacuum booster, remove the master cylinder (see Section 9).

13   Remove the pushrod retaining clip **(see illustration)** and slip the brake light switch and the pushrod off the pin.

14   Remove the four nuts holding the brake booster to the firewall.

15   Slide the booster straight out from the firewall until the studs clear the holes and pull the booster and gasket from the engine compartment.

Installation

16   Installation is the reverse of removal. Be sure to use a new gasket, and tighten the booster mounting nuts and the master cylinder mounting nuts to the torque values listed in this Chapter's Specifications.

17   If you're working on a model with a hydraulic booster, bleed the power steering system as described in Chapter 10. Check the power steering fluid level and add some, if necessary, to bring it up to the appropriate level.

13   Parking brake - adjustment

Refer to illustration 13.4

1   The parking brake is pedal operated and is normally self-adjusting through the automatic adjusters in the rear brake drums. However, supplementary adjustment may be needed in the event of cable stretch, wear in the linkage or after installation of new components.

2   Raise the rear of the vehicle until the wheels are clear of the ground and support it securely on jackstands. Release the parking brake pedal by pulling on the release lever.

3   Apply the parking brake four notches.

4   The adjuster is located on the outside of the frame under the driver's side of the vehicle, just ahead of the rear axle. Hold the cable from turning with locking pliers, then loosen

the locknut and tighten the adjuster nut **(see illustration)** until a slight drag is felt when the rear wheels are turned. **Note:** *If the threads appear rusty, apply penetrating oil before attempting adjustment.*

5   Release the parking brake pedal and make sure there's no longer any drag when the wheels are turned.

6   Tighten the locknut and lower the vehicle to the ground.

14   Brake light switch - replacement

Refer to illustration 14.1

Check

1   The brake light switch **(see illustration)** is located on the side of the brake pedal and is retained by the same clip that retains the booster pushrod. The switch activates the brake lights at the rear of the vehicle when the pedal is depressed.

2   If the brake lights are inoperative, check the fuse first (see Chapter 12).

3   If the fuse is good, check for voltage to

14.1 The brake light switch is mounted on the side of the brake pedal arm

switch on the feed wire (refer to the wiring diagrams at the end of this manual for the proper color wire to check). If no voltage is present, repair the wire between the switch and the fuse box.

4   If voltage is present, depress the brake pedal and check for voltage at the output wire terminal (again, refer to the wiring diagrams). If no voltage is present, replace the switch.

5   If voltage is present, check for power on the brake light wires at the tail light housings (with the brake pedal depressed). If voltage is not present, repair the circuit between the switch and the brake lights.

6   If voltage is present, check for a bad ground; using a jumper wire connected to a good ground, probe the ground wire terminal at the tail light connector. If the brake lights go on, repair the ground circuit (follow the ground wire from the tail light housing).

7   Keep in mind that the brake light bulbs could be burned out, but the likelihood of all the bulbs being burned out is very slim.

Replacement

8   Remove left-side under-dash panel and the heater/air conditioning duct, if not already done.

9   Unplug the electrical connector from the switch.

10   Remove the clip that retains the switch and pushrod to the pin on the brake pedal arm and slip the brake light switch off the pin.

11   To install the new switch, reverse the removal procedure. Make sure the retaining clip is properly installed.

Chapter 10
Suspension and steering systems

Contents

Specifications

Torque specifications

Ft-lbs (unless otherwise indicated)

Front suspension

Shock absorber
  Upper mounting nut
    2002 and earlier models 12
    2003 and later models 15
  Lower mounting bolts
    2002 and earlier models 24
    2003 and later models 18
Upper control arm pivot bolt nuts
  2002 and earlier models 140
  2003 and later models 129
Lower control arm pivot bolt
  2002 and earlier models 115
  2003 and later models 107
Upper balljoint-to-steering knuckle nut
  2002 and earlier models 74
  2003 and later models 37
Lower balljoint-to-steering knuckle nut
  2002 and earlier models 94
  2003 and later models 74
Upper balljoint (replacement)-to-upper control arm nuts 18
Stabilizer bar
  Link nut .... 97 in-lbs
  Clamp bolts (GVW 7300 lbs. or less)
    1500/2500 models 18
  Clamp nuts (GVW 8500 lbs. or more)
    2500/3500 models 34
  Studs (GVW 8500 lbs. or more) 18
Hub/bearing assembly-to-steering knuckle bolts (2003 and later
  models) 133

suspension

f spring-to-axle U-bolt nuts	
2002 and earlier models	
1500	70
2500/3500	115
2003 and later models	
1500	63
2500/3500	103
Leaf spring-to-front spring hanger nut and bolt	
Step 1	80
Step 2	Tighten an additional 200-degrees
Leaf spring-to-rear shackle nut and bolt	
2002 and earlier models	67
2003 and later models	66
Rear shackle-to-frame bracket nut and bolt	
2002 and earlier models	67
2003 and later models	66
Shock absorber upper mounting bolts	
2002 and earlier models	20
2003 and later models	18
Shock absorber lower mounting nut/bolt	
2002 and earlier models	60
2003 and later models	59

Steering

Steering wheel nut	30
Intermediate shaft pinch bolt (to steering gear)	45
Steering gear-to-frame bolts	
Rack-and-pinion type	
1999 and 2000 models	92
2001 and later models	136
Recirculating ball type	
1996 through 2002 models	98
2003 and later models	111
Tie rod end to steering knuckle nut	
1996 through 2002 models	35
2003 and later models	47
Steering linkage (recirculating ball type)	
1996 through 2002 models	
Pitman arm shaft nut	184
Pitman arm-to connecting rod nut	40
Inner tie rod-to-relay rod nut	35
Tie rod adjuster clamp bolts	18
Idler arm-to-relay rod nut	35
Idler arm to frame mounting bolts	74
2003 and later models	
Pitman shaft nut	184
Pitman arm-to relay rod nut	47
Inner tie rod-to-relay rod nut	83
Relay rod-to-idler arm nut	47
Idler arm to frame mounting bolts	111
Power steering pump mounting bolts/nuts	
V8 engines	37
V6 engines	37
Wheel lug nuts	See Chapter 1

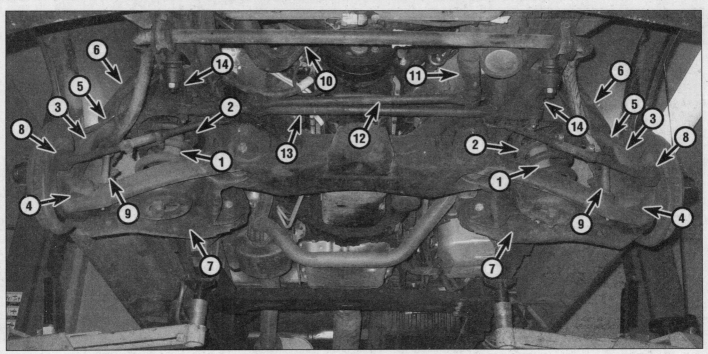

1.1 Front suspension and steering components

1	*Shock absorber*	6	*Upper control arm*	11	*Pitman arm*
2	*Coil spring*	7	*Lower control arm*	12	*Connecting rod*
3	*Steering knuckle*	8	*Tie-rod end*	13	*Relay rod*
4	*Lower balljoint*	9	*Stabilizer bar end link*	14	*Idler arm*
5	*Upper balljoint*	10	*Stabilizer bar link*		

1 General information

Refer to illustrations 1.1 and 1.2

The front suspension **(see illustration)** is fully independent. Each wheel is connected to the frame by a steering knuckle, upper and lower balljoints and upper and lower control arms. Coil springs are independent of the shock absorbers which are bolted to brackets on the frame and the lower control arms. A stabilizer bar connected to the frame and to the two lower control arms reduces body roll during cornering.

The rear suspension consists of a pair of multi-leaf springs and two shock absorbers **(see illustration)**. The rear axle assembly is attached to the leaf springs by U-bolts. The front ends of the springs are attached to the frame at the front hangers, through rubber bushings. The rear ends of the springs are attached to the frame by shackles which allow

1.2 Rear suspension components

1	*Leaf spring*	2	*Shock absorber*	3	*U-bolt*	4	*Spring plate*

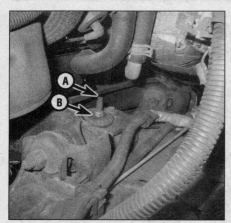

2.3 Hold the shock absorber stem (A) with a wrench to prevent it from turning when the upper mounting nut (B) is loosened

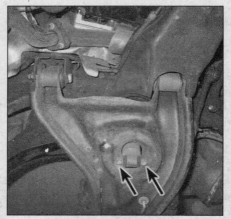

2.5 Shock absorber lower mounting bolts

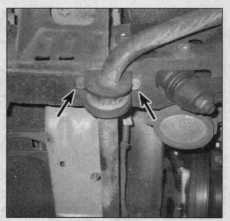

3.2 Remove the bolts attaching the stabilizer bar bracket to the frame

the springs to alter their length as they compress and rebound.

The steering system on some models consists of either a recirculating-ball steering gearbox, Pitman arm, idler arm, relay rod, two adjustable tie-rod assemblies (each consisting of an inner tie-rod, adjuster tube and outer tie-rod) and, on some models, an additional connecting rod and two idler arms instead of one. Generally, when the steering wheel is turned, the gear rotates the Pitman arm which forces the relay rod to one side. The tie-rods, which are connected to the relay rod, transfer steering force to the wheels. The tie-rods are adjustable and are used for toe-in adjustments. The relay rod is supported by the Pitman arm and idler arm. The idler arm pivots on a support attached to the right frame rail.

The steering system on other models consists of a rack-and-pinion steering gear and two adjustable tie-rods. Power assist is standard on all models.

Frequently, when working on the suspension or steering system components, you may come across fasteners which seem impossible to loosen. These fasteners on the underside of the vehicle are continually subjected to water, road grime, mud, etc., and can become rusted or "frozen," making them extremely difficult to remove. In order to unscrew these stubborn fasteners without damaging them (or other components), be sure to use lots of penetrating oil and allow it to soak in for a while. Using a wire brush to clean exposed threads will also ease removal of the nut or bolt and prevent damage to the threads. Sometimes a sharp blow with a hammer and punch is effective in breaking the bond between a nut and bolt threads, but care must be taken to prevent the punch from slipping off the fastener and ruining the threads. Heating the stuck fastener and surrounding area with a torch sometimes helps too, but isn't recommended because of the obvious dangers associated with fire. Long breaker bars and extension, or "cheater," pipes will increase leverage, but never use an extension pipe on a ratchet - the ratcheting mechanism could be

damaged. Sometimes, turning the nut or bolt in the tightening (clockwise) direction first will help to break it loose. Fasteners that require drastic measures to unscrew should always be replaced with new ones.

Since most of the procedures that are dealt with in this Chapter involve jacking up the vehicle and working underneath it, a good pair of jackstands will be needed. A hydraulic floor jack is the preferred type of jack to lift the vehicle, and it can also be used to support certain components during various operations. **Warning:** *Never, under any circumstances, rely on a jack to support the vehicle while working on it.*

Whenever any of the suspension or steering fasteners are loosened or removed they must be inspected and, if necessary, replaced with new ones of the same part number or of original equipment quality and design. Torque specifications must be followed for proper reassembly and component retention. Never attempt to heat or straighten suspension or steering components. Instead, replace any bent or damaged part with a new one.

2   Shock absorber (front) - removal and installation

Refer to illustrations 2.3 and 2.5

1   Loosen the front wheel lug nuts. Raise the front of the vehicle and support it securely on jackstands, then remove the wheel.
2   Support the outer end of the lower control arm with a floor jack (the shock absorber serves as the down-stop for the suspension). The jack must remain in this position throughout the entire procedure.
3   Using a back-up wrench on the stem, remove the shock absorber upper mounting nut **(see illustration)**. **Note:** *Consider going through the splash shield in the wheel well to access the upper mounting nut.*
4   Remove the retainer (metal washer) and grommet (rubber washer).
5   Working underneath the vehicle, remove the two bolts that attach the lower end of the shock absorber to the lower control arm

(see illustration) and pull the shock out from below.
6   Remove the lower grommet and retainer from the stem.
7   Installation is the reverse of removal. Be sure to tighten the upper mounting nut and the lower mounting bolts to the torque listed in this Chapter's Specifications.
8   Install the wheels and lug nuts, lower the vehicle and tighten the lug nuts to the torque listed in the Chapter 1 Specifications.

3   Stabilizer bar - removal and installation

Refer to illustrations 3.2 and 3.3

1   Loosen the front wheel lug nuts. Raise the front of the vehicle and support it securely on jackstands. Apply the parking brake and block the rear wheels to keep the vehicle from rolling off the stands. Remove the front wheels.
2   Remove the stabilizer bar bracket fasteners **(see illustration)**. **Note:** *Heavy duty applications use studs and nuts for the stabilizer bar bracket fasteners and it's possible that the stud may come loose when removing the nut. It this should occur, re-install the stud according to the torque listed in this Chapter's Specifications.*
3   Remove the nuts from the link bolts and then remove the link bolts and parts **(see illustration)**. **Note:** *Be sure to keep the parts for the left and right sides separate.*
4   Remove the stabilizer bar.
5   Remove the rubber bushings.
6   Inspect all parts for wear and damage.
7   When you install the rubber bushings on the stabilizer bar, be sure to position them so the slits face toward the front of the vehicle.
8   Installation is the reverse of removal. Clean the link bolt threads of any old thread lock material and re-apply thread lock compound upon installation (if applicable). Be sure to tighten all fasteners to the torque listed in this Chapter's Specifications. Tighten the wheel lug nuts to the torque listed in the Chapter 1 Specifications.

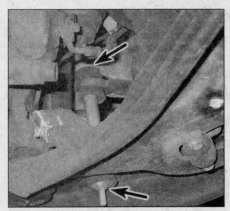

3.3 Stabilizer bar end link nut and bolt

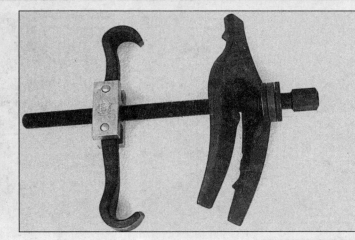

4.5 A typical aftermarket internal spring compressor tool: the hooked arms grip the upper coils of the spring, the plate is inserted below the lower coil, and when the threaded rod is turned, the spring is compressed

4 Coil spring - removal and installation

Removal

Refer to illustration 4.5

1   Loosen the front wheel lug nuts. Raise the front of the vehicle and support it securely on jackstands. Apply the parking brake and block the rear wheels to keep the vehicle from rolling off the stands. Remove the front wheels.
2   Detach the stabilizer bar link from the lower control arm (see Section 3).
3   Support the outer end of the lower control arm with a floor jack.
4   Remove the shock absorber (see Section 2).
5   Install a suitable internal-type spring compressor in accordance with the tool manufacturer's instructions (see illustration). Compress the spring sufficiently to relieve all pressure from the upper spring seat. This can be verified by wiggling the spring. **Note:** *You can buy a suitable spring compressor at most auto parts stores or rent one from a tool rental yard.*
6   Once the spring has been compressed, remove the floor jack, then remove the pivot

bolts from the lower control arm (see Section 5).
7   Carefully move the lower control arm down and remove the compressed spring. **Note:** *Leave the tool on the spring if you are going to re-install it. Otherwise, carefully remove the tool and install it on the replacement spring.*

Installation

8   Place the insulator on top of the coil spring.
9   Install the top of the spring into the spring pocket and the bottom in the lower control arm.
10   Move the lower control arm in position and install the pivot bolts (see Section 5). Support the outer end of the lower control arm with the floor jack, then remove the spring compressor and install the shock absorber (see Section 2).
11   The remainder of installation is the reverse of removal. Tighten all fasteners to the proper torque values. Tighten the wheel lug nuts to the torque listed in the Chapter 1 Specifications.
12   Have the front end alignment checked and, if necessary, adjusted.

5 Control arm - removal and installation

Upper control arm

Refer to illustrations 5.2 and 5.4

1   Loosen the wheel lug nuts, raise the front of the vehicle and support it securely on jackstands. Remove the wheel. Support the outer end of the lower control arm with a floor jack. Raise the jack slightly to take the spring pressure off the upper control arm. **Warning:** *The jack must remain in this position throughout the entire procedure.*
2   Mark the relationship of the adjusting cams to the brackets on the frame (see illustration).
3   Unbolt the brake hose bracket and the wheel speed sensor harness from the upper control arm.
4   Disconnect the upper balljoint from the steering knuckle. Loosen the balljoint stud nut a few turns (be sure to remove the cotter pin on models so equipped). Press the balljoint stud from the steering knuckle (see illustration).
5   Note the direction of the upper control arm pivot bolts and then remove them. Remove the control arm.

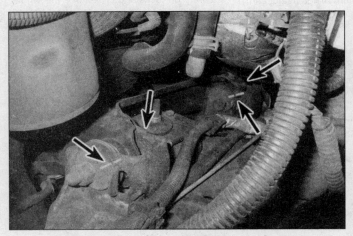

5.2 Mark all four adjusting cams to the frame

5.4 A special tool is required to push the balljoint out of the steering knuckle. An alternative tool can be fabricated from a large bolt, nut, washer and socket.

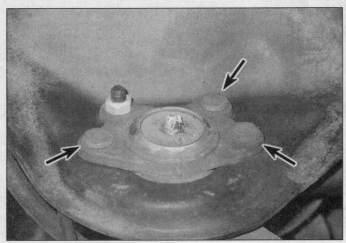

6.8 Remove these three rivets to replace the balljoint

6.13 Using fasteners instead of rivets to attach the balljoint to the upper control arm

6   For installation, position the arm in the frame brackets and install the bolts and nuts. Make sure the marks you made prior to disassembly are aligned and then tighten the nuts to the torque listed in this Chapter's Specifications.

7   Installation is the reverse of removal. Be sure to use a new cotter pin in the balljoint stud (on models so equipped), align the marks made in Step 2, and tighten all fasteners to the torque values listed in this Chapter's Specifications (but don't tighten the pivot bolt nuts until the vehicle is sitting at normal ride height). If it's too hard to get to the nuts with the wheel on, normal ride height can be simulated by raising the outer end of the lower control arm with a floor jack.

8   Install the wheel and lug nuts. Lower the vehicle and tighten the lug nuts to the torque listed in the Chapter 1 Specifications.

9   Have the front end alignment checked and, if necessary, adjusted.

Lower control arm

10   Loosen the wheel lug nuts, raise the vehicle and support it securely on jackstands placed under the frame rails. Remove the wheel.

11   On 2002 and earlier models, remove the brake disc (see Chapter 9).

12   Support the outer end of the lower control arm with a floor jack. Remove the shock absorber (see Section 2).

13   Install a suitable internal type spring compressor in accordance with the tool manufacturer's instructions **(see illustration 4.5)**. Compress the spring sufficiently to relieve all pressure from the upper spring seat. This can be verified by wiggling the spring.

14   Disconnect the stabilizer bar from the lower control arm (see Section 3).

15   If the ballstud is equipped with a cotter pin, remove it. Loosen (but don't remove) the nut on the lower balljoint stud, then disconnect the balljoint from the steering knuckle with a balljoint removal tool. **Note 1:** *On 2002 and earlier models, you could use the same tool*

used for upper balljoint and steering knuckle separation. Make certain that the tool is placed in the proper direction for separating the lower balljoint and steering knuckle **(see illustration 5.4). Note 2:** *If you don't have the proper balljoint removal tool, a "picklefork" type balljoint separator can be used, but keep in mind that this type of tool will probably destroy the balljoint boot.*

16   Lift the knuckle and hub assembly up, then place a block of wood between the upper control arm and the frame to support the assembly out of the way.

17   Pull the lower control arm down, then guide the compressed coil spring out.

18   Remove the bolts that attach the control arm to the frame. Pull the lower arm from its frame brackets.

19   Installation is the reverse of removal. Be sure to use a new cotter pin in the balljoint stud (on models so equipped) and tighten all fasteners to the torque values listed in this Chapter's Specifications (but don't tighten the pivot bolt nuts until the vehicle is sitting at normal ride height). If it's too hard to get to the nuts with the wheel on, normal ride height can be simulated by raising the outer end of the lower control arm with a floor jack.

20   Install the wheel and lug nuts. Lower the vehicle and tighten the lug nuts to the torque listed in the Chapter 1 Specifications.

21   Have the front end alignment checked and, if necessary, adjusted.

---

6   Balljoints - check and replacement

1   Inspect the control arm balljoints for looseness anytime either of them is separated from the steering knuckle. See if you can turn the ballstud in its socket with your fingers. If the balljoint is loose, or if the ballstud can be turned, replace the balljoint. You can also check the balljoints with the suspension assembled as follows.

Upper balljoints
Check
Refer to illustrations 6.8 and 6.13

2   Raise the front of the vehicle and support it securely on jackstands placed under the frame rails. Place a floor jack under the outer end of the lower control arm and raise it slightly.

3   Using a large prybar inserted between the upper control arm and the steering knuckle, pry upwards on the upper control arm. The manufacturer does not give a wear specification for the upper balljoint, but if any freeplay is noticed, the balljoint should be replaced.

Replacement

4   If you're working on a 2003 and later model, and balljoint replacement is indicated, the upper control arm must be replaced (see Section 5).

5   For upper balljoint replacement on 2002 and earlier models, loosen the wheel lug nuts, raise the front of the vehicle and support it securely on jackstands. Remove the wheel. Support the outer end of the lower control arm with a floor jack. Raise the jack slightly to take the spring pressure off the upper control arm. **Warning:** *The jack must remain in this position throughout the entire procedure.*

6   Remove the brake caliper (see Chapter 9).

7   Unbolt the brake hose bracket and the wheel speed sensor harness from the upper control arm.

8   Center-punch the rivet heads that mount the upper balljoint and then carefully drill them out **(see illustration)**. Using a 1/8-inch drill bit, drill a 1/4-inch deep hole in the center of each rivet. Then switch to a 1/2-inch drill bit and finish the job; drill just deep enough to remove the rivet head. **Caution:** *Do not enlarge the holes in the control arm when drilling the rivet heads off.*

9   Use a punch to remove the remaining portion of the rivets.

10 Remove the balljoint stud nut. **Note:** *Discard the cotter pin.*

11 Separate the balljoint from the steering knuckle **(see illustration 5.4)** and then remove the balljoint.

12 Inspect the tapered hole in the steering knuckle where the balljoint stud fits. If it is worn or out of round, the steering knuckle should be replaced (see Section 7).

13 Installation is the reverse of removal. Use the appropriate fasteners to secure the replacement balljoint and tighten them securely **(see illustration). Note:** *The replacement balljoint will usually include the necessary fasteners.* When attaching the balljoint to the steering knuckle, tighten the ballstud nut to the torque listed in this Chapter's Specifications and install a new cotter pin. Tighten the wheel lug nuts to the torque listed in the Chapter 1 Specifications. **Caution:** *Be sure to grease the new balljoint (see Chapter 1).*

Lower balljoints

Check

14 Raise the front of the vehicle and support it securely on jackstands.

15 Place a floor jack under the lower control arm, near the outer end, and raise it until the upper control arm lifts off its rebound bumper.

16 Insert a prybar between the control arm and the steering knuckle and pry up and down. The manufacturer specifies that up to 0.080-inch of vertical movement is allowed; a dial indicator can be used to check for play. If you are unable to accurately measure balljoint play, have the balljoint checked at an automotive repair shop.

Replacement

2002 and earlier models

17 For balljoint replacement on 2002 and earlier models, loosen the wheel lug nuts, raise the front of the vehicle and support it securely on jackstands. Remove the wheel. Support the outer end of the lower control arm with a floor jack. Raise the jack slightly to take the spring pressure off the upper control arm. **Warning:** *The jack must remain in this position throughout the entire procedure.*

18 Remove the brake caliper (see Chapter 9).

19 Separate the lower balljoint from the steering knuckle (see Section 5).

20 Pry the upper control arm up while guiding the lower control arm ballstud out of the steering knuckle with a large screwdriver. Once the control arm is up, place a wooden block between the frame and upper control arm to keep the steering knuckle out of the way.

21 The balljoint is press fit into the lower control arm, which necessitates the use of a special press tool and receiver cup to remove and install the balljoint. Equipment rental yards and some auto parts stores have these tools available for rent. If you don't have access to this tool, you can remove the lower control arm (see Section 5) and have the balljoint replaced by a qualified repair facility. **Note:** *The balljoint replacement tool is similar to a big, heavy-duty C-clamp with special adapters.*

22 Inspect the tapered hole in the steering knuckle where the balljoint stud fits. If it is worn or out of round, the steering knuckle should be replaced (see Section 7).

23 Installation is the reverse of removal. When attaching the balljoint to the steering knuckle, tighten the ballstud nut to the torque listed in this Chapter's Specifications and install a new cotter pin. Tighten the wheel lug nuts to the torque listed in the Chapter 1 Specifications. **Caution:** *Be sure to grease the new balljoint (see Chapter 1).*

2003 and later models

24 For balljoint replacement on 2003 and later models, remove the lower control arm (see Section 8); the balljoint is press fit in the lower control arm and secured by four crimped areas on the balljoint body. To remove the balljoint, the crimped areas must be knocked back with a hammer and chisel, then the balljoint must be pressed out with a hydraulic press. The new balljoint is then pressed into the lower control arm and crimped in four places, just like the old one. If you don't have access to a hydraulic press, take the control arm to an automotive machine shop or other qualified repair facility to have the balljoint replaced.

---

7 Steering knuckle/front hub and bearing - removal and installation

Steering knuckle

1 Loosen the front wheel lug nuts, raise the front of the vehicle and support it securely on jackstands, then remove the wheel.

2 Support the lower control arm with a floor jack. Raise the jack slightly. **Warning:** *The jack must remain in this position throughout the entire procedure.*

3 Disconnect the tie-rod end from the steering knuckle (see Section 11).

4 Remove the brake disc (2002 and earlier models, see Chapter 1, *Front wheel bearing check, repack and adjustment*; 2003 and later models, see Chapter 9).

5 On 2002 and earlier models, remove the steering knuckle seal and the splash shield.

6 On 2003 and later models, remove the hub and bearing assembly and splash shield (see Step 11).

7 Disconnect the upper and lower balljoints from the steering knuckle (see Section 5).

8 Remove the steering knuckle.

9 Installation is the reverse of removal. Be sure to tighten the balljoint and tie-rod end fasteners (and, on 2003 and later models, the hub and bearing assembly bolts) to the torque values listed in this Chapter's Specifications. Tighten the caliper mounting bolts to the

7.13 Fasteners for the wheel bearing/hub assembly (2003 and later models only)

torque values listed in the Chapter 9 Specifications. Tighten the wheel lug nuts to the torque listed in the Chapter 1 Specifications.

Front hub and bearing

2002 and earlier models

10 On these models the front hub and bearing is integral with the brake disc. The removal (and servicing) procedure is covered in Chapter 1, *Front wheel bearing check, repack and adjustment.*

2003 and later models

Refer to illustration 7.13

11 Loosen the front wheel lug nuts, raise the front of the vehicle and support it securely on jackstands, then remove the wheel.

12 Remove the brake disc (see Chapter 9).

13 Remove the bolts securing the hub and bearing assembly to the steering knuckle **(see illustration)**.

14 Installation is the reverse of removal. Be sure to tighten the hub and bearing bolts to the torque listed in this Chapter's Specifications. Tighten the wheel lug nuts to the torque listed in the Chapter 1 Specifications.

---

8 Shock absorber (rear) - removal and installation

Refer to illustration 8.2

1 Raise the rear of the vehicle and support it securely on jackstands placed under the frame rails. Support the rear axle with a floor jack placed under the axle tube on the side being worked on. Don't raise the axle - just support its weight.

2 Remove the bolts that attach the upper end of the shock absorber to the frame and the nut and bolt that attach the lower end of the shock to the axle bracket **(see illustration)**. If the nut won't loosen because of rust, apply some penetrating oil and allow it to soak in for awhile.

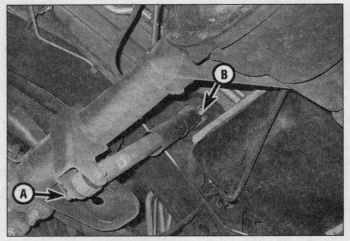

8.2 To detach a rear shock from the axle, remove this nut and bolt (A), then remove the two mounting bolts from the at the top of the shock (B) (one upper bolt not visible in photo)

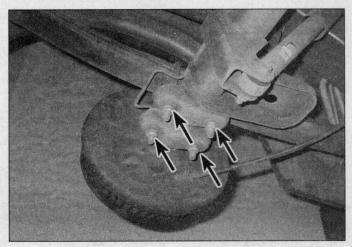

9.2 To remove the spring plate and U-bolts, remove these four nuts

3   Extend the new shock absorber as far as possible. Install new rubber grommets into the shock absorber eyes (if they are not already present).

4   Installation is the reverse of removal. Be sure to tighten the shock absorber mounting fasteners to the torque listed in this Chapter's Specifications.

---

9   Leaf spring/shackle - removal and installation

Removal

Refer to illustrations 9.2, 9.3 and 9.4

1   Loosen the wheel lug nuts, raise the rear of the vehicle and support it securely on jackstands placed under the frame rails. Remove the wheel and support the rear axle with a floor jack placed under the axle tube. Don't raise the axle - just support its weight.

2   Remove the nuts, U-bolts, spring plate, and spring seat that clamp the leaf spring to the axle **(see illustration)**.

3   Remove the leaf spring shackle bolts and the shackle **(see illustration)**.

4   Unscrew the front bolt **(see illustration)** and remove the leaf spring from the vehicle.

Installation

5   To install the leaf spring, position the spring on the axle tube so that the spring center bolt enters the locating hole on the axle tube.

6   Line up the spring front eye with the mounting bracket and install the front bolt and nut.

7   Install the rear shackle, bolts and nuts.

8   Tighten the shackle bolt and the front bolt until all slack is taken up.

9   Install the U-bolts and nuts. Tighten the nuts until they force the spring plate against the axle, but don't torque them yet.

10   Be sure the auxiliary spring, if equipped, aligns with the main spring.

11   Install the wheel and lug nuts. Tighten the lug nuts to the torque listed in the Chapter 1 Specifications. Remove the jackstands

and lower the vehicle.

12   Tighten the U-bolt nuts, front bolt/nut and shackle bolts/nuts to the torque listed in this Chapter's Specifications.

---

10   Steering wheel - removal and installation

Warning: *These models are equipped with airbags. Always disable the airbag system whenever working in the vicinity of any airbag system component to avoid the possibility of accidental airbag deployment, which could cause personal injury (see Chapter 12).*

Removal

Refer to illustrations 10.3a, 10.3b, 10.4, 10.6, 10.7, 10.9 and 10.10

1   Park the vehicle with the front wheels in the straight-ahead position.

2   Disconnect the cable from the negative battery terminal, (see Chapter 5, Section 1).

3   Turn the steering wheel 90-degrees to

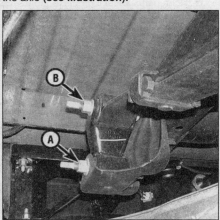

9.3 The shackle-to-bracket bolt/nut (A) and the shackle-to-leaf spring bolt/nut (B)

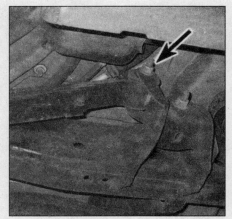

9.4 To detach the front end of the leaf spring from the forward bracket, remove this nut and bolt

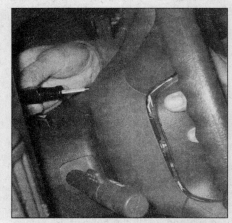

10.3a To release the pins that secure the airbag module to the steering wheel, insert a screwdriver into the holes in the back side of the steering wheel . . .

10.3b . . . and pry each spring clip (arrow) aside to clear the pin (there are two pins; one on each side of the steering wheel) - steering wheel removed for clarity

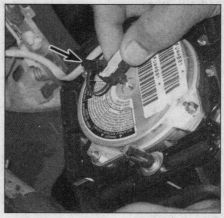

10.4 Pry up the connector lock, then pull the connector out of the airbag module

10.6 To unplug the electrical connector for the horn, push it in and turn it counterclockwise to release it

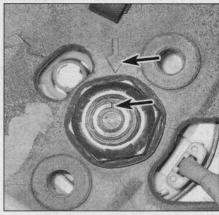

10.7 Check to see if there are alignment marks on the steering wheel and the steering shaft; if there are none, make your own

gain access to the hole in the backside (the side facing the dash) of the steering wheel. Insert a screwdriver into the hole for the spring clip that retains the airbag module **(see illustrations)** and push the spring aside to release the pin. Now turn the steering wheel 180-degrees in the other direction and do the same thing to release the other pin.

4   Lift off the airbag module and unplug the electrical connector for the airbag **(see illustration). Warning:** *Carry the airbag module with the trim cover (upholstered side) facing away from you, and set the airbag module in a safe location with the trim cover facing up.*

5   Center the steering wheel. **Warning:** *Do NOT turn the steering shaft before, during or after steering wheel removal. If the shaft is turned while the steering wheel is removed, a mechanism known as the clockspring can be damaged. The clockspring, which maintains a continuous electrical circuit between the wiring harness and the airbag module, consists of a flat, ribbon-like electrically conductive tape which winds and unwinds as the steering wheel is turned.*

6   Unplug the electrical connector for the horn **(see illustration)**.

7   Mark the relationship of the steering wheel to the steering shaft **(see illustration)**. Remove the steering wheel nut.

8   Use a puller and remove the steering wheel **(see illustration). Caution:** *Any attempt to remove the steering wheel without using a puller can damage the steering column.*

9   If the clockspring requires replacement, see Steps 11 and 12 for the removal, centering and installation procedure.

Installation

Refer to illustrations 10.10, 10.11 and 10.12

10   Before installing the steering wheel, make sure the airbag clockspring is centered **(see illustration)**.

11   If the airbag system clockspring is not centered, remove the steering column covers (see Chapter 11). Remove the snap-ring **(see illustration)** and lift the clockspring off the steering column.

12   To center the clockspring, turn the

clockspring over, depress the lock lever (if equipped) and turn the hub in the direction of the arrow until it stops (don't apply too much force) **(see illustration)**. Then, turn the hub

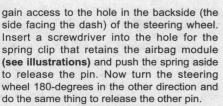

10.8 Remove the steering wheel with a puller that bolts to the hub of the wheel - do not try to hammer the steering wheel off or you will damage the column

10.10 When the clockspring is centered, the arrow on the housing will be aligned with the arrow on the hub

10.11 The clockspring is retained to the steering shaft with a snap-ring

10.12 To center the clockspring, hold it with its underside facing up, depress the spring lock and rotate the hub in the direction of the arrow until it stops, then turn it in the opposite direction 2-1/2 turns

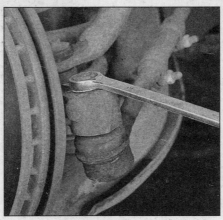

11.2 Loosen - but don't remove - the jam nut on the ballstud (leaving the nut on will prevent the tie-rod end from separating violently)

11.3 Use a two-jaw puller to separate the tie-rod end from the steering knuckle, then remove the jam nut and pull the tie-rod end out of the knuckle

in the opposite direction approximately 2-1/2 turns, aligning the arrows on the front. Release the lock lever and install the clockspring and snap-ring. Secure the wiring harness with a new wire-tie, making sure the harness isn't kinked. Also install the steering column covers.

13   Install the wheel on the steering shaft, aligning the marks.

14   Install the steering wheel nut and tighten it to the torque listed in this Chapter's Specifications.

15   Plug in the horn wire, push down and twist it clockwise to lock it in place.

16   Connect the airbag connector to the back of the airbag module. Make sure the connector lock is securely engaged.

17   Position the airbag module on the steering wheel and push it in until the pins on the module engage with the spring clips.

18   Refer to Chapter 12 for the procedure to enable the airbag system.

11 Steering linkage - removal and installation

Tie-rod ends

Refer to illustrations 11.2 and 11.3

1   Loosen the wheel lug nuts, raise the vehicle and support it securely on jackstands. Remove the wheel.

2   Loosen, but do not remove, the jam nut on the ballstud **(see illustration).**

3   Using a two jaw puller, separate the tie-rod end from the steering knuckle **(see illustration).** Remove the jam nut and pull the tie-rod end from the knuckle.

Non- rack-and-pinion models

Refer to illustrations 11.5, 11.7 and 11.9

4   Remove the nut securing the inner tie-rod end to the relay rod. Separate the inner tie-rod end from the relay rod (see Step 3).

5   If the inner or outer tie-rod end must be replaced, measure the distance from the end of the adjuster tube to the center of

the ballstud and record it **(see illustration).** Loosen the adjuster tube clamp and unscrew the tie-rod end.

6   Lubricate the threaded portion of the tie-rod end with chassis grease. Screw the new tie-rod end into the adjuster tube and adjust the distance from the tube to the ballstud to the previously measured dimension. The number of threads showing on the inner and outer tie-rod ends should be equal within three threads. Don't tighten the clamp yet.

7   To install the tie-rod, connect the outer tie-rod end to the steering knuckle and install the jam nut. Tighten the nut to the torque listed in this Chapter's Specifications. If the ballstud spins when attempting to tighten the nut, force it into the tapered hole with a large pair of pliers **(see illustration).**

8   Insert the inner tie-rod end ballstud into the relay rod until it's seated. Install the nut and tighten it to the torque listed in this Chapter's Specifications.

9   Tighten the clamp nuts. The center of the bolt should be nearly horizontal and the

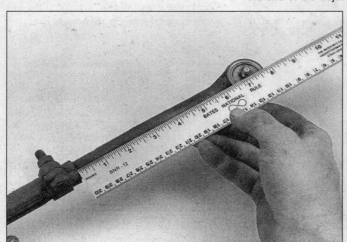

11.5 Measure the distance from the end of the adjuster tube to the center of the ballstud and record the measurement before loosening the adjuster tube clamp and unscrewing the tie-rod end

11.7 If the ballstud spins when you try to tighten the nut, force it into the tapered hole with a large pair of pliers

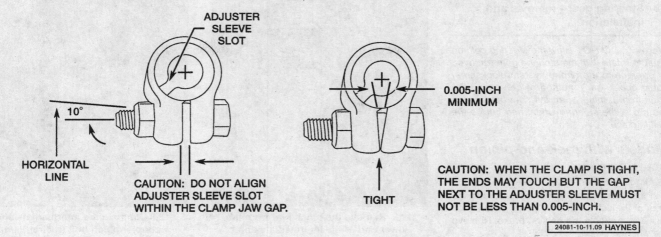

11.9 Note these guidelines when installing the tie-rod ends

adjuster tube slot must not line up with the gap in the clamps **(see illustration).**
10   Install the wheel and lug nuts, lower the vehicle and tighten the lug nuts to the torque listed in the Chapter 1 Specifications. Have the front end alignment checked and, if necessary, adjusted.

Rack-and-pinion models
11   Hold the tie-rod with a pair of locking pliers or wrench and loosen the jam nut enough to mark the position of the tie-rod end in relation to the threads.
12   Unscrew the tie-rod end from the tie-rod.
13   To install the tie-rod end, thread the tie-rod end on to the marked position and insert the stud into the steering knuckle arm. Tighten the jam nut securely.
14   Connect the tie-rod end to the steering knuckle and install the jam nut. Tighten the nut to the torque listed in this Chapter's Specifications.
15   Install the wheel and lug nuts, lower the

vehicle and tighten the lug nuts to the torque listed in the Chapter 1 Specifications. Have the front end alignment checked and, if necessary, adjusted.

Relay rod
16   Loosen the wheel lug nuts, raise the vehicle and support it securely on jackstands. Remove the wheel.
17   Detach the inner tie-rod ends from the relay rod (see Step 4).
18   Loosen but do not remove the Pitman arm-to-relay rod nut.
19   Separate the relay rod from the Pitman arm with a two jaw puller. Remove the nut. Discard the nut - don't reuse it.
20   Loosen but do not remove the idler arm-to-relay rod nut.
21   Separate the relay rod from the Pitman arm with a two jaw puller. Remove the nut. Discard the nut - don't reuse it.
22   Installation is the reverse of the removal procedure. Use new nuts on all of the ballstuds. If the ballstuds spin when attempting to tighten the nuts, force them into the tapered holes with a large pair of pliers. Be

sure to tighten all of the nuts to the torque listed in this Chapter's Specifications.

Idler arm
23   Loosen the wheel lug nuts, raise the vehicle and support it securely on jackstands. Remove the wheel.
24   Loosen but do not remove the idler arm-to-relay rod nut.
25   Separate the idler arm from the relay rod with a two jaw puller. Remove the nut. Discard the nut - don't reuse it.
26   Remove the idler arm-to-frame bolts.
27   To install the idler arm, position it on the frame and install the bolts, tightening them to the torque listed in this Chapter's Specifications.
28   Insert the idler arm ballstud into the relay rod and install a new nut. Tighten the nut to the torque listed in this Chapter's Specifications. If the ballstud spins when attempting to tighten the nut, force it into the tapered hole with a large pair of pliers.

Pitman arm
Refer to illustrations 11.31 and 11.32
29   Raise the vehicle and support it securely on jackstands.
30   Detach the connecting rod or relay rod from the Pitman arm with a puller.
31   Remove the Pitman arm nut and washer and discard the nut - use a new one during installation **(see illustration).** Mark the Pitman arm and the steering gear shaft to ensure proper alignment at reassembly time (only if the same Pitman arm is going to be used).
32   Remove the Pitman arm with a Pitman arm puller or a two-jaw puller **(see illustration).**
33   Inspect the ballstud threads for damage. Inspect the ballstud seal for excessive wear. Clean the threads on the ballstud.
34   Installation is the reverse of removal. Make sure the marks you made on the Pitman arm and Pitman shaft are aligned, and be sure to use a new nut. Tighten the nut to the torque listed in this Chapter's Specifications.

11.31 Use a prybar to hold the Pitman arm and break loose the Pitman arm nut. Be sure to mark the relationship of the Pitman arm to the steering gear shaft before pulling it off (steering gear removed for clarity)

11.32 Remove the Pitman arm with a Pitman arm puller (shown here) or a heavy-duty two-jaw puller

12 Steering gear - removal and installation

Warning: *DO NOT allow the steering column shaft to rotate with the steering gear removed or damage to the airbag system clockspring could occur. As a method of preventing the shaft from turning, wrap the seat belt around the rim of the steering wheel and buckle the belt in place.*

Models with rack-and-pinion steering gear

Refer to illustration 12.2

1   Loosen the front wheel lug nuts, raise the front of the vehicle and support it securely on jackstands. Apply the parking brake. Remove the wheels.

2   Mark the relationship of the intermediate shaft coupler to the steering gear input shaft, then remove the pinch bolt **(see illustration).**

3   Detach the tie-rod ends from the steering knuckles (see Section 11).

4   Position a drain pan under the steering gear. Using a flare-nut wrench, if available, unscrew the power steering pressure and return lines from the steering gear. Cap the lines to prevent leakage.

5   Unscrew the mounting nuts, remove the washers and slide the bolts forward into the frame. Lower the steering gear from the vehicle.

6   Installation is the reverse of removal. Be sure to tighten all fasteners to the torque values listed in this Chapter's Specifications. Tighten the wheel lug nuts to the torque listed in the Chapter 1 Specifications. Check the power steering fluid level and add some, if necessary (see Chapter 1), then bleed the system as described in Section 14.

Models with recirculating ball steering gear

Refer to illustrations 12.8, 12.9 and 12.11

7   Raise the front of the vehicle and support it securely on jackstands. Apply the park-

12.2 Remove the pinch bolt from the lower end of the intermediate shaft (rack-and-pinion steering gear)

ing brake.

8   Mark the relationship of the intermediate shaft coupler to the steering gear input shaft, then remove the pinch bolt from the coupler **(see illustration).**

9   Position a drain pan under the steering gear, then unscrew the power steering lines from the steering gear. Use a flare-nut wrench, if available, to prevent rounding-off the fittings **(see illustration).**

10   Separate the connecting rod or relay rod from the Pitman arm (see Section 11).

11   Support the steering gear and remove the steering gear retaining bolts from the frame rail, then detach the steering gear from the frame and remove it **(see illustration).**

12   If you're installing a new steering gear or a new Pitman arm, remove the Pitman arm from the steering gear sector shaft (see Section 11).

13   Installation is the reverse of removal. Be sure to tighten all fasteners to the torque values listed in this Chapter's Specifications. Check the power steering fluid level and add some, if necessary (see Chapter 1), then bleed the system as described in Section 14.

12.8 Remove the intermediate shaft coupler pinch bolt (recirculating ball steering gear)

13 Power steering pump - removal and installation

Removal

Refer to illustrations 13.4 and 13.7

1   Disconnect the cable from the negative battery terminal (see Chapter 5, Section 1).

2   Remove the upper fan shroud (see Chapter 3).

3   Remove the serpentine drivebelt (see Chapter 1).

4   Using a special power steering pump pulley remover, remove the pulley from the pump **(see illustration).**

5   If you're working on a 2003 or later 4.8L, 5.3L, or 6.0L V8 engine, disconnect the intermediate shaft from the steering gear (see Section 12).

6   Position a drain pan under the power steering pump. Disconnect the pressure and return hoses from the backside of the pump. Plug the hoses to prevent contaminants from entering.

7   Remove the pump mounting fasteners **(see illustration)** and lower the pump from the vehicle.

12.9 Using a flare-nut wrench, unscrew the power steering lines from the steering gear

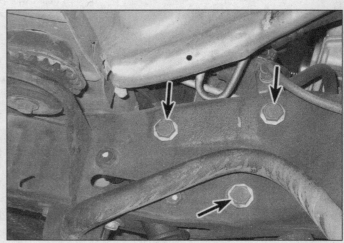

12.11 Remove the steering gear mounting bolts from the frame rail

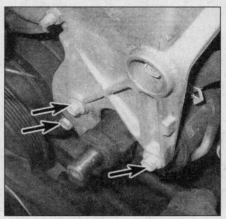

13.4 A special puller is required to remove the power steering pump pulley

13.7 The power steering pump on models with V8 engines is retained by four bolts (the bolt on the back of the pump securing the bracket to the engine is not visible in this photo

13.10 A long bolt with the same thread pitch as the internal threads of the power steering pump shaft, a nut, washer and socket that's the same diameter as the pulley hub can be used to install the pulley on the shaft

Installation

Refer to illustration 13.10

8   Position the pump in the mounting bracket and install the mounting fasteners. Tighten the fasteners securely.

9   Connect the hoses to the pump. Tighten the fittings securely.

10   Press the pulley onto the shaft using a special pulley installer tool. An alternative tool can be fabricated from a long bolt, nut, washer and a socket of the same diameter as the pulley hub **(see illustration)**. Push the pulley onto the shaft until the front of the hub is flush with the shaft, but no further.

11   The remainder of installation is the reverse of the removal procedure. Fill the power steering reservoir with the recommended fluid (see Chapter 1) and bleed the system following the procedure described in the next Section.

14   Power steering system - bleeding

1   The power steering system must be bled whenever a line is disconnected. Bubbles can be seen in power steering fluid that has air in it and the fluid will often have a milky appearance. Low fluid level can cause air to mix with the fluid, resulting in a noisy pump as well as foaming of the fluid.

2   Open the hood and check the fluid level in the reservoir, adding the specified fluid necessary to bring it up to the proper level (see Chapter 1).

3   Start the engine and slowly turn the steering wheel several times from left-to-right and back again. Do not turn the wheel completely from lock-to-lock. Check the fluid level, topping it up as necessary until it remains steady and no more bubbles are visible.

15   Wheels and tires - general information

Refer to illustration 15.1

Most models covered by this manual are equipped with radial tires **(see illustration)** or inch-pattern light truck tires. Use of other size or type of tires may affect the ride and handling of the vehicle. Don't mix different types of tires, such as radials and bias belted tires, on the same vehicle - handling may be seriously affected. It's recommended that tires be replaced in pairs on the same axle, but if only one tire is being replaced, be sure it's the same size, structure and tread design as the other tire on the same axle.

Because tire pressure has a substantial effect on handling and wear, the pressure of all tires should be checked at least once a month or before any extended trips are taken (see Chapter 1).

Wheels must be replaced if they are bent, dented, leak air, have elongated bolt holes, are heavily rusted, out of vertical symmetry or if the lug nuts won't stay tight. Wheel repairs that use welding or peening are not recommended.

Tire and wheel balance are important to the overall handling, braking and performance of the vehicle. Unbalanced wheels can

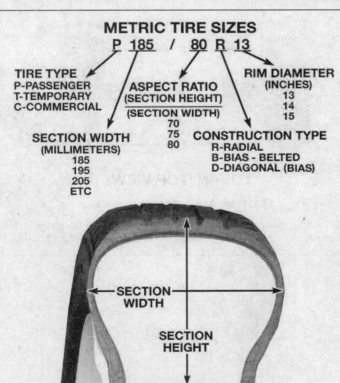

METRIC TIRE SIZES

P 185 / 80 R 13

TIRE TYPE
P-PASSENGER
T-TEMPORARY
C-COMMERCIAL

ASPECT RATIO
(SECTION HEIGHT)
(SECTION WIDTH)
70
75
80

RIM DIAMETER
(INCHES)
13
14
15

SECTION WIDTH
(MILLIMETERS)
185
195
205
ETC

CONSTRUCTION TYPE
R-RADIAL
B-BIAS - BELTED
D-DIAGONAL (BIAS)

SECTION WIDTH

SECTION HEIGHT

15.1 Metric tire size code

adversely affect handling and ride characteristics as well as tire life. Whenever a tire is installed on a wheel, the tire and wheel should be balanced by a shop with the proper equipment and expertise.

16   Wheel alignment - general information

Refer to illustration 16.1

Note: *Since wheel alignment requires special equipment and techniques it is beyond the scope of this manual. This section is intended only to familiarize the reader with the basic terms used and procedures followed during a typical wheel alignment.*

The three basic checks made when aligning a vehicle's front wheels are camber, caster and toe-in **(see illustration)**.

Camber and caster are the angles at which the wheels and suspension are inclined in relation to a vertical centerline. Camber is the angle of the wheel in the lateral, or side-to-side plane, while caster is the tilt between the steering axis and the vertical plane, as viewed from the side. Camber angle affects the amount of tire tread which contacts the road and compensates for changes in suspension geometry as the vehicle travels around curves and over bumps. Caster angle affects the self-centering action of the steering, which governs straight-line stability.

Toe-in is the amount the front wheels are angled in relationship to the center line of the vehicle. For example, in a vehicle with zero toe-in, the distance measured between the front edges of the wheels and the distance measured between the rear edges of the wheels are the same. In other words, the wheels are running parallel with the centerline of the vehicle. Toe-in is adjusted by lengthening or shortening the tie-rods. Incorrect toe-in will cause the tires to wear improperly by allowing them to "scrub" against the road surface.

Proper wheel alignment is essential for safe steering and even tire wear. Symptoms of alignment problems are pulling of the steering to one side or the other and uneven tire wear. If these symptoms are present, check for the following before having the alignment adjusted:

   a) *Loose steering gear mounting bolts*
   b) *Damaged or worn steering gear mounts*
   c) *Worn or damaged wheel bearings*
   d) *Bent tie-rods*
   e) *Worn balljoints*
   f) *Improper tire pressures*
   g) *Mixing tires of different construction*

Front wheel alignment should be left to an alignment shop with the proper equipment and experienced personnel.

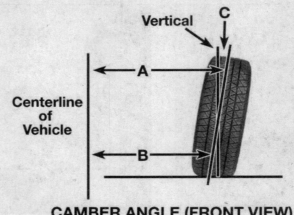

CAMBER ANGLE (FRONT VIEW)

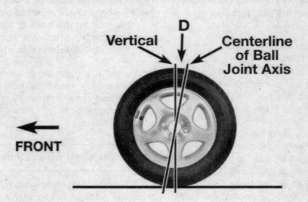

CASTER ANGLE (SIDE VIEW)

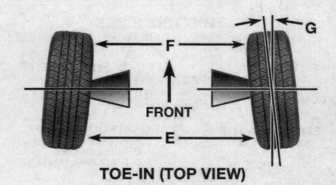

TOE-IN (TOP VIEW)

16.1   Front wheel alignment details

A minus B = C (degrees camber)   *E minus F = toe-in (measured in inches)*
D = degrees caster   *G = toe-in (expressed in degrees)*

Chapter 11
Body

Contents

1   General information

These models feature a body-on-frame construction, using box-sectioned frame side rails welded to boxed front and rear sections, with both welded-in and bolt-in crossmembers.

Certain components are particularly vulnerable to accident damage and can be unbolted and repaired or replaced. Among these parts are the body moldings, bumpers, hood, fenders, doors and all glass.

Certain components are particularly vulnerable to accident damage and can be unbolted and repaired or replaced. Among these parts are the body moldings, bumpers, front fenders, hood, doors and all glass.

Only general body maintenance practices and body panel repair procedures within the scope of the do-it-yourselfer are included in this Chapter.

2   Body - maintenance

1   The condition of your vehicle's body is very important, because the resale value depends a great deal on it. It's much more difficult to repair a neglected or damaged body than it is to repair mechanical components. The hidden areas of the body, such as the wheel wells, the frame and the engine compartment, are equally important, although they don't require as frequent attention as the rest of the body.

2   Once a year, or every 12,000 miles, it's a good idea to have the underside of the body steam-cleaned. All traces of dirt and oil will be removed and the area can then be inspected carefully for rust, damaged brake lines, frayed electrical wires, damaged cables and other problems.

3   At the same time, clean the engine and the engine compartment with a steam cleaner or water-soluble degreaser.

4   The wheel wells should be given close attention, since undercoating can peel away and stones and dirt thrown up by the tires can cause the paint to chip and flake, allowing rust to set in. If rust is found, clean down to the bare metal and apply an anti-rust paint.

5   The body should be washed about once a week. Wet the vehicle thoroughly to soften the dirt, then wash it down with a soft sponge and plenty of clean soapy water. If the surplus dirt is not washed off very carefully, it can wear down the paint.

6   Spots of tar or asphalt thrown up from the road should be removed with a cloth soaked in kerosene. Scented lamp oil is available in most hardware stores and the smell is easier to work with than straight kerosene.

7   Once every six months, wax the body and chrome trim. If a chrome cleaner is used to remove rust from any of the vehicle's plated parts, remember that the cleaner also removes part of the chrome, so use it sparingly. On any plated parts where chrome cleaner is used, use a good paste wax over the plating for extra protection.

3   Vinyl trim - maintenance

Don't clean vinyl trim with detergents, caustic soap or petroleum-based cleaners. Plain soap and water works just fine, with a soft brush to clean dirt that may be ingrained. Wash the vinyl as frequently as the rest of the vehicle.

After cleaning, application of a high quality rubber and vinyl protectant will help prevent oxidation and cracks. The protectant can also be applied to weatherstripping, vacuum lines and rubber hoses, which often fail as a result of chemical degradation, and to the tires.

4   Upholstery and carpets - maintenance

1   Every three months remove the floormats and clean the interior of the vehicle (more frequently if necessary). Use a stiff whisk broom to brush the carpeting and loosen dirt and dust, then vacuum the upholstery and carpets thoroughly, especially along seams and crevices.
2   Dirt and stains can be removed from carpeting with basic household or automotive carpet shampoos available in spray cans. Follow the directions and vacuum again, then use a stiff brush to bring back the "nap" of the carpet.
3   Most interiors have cloth or vinyl upholstery, either of which can be cleaned and maintained with a number of material-specific cleaners or shampoos available in auto supply stores. Follow the directions on the product for usage, and always spot-test any upholstery cleaner on an inconspicuous area (bottom edge of a backseat cushion) to ensure that it doesn't cause a color shift in the material.
4   After cleaning, vinyl upholstery should be treated with a protectant. **Note:** *Make sure the protectant container indicates the product can be used on seats - some products may make a seat too slippery.* **Caution:** *Do not use protectant on steering wheels.*
5   Leather upholstery requires special care. It should be cleaned regularly with saddlesoap or leather cleaner. Never use alcohol, gasoline, nail polish remover or thinner to clean leather upholstery.
6   After cleaning, regularly treat leather upholstery with a leather conditioner, rubbed in with a soft cotton cloth. Never use car wax on leather upholstery.
7   In areas where the interior of the vehicle is subject to bright sunlight, cover leather seating areas of the seats with a sheet if the vehicle is to be left out for any length of time.

5   Body repair - minor damage

Flexible plastic body panels

The following repair procedures are for minor scratches and gouges. Repair of more serious damage should be left to a dealer ser-

vice department or qualified auto body shop. Below is a list of the equipment and materials necessary to perform the following repair procedures on plastic body panels. Although a specific brand of material may be mentioned, it should be noted that equivalent products from other manufacturers may be used instead.

> Wax, grease and silicone removing solvent
> Cloth-backed body tape
> Sanding discs
> Drill motor with three-inch disc holder
> Hand sanding block
> Rubber squeegees
> Sandpaper
> Non-porous mixing palette
> Wood paddle or putty knife
> Curved-tooth body file
> Flexible parts repair material

1   Remove the damaged panel, if necessary or desirable. In most cases, repairs can be carried out with the panel installed.
2   Clean the area(s) to be repaired with a wax, grease and silicone removing solvent applied with a water-dampened cloth.
3   If the damage is structural, that is, if it extends through the panel, clean the backside of the panel area to be repaired as well. Wipe dry.
4   Sand the rear surface about 1-1/2 inches beyond the break.
5   Cut two pieces of fiberglass cloth large enough to overlap the break by about 1-1/2 inches. Cut only to the required length.
6   Mix the adhesive from the repair kit according to the instructions included with the kit, and apply a layer of the mixture approximately 1/8-inch thick on the backside of the panel. Overlap the break by at least 1-1/2 inches.
7   Apply one piece of fiberglass cloth to the adhesive and cover the cloth with additional adhesive. Apply a second piece of fiberglass cloth to the adhesive and immediately cover the cloth with additional adhesive in sufficient quantity to fill the weave.
8   Allow the repair to cure for 20 to 30 minutes at 60-degrees to 80-degrees F.
9   If necessary, trim the excess repair material at the edge.
10   Remove all of the paint film over and around the area(s) to be repaired. The repair material should not overlap the painted surface.
11   With a drill motor and a sanding disc (or a rotary file), cut a "V" along the break line approximately 1/2-inch wide. Remove all dust and loose particles from the repair area.
12   Mix and apply the repair material. Apply a light coat first over the damaged area; then continue applying material until it reaches a level slightly higher than the surrounding finish.
13   Cure the mixture for 20 to 30 minutes at 60-degrees to 80-degrees F.
14   Roughly establish the contour of the area being repaired with a body file. If low areas or pits remain, mix and apply additional adhesive.

15   Block sand the damaged area with sandpaper to establish the actual contour of the surrounding surface.
16   If desired, the repaired area can be temporarily protected with several light coats of primer. Because of the special paints and techniques required for flexible body panels, it is recommended that the vehicle be taken to a paint shop for completion of the body repair.

Steel body panels
See photo sequence

Repair of minor scratches
17   If the scratch is superficial and does not penetrate to the metal of the body, repair is very simple. Lightly rub the scratched area with a fine rubbing compound to remove loose paint and built up wax. Rinse the area with clean water.
18   Apply touch-up paint to the scratch, using a small brush. Continue to apply thin layers of paint until the surface of the paint in the scratch is level with the surrounding paint. Allow the new paint at least two weeks to harden, then blend it into the surrounding paint by rubbing with a very fine rubbing compound. Finally, apply a coat of wax to the scratch area.
19   If the scratch has penetrated the paint and exposed the metal of the body, causing the metal to rust, a different repair technique is required. Remove all loose rust from the bottom of the scratch with a pocket knife, then apply rust inhibiting paint to prevent the formation of rust in the future. Using a rubber or nylon applicator, coat the scratched area with glaze-type filler. If required, the filler can be mixed with thinner to provide a very thin paste, which is ideal for filling narrow scratches. Before the glaze filler in the scratch hardens, wrap a piece of smooth cotton cloth around the tip of a finger. Dip the cloth in thinner and then quickly wipe it along the surface of the scratch. This will ensure that the surface of the filler is slightly hollow. The scratch can now be painted over as described earlier in this Section.

Repair of dents
20   When repairing dents, the first job is to pull the dent out until the affected area is as close as possible to its original shape. There is no point in trying to restore the original shape completely as the metal in the damaged area will have stretched on impact and cannot be restored to its original contours. It is better to bring the level of the dent up to a point which is about 1/8-inch below the level of the surrounding metal. In cases where the dent is very shallow, it is not worth trying to pull it out at all.
21   If the back side of the dent is accessible, it can be hammered out gently from behind using a soft-face hammer. While doing this, hold a block of wood firmly against the opposite side of the metal to absorb the hammer blows and prevent the metal from being stretched.
22   If the dent is in a section of the body

which has double layers, or some other factor makes it inaccessible from behind, a different technique is required. Drill several small holes through the metal inside the damaged area, particularly in the deeper sections. Screw long, self tapping screws into the holes just enough for them to get a good grip in the metal. Now the dent can be pulled out by pulling on the protruding heads of the screws with locking pliers.

23   The next stage of repair is the removal of paint from the damaged area and from an inch or so of the surrounding metal. This is easily done with a wire brush or sanding disk in a drill motor, although it can be done just as effectively by hand with sandpaper. To complete the preparation for filling, score the surface of the bare metal with a screwdriver or the tang of a file or drill small holes in the affected area. This will provide a good grip for the filler material. To complete the repair, see the Section on filling and painting.

Repair of rust holes or gashes

24   Remove all paint from the affected area and from an inch or so of the surrounding metal using a sanding disk or wire brush mounted in a drill motor. If these are not available, a few sheets of sandpaper will do the job just as effectively.

25   With the paint removed, you will be able to determine the severity of the corrosion and decide whether to replace the whole panel, if possible, or repair the affected area. New body panels are not as expensive as most people think and it is often quicker to install a new panel than to repair large areas of rust.

26   Remove all trim pieces from the affected area except those which will act as a guide to the original shape of the damaged body, such as headlight shells, etc. Using metal snips or a hacksaw blade, remove all loose metal and any other metal that is badly affected by rust. Hammer the edges of the hole in to create a slight depression for the filler material.

27   Wire brush the affected area to remove the powdery rust from the surface of the metal. If the back of the rusted area is accessible, treat it with rust inhibiting paint.

28   Before filling is done, block the hole in some way. This can be done with sheet metal riveted or screwed into place, or by stuffing the hole with wire mesh.

29   Once the hole is blocked off, the affected area can be filled and painted. See the following subsection on filling and painting.

Filling and painting

30   Many types of body fillers are available, but generally speaking, body repair kits which contain filler paste and a tube of resin hardener are best for this type of repair work. A wide, flexible plastic or nylon applicator will be necessary for imparting a smooth and contoured finish to the surface of the filler material. Mix up a small amount of filler on a clean piece of wood or cardboard (use the hardener sparingly). Follow the manufacturer's instructions on the package, otherwise the filler will set incorrectly.

31   Using the applicator, apply the filler paste to the prepared area. Draw the applicator across the surface of the filler to achieve the desired contour and to level the filler surface. As soon as a contour that approximates the original one is achieved, stop working the paste. If you continue, the paste will begin to stick to the applicator. Continue to add thin layers of paste at 20-minute intervals until the level of the filler is just above the surrounding metal.

32   Once the filler has hardened, the excess can be removed with a body file. From then on, progressively finer grades of sandpaper should be used, starting with a 180-grit paper and finishing with 600-grit wet-or-dry paper. Always wrap the sandpaper around a flat rubber or wooden block, otherwise the surface of the filler will not be completely flat. During the sanding of the filler surface, the wet-or-dry paper should be periodically rinsed in water. This will ensure that a very smooth finish is produced in the final stage.

33   At this point, the repair area should be surrounded by a ring of bare metal, which in turn should be encircled by the finely feathered edge of good paint. Rinse the repair area with clean water until all of the dust produced by the sanding operation is gone.

34   Spray the entire area with a light coat of primer. This will reveal any imperfections in the surface of the filler. Repair the imperfections with fresh filler paste or glaze filler and once more smooth the surface with sandpaper. Repeat this spray-and-repair procedure until you are satisfied that the surface of the filler and the feathered edge of the paint are perfect. Rinse the area with clean water and allow it to dry completely.

35   The repair area is now ready for painting. Spray painting must be carried out in a warm, dry, windless and dust free atmosphere. These conditions can be created if you have access to a large indoor work area, but if you are forced to work in the open, you will have to pick the day very carefully. If you are working indoors, dousing the floor in the work area with water will help settle the dust which would otherwise be in the air. If the repair area is confined to one body panel, mask off the surrounding panels. This will help minimize the effects of a slight mismatch in paint color. Trim pieces such as chrome strips, door handles, etc., will also need to be masked off or removed. Use masking tape and several thickness of newspaper for the masking operations.

36   Before spraying, shake the paint can thoroughly, then spray a test area until the spray painting technique is mastered. Cover the repair area with a thick coat of primer. The thickness should be built up using several thin layers of primer rather than one thick one. Using 600-grit wet-or-dry sandpaper, rub down the surface of the primer until it is very smooth. While doing this, the work area should be thoroughly rinsed with water and the wet-or-dry sandpaper periodically rinsed as well. Allow the primer to dry before spray-

ing additional coats.

37   Spray on the top coat, again building up the thickness by using several thin layers of paint. Begin spraying in the center of the repair area and then, using a circular motion, work out until the whole repair area and about two inches of the surrounding original paint is covered. Remove all masking material 10 to 15 minutes after spraying on the final coat of paint. Allow the new paint at least two weeks to harden, then use a very fine rubbing compound to blend the edges of the new paint into the existing paint. Finally, apply a coat of wax.

6   Body repair - major damage

1   Major damage must be repaired by an auto body shop specifically equipped to perform body and frame repairs. These shops have the specialized equipment required to do the job properly.

2   If the damage is extensive, the frame must be checked for proper alignment or the vehicle's handling characteristics may be adversely affected and other components may wear at an accelerated rate.

3   Due to the fact that some of the major body components (hood, fenders, doors, etc.) are separate and replaceable units, any seriously damaged components should be replaced rather than repaired. Sometimes the components can be found in a wrecking yard that specializes in used vehicle components, often at considerable savings over the cost of new parts.

7   Hinges and locks - maintenance

Once every 3,000 miles, or every three months, the hinges and latch assemblies on the doors, hood and trunk (or liftgate) should be given a few drops of light oil or lock lubricant. The door latch strikers should also be lubricated with a thin coat of grease to reduce wear and ensure free movement. Lubricate the door and trunk (or liftgate) locks with spray-on graphite lubricant.

8   Windshield and fixed glass - replacement

Replacement of the windshield and fixed glass requires the use of special fast-setting adhesive/caulk materials and some specialized tools and techniques. These operations should be left to a shop specializing in glass work.

9   Hood - removal, installation and adjustment

Note: *The hood is somewhat awkward to remove and install; at least two people should perform this procedure.*

These photos illustrate a method of repairing simple dents. They are intended to supplement *Body repair - minor damage* in this Chapter and should not be used as the sole instructions for body repair on these vehicles.

1 If you can't access the backside of the body panel to hammer out the dent, pull it out with a slide-hammer-type dent puller. In the deepest portion of the dent or along the crease line, drill or punch hole(s) at least one inch apart . . .

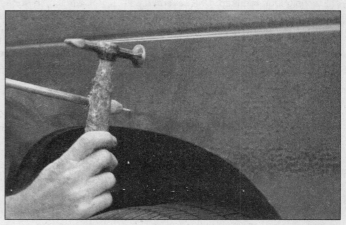

2 . . . then screw the slide-hammer into the hole and operate it. Tap with a hammer near the edge of the dent to help 'pop' the metal back to its original shape. When you're finished, the dent area should be close to its original contour and about 1/8-inch below the surface of the surrounding metal

3 Using coarse-grit sandpaper, remove the paint down to the bare metal. Hand sanding works fine, but the disc sander shown here makes the job faster. Use finer (about 320-grit) sandpaper to feather-edge the paint at least one inch around the dent area

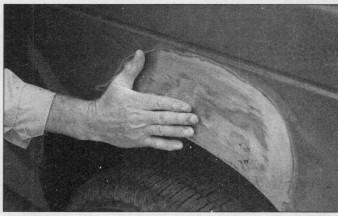

4 When the paint is removed, touch will probably be more helpful than sight for telling if the metal is straight. Hammer down the high spots or raise the low spots as necessary. Clean the repair area with wax/silicone remover

5 Following label instructions, mix up a batch of plastic filler and hardener. The ratio of filler to hardener is critical, and, if you mix it incorrectly, it will either not cure properly or cure too quickly (you won't have time to file and sand it into shape)

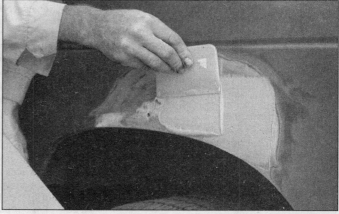

6 Working quickly so the filler doesn't harden, use a plastic applicator to press the body filler firmly into the metal, assuring it bonds completely. Work the filler until it matches the original contour and is slightly above the surrounding metal

7 Let the filler harden until you can just dent it with your fingernail. Use a body file or Surform tool (shown here) to rough-shape the filler

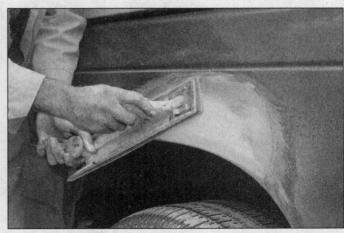

8 Use coarse-grit sandpaper and a sanding board or block to work the filler down until it's smooth and even. Work down to finer grits of sandpaper - always using a board or block - ending up with 360 or 400 grit

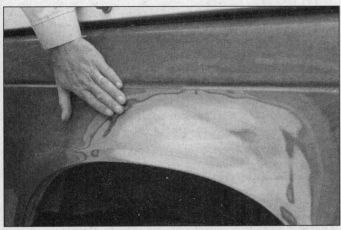

9 You shouldn't be able to feel any ridge at the transition from the filler to the bare metal or from the bare metal to the old paint. As soon as the repair is flat and uniform, remove the dust and mask off the adjacent panels or trim pieces

10 Apply several layers of primer to the area. Don't spray the primer on too heavy, so it sags or runs, and make sure each coat is dry before you spray on the next one. A professional-type spray gun is being used here, but aerosol spray primer is available inexpensively from auto parts stores

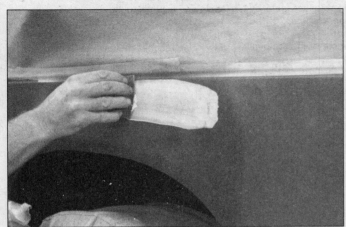

11 The primer will help reveal imperfections or scratches. Fill these with glazing compound. Follow the label instructions and sand it with 360 or 400-grit sandpaper until it's smooth. Repeat the glazing, sanding and respraying until the primer reveals a perfectly smooth surface

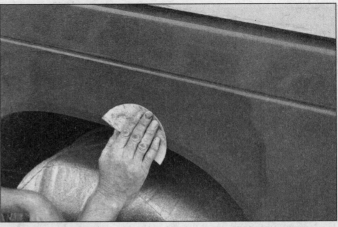

12 Finish sand the primer with very fine sandpaper (400 or 600-grit) to remove the primer overspray. Clean the area with water and allow it to dry. Use a tack rag to remove any dust, then apply the finish coat. Don't attempt to rub out or wax the repair area until the paint has dried completely (at least two weeks)

9.4 Remove the hood hinge bolts

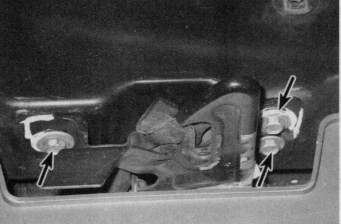
9.6 Scribe a line or make a mark around the latch to use as a reference point. To adjust the hood latch, loosen the retaining bolts, move the latch and retighten bolts, then close the hood to check the fit

Removal and installation

Refer to illustration 9.4
1   Remove the cowl covers (see Section 15).
2   Open the hood, then place blankets or pads over the fenders and cowl area of the body. This will protect the body and paint as the hood is lifted off.
3   Disconnect any cables or wires that will interfere with removal. Disconnect the windshield washer tubing from the nozzles on the hood.
4   Have an assistant support one side of the hood while you support the other. Simultaneously remove the hinge bolts **(see illustration)**, then lift off the hood.
5   Installation is the reverse of removal.

Adjustment

Refer to illustrations 9.6 and 9.7
6   If necessary after installation, the entire hood latch assembly can be adjusted up-and-down as well as from side-to-side on the radiator support so the hood closes securely and flush with the fenders. To make the

9.7 To adjust the vertical height of the leading edge of the hood so that it's flush with the fenders, turn each edge cushion clockwise (to lower the hood) or counterclockwise (to raise the hood)

adjustment, scribe a line or mark around the hood latch mounting bolts to provide a reference point, then loosen them and reposition the latch assembly, as necessary **(see illustration)**. Following adjustment, retighten the mounting bolts.
7   Finally, adjust the hood bumpers on the radiator support so the hood, when closed, is flush with the fenders **(see illustration)**.
8   The hood latch assembly, as well as the hinges, should be periodically lubricated with white, lithium-base grease to prevent binding and wear.

10   Hood latch and release cable - removal and installation

Latch
1   Scribe a line around the latch to aid alignment when reinstalling the latch assembly.
2   Remove the latch retaining bolts securing the latch to the radiator support and remove the latch **(see illustration 9.6)**.
3   Disconnect the hood release cable by disengaging the cable from the back of the latch assembly.
4   Installation is the reverse of the removal

10.7 Carefully pull the kick panel to release the clips

procedure. **Note:** *Adjust the latch so the hood engages securely when closed and the hood bumpers are slightly compressed.*

Cable
Refer to illustrations 10.7 and 10.8
5   Remove the hood latch as described earlier in this Section, then detach the cable from the latch.
6   Working in the engine compartment, detach the cable from all of its retaining clips. It may be necessary to cut some of the clips to free the cable. Attach a length of wire to the cable to assist with the installation of the new cable.
7   Working in the passenger compartment, remove the driver's kick panel to expose the hood latch release cable and handle **(see illustration)**.
8   Remove the screws and detach the hood release cable and handle assembly from the driver's left side hinge pillar **(see illustration)**.
9   Pull the cable through the firewall grommet into the passenger compartment.
10   Disconnect the guide wire from the old cable and fasten it to the new cable.
11   With the new cable attached to the wire, pull the wire back through the firewall until the new cable reaches the latch assembly.

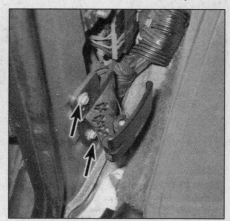
10.8 Remove the hood release handle mounting bolts

11.2 Remove the fasteners securing the grille to the radiator support (left side shown, right side similar)

12.10 Remove the fasteners from both sides of the radiator support

12   The remainder of installation is the reverse of removal. Make sure the latch seats properly in the firewall.

11   Radiator grille - removal and installation

Refer to illustration 11.2

1   Remove the park/turn signal and side marker lamps (see Chapter 12).
2   Detach the screws securing the upper half of the radiator grille **(see illustration).**
3   Lift the radiator grille to disengage the lower half of the grille from the radiator support and remove the grille from the vehicle.
4   Installation is the reverse of the removal procedure.

12   Radiator support - removal and installation

Refer to illustration 12.10

1   Disconnect the cable from the negative battery terminal (see Chapter 5, Section 1).
2   If you're working on a 2003 or later model, remove the battery (see Chapter 5), then remove the battery tray fasteners and remove the tray.
3   Remove the radiator (see Chapter 3).
4   Remove the radiator grille (see Section 11).
5   If you're working on a 2002 or earlier model, remove the headlights (see Chapter 12).
6   If equipped, remove the transmission oil cooler (see Chapter 7).
7   If equipped, remove the engine oil cooler (see Chapter 3).
8   Remove the air conditioning condenser (see Chapter 3).
9   Remove the hood latch from the radiator support (see Section 10).
10   Remove the fasteners securing the radi-

ator support **(see illustration),** then remove the radiator support from the vehicle.
11   Installation is the reverse of the removal procedure.

13   Bumpers - removal and installation

1   Apply the parking brake, raise the vehicle and support it securely on jackstands. Block the wheels at the opposite end of the vehicle.

Front bumper

2   Working from the backside of the bumper, remove the retaining bolts securing the bumper brackets to each frame rail. Then remove the bumper from the vehicle.
3   Installation is the reverse of removal.

Rear bumper

4   Unplug any electrical connectors which would interfere with bumper removal.
5   Working from the backside of the bum-

per, remove the retaining bolts securing the bumper brackets to each frame rail. Then remove the bumper from the vehicle.
6   Installation is the reverse of the removal procedure.

14   Front fender - removal and installation

Refer to illustrations 14.3, 14.4, 14.5 and 14.6

1   Remove the hood (see Section 9).
2   Remove the radiator grille (see Section 11).
3   Remove the plastic filler panel from the fender **(see illustration).**
4   Remove the fender extension panel **(see illustration).**
5   Remove the fender-to-rocker panel bolts and fender-to-door pillar bolts **(see illustration).**
6   Remove the fender-to-radiator support bolts and the remaining fender mounting bolts **(see illustration).**

14.3 Remove the two screws securing the filler panel, then remove the panel

14.4 Remove the fasteners securing the fender extension panel, then remove the panel

14.5 Remove the fasteners securing the fender to the rocker panel and door pillar

7   Detach the fender. It's a good idea to have an assistant support the fender while it's being moved away from the vehicle to prevent damage to the surrounding body panels.
8   Installation is the reverse of the removal procedure.

14.6 Remove the remaining fender mounting bolts

15   Cowl covers - removal and installation

Refer to illustrations 15.2a and 15.2b
1   Remove the windshield wiper arms (see Chapter 12).

2   Remove the screws and clips securing the left hand and right hand cowl covers and weatherstrips **(see illustrations)**.
3   Disconnect the windshield washer hose.
4   Installation is the reverse of the removal procedure.

16   Door trim panels - removal and installation

Front doors

Refer to illustrations 16.1, 16.2a, 16.2b, 16.3 and 16.5
1   On manual window models, remove the window crank **(see illustration)**.
2   Remove all door trim panel retaining screws and door pull/armrest assemblies **(see illustrations)**.
3   Remove the mirror trim cover **(see illustration)**.
4   Pull upward then outward to release the door panel from the door. Disconnect any wiring harness connectors and remove the trim panel from the vehicle.
5   For access to the inner door, carefully

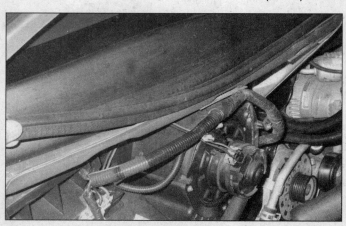

15.2a Remove the cowl cover weatherstrip . . .

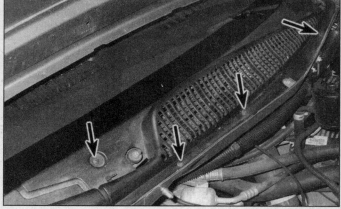

15.2b . . . and the retaining screws (left side shown, right side similar)

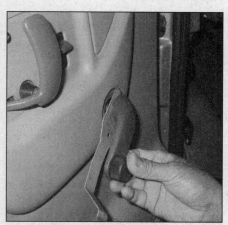

16.1 Use a hooked tool or a special window crank removal tool like this one to remove the retaining clip, then detach the window crank handle

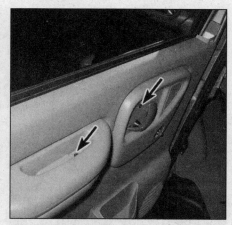

16.2a Remove the screw from the door handle trim plate and the armrest . . .

16.2b . . . then remove the trim plate and the screw underneath

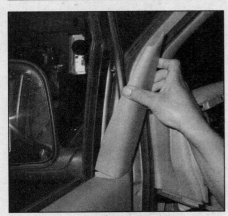

16.3 Pull off the mirror trim cover

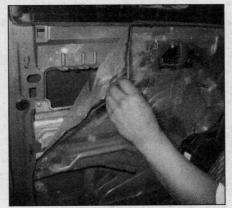

16.5 Carefully peel back the plastic watershield for access to the inner door

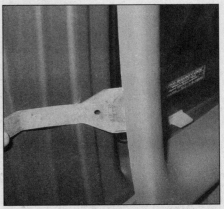

16.9 Carefully pry around the sliding door upper trim panel to release the clips, then remove the trim panel

peel back the plastic watershield **(see illustration)**.

6   Connect the wiring harness connectors and place the panel in position on the door.

7   Press the trim panel straight against the door (slightly higher than the final position) until the tabs on the trim panel align with all the holes in the door, then push down on the panel until the tabs are seated.

8   Install the armrest/door pulls, screws and the window crank.

Sliding door
Refer to illustrations 16.9 and 16.10

9   Remove the sliding door upper trim panel **(see illustration)**.

10   Remove the door handle **(see illustration)**.

11   Pull upward then outward to release the door panel from the door and remove the trim panel from the vehicle.

12   Installation is the reverse of the removal procedure.

Hinged side doors
Side front door
13   Remove the screws securing the door pull handle.

14   Remove the screws securing the door

handle trim bezel, then remove the bezel.

15   Carefully pry around the window trim panel and release the clips securing it to the door.

16   Pull upward then outward to release the door panel from the door and remove the trim panel from the vehicle.

17   Installation is the reverse of the removal procedure.

Side rear door
18   Carefully pry around the window trim panel and release the clips securing it to the door.

19   Pull upward then outward to release the door panel from the door and remove the trim panel from the vehicle.

20   Installation is the reverse of the removal procedure.

Rear doors
21   Carefully pry around the window trim panel and release the clips securing it to the door, then remove the trim panel from the door.

22   If you're working on the right side door, remove the screws securing the door handle trim bezel, then remove the bezel.

23   Pull upward then outward to release the door panel from the door and remove the trim panel from the vehicle.

24   Installation is the reverse of the removal procedure.

17   Door - removal and installation

Front doors
Removal and installation
Refer to illustrations 17.5 and 17.6

Note: *The door is heavy and somewhat awkward to remove and install - at least two people should perform this procedure.*

1   Raise the window completely in the door and disconnect the cable from the negative battery terminal (see Chapter 5, Section 1).

2   Remove the door trim panel and watershield as described in Section 16.

3   Unplug all electrical connections, ground wires and harness retaining clips from the door. **Note:** *It is a good idea to label all connections to aid the reassembly process.*

4   Working through the door opening, detach the rubber conduit between the body and the door. Then pull the wiring harness through the conduit hole and remove it from the door.

5   Remove the bolts securing the door stop **(see illustration)**.

6   With an assistant supporting the door,

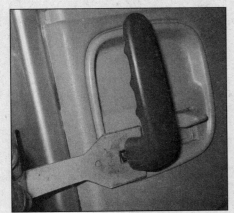

16.10 Use a hooked tool or a special window crank removal tool like this one to remove the retaining clip, then detach the handle

17.5 Remove the door stop mounting bolts

17.6 Use a hammer and punch to drive the pins from the hinges

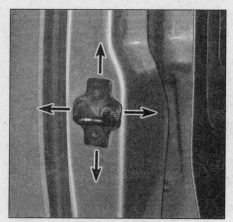

17.11 Adjust the door lock striker by loosening the mounting screws and gently tapping the striker in the desired direction

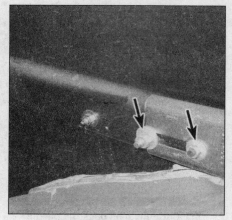

17.13a Remove the two fasteners securing the door stop . . .

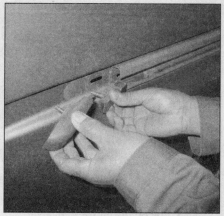

17.13b . . . then remove it from the end of the center track

remove the hinge pins **(see illustration)**.
7   Remove the door from the vehicle. **Note:** *Check the hinge pin bushings for wear. If wear is indicated, replace the bushings with new ones. This can be done by knocking the old ones out with a hammer and punch.*
8   Installation is the reverse of the removal procedure.

Adjustment
Refer to illustration 17.11
9   Having proper door-to-body alignment is a critical part of a well functioning door assembly. First check the door hinge pins for excessive play. Fully open the door and lift up and down on the door without lifting the body. If a door has 1/16-inch or more excessive play, the hinge pin bushings should be replaced.
10   To adjust the door closed position, first check that the door latch is contacting the center of the latch striker. If not, remove the striker and add or subtract shims to achieve correct alignment.
11   Finally, adjust the latch striker as necessary to provide positive engagement with the latch mechanism **(see illustration)** and to align the door panel flush with the rear door or body.

Sliding door
Removal and installation
Refer to illustrations 17.13a, 17.13b, 17.14 and 17.15
Note: *The door is heavy and somewhat awkward to remove and install - at least two people should perform this procedure.*
12   Remove the passenger side rear trim panel (see Section 27).
13   Remove the center track door stop **(see illustrations)**.
14   With an assistant supporting the weight of the door, disconnect the lower roller bracket **(see illustration)**.
15   With the assistant still supporting the weight of the door, remove the sliding door upper trim panel **(see illustration 16.9)**. Outline the upper roller bracket bolt heads then disconnect the upper roller bracket from the door **(see illustration)**.
16   With the help of the assistant, roll the door to the end of the center track, rotate the roller out and lift the door off.
17   Installation is the reverse of the removal procedure.

Adjustment
18   Remove the sliding door upper trim

panel, then loosen the upper bracket bolt heads on the upper roller **(see illustration 17.15)**.
19   Loosen the fasteners on the lower roller bracket **(see illustration 17.14)**.
20   Move the door up or down to obtain the desired position. After the desired position is obtained, tighten all the fasteners securely.
21   Install the sliding door upper trim panel.

Hinged side doors
Refer to illustrations 17.23 and 17.24
Note: *This procedure applies to either hinged side door.*
22   If you're replacing a hinged side door, you'll need to remove the door trim panels (see Section 16) and all handles, latch rods and latches (see Section 18) from the old door and install it on the new door. You can do this now, while the door is still installed, or after removing it.
23   Open the door and locate the check strap **(see illustration)**. Pull the check strap toward the inner side of the door, then swing the door

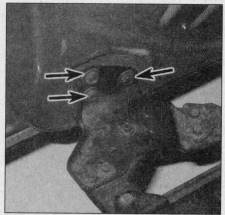

17.14 Remove the fasteners securing the lower roller bracket to the door

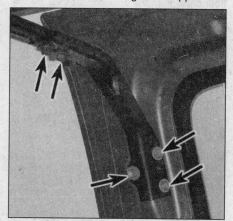

17.15 Remove the fasteners, then disconnect the roller bracket from the door

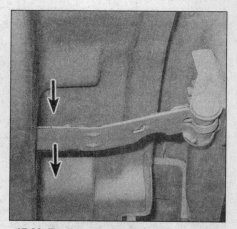

17.23 To disengage the outer end of the check strap from a side door, open the door halfway (at a right angle to the side of the van), then pull the outer end of the check strap toward the inside of the door and open the door all the way

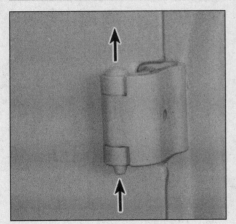

17.24 To remove the door hinge pins, carefully drive them out with a hammer and punch (this is an upper hinge; on the lower hinges the pin is reversed, with the head pointing down)

17.29 Remove the door hinge-to-body bolts (upper hinge shown, lower hinge similar)

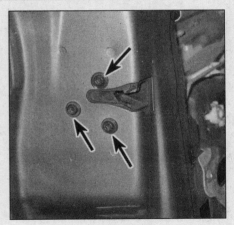

18.3 Latch assembly mounting screws

fully open to disengage the check strap from the door.

24   Remove the door hinge pins **(see illustration)** with a hammer and punch. Be extremely careful not to chip the paint on the hinges.

25   When installing the door, grease the hinge pin before installing it.

Rear doors
Removal and installation
Refer to illustration 17.29

26   Remove the brake light assembly (see Chapter 12).

27   If you're working on the right rear door, remove the door trim panel and watershield as described in Section 16, then unplug all electrical connections, ground wires and harness retaining clips from the door. **Note:** *It is a good idea to label all connections to aid the reassembly process.* Detach the rubber con-

duit between the body and the door, then pull the wiring harness through the conduit hole and remove it from the door.

28   Mark around the door hinges with a pen or scribe to facilitate realignment during assembly.

29   With an assistant supporting the weight of the door, remove the hinge-to-body bolts **(see illustration)** from the upper and lower hinge, then lift the door off.

30   Installation is the reverse of the removal procedure.

---

18   Door latch, lock cylinder and handles - removal and installation

---

Door latch
Refer to illustration 18.3

1   Remove the door trim panel and watershield as described in Section 16.

2   If you're working on the front door, remove the rear glass run channel. If you're

working on a sliding door, remove the door control assembly **(see illustration 18.9).**

3   Remove the screws securing the latch to the door **(see illustration).**

4   Working through the large access hole, position the latch as necessary to disconnect the electrical connector, if equipped, then detach the rods from the latch assembly.

5   Remove the latch assembly from the door.

6   Installation is the reverse of the removal procedure.

Outside door handle and lock cylinder
Refer to illustration 18.9

7   Remove the door trim panel and watershield as described in Section 16.

8   If you're working on the front door, remove the rear glass run channel.

9   If you're working on the sliding door, remove the door control assembly **(see illustration).**

10   Detach the rods from the lock cylinder.

11   Remove the fasteners securing the bracket and handle to the door, then remove the handle from the door.

12   Installation is the reverse of the removal procedure.

Inside door handle - front door
Refer to illustration 18.14

13   Remove the door trim panel and watershield as described in Section 16.

14   Drill out the rivet securing the inside door handle to the door **(see illustration).**

15   Detach the rods from the inside door handle, the remove the handle from the door.

16   Installation is the reverse of the removal procedure.

Hinged side doors

Latch handle (rear side door)
Refer to illustration 18.18

17   Remove the rear side door trim panel, if equipped (see Section 16).

18.9 Remove the fasteners for the door control assembly, then disconnect the rods and remove it from the door

18.14 Drill out the plastic rivet to release the door handle from the door

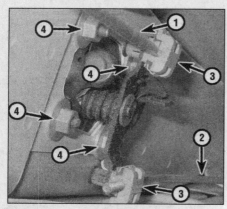

18.18 To remove the latch handle assembly, disengage the upper (1) and lower (2) latch lock rods from the latch handle assembly by opening the clamshell-type plastic connectors (3), then remove the four latch handle mounting nuts (4)

18 Disconnect the latch lock rods (see illustration) from the latch assembly.

19 Remove the latch assembly mounting nuts (see illustration 18.18).

20 Installation is the reverse of removal. Be sure to tighten the latch handle mounting nuts securely.

Upper door latch (rear side door)

Refer to illustration 18.22

21 Remove the rear side door trim panel, if equipped (see Section 16).

22 Disconnect the lock rod from the upper latch (see illustration).

23 Remove the two upper latch mounting screws and remove the upper latch assembly.

24 Installation is the reverse of removal. Be sure to tighten the latch bolts securely.

Lower door latch (rear side door)

Refer to illustration 18.27

25 Remove the rear side door trim panel, if equipped (see Section 16).

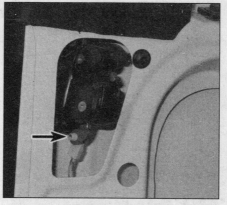

18.22 To remove the upper latch assembly, disconnect the latch rod from the upper latch assembly, then remove the two latch mounting bolts (not visible in this photo; one bolt is located on the upper edge of the door near the upper corner and the other bolt is located on the front edge near the upper corner)

26 Disconnect the lock rod from the lower latch.

27 Remove the four lower latch mounting bolts (see illustration) and the reinforcement from the underside of the door, then remove the upper latch assembly.

28 Installation is the reverse of removal. Be sure to tighten the latch bolts securely.

Upper door latch striker (rear side door)

Refer to illustration 18.29

29 Remove the striker mounting bolts (see illustration) and remove the striker.

30 Installation is the reverse of removal. Be sure to tighten the striker bolts securely.

Lower door latch striker (rear side door)

Refer to illustration 18.32

31 Remove the door step mat.

32 Remove the striker mounting bolts (see

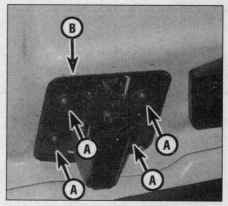

18.27 To detach the lower latch assembly from the door, remove these four mounting bolts (A) and remove the reinforcement plate (B)

illustration) and remove the striker.

33 Installation is the reverse of removal. Be sure to tighten the striker bolts securely.

Check strap (either side door)

Refer to illustration 18.35

34 Disengage the check strap from the side door (see illustration 17.23).

35 Remove the check strap mounting bolts (see illustration) and remove the check strap.

36 Installation is the reverse of removal. Be sure to tighten the check strap bolts securely.

Door latch (front side door)

Refer to illustration 18.38

37 Remove the rear side door trim panel, if equipped (see Section 16).

38 Remove the latch mounting bolts (see illustration).

39 Position the latch as necessary and disconnect the lock rod from the latch.

40 Remove the latch assembly from the door.

41 Installation is the reverse of removal. Be sure to tighten the latch bolts securely.

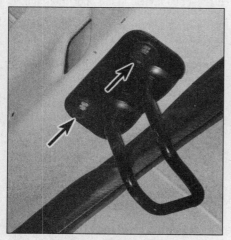

18.29 To detach the upper striker, remove these two bolts

18.32 To remove the lower striker, remove these mounting bolts

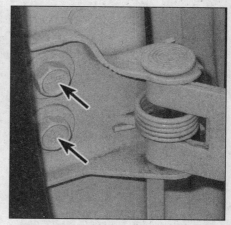

18.35 To detach a check strap, remove these two bolts

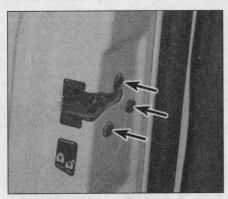

18.38 To detach the door latch from the front side door, remove these three bolts, then reach up inside the door and position the latch assembly as necessary to disconnect the lock rod

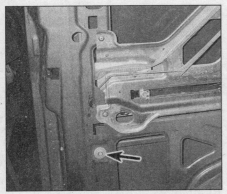

19.4 Loosen the rear glass run channel bolt

Door latch striker (front side door)

Refer to illustration 18.42

Note: *The striker for the front side door latch is located on the front edge of the rear side door.*

42   Remove the striker mounting bolts **(see illustration)** and remove the striker.

43   Installation is the reverse of removal. Be sure to tighten the striker bolts securely.

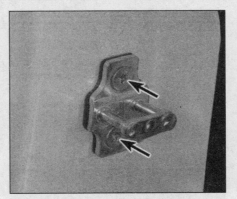

18.42 To detach the latch striker for the front-side door, remove these two bolts

19   Door window glass - removal and installation

Refer to illustrations 19.2 and 19.4

1   Remove the door trim panel and the watershield (see Section 16).

2   Lower the window glass for access to the glass retaining nuts and remove the nuts **(see illustration)**.

3   Carefully pry the inner and outer weatherstripping out of the door window opening.

4   Loosen the rear glass run channel bolt **(see illustration)**.

5   Remove the glass by lifting it out of the door from the outer side of the vehicle.

6   Installation is the reverse of the removal procedure.

20   Door window glass regulator - removal and installation

Refer to illustrations 20.5

1   Remove the door trim panel and the watershield (see Section 16).

2   Unbolt the window glass from the regulator (see Section 19). Push the glass all the way up and tape it to the door frame.

3   On power window equipped models,

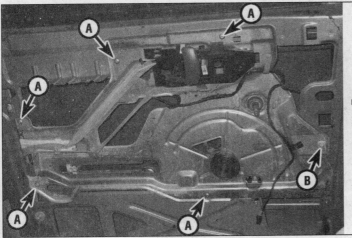

20.5 Drill out the rivets securing the regulator assembly to the door (A), then remove the fastener (B)

unplug the electrical connector.

4   Remove the door handle and disconnect the lock rods (see Section 18).

5   Drill out the rivets securing the window regulator assembly to the door **(see illustration)**. On reassembly, use sheet metal screws in place of the rivets.

6   Remove the regulator from the door.

7   Installation is the reverse of removal.

21   Mirrors - removal and installation

Outside mirrors

Refer to illustration 21.4

1   Remove the mirror trim cover **(see illustration 16.3)**.

2   If you're removing a power mirror, remove the front door trim panel (see Section 16).

3   If you're removing a power mirror, disconnect the electrical connector from the mirror.

4   Remove the mirror retaining fasteners to detach the mirror **(see illustration)**.

5   Installation is the reverse of the removal procedure.

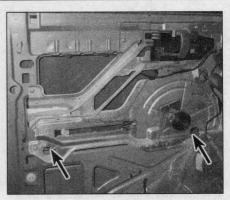

19.2 Raise the window just enough to access the glass retaining nuts through the holes in the door frame

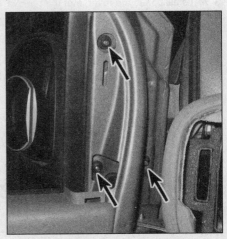

21.4 Remove the fasteners and remove the mirror from the door

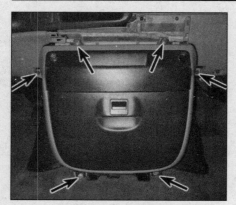

22.1 Remove the fasteners securing the glove box/cup holder to the instrument panel

24.1 Grasp the center trim panel securely and pull it out gently to detach the clips

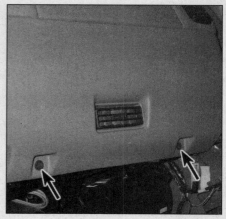

24.4 Remove these fasteners at the bottom of the knee bolster

Inside mirror

6   Remove the setscrew, then slide the mirror up off the support base on the windshield. On models with optional automatic day/night mirror, disconnect the electrical connector.

7   Installation is the reverse of removal.

8   If the support base for the mirror has come off the windshield, it can be reattached with a special mirror adhesive kit available at auto parts stores. Clean the glass and support base thoroughly and follow the directions on the adhesive package.

22   Glove box/cup holder - removal and installation

Refer to illustration 22.1

1   On 2002 and earlier models, remove the center trim panel (see Section 24), then remove the fasteners securing the glove box/cup holder **(see illustration).**

2   On 2003 and later models, open the glove box and remove the fasteners securing the glove box/cup holder, then remove it from the vehicle.

3   Installation is the reverse of the removal procedure.

23   Engine cover - removal and installation

1   Remove the glove box/cup holder (see Section 22).

2   If you're working on a 2003 or later model, remove the passenger seat (see Section 26).

3   On 2002 and earlier models, release the engine cover retaining straps and remove the cover from the vehicle.

4   On 2003 and later models, unlock the four latches and remove the cover from the vehicle.

5   Installation is the reverse of the removal procedure.

24   Dashboard trim panels - removal and installation

Warning: *The models covered by this manual are equipped with Supplemental Restraint Systems (SRS), more commonly known as airbags. Always disable the airbag system before working in the vicinity of any airbag system component to avoid the possibility of*

accidental deployment of the airbags, which could cause personal injury (see Chapter 12).

Center trim panel

Refer to illustration 24.1

1   Grasp the trim panel securely and detach it from the instrument panel by pulling it straight back **(see illustration).**

2   Installation is the reverse of the removal procedure. Make sure the clips are engaged properly before pushing the panel firmly into place.

Knee bolster

Right side

Refer to illustration 24.4

3   On 2002 and earlier models, remove the center trim panel (see Step 1).

4   Remove the fasteners at the bottom of the knee bolster **(see illustration).**

5   Grasp the knee bolster securely and detach it from the instrument panel by pulling it straight back.

6   Installation is the reverse of the removal procedure.

Left side

Refer to illustrations 24.7 and 24.8

7   On 2002 and earlier models, remove the instrument panel cluster trim plate filler **(see illustration)** and the center trim panel **(see illustration 24.1),** then remove the instrument cluster bezel (see Steps 10 thru 14).

8   Remove the two screws at the bottom of the knee bolster and pull it outward, away from the dash **(see illustration).**

9   Installation is the reverse of the removal procedure.

Instrument cluster bezel

Refer to illustration 24.13

10   With the wheels blocked, apply the parking brake and lower the shift lever as far as possible.

11   On 2002 and earlier models, remove the instrument panel cluster trim plate filler **(see illustration 24.7).**

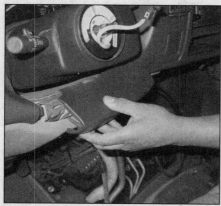

24.7 Grasp the trim plate filler securely and pull it out sharply to detach the clips

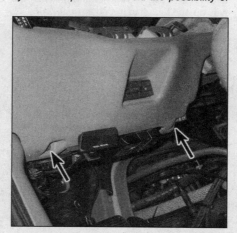

24.8 Remove the fasteners at the bottom of the knee bolster

24.13 Working you're way around the edges of the instrument cluster bezel, carefully detach the clips by pulling the bezel straight out

25.3a Remove the two steering column cover screws from the bottom cover . . .

25.3b . . . and separate the two halves, then remove the two screws securing the top cover

12   On 2003 and later models, remove the two nuts securing the instrument cluster bezel to the instrument panel. The nuts can be found at the bottom of the bezel.

13   Grasp the bezel securely and pull out gently to detach the retaining clips from the instrument panel **(see illustration).**

14   Disconnect any electrical connectors, then remove the bezel.

15   Installation is the reverse of the removal procedure.

25   Steering column covers - removal and installation

Refer to illustrations 25.3a and 25.3b

Warning: *The models covered by this manual are equipped with Supplemental Restraint Systems (SRS), more commonly known as airbags. Always disable the airbag system before working in the vicinity of any airbag system component to avoid the possibility of accidental deployment of the airbags, which could cause personal injury* (see Chapter 12).

1   Remove the steering wheel (see Chapter 10).

2   On tilt steering columns, move the column to the lowest position and remove the tilt lever.

3   Remove the screws, then separate the halves and remove the lower steering column cover **(see illustrations).** Raise the upper steering column cover then remove the ignition key lock cylinder (see Chapter 12). The upper cover can now be removed.

4   Installation is the reverse of the removal procedure.

26   Seats - removal and installation

Front seat

Refer to illustration 26.1

Warning: *The models covered by this manual*

are equipped with Supplemental Restraint Systems (SRS), more commonly known as airbags. Always disable the airbag system before working in the vicinity of any airbag system component to avoid the possibility of accidental deployment of the airbags, which could cause personal injury* (see Chapter 12).

1   Remove the seat bracket-to-floor bolts **(see illustration).**

2   Tilt the seat to access the underside, then disconnect any electrical connectors and lift the seat from the vehicle.

3   Installation is the reverse of the removal procedure.

Rear seats

Refer to illustrations 26.4, 26.5, 26.6 and 26.7

4   Disconnect the lap/shoulder seat belts **(see illustration).**

5   Locate the release handles on the inboard sides of the seats base and release the locking pins **(see illustration).**

6   Lift the rear of the seat and pull rearward

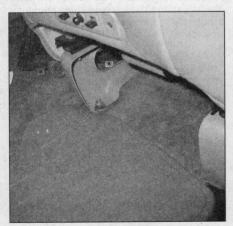

26.1 Remove the fasteners at all four corners of the seat base

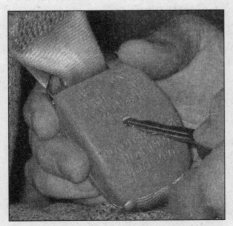

26.4 Insert the tip of a key into the latch to release the belt

26.5 Lift the locking pins up then out to release the seat

26.6 Pull the seat reward and remove it from the floor rails

26.7 Be sure both locking pins are locked in place and the seat is secure

27.2 If you're removing the right side rear trim panel, first pull off the jack storage cover

27.3 Pull the trim panel out to disengage the clips

to remove the seat **(see illustration)**.

7   Installation is the reverse of the removal procedure. Be sure both locking pins are locked into place **(see illustration)**.

27 Rear trim panels - removal and installation

Refer to illustrations 27.2 and 27.3

1   Remove the rear seat (see Section 26).
2   If you're removing the right side rear trim

panel, remove the right rear corner trim panel (the jack storage cover) **(see illustration)**.

3   Using a trim removal tool or a small screwdriver, detach the clips and remove the rear quarter trim panel **(see illustration)**.

4   Installation is the reverse of removal.

Chapter 12
Chassis electrical system

Contents

1 General information

The electrical system is a 12-volt, negative ground type. A lead/acid-type battery that is charged by the alternator supplies power for the lights and all electrical accessories.

This Chapter covers repair and service procedures for the various electrical components not associated with the engine. Information on the battery, alternator, distributor and starter motor can be found in Chapter 5. **Warning:** *When working on the electrical system, disconnect the cable from the negative battery terminal to prevent electrical shorts and/or fires (see Chapter 5, Section 1).*

2 Electrical troubleshooting - general information

Refer to illustrations 2.5a, 2.5b, 2.6, 2.9 and 2.15

A typical electrical circuit consists of an electrical component, any switches, relays, motors, fuses, fusible links or circuit breakers related to that component and the wiring and connectors that link the component to both the battery and the chassis. To help you pinpoint an electrical circuit problem, wiring diagrams are included at the end of this Chapter.

Before tackling any troublesome electrical circuit, first study the appropriate wiring diagrams to get a complete understanding of what makes up that individual circuit. You can often narrow down trouble spots, for instance, by noting whether other components related to the circuit are operating correctly. If several components or circuits fail at one time, chances are that the problem is in a fuse or ground connection, because several circuits are often routed through the same fuse and ground connections.

Electrical problems usually stem from simple causes, such as loose or corroded connections, a blown fuse, a melted fusible link or a failed relay. Visually inspect the condition of all fuses, wires and connections in a problem circuit before troubleshooting the circuit.

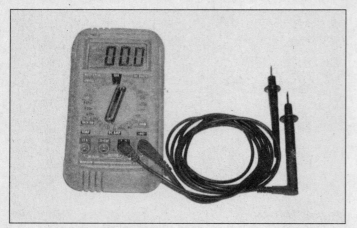

**2.5a The most useful tool for electrical troubleshooting is a
digital multimeter that can check volts, amps, and test continuity**

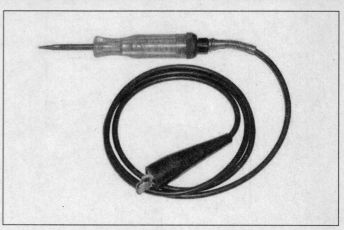

**2.5b A simple test light is a very handy tool used
for testing voltage**

If test equipment and instruments are going to be utilized, use the diagrams to plan ahead of time where you will make the necessary connections in order to accurately pinpoint the trouble spot.

For electrical troubleshooting you'll need a circuit tester or voltmeter, a continuity tester, which includes a bulb, battery and set of test leads, and a jumper wire, preferably with a circuit breaker incorporated, which can be used to bypass electrical components **(see illustrations)**. Before attempting to locate a problem with test instruments, use the wiring diagram(s) to decide where to make the connections.

Voltage checks

Voltage checks should be performed if a circuit is not functioning properly. Connect one lead of a circuit tester to either the negative battery terminal or a known good ground. Connect the other lead to a connector in the circuit being tested, preferably nearest to the battery or fuse **(see illustration)**. If the bulb of the tester lights, voltage is present, which

means that the part of the circuit between the connector and the battery is problem free. Continue checking the rest of the circuit in the same fashion. When you reach a point at which no voltage is present, the problem lies between that point and the last test point with voltage. Most of the time the problem can be traced to a loose connection. **Note:** *Keep in mind that some circuits receive voltage only when the ignition key is in the ACC or RUN position.*

Finding a short

One method of finding shorts in a circuit is to remove the fuse and connect a test light or voltmeter to the fuse terminals. There should be no voltage present in the circuit when it is turned off. Move the wiring harness from side-to-side while watching the test light. If the bulb goes on, there is a short to ground somewhere in that area, probably where the insulation has rubbed through. The same test can be performed on each component in the circuit, even a switch.

Ground check

Perform a ground test to check whether a component is properly grounded. Disconnect the battery and connect one lead of a continuity tester or multimeter (set to the ohm scale), to a known good ground. Connect the other lead to the wire or ground connection being tested. If the resistance is low (less than 5 ohms), the ground is good. If the bulb on a self-powered test light does not go on, the ground is not good.

Continuity check

A continuity check determines whether there are any breaks in a circuit, i.e. whether it's conducting electricity correctly. With the circuit off (no power in the circuit), use a self-powered continuity tester or multimeter to check the circuit. Connect the test leads to both ends of the circuit (or to the "power" end and a good ground). If the test light comes on, the circuit is conducting current correctly **(see illustration)**. If the resistance is low (less than 5 ohms), there is continuity; if the reading is

**2.6 In use, a basic test light's lead is clipped to a known good
ground, then the pointed probe can test connectors, wires or
electrical sockets - if the bulb lights, battery voltage is
present at the test point**

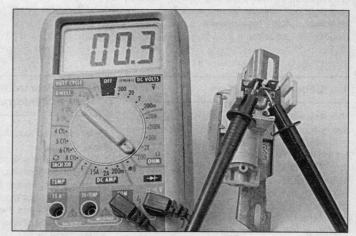

**2.9 With a multimeter set to the ohm scale, resistance can be
checked across two terminals - when checking for continuity,
a low reading indicates continuity, a very high or infinite
reading indicates lack of continuity**

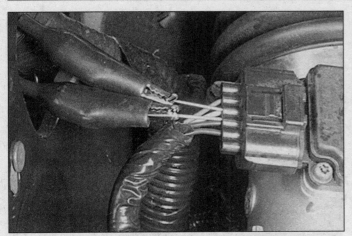

2.15 To backprobe a connector, insert a small, sharp probe (such as a straight-pin) into the back of the connector alongside the desired wire until it contacts the metal terminal inside; connect your meter leads to the probes - this allows you to test a functioning circuit

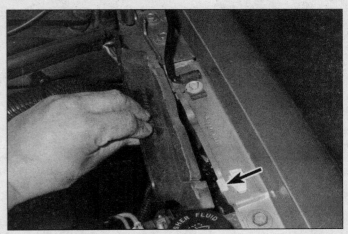

3.1a The underhood fuse and relay box is located at the left front corner of the engine compartment. Before opening the fuse box lid, detach this small trim piece from its mounting clip . . .

10,000 ohms or higher, there is a break somewhere in the circuit. The same procedure can be used to test a switch, by connecting the continuity tester to the switch terminals. With the switch turned on, the test light should come on (or low resistance should be indicated on a meter).

Finding an open circuit

When diagnosing for possible open circuits, it is often difficult to locate them by sight because the connectors hide oxidation or terminal misalignment. Merely wiggling a connector on a sensor or in the wiring harness may correct the open circuit condition. Remember this when an open circuit is indicated when troubleshooting a circuit. Intermittent problems may also be caused by oxidized or loose connections.

Electrical troubleshooting is simple if you keep in mind that all electrical circuits are basically electricity running from the battery, through the wires, switches, relays, fuses and fusible links to each electrical component (light bulb, motor, etc.) and to ground, from which it is passed back to the battery. Any electrical problem is an interruption in the flow of electricity to and from the battery.

Connectors

Most electrical connections on these vehicles are made with multi-wire plastic connectors. The mating halves of many connectors are secured with locking clips molded into the plastic connector shells. The mating halves of large connectors, such as some of those under the instrument panel, are held together by a bolt through the center of the connector.

To separate a connector with locking clips, use a small screwdriver to pry the clips apart carefully, then separate the connector halves. Pull only on the shell, never pull on the wiring harness as you may damage the individual wires and terminals

inside the connectors. Look at the connector closely before trying to separate the halves. Often the locking clips are engaged in a way that is not immediately clear. Additionally, many connectors have more than one set of clips.

Each pair of connector terminals has a male half and a female half. When you look at the end view of a connector in a diagram, be sure to understand whether the view shows the harness side or the component side of the connector. Connector halves are mirror images of each other, and a terminal shown on the right side end-view of one half will be on the left side end view of the other half.

It is often necessary to take circuit voltage measurements with a connector connected. Whenever possible, carefully insert a small straight pin (not your meter probe) into the rear of the connector shell to contact the terminal inside, then clip your meter lead to the pin. This kind of connection is called "backprobing" (see illustration). When inserting a test probe into a male terminal, be careful not to distort the terminal opening. Doing

so can lead to a poor connection and corrosion at that terminal later. Using the small straight pin instead of a meter probe results in less chance of deforming the terminal connector.

---

3 Fuses and fusible links - general information

Fuses

Refer to illustrations 3.1a, 3.1b, 3.1c, 3.2a, 3.2b, 3.2c and 3.3

The electrical circuits of the vehicle are protected by a combination of fuses and circuit breakers. Each fuse protects a specific circuit or two. The location of each fuse, and the circuit(s) protected by that fuse, are designated on the underside of the fuse box cover. The engine compartment fuse and relay box is located on the left side of the engine compartment (see illustrations).

3.1b . . . then release the latches at each end of the lid and remove the lid

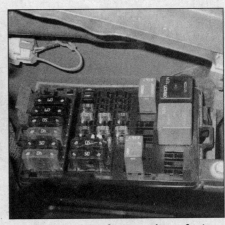

3.1c To locate a fuse or relay, refer to the fuse and relay guide imprinted on the underside of the lid (this information is also available in your owner's manual)

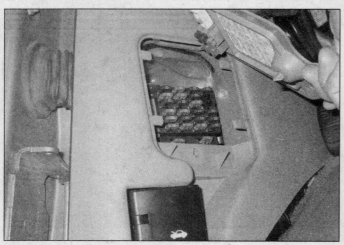

3.2a The passenger compartment fuse box is located in the left kick panel. On the backside of the fuse box cover you'll find a fuse puller, extra fuses and a directory that tells you what circuit each fuse located at this box is protecting

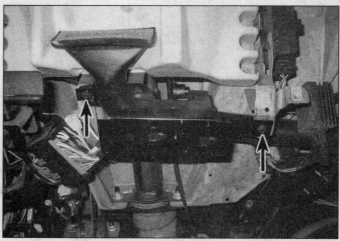

3.2b The instrument panel relay center is located underneath the steering column. To access it, remove the knee bolster (see Chapter 11), then remove these two bolts . . .

The passenger compartment fuse box **(see illustration)** is located in the left kick panel. To access it, simply open and remove the fuse panel cover. The underside of the fuse box cover provides a complete directory of the fuses on this box. The instrument panel relay center **(see illustration)** is bolted to the underside of the steering column. To access the instrument panel relay center, remove the left side knee bolster (see "Dashboard trim panels - removal and installation" in Chapter 11). Then remove the relay center mounting bolts and lower the relay center **(see illustration)** for access to the relays located there.

Different sizes of fuses are employed in the fuse blocks. There are "mini" and "maxi" sizes, with the larger located in the fuse and relay box. The maxi fuses can be removed with your fingers, but the mini fuses require the use of pliers or the small plastic fuse-puller tool found in most fuse boxes. If an electrical component fails, always

check the fuse first. The best way to check the fuses is with a test light. Check for power at the exposed terminal tips of each fuse. If power is present at one side of the fuse but not the other, the fuse is blown. A blown fuse can also be identified by visually inspecting it **(see illustration)**.

Be sure to replace blown fuses with the correct type. Fuses of different ratings are physically interchangeable, but only fuses of the proper rating should be used. Replacing a fuse with one of a higher or lower value than specified is not recommended. Each electrical circuit needs a specific amount of protection. The amperage rating of each fuse is molded into the fuse body.

If the replacement fuse immediately fails, don't replace it again until the cause of the problem is isolated and corrected. In most cases, the cause will be a short circuit in the wiring caused by a broken or deteriorated wire.

Fusible links

The wiring between the battery and the alternator is protected by a fusible link. This link functions like a fuse, in that it melts when the circuit is overloaded, but resembles a large-gauge wire. To replace a fusible link, first disconnect the negative cable from the battery. Disconnect the burned-out link and replace it with a new one (available from your dealer or auto parts store). Always determine the cause for the overload that melted the fusible link before installing a new one.

4 Circuit breakers - general information

Circuit breakers protect certain heavy-load circuits. Depending on the vehicle's accessories, there may be one to three circuit breakers located in the main fuse panel and also in the fuse and relay box.

3.2c . . . and lower the relay center to access the relays located there. (A) indicates the turn signal/hazard flasher relay

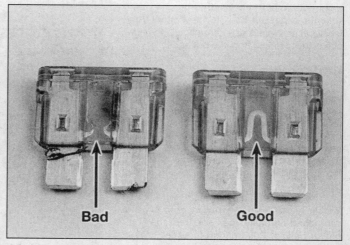

3.3 When a fuse blows, the element between the terminals melts - the fuse on the left is blown, the one on the right is good

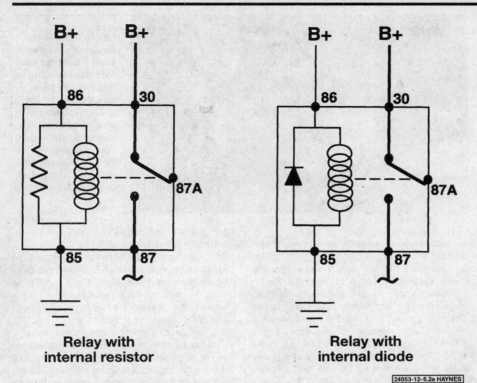

Relay with internal resistor

Relay with internal diode

24053-12-5.2a HAYNES

5.5a Typical ISO relay designs, terminal numbering and circuit connections

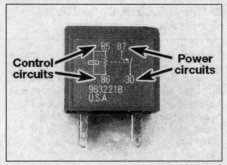

5.5b Most relays are marked on the outside to easily identify the control circuit and power circuits - this one is of the four-terminal type

Because the circuit breakers reset automatically, an electrical overload in a circuit-breaker-protected system will cause the circuit to fail momentarily, then come back on. If the circuit does not come back on, check it immediately.

For a basic check, pull the circuit breaker up out of its socket on the fuse panel, but just far enough to probe with a voltmeter. The breaker should still contact the sockets.

With the voltmeter negative lead on a good chassis ground, touch each end prong of the circuit breaker with the positive meter probe. There should be battery voltage at each end. If there is battery voltage only at one end, the circuit breaker must be replaced.

5   Relays - general information and testing

1   Many electrical accessories in the vehicle utilize relays to transmit current to the component. If the relay is defective, the component won't operate properly.
2   Most relays are located in the engine compartment fuse and relay box (see Section 3).
3   Some relays are located in other parts of the vehicle, primarily in various wiring harnesses underneath the instrument panel.
4   If a faulty relay is suspected, it can be removed and tested using the procedure below or by a dealer service department or a repair shop. Defective relays must be replaced as a unit.

Testing
Refer to illustrations 5.5a and 5.5b

5   Most of the relays used in these vehicles are of a type often called "ISO" relays, which refers to the International Standards Organization. The terminals of ISO relays are numbered to indicate their usual circuit connections and functions. There are two basic layouts of terminals on the relays used in the vehicles covered by this manual (**see illustrations**).
6   Refer to the wiring diagram for the circuit to determine the proper connections for the relay you're testing. If you can't determine the correct connection from the wiring diagrams, however, you may be able to determine the test connections from the information that follows.
7   Two of the terminals are the relay control circuit and connect to the relay coil. The other relay terminals are the power circuit. When the relay is energized, the coil creates a magnetic field that closes the larger contacts of the power circuit to provide power to the circuit loads.
8   Terminals 85 and 86 are normally the control circuit. If the relay contains a diode, terminal 86 must be connected to battery positive (B+) voltage and terminal 85 to ground. If the relay contains a resistor, terminals 85 and 86 can be connected in either direction with respect to B+ and ground.
9   Terminal 30 is normally connected to the battery voltage (B+) source for the circuit loads. Terminal 87 is connected to the ground side of the circuit, either directly or through a

load. If the relay has several alternate terminals for load or ground connections, they usually are numbered 87A, 87B, 87C, and so on.
10   Use an ohmmeter to check continuity through the relay control coil.

a) *Connect the meter according to the polarity shown in* **illustration 5.5a** *for one check; then reverse the ohmmeter leads and check continuity in the other direction.*
b) *If the relay contains a resistor, resistance will be indicated on the meter, and should be the same value with the ohmmeter in either direction.*
c) *If the relay contains a diode, resistance should be higher with the ohmmeter in the forward polarity direction than with the meter leads reversed.*
d) *If the ohmmeter shows infinite resistance in both directions, replace the relay.*

11   Remove the relay from the vehicle and use the ohmmeter to check for continuity between the relay power circuit terminals. There should be no continuity between terminal 30 and 87 with the relay de-energized.
12   Connect a fused jumper wire to terminal 86 and the positive battery terminal. Connect another jumper wire between terminal 85 and ground. When the connections are made, the relay should click.
13   With the jumper wires connected, check for continuity between the power circuit terminals. Now there should be continuity between terminals 30 and 87.
14   If the relay fails any of the above tests, replace it.

6   Turn signal and hazard flasher relay - replacement

1   Remove the left side knee bolster (see "Dashboard trim panels - removal and installation" in Chapter 11).
2   Remove the relay center mounting bolts (**see illustration 3.2b**) and carefully lower the relay center.
3   Remove the turn signal and hazard flasher relay (**see illustration 3.2c**) from the relay center.
4   Installation is the reverse of removal.

7   Key lock cylinder and ignition switch - replacement

Warning: *The models covered by this manual are equipped with a Supplemental Restraint System (SRS), more commonly known as airbags. Always disarm the airbag system before working in the vicinity of any airbag system component to avoid the possibility of accidental deployment of the airbag, which could cause personal injury (see Section 26). Do not use a memory-saving device to preserve the PCM's memory when working on or near airbag system components.*
Note: *If the key is difficult to turn, the problem might not be in the ignition switch or the key lock cylinder. The shift cable might be out of adjustment (see Chapter 7).*

Key lock cylinder
Refer to illustrations 7.6 and 7.7
1   Disconnect the cable from the negative battery terminal (see Chapter 5, Section 1).
2   Wait at least two minutes before proceeding. This gives the airbag system's capacitor (the back-up power supply) time to discharge.
3   On vehicles with a tilt steering column put the steering wheel halfway between the

7.6 To remove the key lock cylinder, insert a bent-tip awl into the retaining pin access hole, turn the key to the START position, depress the retaining pin with the awl, release the key to the RUN position and pull out the lock cylinder

upper and lower tilt stops.
4   Remove the steering wheel (see Chapter 10).
5   Remove the two Torx screws from the lower steering column cover (see *Steering column covers - removal and installation* in Chapter 11) and remove the lower cover. Once you have removed the lower steering column cover, remove the two screws that retain the upper half of the steering column cover. You can't actually remove the upper cover without removing the key lock cylinder,

but you can lift it up far enough to give yourself room to work.
6   Insert a bent-tip awl into the access hole for the key lock cylinder retaining pin **(see illustration)**, turn the key to the START position, depress the lock cylinder retaining pin with the awl, release the key to the RUN position and pull out the lock cylinder.
7   To install the key lock cylinder, insert it through the hole in the upper steering column cover, align the positioning tab and locking tab on the key lock cylinder with the locking tab slot on the lock module **(see illustration)**, then push the lock cylinder into the lock module until the locking tab clicks into place.
8   The remainder of installation is the reverse of removal.

Ignition switch
Refer to illustrations 7.13, 7.14, 7.15 and 7.16
9   Disconnect the cable from the negative battery terminal (see Chapter 5, Section 1).
10   Wait at least two minutes before proceeding. This gives the airbag system's capacitor (the back-up power supply) time to discharge.
11   Remove the steering wheel (see Chapter 10).
12   Remove the upper and lower steering column covers (see Chapter 11).
13   Cut any cable ties securing the ignition switch wiring harness to the multi-function switch wiring harness and remove the bolt that

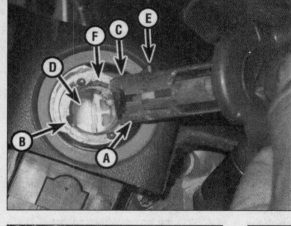

7.7 To install the key lock cylinder, turn the key to the START position and align the following:

A   Align the locator tab . . .
B   . . . with the locator slot inside the lock cylinder bore
C   Align the key buzzer switch . . .
D   . . . with the slot in the upper part of the lock cylinder bore
E   Orient the rectangular lug on the end of the key lock cylinder . . .
F   . . . with the rectangular recess in the bottom of the lock cylinder bore

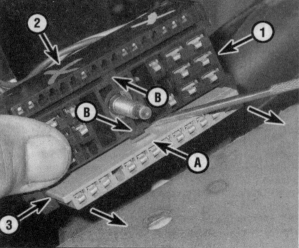

7.13 Cut any cable ties (1) and remove the bolt (2) that secures the ignition switch and multi-function switch electrical connectors

7.14 To detach these three electrical connectors from each other, insert an awl between each of the smaller connectors and the larger central connector, disengage the recess (A) in the smaller connector from the locking tab (B) on the larger connector, then slide out the smaller connector

1   *Ignition switch electrical connector*
2   *Turn signal and multi-function switch electrical connector*
3   *Turn signal and multi-function switch electrical connector*

secures the ignition switch and multi-function switch electrical connectors **(see illustration)**.

14   Separate the ignition switch electrical connector from the turn signal and multi-function switch electrical connectors **(see illustration)**.

15   Disconnect the small electrical connector and the key alarm connector from the lock module assembly **(see illustration)**.

16   Remove the ignition switch mounting screws **(see illustration)** and remove the ignition switch.

17   Installation is the reverse of removal. Be sure to tighten the ignition switch mounting screws to the torque listed in this Chapter's Specifications.

8   Turn signal/multi-function switch - replacement

Refer to illustrations 8.9 and 8.12
Warning: *The models covered by this manual are equipped with a Supplemental Restraint System (SRS), more commonly known as airbags. Always disarm the airbag system before working in the vicinity of any airbag system component to avoid the possibility of accidental deployment of the airbag, which could cause personal injury (see Section 26). Do not use a memory-saving device to preserve the PCM's memory when working on or near airbag system components.*

1   The multi-function switch is located on the steering column. The turn signal/multi-function lever on the left side of the steering column controls the lighting functions such as the headlights and the turn signal lights, as well as the windshield wipers, the windshield washer and, if equipped, the cruise control system.

2   Make sure that the turn signal/multi-function lever is in the OFF (center) position.

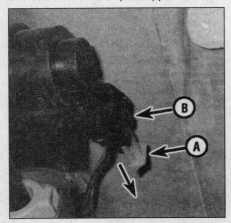

8.9 Remove the Connector Position Assurance (CPA) retainer (A) and disconnect the electrical connector (B) from the Brake Transmission Shift Interlock (BTSI) assembly (the connector and lead for the BTSI assembly are part of the wiring harness for the turn signal/ multi-function switch)

7.15 Disconnect the small electrical connector (A) from the top of the lock module assembly, then rotate the key alarm connector (B) 90-degrees with a small screwdriver and disconnect the key alarm connector

3   Disconnect the cable from the negative terminal of the battery (see Chapter 5, Section 1).

4   Wait at least two minutes before proceeding. This gives the airbag system's capacitor (the back-up power supply) time to discharge.

5   Remove the steering wheel (see Chapter 10).

6   Remove the knee bolster (see *Dashboard trim panels - removal and installation* in Chapter 11).

7   Remove the key lock cylinder (see Section 7).

8   Remove the steering column covers (see Chapter 11).

9   Remove the Connector Position Assurance (CPA) retainer **(see illustration)** from the electrical connector for the Brake Transmission Shift Interlock (BTSI) system and disconnect the electrical connector from the BTSI assembly. (The electrical lead to this connector is routed through the turn signal/multi-function switch connector. When you buy a new turn signal/multi-function switch assembly, the electrical harness includes a new BTSI electrical lead and connector.)

7.16 To detach the ignition switch, remove these two mounting screws

10   Cut any cable ties securing the ignition switch wiring harness to the multi-function switch wiring harness and remove the bolt that secures the ignition switch and multi-function switch electrical connectors **(see illustration 7.13)**.

11   Separate the ignition switch electrical connector from the turn signal and multi-function switch electrical connector **(see illustration 7.14)**.

12   Remove the turn signal/multi-function switch mounting screws **(see illustration)** and remove the switch.

13   Installation is the reverse of removal.

9   Headlight switch - replacement

Refer to illustration 9.2
Warning: *The models covered by this manual are equipped with a Supplemental Restraint System (SRS), more commonly known as airbags. Always disarm the airbag system before working in the vicinity of any airbag system component to avoid the possibility of accidental deployment of the airbag, which could cause personal injury (see Section 26). Do not use a memory-saving device to preserve the PCM's memory when working on or near airbag system components.*

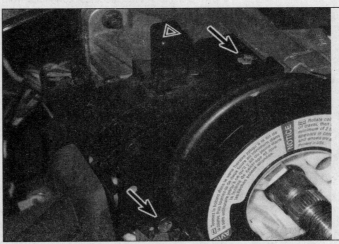

8.12 To detach the turn signal/multi-function switch from the steering column assembly, remove these two screws

9.2 To disengage the headlight switch from the cluster trim bezel, carefully pry these retainers loose and pull out the switch

10.4 To detach the instrument cluster, remove these four mounting screws

1   Remove the instrument cluster bezel (see *Dashboard trim panels - removal and installation* in Chapter 11).

2   To detach the headlight switch from the instrument cluster bezel, disengage the retainer tabs from the switch **(see illustration)** and pull out the switch.

3   Installation is the reverse of removal.

10   Instrument cluster - removal and installation

Refer to illustration 10.4

Warning: *The models covered by this manual are equipped with a Supplemental Restraint System (SRS), more commonly known as airbags. Always disarm the airbag system before working in the vicinity of any airbag system component to avoid the possibility of accidental deployment of the airbag, which could cause personal injury (see Section 26). Do not use a memory-saving device to preserve the PCM's memory when working on or near airbag system components.*

1   Disconnect the cable from the negative battery terminal (see Chapter 5, Section 1).

2   Remove the cluster trim bezel (see *Dashboard trim panels - removal and installation* in Chapter 11).

3   If the vehicle is equipped with a tilt steering column, place the column in its lowest position.

4   Remove the instrument cluster mounting screws **(see illustration)**, pull out the cluster and disconnect the electrical connectors from the backside of the cluster.

5   Installation is the reverse of removal.

11   Windshield wiper motor - replacement

Refer to illustrations 11.3, 11.4, 11.6 and 11.8

1   Make sure that the wipers are in their "parked" position.

2   Disconnect the cable from the negative battery terminal (see Chapter 5, Section 1).

3   Remove the trim covers from the windshield wiper arm retaining nuts **(see illustration)**, remove the wiper arm nuts, disconnect the windshield washer lines and remove the washer line elbows from the cowl covers.

4   Before removing the windshield wiper arms, be sure to mark the relationship of each arm to its shaft **(see illustration)**, then pull off and remove both arms.

5   Remove the cowl covers (see Chapter 11).

6   Disconnect the electrical connector from

the windshield wiper motor **(see illustration)**.

7   Remove the windshield wiper motor and linkage assembly mounting bolts and remove the wiper motor and linkage as a single assembly.

8   If you're going to replace the windshield wiper motor or the windshield wiper arm linkage, pry loose the drive link from the motor crank arm with a trim panel removal tool **(see illustration)** or with some other suitable tool, then remove the crank arm retaining nut, remove the crank arm, remove the motor mounting bolts and separate the motor from its mounting bracket.

9   Installation is the reverse of removal. Be sure to tighten the motor mounting bolts securely.

12   Radio and speakers - removal and installation

Warning: *The models covered by this manual are equipped with a Supplemental Restraint System (SRS), more commonly known as airbags. Always disarm the airbag system before working in the vicinity of any airbag system component to avoid the possibility of*

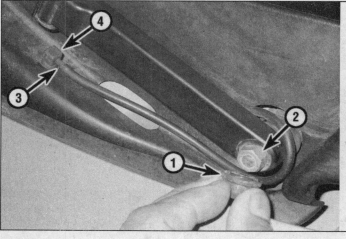

11.3 To detach each windshield wiper arm from its shaft, remove the trim cover (1) from the wiper arm retaining nut, remove the nut (2), disconnect the windshield washer line (3) from the line elbow (4) and remove the elbow from the cowl cover

11.4 Before removing the wiper arms, be sure to mark the relationship of each arm to its shaft

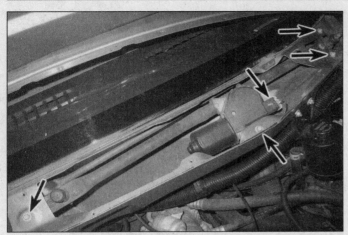

11.6 To detach the windshield wiper motor and linkage assembly from the cowl, disconnect the electrical connector and remove the four mounting bolts

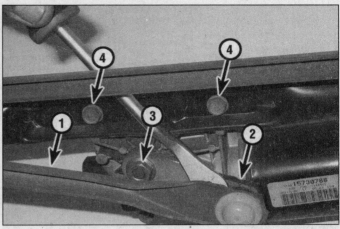

11.8 To replace the wiper motor or the linkage, separate the drive link (1) from the crank arm (2) with a trim removal tool or some other suitable prying tool, remove the crank arm retaining nut (3) and remove the crank arm, then remove the motor mounting bolts (4) and separate the motor from its mounting bracket

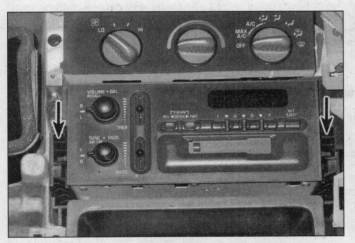

12.3 To detach the radio from the dash, depress these two retaining tabs and pull out the radio

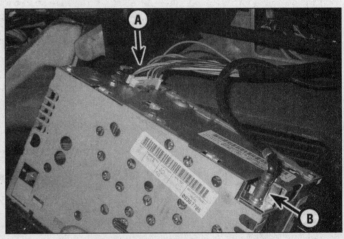

12.4 To remove the radio, disconnect the electrical connectors (A) and the antenna cable (B)

accidental deployment of the airbag, which could cause personal injury (see Section 26). Do not use a memory-saving device to preserve the PCM's memory when working on or near airbag system components.

Radio
Refer to illustrations 12.3 and 12.4
1   Disconnect the cable from the negative battery terminal (see Chapter 5, Section 1).

12.7 To replace a front door speaker, disconnect the electrical connector (A) and remove the four speaker mounting bolts (B). If you're removing the speaker to access the window regulator or some other component inside the door, drill out all four rivets (C) and remove the speaker enclosure (two lower rivets not shown)

2   Remove the instrument cluster bezel (see *Dashboard trim panels - removal and installation* in Chapter 11).
3   Depress the two radio retaining tabs **(see illustration)** and pull the radio out of the dash.
4   Disconnect the electrical connectors and the antenna from the radio **(see illustration)** and remove the radio.
5   Installation is the reverse of removal.

Speakers
Front door speakers
Refer to illustration 12.7
6   Remove the door trim panel (see Chapter 11).
7   To replace just the speaker, disconnect the electrical connector **(see illustration)**, remove the four speaker mounting bolts and remove the speaker.
8   If you need to remove the complete speaker and enclosure in order to access the window regulator or some other compo-

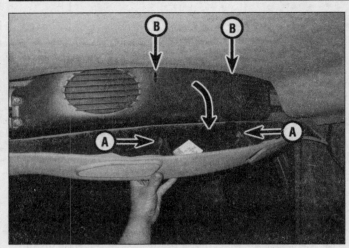

12.15 To detach the rear header trim panel, grasp it firmly, push up slightly to disengage the two retaining hooks (A) from their respective slots (B), then swing it down and remove it

12.16 To detach the rear speaker enclosure, remove these four nuts

nent inside the door assembly, drill out all four speaker enclosure mounting rivets and remove the enclosure.

9   Installation is the reverse of removal. If you removed the speaker enclosures, it's not necessary to rivet them in place. You can use short, self-tapping sheet metal screws instead. But make sure that the screws are short enough that they don't cause any clearance problems inside the door with the window regulator mechanism or with any other moving parts inside the door.

Front door tweeters

10   Remove the door trim panel (see Chapter 11).
11   Disconnect the electrical connectors from the power window switch, power mirror switch and power lock switch, if equipped.
12   Disconnect the electrical connector from the tweeter.
13   Drill out the tweeter mounting rivets and remove the tweeter.
14   Installation is the reverse of removal. It's not necessary to rivet the tweeters in place. You can use short, self-tapping sheet metal screws instead. But make sure that the

screws are short enough that they don't cause any clearance problems inside the door with the window regulator mechanism or with any other moving parts inside the door.

Rear speakers
Refer to illustrations 12.15, 12.16 and 12.17
15   Remove the rear speaker trim panel **(see illustration)**.
16   Remove the rear speaker enclosure **(see illustration)**.
17   If you're removing the rear speaker assembly to access something else, simply disconnect the main speaker harness electrical connector **(see illustration)**. If you're replacing a speaker, disconnect the speaker connector, then remove the speaker mounting screws.
18   Installation is the reverse of removal.

Rear door speakers
19   Remove the rear door trim panel (see Chapter 11).
20   Drill out the speaker mounting rivets.
21   Pull out the speaker and disconnect the electrical connector.
22   Installation is the reverse of removal.

13   Antenna and cable - replacement

Fixed antenna mast
Refer to illustration 13.1
1   Using an antenna wrench or an open wrench, unscrew the antenna mast **(see illustration)**.
2   Installation is the reverse of removal. Be sure to tighten the antenna mast securely.

Power antenna mast
3   Remove the upper antenna mast mounting nut.
4   Turn the ignition key to the ON position, turn on the radio and have an assistant guide the antenna mast as it deploys. When the mast is fully deployed, pull it out of the antenna base the rest of the way and remove it. (Don't forget to turn off the radio and the ignition switch.)
5   To install the antenna mast, turn the ignition key to the ON position, turn on the radio and insert the plastic cable (at the lower end of the antenna mast) into the antenna base. With the serrated side of the plastic cable fac-

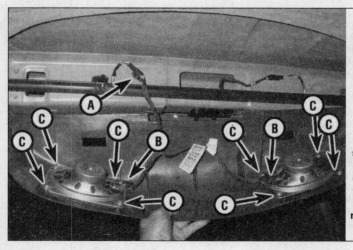

12.17 If you're just removing the speaker/enclosure assembly to access something else, simply disconnect the main speaker harness electrical connector (A). If you're replacing a speaker, disconnect the speaker electrical connector (B) and remove the four speaker mounting screws (C)

13.1 Use an antenna wrench or an open end wrench to unscrew a fixed mast antenna from its mounting base

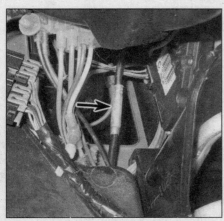

13.20 This coaxial connector, which is located at the right end of the firewall, connects the main antenna cable to the outside antenna lead from the antenna. To remove the main antenna cable, disconnect this connector

ing *toward the power antenna motor* (underneath the fender), insert the cable until you feel resistance. Turn off the radio. The power antenna motor will begin to pull the antenna down into the fender. Have your assistant feed the plastic cable and the mast into the antenna base until it's fully retracted. If the power antenna motor doesn't retract the antenna, rotate the plastic cable clockwise or counterclockwise until the motor engages the plastic cable and pulls it down. Insert the mast into the antenna base and install the upper antenna mast mounting nut. Tighten the nut securely but don't overtighten it.

Power antenna motor

6   Disconnect the antenna cable **(see illustration 13.20)** and the electrical connector for the power antenna motor, both of which are located below the right end of the dash.
7   Push the antenna cable grommet through the cowl panel.
8   Raise the hood.
9   Disconnect the ground strap from the inner fender.
10   Detach the antenna cable retainer from the inner fender.
11   Remove the two power antenna motor mounting bolts.
12   Pull the antenna assembly down until it's disengaged from the fender trim.
13   Remove the antenna base from the top of the fender.
14   Remove the antenna and cable.
15   Installation is the reverse of removal.

Antenna cable
Refer to illustration 13.20
16   Remove the radio (see Section 12).
17   If the vehicle is equipped with a factory-installed CD unit, remove the radio mounting bracket screws and remove the mounting bracket.
18   Remove the engine cover (see Chapter 11).

14.5 When measuring voltage at the rear window defogger grid, wrap a piece of aluminum foil around the positive probe of the voltmeter and press the foil against the wire with your finger

19   Detach the antenna cable clip from the bracket located above the heater/air conditioner outlet.
20   Disconnect the antenna cable connector located in the lower right area of the dash **(see illustration)** and remove the cable.
21   Installation is the reverse of removal.

---

14   Rear window defogger - check and repair

---

1   The rear window defogger consists of a number of horizontal heating elements baked onto the inside surface of the glass. Power is supplied through a relay and fuse from the interior fuse/relay box. A defogger switch on the instrument panel controls the defogger grid.
2   Small breaks in the element can be repaired without removing the rear window.

Check
Refer to illustrations 14.5, 14.6 and 14.8
3   Turn the ignition and defogger switches to the ON position.
4   Using a voltmeter, place the positive probe against the defogger grid positive side and the negative probe against the ground side. If battery voltage is not indicated, check that the ignition switch is On and that the feed and ground wires are properly connected. Check the two fuses, defogger switch, defogger relay and related wiring. The dealer can scan the body control module if necessary. If voltage is indicated, but all or part of the defogger doesn't heat, proceed with the following tests.
5   When measuring voltage during the next two tests, wrap a piece of aluminum foil around the tip of the voltmeter positive probe and press the foil against the heating element with your finger **(see illustration)**. Place the negative probe on the defogger grid ground terminal.
6   Check the voltage at the center of each

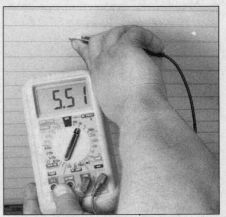

14.6 To determine if a heating element has broken, check the voltage at the center of each element - if the voltage is 6-volts, the element is unbroken

heating element **(see illustration)**. If the voltage is 5 to 6 volts, the element is okay (there is no break). If the voltage is 0 volts, the element is broken between the center of the element and the positive end. If the voltage is 10 to 12 volts, the element is broken between the center of the element and the ground side. Check each heating element.
7   If none of the elements are broken, connect the negative probe to a good chassis ground. The voltage reading should stay the same, if it doesn't the ground connection is bad.
8   To find the break, place the voltmeter negative probe against the defogger ground terminal. Place the voltmeter positive probe with the foil strip against the heating element at the positive side and slide it toward the negative side. The point at which the voltmeter deflects from several volts to zero is the point where the heating element is broken **(see illustration)**.

14.8 To find the break, place the voltmeter negative lead against the defogger ground terminal, place the voltmeter positive lead with the foil strip against the heat wire at the positive terminal end and slide it toward the negative terminal end. The point at which the voltmeter deflects from several volts to zero volts is the point at which the wire is broken

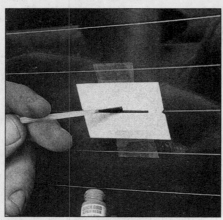

14.14 To use a defogger repair kit, apply masking to the inside of the window at the damaged area, then brush on the special conductive coating

15.1 To remove a sealed beam headlight, remove these four retaining ring screws, remove the retaining ring, pull out the headlight and disconnect the electrical connector

17.1 Headlight adjustment screw locations - sealed beam headlight (left side shown):

A   *Horizontal adjustment screw*
B   *Vertical adjustment screw*

Repair

Refer to illustration 14.14

9   Repair the break in the element using a repair kit specifically for this purpose. The kit includes conductive plastic epoxy.

10   Before repairing a break, turn off the system and allow it to cool for a few minutes.

11   Lightly buff the element area with fine steel wool; then clean it thoroughly with rubbing alcohol.

12   Use masking tape to mask off the area being repaired.

13   Thoroughly mix the epoxy, following the kit instructions.

14   Apply the epoxy material to the slit in the masking tape, overlapping the undamaged area about 3/4-inch on either end **(see illustration)**.

15   Allow the repair to cure for 24 hours before removing the tape and using the system.

15   Headlight bulb (sealed beam headlights) - replacement

Refer to illustration 15.1

1   Remove the four headlight retaining ring screws **(see illustration)** and remove the retaining ring.

2   Pull out the headlight and disconnect the electrical connector.

3   Remove the headlight unit from the vehicle.

4   Installation is the reverse of removal.

16   Headlight bulb (composite headlights) - replacement

Warning: *Halogen bulbs are gas-filled and under pressure and they can shatter if the surface is scratched or the bulb is dropped. Wear eye protection and handle the bulbs carefully, grasping only the base whenever*

possible. Don't touch the surface of the bulb with your fingers because the oil from your skin could cause it to overheat and fail prematurely. If you do touch the bulb surface, clean it with rubbing alcohol.

1   If you're replacing the right-side headlight bulb, remove the battery (see Chapter 5).

2   Rotate the bulb and holder counterclock-

wise to disengage it from the headlight housing.

3   Pull the headlight bulb out of the housing and disconnect the electrical connector from the bulb.

4   Connect the electrical connector to the new headlight bulb.

5   Install the bulb into the headlight housing and turn it clockwise to lock it into place.

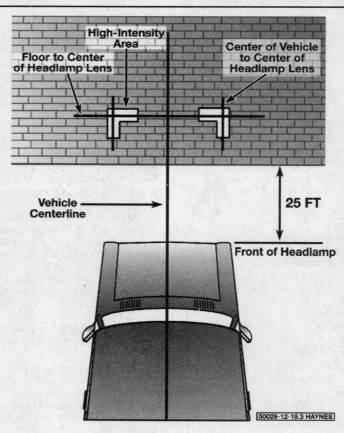

17.2 Headlight adjustment screen details

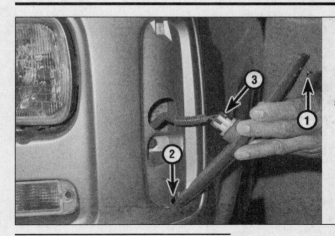

18.1 Details of the front sidemarker light housing

1   *Retaining screw*
2   *Mounting tab*
3   *Electrical connector*

clockwise to lower the beam. On sealed beam headlights, the adjusting screw on the side should be used in the same manner to move the beam left or right.

7   With the high beams on, the high intensity zone should be vertically centered with the exact center just below the horizontal line. **Note:** *It may not be possible to position the headlight aim exactly for both high and low beams. If a compromise must be made, keep in mind that the low beams are the most used and have the greatest effect on safety.*

8   Have the headlights adjusted by a dealer service department at the earliest opportunity.

18   Bulb replacement

Exterior lights
Front sidemarker light bulbs
Refer to illustrations 18.1 and 18.3

1   Remove the screw that secures the sidemarker light housing to the grille fascia, lift up the sidemarker housing to disengage the mounting tab at the lower end of the housing **(see illustration)**, disconnect the electrical connector and remove the sidemarker light housing.

2   To remove the front sidemarker light bulb socket from the sidemarker housing, rotate it counterclockwise and pull it out of the housing.

3   To replace the front sidemarker bulb simply pull it straight out of the socket **(see illustration)**.

4   To install the new bulb push it straight into the bulb holder until it's fully seated.

5   Installation is the reverse of removal.

Front park/turn signal light bulbs
Refer to illustrations 18.6, 18.7 and 18.8

6   Remove the screws that attach the park/turn signal light housing to the grille **(see illustration)** and pull the housing out of the grille.

7   To remove a front park/turn signal light bulb socket, press the release tab **(see illustration)**, turn it counterclockwise and pull it out.

17   Headlights - adjustment

Refer to illustrations 17.1 and 17.2
Warning: *The headlights must be aimed correctly. If adjusted incorrectly, they could temporarily blind the driver of an oncoming vehicle and cause an accident or seriously reduce your ability to see the road. The headlights should be checked for proper aim every 12 months and any time a new headlight is installed or front-end bodywork is*

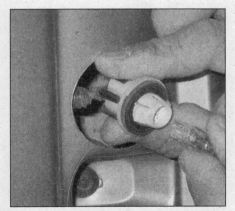

18.3 To remove a front sidemarker light bulb from the bulb socket, simply pull it straight out of the socket

performed. The following procedure is only intended to provide temporary adjustment until you can have the headlights professionally adjusted by a dealer service department.

1   Sealed beam headlights have an adjusting screw for horizontal adjustments and a screw for vertical adjustments **(see illustration)**. Composite headlights only have a vertical adjusting screw.

2   There are several methods of adjusting the headlights. The simplest method requires an open area with a blank wall and a level floor **(see illustration)**.

3   Position masking tape vertically on the wall in reference to the vehicle centerline and the centerlines of both headlights.

4   Position a horizontal tape line in reference to the centerline of the headlights. **Note:** *It might be easier to position the tape on the wall with the vehicle parked only a few inches away.*

5   Adjustment should be made with the vehicle parked 25 feet from the wall, sitting level, the gas tank full and no unusually heavy load in the vehicle.

6   Starting with the low beam adjustment, position the high intensity zone so it is two inches below the horizontal line and two inches to the side of the headlight vertical line, away from oncoming traffic. Adjustment is made by turning the top adjusting screw clockwise to raise the beam and counter-

18.6 To detach a front park/turn signal light housing from the grille, remove these two screws, then pull out the housing

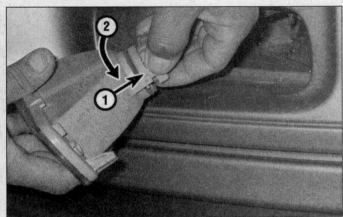

18.7 To remove the front park/turn signal bulb socket, press the release tab (1) and turn the socket counterclockwise (2)

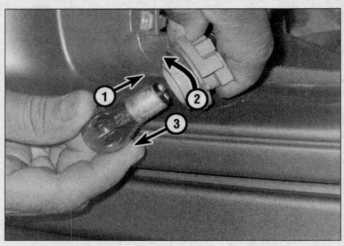

18.8 To remove the front park/turn signal bulb from its socket, press the bulb into the socket (1), rotate it counterclockwise (2) and pull it out (3)

18.11 To detach the center high-mounted brake light housing from the roof, remove these two screws

8   To remove a front park/turn signal light bulb from its socket, push the bulb into the socket, turn it counterclockwise and pull it out **(see illustration)**.
9   To install a new bulb, push it into the socket, turn it clockwise until it stops, then release it.
10   Installation is otherwise the reverse of removal.

Center high-mounted brake light bulbs
Refer to illustrations 18.11, 18.12 and 18.13
11   Remove the screws that attach the center high-mount brake light housing **(see illustration)** and flip up the housing to access the bulb sockets.
12   To remove a bulb holder from the center high-mounted brake light housing, rotate the bulb holder counterclockwise, then remove it from the housing **(see illustration)**.
13   To remove a center high-mounted brake light bulb from its socket simply pull it straight out of the socket **(see illustration)**.
14   To install a new bulb push it straight into the bulb socket.
15   Installation is the reverse of removal.

Taillight bulbs
Refer to illustrations 18.16, 18.17 and 18.18
16   Open the rear doors, then remove the two push fasteners that secure the taillight access cover and remove the cover **(see illustration)**.

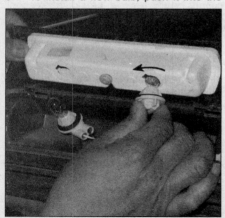

18.12 To remove a bulb holder from the center high-mounted brake light housing, rotate the bulb holder counterclockwise, then pull it out of the housing

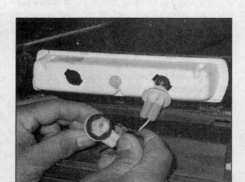

18.13 To remove a center high-mounted brake light bulb from its socket, simply pull it straight out of the socket

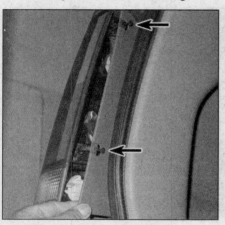

18.16 To remove the taillight access cover, pull out these two push fasteners

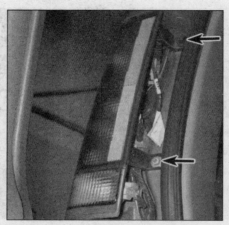

18.17 To detach the taillight housing from the body, remove these two nuts

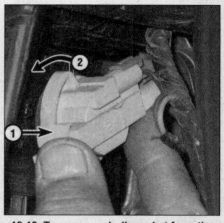

18.18 To remove a bulb socket from the taillight housing, depress the release tab (1), rotate the socket counterclockwise (2) and pull it out of the housing

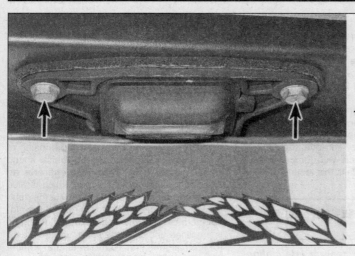

18.21 To detach the license plate light housing, remove these two bolts

18.22 To remove the bulb socket from the license plate light housing, rotate it counterclockwise until the lugs on the socket are aligned with the slots in the housing, then pull it out

17   Remove the taillight housing mounting nuts **(see illustration)** and remove the taillight housing.

18   Remove the socket for the bulb that you want to replace **(see illustrations)**. (There are three taillight bulbs: The upper bulb is the turn signal bulb, the middle bulb is the brake light bulb and the lower bulb is the back-up light bulb.)

19   To remove the bulb from its socket, push it into the socket, turn it counterclockwise and pull it out **(see illustration 18.8)**. To install a new bulb into the socket, push it into the socket, turn it clockwise and release.

20   Installation is otherwise the reverse of removal.

License plate light bulbs

Refer to illustrations 18.21 and 18.22

21   To remove the license plate light housing remove the two housing mounting bolts **(see illustration)** and remove the housing.

22   To remove a license plate light bulb holder, rotate it counterclockwise until the lugs on the socket are aligned with the slots in the housing and pull it out **(see illustration)**.

23   To remove the bulb from its socket, pull it straight out.

24   To install a new bulb in the socket push it straight into the socket.

25   Installation is the reverse of removal.

Interior lights

Warning: *The models covered by this manual are equipped with a Supplemental Restraint System (SRS), more commonly known as airbags. Always disarm the airbag system before working in the vicinity of any airbag system component to avoid the possibility of accidental deployment of the airbag, which could cause personal injury (see Section 26). Do not use a memory-saving device to preserve the PCM's memory when working on or near airbag system components.*

Dome light

Refer to illustrations 18.26 and 18.27

26   Using a small flat-bladed screwdriver, carefully pry loose either end of the dome light lens **(see illustration)** and remove the lens.

27   Remove the dome light bulb from the dome light housing **(see illustration)**. **Warning:** *If it's necessary to pry the bulb from its contacts, pry only on the metal end of the bulb.*

28   Insert a new dome light bulb in the dome light housing. Make sure that it's centered and

fully seated.

29   Installation is otherwise the reverse of removal.

Instrument cluster light bulbs

30   Remove the instrument cluster (see Section 10).

31   To remove a bulb socket from the instrument cluster turn the socket counterclockwise and pull it out.

32   To remove the bulb from the socket pull it straight out.

33   To install a new bulb in the socket push it straight in.

34   Install the instrument cluster (see Section 10).

---

19   Horn - replacement

Refer to illustration 19.2

1   The horns are located in the left front corner of the engine compartment, behind and below the left headlight.

2   Disconnect the electrical connector from the horns **(see illustration)**.

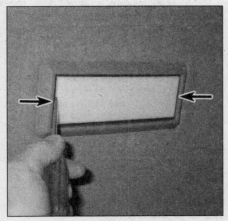

18.26 The dome light lens is secured to the dome light housing by a pair of small tabs at each end of the lens. To remove the lens, simply pry loose either tab

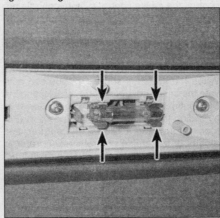

18.27 To remove the dome light bulb, simply pull it straight down from the terminals at each end

19.2 To replace the horn(s), disconnect the electrical connector (1) and remove the horn mounting nut (2)

3   Remove the horn mounting nuts and remove the horns from their mounting bracket.

4   Installation is the reverse of removal.

20 Electric side-view mirrors - general information

1   The optional electric side-view mirrors can be adjusted up-and-down and left-to-right by a driver's side switch located on the left door trim panel. To adjust the left mirror, turn the switch clockwise. To adjust the right mirror, turn the switch counterclockwise. The mirror control switch has four arrows on it. After selecting which mirror you wish to adjust, push on each arrow until the mirror is where you want it. With the ignition switch in the ACC position, roll down the windows and operate the mirror control switch through all functions (left-right and up-down) for both the left and right side-view mirrors.

2   On models with factory-installed dual power mirrors, each mirror is also equipped with a defroster grid behind the mirror glass to clear the mirror surface of fog, ice or snow. To activate the mirror defroster grids, push the button located to the left of the heater/air conditioning controls. On these models, the mirror defroster grid is an integral component of each mirror. If a defroster grid fails, replace the mirror (see Chapter 11). The heater grid switch is located on the dash, to the left of the headlight switch. The fuse for the mirror defroster circuit is located in the passenger compartment fuse box (see Section 3).

3   Listen carefully for the sound of the electric motors running in the mirrors.

4   If you can hear the motors but the mirror glass doesn't move, the problem is probably a defective drive mechanism inside the mirror, which will necessitate replacement of the mirror.

5   If the mirrors don't operate and no sound comes from the mirrors, check the fuse in the passenger compartment fuse box (see Section 3).

6   If the fuse is OK, refer to Chapter 11 and remove the door panel for access to the back of the mirror control switch, without disconnecting the wires attached to it. Turn the ignition ON and check for voltage at the switch. There should be voltage at one terminal. If there's no voltage at the switch, check for an open in the wiring between the fuse panel and the switch.

7   If there's voltage at the switch, disconnect it. Check the switch for continuity in all its operating positions. If the switch does not have continuity, replace it.

8   Reconnect the switch. Locate the wire going from the switch to ground. Leaving the switch connected, connect a jumper wire between this wire and ground. If the mirror works normally with this wire in place, repair the faulty ground connection.

9   If the mirror still doesn't work, remove the mirror and check the wires at the mirror for voltage. Check with the ignition key turned to ON and the mirror selector switch on the appropriate side. Operate the mirror switch in all its positions. There should be voltage at one of the switch-to-mirror wires in each switch position, except the neutral (off) position.

10   If voltage is not present in each switch position, check the wiring between the mirror and control switch for opens and shorts.

11   If there's voltage, remove the mirror and test it off the vehicle with jumper wires. Replace the mirror if it fails this test.

21 Cruise control system - general information

Note: *The following general information applies to all vehicles with 4.3L V6 and 5.0L and 5.7L V8 engines. It also applies to vehicles with 4.8L, 5.3L and 6.0L V8 engines without Throttle Actuator Control (TAC), but not to those same vehicles that are TAC-equipped. On TAC-equipped vehicles there is no standalone cruise control system; the Powertrain Control Module (PCM) controls the cruise control system electronically. If you have problems with the cruise control system on a TAC-equipped vehicle, have it checked by a dealer service department.*

1   When it's activated, the optional cruise control system maintains a constant vehicle speed without having to keep your foot on the accelerator pedal. The system consists of the multi-function switch control lever, the cruise control module, the Powertrain Control Module (PCM), the Vehicle Speed Sensor (VSS), the brake release switch, and the wiring connecting all of these components. System diagnosis and troubleshooting require the use of a scan tool and diagnostic procedures that are beyond the scope of the home mechanic. A general description of the important components follows, as well as some general procedures that might help you identify common problems.

2   If the vehicle is equipped with cruise control, the cruise control system controls are located on the **multi-function switch control lever**, which has a sliding switch that can be set to OFF, ON or R/A (resume/accelerate). When the sliding switch is set to OFF, the cruise control system cannot be activated. When the switch is set to ON, you can activate the cruise control system by selecting the SET button on the end of the control lever or by sliding the switch to the R/A position. (For more information about all the features and modes of the cruise control system, refer to your owner's manual.) A defective multi-function switch and/or control lever could cause problems with the cruise control system. If the multi-function switch or the control lever is defective, replace the multi-function switch (see Section 8).

3   The **cruise control module**, which is located on the firewall near the brake master cylinder, houses a stepper motor that changes throttle position. When you select the speed that you want, press the SET button on the end of the multi-function lever. This command is sent to the cruise control module, which monitors the actual vehicle speed through the Vehicle Speed Sensor (VSS), then uses its stepper motor to open and close the throttle plate inside the throttle body to produce the speed that you've selected.

4   The **Vehicle Speed Sensor (VSS)**, which is located on the extension housing of the transmission, generates the vehicle speed signal for the PCM. The VSS generates an alternating current (AC) signal, which is also referred to as an "analog" signal. As the vehicle speed increases the frequency of the signal increases. At the PCM this analog signal is amplified and converted to a "square-wave" (digital) signal that represents the vehicle speed in pulses-per-mile. The PCM produces a 4000 pulses-per-mile signal to the cruise control module and to the speedometer in the instrument cluster.

5   The **brake release switch** is an integral part of the brake light switch, which is located at the top of the brake pedal. The brake release switch contains a normally open switch contact and a normally closed contact. When you depress the brake pedal, these two contacts change their input state at the cruise control module, which interprets this change as braking and it shuts off the cruise control system. If the brake release switch fails, replace the brake light switch (see Chapter 9).

6   To functionally test the cruise control system, test drive the vehicle and, using your owner's manual as a guide verify that the cruise control is working correctly. If any function of the system is not working as described in your owner's manual, have it diagnosed and repaired by a dealer service department.

22 Power window system - general information

1   The optional power window system controls the electric motors, mounted inside the doors, that lower and raise the windows. The power window system consists of the fuse, the control switches, the motors, the window "regulators" (the mechanisms that raise and lower the window glass) and the wiring connecting the switches to the motors. When the ignition switch is turned to ON, current flows through the power window fuse in the instrument panel fuse box to the power window switches.

2   The power windows are wired so that they can be lowered and raised from the master control switch by the driver or by passengers using remote switches located at each passenger window. Each window has a separate motor that is reversible. The position of the control switch determines the polarity and therefore the direction of operation.

3   The power window system will only operate when the ignition switch is turned to ON.

4   The following troubleshooting procedures are general in nature, so if you can't find the problem using them, take the vehicle to a dealer service department.

5   If the power windows don't work at all, check the fuse, which is located in the passenger compartment fuse box (see Section 3).

6   Check the wiring between the switches and the fuse for continuity. Repair the wiring, if necessary.

7   If only one window is inoperative from the master control switch, try the control switch *at the window that doesn't work.* **Note:** *This doesn't apply to the driver's door window.*

8   If the same window works from one switch, but not the other, check the switch for continuity.

9   If the switch tests OK, check for a short or open in the wiring between the affected switch and the window motor.

10   If one window is inoperative from both switches, remove the trim panel from the affected door (see Section 16 in Chapter 11), then check for voltage at the switch and at the motor while operating the switch. First check for voltage at the electrical connectors for the circuit. With the ignition key turned to ON and the connectors all connected, backprobe at the designated wire (see the wiring diagrams at the end of this Chapter) with a grounded test light. Pushing the driver's window switch to the DOWN position, there should be voltage at one terminal. Pushing the same switch to the UP position, there should be voltage at another terminal. If these voltage checks are OK, disconnect the electrical connector at the driver's motor, and check it for voltage when the switch is operated.

11   If voltage is reaching the motor and the switch is OK, disconnect the door glass from its regulator (see Chapter 11). Move the window up and down by hand while checking for binding and damage. Also check for binding and damage to the regulator. If the regulator is not damaged and the window moves up and down smoothly, replace the motor. If there's binding or damage, lubricate, repair or replace parts, as necessary.

12   If voltage isn't reaching the motor, check the wiring in the circuit for continuity between the switches and motors (see the wiring diagrams at the end of this Chapter).

13   If you have to replace the main power window switch, pry it out of the door trim panel (see Section 16 in Chapter 11), then disconnect the electrical connector(s) from the switch.

14   When you're done test the windows to confirm that the window system is functioning correctly.

23   Power door lock system - general information

1   The optional power door lock system operates the power door motors, which are integral components of the door latch units

in each door. The system consists of a fuse (in the passenger compartment fuse box), the control switches (in each of the front doors), the power door motors and the electrical wiring harnesses connecting all of these components.

2   The lock mechanisms in the door latch units are actuated by a reversible electric motor in each door. When you push the LOCK part of the door lock switch, the motor operates one way and locks the latch mechanism. When you push the UNLOCK part of the door lock switch, the motor operates in the other direction, unlocking the latch mechanism. Because the motors and lock mechanisms are an integral part of the door latch units, they cannot be repaired. If a door lock motor or lock mechanism fails, replace the door latch unit (see Chapter 11).

3   Some vehicles have an optional keyless entry system that allows you to lock and unlock the doors from outside the vehicle. The keyless entry system consists of the transmitter (the electronic push-button "key") and a receiver located in the dash.

4   At-home repairs are limited to inspecting the wiring for bad connections and for minor faults that can be easily repaired. If you are unable to locate the trouble using the following general steps, consult your dealer service department.

5   Always check the circuit fuse (in the passenger compartment fuse box) first.

6   When depressed, each power door lock switch locks or unlocks *all* of the doors. The easiest way to verify that each door lock switch is operating correctly is to watch the door lock button in each door as you operate the switch. The door lock buttons should all go down when you push the door lock switch to the LOCK position, and go up when you push the door lock switch to the UNLOCK position. Also, with the engine turned off so that you can hear better, operate the door lock switches in both directions and listen for the faint click of the motors locking and unlocking the latch mechanisms.

7   If there's no click, check for voltage at the switches. If no voltage is present, check the wiring between the fuse and the switches for shorts and opens (see the wiring diagrams at the end of this chapter).

8   If voltage is present, but no clicking sound is apparent, remove the switch from the door trim panel (see Section 16 in Chapter 11) and test it for continuity. If there is no continuity in either direction, replace the switch.

9   If the switch has continuity but the latch mechanism doesn't click, check the wiring between the switch and the motor in the latch mechanism for continuity. If the circuit is open between the switch and the motor, repair the wiring.

10   If all but one of the motors is operating, remove the trim panel from the affected door (see Section 16 in Chapter 11) and check for voltage at the motor while operating the lock switch. One of the wires should have voltage

in the LOCK position; the other should have voltage in the UNLOCK position.

11   If the inoperative motor is receiving voltage, replace the latch mechanism.

12   If the inoperative motor isn't receiving voltage, check for an open or a short in the circuit between the switch and the motor. **Note:** *It's common for wires to break in the harness between the body and the door because repeatedly opening and closing the door fatigues and eventually breaks the wires.*

24   Power seats - general information

Warning: *The models covered by this manual are equipped with a Supplemental Restraint System (SRS), more commonly known as airbags. Additionally, some models are equipped with seat belt pre-tensioners, which are explosive devices. Always disarm the airbag/restraint system before working in the vicinity of any airbag/restraint system component to avoid the possibility of accidental deployment of the airbag/seat belt pre-tensioners, which could cause personal injury (see Section 26). Do not use a memory-saving device to preserve the PCM's memory when working on or near airbag system components.*

1   Some models feature an optional eight-way power seat system that allows the driver and passenger to adjust the front seats up, down, front up, front down, rear up, rear down, forward and rearward. The system consists of the fuse (in the passenger compartment fuse box), the driver's power seat switch, the passenger power seat switch, the driver's power seat track and the passenger power seat track.

2   The seats are powered by three reversible motors that are attached to the upper half of the power seat track assembly. The forward/rearward motor moves the seat forward and backward. The front tilt motor moves the front of the seat up and down. The rear tilt motor moves the rear of the seat up and down. The motors are an integral part of the power seat track assembly and cannot be repaired or replaced separately. If a motor fails, replace the power seat track assembly.

3   These motors are controlled by the power seat switches, which are located on the outboard side of the seat cushions, on the seat cushion side panels. Each switch changes the direction of seat travel by reversing polarity to the drive motor. Refer to your owner's manual for instructions regarding switch functions. Individual switches in the power seat switch assemblies cannot be repaired or replaced separately. If one of the switches in a power seat switch assembly fails, replace the entire switch assembly.

4   The circuit between each switch and the motor that it controls is protected by an automatically resetting thermal circuit breaker. If a seat is being adjusted and it encounters some sort of obstruction, the circuit breaker will heat

up and open the circuit. Current flow ceases and the circuit breaker cools down. When it has cooled down sufficiently, it closes the circuit again.

5   Diagnosis is usually a simple matter, using the following procedures.

6   Look under the seat for any object which may be preventing the seat from moving.

7   If the seat won't work at all, check the fuse, which is located in the passenger compartment fuse box.

8   With the engine off to reduce the noise level, operate the seat controls in all directions and listen for sound coming from the seat motors.

9   If the motor doesn't work or make noise, check for voltage at the motor while an assistant operates the switch.

10   If the motor is getting voltage but doesn't run, test it off the vehicle with jumper wires. If it still doesn't work, replace it. The individual components are not available separately. The whole power-seat track must be purchased as an assembly.

11   If the motor isn't getting voltage, remove the seat side panel to access the switch and check for voltage. If there's no voltage at the switch, check the wiring between the fuse and the switch. If there's voltage at the switch, check for a short or open in the wiring between the switch and the motor. If that circuit is okay, replace the switch. No further testing is recommended. If the power seat system is still malfunctioning at this point, have the system checked out by a dealer service department.

25 Daytime Running Lights (DRL) - general information

Some domestic and all Canadian models are equipped with Daytime Running Lights (DRL). The DRL system illuminates the headlights whenever the engine is running and the parking brake is disengaged. The DRL system provides reduced power to the headlights so that they won't be too bright for daytime use and it prolongs the headlight bulbs' service life. It does this by modulating the pulse-width of the power to the headlights. The duration and interval of these power pulses is determined by the DRL Control Module, which is located on the left knee bolster mounting bracket, to the left of the steering column. If your vehicle is equipped with DRL, and if there seems to be a problem with it, have it serviced by a dealer.

26 Airbag system - general information

These models are equipped with a Supplemental Restraint System (SRS), more commonly called an airbag system. The SRS system consists of the Sensing and Diagnostic Module (SDM), the steering wheel airbag module, the steering wheel airbag module

coil, the passenger airbag module, the front end discriminating sensor and the AIR BAG warning light on the instrument cluster. There are at least two airbags, one for the driver and one for the front seat passenger, on all models. The SRS system is designed to protect the driver and passenger from serious injury in the event of a head-on or frontal collision.

Airbag modules

The airbag module houses the airbag and the inflator unit. The inflator unit is mounted on the back of the housing over a hole through which gas is expelled, inflating the bag almost instantaneously when an electrical signal is received from the airbag control module. On the driver's airbag, the specially wound wire that carries this signal to the module is called a "clockspring." The clockspring is a flat, ribbon-like electrically conductive tape that winds and unwinds as the steering wheel is turned so it can transmit an electrical signal regardless of wheel position. The procedure for removing the driver's airbag is part of *Steering wheel - removal and installation* in Chapter 10.

The passenger airbag is located in the top of the dashboard, above the glove box. We don't recommend removing the passenger airbag because there is no reason to do so unless it has been activated during an accident and needs to be replaced afterward.

Sensing and Diagnostic Module (SDM)

The SDM is the microprocessor that monitors and operates the airbag system. It contains a special sensing device known as an "accelerometer" that converts changes in vehicle velocity to an electrical signal. The SDM compares this electrical signal to a value stored in its memory. If the generated signal exceeds the value in the SDM's memory, the SDM closes the circuits to the airbag inflator units, which deploy the airbags. The front end discriminating sensor assists the SDM in determining whether to deploy the airbags by providing an external input signal to the SDM that is also processed and compared to the SDM's threshold value in memory.

The SDM checks the system every time the vehicle is started. When you start the car, an AIRBAG indicator light comes on for about six seconds, then goes off, if the system is operating correctly. If there is a fault in the system, the SDM stores a Diagnostic Trouble Code (DTC) and illuminates the AIRBAG indicator light, which remains on until the problem is repaired and the SDM's memory is cleared of any DTCs. If the AIRBAG indicator light comes on at any time other than the bulb test and remains on, or doesn't come on at all, there's a problem in the system. A special GM scan tool and multimeter are the only means by which the system can be diagnosed. Take the vehicle to your dealer immediately and have the system professionally diagnosed and repaired.

Servicing components near the SRS system

There are times when you need to remove the steering wheel, the instrument cluster, the radio, the heater/air conditioning control assembly or other components on or near the dashboard. At these times you'll be working around components and wire harnesses for the SRS system. Do not use electrical test equipment on airbag system wires; it could cause the airbag(s) to deploy. **ALWAYS DISABLE THE SRS SYSTEM BEFORE WORKING NEAR THE SRS SYSTEM COMPONENTS OR RELATED WIRING.**

Disabling the system

Whenever working in the vicinity of the steering wheel, steering column, floor console or near other components of the airbag system, the system should be disarmed. To do this perform the following steps:

a) *Turn the ignition switch to the OFF position.*

b) *Disconnect the cable from the negative battery terminal (see Chapter 5, Section 1).*

c) *WAIT FOR AT LEAST TWO MINUTES before beginning work (during this two-minute interval the capacitor that provides emergency back-up power to the system loses its charge).*

Enabling the system

To enable the airbag system, perform the following steps:

a) *Turn the ignition switch to the OFF position.*

b) *Connect the cable to the negative battery terminal.*

c) *Without putting your body in front of either airbag, turn the ignition switch to the ON position. Note whether the airbag indicator light glows for six seconds, then goes out. If it does, this indicates that the system is functioning properly.*

27 Wiring diagrams - general information

Since it isn't possible to include all wiring diagrams for every year covered by this manual, the following diagrams are those that are typical and most commonly needed.

Prior to troubleshooting any circuits, check the fuse and circuit breakers (if equipped) to make sure they are in good condition. Make sure the battery is properly charged and has clean, tight cable connections (see Chapter 1).

When checking the wiring system, make sure that all electrical connectors are clean, with no broken or loose pins. When disconnecting an electrical connector, do not pull on the wires, only on the connector housings.

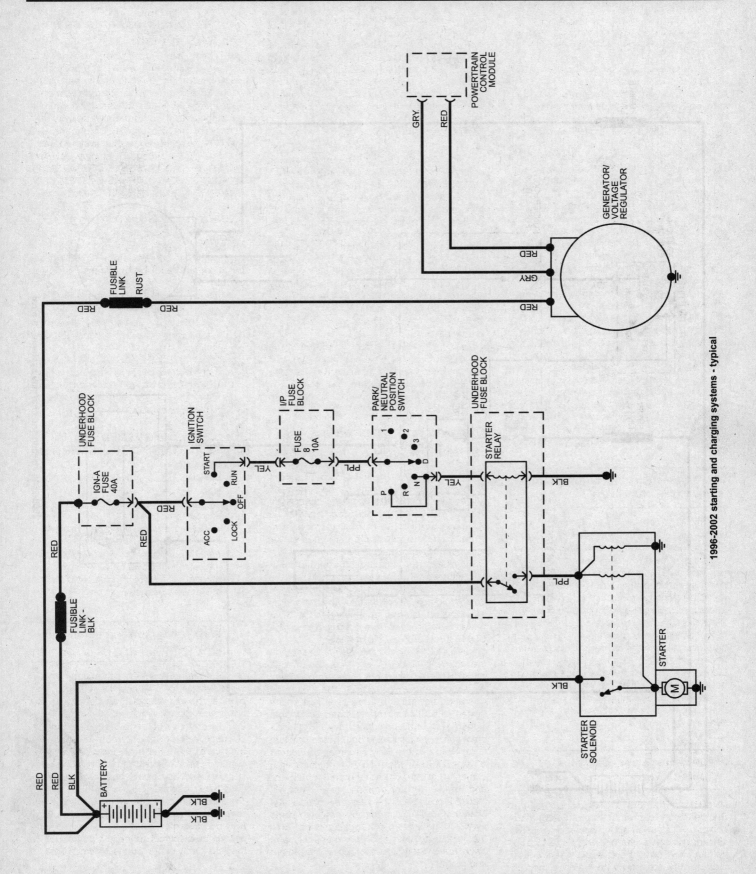

1996-2002 starting and charging systems - typical

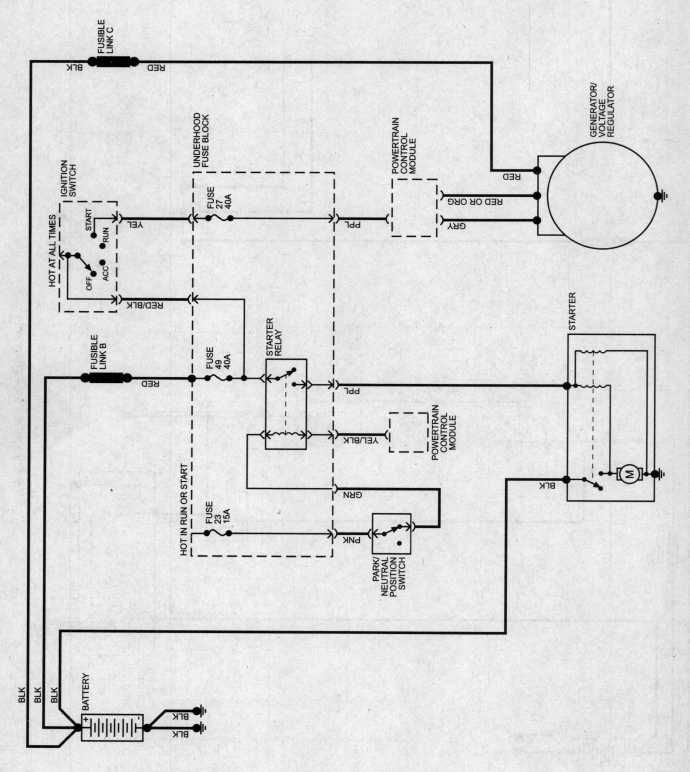

2003-2005 starting and charging systems - typical

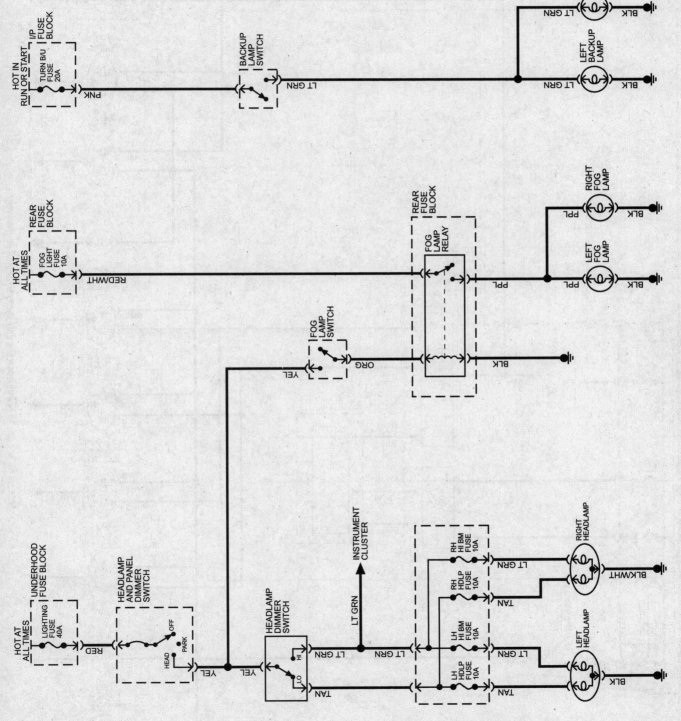

1996-2002 exterior lighting system (1 of 2) - typical

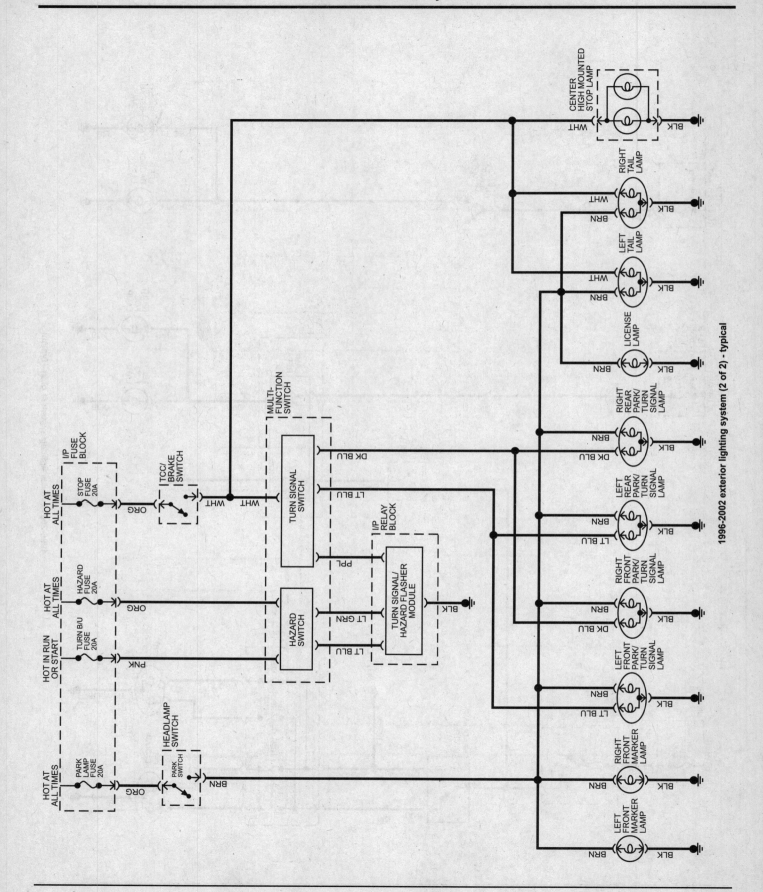

1996-2002 exterior lighting system (2 of 2) - typical

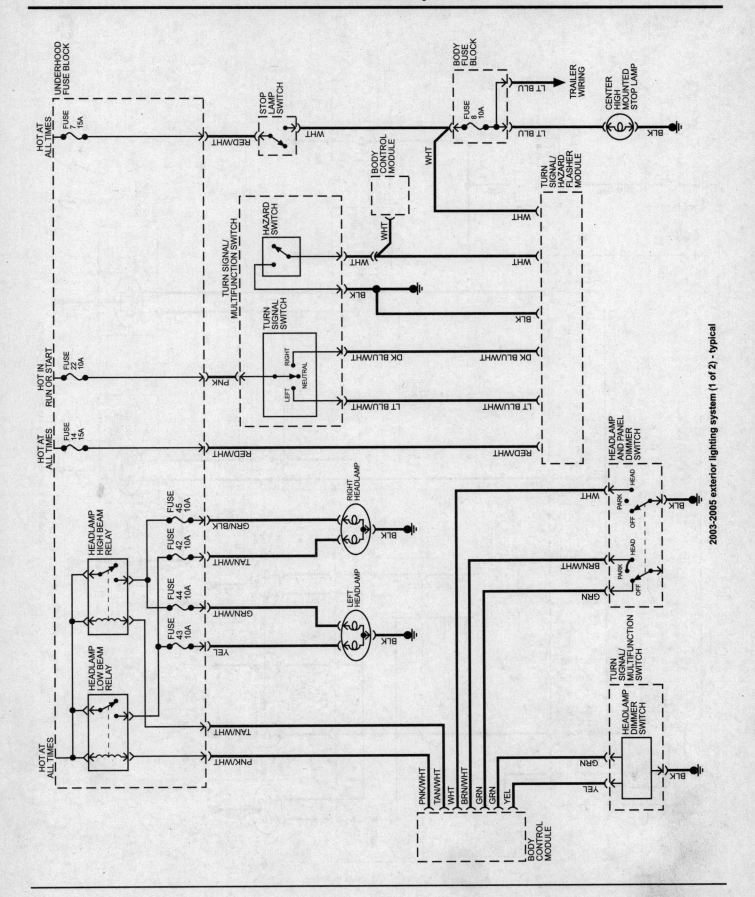

2003-2005 exterior lighting system (1 of 2) - typical

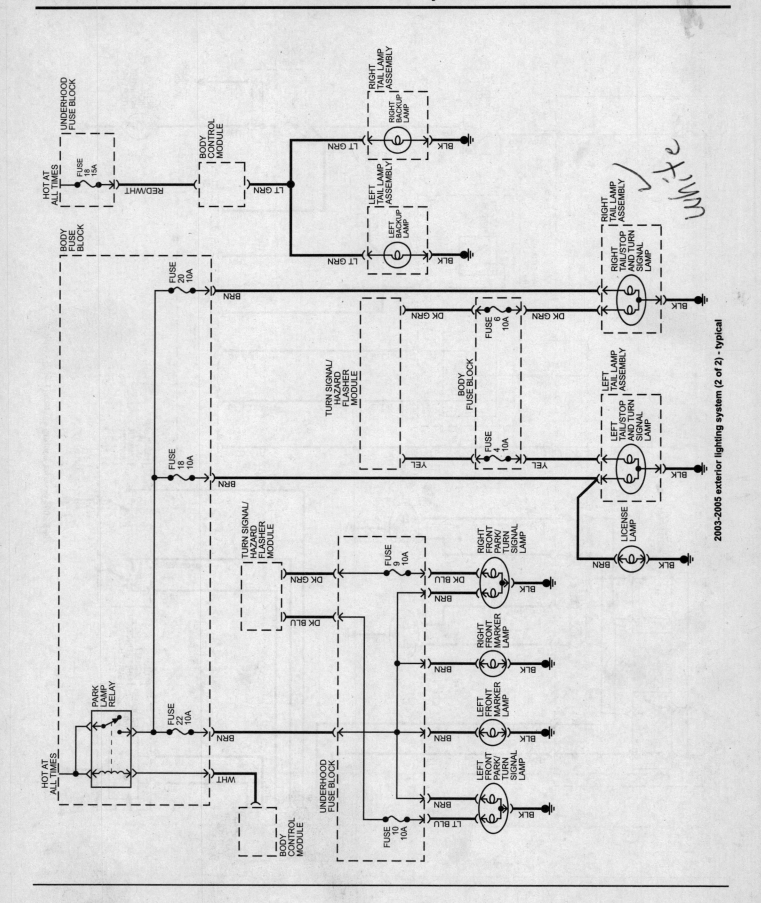

2003-2005 exterior lighting system (2 of 2) - typical

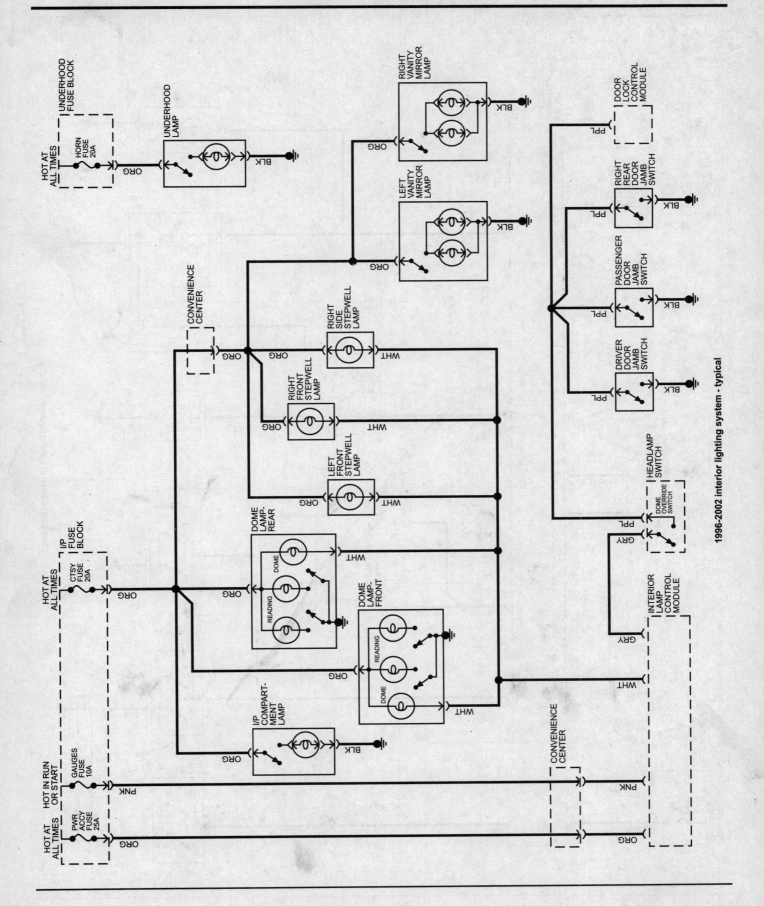

1996-2002 interior lighting system - typical

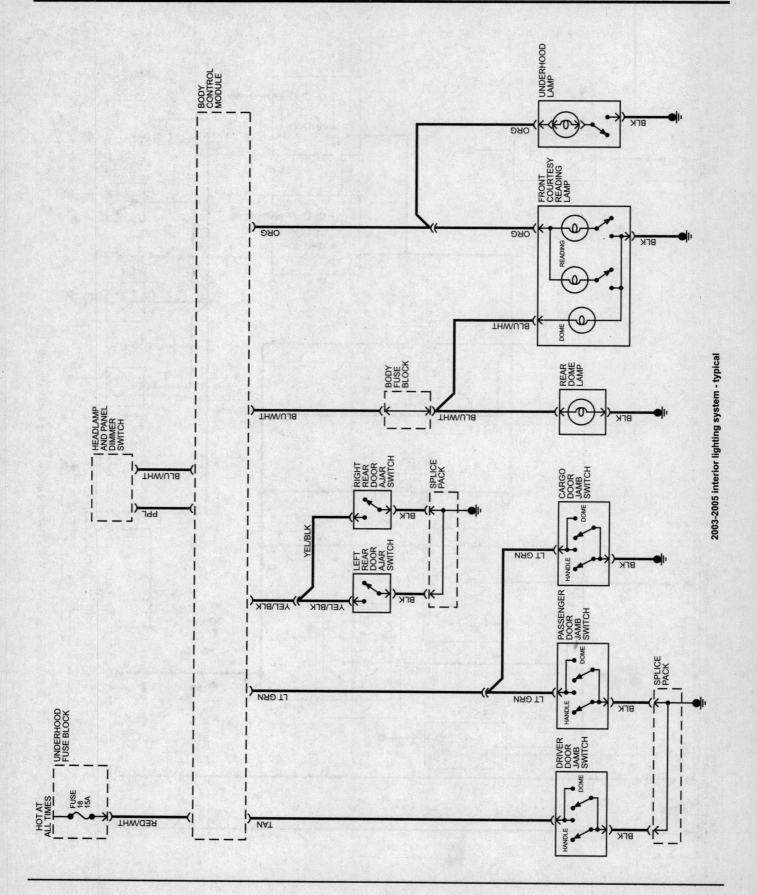

2003-2005 interior lighting system - typical

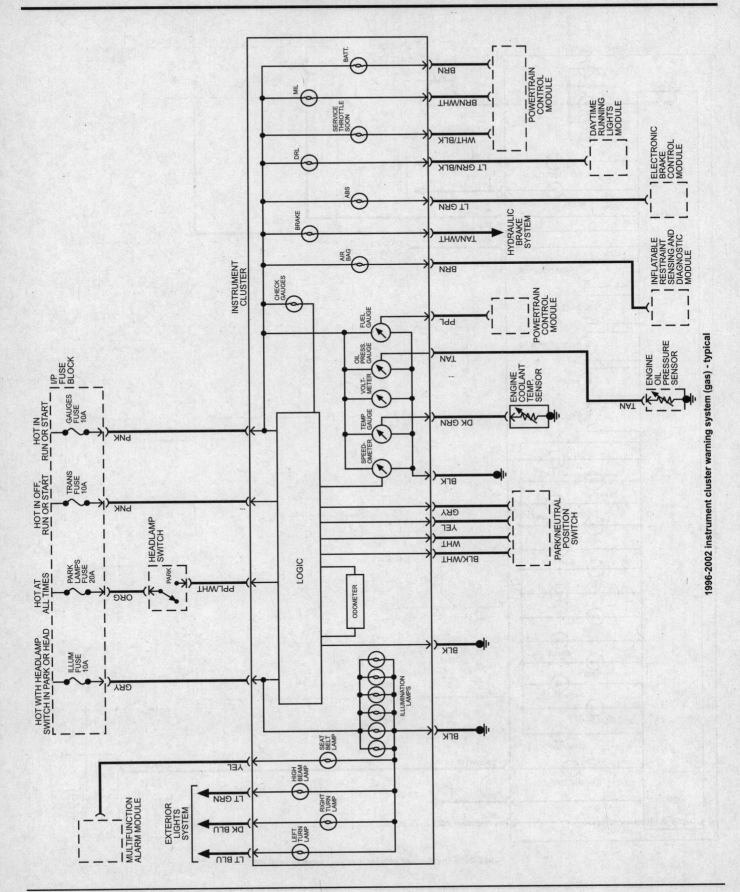

1996-2002 instrument cluster warning system (gas) - typical

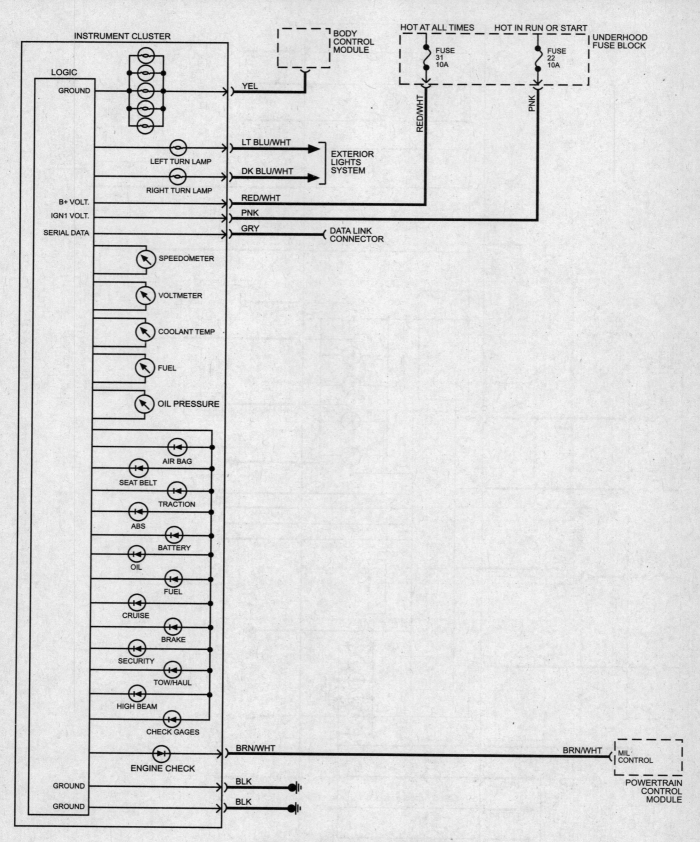

2003-2005 instrument cluster warning system - typical

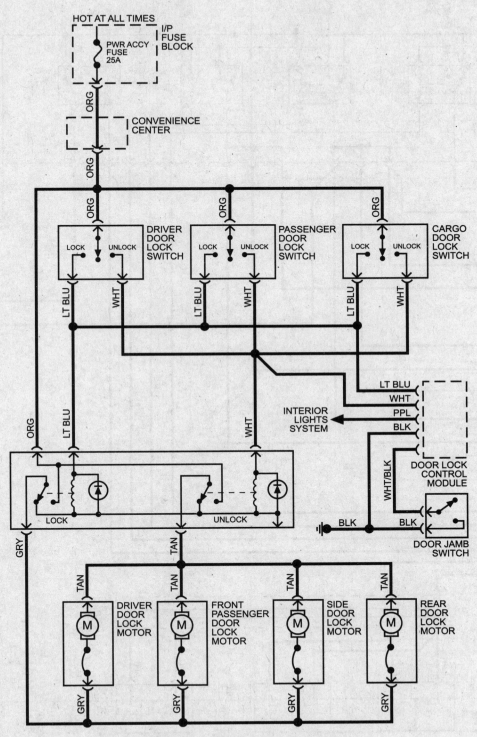

1996-2002 power door lock system - typical

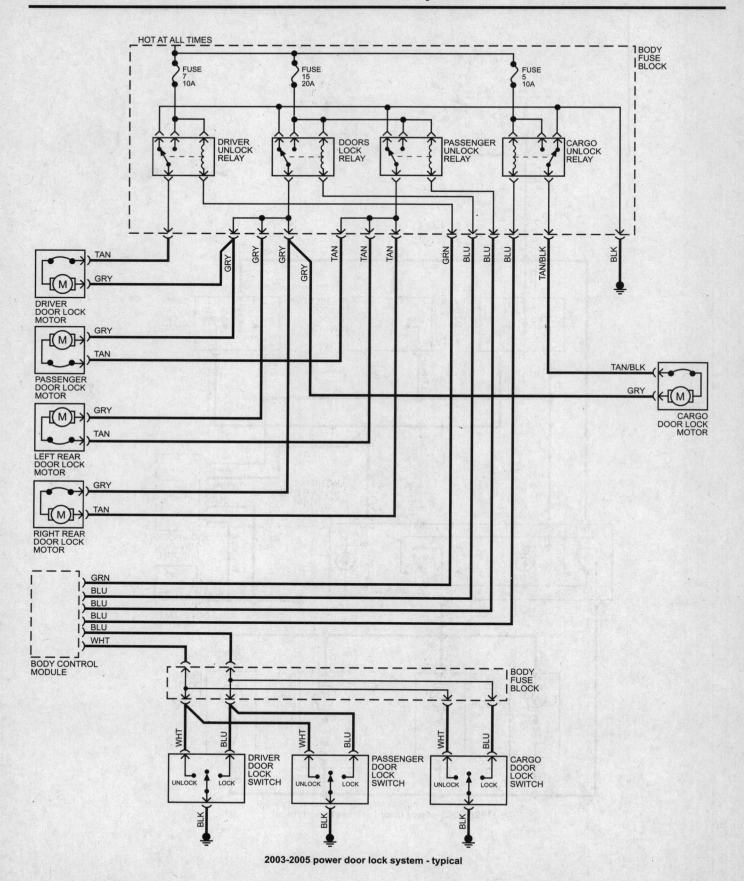

2003-2005 power door lock system - typical

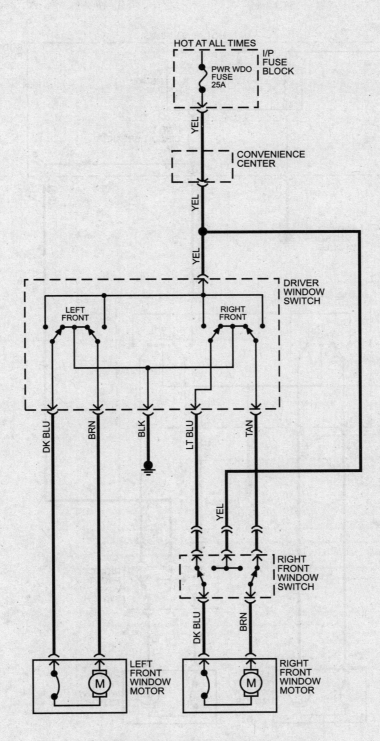

1996-2002 power windows system - typical

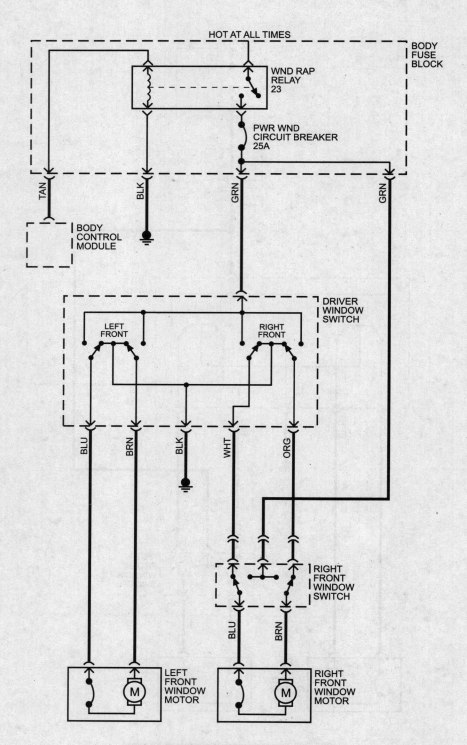

2003-2005 power windows system - typical

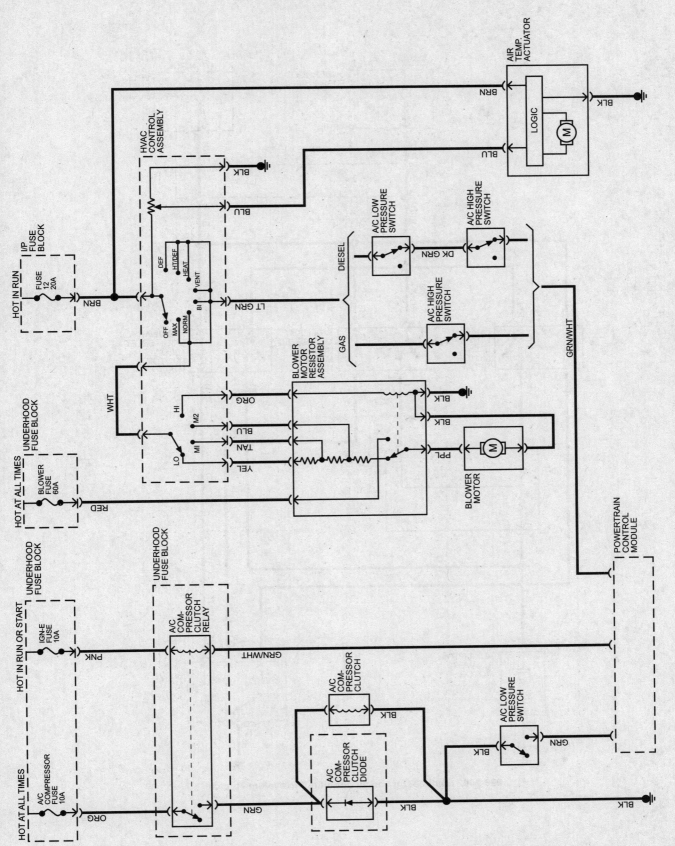

1996-2002 heating and air conditioning system - typical

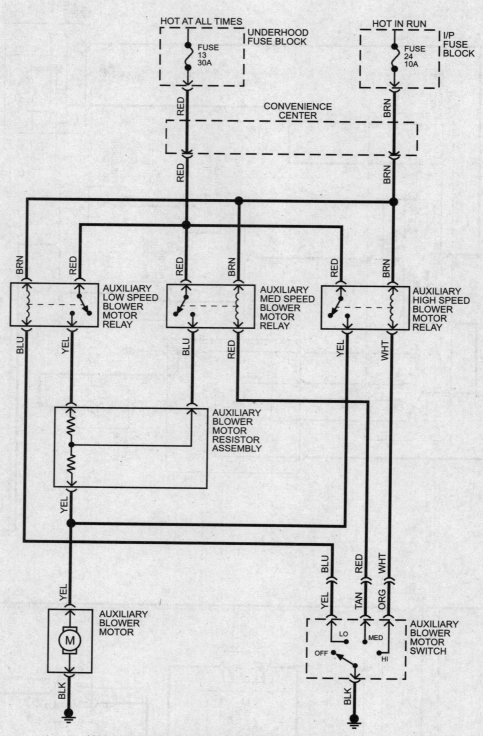

1996-2002 rear heating and air conditioning system - typical

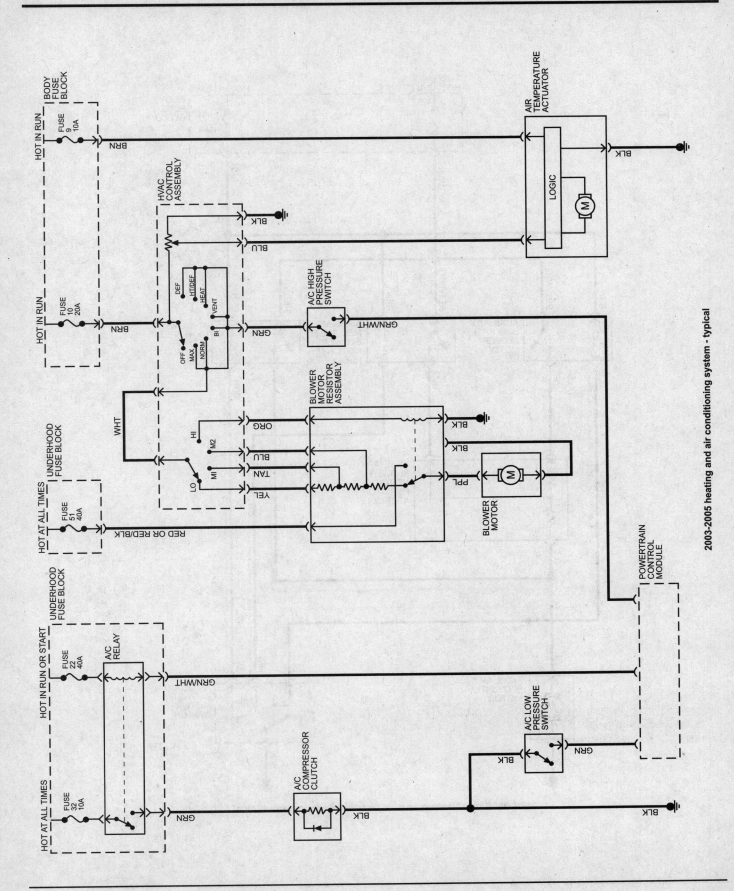

2003-2005 heating and air conditioning system - typical

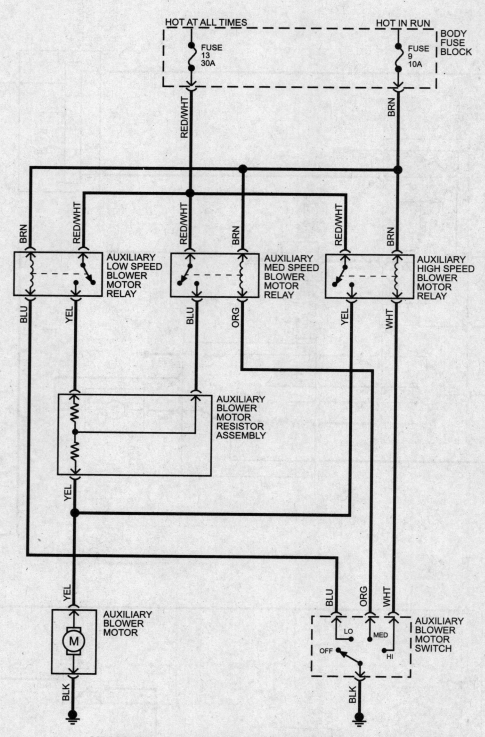

2003-2005 rear heating and air conditioning system - typical

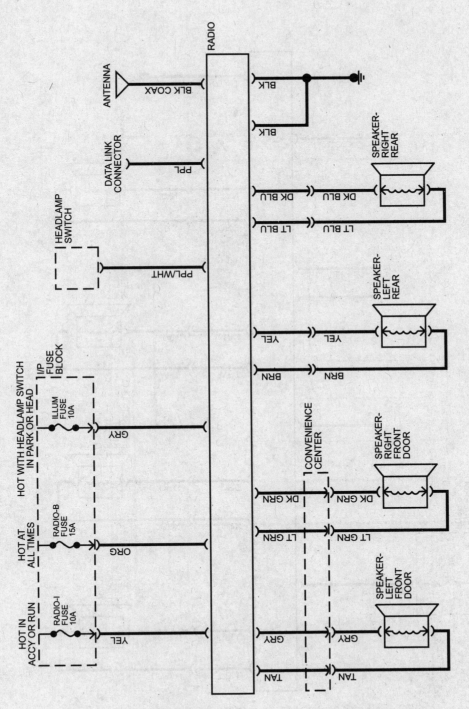

1996-2002 Radio - typical

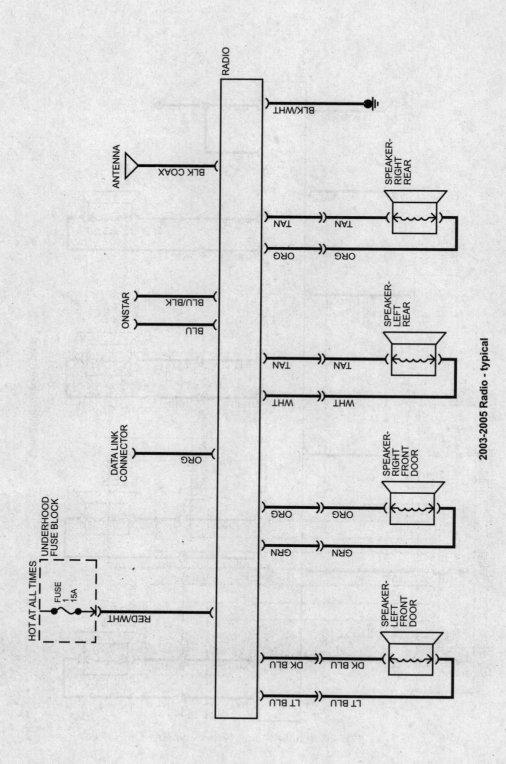

RADIO

BLK/WHT

ANTENNA

BLK COAX

SPEAKER-
RIGHT
REAR

TAN   TAN

ORG   ORG

ONSTAR

BLU/BLK

BLU

SPEAKER-
LEFT
REAR

TAN   TAN

WHT   WHT

DATA LINK
CONNECTOR

ORG

SPEAKER-
RIGHT
FRONT
DOOR

ORG   ORG

GRN   GRN

UNDERHOOD
FUSE BLOCK

HOT AT ALL TIMES

FUSE
1
15A

RED/WHT

SPEAKER-
LEFT
FRONT
DOOR

DK BLU   DK BLU

LT BLU   LT BLU

2003-2005 Radio - typical

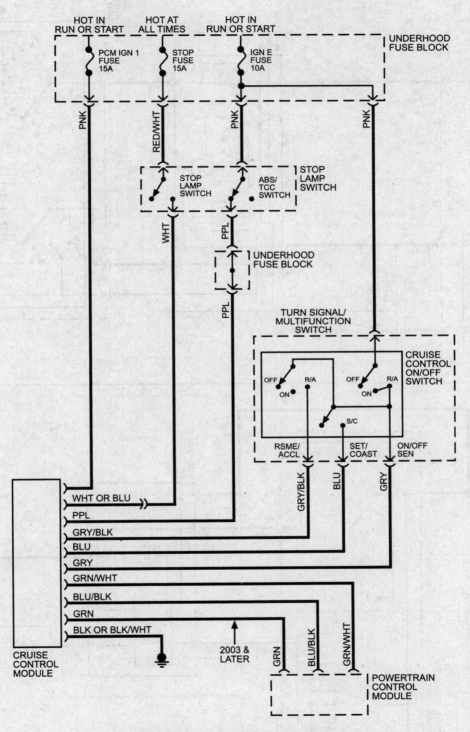

1996-2005 cruise control system - typical

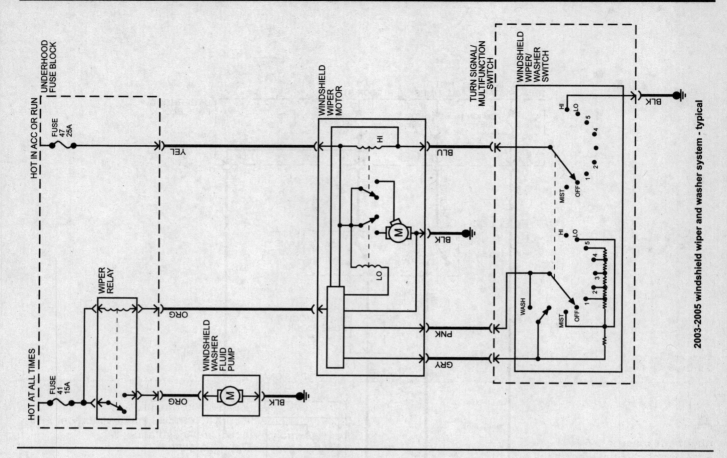

2003-2005 windshield wiper and washer system - typical

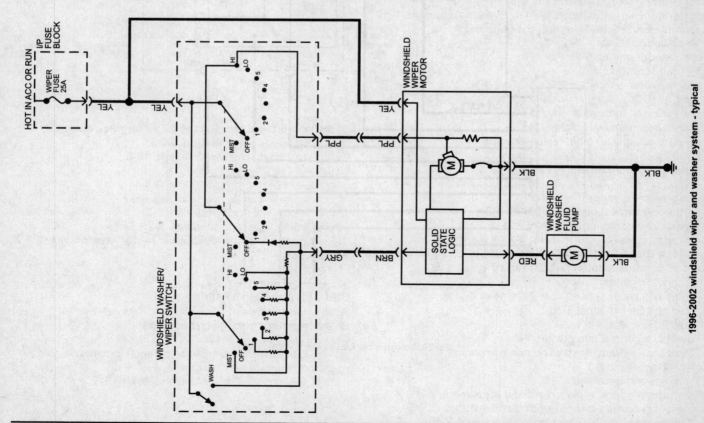

1996-2002 windshield wiper and washer system - typical

Index

Haynes Automotive Manuals

NOTE: If you do not see a listing for your vehicle, consult your local Haynes dealer for the latest product information.

HAYNES XTREME CUSTOMIZING
11101 Sport Compact Customizing
11102 Sport Compact Performance
11110 In-car Entertainment
11150 Sport Utility Vehicle Customizing
11213 Acura
11255 GM Full-size Pick-ups
11314 Ford Focus
11315 Full-size Ford Pick-ups
11373 Honda Civic

ACURA
12020 Integra '86 thru '89 & Legend '86 thru '90
12021 Integra '90 thru '93 & Legend '91 thru '95

AMC
Jeep CJ - see *JEEP (50020)*
14020 Mid-size models '70 thru '83
14025 (Renault) Alliance & Encore '83 thru '87

AUDI
15020 4000 all models '80 thru '87
15025 5000 all models '77 thru '83
15026 5000 all models '84 thru '88

AUSTIN-HEALEY
Sprite - see *MG Midget (66015)*

BMW
18020 3/5 Series not including diesel or all-wheel drive models '82 thru '92
18021 3-Series incl. Z3 models '92 thru '98
18022 3-Series, E46 chassis '99 thru '05, Z4 models '03 thru '05
18025 320i all 4 cyl models '75 thru '83
18050 1500 thru 2002 except Turbo '59 thru '77

BUICK
19010 Buick Century '97 thru '05
Century (front-wheel drive) - see *GM (38005)*
19020 Buick, Oldsmobile & Pontiac Full-size (Front-wheel drive) '85 thru '05
Buick Electra, LeSabre and Park Avenue; Oldsmobile Delta 88 Royale, Ninety Eight and Regency; Pontiac Bonneville
19025 Buick Oldsmobile & Pontiac Full-size (Rear wheel drive)
Buick Estate '70 thru '90, Electra '70 thru '84, LeSabre '70 thru '85, Limited '74 thru '79
Oldsmobile Custom Cruiser '70 thru '90, Delta 88 '70 thru '85, Ninety-eight '70 thru '84
Pontiac Bonneville '70 thru '81, Catalina '70 thru '81, Grandville '70 thru '75, Parisienne '83 thru '86
19030 Mid-size Regal & Century all rear-drive models with V6, V8 and Turbo '74 thru '87
Regal - see *GENERAL MOTORS (38010)*
Riviera - see *GENERAL MOTORS (38030)*
Roadmaster - see *CHEVROLET (24046)*
Skyhawk - see *GENERAL MOTORS (38015)*
Skylark - see *GM (38020, 38025)*
Somerset - see *GENERAL MOTORS (38025)*

CADILLAC
21030 Cadillac Rear Wheel Drive all gasoline models '70 thru '93
Cimarron - see *GENERAL MOTORS (38015)*
DeVille - see *GM (38031 & 38032)*
Eldorado - see *GM (38030 & 38031)*
Fleetwood - see *GM (38031)*
Seville - see *GM (38030, 38031 & 38032)*

CHEVROLET
24010 Astro & GMC Safari Mini-vans '85 thru '03
24015 Camaro V8 all models '70 thru '81
24016 Camaro all models '82 thru '92
24017 Camaro & Firebird '93 thru '02
Cavalier - see *GENERAL MOTORS (38016)*
Celebrity - see *GENERAL MOTORS (38005)*
24020 Chevelle, Malibu & El Camino '69 thru '87
24024 Chevette & Pontiac T1000 '76 thru '87
Citation - see *GENERAL MOTORS (38020)*
24027 Colorado & GMC Canyon '04 thru '06
24032 Corsica/Beretta all models '87 thru '96
24040 Corvette all V8 models '68 thru '82
24041 Corvette all models '84 thru '96
10305 Chevrolet Engine Overhaul Manual
24045 Full-size Sedans Caprice, Impala, Biscayne, Bel Air & Wagons '69 thru '90
24046 Impala SS & Caprice and Buick Roadmaster '91 thru '96
Impala - see *LUMINA (24048)*
Lumina '90 thru '94 - see *GM (38010)*
24048 Lumina & Monte Carlo '95 thru '05
Lumina APV - see *GM (38035)*

24050 Luv Pick-up all 2WD & 4WD '72 thru '82
Malibu '97 thru '00 - see *GM (38026)*
24055 Monte Carlo all models '70 thru '88
Monte Carlo '95 thru '01 - see *LUMINA (24048)*
24059 Nova all V8 models '69 thru '79
24060 Nova and Geo Prizm '85 thru '92
24064 Pick-ups '67 thru '87 - Chevrolet & GMC, all V8 & in-line 6 cyl, 2WD & 4WD '67 thru '87; Suburbans, Blazers & Jimmys '67 thru '91
24065 Pick-ups '88 thru '98 - Chevrolet & GMC, full-size pick-ups '88 thru '98, C/K Classic '99 & '00, Blazer & Jimmy '92 thru '94; Suburban '92 thru '99; Tahoe & Yukon '95 thru '99
24066 Pick-ups '99 thru '06 - Chevrolet Silverado & GMC Sierra '99 thru '06, Suburban/Tahoe/Yukon/Yukon XL/Avalanche '00 thru '06
24070 S-10 & S-15 Pick-ups '82 thru '93, Blazer & Jimmy '83 thru '94,
24071 S-10 & Sonoma Pick-ups '94 thru '04, Blazer & Jimmy '95 thru '04, Hombre '96 thru '01
24072 Chevrolet TrailBlazer & TrailBlazer EXT, GMC Envoy & Envoy XL, Oldsmobile Bravada '02 thru '06
24075 Sprint '85 thru '88 & Geo Metro '89 thru '01
24080 Vans - Chevrolet & GMC '68 thru '96
24081 Chevrolet Express & GMC Savana Full-size Vans '96 thru '06

CHRYSLER
25015 Chrysler Cirrus, Dodge Stratus, Plymouth Breeze '95 thru '00
10310 Chrysler Engine Overhaul Manual
25020 Full-size Front-Wheel Drive '88 thru '93
K-Cars - see *DODGE Aries (30008)*
Laser - see *DODGE Daytona (30030)*
25025 Chrysler LHS, Concorde, New Yorker, Dodge Intrepid, **Eagle Vision,** '93 thru '97
25026 Chrysler LHS, Concorde, 300M, Dodge Intrepid, '98 thru '04
25027 Chrysler 300, Dodge Charger & Magnum '05 thru '07
25030 Chrysler & Plymouth Mid-size front wheel drive '82 thru '95
Rear-wheel Drive - see *Dodge (30050)*
25035 PT Cruiser all models '01 thru '03
25040 Chrysler Sebring, Dodge Avenger '95 thru '05 Dodge Stratus '01 thru 05

DATSUN
28005 200SX all models '80 thru '83
28007 B-210 all models '73 thru '78
28009 210 all models '79 thru '82
28012 240Z, 260Z & 280Z Coupe '70 thru '78
28014 280ZX Coupe & 2+2 '79 thru '83
300ZX - see *NISSAN (72010)*
28018 510 & PL521 Pick-up '68 thru '73
28020 510 all models '78 thru '81
28022 620 Series Pick-up all models '73 thru '79
720 Series Pick-up - see *NISSAN (72030)*
28025 810/Maxima all gasoline models, '77 thru '84

DODGE
400 & 600 - see *CHRYSLER (25030)*
30008 Aries & Plymouth Reliant '81 thru '89
30010 Caravan & Plymouth Voyager '84 thru '95
30011 Caravan & Plymouth Voyager '96 thru '02
30012 Challenger/Plymouth Saporro '78 thru '83
30013 Caravan, Chrysler Voyager, Town & Country '03 thru '06
30016 Colt & Plymouth Champ '78 thru '87
30020 Dakota Pick-ups all models '87 thru '96
30021 Durango '98 & '99, Dakota '97 thru '99
30022 Dodge Durango models '00 thru '03 Dodge Dakota models '00 thru '04
30023 Dodge Durango '04 thru '06, Dakota '05 and '06
30025 Dart, Demon, Plymouth Barracuda, Duster & Valiant 6 cyl models '67 thru '76
30030 Daytona & Chrysler Laser '84 thru '89 Intrepid - see *CHRYSLER (25025, 25026)*
30034 Neon all models '95 thru '99
30035 Omni & Plymouth Horizon '78 thru '90
30036 Dodge and Plymouth Neon '00 thru '05
30040 Pick-ups all full-size models '74 thru '93
30041 Pick-ups all full-size models '94 thru '01
30042 Dodge Full-size Pick-ups '02 thru '05
30045 Ram 50/D50 Pick-ups & Raider and Plymouth Arrow Pick-ups '79 thru '93
30050 Dodge/Plymouth/Chrysler RWD '71 thru '89
30055 Shadow & Plymouth Sundance '87 thru '94
30060 Spirit & Plymouth Acclaim '89 thru '95
30065 Vans - Dodge & Plymouth '71 thru '03

EAGLE
Talon - see *MITSUBISHI (68030, 68031)*
Vision - see *CHRYSLER (25025)*

FIAT
34010 124 Sport Coupe & Spider '68 thru '78
34025 X1/9 all models '74 thru '80

FORD
10355 Ford Automatic Transmission Overhaul
36004 Aerostar Mini-vans all models '86 thru '97
36006 Contour & Mercury Mystique '95 thru '00
36008 Courier Pick-up all models '72 thru '82
36012 Crown Victoria & Mercury Grand Marquis '88 thru '06
10320 Ford Engine Overhaul Manual
36016 Escort/Mercury Lynx all models '81 thru '90
36020 Escort/Mercury Tracer '91 thru '00
36022 Ford Escape & Mazda Tribute '01 thru '03
36024 Explorer & Mazda Navajo '91 thru '01
36025 Ford Explorer & Mercury Mountaineer '02 thru '06
36028 Fairmont & Mercury Zephyr '78 thru '83
36030 Festiva & Aspire '88 thru '97
36032 Fiesta all models '77 thru '80
36034 Focus all models '00 thru '05
36036 Ford & Mercury Full-size '75 thru '87
36044 Ford & Mercury Mid-size '75 thru '86
36048 Mustang V8 all models '64-1/2 thru '73
36049 Mustang II 4 cyl, V6 & V8 models '74 thru '78
36050 Mustang & Mercury Capri all models Mustang, '79 thru '93; Capri, '79 thru '86
36051 Mustang all models '94 thru '04
36052 Mustang '05 thru '07
36054 Pick-ups & Bronco '73 thru '79
36058 Pick-ups & Bronco '80 thru '96
36059 F-150 & Expedition '97 thru '03, F-250 '97 thru '99 & Lincoln Navigator '98 thru '02
36060 Super Duty Pick-ups, Excursion '99 thru '06
36061 F-150 full-size '04 thru '06
36062 Pinto & Mercury Bobcat '75 thru '80
36066 Probe all models '89 thru '92
36070 Ranger/Bronco II gasoline models '83 thru '92
36071 Ranger '93 thru '05 & Mazda Pick-ups '94 thru '05
36074 Taurus & Mercury Sable '86 thru '95
36075 Taurus & Mercury Sable '96 thru '05
36078 Tempo & Mercury Topaz '84 thru '94
36082 Thunderbird/Mercury Cougar '83 thru '88
36086 Thunderbird/Mercury Cougar '89 and '97
36090 Vans all V8 Econoline models '69 thru '91
36094 Vans full size '92 thru '05
36097 Windstar Mini-van '95 thru '03

GENERAL MOTORS
10360 GM Automatic Transmission Overhaul
38005 Buick Century, Chevrolet Celebrity, Oldsmobile Cutlass Ciera & Pontiac 6000 all models '82 thru '96
38010 Buick Regal, Chevrolet Lumina, Oldsmobile Cutlass Supreme & Pontiac Grand Prix (FWD) '88 thru '05
38015 Buick Skyhawk, Cadillac Cimarron, Chevrolet Cavalier, Oldsmobile Firenza & Pontiac J-2000 & Sunbird '82 thru '94
38016 Chevrolet Cavalier & Pontiac Sunfire '95 thru '04
38017 Chevrolet Cobalt & Pontiac G5 '05 thru '07
38020 Buick Skylark, Chevrolet Citation, Olds Omega, Pontiac Phoenix '80 thru '85
38025 Buick Skylark & Somerset, Oldsmobile Achieva & Calais and Pontiac Grand Am all models '85 thru '98
38026 Chevrolet Malibu, Olds Alero & Cutlass, Pontiac Grand Am '97 thru '03
38027 Chevrolet Malibu '04 thru '07
38030 Cadillac Eldorado '71 thru '85, Seville '80 thru '85, Oldsmobile Toronado '71 thru '85, Buick Riviera '79 thru '85
38031 Cadillac Eldorado & Seville '86 thru '91, DeVille '86 thru '93, Fleetwood & Olds Toronado '86 thru '92, Buick Riviera '86 thru '93
38032 Cadillac DeVille '94 thru '05 & Seville '92 thru '04
38035 Chevrolet Lumina APV, Olds Silhouette & Pontiac Trans Sport all models '90 thru '96
38036 Chevrolet Venture, Olds Silhouette, Pontiac Trans Sport & Montana '97 thru '05
General Motors Full-size Rear-wheel Drive - see *BUICK (19025)*

GEO
Metro - see *CHEVROLET Sprint (24075)*
Prizm - '85 thru '92 see *CHEVY (24060)*, '93 thru '02 see *TOYOTA Corolla (92036)*

(Continued on other side)

Haynes North America, Inc., 861 Lawrence Drive, Newbury Park, CA 91320-1514 • (805) 498-6703

Haynes Automotive Manuals (continued)

NOTE: If you do not see a listing for your vehicle, consult your local Haynes dealer for the latest product information.

40030 Storm all models '90 thru '93
Tracker - see SUZUKI Samurai (90010)

GMC
Vans & Pick-ups - see CHEVROLET

HONDA
42010 Accord CVCC all models '76 thru '83
42011 Accord all models '84 thru '89
42012 Accord all models '90 thru '93
42013 Accord all models '94 thru '97
42014 Accord all models '98 thru '02
42015 Honda Accord models '03 thru '05
42020 Civic 1200 all models '73 thru '79
42021 Civic 1300 & 1500 CVCC '80 thru '83
42022 Civic 1500 CVCC all models '75 thru '79
42023 Civic all models '84 thru '91
42024 Civic & del Sol '92 thru '95
42025 Civic '96 thru '00, CR-V '97 thru '01,
Acura Integra '94 thru '00
42026 Civic '01 thru '04, CR-V '02 thru '04
42035 Honda Odyssey all models '99 thru '04
42037 Honda Pilot '03 thru '07, Acura MDX '01 thru '07
42040 Prelude CVCC all models '79 thru '89

HYUNDAI
43010 Elantra all models '96 thru '01
43015 Excel & Accent all models '86 thru '98

ISUZU
Hombre - see CHEVROLET S-10 (24071)
47017 Rodeo '91 thru '02; Amigo '89 thru '94 and
'98 thru '02; Honda Passport '95 thru '02
47020 Trooper & Pick-up '81 thru '93

JAGUAR
49010 XJ6 all 6 cyl models '68 thru '86
49011 XJ6 all models '88 thru '94
49015 XJ12 & XJS all 12 cyl models '72 thru '85

JEEP
50010 Cherokee, Comanche & Wagoneer Limited
all models '84 thru '01
50020 CJ all models '49 thru '86
50025 Grand Cherokee all models '93 thru '04
50029 Grand Wagoneer & Pick-up '72 thru '91
Grand Wagoneer '84 thru '91, Cherokee &
Wagoneer '72 thru '83, Pick-up '72 thru '88
50030 Wrangler all models '87 thru '03
50035 Liberty '02 thru '04

KIA
54070 Sephia '94 thru '01, Spectra '00 thru '04

LEXUS
ES 300 - see TOYOTA Camry (92007)

LINCOLN
Navigator - see FORD Pick-up (36059)
59010 Rear-Wheel Drive all models '70 thru '05

MAZDA
61010 GLC Hatchback (rear-wheel drive) '77 thru '83
61011 GLC (front-wheel drive) '81 thru '85
61015 323 & Protogé '90 thru '00
61016 MX-5 Miata '90 thru '97
61020 MPV all models '89 thru '94
Navajo - see Ford Explorer (36024)
61030 Pick-ups '72 thru '93
Pick-ups '94 thru '00 - see Ford Ranger (36071)
61035 RX-7 all models '79 thru '85
61036 RX-7 all models '86 thru '91
61040 626 (rear-wheel drive) all models '79 thru '82
61041 626/MX-6 (front-wheel drive) '83 thru '92
61042 626 '93 thru '01, MX-6/Ford Probe
'93 thru '01

MERCEDES-BENZ
63012 123 Series Diesel '76 thru '85
63015 190 Series four-cyl gas models, '84 thru '88
63020 230/250/280 6 cyl sohc models '68 thru '72
63025 280 123 Series gasoline models '77 thru '81
63030 350 & 450 all models '71 thru '80

MERCURY
64200 Villager & Nissan Quest '93 thru '01
All other titles, see FORD Listing.

MG
66010 MGB Roadster & GT Coupe '62 thru '80
66015 MG Midget, Austin Healey Sprite '58 thru '80

MITSUBISHI
68020 Cordia, Tredia, Galant, Precis &
Mirage '83 thru '93

68030 Eclipse, Eagle Talon & Ply. Laser '90 thru '94
68031 Eclipse '95 thru '01, Eagle Talon '95 thru '98
68035 Mitsubishi Galant '94 thru '03
68040 Pick-up '83 thru '96 & Montero '83 thru '93

NISSAN
72010 300ZX all models including Turbo '84 thru '89
72015 Altima all models '93 thru '04
72020 Maxima all models '85 thru '92
72021 Maxima all models '93 thru '04
72030 Pick-ups '80 thru '97 Pathfinder '87 thru '95
72031 Frontier Pick-up '98 thru '04, Xterra '00 thru
'04, Pathfinder '96 thru '04
72040 Pulsar all models '83 thru '86
Quest - see MERCURY Villager (64200)
72050 Sentra all models '82 thru '94
72051 Sentra & 200SX all models '95 thru '04
72060 Stanza all models '82 thru '90

OLDSMOBILE
73015 Cutlass V6 & V8 gas models '74 thru '88
For other OLDSMOBILE titles, see BUICK,
CHEVROLET or GENERAL MOTORS listing.

PLYMOUTH
For PLYMOUTH titles, see DODGE listing.

PONTIAC
79008 Fiero all models '84 thru '88
79018 Firebird V8 models except Turbo '70 thru '81
79019 Firebird all models '82 thru '92
79040 Mid-size Rear-wheel Drive '70 thru '87
For other PONTIAC titles, see BUICK,
CHEVROLET or GENERAL MOTORS listing.

PORSCHE
80020 911 except Turbo & Carrera 4 '65 thru '89
80025 914 all 4 cyl models '69 thru '76
80030 924 all models including Turbo '76 thru '82
80035 944 all models including Turbo '83 thru '89

RENAULT
Alliance & Encore - see AMC (14020)

SAAB
84010 900 all models including Turbo '79 thru '88

SATURN
87010 Saturn all models '91 thru '02
87011 Saturn Ion '03 thru '07
87020 Saturn all L-series models '00 thru '04

SUBARU
89002 1100, 1300, 1400 & 1600 '71 thru '79
89003 1600 & 1800 2WD & 4WD '80 thru '94
89100 Legacy all models '90 thru '99
89101 Legacy & Forester '00 thru '06

SUZUKI
90010 Samurai/Sidekick & Geo Tracker '86 thru '01

TOYOTA
92005 Camry all models '83 thru '91
92006 Camry all models '92 thru '96
92007 Camry, Avalon, Solara, Lexus ES 300 '97 thru '01
92008 Toyota Camry, Avalon and Solara and
Lexus ES 300/330 all models '02 thru '05
92015 Celica Rear Wheel Drive '71 thru '85
92020 Celica Front Wheel Drive '86 thru '99
92025 Celica Supra all models '79 thru '92
92030 Corolla all models '75 thru '79
92032 Corolla all rear wheel drive models '80 thru '87
92035 Corolla all front wheel drive models '84 thru '92
92036 Corolla & Geo Prizm '93 thru '02
92037 Corolla models '03 thru '05
92040 Corolla Tercel all models '80 thru '82
92045 Corona all models '74 thru '82
92050 Cressida all models '78 thru '82
92055 Land Cruiser FJ40, 43, 45, 55 '68 thru '82
92056 Land Cruiser FJ60, 62, 80, FZJ80 '80 thru '96
92065 MR2 all models '85 thru '87
92070 Pick-up all models '69 thru '78
92075 Pick-up all models '79 thru '95
92076 Tacoma '95 thru '04, 4Runner '96 thru '02,
& T100 '93 thru '98
92078 Tundra '00 thru '05 & Sequoia '01 thru '05
92080 Previa all models '91 thru '95
92081 Prius all models '01 thru '08
92082 RAV4 all models '96 thru '05
92085 Tercel all models '87 thru '94
92090 Toyota Sienna all models '98 thru '02
92095 Highlander & Lexus RX-330 '99 thru '06

TRIUMPH
94007 Spitfire all models '62 thru '81
94010 TR7 all models '75 thru '81

VW
96008 Beetle & Karmann Ghia '54 thru '79
96009 New Beetle '98 thru '05
96016 Rabbit, Jetta, Scirocco & Pick-up gas
models '75 thru '92 & Convertible '80 thru '92
96017 Golf, GTI & Jetta '93 thru '98
& Cabrio '95 thru '98
96018 Golf, GTI, Jetta & Cabrio '99 thru '02
96020 Rabbit, Jetta & Pick-up diesel '77 thru '84
96023 Passat '98 thru '01, Audi A4 '96 thru '01
96030 Transporter 1600 all models '68 thru '79
96035 Transporter 1700, 1800 & 2000 '72 thru '79
96040 Type 3 1500 & 1600 all models '63 thru '73
96045 Vanagon all air-cooled models '80 thru '83

VOLVO
97010 120, 130 Series & 1800 Sports '61 thru '73
97015 140 Series all models '66 thru '74
97020 240 Series all models '76 thru '93
97040 740 & 760 Series all models '82 thru '88
97050 850 Series all models '93 thru '97

TECHBOOK MANUALS
10205 Automotive Computer Codes
10206 OBD-II & Electronic Engine Management
Systems
10210 Automotive Emissions Control Manual
10215 Fuel Injection Manual, 1978 thru 1985
10220 Fuel Injection Manual, 1986 thru 1999
10225 Holley Carburetor Manual
10230 Rochester Carburetor Manual
10240 Weber/Zenith/Stromberg/SU Carburetors
10305 Chevrolet Engine Overhaul Manual
10310 Chrysler Engine Overhaul Manual
10320 Ford Engine Overhaul Manual
10330 GM and Ford Diesel Engine Repair Manual
10333 Building Engine Power Manual
10340 Small Engine Repair Manual, 5 HP & Less
10341 Small Engine Repair Manual, 5.5 - 20 HP
10345 Suspension, Steering & Driveline Manual
10355 Ford Automatic Transmission Overhaul
10360 GM Automatic Transmission Overhaul
10405 Automotive Body Repair & Painting
10410 Automotive Brake Manual
10411 Automotive Anti-lock Brake (ABS) Systems
10415 Automotive Detailing Manual
10420 Automotive Electrical Manual
10425 Automotive Heating & Air Conditioning
10430 Automotive Reference Manual & Dictionary
10435 Automotive Tools Manual
10440 Used Car Buying Guide
10445 Welding Manual
10450 ATV Basics
10452 Scooters, Automatic Transmission 50cc
to 250cc

SPANISH MANUALS
98903 Reparación de Carrocería & Pintura
98904 Carburadores para los modelos
Holley & Rochester
98905 Códigos Automotrices de la Computadora
98910 Frenos Automotriz
98913 Electricidad Automotriz
98915 Inyección de Combustible 1986 al 1999
99040 Chevrolet & GMC Camionetas '67 al '87
Incluye Suburban, Blazer & Jimmy '67 al '91
99041 Chevrolet & GMC Camionetas '88 al '98
Incluye Suburban '92 al '98, Blazer &
Jimmy '92 al '94, Tahoe y Yukon '95 al '98
99042 Chevrolet & GMC Camionetas
Cerradas '68 al '95
99055 Dodge Caravan & Plymouth Voyager '84 al '95
99075 Ford Camionetas y Bronco '80 al '94
99077 Ford Camionetas Cerradas '69 al '91
99088 Ford Modelos de Tamaño Mediano '75 al '86
99091 Ford Taurus & Mercury Sable '86 al '95
99095 GM Modelos de Tamaño Grande '70 al '90
99100 GM Modelos de Tamaño Mediano '70 al '88
99106 Jeep Cherokee, Wagoneer & Comanche
'84 al '00
99110 Nissan Camioneta '80 al '96, Pathfinder '87 al '95
99118 Nissan Sentra '82 al '94
99125 Toyota Camionetas y 4Runner '79 al '95

Over 100 Haynes
motorcycle manuals
also available

10-07

Haynes North America, Inc., 861 Lawrence Drive, Newbury Park, CA 91320-1514 • (805) 498-6703